www.mcgrawhill.ca/olc/thecore

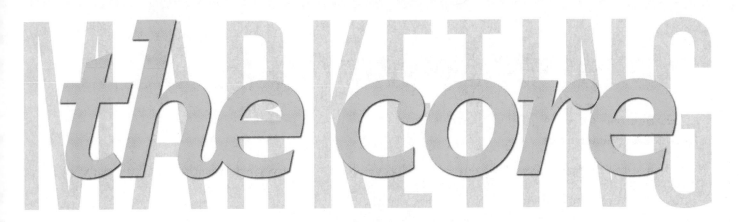

MARKETING the core

SECOND CANADIAN EDITION

ROGER A. KERIN
Southern Methodist University

STEVEN W. HARTLEY
University of Denver

WILLIAM RUDELIUS
University of Minnesota

CHRISTINA CLEMENTS
Humber College Institute of Technology & Advanced Learning

HARVEY SKOLNICK
Sheridan Institute of Technology and Advanced Learning

Revised from the First Canadian Edition co-authored by Roger A. Kerin, Steven W. Hartley,
William Rudelius, and **Gerard Edwards**, *Douglas College*, and **Carla Gail Tibbo**, *Douglas College*.

McGraw-Hill Ryerson

Toronto   Montréal   Boston   Burr   Ridge, IL   Dubuque, IA   Madison, WI   New York
San Francisco   St. Louis   Bangkok   Bogotá   Caracas   Kuala   Lumpur   Lisbon   London
Madrid   Mexico City   Milan   New Delhi   Santiago   Seoul   Singapore   Sydney   Taipei

ISBN-13: 978-0-07-097426-5
ISBN-10: 0-07-097426-8

5 6 7 8 9 10 TCP 1 9 8 7 6 5 4 3 2 1

Printed and bound in Canada.

Vice-President and Editor-in-Chief: Joanna Cotton
Executive Sponsoring Editor: Leanna MacLean
Executive Marketing Manager: Joy Armitage Taylor
Senior Developmental Editor: Denise Foote
Supervising Editor: Kara Stahl
Photo/Permission Research: Tracy Leonard
Copy Editor: Michael Kelly
Team Lead, Production: Paula Brown
Cover Design: Valid Design & Layout/Dave Murphy
Cover Image Credit: © Masterfile/Brad Wrobleski
Interior Design: Valid Design & Layout/Dave Murphy
Page Layout: Valid Design & Layout/Dave Murphy
Printer: Transcontinental Printing Group

Library and Archives Canada Cataloguing in Publication

Marketing : The Core / Roger A. Kerin ... [et al.]. — 2nd Canadian ed.

Includes bibliographical references and indexes.
ISBN 978-0-07-097426-5

1. Marketing--Textbooks. I. Kerin, Roger A.

HF5415.M374 2009   658.8   C2008-907151-4

Author Profiles

Roger A. Kerin is the Harold C. Simmons Distinguished Professor of Marketing at the Edwin L. Cox School of Business, Southern Methodist University in Dallas, Texas. Professor Kerin holds a B.A. (magna cum laude), M.B.A., and Ph.D. from the University of Minnesota. His teaching and research interests lie in marketing planning and strategy, product management, financial aspects of marketing, and marketing research. Professor Kerin is a frequent participant in executive development programs and is also an active consultant on matters of marketing planning and strategy. Professor Kerin has published and authored several texts and many articles on marketing. He also serves on numerous journal editorial review boards and is currently a member of the Board of Governors of the Academy of Marketing Science.

Steven W. Hartley is Professor of Marketing in the Daniels College of Business at the University of Denver. He holds Bachelor of Mechanical Engineering, M.B.A., and Ph.D. degrees from the University of Minnesota. Dr. Hartley was formerly the chair of the Department of Marketing at the University of Denver, and has taught at the University of Colorado, the University of Minnesota, and in several executive development programs. His teaching interests include principles of marketing, marketing research, and marketing planning. Dr. Hartley's research has appeared in many leading marketing publications. He is an active consultant to several prominent U.S. corporations and is active in many professional organizations including the American Marketing Association, the Academy of Marketing Science, and the Marketing Educators' Association.

William Rudelius holds the Endowed Chair in Global Marketing at the Graduate School of Business of the University of St. Thomas in Minnesota. He holds a B.S. degree in Mechanical Engineering from the University of Wisconsin and an M.B.A. in Marketing and Ph.D. in Applied Economics from the Wharton School of the University of Pennsylvania. Professor Rudelius has co-authored other marketing textbooks. His articles have appeared in leading academic journals. During the past ten years, he has taught extensively in Europe; he serves on the board of directors for several business and not-for-profit organizations.

Christina Clements is an award-winning professor from the Business School at Humber College Institute of Technology & Advanced Learning in Ontario. She is renowned for the creativity and knowledge she brings to the field of marketing education and was recently presented with the Leadership in Faculty Teaching Award, honouring Ontario's best university and college faculty, by the Ministry of Training, Colleges and Universities. She holds an M.B.A. from the Bradford University Management Centre in the U.K. and has extensive experience in marketing and advertising from both client and agency perspectives. Her experience spans two continents and covers a variety of industries including consumer packaged goods, cosmetics, food service, and personal care. She now channels her practical experience, knowledge, and creativity into the field of education, developing written materials, online resources, and educational tools that bring the subject of marketing alive. She is frequently called upon to mentor others in the field of education.

Harvey Skolnick is a marketing professor in the School of Business at the Sheridan Institute of Technology and Advanced Learning. He is the author of many articles that have appeared in *Marketing* magazine and other business publications. He holds an M.B.A. from the University of Toronto, specializing in marketing, and a B.Sc. from McGill University, specializing in psychology. Professor Skolnick's teaching interests include principles of marketing, consumer behaviour, integrated marketing communications, and marketing management. He has also previously taught at York University and the University of Toronto.

Brief Contents

Preface xii

PART 1 Understanding Marketing
Chapter 1 Marketing Fundamentals 2
Chapter 2 The Marketing Environment 22

PART 2 Understanding Markets and Their Behaviour
Chapter 3 Consumer Behaviour 40
Chapter 4 B2B Marketing 62
Chapter 5 Market Research 80
Chapter 6 Segmentation and Targeting 98

PART 3 Designing Marketing Strategies and Marketing Mix Elements
Chapter 7 Products and Brands 116
Chapter 8 New Product Development 134
Chapter 9 Pricing 156
Chapter 10 Distribution and Supply Chain 180
Chapter 11 Retailing and Wholesaling 202
Chapter 12 Integrated Marketing Communications and Interactive Marketing 224
Chapter 13 Promotional Tools 250
Chapter 14 Customer Relationship Management 276

PART 4 Putting It All Together
Chapter 15 Marketing & Strategic Planning 288

Appendix A Creating an Effective Marketing Plan
    See the Online Learning Centre: www.mcgrawhill.ca/olc/thecore

Glossary 307

Chapter Notes 315

Credits 323

Name Index 325

Company/Product Index 327

Subject Index 333

Contents

Preface xii

Part 1 Understanding Marketing

Chapter 1 Marketing Fundamentals 2

The Essence of Marketing 5
Focusing on Consumer Needs 5
Creating Customer Value 6
Appealing to Target Markets 6
Coordinating the Marketing Mix 6
The Marketing Process 8
What Can Be Marketed? 9
What Is a Market? 10
**The Evolution of Business
Philosophies 10**
**The Progression of Marketing
and Evolving Areas 12**
Customer Relationship
Management 13
Experiential Marketing 13
Corporate Social Responsibility 14
Marketing Careers 17
Summary 20
Key Terms and Concepts 20
Digital Marketing NewsFlash: HMV Reinvents Itself 8
Marketing NewsFlash: Marketing Ideas: Earth Hour 11
Marketing NewsFlash: CTV Helps the Idols Build a House 17
Online Video Case: Earth Hour

Chapter 2 The Marketing Environment 22

The Marketing Environment 25
A Marketing Environmental Scan 25
Demographic Forces 26
Socio-Cultural Forces 30
Economic Forces 32
Technological Forces 33
Competitive Forces 34
Regulatory Forces 36
A Marketing Environmental Scan in Practice 38
Summary 39
Key Terms and Concepts 39
Marketing NewsFlash: Baby Boomers' Interests 27
Digital Marketing NewsFlash: Flick-Fest's Focus on Global Warming 31
Focus on Ethics: Advertising Junk Food to Kids 37
Online Video Case: iPod Baby

Part 2 Understanding Markets and Their Behaviour

Chapter 3 Consumer Behaviour 40

Consumer Purchase Decision Process 42
Problem Recognition: Perceiving a Need 42
Information Search: Seeking Value 42
Alternative Evaluation: Assessing Value 43
Purchase Decision: Buying Value 44
Post-purchase Behaviour: Value in Consumption or Use 44
Involvement and Problem-Solving Variations 45
Situational Influences 46
**Psychological Influences on Consumer
Behaviour 46**
Motivation and Personality 47
Perception 48
Learning 49
Values, Beliefs, and Attitudes 50
Lifestyle 51
**Socio-Cultural Influences on
Consumer Behaviour 52**
Personal Influence 52
Reference Groups 54
Family Influence 54
Cultural and Subculture 56
Global Cultural Diversity 59
Summary 61
Key Terms and Concepts 61
*Digital Marketing NewsFlash:
Shopping Carts Abandoned 44*
*Focus on Ethics: The Power
of Word of Mouth 55*
*Marketing NewsFlash:
Companies Turn to
Blogging as a Tool of
Social Marketing 58*
Online Video Case: Best Buy

Chapter 4 B2B Marketing 62

The Nature and Size of Organizational Markets 64
Industrial Markets 64
Reseller Markets 66
Government Markets 66
Non-Profit Organizations 66
**Measuring Industrial, Reseller, Government, and
    Non-Profit Markets 67**
Characteristics of Organizational Buying 68
Derived Demand 68
Inelastic Demand 69
Fluctuating Demand 69
Size of the Order or
    Purchase 69
Number of Potential
    Buyers 70
Organizational Buying
    Objectives 70
Organizational Buying Criteria 70
Buyer–Seller Relationships and Supply Partnerships 71
**The Organizational Buying Process
    and the Buying Centre 72**
Stages in the Organizational Buying Process 72
The Buying Centre: A Cross-Functional Group 72
Online Buying in Organizational Markets 75
Prominence of Online Buying in Organizational
    Markets 75
E-Marketplaces: Virtual Organizational Markets 75
Online Auctions in Organizational Markets 77
Summary 78
Key Terms and Concepts 79
Marketing NewsFlash: Kodiak Comes Home 66
Marketing NewsFlash: Product Recalls 71
Digital Marketing NewsFlash: Companies Embrace Social Networking 76
Online Video Case: Lands' End

Chapter 5 Market Research 80

**Marketing Information Systems and Market
    Research 82**
What Is Market Research? 83
Research Classifications 84
The Six-Step Market Research Approach 86
Step 1: Define the Problem/Issue/Opportunity 86
Step 2: Define the Research Plan 87
Step 3: Conduct Exploratory Research 88
Step 4: Collect Quantitative Research Information 92
Step 5: Compile, Analyze, and Interpret Data 94
Step 6: Generate Report and Recommendations 94
The Future of Market Research 95
Summary 96
Key Terms and Concepts 96
Marketing NewsFlash: New Advertising Research Centre 85

Marketing NewsFlash: Tostitos Uses Market Research 92
Digital Marketing NewsFlash: Research Supports Pepsi Sponsorship 95
Online Video Case: 3M

Chapter 6 Segmentation and Targeting 98

Market Segmentation 101
Forms of Market Segmentation 102
Steps in Market Segmentation 105
Target Market Profiles 107
Geographics 107
Demographics 108
Psychographics 108
Behaviouristics 108
Product Positioning 110
Repositioning 111
Positioning Maps 112
**Market Segmentation, Target Markets, and
    Product Positioning in Practice 114**
Summary 115
Key Terms and Concepts 115
Digital Marketing NewsFlash: Koodo's Youth Market 102
*Marketing NewsFlash: A Healthy Twist for Clearly Canadian
    Beverages 111*
Marketing NewsFlash: McDonald's Makeover 113
Online Video Case: The Running Room

Part 3 Designing Marketing Strategies and Marketing Mix Elements

Chapter 7 Products and Brands 116

Types of Products 118
The Uniqueness of Services 119
Product Elements 121
The Total Product Concept 121
Packaging 121
Product Lines and Product Mixes 122

The Classification of Consumer and Business Products 123
Consumer Products 123
Business Products 124
Branding 125
Brand Loyalty 126
Brand Personality 127
Brand Name 127
Types of Brands 129
A Practical Look at Marketing Products and Brands 131
Summary 133
Key Terms and Concepts 133
Marketing NewsFlash: A Facelift for Sun-Rype 122
Focus on Ethics: Problems with the Scrabble Trademark? 127
Marketing NewsFlash: New TV Spokesperson for President's Choice 130
Online Video Case: Canada's Brands: Can They Compete?

Chapter 8 New Product Development 134
The Product Life Cycle 136
Introduction Stage 138
Growth Stage 138
Maturity Stage 139
Decline Stage 140
Shape of the Product Life Cycle 141
Extending the Product Life Cycle 142
Targeting Current Users with Extended Usage Strategies 142
Targeting New Consumers through New Marketing Approaches 142
Revitalizing a Product with Product Improvements and Line Extensions 143
Repositioning a Product 144
Introducing a New Product 144
Finding New Uses for a Product 144
New Product Innovation 145
The Adoption Curve 146
Why New Products Succeed or Fail 147
New Product Development 149
Approaches to New Product Development 149
The New Product Development Process 150
Summary 154

Key Terms and Concepts 155
Marketing NewsFlash: TSN Keeps Its Product Line Fresh 139
Digital Marketing NewsFlash: New Pittsburgh Arena Meets Youth Demographic 143
Marketing NewsFlash: Guinness Christmas Puddings—Success or Failure? 146
Online Video Case: BMW

Chapter 9 Pricing 156
Nature and Importance of Price 158
What Is a Price? 158
Price as an Indicator of Value 160
Price in the Marketing Mix 160
General Pricing Approaches 160
Demand-Oriented Approaches 160
Cost-Oriented Approaches 163
Profit-Oriented Approaches 164
Competition-Oriented Approaches 165
Estimating Demand and Revenue 166
Fundamentals of Estimating Demand 166
Fundamentals of Estimating Revenue 168
Determining Cost, Volume, and Profit Relationships 168
The Importance of Controlling Costs 168
Break-Even Analysis 169
Pricing Objectives and Constraints 170
Identifying Pricing Objectives 170
Identifying Pricing Constraints 172
Legal and Ethical Considerations 173
Global Pricing Strategy 174
Setting a Final Price 175
Step 1: Select an Approximate Price Level 175
Step 2: Set the List or Quoted Price 175
Step 3: Make Special Adjustments to the List or Quoted Price 176
Step 4: Monitor and Adjust Prices 178
Summary 178
Key Terms and Concepts 179
Marketing NewsFlash: The Alligator's New Look 162
Digital Marketing NewsFlash: iTunes in Battle with Wal-Mart 165
Focus on Ethics: Retailer Fined $1.2 Million for Misleading Sale Prices 174
Online Video Case: Washburn Guitars

Chapter 10 Distribution and Supply Chain 180

Nature and Importance of Marketing Channels 182

What Is a Marketing Channel? 182

Value Created by Intermediaries 183

Channel Structure and Organization 185

Marketing Channels for Consumer Goods and Services 185

Marketing Channels for Business Goods and Services 186

Electronic Marketing Channels 186

Multiple Channels and Strategic Alliances 187

Multichannel Marketing to the Online Consumer 187

Global Channel Strategy 189

Vertical Marketing Systems 190

Channel Choice and Management 193

Factors in Choosing a Marketing Channel 193

Channel Relationships: Conflict and Cooperation 194

Logistics and Supply Chain Management 195

Supply Chains versus Marketing Channels 196

Sourcing, Assembling, and Delivering a New Car: The Automotive Supply Chain 196

Supply Chain Management and Marketing Strategy 197

Two Concepts of Logistics Management in a Supply Chain 199

Total Logistics Cost Concept 199

Customer Service Concept 199

Summary 201

Key Terms and Concepts 201

Marketing NewsFlash: Wal-Mart Unveils Plan to Reduce Packaging 185

Digital Marketing NewsFlash: Reebok Website Allows Brand to Spend More Time with Consumers 188

Marketing NewsFlash: American Apparel Practises Backward Integration 192

Online Video Case: Christine Magee

Chapter 11 Retailing and Wholesaling 202

The Value of Retailing 204

Consumer Utilities Offered by Retailing 205

The Canadian Retail Scene 205

The Global Retail Picture 206

Retailing Strategy 207

Selecting a Target Market 207

Classifying Retail Outlets 207

Retailing Mix 212

Non-store Retailing 215

Online Retailing 217

The Changing Nature of Retailing: The Retail Life Cycle 219

The Retail Life Cycle 220

Wholesaling 220

Merchant Wholesalers 220

Agents and Brokers 221

Manufacturer's Branches and Offices 222

Summary 223

Key Terms and Concepts 223

Marketing NewsFlash: Tim's Takes on America 206

Marketing NewsFlash: Holt Renfrew Pampers Customers 211

Digital Marketing NewsFlash: The Long-Distance Journey of a Fast-Food Order 222

Online Video Case: Cora Mussely Tsouflidou

Chapter 12 Integrated Marketing Communications and Interactive Marketing 224

Developments in Marketing Communications 226

The Communications Process 229

Encoding and Decoding 229

Feedback 229

Noise 230

Promotional Tools 230

Advertising 230

Personal Selling 232

Public Relations 233

Sales Promotion 234
Direct Response 234
The IMC Promotional Mix 235
Integrated Marketing Communications 235
Creating IMC Promotional Programs 239
Developing the IMC Promotional Program 239
Interactive Marketing 242
Customer-Value and E-Commerce 243
Components of Interactive Marketing 245
Marketing on the Web 246
Components of Good Web Design 246
Webspeak for the Interactive Marketer 246
Summary 249
Key Terms and Concepts 249
Digital Marketing NewsFlash: Attention! Blogs and Social Media 232
Marketing NewsFlash: A Musical Campaign for Cheese 236
Marketing NewsFlash: Grolsch—Building Business on a Small Budget 238
Online Video Case: Las Vegas

Chapter 13 Promotional Tools 250
Developments in Promotion 252
Developing the IMC Promotional Program 254
Advertising 254
Key Considerations in
    Advertising Planning 255
Advertising Media
    Choices 257
Sales Promotion 263
Consumer-Oriented Sales
    Promotion 264
Trade-Oriented Sales
    Promotion 265
Public Relations 266
Public Relations Tools 267
**Direct Response
    Marketing 267**
Personal Selling 270
Order Taking 271
Order Getting 271
Developments in the Sales Industry 272
Summary 275
Key Terms and Concepts 275
Digital Marketing NewsFlash: Dove "Evolution" Goes Viral 261
Focus on Ethics: Greenpeace Takes on Unilever 266
Marketing NewsFlash: Purina's Pet Community & Discovery Centre 268
Online Video Cases: (1) New Media: Friend or Foe? (2) Dove Evolution

Chapter 14 Customer Relationship
Management 276
Customer Relationship Management 278
CRM Entails Cultural Changes 279
Customer Acquisition 281
Customer Retention 281

Loyalty Programs 281
Data Mining 282
Customer Lifetime Value 283
Customer Service Component of CRM 284
The Worth of Retaining Marginal Customers 284
CRM and Customer Reaquisition 284
Summary 287
Key Terms and Concepts 287
Digital Marketing NewsFlash: The Power of Moms 280
Marketing NewsFlash: The Popularity of Loyalty Cards 283
Focus on Ethics: WestJet Walks the Talk 285
Online Video Case: Razor Suleman

Part 4 Putting It All Together

Chapter 15 Marketing & Strategic
Planning 288
Organizations and Their Levels of Strategy 290
Levels in Organizations and How Marketing Links to
    Them 291
Strategic Issues in Organizations 291
Setting Strategic Directions 294
A Look Around: Where Are We Now? 294
Growth Strategies: Where Do We Want to Go? 295
The Strategic Marketing Process 298
Strategic Marketing Process: The Planning Phase 298
Strategic Marketing Process: The Implementation Phase 302
Strategic Marketing Process: The Evaluation Phase 303
Summary 304
Key Terms and Concepts 304
Focus on Ethics: Consumer Confusion over Green Products 292
Digital Marketing NewsFlash: Nintendo Captures Adult Market 296
Marketing NewsFlash: Famous Canadian Brands 302
Online Video Case: Starbucks

Appendix A Creating an Effective Marketing Plan
    See the Online Learning Centre: www.mcgrawhill.ca/olc/thecore

Glossary 307

Chapter Notes 315

Credits 323

Name Index 325

Company/Product Index 327

Subject Index 333

Preface

Welcome to the exciting, dynamic, and challenging field of marketing! If you've been on the web, in a store, working in a company, or a consumer of any of the thousands of products and services available in our marketplace, you are already involved with marketing, and you have probably already noticed many of the extraordinary changes taking place. You are most likely familiar with online social networking sites such as Facebook and MySpace. Some of you read blogs and listen to podcasts. Marketers are interested in learning more about these types of communication vehicles, and they want to make a presence there, "joining in the conversation," so to speak, with consumers. Personalized advertising, multichannel retailing, cashless vending, customized products, online coupons, web-based surveys, and interactive media are just a few of the other indications that marketing is racing into a new era. At the same time, many traditional elements of the discipline, such as segmentation, new product development, and pricing, are growing in importance and use. The combination of the current and the traditional elements of marketing creates a truly exceptional topic to study and understand. We are all marketed to, and we find marketing all around us, every day of our lives.

Our goal with the Second Canadian Edition of this text is to present the concepts essential to an introductory marketing course in an engaging magazine-like format to better reflect this dynamic, ever-changing field.

What *is* our pedagogical framework? First, we use an active-learning approach that involves students in the text by combining facts, figures, information, questions, and photos in an engaging, experiential fashion. Second, we incorporate many current examples using products and services that students will recognize and may have purchased as consumers. Third, our in-chapter study aids and design elements—such as "Ask Yourself" concept checks and easy-to-read figures—were developed to match the learning styles of today's students.

We are gratified by the growing interest in this approach to the study of marketing. Feedback from students and instructors continues to reinforce our pedagogical style. We hope that you will find *Marketing: The Core,* Second Canadian Edition, a key factor in your exploration of the knowledge, skills, and tools of the marketing discipline.

Distinctive Features of *The Core* for Marketing Students

We have developed many important, student-focused features that are prominent in every chapter. The text is very current, very Canadian, and very inviting with its new magazine-style format. It is full of up-to-date, newsworthy facts and information to which students can relate. It invites and entices students to want to read and find out more.

- *Magazine-style format.* The text has been designed in a dynamic magazine look to appeal to Canadian students. Each chapter contains new features developed to keep students reading, including an opening vignette, Marketing NewsFlash boxes (two to three per chapter, including one with a digital focus), Focus on Ethics boxes, Marketing Tips from experts in the field, pulled quotes that highlight key chapter elements, interesting quick-hit numbers in Marketing Meters and Data Boxes, and the adAlyze feature, which asks students to critically evaluate a current advertisement.

- *Engaging writing style.* Our easy-to-read writing style is designed to engage students through active-learning techniques, timely and interesting examples, and challenging applications.

- *Personal look at marketing professionals.* Each chapter begins with a marketing vignette that provides vivid and accurate descriptions of Canadian marketing professionals in action. The vignettes allow students to personalize marketing and identify possible career interests and role models.

- *Contemporary and classic real-world examples.* We use the most current Canadian examples—examples that students are likely to recognize from their own experiences in the marketplace.

- *Built-in learning aids.* Learning Objectives, "Ask Yourself" concept check questions, key terms, and chapter summaries are found in each chapter. Internet exercises, discussion forums, and application questions on the Online Learning Centre reinforce learning and allow students to assess their progress.

- *In-class activities.* The Instructor's Manual contains chapter-by-chapter in-class discussion questions for each Marketing NewsFlash, with worksheets for instructors to include in class as written activities.
- *Up-to-date videos.* There is a written video case and video for each chapter on the Online Learning Centre. The videos add an exciting visual perspective to the companies, products, and marketing decision makers discussed in the cases. Questions at the end of each video case, with suggested responses and in-class worksheets found in the Instructor's Manual, make them even more interactive.

Organization and Content of *The Core*

Marketing: The Core, Second Canadian Edition, is divided into four parts. Part 1, "Understanding Marketing," looks first at what marketing is and how it creates customer value and customer relationships (Chapter 1). Chapter 2 analyzes the major environmental factors in our changing marketing environment.

Part 2, "Understanding Markets and Their Behaviour," first describes, in Chapter 3, how individual consumers reach buying decisions. Chapter 4 looks at industrial and organizational buyers and how they make purchase decisions. Chapter 5 examines the marketing research function and how information about prospective consumers is linked to marketing strategy and decisions. The process of segmenting and targeting markets and positioning products appears in Chapter 6.

Part 3, "Designing Marketing Strategies and Marketing Mix Elements," covers the four Ps of marketing: product, price, placement, and promotion. The product element is divided into two chapters. Chapter 7 looks at the way existing products, services, and brands are managed. Chapter 8 discusses the development of new products and the product life cycle. Pricing is discussed focusing on the way organizations set prices (Chapter 9). Two chapters address the place aspects of marketing: "Distribution and Supply Chain" (Chapter 10) and "Retailing and Wholesaling" (Chapter 11). Chapter 12 discusses integrated marketing communications and interactive marketing, topics that have grown in importance in the marketing discipline recently. The primary forms of communication—advertising, sales promotion, public relations, direct response marketing, and personal selling are covered in detail in "Promotional Tools" (Chapter 13). Chapter 14, "Customer Relationship Management,"

examines the three stages of CRM: customer acquisition, customer retention, and customer reacquisition.

Part 4, "Putting It All Together," provides an overview of the strategic marketing process that occurs in an organization.

Finally, Appendix A on the Online Learning Centre provides a guide to preparing a marketing plan.

New to the Second Canadian Edition

Marketing: The Core, Second Canadian Edition, has been redesigned to be a real and tangible reflection of current marketing practices in Canada. The material is not only extremely current but also borrows from the techniques used in the magazine industry to provide an interesting and engaging read. This book, with all its interesting content and visual appeal, encourages the student to read . . . and keep reading!

In line with this new approach, most chapter titles have been given more direct names, and the following changes have occurred:

- Two chapters have been deleted: "Ethics and Social Responsibility in Marketing" and "Reaching Global Markets." These topics have been woven throughout the text in a number of Marketing NewsFlash and Focus on Ethics boxes, with further emphasis included within the chapters.
- Two chapters have been combined: "Advertising, Sales Promotion, and Public Relations" and "Direct Marketing and Personal Selling." This leaves the book with two full chapters on promotion and expanded coverage of the Internet.
- Two chapters have changed sequencing within the text to provide a more logical flow: "Marketing and Strategic Planning" is now at the end of the book to facilitate teaching of this subject, while "New Product Development" follows the chapter on "Products and Brands," in line with the emphasis in the industry.
- A new chapter on the increasingly important area of "Customer Relationship Management" has been added to introduce students to this newly evolving area.

In addition, a number of changes have been made within the chapters to guarantee currency:

Chapter 1: Marketing Fundamentals

This chapter has been rewritten to provide a vibrant introduction to the book, covering topics essential to the understanding of marketing and recent developments in the field. The following elements have been added:

- New opening vignette on the launch of a new cell-phone in Canada by LG
- New section on "The Progression of Marketing and Evolving Areas"
- New section on "Experiential Marketing"
- New section on "Corporate Social Responsibility"
- New section on "Marketing Careers"

In addition, the section on "Customer Relationship Management" has been expanded and clarified.

Chapter 2: The Marketing Environment

This chapter has been revised to clearly group the marketing environmental factors and provide current, relevant examples on how these factors are used by marketers. The following elements have been added:

- New opening vignette on the use of the Internet by the Childhood Cancer Foundation Candlelighters Canada
- New section on "Socio-Cultural Forces"
- New section on "Marketing Environmental Scan in Practice"

In addition, the section on culture has been moved from demographics to the new section on "Socio-Cultural Forces."

Chapter 3: Consumer Behaviour

This chapter has been updated to touch on global culture. Modifications include the following:

- New opening vignette on the use of consumer touch points by the advertising agency ZenithOptimedia
- New section on the importance and elements of "Global Cultural Diversity"

Chapter 4: B2B Marketing

This chapter has been modified to include the following:

- New opening vignette on IBM's approach to the business-to-business market
- New concepts of "Fluctuating Demand" and "Inelastic Demand"

Chapter 5: Market Research

This chapter has been streamlined to provide a clear focus and sequence to the market research process. The following elements have been added:

- New opening vignette on the market research firm Sklar Wilton & Associates
- Explanation of qualitative and quantitative research

- Heightened focus on secondary online research resources
- New section on "The Future of Market Research"

In addition, this chapter incorporates the topic of sampling within the market research process, and the topic of sales forecasting has been removed.

Chapter 6: Segmentation and Targeting

This chapter includes a revamping of the steps of the market segmentation process. The following elements have been added:

- New opening vignette on Atomic Skis' approach to segmenting the ski-equipment market
- New section on "Individualized Marketing"
- Increased focus on SWOT analysis
- Newly revamped section on "Steps in Market Segmentation"
- New section on "Target Market Profiles"
- New section on "Market Segmentation, Target Markets, and Product Positioning in Practice"
- New section on "Repositioning"

In addition, a more practical emphasis has been added to the topics of market segmentation, target markets, and positioning.

Chapter 7: Products and Brands

This chapter now focuses on products and brands, switching places with the chapter on new products. These two chapters have been reorganized to ensure that the material pertinent to products and brands is grouped together in Chapter 7, while the new product material is found together in Chapter 8. The following elements have been moved, or added, to this chapter on products and brands:

- New opening vignette on the San Diego Chargers explaining the relevance of products to the sports/entertainment industry
- New section on "Types of Products"
- New section on "The Total Product Concept"
- New section on "The Classification of Consumer and Business Products"
- New discussion of trademarks, patents, and copyrights
- New section on "A Practical Look at Marketing Products and Brands"

In addition to the above, the topics of "The Product Life Cycle" and "Managing the Product Life Cycle" have been removed from this chapter and reworked into Chapter 8.

Chapter 8: New Product Development

This chapter has been reorganized to group all the new product information together in a single chapter. The changes are as follows:

- New opening vignette on President's Choice's approach to product innovation
- New section on "The Product Life Cycle"
- New section on "The Adoption Curve"

In addition to the above, the sections on "The Product—Total Product Concept," "The Variations of Products," and "Classifying Goods and Services" have been removed from this chapter and reworked into Chapter 7.

Chapter 9: Pricing

This chapter has been updated to touch on global pricing issues. Modifications are as follows:

- New opening vignette on Nearly Famous Enterprises and its approach to pricing
- New section on "Global Pricing Strategy"

Chapter 10: Distribution and Supply Chain

This chapter has been updated to touch on global marketing channels. Modifications are as follows:

- New opening vignette on Sleep Country Canada
- New section on "Global Channel Strategy"

Chapter 11: Retailing and Wholesaling

This chapter updates facts on the retail market in Canada and has the following new element:

- New opening vignette on Cadillac Fairview's new lifestyle centre at the Shops at Don Mills

Chapter 12: Integrated Marketing Communications and Interactive Marketing

This chapter provides a more detailed look at integrated marketing communications programs and the role of the Internet in promotion. New to this chapter are the following:

- New opening vignette on product integration in CTV's *Canadian Idol*
- New section on "Developments in Marketing Communications"
- New coverage on "Marketing on the Web" and "Components of Good Web Design"
- Expanded coverage on the use of the Internet in promotional programs

In addition to the above, the discussions of both integrated marketing communications and interactive marketing have been expanded to reflect their increased role in promotion. The chapter also presents a more balanced view of all the promotional tools available to marketers.

Chapter 13: Promotional Tools

This chapter provides a detailed review of each promotional element. Two chapters from the previous edition on this subject have been combined to provide a more cohesive and streamlined approach to teaching this subject. The changes are as follows:

- New opening vignette on *doug agency inc.* and its campaigns for Oxfam and York University
- Combined Chapter 16 ("Advertising, Sales Promotion, and Public Relations") and Chapter 17 ("Personal Selling and Sales Management") from the previous edition
- New section on "Developments in Promotion"
- New section on "Key Considerations in Advertising Planning"
- Explanations for each type of direct response marketing tool

In addition to the above, this chapter has been updated with Canadian facts, and the Internet section has been revamped to include new terms.

Chapter 14: Customer Relationship Management

This chapter is new to this edition and looks at the increasingly important area of customer relationship management. It starts with a glimpse into the world of loyalty programs and includes the following:

- Opening vignette on Alliance Data and customer relationship management
- Section on "Customer Relationship Management"
- Section on "Customer Acquisition"
- Section on "Customer Retention"
- Section on "Loyalty Programs"
- Section on "Data Mining"
- Section on "Customer Lifetime Value"
- Section on "Customer Service"
- Section on "Customer Reacquisition"

Chapter 15: Marketing & Strategic Planning

This chapter looks at strategic marketing planning. It has been placed at the end of the text to allow students to gain a greater understanding of marketing before embarking on this more complex topic. This chapter has been updated with the following:

- New opening vignette on the strategic planning process at the Humber River Regional Hospital

A Student's Guide to *Marketing: The Core*

Marketing: The Core offers an array of features to help you learn and apply the concepts.

Chapter-Opening Vignettes

Each chapter hooks you with a vignette that focuses on the programs of top Canadian marketers. No revamp of an article here—only current facts, real approaches, and tangible examples from one-on-one interviews! The topics are vibrant, selected intentionally for students, and cover companies and products such as LG cellphones, Atomic Skis, the San Diego Chargers, President's Choice, *Canadian Idol*, and the advertising agency *doug agency inc.,* just to name a few. The chapter-opening example is then often integrated into parts of the narrative and exhibits throughout the chapter.

The Core

This unique feature is introduced at the beginning of each chapter, designed to guide you through your study of introductory marketing. We created this model to show the essentials of each chapter and the progression of topics as you move through the book.

Marketing NewsFlashes

This feature provides exciting, current examples of marketing applications in action, making the material relevant and memorable. You will find two to three Marketing NewsFlashes in each chapter.

A Student's Guide to *Marketing: The Core*

Focus on Ethics

These boxes increase your awareness and assessment of current topics of ethical and social concern.

Marketing Tips

These valuable thoughts from the experts—real-world marketers—are relevant to the topics discussed in each chapter.

Marketing ▶ tip

"The attributes of quality and consumer confidence come from a consistent marketing approach based on a solid brand positioning. Developing and growing a brand becomes an essential part of a marketer's responsibility in growing the business."

Ken Derrett, vice president and chief marketing officer, San Diego Chargers

Marketing ▶ tip

"Innovation is about the journey and applying your learning over time to create successful products and brands."

Ian Gordon, senior vice president, Loblaw Companies Ltd.

Data Boxes

These boxes sprinkle the text with interesting, engaging facts.

Top Worldwide Brand Rankings (2008)

Ranking	Brand	Brand Value (US$ millions)
1	Coca-Cola	66,667
2	IBM	59,007
3	Microsoft	59,031
4	GE	53,086
5	Nokia	35,942
6	Toyota	34,050

Source: Interbrand, "Best Global Brands: 2008 Rankings," accessed at www.interbrand.com/best_global_brands.aspx.

Top 10 Canadian Brands (2008)

Ranking	Brand	Brand Value (C$ million)
1	BlackBerry	5,607.7
2	RBC	4,141.1
3	TD Canada Trust	3,779.6
4	Shoppers Drug Mart	3,137.5
5	Petro-Canada	3,132.6
6	Manulife	2,550.9
7	Bell	2,537.0
8	Scotiabank	1,870.4
9	Canadian Tire	1,828.5
10	Tim Hortons	1,604.6

Source: Interbrand, *Competing in the Global Brand Economy: Best Canadian Brands 2008*, June 2008, accessed, at www.ourfishbowl.com/images/surveys/BestCanadianBrands2008.pdf.

Marketing Meters

These elements feature unique, relevant, facts that you'll want to share with friends.

Research on the impact of the writers' strike on TV viewing

Watching the same 72%   Watching less   Watching more 3%

Number of Branded Products Appearing in Movies Released in 2008

Sex and the City **94** brands   Iron Man **42** brands   The Dark Knight **17** brands   Kung Fu Panda **0** brands

marketing meter

Source: Brandchannel.com, "Leading brand appearances this year," *Brandcameo—brands*, 2008, accessed, at www.brandchannel.com/brandcameo_brands.asp?brand_year=2008#brand_list.

Supplement Guide to
Marketing: The Core

To help instructors and students meet today's teaching and learning challenges, *Marketing: The Core*, Second Canadian Edition, offers a complete, integrated supplements package.

For Instructors

Superior Service Service takes on a whole new meaning with McGraw-Hill Ryerson and *Marketing: The Core*. More than just bringing you the textbook, we have consistently raised the bar in terms of innovation and educational research. These investments in learning and the educational community have helped us to understand the needs of students and educators across the country and allowed us to foster the growth of truly innovative, integrated learning.

Integrated Learning Your Integrated Learning Sales Specialist is a McGraw-Hill Ryerson representative who has the experience, product knowledge, training, and support to help you assess and integrate any of our products, technology, and services into your course for optimum teaching and learning performance. Whether it's using our test bank software, helping your students improve their grades, or putting your entire course online, your iLearning Sales Specialist is there to help you do it. Contact your local iLearning Sales Specialist today to learn how to maximize all of McGraw-Hill Ryerson's resources!

iLearning Services Program McGraw-Hill Ryerson offers a unique *i*Services package designed for Canadian faculty. Our mission is to equip providers of higher education with superior tools and resources required for excellence in teaching. For additional information, visit www.mcgrawhill.ca/highereducation/*i*services.

Teaching, Learning & Technology Conference Series The educational environment has changed tremendously in recent years, and McGraw-Hill Ryerson continues to be committed to helping you acquire the skills you need to succeed in this new milieu. Our innovative Teaching, Technology, & Learning Conference Series brings faculty together from across Canada with 3M Teaching Excellence award winners to share teaching and learning best practices in a collaborative and stimulating environment. Pre-conference workshops on general topics such as teaching large classes and technology integration are also offered. In addition, we will work with you at your own institution to customize workshops that best suit the needs of your faculty.

CourseSmart CourseSmart brings together thousands of textbooks across hundreds of courses in an eTextbook format providing unique benefits to students and faculty. By purchasing an eTextbook, students can save up to 50 percent off the cost of a print textbook, reduce their impact on the environment, and gain access to powerful Web tools for learning including full text search, notes and highlighting, and e-mail tools for sharing notes between classmates. For faculty, CourseSmart provides instant access to review and compare textbooks and course materials in their discipline area without the time, cost, and environmental impact of mailing print copies. For further details contact your iLearning Sales Specialist or go to www.coursesmart.com.

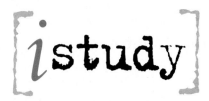

iInteract iLearn iSucceed

iStudy (www.istudymarketing.ca)

In partnership with Youthography, a Canadian youth research company, and hundreds of students from across Canada, McGraw-Hill Ryerson conducted extensive student research on student study habits, behaviours, and attitudes—we asked questions and listened . . . and we heard some things we didn't expect. We had two goals: to help faculty be more efficient in and out of the classroom by providing a study tool that would help them improve student engagement and to help students learn their course material and get better grades. Through this research, we gained a better understanding of how students study—and how we could make vast improvements to our current online study tools. The result is a study tool that students overwhelmingly said is *better* and there's *nothing else like it out there*. iStudy really is the first study tool built by students for students. Getting better grades really is only a click away!

- *Study Plan.* An innovative tool that helps students customize their own learning experience. Students can diagnose their knowledge with pre- and post-tests and search contents of the entire learning package for content specific to the topic they're studying to add these resources to their study plan. Students told us the act of creating a study plan is how they actually study and that having the opportunity to have everything in one place, with the ability to search, customize and prioritize the class resources, was critical. No other publisher provides this type of tool and students told us without a doubt, the "Study Plan" feature is the most valuable tool they have used to help them study.

- *eText.* Now students can search the textbook online, too! When struggling with a concept or reviewing for an exam, students can conduct key word searches to quickly find the content they need.

- *Homework Assessment.* iStudy assessment activities don't stop with students. There is material for instructors to leverage as well. For *Marketing: The Core*, this includes quizzes you can use in class, assign as homework, or add to exams.

Online Learning Centre (www.mcgrawhill.ca/olc/thecore)

The Online Learning Centre includes a password-protected website for instructors that features additional in-class materials, including questions and discussions, Internet exercises, video case studies, Ask Yourself and adAlyze answers, and the "Creating a Successful Marketing Plan" appendix (see the Student Online Learning Centre below for more details on all of these features), and offers all the necessary instructor supplements:

- *Instructor's Manual.* The thoroughly revised Instructor's Manual includes lecture notes; a new "Bring it to Life" section with discussion questions, teaching notes, and teaching suggestions for the Marketing NewsFlash boxes, Focus on Ethics boxes, video cases, and other in-class activities. It also provides answers to "Ask Yourself," adAlyze, Applying Marketing Concepts and Perspectives, and Discussion Forum questions.

- *Microsoft® PowerPoint® presentations and digital assets.* These incorporate high-quality images, including figure slides, product shots, and advertisements.

- *Computerized Test Bank.* This tool contains questions categorized by topic and level of learning (definitional, conceptual, or application). The EZ Test program allows you to select any of the questions, make changes if desired, and add new questions—and quickly print out a finished set, customized to your course.

- *Video case studies.* A unique series of 16 contemporary marketing cases is available. Each video case corresponds with chapter-specific topics and a written case.

Course Management

Content cartridges are available for the course management systems WebCT and Blackboard. These platforms provide instructors with user-friendly, flexible teaching tools. Please contact your local McGraw-Hill Ryerson iLearning Sales Specialist for details.

 ## For Students

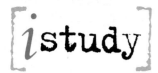

iStudy Marketing (www.istudymarketing.ca)

This tool was developed to help students master concepts and achieve better grades with all the learning tools they've come to expect, plus a lot more! Some of the key features include pre- and post-tests tied to the chapter learning objectives, to assess mastery and monitor improvement, additional quizzing material, marketing videos, and an e-Book for easy reference. iStudy offers the best, most convenient way to learn, interact, and succeed.

Online Learning Centre (www.mcgrawhill.ca/olc/thecore)

The Online Learning Centre for the text offers chapter outlines, multiple-choice quizzes, and other study tools, including:

- *Questions and discussion.* Two features allow you to test your knowledge and your capability to apply the material covered in each chapter. *Questions: Applying Marketing Concepts and Perspectives* asks you to think about the marketing material and check yourself on your comprehension of it. *Discussion Forum* presents a thought-provoking scenario for you to discuss with other students.

- *Internet exercises.* These exercises ask you to think critically about a specific company's use of the Internet—helping you apply your knowledge of key chapter concepts, terms, and topics, as well as evaluate the success or failure of the company's efforts.

- *Video case studies.* The Online Learning Centre feature provides an up-close look at a company example—reinforcing the chapter content, while bringing the material to life. Earth Hour, iPod, The Running Room, and Sleep Country Canada are just a few of the exciting video cases incorporated into *Marketing: The Core*, Second Canadian Edition.

- *Appendix A: Creating a Successful Marketing Plan.* Also on the Online Learning Centre, this guide to planning, researching, and writing a winning marketing plan is a resource that you can use in a number of ways, throughout your use of this text and beyond. It incorporates the marketing plan rationale, detailed plan contents, and effective design and execution of the plan, as well as checklists for implementing and evaluating the marketing plan.

Acknowledgements

Special words of appreciation go out to the following individuals, marketers, and business people who spent their valuable time imparting interesting insights on the world of marketing. Your passion for the industry and your interest in helping to educate up-and-coming marketers is a credit to each of you. You have helped make this book fresh, spirited, real, and dynamic. We thank you:

Andrew Barrett
Lucy Brun
Barbara Collins
Ken Derrett
Neil Everett
Ian Gordon
Ruth Klostermann
Mary Kreuk
Christine Magee
Brandy Martin
Deborah McKenzie
Anabella Mandel
Rob Morash
Anne Morash
Luke Sklar
Judith Shaw
David Stones, and
Mike Welling.

In addition, we would like to thank Anna Bligh and Tara Wood, from the World Wildlife Fund (WWF), and Kim Feinberg, from Tomorrow Trust, for their multimedia materials and helpful insights, which take us further afield into non-profit marketing in South Africa, Australia, and back again into the Canadian market. Special thanks also go to Janet Kestin and Coby Shuman at Ogilvy & Mather for their assistance in securing the Unilever Dove "Evolution" multimedia materials. To the companies who have provided us with visuals to include in the book we extend our appreciation.

We also extend our gratitude to the people at McGraw-Hill Ryerson for their professionalism, namely Leanna MacLean (executive sponsoring editor) and Denise Foote (senior developmental editor), who managed to cheerfully keep the process moving forward. Kara Stahl (supervising editor) and Mike Kelly (copy editor) were invaluable in their attention to detail and ability to juggle so many elements. We would be remiss if we did not acknowledge the contributions of the design team at Valid Design.

Finally, we would like to recognize the work that was put into the First Canadian Edition of *Marketing: The Core* by Gerard Edwards and Carla Gail Tibbo, both of Douglas College, and the suggestions and insights provided by the following reviewers. These comments have helped guide and steer this Second Canadian Edition.

Cathy Ace, *Simon Fraser University*
Edmund Baumann, *Humber College Institute of Technology & Advanced Learning*
Laura Brideau, *New Brunswick Community College*
Peter Burgess, *George Brown College*
Brahm Canzer, *John Abbott College*
Morai Forer, *Saskatchewan Institute of Applied Science and Technology*
Paula Greaves, *George Brown College*
Allan Green, *Red River College*
Robert Krider, *Simon Fraser University*
Melanie Lang, *University of Guelph*
Donna Lazdowski, *Mount Royal College*
Susan Myrden, *Memorial University of Newfoundland*
Marg O'Brien, *Algonquin College*
Christine W. Oldfield, *Centennial College*
Beth Pett, *Niagara College*
Saba Safdar, *University of Guelph*
Diana Serafini, *Dawson College*
Janice Shearer, *Mohawk College*
Dea Watson, *Conestoga College*
Barb Watts, *Georgian College*

We are truly grateful to each of you, and of course to our families for their enthusiasm and support. Thank you.

Christina Clements and Harvey Skolnick

Marketing Fundamentals

In 2008, LG Canada brashly launched a new line of cellphones with a marketing program that beat Apple's iPhone to the punch. "The essence of marketing is discovering consumer insights," says Andrew Barrett, vice president of marketing for LG Canada. Barrett explains that you must be "relevant and engaging enough for consumers to choose your product or service," and with that in mind, LG Canada launched the LG Vantage, Venus, and Vu touch phones with a marketing program that could not be missed. The program's purpose was to create awareness and hype for the new products, prompt support from retailers, and encourage consumers to gather information and buy the product. LG flirted with consumers and encouraged them to experience and buy the phones. This resulted in revenues for LG and an example of marketing that works.

The youthful *target market* for the touch phones was the style-conscious and techno-savvy university and college crowd. All launch elements of the new LG cellphones were designed with these Canadian consumers in mind—no quick launch of a U.S. product here. Research determined *product* needs, that is, which features were most appealing, what technology was required, and which product names should be used. The *price* was established based on a competitive evaluation and the fact that expensive data plans were an issue with consumers. Importantly, *distribution* was worked through with the cellphone carriers, Bell, Rogers, and Telus, whose support was needed for the product to be carried at retail and displayed in stores. Once these elements were finalized, a *promotional* campaign was crafted to fit the needs of the target audience and create a buzz in the market.

Three sleekly designed phones with intuitive touch screens surfaced. Their features included instant messaging and the ability to listen to the radio, watch mobile TV, and access video on demand—all features designed to appeal to the target market's desire for technology, style, and entertainment. To address consumer concerns that perhaps the

LEARNING OBJECTIVES

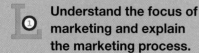 Understand the focus of marketing and explain the marketing process.

 Define the marketing mix.

 Understand the difference between goods, services, and ideas.

L₄ Describe the evolution of different business philosophies and understand how marketing has evolved.

L₅ Understand what careers exist in marketing.

phone was not heeding their commands, LG introduced "vibe-feedback technology": The phone now shuddered slightly, indicating that the phone was responding. A faster processor was also included to make it the fastest downloading phone in Canada, even faster than home-based high-speed Internet. Best of all, it did not require consumers to purchase expensive data plans, an issue with competing products.

The launch platform was crafted to pique consumer interest and encourage purchase. The promotional campaign stood out from the crowd in that it considered the target market's social interests, activities, and media habits. The campaign included public relations, advertising, and point-of-sale efforts.

Public relations: Media journalists were invited to attend a lunchtime launch event staged at Sultan's Tent, a Toronto restaurant. The event treated guests to massages, capitalizing on the touch theme, piquing their interest with facts about things that most consumers are unlikely to touch, such as wet cement or a luxury car. Ultimately, the new touch phones were unveiled exposing their chic designs and features. The event resulted in valuable press mentions.

TV advertising: Following the launch, LG kicked off its advertising campaign with TV spots airing on primetime TV shows such as *American Idol, The Late Show with David Letterman,* and *Pussycat Dolls Present: Girlicious*—all shows watched by the target market. The spots focused on a typical young man, forbidden all his life to touch things, until along came the LG touch phones. The spots intentionally used humour to resonate with this group and drive them to a website to interact with the product.

Print-based advertising: A number of provocative washroom ads were created to appear in bars and restaurants in major Canadian cities. Nine ads were rotated to keep them fresh and engaging for this particular demographic. Headlines that raised eyebrows included "Unbutton your phone," "Another good reason to wash your hands," and "You're going to want a daily manicure." A superboard appeared across a major highway getting the attention of daily commuters.

Online advertising: Online banner ads, a keyword search program, and a microsite were designed to intrigue the target audience. At the microsite visitors could interact with the phone, be enticed by its design, and be amused by the advertising. In addition, e-mail alerts were sent to LG's database of customers, which had been built to develop these important linkages.

Point-of-sale material: Finally, point-of-sale signage was created in collaboration with the phone carriers—Bell, Rogers, and Telus—for display at retail.

All in all, LG successfully launched its Vantage, Venus, and Vu touch phones with a marketing program that stood out. All elements of the marketing mix—product, price, place, and promotion—were carefully crafted to meet consumer needs and appeal distinctly to the target audience. Andrew Barrett, a long-time Canadian marketer, tells us that marketing success is rooted in understanding consumer needs and delivering on those needs. He points to the 2008 Leger Corporate Reputation Survey, in which LG Canada moved up an unprecedented 26 spots in the rankings to no. 39, a feat that Barrett attributes to the company's increased focus on marketing. "Consumers are busy in their worlds and not in our worlds, so to capture their attention we must be highly creative in what we do," he says. Barrett explains that you must never lose sight of your consumer, or you may miss your window of opportunity.

LG's marketing program kept a watchful eye on the competition, while considering the needs of target consumers every step of the way. It created *products* that Canadians wanted to buy, worked to ensure that *pricing* was in line with consumer needs, and put *distribution* plans in place so that consumers could purchase the product at retail. LG's creative *promotional program* was the final element used to capture consumers' interest and pique their curiosity with initiatives that were daring and imaginative. The program allowed LG to dance with consumers, satisfy their needs, and ultimately sell product. It shows us the marketing concept in action. 🍎

The Essence of Marketing

L① Marketing success is rooted in focusing on consumers and providing them with value through products and services that meet their needs. The challenge is to craft marketing programs that create a distinct image for the product, setting it apart from the competition, while also appealing to consumers' needs. The Canadian market is very competitive and if you, as a marketer, do not focus on providing consumers with products and services that meet their needs, a competitor will do so. The launch of LG touch phones is a prime example. Canadians had been waiting for Apple to launch its iPhone for over a year. There was pent-up demand and consumers were going to extreme lengths to purchase the iPhone from the U.S. LG rose to the occasion, did its research, and met consumer needs head-on by launching a product tailored to the Canadian marketplace.

It is important to understand that marketers' ultimate objectives are to realize a profit, or, if working in the non-profit sector, to generate revenue to fund their programs and run their operations. In this chapter, we will focus on the "for-profit" sector.

Focusing on Customer Needs

Successful marketing programs focus on consumer needs and try to develop programs that delight the consumer and encourage customer loyalty. Frequently, the challenge is to clearly determine these needs and to understand how they can best be met with meaningful marketing approaches. This may appear easy, but in reality it is often faced with challenges: Consumers do not always know what they want; consumers do not always want to articulate their feelings; and, in some cases, consumers are unable to communicate and rationalize their preferred choices. In many product categories, such as fragrances or luxury cars, choices are not entirely rational, but partly based on self-image and emotional attachment to a brand. In these

The Core: Chapter 1

The focus of marketing is satisfying consumers' needs.

Target Customers

In marketing, the consumer is central to everything you do.

cases, consumers may find it difficult to articulate their preferences, and marketers may become misguided in their observations and conclusions.

Research can often be a difficult area to navigate for marketers. It requires insight into where a brand should be heading, together with the flexibility and clarity of thought to discern good ideas from bad. Often the results are not crystal clear and this requires marketers to take calculated risks in their marketing approaches. Sometimes marketers may not be asking consumers the right questions, which can result in important oversights. Take, for example, the Sony Walkman. This idea initially failed in consumer research because Sony's line of questioning focused on technology rather than on teenagers' lifestyles and their love of music.

Research can be further complicated when dealing with certain target groups that may be difficult to find, or that may be unable to express their thoughts. Take, for instance, a situation where a toy company requires feedback from young children. Members

The essence of marketing is focusing on the consumer.

of this target group will be unable to crystallize their thoughts and clearly communicate their ideas. Consider another situation where a company needs to get feedback from doctors about an anti-smoking marketing program. This target group may be too busy to provide feedback to the marketing group.

Creating Customer Value

Developing customer loyalty is prompting many firms to focus on customer value by providing customers with products and services that have added value. This is often achieved by delivering outstanding value through a combination of (1) pricing strategies, (2) product design, and (3) service elements. Companies such as Zellers focus on providing the lowest prices; Mountain Equipment Co-op claims to provide the best products; and companies such as Pizza-Pizza pioneered their fast delivery service as a point of difference. Apple uses a combination of unique product design and superior service levels to market their iPods as premium quality products. For our purposes, customer value is the unique combination of benefits received by targeted buyers that includes quality, price, convenience, on-time delivery, and both before-sale and after-sale service. Marketers work diligently to deliver this value by carefully managing each element of the marketing mix (product, price, place, and promotion) so that this value is evident to consumers who in turn purchase the product. On-going marketing programs then come into play, encouraging these consumers to become long-term loyal customers.

Appealing to Target Markets

In a competitive marketplace, companies cannot satisfy everyone's needs with a single product, and so they design their products to appeal to specific target markets. Marketing follows the principle that with limited funds, it is better to channel your resources toward the groups of consumers that are most interested in purchasing your product, rather than target everyone and squander funds on those who have no interest at all. This approach results in marketers tailoring products to meet the specific needs of different target markets. A target market can be formally defined as the specific group of existing and potential consumers to which a marketer targets its marketing efforts. Marketing efforts are geared to appeal to a product's specific target market, ensuring that each element of the marketing mix appeals to the characteristics of the target group.

Coordinating the Marketing Mix

The elements of the marketing mix—product, price, place, and promotion—need to be carefully managed by marketers to ensure that they are well coordinated and that each appeals to the distinct characteristics of the target market for the product. There is no point in having an amazing product if consumers cannot find it at the retail stores they

> ## MARKETERS NEED TO UNDERSTAND WHAT MAKES THEIR CONSUMERS TICK: WHAT DELIGHTS THEM AND WHAT DOES NOT.

frequent. If the product is priced too high or too low for the target market, it will be unaffordable or will simply portray the wrong image. If marketers promote the product only in newspapers and the target market does not read newspapers, then the message will not be received. In all instances, marketers need to understand what makes their consumers tick: what delights them and what does not. This is determined by market research and a constant evaluation of marketing programs to understand how marketing efforts can best meet consumer needs. Marketers pick up

on these consumer preferences, and they design marketing programs that coordinate each element of the marketing mix to meet their specific target market needs.

The elements of the marketing mix can be simply described as follows:

1. **Product.** All the attributes that make up a good, a service, or an idea, including product design, features, colour, packaging, warrantee, and service levels.

2. **Price.** The expected retail shelf price and sale price of the product.

3. **Place.** The distribution channels and retailers required to sell the product.

4. **Promotion.** The communication tools needed to inform consumers about the product, including advertising, sales promotion, public relations, direct marketing, and personal selling.

Now, we look at two Nestlé products, Smarties and After Eight Straws, to find out how marketers at this company carefully craft each element of the marketing mix to appeal to distinct target groups. Smarties, targeting families, are brightly coloured candy-coated chocolates that come in a bright blue package with colourful, fun graphics. The product also comes in bite-sized pieces that are easy to share. The product

continues its appeal to families through a fun promotional program at www.smarties.ca, where images of Smarties are used in an online computer game. The product is also sold at a relatively inexpensive price, approximately $1.09 for 50 grams, making it affordable. Finally, the product is merchandised at retail, close to cash registers to stand as a visual reminder of this family treat and prompt impulse purchases.

On the other hand, After Eight Straws, launched in 2006, are a twist on classic dark chocolate mints and are geared to adults. The product is designed to be sleek and stylish and comes in an upscale silver cylinder with muted grey tones and subdued graphics. The package contains 20 thin After Eight Straws, which are filled with a delicate mint-cream filling. The product combines a bitter, dark chocolate with a minty flavour that appeals to adults. The product is sold at a premium price of $3.99 for a 90-gram package, reflecting its high-quality image and adult target market. This product is not merchandised at the cash register. Instead, it is typically found on the shelves of many grocery stores and drug retailers, but also enjoys wider seasonal distribution during the winter holidays when the product is popular for entertaining and is thus prominently displayed in store. In 2007, the product was promoted at Toronto Symphony Orchestra events to reflect its image as a product for adult entertaining.

In both instances, Nestlé moulded each element of the marketing mix to appeal to its specific target group. Neither product is geared to appeal to everyone in the market. Instead, Smarties targets families, and After Eight Straws targets only adults. It is important to note that over time, marketers gather extensive information on their target markets, being able to identify purchase motivation

product
Attributes that make up a good, a service, or an idea, including product design, features, colour, packaging, warrantee, and service levels

price Expected retail shelf price and sale price of the product

place Distribution channels and retailers required to sell the product

promotion
Communication tools needed to inform consumers about the product, including advertising, sales promotion, public relations, direct marketing, and personal selling

that goes beyond age and gender into behavioural and psychological motivation, which is an important determinant in many purchases. In this way, marketers define their target markets in more complex terms, including elements such as their target group's likes and dislikes, motivation, interests, and concerns.

The communications program for LG's touch phone also demonstrates how marketers appeal to specific target groups. Did you notice that LG put its ads in restaurants and bars, and that the ads were humorous? This was an intentional approach taken by LG to appeal to its target market, who spends time socializing in these venues and enjoys this sense of humour. The ads were designed to appear in the washrooms of restaurants and bars and were intentionally created to use irreverent headlines to stimulate a buzz with this target group. In addition, the ads were frequently changed—LG created a total of nine ads—so that the college and university target group would notice the latest clever headline and, once again, notice the product.

ask yourself

1. What is the essence of marketing?

2. What is a target market?

3. What is the marketing mix?

The Marketing Process

The marketing process is a continuous one that requires marketers to pay attention to detail and apply their strategic, analytical, and creative-thinking skills. In short, the **marketing process** involves (1) identifying consumer needs, (2) managing the marketing mix to meet these needs, and (3) realizing profits (see Figure 1–1 on page 10). Throughout the cycle, marketers constantly evaluate the success of their programs, implementing and recommending future changes to make the programs more competitive and alluring to their consumers.

HMV Reinvents Itself

Marketing **NewsFlash**

In recent years, HMV has been forced to change its tune. HMV Canada Inc. is the country's leading music retailer, but it has found itself evolving its focus in recent years to better reflect the changing habits of the buying public. The music industry was a $1.3 billion business in Canada as recently as 1999, but by 2006 sales had plummeted to roughly half that at $679 million. Only 39.9 million physical albums were sold in 2007, a decrease of 12.1 percent since 2006.

HMV has been changing to meet the needs of a new kind of consumer, one that forgoes going into a store and buying a CD for the convenience of downloading the material and playing it on an MP3 player. Recently, HMV has begun to sell the Sony BMG Platinum MusicPass, a card that enables a user to buy and download albums plus bonus material to play on any MP3 player.

Downloading music, both legally and illegally, has vastly outstripped the purchasing of physical CDs

by teenage consumers. HMV has responded by expanding its product base to include DVDs and video games, as well as MP3 players and other related accessories. HMV locations in the United Kingdom have also expanded in this direction, opening stores that have digital download hubs, gaming stations, and smoothie bars. HMV Canada is also evolving, moving to encompass not only music, but all forms of entertainment.

Source: Matt Semansky, "Record Shift." *Marketing* magazine, March 10, 2008: 17–20; "iPod is making beautiful music at HMV," HMV press release, December 3, 2007, accessed at www.newswire.ca/en/releases/archive/December2007/03/c6524.html; "Record-breaking DVD sales expected this Tuesday," HMV press release, December 6, 2007, accessed at www.cnw.ca/en/releases/archive/December2007/06/c7933.html; and HMV website, 2009, accessed at www.hmv.ca/hmvcaweb/en_CA/navigate.do?pPageID=100000035.

It is imperative to understand that marketers are ultimately responsible for generating company profits or revenues, and that marketing programs are designed with this end in mind. On occasion, students have the misconception that marketing is all about advertising or selling, when in fact it is about managing *all* the elements of the marketing mix and using research to help generate profits or revenues for an organization. Formally, **marketing** is described as the process of planning goods, services, or ideas to meet consumer needs and organizational objectives. It includes the conception of these products, and the pricing, promotion, and distribution programs designed to make a profit.[1] The objectives of both buyers and sellers must be met for exchanges to occur and for profits to be realized.

Exchange is the trade of things of value between buyers and sellers so that each benefits. Typically, the trade is money for a product or service, however, there is more to exchange than just money. A consumer may volunteer time with a non-profit organization such as the Heart and Stroke Foundation, which in return may satisfy the consumer's need to support the cause. Additionally, customers may provide referrals to a tutoring service or a fitness club in return for discounts or more services.

What Can Be Marketed?

In marketing, the term product encompasses goods, services, and ideas. These can all be marketed to encourage people to buy, or as in the case of ideas, to support a cause.

A **good** is a product you can touch and own. An example is a pair of Adidas running shoes or a can of Red Bull energy drink. Red Bull energy drink is a tangible product that is marketed in two varieties, sold at a premium price, merchandised in-store, promoted on TV with humorous ads, and publicized through the sponsorship of extreme sporting events.

A **service** is an intangible product you cannot touch. It does not result in something you take home. A physiotherapy session, a holiday, or going to a movie are examples of services. When you watch a movie at Cineplex Odeon, marketers have worked to ensure that your experience encourages you to come back. Movie selection, theatre layout, seating, and concession items have all been carefully selected with the comfort and needs of the target market in mind.

Ideas can also be marketed. An **idea** is a concept that typically looks for your support. An example is the Earth Hour campaign promoted by the World Wildlife Fund (WWF), which encouraged Canadians to all turn out their lights from 8 to 9 p.m. on March 29, 2008. It worked; the WWF successfully marketed the idea and garnered support for the cause.

**Be a walker.
Be an end to MS.**

Join over 70,000 walkers across Canada in the movement to end multiple sclerosis. Step up and make your mark in 2009.

register for 2009
www.mswalks.ca

MS. WALK
EVERY STEP MATTERS.

Marketing ideas can encourage people to support causes.

marketing
The process of planning goods, services, or ideas to meet consumer needs and organizational objectives. It includes the conception of these products and the pricing, promotion, and distribution programs designed to make a profit

exchange The trade of things of value between buyers and sellers so that each benefits

good A product you can touch and own

service A good that is intangible, that you cannot touch

idea A concept that typically looks for your support

CD/Cassette Sales in Canada (in $000)

2000 $1,130,700

2002 $922,500

2004 $806,800

2006 $678,745

marketing meter

Source: Matt Semansky, "Record Shift," *Marketing*, March 10, 2008: 17-20.

Figure 1–1
The Marketing Process

| Identify consumer needs | Manage the marketing mix to meet consumer needs | Realize profits for the company |

A logical process that focuses on consumer needs

What Is a Market?

The term **market** is used in marketing to describe the potential consumers who have both the *willingness* and *ability* to buy a product. Importantly, just being willing to buy does not constitute a market. For example, Fisher Price's Smart Cycle, the Toy Industry Association's Toy of the Year for 2008, is a stationary bike that plugs into your TV. It is made for children three to six years old. When children sit on the bike and pedal, they can play and learn through interactive arcade-type games—exercise and fun all rolled into one. The children, however, are not considered the market because they do not have the money or the physical means to buy the product. The market consists of parents with young children in that age group.

This product touches on an interesting marketing issue: Sometimes the market, target market, and consumers are different groups of people, and marketers need to decide on a balance of who should be targeted with their programs. While the *market* for Fisher Price's Smart Cycle is the parents with children three to six years old, the marketing also needs to focus on the children who may exert some influence over their parents. Therefore, we see the *target market* for the product including both children and parents. Finally, the *consumers* of the product, in this case the users, are the children, not the parents, and marketers need to ensure that the product is designed with their interests in mind without overlooking the parents, who are the main decision makers in the purchase process.

ask yourself

1. What steps are involved in the marketing process?

2. What are the differences between goods, services, and ideas?

3. Are credit cards goods, services, or ideas?

The Evolution of Business Philosophies

Marketing was not always the driving force in business philosophy. Up until the 1930s, businesses were in the **production orientation** stage. This stage focused on manufacturing, which until the industrial revolution was not a widespread phenomenon. Manufactured goods tended to sell, regardless of their quality, because they were in short supply. Consumer needs were not a priority. The second stage, from the 1930s to the 1960s, was the **sales orientation** stage. This stage focused on selling as many products as possible. The market had become more competitive, production had become more efficient, and products were in abundance. Companies started to hard-sell to make a profit, and consumer needs were still not a major consideration. As the

Marketing Ideas: Earth Hour

At 8:00 p.m. on March 29, 2008, the lights went out. Not for everyone, perhaps, but for enough people to send a strong message to the government of Canada, and governments around the world. This was not a blackout, but an extremely successful marketing campaign: the World Wildlife Fund's Earth Hour. Organized to raise awareness of climate change, Earth Hour is a largely grassroots campaign highlighting the simple measures that people can take to cut emissions by urging them to pledge to turn off their lights for just one hour—from 8:00 to 9:00 p.m. local time.

When Earth Hour was first celebrated in Sydney, Australia, in 2007, the city reported a 10.2 percent decrease in energy use—the equivalent of taking 48,000 cars off the road for the hour. In 2008, Earth Hour went global, spreading from Sydney to more than 300 towns and cities in two dozen countries. Designed as a symbolic event to show concern and inspire long-term action, Earth Hour doesn't ask participants to trade their SUVs for hybrid cars, or move into the wilderness. Rather, the Earth Hour campaign seeks just a small commitment to show the world how easy reducing emissions can be.

For the 2008 event, Canadians in about 150 communities pledged to turn off their lights for the hour. Across Canada, restaurants offered candlelight dining. Toronto's City Hall, CN Tower, and Air Canada Centre were dimmed to darkness. The clock on Parliament's Peace Tower in Ottawa went dark as Canada marked its participation. Darkness spread worldwide, starting earlier that day in New Zealand and rolling through 14 time zones before ending on North America's West Coast. The Sydney Opera House, Rome's Colesseum, and Coke's billboard in Times Square were all plunged into darkness as 8 p.m. local time moved across the world. In total, approximately 100,000 Canadians registered online for the event—roughly one third of the 300,000 registered worldwide. ●

Marketing NewsFlash

Sources: "Earth Hour," WWF-Canada website, 2009, accessed at www.wwf.ca/earthhour; "Canadians go dark with world for Earth Hour," CBC News, March 29, 2008, accessed at www.cbc.ca/world/story/2008/03/29/earth-hour.html; and Jennifer MacMillan, "Canadians embrace Earth Hour," *The Globe and Mail*, March 27, 2008, accessed at www.theglobeandmail.com/servlet/story/RTGAM.20080327.wearthhour0327/BNStory/National/?page=rss&id=RTGAM.20080327.wearthhour0327.

---

marketplace got more competitive, businesses became more sophisticated and the basic marketing stage evolved in the 1960s. At this point, consumer needs became paramount, and the marketing concept arose and became the focus of businesses. The **marketing orientation** stage focuses on the idea that an organization should strive to satisfy the needs of consumers while also trying to achieve the organization's goals. The **marketing concept** follows this idea. An organization that has a marketing orientation focuses its efforts on continuously collecting information about customers' needs, sharing this information across departments, and using it to create customer value.[2]

In the last decade, marketing has evolved from a discipline that had more of a short-term focus on transactions to one that now focuses on building long-term customer relationships. This **relationship marketing** approach now sees organizations considering the lifetime value of its customers as they strive to offer better services, deliver consistent product quality, and develop long-term relationships with their customers. This approach emphasizes customer retention and on-going customer satisfaction rather than short-term sales transactions. It carefully uses information on customer interests to develop relationships with customers and retain their loyalty. Improved customer relationships can result in increased customer loyalty, improved customer retention levels, and greater profits for the organization. Formally, the concept of relationship marketing is when organizations create long-term links with their customers, employees, suppliers, and other partners to increase loyalty and customer retention.

marketing orientation
The idea that an organization should strive to satisfy the needs of consumers while also trying to achieve organizational goals

marketing concept
Focusing organizational efforts to collect and use information about customers' needs to create customer value

relationship marketing
When organizations create long-term links with customers, employees, suppliers, and other partners to increase loyalty and customer retention

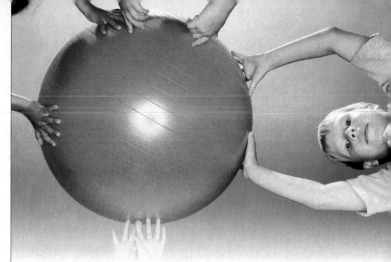

(Figure 1–2 summarizes this evolution of business philosophies.)

It is important to understand that relationship marketing involves a personal, on-going relationship between an organization and its customers that often starts before a sale occurs, and lasts well beyond the point when a sale has concluded. The automobile industry has used this approach for many years, seeing the value of a satisfied customer play out in future purchases. A Saab dealership in Toronto, for example, regularly phones its customers with invitations to events, sends out mailings with car maintenance information, and distributes a high-quality magazine for customers to enjoy.

Saab's vision for the future

Internet technology and database marketing have surfaced as ways to facilitate relationship marketing and create a whole new focus on *customer relationship management (CRM)* for the marketing industry. This approach is grounded in the fact that it is less expensive to service and maintain current customers rather than obtain new ones. CRM involves a systematic and active company approach to managing and retaining satisfied customers by efficiently and accurately identifying the elements that lead to satisfied customers and increased company profits. This approach is partly facilitated by CRM computer software that tracks customer choices, preferences, and complaints, allowing marketers to customize sales and marketing tools to better fit customer needs. Returning to the example of the automobile industry, CRM software is a useful tool that can track whether customers buy or lease a vehicle, how often they are in the market to purchase a vehicle, what type of financing arrangements are used, and the features they prefer in a car. The challenge is then to use this data to help manage current customer needs and to become forward thinking by pre-empting their customers' future needs. CRM is discussed in more detail in the following section and reviewed at length in Chapter 14.

The Progression of Marketing and Evolving Areas

LO4 Marketing thinking has progressed over the last decade due to changes in consumer expectations, societal pressures, technological changes, and the philosophy of doing business. Marketing is moving from purely focusing on consumers

---

Figure 1–2
The Evolution of Business Philosophies

Production orientation → **1930s** → Sales orientation → **1960s** → Marketing orientation → **1990s** → Relationship marketing orientation and company profits to developing relationships with customers and giving back to society. Some of the latest evolving areas are (1) customer relationship management, (2) experiential marketing, and (3) corporate social responsibility.

Customer Relationship Management

Customer relationship management (CRM) focuses on identifying a firm's most-valued customers and building programs to appeal to their needs while fostering long-term customer relationships and loyalty. This approach can use a number of different methods to encourage customer loyalty. When used successfully, the concept of CRM permeates an organization, which then implements policies, processes, and strategies to maximize customer satisfaction by tracking customer information and using this data to anticipate and meet customer needs. Formally, CRM is defined as the overall process of building and maintaining profitable customer relationships by delivering superior customer value and satisfaction.[3]

We look at the Canadian retail industry to better understand this concept and see how CRM can be applied. In practical terms, CRM can take many forms in the retail environment. In one of its most basic forms, CRM can involve the occasional phone call to customers or the use of customer lists to make customers aware of new product offers. In a more advanced state, it can include customer incentives such as customer loyalty cards to reward consumers with collectable points for their purchases. These points can then be redeemed by customers for items such as merchandise or other in-store purchases. For the retailer, these cards can in turn track the purchase patterns of individual consumers, providing valuable data to marketers who can use sophisticated software and highly qualified personnel to determine and develop individualized consumer programs to encourage customer loyalty. This approach has been pioneered in Canada by retailers such as HBC, with the HBC Rewards Card, and Shoppers Drug Mart with the Optimum card. Loyalty programs such as Air Miles use a host of partner-brands to reward members with travel rewards. Air Miles uses companies such as the Loyalty Group, which specialize in CRM, to help manage its CRM programs.

Advanced CRM can take into consideration the value of specific customers over their lifetime and what offers are most suited to their stage in life. Let's look at a simple example to demonstrate this concept. If a pregnant woman buys pre-natal vitamins at a store that uses CRM tracking software such as loyalty cards,

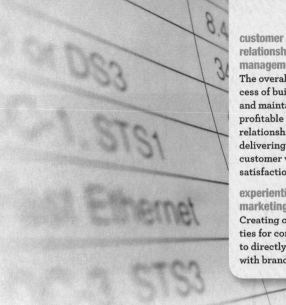

in time she may start receiving coupons for diapers, baby food, and tips on infant nutrition; her pre-natal purchase has triggered sophisticated computer programs to recognize her eventual need for baby products. As this woman's needs evolve, and as the children get older, the offers may change to include over-the-counter medications for toddlers or school supplies for youths. This is one of the ways that companies can use CRM to encourage customer loyalty.

Another simple example of how the concept of CRM can be applied at retail is in the area of store design. Retailers can use customer purchase data to analyze departmental purchases to improve store design and maximize their profitability. If, for instance, CRM identifies organic foods as a highly purchased product for a store's catchment area, when the store is being refurbished, the section for these products may be expanded and given more prominence within the store. CRM is covered in more detail in Chapter 14.

Experiential Marketing

Experiential marketing is an approach where marketers create opportunities for their consumers to interact directly with a brand. Instead of relying on mass media, a brand creates an occasion for a few consumers to interact personally with the brand and spread the word to their friends. This generates word-of-mouth awareness and often free publicity for the brand. The brand goes from being passive to actively interacting with the target market. A brand can follow a number of approaches, often using a combination of public relations, event marketing, viral marketing, and promotions to break through the clutter of competing marketing messages. A well-known example, touted around the world, relates to Absolut Vodka's launch of

its CUT brand in Australia. No media was used during the launch. Instead, the brand rented two major nightclubs and created a free entertainment spot for people to try the product and spread the word about the new brand to their friends.

LG's launch event for its touch phones is another example of experiential marketing. Guests from the media, influencers in the fashion and entertainment world, and key customers were invited to experience the brand and spread the word to others. Over 170 people attended the event, with good representation from the media; attendance by executives from Bell, Rogers, and Telus; and involvement of key influencers in the hospitality, fashion, and entertainment industry. These people were targeted by LG to spread the word

about the new LG phones into the market so that interest and hype would be generated.

Corporate Social Responsibility

Corporate social responsibility (CSR) is a concept where organizations voluntarily consider the well-being of society by taking responsibility for how their businesses impact consumers, customers, suppliers, employees, shareholders, communities, the environment, and society in general.

Many organizations now include a CSR component in their business plans. CSR initiatives can range from the simple to the complex, and typically include one of three approaches. In its simplest forms, CSR can involve (1) the sponsorship and/or spearheading of community programs, and (2) the sponsorship and/or involvement in major fundraising initiatives for charitable organizations. In its most advanced form, CSR is used as a business philosophy that permeates the organization. Here are some examples that we see in Canada today:

- Tim Hortons stands as an example of a company that uses its CSR efforts to support the community in a number of ways. In 1974, Tim Hortons established the Tim Horton Children's Foundation to honour the memory of Tim Horton, his love of children, and his desire to help the less fortunate.

What Would Canadians Like to Touch?

As a part of the marketing campaign for the LG touch phones, LG commissioned Ipsos Reid Canada to poll Canadians on what they would most like to touch.

The very top of an Egyptian pyramid	45%
Freshly poured sidewalk cement	29%
The Stanley Cup	18%
The Hope Diamond	11%

Source: "LG Launches the First True Touch Phone Series In Canada," LG Canada press release, March 27, 2008, accessed at http://ca.lge.com/en/about/press_release/detail/ PRE|MENU_5630.jhtml.

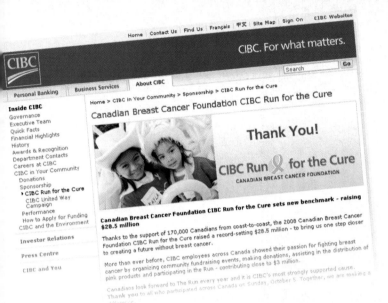

Annually, the foundation provides economically disadvantaged children with a fun-filled camp experience. In 2008, the foundation helped 13,000 under-privileged children participate. Tim Hortons also sponsors local children's house leagues for hockey, soccer, lacrosse, T-ball, and baseball. Visit www.timhortons.com to find out more about their other CSR programs.

- CIBC is a Canadian financial institution that implements CSR by sponsoring major charitable institutions. CIBC has supported breast cancer research, education, and awareness for over 12 years as the lead sponsor for the annual CIBC Run for the Cure fundraiser. In 2008, this charitable event involved over 170,000 participants and raised more than $28 million for the cause. CIBC alone contributed close to $3 million through pink ribbon merchandise, employee fundraising events, and the collection of pledges. Visit www.cibc.com to see the results of its latest fundraiser for the Canadian Breast Cancer Foundation.

- HBC (The Bay, Zellers, Home Outfitters, and Fields stores) uses CSR as a philosophy of doing business. Annually, since 2002, HBC issues a "Corporate Social Responsibility Report" as a means of reporting, measuring, and delivering on its promises to support the well-being of society. HBC's CSR efforts focus on four key areas: the environment, wellness, community investment, and ethical sourcing. The result has been very positive, with HBC launching initiatives such as the September 2008 launch of its first environmentally friendly Bay store in Conestoga, Ontario. This 120,000-square-foot store boasts the use of solar panels, energy-efficient lighting, recyclable carpet, thermal-reduction roofing, waterless urinals, touchless water faucets, touchless toilets, and an automated energy-management system to reduce energy consumption. HBC has delivered on numerous other CSR initiatives. In 2007, its head office became the first office tower in Canada to be certified zero waste, and in that same year, HBC stores achieved the goal of diverting most clean plastic, fine paper, plastic hangers, corrugated cardboard, cafeteria grease, and store-use print cartridges from landfills. Visit www.hbc.com to learn more about HBC's CSR initiatives.

   FIELDS

The marketing community is also putting an increased focus on the well-being of society and the environment. It is commonplace to now see marketing programs include a component that addresses these needs, an approach described as the **societal marketing concept.** An example is when Maxwell House coffee instituted its "Brew Some Good" marketing program in 2008, raising awareness for Habitat for Humanity and earmarking over $200,000 for charitable donations. Similarly, in 2007, CTV's *Canadian Idol* TV show used a marketing initiative that marshalled the proceeds from the sales of a *Canadian Idol* song to Ronald McDonald House Charities for children with serious illnesses or

Marketing tip

"*The consumer's decision to purchase a product or service is part of a journey of discovery that the consumer travels along. Sometimes it is as short as minutes when we buy on impulse, and other times it is months or years for major purchases. Market research is a key tool to understanding consumer buying behaviour.*"

Andrew Barrett, vice president of marketing, LG Canada

disabilities. Another example of the societal marketing concept is the new social networking site created in 2008 by Mountain Equipment Co-op and the Canadian Parks and Wilderness Society at www.thebigwild.org. This site promotes conservation programs by encouraging people to share their outdoor experiences about places that need protection. People post their stories, comments, and photos on the site to gain support. This initiative was launched with a marketing program that saw outdoor enthusiasts such as mountain bikers, kayakers, and rock climbers participate in parades in major cities across Canada. At the store level, Mountain Equipment Co-op customers were encouraged to participate with a small donation toward the cause. Customers then received green shoelaces and were encouraged to wear just one lace to raise awareness for the cause.[4]

A Focus on Ethics Companies and marketers are increasingly focusing on society, understanding that they can play a major role and have a strong impact on its well-being. Nonetheless, not all organizations or marketers are focused on CSR or the societal marketing concept. This orientation requires financial commitment and long-term support from the organization and its employees. To protect society and the environment from the adverse effect of businesses, regulations are imposed (see Chapter 2) as a basic safeguard for our communities. This can take many forms such as pollution-emission thresholds, food and safety regulations, advertising standards, telemarketing regulations, and water safety guidelines, just to name a few. A recent example is the CRTC's (Canadian Radio-television and Telecommunications Commission) telemarketing initiative that launched a "National Do Not Call List" in September 2008, allowing the public to sign up to reduce the number of telemarketing calls to their phones. Consumer groups also exert pressure on government bodies to protect society. This was seen in 2008 with the Maple Leaf Foods listeria contamination issue prompting consumer advocates to demand stricter government regulations on food processing.

In addition to government regulations, many companies, industries, and professional associations have guidelines and codes of ethics to provide direction to their employees and members. The Canadian Marketing Association (CMA) is the professional body for the marketing industry, and it responds to legislative issues and sets guidelines on areas such as responsible business practices, ethics, and privacy policy. The CMA has dealt with policy issues concerning telemarketing fraud, electronic commerce, and privacy policy. It consists of over 800 corporate members from major financial institutions, insurance companies, publishers, retailers, charitable organizations, agencies, relationship marketers, and those involved in e-business and Internet marketing.

The CMA has a code of ethics with which all members must comply. Its purpose is to encourage ethical and legal marketing practices by the marketing community. It covers topics such as accurate representations, truthfulness in marketing communications, price claims, fulfillment practices, privacy policy, marketing to children, and direct marketing approaches, just to name a few. The CMA's website contains a wealth of information for marketers, including its code of ethics, marketing tips, case studies, news releases, educational courses, and job postings. Visit www.the-cma.org to become familiar with this important marketing association.

ask yourself

1. What are the stages involved in the evolution of business philosophies?

2. What is involved in a relationship marketing orientation?

3. In your own words explain experiential marketing?

4. What is CSR?

MARKETERS ARE DEVELOPING PROGRAMS THAT ADDRESS THE WELL-BEING OF SOCIETY.

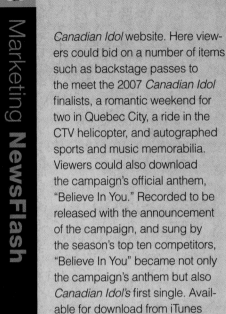
CTV Helps the Idols Build a House

After five years on television, in 2007, Canada's most-watched summer series, *Canadian Idol*, brought something new to viewers. For the first time, CTV's hit series became involved with a charitable venture. Teaming up with McDonald's Restaurants of Canada Limited, *Canadian Idol* launched the "Help the Idols Build a House" campaign.

Since 1974, Ronald McDonald Houses around the world have offered free lodging to out-of-town families of children undergoing treatment at local hospitals. In 2007, thanks to the donation of a two-acre plot of land on Vancouver Island's Bear Mountain Resort,

Ronald McDonald House Charities of Canada embarked on an extension of the charity's central concept: to build the first North American Ronald McDonald Family Retreat. Here, families who have previously stayed at one of Canada's 12 Ronald McDonald Houses would be given the opportunity to spend quality time together, free of charge, to focus on their emotional needs and get their lives back on track. Run during the show's 2007 summer season, the "Help the Idol's Build a House" campaign offered viewers a number of opportunities to support the charity.

The viewers' first opportunity to "Help the Idols Build a House" was an online auction run on the

Canadian Idol website. Here viewers could bid on a number of items such as backstage passes to the meet the 2007 *Canadian Idol* finalists, a romantic weekend for two in Quebec City, a ride in the CTV helicopter, and autographed sports and music memorabilia. Viewers could also download the campaign's official anthem, "Believe In You." Recorded to be released with the announcement of the campaign, and sung by the season's top ten competitors, "Believe In You" became not only the campaign's anthem but also *Canadian Idol's* first single. Available for download from iTunes and other online music stores, net proceeds from sales of the single were donated to Ronald McDonald House Charities.

Sources: "Sales from first Idol single to benefit children in need," CTV's Canadian Idol website, 2007, accessed at www.ctv.ca/mini/idol2007/static/bearmountain.html; "Canadian Idol to Support Ronald McDonald House Charities® of Canada," CTV press release, July 9, 2007, accessed at www.ctv.ca/servlet/ArticleNews/story/CTVNews/20070709/ctv_release_20070709/20070709?s_name=idol2007&no_ads=; and "Top 8 Revealed: Khalila Glanville is Next Eliminated Canadian Idol Finalist," Channel Canada, July 25, 2007, accessed at www.channelcanada.com/Article1931.html.

Marketing Careers

Many students wonder whether there are jobs in the marketing field. As in any business, it is somewhat dependent of the strength of the economy, and entry-level jobs exist for college and university graduates. The starting point is to get an education and, while studying, to create a network of business professionals to contact upon graduation. Creating this network can be done through summer jobs and volunteering in areas that might be of interest. Networking with guest speakers who may visit your institution is also an important avenue to pursue. These strategies are a wonderful way to gain exposure to the marketing discipline. Be sure to also bookmark Canadian marketing job-search websites and track job postings. Examples of such sites are www.nabs.org, www.marketingmag.ca, www.strategymag.com, www.the-cma.org, www.aimscanada.com, and www.media-jobsearchcanada.com.

Entry-level positions exist in sales, marketing, and promotions in a variety of fields. Job titles vary from

company to company, but typical jobs include marketing coordinators, marketing analysts, marketing assistants, sales representatives, and account coordinators. These entry-level jobs usually include on-the-job training, the creation of analytical reports, liaison with other departments within the company, exposure to marketing program development, and the potential to move up within the company. Areas of growth are in promotions and Internet service businesses. Opportunities exist in small, medium, and large organizations, and can be found in the private sector, in the non-profit sector, and in the government. In the private sector, marketers are required in consumer marketing and in the business-to-business market. For students who have the advantage of a foreign language, this language can be leveraged with companies dealing in foreign markets, or in Canada, with multicultural target groups. Companies are often looking for employees with language skills.

Students wanting to get into the marketing field need to be analytical, be able to work with others, be capable of working in teams, and have strong communication skills in both written and verbal contexts.

As a marketer, you need to keep your finger on the pulse of the consumer. This requires you to stay current, to be intellectually curious, and to be involved in the conversation of life. Marketers need to read newspapers and magazines, surf the Internet, watch TV, listen to the radio, and absorb the trends that are evolving in society and around the world. Publications such as *Marketing* magazine, *Strategy* magazine, *Canadian Business,* and *Maclean's* magazine are highly recommended.

Marketers often spend part of their careers working in a sales or promotional role, and moving into marketing with this relevant and valuable experience. A recent college marketing graduate, Brandy Martin armed herself with knowledge about the industry and found her initial passion working in the confectionery business. While still completing her studies, she networked with a number of guest speakers to gain part-time employment in the Internet industry, helping to create search words for a behavioural marketing Internet company. Upon graduation, assisted by her experience gained through part-time jobs, and prompted by post-secondary networking opportunities, she secured a position as an insight analyst with Cadbury Adams. In a few months, Brandy moved on to become a go-to-market coordinator, a position that required her to liaise with both the marketing and sales departments. "Working at Cadbury Adams was the best possible experience for

me," explains Brandy. "I gained valuable insight into the consumer packaged goods' industry and how a marketing department functions in a major corporation." Since her initial position as an insight analyst, this marketing graduate has moved on to work at the top lawn and garden care company in the world, The Scotts Miracle-Gro Company. She now works as the program coordinator for the national field sales team, again liaising with the marketing department, but also managing her own sales territory. "My job is insanely busy," explains Brandy in the midst of creating multimedia e-learning sales support materials for the company's entire Canadian sales force. We asked Brandy to pass along her insights into what it takes to work in marketing and how to get a job in the field. She tells us, "Networking really is the key! Meet as many people as possible, stay in touch, and never burn a bridge." Her path tells marketing students to take full advantage of those networking opportunities that come their way while studying at college or university. These can become invaluable door openers. As for working in the marketing field, she tells us, "It takes creativity, passion, and the desire for knowledge. Learning doesn't stop once you finish school, and if you are no longer learning, it might be time to move on."

Brandy Martin enjoys the fast pace of the sales and marketing world in which she works. It provides her with the opportunity to be creative, apply her knowledge, and use her analytical skills to help build a business. Marketing is an exciting area where change is the norm and being able to rise to the challenge is imperative. Learn the fundamentals through education, apply your knowledge through part-time employment, and enjoy the ride by working full-time in the industry! Good luck Brandy Martin.

Worldwide Market Share of Cellphones (Q1, 2008)

1. Nokia		40.9%
2. Samsung		16.4%
3. Motorola		9.7%
4. LG		8.6%
5. Apple		0.6%

Source: CBC News, "Mobile phone sales jump in Q1," April 25, 2008, www.cbc.ca/technology/story/2008/04/25/tech-mobile-sales.html.

[adAlyze]

Summary...*just the facts*

- The essence of marketing is to focus on consumer needs.
- The marketing process follows three main steps: (1) identifying consumer needs, (2) managing the marketing mix to meet consumer needs, and (3) realizing revenues or profits.
- The marketing mix, also known as the 4 Ps, consists of product, price, place, and promotion.
- Product refers to all the attributes that make up a good, a service, or an idea. Product elements include areas such as product design, product features, colour, packaging, warrantee, and service levels.
- Price refers to the retail-shelf price and sale price of a product.
- Place refers to the distribution channels and retailers required to sell the product.

- Promotion refers to the communication tools needed to communicate to consumers, such as advertising, sales promotion, public relations, direct marketing, and personal selling.
- Marketers are responsible for bringing profits and revenues into the company.
- The evolution of marketing has progressed from a production orientation stage, to a sales orientation stage, on to a marketing orientation stage, and finally to a relationship marketing stage.
- New evolving areas in marketing are customer relationship management (CRM), experiential marketing, and corporate social responsibility (CSR).
- The Canadian Marketing Association (CMA) is the professional body for the marketing industry that responds to legislative issues and sets guidelines on responsible business practices.

Key Terms and Concepts...*a refresher*

corporate social responsibility (CSR) *p. 14*
customer relationship management (CRM) *p. 13*
customer value *p. 6*
exchange *p. 9*
experiential marketing *p. 13*
good *p. 9*
idea *p. 9*

market *p. 10*
marketing *p. 9*
marketing concept *p. 11*
marketing mix *p. 6*
marketing orientation *p. 11*
marketing process *p. 8*
place *p. 7*
price *p. 7*
product *p. 7*

production orientation *p. 10*
promotion *p. 7*
relationship marketing *p. 11*
sales orientation *p. 10*
service *p. 9*
societal marketing concept *p. 15*
target market *p. 6*

Check out the Online Learning Centre at **www.mcgrawhill.ca/olc/thecore**
for chapter application questions, discussion activities, Internet exercises, and video cases.

the marketing
environment

I n marketing, being aware of the world in which we live is important. Keeping your finger on the pulse of the consumer allows marketers to capitalize on new opportunities and thwart potential threats. In Chapter 2, we focus on these areas of change and explain

how they impact on marketing decisions. We start by looking at a non-profit organization, the Childhood Cancer Foundation Candlelighters Canada (CCFC), to see that recognizing changes in consumer behaviour can create opportunities to better deliver services. In this instance, technology is the main area of change.

The CCFC is a national charitable foundation, established in 1987, run by a small group of staff and volunteers. It provides support for children, and their families, facing cancer, and raises funds to support childhood cancer research across Canada. It does this without government funding and finds that communicating effectively and efficiently with its target group is imperative to its success. This charity functions in the non-profit sector where there are three main target groups: (1) the users of the service, (2) the volunteers of the organization, and (3) the contributors to the cause. Here we examine the Internet's impact on CCFC's contributors and volunteers, and a specific user group, teenagers.

"The Internet has revolutionized the world of not-for-profit organizations and charitable foundations," states David Stones, the CCFC's president and CEO as he recalls the 1990s and having to work diligently to persuade non-profit organizations to invest in website

technology. "Hard to believe," he says, "In just 12 years or so, websites and the Internet have become pivotal in terms of marketing and communications strategy." Websites have gone from being carriers of static brochure-ware, to being user-friendly, interactive sites. The Internet is now an interactive and sophisticated tool that narrowly targets individuals and companies alike. Now consumers intuitively use the Internet to gather information, purchase products, download music, watch movies, and pledge donations.

The CCFC looked at the marketing environment and saw an opportunity for a web-based fundraising tool. It realized target groups wanted online registration and a sense of participation in the event. People also wanted the ease of online registration, the ability to be involved in the experience, and instant tax receipts. The CCFC recognized an opportunity to make fundraising a more personal and rewarding experience that could allow contributors to connect with the cause on an emotional level. The charity introduced its Small Hands initiative.

The CCFC's Small Hands program is a fundraising campaign that works with individual volunteers and families who wish to raise money for the cause. It uses an off-the-shelf Internet-based fundraising tool to connect with individuals and small groups of people who wish to raise funds for the CCFC. Now these people can sign up online and receive a personalized web page that allows their supporters to pledge funds, monitor progress of the fundraiser, and receive instant tax receipts. An online thermometer monitors, in real-time, how much money has been raised for the initiative, providing instant gratification for the donor and fundraiser. These personal web pages use templates to enable users to easily upload images, tell their story, and monitor contributions to their fundraising efforts. It provides the individual fundraiser with a personal web link, which they then give to their friends and supporters for online donations.

The success of the Small Hands program can be seen in the CCFC's "Shave for the Cure" event, run annually by the medical students at the University of Ottawa. In 2008, this event went from the traditional paper-based pledge system to using the CCFC's Small Hands interface. The result was that contributions more than doubled over previous years to yield over $60,000. This new Internet-based approach was enormously successful for the CCFC. It tied into contributor and volunteer needs, and made initiatives relevant to how consumers use the Internet today. Individual fundraising initiatives became an emotional experience for both the fundraiser and contributor,

resulting in increased revenue for the CCFC and a greater sense of fulfillment for all. For more about Small Hands, go to www.smallhands.ca.

The second example of how the CCFC tapped into its target groups' use of new technology involves helping teenagers with cancer. David Stones explains that teenagers are at a tumultuous age, and a diagnosis of cancer requires unique support that involves friends, online communities, and a need to connect with someone who has gone through the same experience. The CCFC recognizes that teens have a special affinity with the Internet and want to ensure that they use this communication tool to help teens get through this difficult time. Currently, the CCFC is pursuing a new Teen Network Internet initiative, looking for an injection of funds to help support teenagers with cancer. The Teen Network will provide teens with the opportunity to connect with other teens with similar experiences. It will allow them to use the Internet, often their communication tool of choice, to provide that critical emotional support. The CCFC is looking to popular social networking sites such as Facebook and MySpace to understand what design elements are crucial to the success of this website. The CCFC has learned that customizable elements are key, and the organization will build the new initiative with this in mind so that teens can create their own websites that reflect their personality. Themes, backgrounds, colours, and many features will be customizable. Teens will be able to upload as much, or as little, information as they wish, and organize their site to stay in touch with their friends and mentors. The CCFC is planning to include areas for blogs, music, travel, friends, and instant messaging. The CCFC is harnessing the power of the Internet to enable teenagers to connect with as many teen mentors as possible, creating online communities that help. The CCFC's corporate website can be found at www.childhoodcancer.ca.

The CCFC's David Stones is forward-thinking and understands the need to relate to consumers on their terms. The CCFC is careful to ensure that it understands the environment in which it functions, and to tie in to evolving changes and uses of technology. Its target groups are on the Internet and expect to be able to use web-based technology to communicate and support initiatives. The CCFC realizes the Internet has changed the way consumers collect information, communicate with each other, and contribute to causes, and it taps into this consumer insight in exciting new ways, creating personal connections that count. This is non-profit marketing making its mark by heeding the environment in which it functions. 🍎

The Marketing Environment

Chapter 2 focuses on understanding the environment that affects marketing decisions. Marketers do not function in a vacuum and need to channel their ideas and programs on meaningful consumer needs that address changes that are occurring in the marketplace. The Childhood Cancer Foundation Candlelighters Canada recognized how technology is changing its target groups' expectations and seized the opportunity to tap into the power of the Internet. Other business sectors also follow this approach and stay abreast of changes that affect their consumers. Marketers constantly monitor the marketing environment with a view to capitalizing on new opportunities and thwarting potential threats that may surface in their businesses. In short, marketers scan the marketing environment in six key areas, looking for factors that are important or changing. They are looking at (1) demographic forces (2) socio-cultural forces (3) economic forces (4) technological forces (5) competitive forces, and (6) regulatory forces. This chapter looks at developments in these areas, providing a wide array of examples that demonstrate how heeding and responding to these changes results in more relevant marketing programs.

Marketers constantly monitor the marketing environment with a view to capitalizing on new opportunities and thwarting potential threats.

Traditional fundraising combines with new technology.

The Core: Chapter 2

A marketing environmental scan helps marketers know what affects consumers.

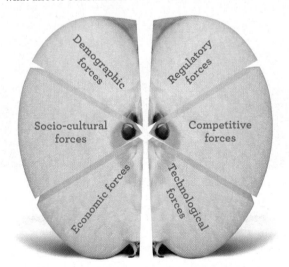

A marketer looks at opportunities and threats that stem from the world around the consumer.

A Marketing Environmental Scan

A **marketing environmental scan** is the process of continually acquiring information on events occurring outside the organization to identify trends, opportunities, and threats to a business. Marketers use this knowledge to ensure that their products, services, and ideas are relevant and meaningful. Managed properly, this knowledge translates into competitive marketing programs that meet consumer needs and bring revenues into the company. A marketing environmental scan looks at the forces identified in "The Core" image (opposite), namely demographic forces, socio-cultural forces, economic forces, technological forces, competitive forces, and regulatory forces.

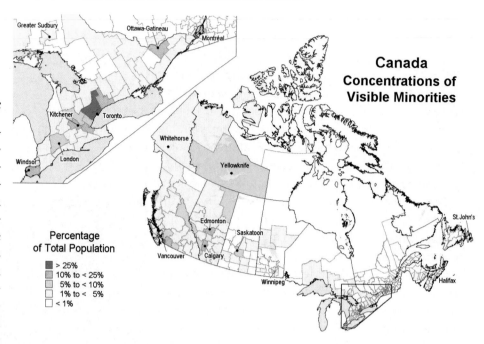

Figure 2–1
Geographic concentration of visible minorities in Canada

Canada Concentrations of Visible Minorities

Percentage of Total Population

- ☐ > 25%
- ☐ 10% to < 25%
- ☐ 5% to < 10%
- ☐ 1% to < 5%
- ☐ < 1%

Source: Statistics Canada 2001 Census of Population Topic Based Tabulation catalogue number 95F0363XCB01001.

Demographic Forces

The statistical study of populations is referred to as **demographics**. It looks at characteristics such as age, gender, ethnicity, income, and occupation of a group of people. Marketers can access demographic information through Statistics Canada or through their own surveys and databases of information. It is important for marketers to clearly understand changes that are occurring in the demographic arena to ensure marketing efforts are well placed.

Statistics Canada provides demographic data through its census information. The Census of Canada indicates that the Canadian population is growing older, contains diverse generations, is settling in the suburbs of large cities, is becoming more ethnically mixed (see Figure 2–1), and is increasingly living in non-traditional families.[1] We look at these trends and identify their impact on marketing efforts.

An Aging Population

The 2006 Census of Canada shows that Canada is populated by approximately 31.6 million people, of which 3.7 million, or 11.7 percent, are between the ages of 55 and 64, an all-time high.[2] The percentage of the population over the age of 55 continues to increase due to low birth rates and better health care. An important fact is that people over the age of 50 control 75 percent of the net worth of Canadian households.[3]

Marketers are rising to the occasion and addressing this greying market with new products and services geared to this target group. The older populations in Canada are likely to spend their resources on travel and electronics. Health-related products are also popular. Tylenol is an example of a health care brand specifically addressing the aging population. Noting that arthritis was becoming more prevalent due to the aging population, it developed Tylenol Arthritis Pain to help relieve pain symptoms. Tylenol advertises this product in magazines such as *CAA,* which focuses on older Canadians who travel.

Who's Who in Canada?

	Population
Baby Boomers	9.6 million
Generation X	3.9 million
Generation Y	8.7 million

Source: Statistics Canada, 2006 Census of Population, Statistics Canada catalogue no. 97-551-XCB2006009.

> **THE ELDERLY POPULATIONS IN CANADA ARE LIKELY TO SPEND THEIR RESOURCES ON TRAVEL AND HEALTHCARE.**

"Knowing your customer is both the start and end point of effective marketing and communications in both the profit and not-for-profit sectors."

David Stones, president and CEO, Childhood Cancer Foundation Candlelighters Canada

Diverse Generations Marketers note three main generational groups of consumers: baby boomers, Generation X, and Generation Y. **Baby boomers** are the main reason for the greying of North America. During the baby boom (people born between 1946 and 1965), families had an average of 4 children versus the current average of 1.54.[4] This group now accounts for approximately 60 percent of expenditures on consumer goods and services, and will continue to be a key force as they move into their senior years.[5] Baby boomers are currently redefining the concept of aging with a keen interest in health, self-image, and retirement. Marketers have noted these interests and are developing products to address these needs. Examples that we see in the marketplace are the host of anti-wrinkle creams and grey hair dye products that have saturated the personal care arena.

Generation X is the group of people born after the baby boomers, between 1966 and 1974. In Canada, this generation numbers 3.9 million, accounting for 12 percent of the population.[6] These consumers differ from baby boomers in that they are not as brand loyal and tend to be more self-reliant, entrepreneurial, and better educated. They are less prone to materialism and extravagance than the baby boomers. Generation X is becoming a key influence in the market.[7]

Generation Y is the group of people born between 1975 and 1995.[8] These are mostly children of baby boomers, and are referred to as the echo boom. They number 8.7 million and account for 27.5 percent of the Canadian population.[9] Music, video games, sports, and computer purchases are key products developed to meet the needs of this demographic group. In time, this generation is expected to become as influential as their baby-boom parents.

Each of these three generations has very different tastes, consumption patterns, and attitudes. For each generation, marketers need to develop distinct marketing programs, products, and services. For example, each of these generations uses the media quite differently, and marketers have to carefully select

baby boomers
Generation of people born between 1946 and 1964

Generation X
People born between 1965 and 1976

Generation Y
People born between 1975 and 1995

Baby Boomers' Interests

They have the money. They want to spend it. But nobody seems to want it. In terms of sheer population, baby boomers are the spine of Canadian consumer culture. Those born in the years following World War II—1946 through 1965—represent the bulk of the country's money and buying power, but according to a 2008 Ipsos Reid poll conducted for the Canadian Newspaper Association, they feel they are being overlooked by advertisers who focus on younger consumers.

Boomer spending priorities tend to come with high price tags. Those polled list the following among their priorities for the coming year: vacations (39 percent), home electronics (35 percent), mutual funds or investments (31 percent), appliances (24 percent), and a car (23 percent). Canadians 44 and older control more than 77 percent of the country's wealth, according to Statistics Canada. In 2007, the group was responsible for 58 percent of all cars sold and 80 percent of all health care product purchases. Of those aged 44 and older, 73 percent have a household income of over $100,000, and 83 percent of households have savings or securities surpassing

$500,000. However, despite all this, the Ipsos Reid survey found that nearly three-quarters—74 percent—of advertising dollars were being spent on consumers aged 25 to 54.

Canadian Newspaper Association president and CEO Anne Kothawala says, "Clearly, there's a disconnect between who advertisers think they should be marketing to, and who actually has the resources and intention to spend. In other words, fistfuls of ad dollars are missing the boat."

Sources: Terry Poulton, "Boomers ready to spend: Ipsos Reid," *Media in Canada*, May 9, 2008, accessed at www.mediaincanada.com/articles/mic/20080509/boomers.html; and Chris Powell, "Marketers missing boomer boat: CNA study," *Marketing* magazine, May 09, 2008, accessed at www.marketingmag.ca/english/news/media/article.jsp?content=20080509_777333_2521.

which communication tools will effectively communicate with their target market. If communicating with Generation X and Y, a marketer will likely include an Internet component in its media mix. However, if communicating with the older baby boomers, the marketing communications program may rely on more traditional communications tools such as print- and TV-based advertising.

Big City Dwelling Canada is one of the most urbanized nations in the world. In 2006, more than 80 percent of Canadians lived in urban areas or their suburbs. Statistics indicate that cities are growing much faster than rural areas, which lag behind the rest of the country in growth rates. Between 2001 and 2006, the overall population of Canada grew by 5.4 percent compared to rural areas, which only grew by 1.0 percent.[10]

Canadian cities are not the vast metropolitan areas we see in many other countries. There are only six urban areas in Canada with populations over 1 million people: Toronto, Montreal, Vancouver, Ottawa-Gatineau, Calgary, and Edmonton. Interestingly, in

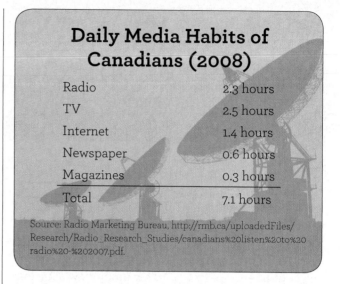

Daily Media Habits of Canadians (2008)

Radio	2.3 hours
TV	2.5 hours
Internet	1.4 hours
Newspaper	0.6 hours
Magazines	0.3 hours
Total	7.1 hours

Source: Radio Marketing Bureau, http://rmb.ca/uploadedFiles/Research/Radio_Research_Studies/canadians%20listen%20to%20radio%20-%202007.pdf.

the biggest cities, the city centres are growing more slowly than the suburbs. Over the five-year period from 2001 to 2006, the cities with the highest growth rates were Barrie, Ontario, at 19.2 percent, and Calgary, Alberta, at 13.4 percent. Population declines were seen in Saint John, New Brunswick, and Saguenay, Quebec.

Figure 2–2
Canadian cities—which ones have grown, which ones have lost population in the 2001–2006 period

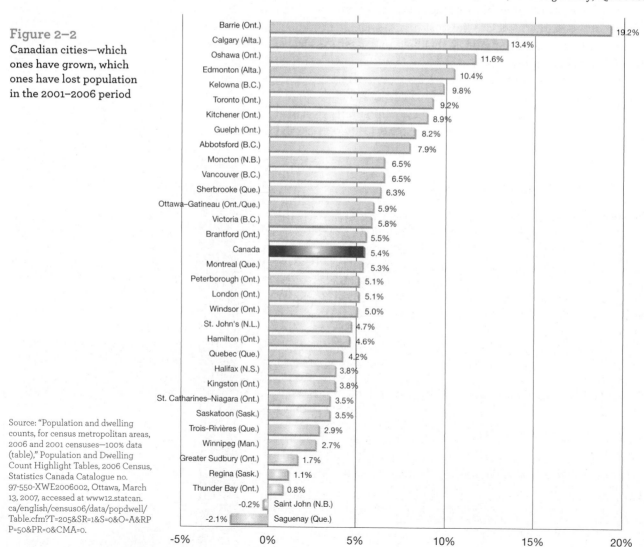

Source: "Population and dwelling counts, for census metropolitan areas, 2006 and 2001 censuses—100% data (table)," Population and Dwelling Count Highlight Tables, 2006 Census, Statistics Canada Catalogue no. 97-550-XWE2006002, Ottawa, March 13, 2007, accessed at www12.statcan.ca/english/census06/data/popdwell/Table.cfm?T=205&SR=1&S=0&O=A&RPP=50&PR=0&CMA=0.

Figure 2–3
Annual number of immigrants admitted to Canada, 1901–2001

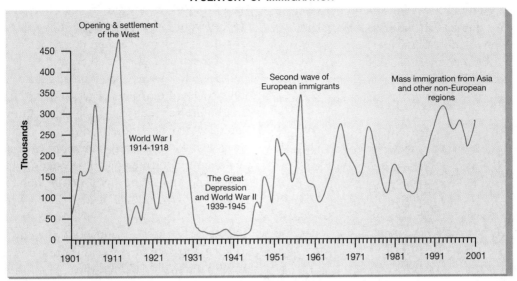

A CENTURY OF IMMIGRATION

Source: Citizenship and Immigration Canada

Figure 2-2 (see page 28) shows metropolitan growth levels over this five-year period.[11]

Ethnic Diversity   Canada prides itself on being a multicultural country (see Figure 2-3). Two-thirds of the nation's growth between 2001 and 2006 was due to immigration, with most new immigrants coming from Asia (58 percent). In 2006, there were 6.2 million foreign-born people living in Canada, with one in five people citing their mother tongue as neither English nor French.[12] Other than English or French, the top two languages used at home were the Chinese languages and Punjabi.

This multicultural mix creates an interesting array of opportunities for marketers. These specific ethnic groups have their own particular interests and habits, which can be addressed in unique ways. Companies such as Rogers Communications have risen to this challenge, offering a diverse list of foreign-based TV stations to people in Canada. A person can watch Greek TV stations, Korean TV programs, and movies from India, just to mention a few.

Non-traditional Families   The traditional nuclear family of two parents and two children has changed over time. Family size has decreased with families having between one and two children each. The structure

"IN 2006, THERE WERE 6.2 MILLION FOREIGN-BORN PEOPLE LIVING IN CANADA."

of the family has also changed with evidence of more common-law relationships, single-parent families, and blended families. In the last few years, same-sex marriages have also surfaced.

This change in family structure impacts on marketers who need to determine whether these new trends will affect their market. An interesting example is DeBeers Canada, which took these societal changes and used them as an opportunity to develop products to address evolving needs. DeBeers continued to market its diamond engagement rings to traditional groups, but also expanded into diamond pendants and anniversary bands, and also developed a celebratory Three-Stone Ring, to symbolize the past, the present, and the future for less traditional target groups.

CHAPTER 2 THE MARKETING ENVIRONMENT 29

socio-cultural forces Cultural values, ideas, and attitudes, as well as society's morals and beliefs

World Markets The world population is showing growth in underdeveloped areas such as Africa, Asia, and India.[13] China and India alone are home to 2.5 billion people, 38 percent of the world's population. These areas represent future opportunities for marketers seeking to expand into foreign markets.[14] The sheer size of these countries presents an opportunity to sell products and services.

Socio-Cultural Forces

Socio-cultural trends are more difficult to pinpoint than demographic changes. It is not easy to identify societal and cultural shifts in attitudes, or to track newly evolving trends. Socio-cultural changes tend to be gradual, over a prolonged period of time, and sometimes very subtle. Statistical data is not as readily available on these areas, but good marketers are able to observe changes in society and identify evolving trends and opportunities. Sometimes, identifying these trends involves consumer research; other times it involves a keen eye and good intuition.

Top 5 Population Hot Spots (2008)

1. China	1,330,044,605
2. India	1,147,995,898
3. United States	303,824,646
4. Indonesia	237,512,355
5. Brazil	191,908,598

Source: U.S. Census Bureau, International Data Base, www.census.gov/cgi-bin/ipc/idbrank.pl.

When we discuss **socio-cultural forces**, we are referring to cultural values, ideas, and attitudes that are learned and shared among a group of people. It also includes society's morals and beliefs. Canadians are known to be trustworthy, family oriented, worldly, organized, reliable, socially conscious, and conservative. Canadian society is tolerant of different cultural beliefs; welcomes new ideas and perspectives; and values honesty, integrity, fairness, and hard work. Marketers monitor changes in these areas so that they can capitalize on new opportunities in their marketing programs. Most recently, marketers are responding to socio-cultural changes as they relate to ethnic foods, health and fitness, the environment, and the changing role of women in society.

Ethnic Foods Consumers in Canada are exposed to a wide variety of spices, flavours, and dishes from around the world. We find these in our homes, in restaurants throughout the country, and in the multicultural communities where we live. This exposure has trickled down to the types of foods people enjoy and wish to purchase in grocery stores. Marketers in the food industry have noted these trends and launched a wide range of pre-prepared foods and sauces to cater to these evolving tastes. Examples are Patak's, which markets a full line of Indian sauces in mainstream supermarkets, and McCormick & Co., which developed the Thai Kitchen brand of meal-kits and ingredients for consumers to use at home.

Cultural diversity stimulates the creation of new products.

Health and Fitness An increased media focus on health issues and the need to remain active and fit has encouraged Canadians to demand smarter choices in their lives. Companies that recognize this shift in socio-cultural focus are introducing products that are healthier and better for Canadians. Cadbury is meeting consumer needs for smaller, low-calorie portions with its Cadbury Thins® line of smaller chocolate bars, while Kraft, with a low-fat line of Cracker Barrel cheese is meeting consumer demands for healthier choices.

Environmental Awareness Global warming has received enormous attention in the press, rallying Canadians around the cause to reduce pollution and save the environment. Canadians are showing a keen interest in being less wasteful and making choices that do not negatively impact the environment. Companies such as Canadian Tire are rising to the challenge and encouraging people to be less wasteful. Canadian Tire has introduced their Smart Energy Solutions, which promotes its ability to help homeowners save electricity and reduce pollution to save the environment.

Changing Gender Roles Over the past 30 years, one of the most notable socio-cultural changes in Canada has been the changing role of women and men in society. Increasingly, women are working full-time and men are becoming more involved in household duties. This has resulted in dual-income families who are time-starved. Marketers and companies have identified an opportunity to address this issue with more convenience products and better services to help busy families. Increasingly, we see companies offering flexible hours for employees and the continued growth of

Flick-Fest's Focus on Global Warming

Launched in 2005 to encourage the fight against global warming, Flick Off partnered with Virgin Mobile Canada, MuchMusic, Roots Canada, the David Suzuki Foundation, and the Government of Ontario. Designed around its website, www.flickoff.com, which educates Canadians about the effects of global warming and attempts to motivate change, Flick Off stands behind a simple message: Worrying about global warming isn't enough; we have to take action. Targeting youth who are worried about the environment but intimidated by the overwhelming challenges of eco-consciousness, the Flick Off campaign focuses on practical steps that can be taken by

individuals. "If they go and tell their friends about what they did to make a difference, and they tell their family, we collectively as a community, and collectively as a country, can continue to bring the issue to a head and really make a difference," says Andrew Bridge, Virgin Mobile's director of communications.

In 2007, Flick Off announced the inaugural Flick-Fest a free, carbon-neutral music festival that would be offered as a reward to the community in Canada most concerned with its energy footprint. The winner was Estevan, Saskatchewan, a town with a population of about 10,000. Ironically known as Saskatchewan's "energy city" for its robust

power-generation industries, Estevan had the most residents per capita of the communities that registered their carbon footprint on the Flick Off website, narrowly beating out Duncan, British Columbia, and Wolfville, Nova Scotia.

Partially funded by a grant from Canada's Ministry of the Environment, the concert was held in Estevan on May 30, 2008, and attracted about 1,000 concert-goers. Besides on-site recycling, the grounds of Estevan's Civic Auditorium were patrolled by "Green Angels," whose job was to ensure nothing recyclable found its way into trash cans. "A lot of the awareness happens in the big cities, so it's really great to get the awareness in a smaller town," said event coordinator Lorne Cooperberg. ●

Marketing NewsFlash

Sources: "Flick-Fest announces new hot act for Estevan," Flick Off press release, May 16, 2008, accessed at www.flickoff.org/aboutus/mediareleases; and "Environmental Defence, Virgin Mobile Canada, MuchMusic, Roots Canada and the Province of Ontario Tell Canadians To... FLICK OFF!" Environmental Defence press release, April 25, 2007, accessed at www.environmentaldefence.ca/pressroom/viewnews.php?id=42.

the home office. Supermarkets cater to this same socio-cultural change by offering prepared foods and expanded areas that merchandise these items. Loblaws recently introduced an upscale line of freshly prepared gourmet salads for these busy, time-starved individuals. Many restaurants also address these needs by providing delivery services within their catchment areas. Small businesses have even developed gourmet meal-kits, complete with all the fresh ingredients, allowing consumers to more easily make gourmet meals without the hassle of finding a recipe and separately purchasing ingredients.

Economic Forces

The **economy** is another area in a marketing environmental scan that marketers need to note. The economic ability of a consumer to purchase a product is what interests marketers. If there is a significant change in the economy, this will impact on a household's income and ability to purchase. If people become unemployed, they will likely defer the purchase of a new car and concentrate their purchases on life's necessities. When the economy slows down, and people do not feel secure in their jobs, many higher-priced purchases are delayed. In an economic downturn, the automotive sector is one of the first industries to suffer.

Marketers need to recognize how the economy impacts on the purchase behaviour of their specific target group. Some products such as flour do better in a poor economy, with consumers making their own cookies and muffins rather than spending the extra money to buy more expensive ready-to-eat items. However, as noted earlier, the purchase of automobiles tends to suffer in a worsening economy.

The economy consists of macroeconomic forces and microeconomic forces. **Macroeconomic forces** refer to the state of a country's economy as a whole. Indicators of strength and weakness should be on a marketer's radar screen so that they can react quickly

to changes that affect their consumers. A country's key economic indicators are its inflation rate, its unemployment rate, and its economic growth rate. Consumer confidence is also an important indicator of the economy's health, showing how people feel about their long-term economic prospects.

One key economic indicator is **inflation**, a period when the cost to produce and buy products and services gets higher as prices rise. From a marketing standpoint, if prices rise faster than consumer income, consumer purchasing power decreases.

A **recession** is a time of slow economic activity with two consecutive periods of negative growth. During recessions, production levels decline, unemployment levels rise, and many consumers have less money to spend. At these times, consumers tend to focus their spending on life's necessities.

A country's business cycle fluctuates between different levels of growth depending on the state of the economy, international economic factors, and global pressures. Canada's growth is described by the Organisation for Economic Co-operation and Development (OECD) as strong due to its strength in productivity, investment levels, the Canadian dollar, and technological advances. Canada's economy is outperforming that of the United States, posting an estimated 2.5 percent increase in 2007, compared to 2.1 percent for the U.S. During the 2009 economic downturn, Canada is expected to perform relatively well compared to other Western nations. By watching these key economic indicators, marketers

ask yourself

1. What do we mean by time-starved?

2. What are the marketing implications of ethnic diversity in Canada?

3. How are important values such as health and fitness reflected in the marketplace today?

can have an understanding of whether they can expect a downturn or upswing in the economy and forecast how this will affect their consumers and ultimately their business.

Microeconomic forces directly refer to the supply and demand of goods and services and how this is impacted by individual, household, and company decisions to purchase. A marketer needs to be alerted to how these areas affect their consumers' buying power. Here are some terms you need to know (see Figure 2–4):

● **Gross income.** This is the total amount of money made in one year by a person, household, or family unit including taxes.

● **Disposable income.** This is the after-tax income that consumers have left for spending and savings. Typical purchases are for rent, clothing, and transportation. If taxes rise at a faster rate than income, consumers have less disposable income with which to pay the bills.

● **Discretionary income.** This is the after-tax income a consumer has left after paying for necessities such as food, shelter, and clothing. This income is used for discretionary purchases that are not deemed a necessity. Examples include going to a movie, eating at a restaurant, buying a computer, or going on a vacation.

Figure 2–4
Three levels of consumer income

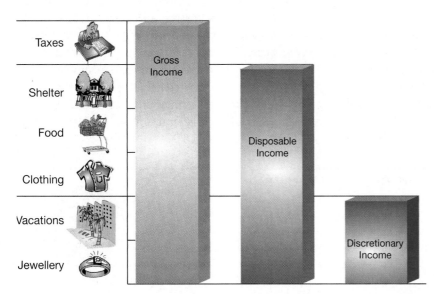

Technological Forces

Changes in how consumers use technology must be understood by marketers. This is another area in a marketing environmental scan that must be noted or the results can be problematic. Marketers need to know not only what new inventions are coming on the scene but also how consumers are integrating technology into their daily lives. The Childhood Cancer Foundation Candlelighters Canada is a prime example of an organization where understanding the usage of technology prompted changes to the delivery of its programs.

Technological forces refer to inventions or innovations that stem from scientific or engineering research. Each new wave of technology can replace existing products, and companies need to be aware of technological changes to ensure that their products do not become obsolete. An example of technological change can be seen with the Internet and how it is changing the way viewers watch TV programs. The younger generations are watching TV programs online and demanding to use this format to satisfy their viewing needs. The major Canadian TV networks such as Global and CTV are responding to these changes in technology and consumer usage patterns by streaming more and more shows on the Internet. Global TV is broadcasting 17 programs on TV and on the Internet during the 2008–2009 season. Shows such as *90210*, *Knight Rider*, *Heroes*, and *The Office* are all being streamed at www.globalTV.com. CTV also provides streaming video of its popular programs, including *Gossip Girl*,

microeconomic forces The supply and demand of goods and services and how this is impacted by individual, household, and company decisions to purchase

gross income Total amount of money made in one year by a person, household, or family unit, including taxes

disposable income Balance of income left after paying taxes; income that is used for spending and savings

discretionary income Money that consumers have left after paying taxes and buying necessities

technological forces Inventions from applied science or engineering research

> *Changes in how consumers use technology must be understood by marketers.*

Desperate Housewives, and *The Daily Show.* These can be seen at www.ctv.ca.

Some of the most recent technological advances that have changed how consumers conduct their daily lives are noted below:

- The Internet and search engines are replacing bricks-and-mortar libraries as instant sources of information.
- E-mail, text messaging, and instant messaging are reducing the need for traditional mail delivery systems.
- Social networking sites such as Facebook and My-Space are surfacing as new virtual meeting places.
- Video-sharing sites such as YouTube are allowing people to create and share their own video content.
- Music and video download sites such as LimeWire and iTunes are replacing traditional music and DVD retailers.
- Blogs are allowing people to create their own content and voice opinions.
- High-speed Internet connections are facilitating the viewing of TV online.
- Cellphones are replacing land-line phones.

An example of how marketers are using new technology to meet consumer needs can be seen in the automotive industry. General Motors offers OnStar, a comprehensive in-vehicle safety, security, and convenience service including built-in navigation, vehicle diagnostics, and automatic crash response that gets help to your exact location in the event of a collision. Under development are radar-like collision-avoidance systems that disengage cruise control and reduce engine speed. Honda, GM, and Volkswagen are all developing self-piloting cars.

Marketing ▶ tip

"The not-for-profit world is highly competitive today. Only the fittest will do well and mastering the Internet is at the core of success for not-for-profits."

David Stones, president and CEO, Childhood Cancer Foundation Candlelighters Canada

Competitive Forces

L❸ Another important element in the marketing environmental scan is competition, with a focus on **competitive forces**, which refer to alternative products that can satisfy a specific market's needs. There are various types of competition, and each company must consider its present and potential competitors when designing its marketing strategy. A company must first look at its most obvious competitors, **direct competitors** that offer very similar products in the same category, and must then examine those competitors that

Hours spent on the Internet (monthly)

Canada **46**   United States **32**   Sweden **31**

marketing meter

Source: *Canadian Media Directors' Council Media Digest 2008/2009,* p. 64, www.cmdc.ca/pdf/2008_09_media_digest.pdf.

compete for the same buying dollar in a slightly different market, **indirect competitors**. Consider, for example, Pizza Hut. If Pizza Hut wanted to review its direct competitors, it may focus on Domino's and Pizza Pizza. However, an indirect competitor such as Swiss Chalet should not be ignored as it provides home-delivery service. Pizza Hut must also consider the frozen pizza market, which competes in this segment with competitors such as Kraft's Delissio pizza. A consumer can order a pizza, go to a pizza parlour, take one out of the freezer, or buy something altogether different. When analyzing the competitive environment, a competitor needs to also take its direction from its consumers and understand how they choose among competitive offerings.

Marketers need to be intimately familiar with competitive products and try to anticipate competitive moves in the marketplace. This will help avoid the pitfalls that can surface from underestimating the competition.

Using new technology to meet consumer needs

Apart from intimately understanding direct and indirect competitors, marketers need to have a clear understanding of the competitive nature of the industry in which they function. Figure 2–5 shows the four basic types of competition as identified by economists.

At one end is **perfect competition** where there are many sellers with nearly identical products and little differentiation. Companies that deal in commodities, that is, products such as grains, vegetables, or coal, often function in an environment where perfect competition exists. In this instance, marketers need to know that pricing plays a key role in securing business, and that the focus will be on cost reduction in every element of the business.

The second point on the continuum is **monopolistic competition**. This is where a large number of sellers compete with each other, offering customers similar or substitute products. Marketers need to know that in this instance branding plays an important role, as does product differentiation and

Figure 2–5
Types of competitions

Perfect Competition
Many firms, identical products
Example: apple farmers

Monopolistic Competition
Many firms, similar products
Example: blue-jean manufacturers

Oligopoly
Few firms
Example: airlines

Monopoly
One firm
Example: local cable service providers

added-value activities to draw consumers to the product. Being in touch with consumer needs and adjusting the marketing mix to meet these needs is crucial for long-term survival. The market for jeans is a good example. This market is dominated by major brands such as Levi's and Calvin Klein, but there are also many premium specialty brands such as Seven, Guess, and Diesel, and many lower-priced offerings that marketers need to keep in mind when marketing their products.

The third type of competition is an **oligopoly**, which occurs when a few companies control a market. In Canada, this situation exists with oil companies that control the gasoline industry. Companies such as Shell, Petro Canada, Chevron, and Esso dominate the market. Because there is limited competition, these companies can easily control prices and are often criticized for price collusion (fixing prices among competitors). This has yet to be proven in the oil industry. Marketers who function in an oligopoly need to be acutely aware of competitive moves and, particularly, changes in price. An unnecessary price cut that is followed by the entire industry may result in profits being taken out of the category for everyone.

The fourth type of competition is a **monopoly**. A monopoly exists when there is only one company selling in the market. Monopolies are not illegal in Canada but they are carefully monitored by the Competition Bureau to ensure that consumers are not charged excessive prices. Governments do not like to see unregulated monopolies, and actively seek to reduce their control of the market through regulation and by encouraging competition.

Regulatory Forces

LO ④ The final area involved in a marketing environmental scan relates to **regulations**, which are restrictions placed on marketing practices by different levels of government and industry associations. These regulations are put in place to protect consumers from unscrupulous business practices, to set acceptable standards of practice, and to encourage fair competition.

The key regulatory groups that affect marketing practices in Canada are the Competition Bureau, the Canadian Radio-television and Telecommunications Commission (CRTC), Advertising Standards Canada (ASC), the Canadian Marketing Association (CMA), and the Better Business Bureau (BBB). In addition to these general regulatory bodies, a marketer needs to investigate other regulatory bodies specific to its industry, or those that apply in other countries where they conduct business.

The **Competition Bureau** is responsible for the administration and enforcement of the *Competition Act,* the *Consumer Packaging and Labelling Act,* the *Textile Labelling Act,* and the *Precious Metals Marking Act,* just to name a few. The bureau's role is to promote and maintain fair competition so that Canadians can benefit from lower prices, product choice, and quality services. Prohibited practices among business competitors include, among other things, price fixing among competitors, predatory pricing by large competitors to run a small company out of business, and bid-rigging among competitors to inflate prices on government contracts. Prohibited practices to lure consumers include bait-and-switch advertising practices, fraudulent advertising claims, and misleading pricing practices. Failure to abide by these rules can result in fines and jail time, if appropriate. For a complete list of regulations from the Competition Bureau, go to www.cb-bc.gc.ca.

The **Canadian Radio-television and Telecommunications Commission (CRTC)** is another government agency that enforces regulations on Canadian businesses. It administers the *Broadcast and Telecommunications Act,* setting guidelines for broadcast standards, adjudicating on the ownership of media outlets, and approving broadcast licences for TV

ask yourself

1. What is the difference between a consumer's disposable and discretionary income?

2. What is the most common form of competition?

3. What are the indirect competitors to a bag of Doritos chips?

and radio stations. It also sets guidelines for the broadcast of Canadian content and sets the number of minutes of advertising permitted hourly on TV. As an example, starting in 2007, the CRTC permitted the number of minutes of advertising to be gradually increased from 12 minutes per hour to being unregulated by 2009.

Advertising Standards Canada is a non-government agency run by professionals from the advertising, media, and marketing communities. It is self-regulating, meaning that the government does not impose its ideas. Instead, the industry sets and imposes its own guidelines and members of the marketing, advertising, and media communities agree to abide by these standards. These guidelines address issues such as comparative advertising, accuracy, safety, decency, and advertising to children. For a complete set of guidelines, visit www.asc.ca.

The **Canadian Marketing Association (CMA)** represents companies involved in marketing in Canada. It acts as a voice for Canadian marketers and deals with issues such as privacy, identity theft, mobile marketing, spam, and fraud prevention. Its members must follow its Code of Ethics and Standards of Practice. For information on this organization, visit www.the-cma.org.

The **Better Business Bureau (BBB)** is a voluntary alliance of businesses whose members are committed to being fair and honest in their dealings, to promoting self-regulatory practices, and to collecting and dispensing information to help businesses and consumers make sound decisions. The BBB provides an extensive selection of services for its members, businesses, and the general public. For a complete list of these services visit www.bbb.org.

ask yourself

1. What role does the Canadian Radio-television and Telecommunications Commission (CRTC) play in Canadian marketing regulations?

2. Do you think the Canadian Children's Food and Beverage Advertising Initiative will have any impact?

3. Does self-regulation work? Why or why not?

Advertising Junk Food to Kids

Focus on Ethics

In 2006, Kellogg's was under pressure by consumer advocacy groups, which threatened to sue the company for advertising junk food to children. So, when Kellogg's announced in 2007 that it would no longer market foods failing to meet its new nutritional criteria to preteens, the advocacy groups were suitably impressed.

Kellogg Canada is a charter participant in the Canadian Children's Food and Beverage Advertising Initiative, a voluntary initiative by 16 of Canada's food and beverage companies.

In 2007, participants began a campaign to use their marketing activities to promote healthy lifestyle and dietary choices to children under 12 years of age. Shifting advertising to emphasize foods and drinks consistent with sound nutrition guidance, the initiative boasts companies such as Nestlé Canada, Coca-Cola Canada, Kraft Canada, and McDonald's Restaurants of Canada, among others. Participants pledge to devote at least half of their advertising directed at preteens to the initiative, to incorporate only health-concerned

messages in interactive games aimed at children under 12, and to pursue several other core principles. The initiative is monitored by a transparent, accountable compliance auditing process directed by Advertising Standards Canada to check participants' compliance and publicly report annual results.

Whether this move will actually change children's eating habits remains to be seen, but Kellogg's, at least, is committed to its move. It has announced that if it can't reformulate its products—including Pop-Tarts and Corn Pops—to bring them in line with the nutritional criteria, it won't advertise them to children. ●

Sources: "About the Initiative," Canadian Children's Food and Beverage Advertising Initiative website, accessed at http://adstandards.ca/en/childrensinitiative/default.asp; "Canada's Food and Beverage Industry Unveils Integrated Children-Focused Initiatives: New Social Marketing Campaign and Advertising Commitment Focused on Healthy Active Living," Food and Consumer Products of Canada press release, April 16, 2007, accessed at www.fcpmc.com/mediaroom/releases/2007/ca041607-eng.pdf; and Elaine D. Kolish, "Progress In Action: Children's Food & Beverage Advertising Self Regulation: A Report From the BBB FTC/HHS Forum, July 18, 2007, accessed at www.ftc.gov/bcp/workshops/childobesity/presentations/kolish.pdf.

A Marketing Environmental Scan in Practice

A group of students were recently asked to conduct a marketing environmental scan on Fisher Price's Smart Cycle. This is a stationary bike, made for children between the ages of 3 and 6 years, that plugs into a TV. It was named Toy of The Year in 2008 by the Toy Industry Association. When a child sits on the bike and pedals, he or she can play and learn through interactive arcade-type games. The product allows children to have fun and be active while also playing video games! The students were tasked to scan the marketing environment for the toy, and consider opportunities and threats with a view to recommending changes to its marketing program for the next toy marketing season.

After a review and brainstorming session, the students identified the facts and marketing ideas for the next season, which are presented in Figure 2–6.

The students recommended a number of changes for the next season in order to strengthen the product and meet evolving consumer needs. Ideas related to introducing new games that addressed basic reading, math, and language skills. These games were to include language options such as English, French, Punjabi, Spanish, and Mandarin. From a pricing perspective, the price of the toy was to be reduced if a consumer selected the option of downloading games from the Internet. The technology would be fast-loading, with fun, contemporary graphics and cartoon characters from kids' TV shows. A website would be created to accompany the toy with additional fun activities. Finally, in terms of safety standards, the students recommended rigorous regulations be imposed on offshore and local manufacturing. This is a marketing environmental scan in action.

Figure 2–6
Marketing Environmental Scan: Fisher Price Smart Cycle

MARKETING ENVIRONMENTAL SCAN		
	FACTS	MARKETING IDEAS
Demographic factors	Time-starved parents Multicultural families More single-parent families	Create games with language options to help kids learn their parent's language.
Socio-cultural factors	Concerns with health and the environment Kids inactive Kids watch too much TV Kids like computer games Concerns with education	Create games focusing on basic reading and math skills to help time starved parents. Pick themes and characters that are in TV shows. Ensure that games continue to encourage physical activity.
Economic factors	Concerns about the economy More single-parent families	Allow parents to download games to reduce costs and save on packaging.
Technological factors	Kids play computer games Kids surf the Internet Kids embrace technology	Create a website to add more fun and games.
Competitive factors	Traditional toys compete with computer games, video games, and online activities	Consider a licensing agreement.
Regulatory factors	Concerns with toy safety and off-shore production	Enforce strong regulatory standards on suppliers.

Summary...*just the facts*

- A marketing environmental scan is the process of continually acquiring information on events outside the organization to identify trends, opportunities, and threats.

- Demographics are the statistical study of populations, looking at characteristics such as gender, age, ethnicity, income, and occupation.

- Socio-cultural forces look at cultural values, ideas, and attitudes as they relate to society's trends and beliefs.

- Economic forces are important in terms of personal income and the health of the economy.

- Technological forces relate to scientific inventions and innovations that affect the running of the business or target-group behaviour.

- Competitive forces refer to direct and indirect competitors and also the competitive nature of the market in which they function.

- Regulatory forces are the restrictions placed on a business, product, or service by the government or industry association.

Key Terms and Concepts...*a refresher*

baby boomers *p. 27*
competitive forces *p. 34*
demographics *p. 26*
direct competitors *p. 34*
discretionary income *p. 33*
disposable income *p. 33*
economy *p. 32*
Generation X *p. 27*

Generation Y *p. 27*
gross income *p. 33*
indirect competitors *p. 35*
inflation *p. 32*
macroeconomic forces *p. 32*
marketing environmental scan *p. 25*
microeconomic forces *p. 33*
monopolistic competition *p. 35*

monopoly *p. 36*
oligopoly *p. 36*
perfect competition *p. 35*
recession *p. 32*
regulations *p. 36*
socio-cultural forces *p. 30*
technological forces *p. 33*

consumer behaviour

Advertising agency ZenithOptimedia (ZO) prides itself on researching consumer behaviour to better understand the target markets of the products the agency advertises, and ultimately to create more effective marketing communications programs. ZO created Touchpoints ROI Tracker, a research tool that identifies the points of contact (called consumer touch points) that consumers have with products. ZO works to identify the role of consumer touch

points in purchase behaviour and how they can best be used to communicate with consumers. These touch points refer to areas such as the media that a person uses, the items that a consumer uses to gather information, or the activities consumers do when socializing. Specifically, ZO measures all forms of consumer contact with the brand, such as when the product is used, and specific influences, such as salespeople, word of mouth, event marketing, the Internet, and mass media.

In January 2004, under the guidance of Ruth Klostermann, vice president of strategic resources, ZO introduced the Touchpoints ROI Tracker in Canada. Since then, the agency has interviewed over 30,000 Canadians about 216 brands. Klostermann explains that creating this body of research helps the agency determine which communications programs best serve their individual clients and what combination of tools may elicit the greatest return on investment: "At ZenithOptimedia, we believe that by creating powerful connections with our consumers, we will deliver the best return on investment for our clients."[1]

Looking internationally at this research tool, the database confirms that the Internet is now central to marketing communications programs and that the Internet is starting to play a more important role with aging consumers. However, recommendations from friends and families appear to be the most influential factor on brand choice around the world. In fact, these recommendations are 22 percent more impactful than television advertising. Comparing different regions around the world, marketing communications programs have much higher awareness in the Asia Pacific region than in North America or Europe. Television advertising surfaces as 20 percent more influential in the Asia Pacific region than in North America.[2]

LEARNING OBJECTIVES

 Describe the stages in the consumer decision process.

 Distinguish among three variations of the consumer decision process: routine, limited, and extended problem solving.

 Describe how situational influences affect the purchase decision process.

L⓸ Explain how psychological influences affect consumer behaviour, particularly purchase decision processes.

L⓹ Identify major socio-cultural influences on consumer behaviour and their effects on purchase decisions.

L⓺ Understand how marketers can use knowledge of consumer behaviour to better understand and influence individual and family purchases.

Klostermann further notes that "Touchpoints ROI Tracker has generated a huge body of learning that spans a wide range of consumers, categories and countries, and has greatly enhanced our holistic, consumer-centric approach to communications planning." This approach to marketing communications emphasizes that we need to understand our consumers clearly in order to allocate marketing resources effectively and efficiently. Advances in technology now allow marketers to create databases of information that can effectively evaluate the impact of marketing programs on consumer behaviour. We will increasingly see marketers turn to such sophisticated research tools in the future, using these techniques to help plan and evaluate their marketing programs.

This chapter's focus is on **consumer behaviour**, from the psychological and socio-cultural points of view. Effective marketers keep an eye on their target market, and work to understand them and satisfy consumers' wants and needs. 🍎

Consumer Purchase Decision Process

LO 1 Behind the visible act of making a purchase lies an important decision process. The stages that a buyer passes through when making choices about which products and services to buy is the **purchase decision process**. This process has the five stages, as shown in Figure 3–1 (see page 43): problem recognition, information search, alternative evaluation, purchase decision, and post-purchase behaviour.

Problem Recognition: Perceiving a Need

Problem recognition, the initial step in the purchase decision, occurs when a person realizes that the difference between what he or she has and what he or she would like to have is big enough to actually do something about it.[3] The process may be triggered by a situation as simple as finding an empty milk carton in the refrigerator; noting, as a first-year university student, that your high school clothes are not in the style that other students are wearing; or realizing that your laptop computer may not be working properly.

In marketing, advertisements or salespeople can activate a consumer's decision process by showing the shortcomings of competing (or currently owned) products. For instance, an advertisement for an MP3 player could stimulate problem recognition by emphasizing the features, versatility, and storage capacity of new MP3 players over the CD player you may now own.

Information Search: Seeking Value

After recognizing a problem, consumers begin to search for information about what product or service might satisfy the newly discovered need. First, they may scan their memory for knowledge of or previous experiences with products or brands.[4] This action is called *internal search.* For frequently purchased products such as shampoo and conditioner, this may be enough. Or a consumer may undertake an *external search* for information.[5] This is especially needed when one does not have much past experience or knowledge, the risk of making a bad decision is high, and the cost of gathering information is low. The primary sources of external information are *personal sources,* such as relatives and friends who the consumer trusts; *public sources,* such as the Internet, including various product-rating organizations such as *Consumer Reports* or government agencies; and *marketer-dominated sources,* such

The Core: Chapter 3

Marketers understand what influences consumers' purchase decisions.

Psychological influences

Socio-cultural influences

Effective marketers keep an eye on their target market, and work to understand them and satisfy consumers' wants and needs.

Figure 3–1
Purchase decision process

| Problem recognition: Perceiving a need | → | Information search: Seeking value | → | Evaluation of alternatives: Assessing value | → | Purchase decision: Buying value | → | Post-purchase behaviour: Value in consumption or use |

as information from sellers that include advertising, company websites, salespeople, and point-of-purchase displays in stores. These sources of external information are examples of consumer touch points, which we described in this chapter's opening vignette.

Suppose you consider buying your first MP3 player. You will probably tap several of these information sources: friends and relatives, advertisements for MP3 players, brand and company websites, and stores carrying MP3 players (for demonstrations).

Alternative Evaluation: Assessing Value

The information search stage clarifies the problem for the consumer by suggesting criteria, or points to consider, for the purchase; providing brand names that might meet the criteria; and developing consumer value perceptions. What selection criteria would you use in buying a portable MP3 player? Would you use price, ease of using the controls, or some other combination?

Consider all the factors you may consider when evaluating portable MP3 players. These factors are a consumer's *evaluative criteria,* which represent both the objective attributes of a brand (such as sound quality) and the subjective ones (such as prestige) you use to compare different products and brands.[6] Firms try to identify and make the most of both types of evaluative criteria to create the best value for consumers. These criteria are often emphasized in advertisements.

For a product like a portable MP3 player, the information search process would probably involve visiting retail stores, seeing different brands in magazines, viewing promotions on a home shopping television channel, or visiting a seller's website. Consumers often have several criteria for comparing products. For example, among the evaluative criteria you might think of, suppose that you use three in considering brands of portable MP3 players: a list price under $400, a battery life of more than 20 hours, and ease of use. These criteria establish the brands in your *evoked set*—the group of brands that a consumer would consider acceptable from among all the brands in the product class of which he or she is aware.[7] Your three evaluative criteria may result in four models and three brands (Sony, Panasonic, and Apple) in your evoked set. If these alternatives don't satisfy you, you can change your evaluative criteria to create a different evoked set of models and brands.

iPod Sales by Year

2002	376,000
2003	937,000
2004	4,416,000
2005	22,497,000
2006	39,409,000
2007	51,630,000
2008	32,765,000

Source: "iPod," Wikipedia, based on press releases retrieved from Apple Inc., January 2002 to October 2008, accessed at http://en.wikipedia.org/wiki/File:IPodsales_2008Q3.svg.

Purchase Decision: Buying Value

Having examined the alternatives in the evoked set, you are almost ready to make a purchase decision. Three choices remain: the chosen brand, from whom to buy, and when to buy. The choice of which seller to buy from will depend on such considerations as the seller's location, your past experience buying from the seller, and the return policy.

Deciding when to buy is frequently determined by a number of factors. For instance, you might buy sooner if one of your preferred brands is on sale or its manufacturer offers a rebate. Other factors such as the store atmosphere, pleasantness of the shopping experience, salesperson persuasiveness, time pressure, and financial circumstances could also affect whether a purchase decision is made or postponed. If your decision is the iPod, you may decide to buy it at the Apple Store because it's a cool place to shop.

Use of the Internet to gather information, evaluate alternatives, and make buying decisions adds a technological dimension to the consumer purchase decision process.

Post-purchase Behaviour: Value in Consumption or Use

After buying a product, the consumer compares it with his or her expectations and is either satisfied or dissatisfied. A company's sensitivity to a customer's consumption experience strongly affects the value a customer perceives after the purchase. Studies show that satisfaction or dissatisfaction affects consumer communications and repeat-purchase behaviour. Satisfied buyers tell three other people about their experience. Dissatisfied buyers complain to nine people![8] Satisfied

Shopping Carts Abandoned

Marketing NewsFlash

It's a common online scenario: A customer visits a website and browses through its products, selecting various items and placing them in the customer's virtual shopping cart. At the end of the shopping trip, however, the visitor exits the site without finishing the transaction, leaving the cart and the items within it. Such abandonment of online shopping carts is a major problem with online retailers, causing companies to pursue changes in the way that their websites operate. A consumer often fills a virtual shopping cart in order to calculate shipping costs or to get prices for comparison-shopping, and after obtaining this information, customers frequently leave the site without actually ordering the items, causing vendors to lose potential revenue. Customers abandon shopping carts

when faced with website barriers such as site registrations, where in order to actually purchase the items that they have selected, they must register at the site; many customers instead choose to purchase from another location rather than register, often due to privacy concerns or time issues.

In order to fix these recurring issues, many vendors are seeking changes in their websites, redesigning sites to make the shopping process an easier one. Some of these changes include showing content summaries that appear on the screen as the customer is shopping, allowing them to see what their shipping costs will be before they check out, and stock control features that tell consumers whether the item they're shopping for is available before they attempt to buy it. Vendors are streamlining registration

processes to make customers more comfortable with using their website. Companies have also improved their customer service features, making contact information easily available to online users. With the implementation of these changes, companies hope to increase the confidence that visitors will have in their sites and in their company, confidence that will turn browsers into buyers.

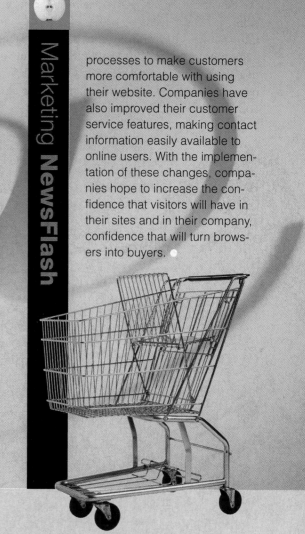

buyers also tend to buy from the same seller each time a purchase occasion arises. The financial impact of repeat-purchase behaviour is significant.[9] Accordingly, firms such as General Electric (GE), Johnson & Johnson, Coca-Cola, and British Airways focus attention on post-purchase behaviour to maximize customer satisfaction and retention.[10] These firms, among many others, now provide toll-free telephone numbers, offer liberalized return and refund policies, and engage in staff training to handle complaints, answer questions, and record suggestions. Lands' End has a particularly interesting way of maximizing customer satisfaction: with its guarantee. Instead of having pages and paragraphs of legal-sounding explanations of the limitations of the guarantee, Lands' End makes it simple: "Guaranteed. Period."[11] This simplicity gives consumers peace of mind and a feeling that Lands' End is a consumer-friendly place to shop.

Often, a consumer is faced with two or more highly attractive alternatives, such as choosing between a Sony MP3 player or an iPod. If you choose the Sony, you may think, "Should I have purchased the iPod?" This feeling of post-purchase psychological tension or anxiety is called *cognitive dissonance*. To alleviate it, consumers often attempt to applaud themselves for making the right choice. So, after purchase, you may seek information to confirm your choice by asking friends questions like, "Don't you like my new MP3 player?" or by reading ads of the brand you chose. You might even look for negative features about the brand you didn't buy. Firms often use ads or follow-up calls from salespeople in this post-purchase stage to assure buyers that they made the right decision.

> Satisfied buyers tell three other people about their experience. Dissatisfied buyers complain to nine people!

involvement
Personal, social, and economic significance of a purchase to the consumer

Involvement and Problem-Solving Variations

L2 Sometimes consumers don't engage in the five-step purchase decision process. Instead, they skip or minimize one or more steps depending on the level of involvement. The level of involvement that a consumer has in a particular purchase depends on the personal, social, and economic consequences of that purchase to the consumer.[12] Items such as soft drinks or toothpaste may have such a low level of involvement for consumers that they may skip or minimize one or more steps in the process. But they may do just the opposite for a high-involvement purchase like a computer or an automobile.

High-involvement purchase occasions typically have at least one of three characteristics: the item to be purchased is expensive; it can have serious personal consequences; or it could reflect on one's social image. For these occasions, consumers engage in extensive information search, consider many product attributes and brands, form attitudes, and participate in word-of-mouth communication. Researchers have identified three general variations in the consumer purchase process based on consumer involvement and product knowledge. Figure 3–2 summarizes some of the important differences between the three problem-solving variations.[13]

Figure 3–2
Comparison of problem-solving variations

CHARACTERISTICS OF PURCHASE DECISION PROCESS	LOW ← CONSUMER INVOLVEMENT → HIGH		
	ROUTINE PROBLEM SOLVING	LIMITED PROBLEM SOLVING	EXTENDED PROBLEM SOLVING
Number of brands examined	One	Several	Many
Number of sellers considered	Few	Several	Many
Number of product attributes evaluated	One	Moderate	Many
Number of external information sources used	None	Few	Many
Time spent searching	Minimal	Little	Considerable

Routine Problem Solving For products such as table salt and milk, consumers recognize a problem, make a decision, and spend little effort seeking external information and evaluating alternatives. The purchase process for such items is virtually a habit and typifies low-involvement decision making. Routine problem solving is typically the case for low-priced, frequently purchased products.

Limited Problem Solving In limited problem solving, consumers typically seek some information or rely on a friend to help them evaluate alternatives. In general, several brands might be evaluated using a moderate number of different attributes. You might use limited problem solving in choosing a pair of jeans, deciding on a restaurant for dinner, and other purchase situations in which you have little time or effort to spend researching options.

Extended Problem Solving In extended problem solving, each of the five stages of the consumer purchase decision process is used in the purchase, including considerable time and effort on external information search and in identifying and evaluating alternatives. Several brands are in the evoked set, and these are evaluated on many attributes. Extended problem solving exists in high-involvement purchase situations for items such as automobiles, houses, and financial investments.

Figure 3–3 (see page 47) shows the many influences that affect the consumer purchase decision process. The decision to buy a product also involves important situational, psychological, and sociocultural influences, the topics discussed during the remainder of this chapter. Marketing mix influences are described later in Part 3 of the book.

Situational Influences

Often the purchase situation will affect the purchase decision process. Five *situational influences* have an impact on your purchase decision process: the purchase task, social surroundings, physical surroundings, temporal effects, and antecedent states.[14]

1. The *purchase task* is the reason for engaging in the decision in the first place. Information searching and evaluating alternatives may differ depending on whether the purchase is a gift, which often involves social visibility, or for the buyer's own use.

2. *Social surroundings,* including the other people present when a purchase decision is made, may also affect what is purchased.

3. *Physical surroundings* such as decor, music, and crowding in retail stores may alter how purchase decisions are made.

4. *Temporal effects,* such as time of day or the amount of time available, will influence where consumers have breakfast and lunch and what is ordered.

5. Finally, *antecedent states,* which include the consumer's mood or the amount of cash on hand, can influence purchase behaviour and choice.

ask yourself

1. What is the first stage in the consumer purchase decision process?

2. The grouping of brands that a consumer considers buying out of the set of brands in a product class is called the _____.

3. What is the term for post-purchase anxiety?

Psychological Influences on Consumer Behaviour

Psychology helps marketers understand why and how consumers behave as they do. In particular, concepts such as motivation and personality; perception; learning; values, beliefs, and attitudes; and lifestyle are useful for interpreting buying processes and directing marketing efforts.

motivation
Energizing force that stimulates behaviour to satisfy a need

personality
A person's consistent behaviours or responses to recurring situations

Motivation and Personality

Motivation and personality are two familiar psychological concepts that have specific meanings and marketing implications. They are both used frequently to describe why people do some things and not others.

Motivation **Motivation** is the energizing force that stimulates behaviour to satisfy a need. Because consumer needs are the focus of the marketing concept, marketers try to arouse these needs.

An individual's needs are boundless. People have physiological needs for basics such as water, food, and shelter. They also have learned needs, including esteem, achievement, and affection. Psychologists point out that these needs are hierarchical; that is, once physiological needs are met, people seek to satisfy their learned needs. Figure 3–4 (see page 48) shows one need hierarchy and classification scheme that contains the following five need classes:[15]

1. *Physiological needs* are basic to survival and must be satisfied first. A Burger King advertisement featuring a juicy hamburger attempts to activate the need for food.

2. *Safety needs* involve self-preservation and physical well-being. Smoke detector and burglar alarm manufacturers focus on these needs.

3. Social needs are concerned with love and friendship. Dating services and fragrance companies try to arouse these needs.

4. *Personal needs* are represented by the need for achievement, status, prestige, and self-respect. The American Express Gold Card and Holt Renfrew appeal to these needs. Sometimes firms try to arouse multiple needs to stimulate problem recognition. Michelin combines security with parental love to promote tire replacement for automobiles.

5. *Self-actualization needs* involve personal fulfillment. For example, travel providers offer specialized educational and exotic trips.

Personality **Personality** refers to a person's consistent behaviours or responses to recurring situations. Although numerous personality theories exist, most identify key traits such as assertiveness, extroversion, compliance, dominance, and aggression, among others. Research suggests that compliant people prefer known brand names and use more

Figure 3–3
Influences on the consumer purchase decision process

Marketing mix influences
- Product
- Price
- Promotion
- Place

Psychological influences
- Motivation
- Personality
- Perception
- Learning
- Values, beliefs, and attitudes
- Lifestyle

Consumer purchase decision process
Problem recognition

Information search

Alternative evaluation

Purchase decision

Post-purchase behaviour

Sociocultural influences
- Personal influence
- Reference groups
- Family
- Culture
- Subculture

Situational influences
- Purchase task
- Social surroundings
- Physical surroundings
- Temporal effects
- Antecedent states

mouthwash and toilet soaps. In contrast, aggressive types use razors, not electric shavers; apply more cologne and after-shave lotions; and purchase signature goods such as Gucci, Yves St. Laurent, and Donna Karan as an indicator of status.[16]

Personality characteristics are often revealed in a person's *self-concept,* which is the way people see themselves and the way they believe others see them. Marketers recognize that people have an actual self-concept and an ideal self-concept. The actual self refers to how people actually see themselves. The ideal self describes how people would like to see themselves. These two self-images are reflected in the products and brands a person buys, including automobiles, home appliances and furnishings, magazines, clothing, grooming and leisure products, and in the stores where a person shops. The importance of self-concept is summed up by a senior executive at Barnes & Noble: "People buy books for what the purchase says about them—their taste, their cultivation, their trendiness."[17]

Perception

One person sees a Porsche as a mark of achievement; another sees it as showing off. This is the result of **perception**—the process by which an individual selects, organizes, and interprets information to create a meaningful picture of the world.

Figure 3–4
Hierarchy of needs

Self-actualization needs:
Fulfillment of ambitions and hopes

Personal needs:
Status, respect, prestige

Social needs:
Friendship, belonging, love

Safety needs:
Freedom from harm, financial security

Physiological needs:
Food, water, shelter

Selective Perception The average consumer operates in a complex, information-rich environment. The human brain organizes and interprets all this information with a process called *selective perception,* which filters the information so that only some of it is understood or remembered or even available to the conscious mind. *Selective exposure* occurs when people pay attention to messages that are consistent with their attitudes and beliefs and ignore messages that are inconsistent. Selective exposure often occurs in the post-purchase stage of the consumer decision process, when consumers read advertisements for the brand they just bought. It also occurs when a need exists—you are more likely to "see" a McDonald's advertisement when you are hungry rather than after you have eaten a pizza.

Selective comprehension involves interpreting information so that it is consistent with your attitudes and beliefs. A marketer's failure to understand this can have disastrous results. For example, Toro introduced a small, lightweight snow-blower called the Snow Pup. Even though the product worked, sales failed to meet expectations. Why? Toro later found out that consumers perceived the name to mean that Snow Pup was a toy or too light to do any serious snow removal. When the product was renamed Snow Master, sales increased sharply.[18]

> *Research suggests that compliant people prefer known brand names and use more mouthwash and toilet soaps.*

Selective retention means that consumers do not remember all the information they see, read, or hear, even minutes after exposure to it. This affects the internal and external information search stage of the purchase decision process. This is why furniture and automobile retailers often give consumers product brochures to take home after they leave the showroom.

Perceived Risk Consumers' beliefs about the potential negative consequences of a product or service strongly affect their purchasing decisions. **Perceived risk** represents the anxieties felt because the consumer cannot anticipate the outcomes of a purchase but believes that there may be negative consequences. Examples of possible negative consequences are the price of the product (Can I afford $300 for those skis?), the risk of physical harm (Is bungee jumping safe?), and the performance of the product (Will the hair colouring work?). Sometimes the consequence is psychosocial (What will my friends say if I wear that fur coat?). Perceived risk affects the information search stage: the greater the perceived risk, the more extensive the external search is likely to be.

Recognizing the importance of perceived risk, companies develop strategies to make consumers feel more at ease about their purchases. Strategies and examples of firms using them include the following:

- *Obtaining seals of approval.* The Good Housekeeping seal that appears on many brands
- *Securing endorsements from influential people.* The National Fluid Milk Processor Promotion Board's "Got Milk" advertising campaign
- *Providing free trials of the product.* Samples of Mary Kay's Velocity fragrance
- *Giving extensive usage instructions.* Clairol hair colouring
- *Providing warranties and guarantees.* BMW's two-year, unlimited-mileage warranty on all of their automobiles.[19]

Learning

Why do consumers behave in the marketplace as they do? Over consumers' lifetimes, they learn behaviours, and they also learn responses to those behaviours—this learning is a continual process. Consumers learn which sources to use for information about products and services, which evaluative criteria to use when assessing alternatives, and how to make purchase decisions. **Learning** refers to those behaviours that result from repeated experience and reasoning.

Behavioural Learning *Behavioural learning* is the process of developing automatic responses to a type of situation built up through repeated exposure to it. Four variables are central to how one learns from repeated experience: drive, cue, response, and reinforcement. A *drive* is a need, such as hunger, that moves an individual to action. A *cue* is a stimulus or symbol that one perceives. A *response* is the action taken to satisfy the drive, and a *reinforcement* is the reward. Being hungry (a drive), a consumer sees a cue (a billboard), takes action (buys a hamburger), and receives a reward (it tastes great!). If what the consumer experiences upon responding to a stimulus is not pleasant (I feel sick now!), then *negative reinforcement* has occurred. Behavioural learning plays a major role in consumer decision making—in this case, causing the consumer to avoid the behavioural response rather than repeat it.

Marketers use two concepts from behavioural learning theory. *Stimulus generalization* occurs when a response brought about by one stimulus (cue) is generalized to another stimulus. Using the same brand name to launch new products is one common application of this concept, as when the makers of Tylenol followed up their original pain reliever with Tylenol Cold, Tylenol Flu, Tylenol Sinus, and others. Consumers familiar with one product will often transfer their feelings to others that seem similar—whether the

perceived risk
Anxiety felt when a consumer cannot anticipate possible negative outcomes of a purchase

learning
Behaviours that result from repeated experience or reasoning

similarity is in a brand name or in the shape and colour of the packaging. Are you familiar with President's Choice Cola or Costco's Simply Soda? They use red cans, similar in colour to Coca-Cola cans—this is stimulus generalization in action!

Stimulus discrimination refers to one's ability to perceive differences among similar products. Consumers may do this easily with some groups of products, such as automobiles. But in many cases, such as low-involvement purchases, advertisers work to point out the differences. For example, consumers' tendency to perceive all light beers as being alike led to Budweiser Light commercials that distinguished between many types of lights and Bud Light.

Cognitive Learning
Consumers also learn without direct experience—through thinking, reasoning, and mental problem solving. This type of learning, called *cognitive learning,* involves making connections between two or more ideas or simply observing the outcomes of others' behaviours and adjusting your own accordingly. Firms also influence this type of learning. Through repetition in advertising, messages such as "Advil is a headache remedy" attempt to link a brand (Advil) and an idea (headache remedy) by showing someone using the brand and finding relief.

Brand Loyalty
Learning is also important to marketers because it relates to habit formation. Developing habits means that a consumer is solving problems (such as what to do when she's hungry) routinely and consistently, without much thought. Not surprisingly, there is a close link between habits and **brand loyalty**, which is a favourable attitude toward and consistent purchase of a single brand over time. Brand loyalty results from positive reinforcement. If a consumer is satisfied with a product, he reduces his risk and saves time by consistently purchasing that same brand.

> "CONSUMERS FAMILIAR WITH ONE PRODUCT WILL OFTEN TRANSFER THEIR FEELINGS TO OTHERS THAT SEEM SIMILAR— WHETHER THE SIMILARITY IS IN A BRAND NAME OR IN THE SHAPE AND COLOUR OF THE PACKAGING."

Values, Beliefs, and Attitudes

Values, beliefs, and attitudes play a central role in consumer decision making.

Attitude Formation
An **attitude** is a "learned predisposition to respond to an object or class of objects in a consistently favourable or unfavourable way."[20] Attitudes are shaped by our values and beliefs, which we develop in the process of growing up. For example, we speak of core values, including material well-being and humanitarianism. We also have personal values, such as thriftiness and ambition. Marketers are concerned with both, but focus mostly on personal values. Personal values affect attitudes by influencing the importance assigned to specific product attributes, or features. Suppose thriftiness is one of your personal values. When you evaluate cars, fuel economy (a product attribute) becomes important. If you believe a specific car has this attribute, you are likely to have a favourable attitude toward it.

Beliefs also play a part in attitude formation. In consumer terms, **beliefs** are one's perception of how a product or brand performs on different attributes. Beliefs are based on personal experience, advertising, and discussions with other people. Beliefs about product attributes are important because, along with personal values, they create the favourable or unfavourable attitude the consumer has toward certain products and services.

Attitude Change
Marketers use three approaches to try to change consumer attitudes toward products and brands, as shown in the following examples.[21]

1. *Changing beliefs about the extent to which a brand has certain attributes.* To reduce consumer concern that Aspirin use causes an upset stomach, Bayer Corporation successfully promoted the gentleness of its Extra Strength Bayer Plus Aspirin.

2. *Changing the perceived importance of attributes.* Pepsi-Cola made freshness an important product attribute when it stamped

freshness dates on its cans. Prior to doing so, few consumers considered cola freshness an issue. After Pepsi spent about $25 million on advertising and promotion, a consumer survey found that 61 percent of cola drinkers believed freshness dating was an important attribute.

3. *Adding new attributes to the product.* Colgate-Palmolive included a new antibacterial ingredient, triclosan, in its Colgate Total toothpaste and spent $100 million marketing the brand. The result? Colgate replaced Crest as the market leader for the first time in 25 years.

Lifestyle

Lifestyle is a way of living that is identified by how people spend their time and resources (activities), what they consider important in their environment (interests), and what they think of themselves and the world around them (opinions). The analysis of consumer

lifestyles, called *psychographics*, has produced many insights into consumer behaviour. For example, lifestyle analysis has proven useful in segmenting and targeting consumers for new and existing products.

One of the most popular examples of psychographic analysis is the VALS™ Program developed by SRI International.[23] The VALS Program identifies eight interconnected categories of adult lifestyles based on a person's self-orientation and resources. Self-orientation describes the patterns of attitudes and activities that help a person reinforce his or her social self-image. Three patterns have been uncovered, which are oriented toward principles, status, and action. A person's resources range from minimal to abundant and include income, education, self-confidence, health, eagerness to buy, intelligence, and energy level. Each of these categories exhibits different buying behaviour and media preferences.

VALS is an American-based system, and the psychographics of Americans differ significantly from those of Canadians. When some market researchers have tried to use American values and lifestyles to describe Canadians, they have not succeeded. The firm Millward Brown Goldfarb created psychographic groups based on an extensive survey of Canadian values, ethics, opinions and interests over a three-year period. Figure 3–5 (see page 52) shows their nine segments and the percentage of the Canadian adult population that matches the characteristics of each group. The axes of the chart show orientations towards key traits: for example, a "Tie-dyed Grey" is more oriented toward individuals, while a "Contented Traditionalist" considers family or other close group as more important.

Figure 3–6 (see page 53) summarizes the nine lifestyle types and highlights selected behavioural characteristics of each and their implications for marketers, who can use this information in a variety of ways.

Attitudes toward Colgate toothpaste and Extra Strength Bayer Aspirin were successfully changed by these ads. How? Read the text to find out how marketers can change consumer attitudes toward products and brands.

Figure 3–5
Goldfarb psychographic
market segments for
Canada

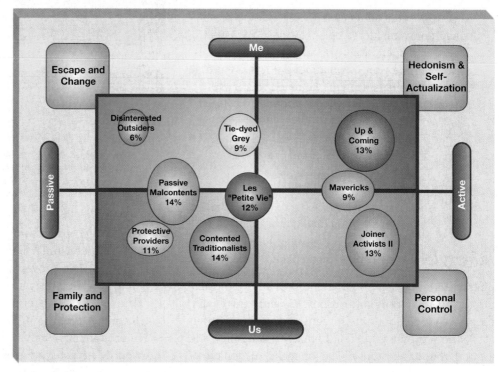

Source: Consumer TrendZ Report, Millward Brown Goldfarb

ask yourself

1. The problem with the Toro Snow Pup was an example of selective _____.

2. What three attitude-change approaches are most common?

3. What does the concept of lifestyle mean?

Socio-Cultural Influences on Consumer Behaviour

Socio-cultural influences, which evolve from a consumer's formal and informal relationships with other people, also have an impact on consumer behaviour. These include personal influence, reference groups, family, culture, and subculture.

Personal Influence

A consumer's purchases are often influenced by the views, opinions, or behaviours of others. Two aspects of personal influence are important to marketing: opinion leadership and word-of-mouth activity.

Opinion Leadership   Individuals who have social influence over others are called **opinion leaders**. Opinion leaders are more likely to be important for products that provide a form of self-expression. Automobiles, clothing, and club memberships are products affected by opinion leaders, but appliances usually are not.[23]

A small percentage of adults—from influential community leaders and business executives to movie stars—are opinion leaders.[24] Identifying, reaching, and influencing opinion leaders is a major challenge for companies. Some firms use sports figures or celebrities as spokespersons to represent their products, such as Wayne Gretzky for Ford, in the hope that they are opinion leaders.

Word of Mouth   People influencing each other during conversations is called **word of mouth**. Word of mouth is perhaps the most powerful information source for consumers, because it typically involves friends or family who are viewed as trustworthy.

Figure 3–6
Goldfarb psychographic market segments for Canada

SEGMENT	PERCENTAGE OF CANADIAN POPULATION	DESCRIPTION	MARKETING IMPLICATIONS
Disinterested Outsiders	6%	Materialistic, price conscious, willing to bend rules, younger, fewer married, lower education, lack respect for authority, not intellectually curious, less into technology, dislike change	Materialistic yet price conscious, low income (offer financing, incentives, and discounts), need to know immediate benefits, like irreverent tone of communications, want non-mainstream items, TV is a good way to reach them
Tie-Dyed Grey	9%	Older, lower income, more unmarried (single, divorced), urban dwellers, few with children, open minded, environmentally conscious, slightly uncomfortable with technology, like cultural events, independent	Do not respond well to family focus or romantic appeals, big readers (like newspapers, TV, magazines, current affairs shows), natural market for travel/holiday packages, marketing should have little jargon and technospeak, like personal touch in services
Passive Malcontents	14%	Older, maybe ethnic, patriotic, lack self-confidence, trusting, not too health conscious, participate in on-line chat	Unhappy (may respond well to products that improve), full-service offerings, health concerns, stress "made in Canada," respectful of authority figures, enjoy reading (magazine & newspaper ads appeal to them), very loyal
Protective Providers	11%	Hard-working, personal initiative, committed to family, financial pressures, distrustful, dislike change, enjoy outdoor activities, married with children, patriotic and proud, not highly educated	Very price conscious, looking for best value and incentives, home improvement and children's products appeal to them, brand names important, respond to respectful promotion, reinforce ideas of safety and security for family to attract them, use TV
Contented Traditionalists	12%	Older, married, religious focus, family oriented, conservative, ethical, respectful of authority, organized, brand loyal, not materialistic	Products/brands with a clean image, tone not irreverent or disrespectful, appreciate products that promote healthy living and family togetherness, like full service offerings, like to take care of future, need reassurance
Up & Comers	12%	Younger, many visible minorities or foreign-born, materialistic, outgoing, looking for quick gratification, optimistic, value friendships	Latest trends and gadgets, entertainment and sports-related products, brand names important, conservative advertising tastes, reach through TV and cinema ads, not newspapers/magazines
Mavericks	9%	Higher household income, solid employment, natural leaders, enjoy challenge, seek wealth, conservative views on family issues	Early adopters, voracious consumers, willing to pay, time poor, like to see benefits emphasized, technology is important to them and high-tech items, make them feel in control and empowered
Joiner Activists II	13%	Married, younger, higher income, optimistic, financially sound, non-religious, environmentalists, health conscious, like cultural activities, comfortable with online purchases	Crave information, like details, interested in new experiences/products, good quality and unique, upscale products, expect intelligent and sophisticated promotions, socially responsible companies attract them, early adopters
Les "Petite Vie"	12%	Friends and family very important, relaxed life, not leaders, respect business leaders, support government, open-minded, many French-speaking, low university attendance	Watch lots of TV, do not trust outsiders, not materialistic, believe spokespeople or experts, brand names are important, do not respond well to "new and improved" (instead they like tried and true)

Source: Consumer TrendZ Report, Millward Brown Goldfarb

Canadians' Online Shopping Habits

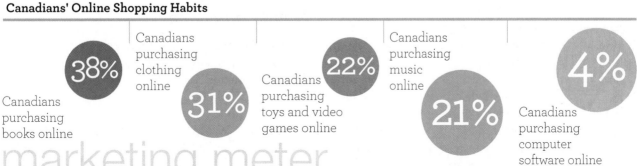

38% Canadians purchasing books online

Canadians purchasing clothing online

31% Canadians purchasing toys and video games online

22% Canadians purchasing music online

21% Canadians purchasing computer software online

4%

marketing meter

Source: Ipsos Reid, "The 2007 Ipsos CanadianInter@ctive Reid Report—Fact Guide: The Definitive Resource on Canadians and the Internet," accessed at www.ipsos.ca/pdf/CIFG.pdf.

The power of personal influence has prompted firms to make efforts to increase positive and decrease negative word of mouth.[25] For instance, "teaser" advertising campaigns are run in advance of new-product introductions to stimulate conversations. Other techniques such as advertising slogans, music, and humour also heighten positive word of mouth. On the other hand, rumours about McDonald's (worms in hamburgers) and Corona Extra beer (contaminated beer) have resulted in negative word of mouth, none of which was based on fact. Overcoming negative word of mouth is difficult and costly. Firms have found that supplying factual information, providing toll-free numbers for consumers to call the company, and giving appropriate product demonstrations also have been helpful.

The term *buzz marketing* refers to a brand becoming popular as a result of people talking about it to friends and neighbours. Another way that a company can create buzz is by hiring an outside agency. Word-of-mouth agencies such as Matchstick specialize in product seeding programs. Product seeding consists of hiring people to talk up a brand to others. The Word of Mouth Marketing Association (WOMMA) has issued ethical guidelines on product seeding, including the guideline that brand representatives must always disclose their relationship to the brand when promoting it to others.

The power of word of mouth has been magnified by the Internet and e-mail. The online version of word of mouth is called *viral marketing*. This includes the use of messages that consumers pass along to others through online forums, social networks, chat rooms, bulletin boards, blogs, and e-mails.

Reference Groups

Reference groups are people to whom an individual looks as a basis for self-appraisal or as a source of personal standards. For example, you might consider your family or the other students in your school as a reference group. Reference groups affect consumer purchases because they influence the information, attitudes, and aspiration levels that help set a consumer's standards. Reference groups have an important influence on the purchase of luxury products but not of necessities—reference groups exert a strong influence on the brand chosen when its use or consumption is highly visible to others.[26]

> ## PRODUCT SEEDING CONSISTS OF HIRING PEOPLE TO TALK UP A BRAND TO OTHERS.

Consumers have many reference groups, but three groups have clear marketing implications.

- *Membership group.* One to which a person actually belongs, including fraternities and sororities, social clubs, and the family. Such groups are easily identifiable and are targeted by firms selling insurance, insignia products, and vacation packages.

- *Aspiration group.* One that a person wishes to be a member of or wishes to be identified with, such as a professional society. Firms frequently rely on spokespeople or settings associated with their target market's aspiration group in their advertising.

- *Dissociative group.* One that a person wishes to maintain a distance from because of differences in values or behaviours.

Family Influence

Family influences on consumer behaviour result from three sources: consumer socialization, passage through the family life cycle, and decision making within the family or household.

Consumer Socialization The process by which people acquire the skills, knowledge, and attitudes necessary to function as consumers is *consumer socialization*.[27] Children learn how to purchase by

The Power of Word of Mouth

One of the most powerful forms of marketing is the result of one of the most natural activities: talking. Word-of-mouth marketing is an extraordinary tool for marketers to use as they spread their brands, as it is the most effective form of marketing available—and the simplest. The Word of Mouth Marketing Association (WOMMA) is the official trade association for word-of-mouth marketers and is a coalition comprised of top marketers who are interested in learning how to encourage and utilize word of mouth while respecting and protecting its integrity.

WOMMA aids its members with the implementation of word of mouth using training, best practices, standards and metrics, and mainstreaming. WOMMA provides outreach and education, aids marketers in creating sustainable word-of-mouth programs, creates accountability for practices, and works at bringing word of mouth into the centre of the marketing world. WOMMA's mission is to improve word-of-mouth marketing by "Promoting 'best practices' to ensure more effective marketing; protecting consumers and the industry with strong ethical guidelines; evangelizing word of mouth as an effective marketing tool; and setting standards to encourage its use."

Recently, WOMMA developed a code of ethics for word-of-mouth marketing.

Source: Word of Mouth Marketing Association (WOMMA), www.womma.org.

Focus on Ethics

These guidelines are meant to protect the consumer during the use of and participation in word-of-mouth marketing. The code focuses on openness between consumers, advocates, and marketers: Advocates are encouraged to be open with consumers about their relationship with the marketers. Advocates are also encouraged to be honest with their opinions about the products that they are marketing and to disclose their identity to the consumers. WOMMA created the code of ethics in order to help marketers see what practices they should be supporting and to allow the word-of-mouth industry to set clear standards for itself. ●

---

interacting with adults in purchase situations and through their own purchasing and product usage experiences. Research demonstrates that children show signs of brand preferences as early as age two, and these preferences often last a lifetime. This knowledge prompted Sony to introduce My First Sony, a line of portable audio equipment for children, and Time, Inc., to launch *Sports Illustrated for Kids*. The brand of toothpaste, laundry detergent, or soft drink used in your home will very likely influence your brand choice when you purchase these items for yourself.

Family Life Cycle Consumers act and purchase differently as they go through life. The **family life cycle** concept describes the distinct phases that a family progresses through from formation to retirement, each phase bringing with it identifiable purchasing behaviours.[28] Today, the traditional family—married couples with children younger than 25 years—constitute just over 30 percent of all Canadian households. Nearly 26 percent are single-person households, and another 28 percent are couples without children (or with older children over the age of 25). Multiple-family households, single-parent households, and other groupings account for 16 percent.[29]

Young single consumers' buying preferences are for nondurable items, including prepared foods, clothing, personal care products, and entertainment. They represent a significant target market for recreational travel, automobile, and consumer electronics firms. Young married couples without children are typically more affluent than young singles because usually both spouses are employed. These couples exhibit preferences for furniture, housewares, and gift items for each other. Young marrieds with children are driven by the needs of their children. These families make up a sizable market for life insurance, various children's products, and home furnishings. Single parents with children are the least financially secure type of households. Their buying preferences are usually affected by a limited economic status and tend toward convenience foods, child care services, and personal care items.

> **family life cycle**
> A family's progression from formation to retirement, with each phase bringing distinct needs and purchasing behaviours

Middle-aged married couples with children are typically better off financially than their younger counterparts. They are a significant market for leisure products and home improvement items. Middle-aged couples without children typically have a large amount of discretionary income. These couples buy better home furnishings, status automobiles, and financial services. Persons in the last two phases—older married and older unmarried—make up a sizable market for prescription drugs, medical services, vacation trips, and gifts for younger relatives.

Family Decision Making A third family-based influence on consumer decision making occurs in the context of the relationship dynamics of the household. Two decision-making styles exist: spouse-dominant and joint decision making. With a joint decision-making style, most decisions are made by both husband and wife. Spouse-dominant decisions are those for which either the husband or the wife has more influence in the purchase decision. Research indicates that wives tend to have the most say when purchasing groceries, children's toys, clothing, and medicines. Husbands tend to be more influential in home and car maintenance purchases. Joint decision making is common for cars, vacations, houses, home appliances and electronics, medical care, and long-distance telephone services. As a rule, joint decision making increases with the education of the spouses.[30]

Roles of individual family members in the purchase process are another element of family decision making. Five roles exist: information gatherer, influencer, decision maker, purchaser, and user. Family members assume different roles for different products and services.[31] For example, 89 percent of wives either influence or make outright purchases of men's clothing. Knowing this, Haggar Clothing, a menswear marketer, advertises in women's magazines such as *Vanity Fair* and *Redbook*. Even though women are often the grocery decision makers, they are not necessarily the purchaser. Husbands do about one-half of food shopping. Increasingly, preteens and teenagers are the information gatherers, influencers, decision makers, and purchasers of products and services items for the family, given the prevalence of working parents and single-parent households. Children and teenagers directly influence billions of dollars in annual family purchases. These figures help explain why, for example, Johnson & Johnson, Apple, Kellogg, P&G, Sony, and Oscar Mayer, among countless other companies, spend billions annually in media that reach preteens and teens.[32]

> *"Even though women are often the grocery decision makers, they are not necessarily the purchaser. Husbands do about one-half of food shopping."*

Culture and Subculture

Culture refers to the set of values, ideas, and attitudes that are learned and shared among the members of a group. Thus we often refer to Canadian culture, American culture, or Japanese culture.

Subgroups within the larger, or national, culture with unique values, ideas, and attitudes are referred to as **subcultures**. Subcultures can be defined by regions, by demographic groups, or by values. The most prominent types of subcultures are racial and ethnic, and many of these exist within the Canadian mosaic of people. French, German, Italian, Chinese, and Ukrainian subcultures are the ones we see most in Canada, and they make up nearly 40 percent of the Canadian population. Each one exhibits unique buying patterns and socio-cultural behaviours.

Canada's outlook on ethnicity is that cultural and ethnic groups are welcome to continue with their traditions, languages, and values. We are a nation of many faces, and people have been immigrating to Canada continually over many decades. A person may regard themselves as Italian, yet never have been to Italy—their grandparents may have immigrated here many years ago. If Italian customs have been maintained by the family, this person may behave much like a recently arrived Italian. Some countries encourage

In the **female** the ability to match colors comes at an early age. In the **male** it comes when he marries a female.

The City Casuals three-button, crepe jacket, 100% cotton, French-yarn shirt, Bedford cord pants, and a touch of color.

HAGGAR
Stuff you can work with.

immigrants to join the mainstream national culture, while in Canada we encourage diversity.

Our ethnic composition, and the philosophy that we take towards it, has led to the creation of many ethnic neighbourhoods in our cities. As our population becomes more diverse, people immigrating here bring foods from their native lands. Canadians do not have a lot of native food and preparation styles, so the country has been particularly welcoming of cuisine from around the world. Immigration has had a major influence on Canada's food market, both in the many restaurants and in the food items available from all corners of the globe. Not only food consumption is affected by immigration but also many cultural events have become mainstream, and many local happenings are the result of a tradition or celebration brought here by some new Canadians.

Ethnic Groups in Canada

British descent	28%
French descent	23%
Other European descent	15%
Native descent	2%
Other	6%
Mixed descent	26%

Source: "Canada," Central Intelligence Agency, The World Factbook website, accessed at https://www.cia.gov/library/publications/the-world-factbook/print/ca.html.

French-Canadian Subculture There are more than 9 million French-speaking Canadians in this country, about 30 percent of the population.[33] By far the largest majority of them live in the province of Quebec. Research shows that French-speaking Quebecers do exhibit different consumption behaviour from the rest of Canada.[34] French Quebecers link price to perceived value but will decide against buying rather than buy on credit. They are more willing to pay higher prices for convenience and premium brands, and they believe advertising more than the average Canadian.

French Quebecers are cautious about new products and often postpone trying something new until they see that the product has proven itself. They exhibit brand loyalty, but they will switch brands if offered a special. They also prefer convenience and health food stores over food warehouses and local grocery stores. French Quebecers are less likely to buy grocery items on impulse, and are increasingly calculating in their food purchases. Some grocery chains have responded to this characteristic by offering more discount coupons, weekly specials, and money-saving tips. Personal grooming and fashion are more important to French Quebecers than to the average Canadian, and they are more likely to shop in specialty clothing boutiques.

French Quebec has a higher percentage of wine and beer drinkers and more smokers; while Quebecers enjoy their beer, Molson says its research indicates that French Quebecers prefer a stronger beer, so it launched the O'Keefe 6.2 brand (which contains

6.2 percent alcohol) exclusively for the Quebec market. There are fewer golfers, joggers, and gardeners in Quebec, and the proportion of people who entertain at home or go to movies is also lower. By contrast, Quebec has more cyclists, skiers, and live theatre fans.

French Quebecers are big buyers of lottery tickets and more likely to subscribe to book clubs, but they make fewer long-distance phone calls. They travel less, whether for business or pleasure. More French Quebec adults hold life insurance policies, but they are less likely to have a credit card. They also tend to use the services of credit unions (*caisses populaires*) rather than banks.

Some people feel that French Quebec can be characterized by a set of values that are traditional, consistent, and relatively static, but changes are evident. While values are still strong regarding family life, having children in a marriage, and about giving the children religious training, the use of birth control is rising, and the marriage rate is below the national average.

Marketers must realize that certain products and other elements of the marketing mix may have to be modified in order to be successful in French Quebec. In addition to cultural differences, there are other issues that marketers must address. Commercial advertising to children is prohibited and greater restrictions exist for alcohol advertising. Provincial regulations also require that labels and packages must be both English and French, while storefront signage must be in French, not English. Good investigation and analysis of this market is a requirement for all companies wishing to do business in this province.

Chinese-Canadian Subculture   The Chinese comprise the largest visible minority group in Canada, and more than a million people (3.5 percent of the population) represent this ethnic group. There were restrictions on immigration from China up until the 1960s, but since then the Chinese have become one of Canada's fastest-growing ethnic populations. Many of them reside in Vancouver, which has the largest proportion of Chinese of any Canadian metropolitan area at 343,000 (17 percent of the metropolitan area's population). Another 409,000 Chinese residents live in Toronto, to comprise 9 percent of the population.[35]

Chinese-Canadians have unique characteristics and values. While most Canadians value straight-line thinking (logic), the Chinese value circular thinking (what goes around, comes around). They value work, family, and education. Their purchasing patterns are quite different from those of the average Canadian, and they often perceive products differently. Many prefer to be communicated with in their own language, and this has caused many companies to produce ads in Mandarin or Cantonese and run them in specialty Chinese newspapers, such as Toronto's *Sing Tao* or Vancouver's *Ming*

Companies Turn to Blogging as a Tool of Social Marketing

Many major corporations are turning to social marketing as a tool for reaching out to their consumers in a more informative and casual manner. Some companies are turning to official corporate blogs in order to communicate with their customers on a personal and interactive level. While only 12 percent of Fortune 500 corporations currently run a corporate blog, the companies that have embraced the concept (including Dell, Eastman Kodak, IBM, and Intel) have begun to utilize blogs as a way to hold open dialogues

with their customers. Companies have begun to make blogging a central function of their marketing teams, and a recent trend has developed toward creating chief bloggers, employees whose job it is to represent the company via its official blog. A growing element of this trend has been the slow emergence of the blogger role as an official job title, not merely a side task of an executive.

Blogs are increasingly becoming legitimate means of passing information, and it is little wonder that many corporations choose to have a blogging presence.

Corporate blogs feature interactive content such as commenting, tagging, forums, and feeds that allow readers to share their opinions on company products and policies, as well as giving corporations a better view into who makes up their consumer base. ●

Marketing NewsFlash

Sources: Rich Karpinski, "Businesses embrace blogging," *B to B*, Vol. 93, Iss. 8 (Jun 9, 2008): 1–2; Nancy Davis Kho, "The Blogging Business," *EContent*, Vol. 31, Iss. 6 (Jul/Aug 2008): 24–25.

Pao. The average Chinese-Canadian has a higher income, is better educated, and is less likely to be unemployed than the general Canadian population.

Chinese-Canadians have a preference for luxury vehicles, and many car dealerships see them as good potential customers for new cars. In general, they tend to eat out at restaurants more than the average Canadian, and there has been significant growth in the number of Chinese restaurants in Canada, and particularly in Vancouver and Toronto, over the past 10 years. For these, and a number of other factors, many marketers cater to the Chinese market as they see them as being good prospective customers.

Chinese New Year celebrations take place in Vancouver each year and have become an integral part of the city's cultural fabric.

cross-cultural analysis Study of similarities and differences among consumers in two or more societies

values Socially preferable modes of conduct or states of existence that tend to persist over time

customs Norms and expectations about the way people do things in a specific country or culture

Global Cultural Diversity

Canada has become increasingly multi-ethnic and multi-cultural, making it one of the most diverse countries in the world. Different countries take different approaches to admitting immigrants and integrating them into society. Canada's approach is often referred to as a mosaic, meaning that people who come to the country from another are welcome to maintain their cultural identities and customs—the belief is that this will create a situation where all Canadians can learn from the rich variety of over 200 cultures that make up the citizenry of the country. This environment works to increase Canadian companies' sensitivity and orientation towards other cultures, so the transition to global activities and relationships is facilitated.

Just as marketers must be sensitive to subcultures in Canada, they must appreciate the cultural differences of people in other countries if they want to market products and services to them. A necessary step in this process is **cross-cultural analysis**, which involves the study of similarities and differences among consumers in two or more nations or societies.[36] A thorough cross-cultural analysis involves an understanding of and an appreciation for the values, customs, symbols, and language of other societies.

Values A society's **values** represent socially preferable modes of conduct or states of existence that tend to persist over time. Understanding and working with these aspects of a society are important factors in global marketing. For example,[37]

- McDonald's does not sell hamburgers in its restaurants in India because the cow is considered sacred by almost 85 percent of the population. Instead, McDonald's sells the McMaharajah: two all-mutton patties, special sauce, lettuce, cheese, pickles, onions on a sesame-seed bun.

- Germans have not responded to the promotion of credit cards such as Visa or MasterCard, nor to the idea of borrowing to purchase goods and services. The German word for "debt," *Schuld*, is the same as the German word for "guilt."

Customs **Customs** are what is considered normal and expected about the way people do things in a specific country or culture. Clearly, customs can vary significantly from country to country. Some customs may seem unusual to Canadians. Consider, for example, that in France men wear more than twice the number of cosmetics that women do, and that the Japanese consider slurping their food to be a sign of approval and appreciation to the chef.

The custom of giving token business gifts is popular in many countries where they are expected and accepted. However, bribes, kickbacks, and payoffs offered to entice someone to commit an illegal or improper act on behalf of the giver for economic gain is considered corrupt in most cultures. The widespread use of bribery in global marketing has led to an agreement among the world's major exporting nations to make bribery of foreign government officials a criminal offence.

The Organisation for Economic Cooperation and Development (OECD) is an international body whose goal is to foster democratic government and a market-driven economy. With its global reach, OECD addresses issues of general interest to its members and affiliates. Corruption has become an issue of major importance in the past decade, and the OECD has taken action to set guidelines and procedures for preventing international bribery and corruption. Canada has adopted the OECD's anti-corruption convention and has made bribery of foreign public officials a criminal offence.[38]

Bribery paid to foreign companies is another matter. In France and Greece, bribes paid to foreign companies are a tax-deductible expense!

Cultural Symbols

Cultural symbols are objects, ideas, or processes that represent a particular group of people or society. Symbols and symbolism play an important role in cross-cultural analysis because different cultures attach different meanings to things. By cleverly using cultural symbols, global marketers can tie positive symbolism to their products and services to enhance their attractiveness to consumers. However, improper use of symbols can spell disaster. A culturally sensitive global marketer will know that[39]

What cultural lesson did Coca-Cola executives learn when they used the Eiffel Tower and the Parthenon in a recent global advertising campaign?

- North Americans are superstitious about the number 13, and Japanese feel the same way about the number 4. *Shi,* the Japanese word for "four," is also the word for "death." Knowing this, Tiffany & Company sells its fine glassware and china in sets of five, not four, in Japan.

- "Thumbs-up" is a positive sign in Canada. However, in Russia and Poland, this gesture has an offensive meaning when the palm of the hand is shown, as AT&T learned. The company reversed the gesture depicted in ads, showing the back of the hand, not the palm.

Cultural symbols stir up deep feelings. Consider how executives at Coca-Cola's Italian office learned this lesson. In a series of advertisements directed at Italian vacationers, the Eiffel Tower, Empire State Building, and the Tower of Pisa were turned into the familiar Coca-Cola bottle. However, when the white marble columns in the Parthenon that crowns Athens's Acropolis were turned into Coca-Cola bottles, the Greeks were outraged. Greeks refer to the Acropolis as the "holy rock," and a government official

said the Parthenon is an "international symbol of excellence" and that "whoever insults the Parthenon insults international culture." Coca-Cola apologized for the ad.[40]

Language Global marketers should know not only the basics of the native tongues of countries in which they market their products and services but also the subtleties and unique expressions of the language. About 100 official languages exist in the world, but anthropologists estimate that at least 3,000 different languages are actually spoken. There are 11 official languages spoken in the European Union, and Canada has two official languages (English and French). Seventeen major languages are spoken in India alone.

English, French, and Spanish are the principal languages used in global diplomacy and commerce. However, the best language with which to communicate with consumers is their own, as any seasoned global marketer will agree. Language usage and translation can present challenges. Unintended meanings of brand names and messages have ranged from the absurd to the obscene:

- When the advertising agency responsible for launching Procter & Gamble's successful Pert shampoo in Canada realized that the name means "lost" in French, it substituted the brand name Pret, which means "ready."

- The Vicks brand name common in North America is German slang for sexual intimacy; therefore, Vicks is called Wicks in Germany.

Experienced global marketers use **back translation**, where a translated word or phrase is retranslated back into the original language by a different interpreter to catch errors.[41] IBM's first Japanese translation of its "Solution for a small planet" advertising message yielded "Answers that make people smaller." The error was caught by back translation and corrected.

ask yourself

1. What are the two primary forms of personal influence?

2. What challenges do marketers face when marketing to ethnic subcultural groups?

Summary...*just the facts*

- When a consumer buys a product, it is not an act but a process. There are five stages in the purchase decision process: problem recognition, information search, alternative evaluation, purchase decision, and post-purchase behaviour.

- Consumers evaluate alternatives on the basis of attributes. Identifying which attributes are most important to consumers, along with understanding consumer beliefs about how a brand performs on those attributes, can make the difference between successful and unsuccessful products.

- Consumer involvement with what is bought affects whether the purchase decision process involves routine, limited, or extended problem solving. Situational influences also affect the process.

- Perception is important to marketers because of the selectivity of what a consumer sees or hears, comprehends, and retains.

- Much of the behaviour that consumers exhibit is learned. Consumers learn from repeated experience and reasoning. Brand loyalty is a result of learning.

- Attitudes are learned predispositions to respond to an object or class of objects in a consistently favourable or unfavourable way. Attitudes are based on a person's values and beliefs concerning the attributes of products or services.

- Personal influence takes two forms: opinion leadership and word-of-mouth activity. A specific type of personal influence exists in the form of reference groups.

- Family influences on consumer behaviour result from two sources: family life cycle and decision making within the household.

- Within Canada there are subcultures that affect consumer values and behaviour. Marketers must be sensitive to these influences when developing a marketing mix.

Key Terms and Concepts...*a refresher*

attitude *p. 50*
back translation *p. 60*
beliefs *p. 50*
brand loyalty *p. 50*
consumer behaviour *p. 42*
cross-cultural analysis *p. 59*
cultural symbols *p. 60*
culture *p. 56*

customs *p. 59*
family life cycle *p. 55*
involvement *p. 45*
learning *p. 49*
motivation *p. 47*
opinion leaders *p. 52*
perceived risk *p. 49*
perception *p. 48*

personality *p. 47*
purchase decision process *p. 42*
reference groups *p. 54*
subcultures *p. 56*
values *p. 59*
word of mouth *p. 52*

B2B
marketing

Business-to-business (B2B) marketing requires a slightly different approach than consumer marketing. B2B customers often have more specialized needs that must be addressed to secure their business. The sales channel generally plays a greater role and works more closely with marketing to address customer needs and provide business solutions. We gain insights into the B2B market by talking to Deborah McKenzie, global marketing manager for IBM Canada, and responsible for delivering consistent marketing strategy and

programs, with the directive to increase market share and meet revenue objectives for her business. Specifically, McKenzie explains that the approach in B2B marketing is more direct than in the consumer field, focusing more on individual customers and their particular needs. A solutions-based approach is important, and marketers work to understand customer "pain points" and to provide solutions that add value. A team approach is important from the very start of the process with marketing, sales, and business strategists coming together to ensure that the value proposition exists from the onset. Marketers then go to market with client solutions and flexible approaches rather than a definitive product that typically exists in consumer marketing.

McKenzie explains that in the B2B market, a successful approach encompasses four important elements: (1) focusing on business solutions for their customers, (2) using 360-degree integrated marketing communications tactics, (3) communicating marketing programs to all distribution channels, and (4) establishing marketing metrics to evaluate marketing and sales. Typically, IBM uses a multi-touch approach to B2B marketing, initially sending out two forms of communication—*one-to-many* and *one-to-few*—and then following up with a *one-to-one* communication approach.

One-to-many communication focuses on building awareness of IBM in the business community, and reinforcing IBM as the leader in B2B technology solutions. This relies on public relations, print advertising, Internet-based viral marketing, search word advertising, websites, trade shows, newsletters, and speakers' bureaus to establish IBM as an industry leader. One-to-few

LEARNING OBJECTIVES

LO 1 Identify the distinguishing characteristics of industrial, reseller, government, and non-profit markets.

LO 2 Understand how to measure industrial, reseller, government, and non-profit markets.

LO 3 Recognize the key characteristics of organizational buying that make the process different from consumer buying.

Let IBM help reduce the carbon in your business.

Breathe life into your business with IBM's Carbon Management Solutions. IBM has business insights and innovative technologies to locate, analyze and act on areas within your business that are creating more than their fair share of carbon. Reducing carbon is good for business and good for the environment. A greener world starts with greener business. Greener business starts with IBM.

STOP TALKING **START DOING.** Go to ibm.com/green/ca

 Understand how buying centres and buying situations influence organizational purchasing.

 Understand the growing importance of and the approaches in online buying for industrial, reseller, and government markets.

communication looks to generate sales leads through a more targeted approach, relying on direct marketing tools such as targeted direct mail, closed-access web portals, specialized IBM events, and e-newsletters to generate sales leads for the follow-up one-to-one approach. The one-to-one phase focuses on closing the potential sale using both formal and informal customer-closing events to finalize the business, along with special sales promotions and financing options.

This multifaceted marketing strategy and execution approach allows IBM to focus on solutions-based tactics that directly address customer needs and to deliver in a B2B environment that requires flexibility.

Just as Chapter 3 focuses on consumer behaviour, Chapter 4 focuses on the organizational consumer. Marketers identify, analyze, and seek to satisfy their organizational target markets. 🍎

The Nature and Size of Organizational Markets

L₁ Understanding organizational markets and buying behaviour is necessary for effective business marketing. Business marketing is the marketing of products to companies, governments, or non-profit organizations for use in the creation of goods and services that they then produce and market to others.[1] It is also referred to as business-to-business (B2B) marketing. So many firms engage in business marketing that it is important to understand the characteristics of organizational buyers and their buying behaviour, as they differ from consumer buying behaviour.

Organizational buyers are those manufacturers, wholesalers, retailers, and government agencies that buy goods and services for their own use or for resale. For example, these organizations buy computers and smartphones such as the BlackBerry for their own use. Manufacturers buy raw materials and parts that they reprocess into the finished goods they sell, and wholesalers and retailers resell the goods they buy without reprocessing them. Organizational buyers include all buyers in a nation except ultimate consumers. These organizational buyers purchase and lease large volumes of equipment, raw materials, manufactured parts, supplies, and business services. They often buy raw materials and parts, process them, and sell them. This upgraded

The Core: Chapter 4

Business marketers recognize that their customers require specialized needs.

Effective marketers provide business solutions to customers in order to secure their business.

product may pass through several different organizations (as it is bought and resold by different levels of manufacturers, distributors, wholesalers, and retailers) before it is purchased by the final organizational buyer or final consumer. So the total purchases of organizational buyers in a year are far greater than those of ultimate consumers.

Organizational buyers are divided into three different markets: industrial, reseller, and government markets (see Figure 4–1 on page 65).[2]

Industrial Markets

There are over 1.6 million firms in the industrial, or business, market. These *industrial firms* in some way reprocess a product or service they buy before selling it again to the next buyer. This is certainly true

"Testing a concept is extremely important. It ensures the enthusiasm of an idea can become reality."

Deborah McKenzie, global marketing manager, CIO program, IBM Canada

of Nortel Networks Limited, a prominent Canadian producer of telecommunications equipment, which assembles optical network systems from parts they manufacture themselves, as well as some they source from other companies. More than 75 percent of all North American backbone Internet traffic travels on Nortel Network optical systems.[3] It is also true (if you stretch your imagination) of a selling service, such as a bank that takes money from its depositors, "stores" it, and "sells" it as loans to borrowers.

The importance of services in Canada today is emphasized by the composition of the industrial markets shown in Figure 4–1. Primary industries (agriculture, fishing, mining, and forestry), utilities, manufacturers, and construction sell physical products and represent 33 percent of all of the industrial firms, or about 546,000. The service market sells diverse services such as legal advice, auto repair, and dry cleaning. Along with finance, insurance, and real estate businesses; transportation, communication, and public utility firms; and non-profit associations, these service firms represent about 67 percent of all industrial firms, or about 1.1 million.

Figure 4–1

Type and number of organizational customers, as reported by Statistics Canada

BUSINESS MARKETS IN CANADA

KIND OF BUSINESS MARKET	TYPE OF ORGANIZATION	NUMBER OF FIRMS IN CANADA
All industries		2,024,508
Industrial markets: 1,641,170	Primary industries (agriculture, fishing, mining, forestry)	209,657
	Utilities	4,926
	Manufacturers	105,256
	Construction	225,837
	Services	691,779
	Transportation, storage, and communications	102,168
	Finance, insurance, and real estate	301,547
Reseller markets: 375,538	Wholesale trade	132,666
	Retail trade	242,872
Government markets: 7,800	Public administration (federal, provincial, municipal, regional)	7,800

Source: Statistics Canada (www.statcan.ca/english/Pgdb/econ18.htm).

Kodiak Comes Home

In 2006, the Kodiak Original, an iconic Canadian work boot was re-released and returned not only to Canadian markets but also to Canadian plants. For six years, Kodiak boots, a staple of workers and teenagers alike for over 50 years, had been making their way to the feet of Canadian consumers from manufacturing locations in China, Vietnam, and Thailand. However, when the time came to re-release the Original, Kodiak decided to move production of the boots to its plants in Markham, Ontario, and Harbour Grace, Newfoundland, in order to expedite the delivery of the boots to the public (turnaround in the Canadian plants can be as little as 21 days, compared to the 90 days of the Asian plants). This repatriation is a unique occurrence in today's markets, where much production has been outsourced overseas.

The company hoped that this homecoming would signify a connection to the brand's roots, separating Kodiak from other branded merchandisers. The company also took into consideration its core market and their desire to see a made-in-Canada label on the products that they buy. The move to Canadian production helped to solidify Kodiak's authenticity as an iconic Canadian work boot. ●

Sources: "Kodiak originals come home," *National Post*, May 1, 2006, p. G2; Gordon Pitts, "Kodiak Comes Home," *The Globe and Mail*, May 15, 2006, p. B1.

Reseller Markets

Wholesalers and retailers that buy physical products and resell them again without any reprocessing are *resellers*. In Canada, there are almost 243,000 retailers and 133,000 wholesalers. In this chapter, we look at these resellers mainly as organizational buyers in terms of how they make their own buying decisions and which products they choose to carry.

Government Markets

Government units are the federal, provincial, regional, and municipal agencies that buy goods and services for the constituents that they serve. With a spending budget of close to $180 billion annually, the federal government is a major customer, possibly the largest in Canada.[5] In addition to specialized purchases for the military, government agencies also buy almost everything that regular consumers buy, from toilet paper to chewing gum to cars for federal prisons, hospitals, and schools. At the federal government level, the bulk of the purchasing is done by Public Works and Government Services Canada. Provincial and municipal governments typically have government departments that do the buying for them. In addition, hundreds of government departments, agencies, and Crown corporations (owned by the government on behalf of the people of Canada) such as CBC, VIA Rail, and the Royal Canadian Mint purchase supplies and services to operate. An example of a very successful Canadian company is Bombardier. Over the years, it has produced regional aircraft, business jets, mass transportation equipment such as subways and passenger rail vehicles, and recreational equipment. Many of its sales are to governments.

Non-Profit Organizations

Organizations that operate without having financial profit as a goal, and which seek to provide goods and services for the good of society, are called *non-profit organizations*. They are also known as charitable organizations, and some 83,000 of them are registered with Canada Revenue Agency.[5] Tax advantages make it beneficial for this type of organization to register with the federal government.

You are probably familiar with many non-profit organizations. Were you a member of the Boy Scouts or Girl Guides? Have you participated in a Canadian Cancer Society run or marathon? Have you been asked for a donation to the United Way? Hospitals, arts organizations, cultural groups, and some research institutes can be classified as non-profit organizations. In your school, you may have a foundation office that raises money for student awards and aid; this too is a non-profit organization. In the past, marketing in these organizations has

North American Industry Classification System (NAICS) Provides common industry definitions for Canada, Mexico, and the United States

services, competition from imports in domestic markets, and similar studies. The NAICS designates industries with a numerical code in a defined structure. A six-digit coding system is used. The first two digits designate a sector of the economy, the third digit designates a subsector, and the fourth digit represents an industry group. The fifth digit designates a specific industry and is the most detailed level at which comparable data is available for Canada, Mexico, and the United States. The sixth digit designates individual country-level national industries. Figure 4-2 (see page 68) presents an abbreviated breakdown within the Arts, Entertainment, and Recreation Sector (code 71) to illustrate the classification scheme.

The NAICS permits a firm to find the NAICS codes of its present customers and then obtain NAICS-coded lists of similar firms. Also, it is possible to monitor NAICS categories to determine the growth in various sectors and industries to identify promising marketing opportunities. However, NAICS codes, like the earlier SIC codes, have important limitations. The NAICS assigns only one code to each organization based on its major economic activity, but large firms

been limited, but increasingly they are adopting the same types of marketing techniques that other business firms employ, and with good success. As purchasers, this sector of business buys a wide array of goods and services to conduct their operations.

Measuring Industrial, Reseller, Government, and Non-Profit Markets

LO2 The measurement of industrial, reseller, government, and non-profit markets is an important first step for a firm interested in determining the size of one, two, or all of these markets in Canada and around the world. This task has been made easier with the North American Industry Classification System (NAICS).[6] The NAICS provides common industry definitions for Canada, Mexico, and the United States, which facilitate the measurement of economic activity in the three member countries of the North American Free Trade Agreement (NAFTA). The NAICS replaced the Standard Industrial Classification (SIC) system, a version of which had been in place for more than 50 years in the three NAFTA member countries. The SIC neither permitted comparability across countries nor accurately measured new or emerging industries. Furthermore, the NAICS is consistent with the International Standard Industrial Classification of All Economic Activities, published by the United Nations, to help measure global economic activity.

The NAICS groups economic activity to permit studies of market share, demand for goods and

World's Largest Exporters

China has passed the United States as the world's second largest exporter.

1. Germany
2. China
3. United States
4. Japan
5. France
6. Netherlands
7. Italy
8. United Kingdom
9. Belgium
10. Canada

Source: "World Trade 2007, Prospects for 2008: WTO, developing, transition economies cushion trade slowdown," World Trade Organization, press release, April 17, 2008 (www.wto.org/english/news_e/pres08_e/pr520_e.htm).

derived demand
Demand for industrial products and services driven by demand for consumer products and services

that engage in many different activities are still given only one NAICS code. A second limitation is that five-digit national industry codes are not available for all three countries because the respective governments will not reveal data when too few organizations exist in a category. Despite these limitations, the NAICS represents yet another effort toward economic integration in North America and the world.

ask yourself

1. Organizational buyers are divided into three different markets. What are they?

2. What is the North American Industry Classification System (NAICS)?

Characteristics of Organizational Buying

L3 Organizations are different from individuals in the way they purchase goods and services, so buying for an organization is different from buying for yourself and your family. In both cases the objective in making the purchase is to solve the buyer's problem—to satisfy a need or want. Unique objectives and policies of an organization put special constraints on how it makes buying decisions. Understanding the characteristics of organizational buying is essential in designing effective marketing

programs to reach these buyers. Key characteristics of organizational buying are listed in Figure 4–3 (see page 69) and discussed next.[7]

Derived Demand

Consumer demand for products and services is affected by their price and availability and by consumers' personal tastes and discretionary income. By comparison, industrial demand is derived. **Derived demand** means that the demand for industrial products and services is driven by, or derived from, demand for consumer products and services, as demonstrated in Figure 4–4 (on page 70). For example, the demand for Weyerhaeuser's pulp and paper products is based on consumer demand for newspapers, Domino's "keep warm" pizza-to-go boxes, FedEx packages, and disposable diapers. Derived demand is often based on expectations of future consumer demand. For instance, Whirlpool purchases parts for its washers and dryers in anticipation of consumer demand, which is affected by the replacement cycle for these products and by consumer income. Another example of derived demand is the car industry. Demand for auto parts is driven by new car sales. Magna International Inc. is a Canadian company based in Aurora, Ontario. It is Canada's largest automobile parts manufacturer, and one of the country's largest companies.

Figure 4–2
NAICS breakdown for the Arts, Entertainment, and Recreation Sector: NAICS code 71 (abbreviated)

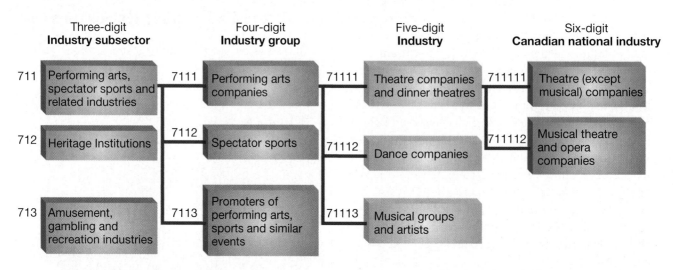

Source: Statistics Canada.

Marketing tip

"Knowing that Magna is going there, and how big and sophisticated they are, you know that the market is there and expanding."

Gerry Fedchun, president of Canada's Automotive Parts Manufacturers' Association, referring to Magna International producing auto parts for the Russian auto market, in The National Post, *May 22, 2008*

Inelastic Demand

Inelastic demand means that regardless of whether there is an increase or decrease of the price of a B2B product, customers will buy the same quantity. For example, if the price of brake pads goes up, a car manufacturer will still order the same quantity. A single business product, such as a brake pad is only one of many parts that go into making the final product, and is only a minor portion of the price of the car.

Fluctuating Demand

Small changes in demand for consumer products can result in large increases or decreases in demand for the facilities and equipment needed to make the consumer product. This is referred to as **fluctuating demand**. A product's life expectancy also has a bearing in this type of demand. For example, business products such as large machinery are purchased infrequently. Demand for such products can be high one year when they are wearing out but low in the following year if the old machinery is operating satisfactorily.

inelastic demand Demand for products does not change because of increases or decreases in price

fluctuating demand Demand for business products and services fluctuates more than demand for consumer products and services

Size of the Order or Purchase

The size of the purchase involved in organizational buying is typically much larger than that in consumer buying. The dollar value of a single purchase made by an organization often runs into the thousands or millions of dollars. For example, in 2002, Nortel Networks, Canada's largest phone equipment supplier, won a $500 million contract to upgrade the wireless network of Cingular Wireless in the U.S. and Puerto Rico.[8]

Figure 4–3
Key characteristics of organizational buying behaviour

CHARACTERISTICS	DIMENSIONS
Market characteristics	• Demand for industrial products and services is derived. • The number of business customers is typically small, and their purchase orders are typically large.
Product or service characteristics	• Products or services are technical in nature and purchased on the basis of specifications. • Many goods purchased are raw or semifinished. • Heavy emphasis is placed on delivery time, technical assistance, and postsale service.
Buying process characteristics	• Technically qualified and professional buyers follow established purchasing policies and procedures. • Buying objectives and criteria are typically spelled out, as are procedures for evaluating sellers and their products or services. • There are multiple buying influences, and multiple parties participate in purchase decisions. • There are reciprocal arrangements, and negotiation between buyers and sellers is commonplace. • Online buying over the Internet is widespread.
Marketing mix characteristics	• Personal selling to organizational buyers is used extensively, and distribution is very important. • Advertising and other forms of promotion are technical in nature. • Price is often negotiated, evaluated as part of broader seller and product or service qualities, and frequently affected by quantity discounts.

Figure 4–4
Direct versus derived demand

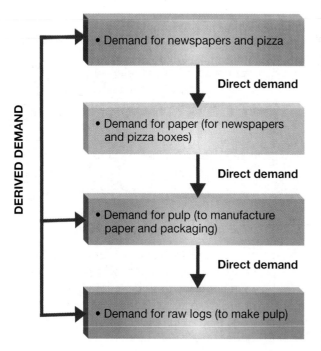

DERIVED DEMAND

- Demand for newspapers and pizza

Direct demand

- Demand for paper (for newspapers and pizza boxes)

Direct demand

- Demand for pulp (to manufacture paper and packaging)

Direct demand

- Demand for raw logs (to make pulp)

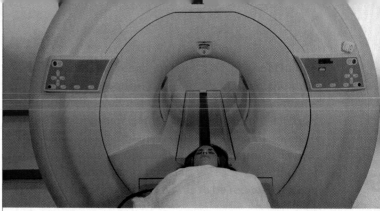

With so much money at stake, most organizations place constraints on their buyers in the form of purchasing policies or procedures. Buyers must often get competitive bids from at least three prospective suppliers when the order is above a specific amount, such as $5,000. When the order is above an even higher amount, such as $50,000, it may require the review and approval of a vice president or even the president of the company. Knowing how the size of the order affects buying practices is important in determining who participates in the purchase decision and makes the final decision and also the length of time required to arrive at a purchase agreement.

Number of Potential Buyers

Firms selling consumer products or services often try to reach thousands or millions of individuals or households. For example, your local supermarket or bank probably serves thousands of people, and Kellogg tries to reach millions of Canadian households with its breakfast cereals and probably succeeds in selling to a third or half of these in any given year. In contrast, firms selling to organizations are often restricted to far fewer buyers. Bombardier Aerospace can sell its Challenger business jets to a few thousand organizations throughout the world, and B. F. Goodrich sells its original equipment tires to fewer than 10 car manufacturers.

Organizational Buying Objectives

Organizations buy products and services for one main reason: to help them achieve their objectives. For business firms, the buying objective is usually to increase profits through reducing costs or increasing sales. 7-Eleven buys automated inventory systems to increase the number of products that can be sold through its convenience stores and to keep them fresh. Nissan Motor Company switched its advertising agency because it expects the new agency to devise a more effective ad campaign to help it sell more cars and increase sales. To improve executive decision making, many firms buy advanced computer systems to process data.

The objectives of non-profit firms and government agencies are usually to meet the needs of the groups they serve. Thus, a hospital buys a high-technology diagnostic device to serve its patients better. Understanding buying objectives is a necessary first step in marketing to organizations.

Organizational Buying Criteria

In Chapter 3, we discussed the criteria that consumers use when purchasing a product. Businesses also use criteria in their purchasing: They specify *organizational buying criteria*, which are detailed specifications for the products and services they want to buy and the characteristics of the suppliers that will supply them. When suppliers are selected, their products and their firm's characteristics are evaluated using these criteria. The following lists some of the most commonly used criteria:

- Price
- Ability to meet the quality specifications required
- Ability to meet the required delivery schedules
- Technical capability
- Warranties and claim policies
- Past performance on previous contracts
- Production facilities and capacity

Suppliers that meet or exceed the criteria create customer value for the business doing the purchasing.

Many organizational buyers today are transforming their buying criteria into specific requirements that are communicated to suppliers. This practice, called *reverse marketing*, means that organizational buyers are attempting to work with suppliers to make their products, services, and capabilities fit the buyer's needs. Working closely and collaboratively like this with suppliers also helps build buyer-seller relationships and leads to supply partnerships.

Buyer–Seller Relationships and Supply Partnerships

Another distinction between organizational and consumer buying behaviour lies in the nature of the relationship between organizational buyers and suppliers. Specifically, organizational buying is more likely to involve complex and lengthy negotiations concerning delivery schedules, price, technical specifications, warranties, and claim policies. These negotiations can last for more than a year.

Reciprocal arrangements also exist in organizational buying. Reciprocity is an industrial buying practice in which two organizations agree to purchase each other's products and services. Governments frown on reciprocal buying because it restricts the normal operation of the free market. However, the practice exists and can limit the flexibility of organizational buyers in choosing alternative suppliers.

In some cases, buyer–seller relationships develop into supply partnerships.[12] A **supply partnership** exists when a buyer and its supplier adopt mutually beneficial objectives, policies, and procedures for the purpose of lowering the cost or increasing the value of products and services delivered to the ultimate consumer. Intel, the world's largest manufacturer of microprocessors and famous for the "intel inside" sticker on most personal computers, is a case in point. Intel supports its suppliers by offering them quality management programs and by investing in supplier equipment that

> **supply partnership**
> Relationship between a buyer and supplier that adopt mutually beneficial objectives, policies, and procedures

> # "UNDERSTANDING BUYING OBJECTIVES IS A NECESSARY FIRST STEP IN MARKETING TO ORGANIZATIONS."

Product Recalls

Marketing **NewsFlash**

Over the past year, numerous products exported from China were withdrawn from shelves due to health concerns. In June 2007, toothpaste that shipped from China and was sold in Canadian and U.S. discount stores was found to contain diethylene glycol, a toxic chemical used in antifreeze. Also in June 2007, 180 Chinese factories were closed after inspectors found industrial chemicals being used in food products. Immediately after this, the U.S. banned farmed Chinese catfish, shrimp, basa, dace, and eel after discovering drug contamination. Toys made using paint that contained dangerous levels of lead, toys with loose magnets, and melamine-laced dog food and milk were among the products involved in high-level product withdrawals costing manufacturers millions of dollars. These events have also created deepening distrust among consumers for products that come from China, as well as known big-brand operations that utilize Chinese production resources.

The pet food scandal (in which pets across North America died after eating food that contained melamine-tainted Chinese wheat gluten) revealed that many companies use the same international sources regardless of the name on the label. The tainted wheat gluten shipped to a single source: Menu Foods in Mississauga, Ontario, and from there found its way into national, discount, and private-label pet food brands. This showed that while premium brands promote their use of high-quality ingredients, they source from the same suppliers as the discount labels and are therefore just as susceptible to receiving tainted products. ●

Source: Jeremy Lloyd, "Wake Up and Smell the Lead," *Marketing* magazine, September 2007.

produces fewer product defects and boosts supplier productivity. Suppliers, in turn, provide Intel with consistent high-quality products at a lower cost for its customers, the makers of personal computers, and finally you, the ultimate customer. Retailers, too, are developing partnerships with their suppliers. Wal-Mart has such a relationship with Procter & Gamble (P&G) for ordering and replenishing P&G's products in their stores. By using computerized cash register scanning equipment and direct electronic linkages to P&G, Wal-Mart can tell P&G what merchandise is needed, along with how much, when, and to which store to deliver it on a daily basis.

The Organizational Buying Process and the Buying Centre

LO 4 Organizational buyers, like consumers, engage in a decision process when selecting products and services. **Organizational buying behaviour** is the decision-making process that organizations use to establish the need for products and services and identify, evaluate, and choose among alternative brands and suppliers. There are important similarities and differences between the two decision-making processes. To better understand the nature of organizational buying behaviour, we first compare it with consumer buying behaviour. We then describe a unique feature of organizational buying: the buying centre.

Stages in the Organizational Buying Process

As shown in Figure 4–5 (see page 73), the five stages that a student might use in buying a portable MP3 player also apply to organizational purchases. However, comparing the two right-hand columns in Figure 4–5 reveals some key differences. For example, when a portable MP3 player manufacturer buys earphones for its units from a supplier, more individuals are involved,

supplier capability becomes more important, and the post-purchase evaluation behaviour is more formal. The earphone-buying decision process is typical of the steps made by organizational buyers.

The Buying Centre: A Cross-Functional Group

For routine purchases with a small dollar value, a single buyer or purchasing manager often makes the purchase decision alone. In many instances, however, several people in the organization participate in the buying process. The individuals in this group, called a **buying centre**, share common goals, risks, and knowledge important to purchase decisions. For most large multistore chain resellers, such as Sears, 7-Eleven convenience stores, or Safeway, the buying centre is very formal and is called a *buying committee*. However, most industrial firms or government units use informal groups of people or call meetings to arrive at buying decisions.

A firm marketing to industrial firms and government units must understand the structure, technical and business functions represented, and the behaviour of the buying centre. One researcher has suggested four questions to provide guidance in understanding the buying centre in these organizations:[10]

- Which individuals are in the buying centre for the product or service?
- What is the relative influence of each member of the group?

ask yourself

1. What is derived demand?
2. A supply partnership exists when _____.

Canadian Opinions on Chinese Imports

Very safe	4%
Safe	28%
Not all that safe	33%
Not safe at all	28%
Other	7%

Source: "Chinese Imports: Safety Questions," News release about Canadian Press/Decima Research poll, June 21–24, 2007 (www.harrisdecima.com/en/downloads/pdf/news_releases/070703E.pdf).

- What are the buying criteria of each member?
- How does each member of the group perceive the potential supplier, its products and services, and its salespeople?

People in the Buying Centre Who makes up the buying centre in a given organization depends on the specific item being bought. Although a buyer or purchasing manager is almost always a member of the buying centre, individuals from other functional areas are included, depending on what is to be purchased.

In buying a million-dollar machine tool, the president (because of the size of the purchase) and the production vice president would probably be members. For key components to be included in a final manufactured product, a cross-functional group of individuals from research and development (R&D), engineering, and quality control are likely to be added. For new word-processing software, experienced office staff who will use the equipment would be members. Still, a major question in understanding the buying centre is finding and reaching the people who will initiate, influence, and actually make the buying decision.

> *Still, a major question in understanding the buying centre is finding and reaching the people who will initiate, influence, and actually make the buying decision.*

Figure 4–5

Comparing the stages in a consumer and organizational purchase decision process reveals subtle differences.

STAGE IN THE BUYING DECISION PROCESS	CONSUMER PURCHASE: PORTABLE MP3 PLAYER FOR A STUDENT	ORGANIZATIONAL PURCHASE: EARPHONES FOR A PORTABLE MP3 PLAYER
Problem recognition	Student doesn't like the features of the portable MP3 player now owned and desires a new portable MP3 player.	Marketing research and sales departments observe that competitors are improving the earphones on their portable MP3 models. The firm decides to improve the earphones on their own new models, which will be purchased from an outside supplier.
Information search	Student uses past experience, that of friends, ads, the Internet, and magazines to collect information and uncover alternatives.	Design and production engineers draft specifications for earphones. The purchasing department identifies suppliers of portable MP3 player earphones.
Alternative evaluation	Alternative portable MP3 players are evaluated on the basis of important attributes desired in a portable MP3 player, and several stores are visited.	Purchasing and engineering personnel visit with suppliers and assess facilities, capacity, quality control, and financial status. They drop any suppliers not satisfactory on these factors.
Purchase decision	A specific brand of portable MP3 player is selected, the price is paid, and the student leaves the store.	They use quality, price, delivery, and technical capability as key buying criteria to select a supplier. Then they negotiate terms and award a contract.
Post-purchase behaviour	Student reevaluates the purchase decision, may return the portable MP3 player to the store if it is unsatisfactory.	They evaluate the supplier using a formal vendor rating system and notify the supplier if earphones do not meet their quality standard. If the problem is not corrected, they drop the firm as a future supplier.

Figure 4–6
Roles in the Buying Centre

Roles in the Buying Centre

Researchers have identified five specific roles that an individual in a buying centre can play (see Figure 4–6).[11] In some purchases, the same person may perform two or more of these roles.

- *Users* are the people in the organization who actually use the product or service, such as office staff who will use new word-processing software.

- *Influencers* affect the buying decision, usually by helping define the specifications for what is bought. They usually have specialized knowledge. The information systems manager would be a key influencer in the purchase of a new computer network.

- *Buyers* have formal authority and responsibility to select the supplier and negotiate the terms of the contract. The purchasing manager probably would perform this role in the purchase of a computer network.

- *Deciders* have the formal or informal power to select or approve the supplier that receives the contract. Whereas in routine orders the decider is usually the buyer or purchasing manager, in important technical purchases it is more likely to be someone from R&D, engineering, or quality control. The decider for a key component being included in a final manufactured product might be any of these three people.

- *Gatekeepers* control the flow of information in the buying centre. Purchasing personnel, technical experts, and office staff can all help or prevent salespeople (or information) from reaching people performing the other four roles.

Buying Situations and the Buying Centre

The number of people in the buying centre largely depends on the specific buying situation. Researchers who have studied organizational buying identify three types of buying situations, called **buy classes**. These buy classes vary from the routine reorder, or *straight rebuy*, to the completely new purchase, termed *new buy*. In between these extremes is the *modified rebuy*. Some examples will clarify the differences.[12]

- *Straight rebuy.* Here the buyer or purchasing manager reorders an existing product or service from thse list of acceptable suppliers, probably without even checking with users or influencers from the engineering, production, or quality control departments. Office supplies and maintenance services are usually obtained as straight rebuys.

- *Modified rebuy.* In this buying situation, the company is purchasing a product that it has experience purchasing, such as new laptops for salespeople, but it wants to change the product specifications, price, delivery schedule, or supplier. The changes usually mean involving users, influencers, and/or

> AT GENERAL ELECTRIC, ONLINE BUYING HAS CUT THE COST OF A TRANSACTION FROM $50 TO $100 PER PURCHASE TO ABOUT $5.

deciders in the buying decision—more input than would be necessary for a straight rebuy.

- *New buy.* In this situation, the company is buying the product or service for the first time. This purchase involves greater potential risk and is more complex than other buying situations. The buying centre is larger, comprised of people representing those parts of the organization having a stake in the new buy. Procter & Gamble's purchase of a multimillion-dollar fibre-optic network from Corning, Inc., linking its corporate offices, represented a new buy.[13]

Figure 4–7 summarizes how buy classes affect buying centre tendencies in different ways.[14]

Online Buying in Organizational Markets

L5 Organizational buying behaviour and business marketing continue to change with the use of the Internet and e-commerce. Organizations vastly outnumber consumers both in terms of online transactions made and purchase volume.[15] In fact, organizational buyers account for about 80 percent of the total worldwide dollar value of all online transactions. Online organizational buyers around the world will purchase between $8 and $10 trillion worth of products and services by 2010. Organizational buyers in North America will account for about 60 percent of these purchases.

Prominence of Online Buying in Organizational Markets

Online buying in organizational markets is prominent for three major reasons.[16] First, organizational buyers depend heavily on timely supplier information that describes product availability, technical specifications, application uses, price, and delivery schedules. This information can be conveyed quickly online. Second, web-based technology has been shown to substantially reduce buyer order-processing costs. At General Electric, online buying has cut the cost of a transaction from $50 to $100 per purchase to about $5. Third, business marketers have found that web-based technology can reduce marketing costs, particularly sales and advertising expense, and broaden their potential customer base for many types of products and services. For these reasons, online buying is popular in all three kinds of organizational markets. For example, airlines order over $400 million in spare parts from the Boeing Company website each year. Customers of Provigo, a large Canadian food wholesaler, can buy online; provincial and municipal governments across Canada also engage in online purchasing.

E-Marketplaces: Virtual Organizational Markets

A significant development in organizational buying has been the creation and growth of online trading communities, called **e-marketplaces**, that bring together buyers and supplier organizations.[17] These

e-marketplaces Online trading communities that bring together buyers and supplier organizations

Figure 4–7

How the buying situation affects buying centre behaviour

BUYING CENTRE DIMENSION	BUY-CLASS SITUATION		
	STRAIGHT REBUY	**MODIFIED REBUY**	**NEW BUY**
People involved	1	2–3	Many
Decision time	Short	Short	Long
Problem definition	Well-defined	Minor modifications	Uncertain
Buying objective	Low-priced supplier	Low-priced supplier	Good solution
Suppliers considered	Present	Present	New/present
Buying influence	Purchasing agent	Purchasing agent and others	Technical/operating personnel

Companies Embrace Social Networking

Social networking on the Internet has become an intrinsic part of everyday life for people around the world. With the introduction of Web 2.0, brands are becoming better able to interact with their consumers via social networking sites such as Facebook, LinkedIn, and Twitter. A crucial part of any brand's success is the loyalty of its customer base, and in order to develop this, a brand must demonstrate its core values in a consistent and targeted manner toward its core audience. Social networking sites provide a platform for a brand to reach out to its customer base and determine what its consumers want from the brand's products. Companies are no longer able to create brands in a vacuum. Consumers are a part of the evolution of brands in numerous ways due to the Internet (especially social networking sites like Facebook and sharing sites such as YouTube) and word of mouth.

Over time, many brands develop a culture amongst their consumers. These brands, such as Apple and Harley Davidson, among others, have become more and more shaped by their fan base and less by their marketers. Marketers have taken advantage of this by reaching out for customer input on company blogs, asking for idea submissions, and looking out for what consumers are saying about their brands via word of mouth and on social sites. ●

Sources: Naomi Grossman, "The Business Value of Social Networking," Forbes.com, July 18, 2008 (www.forbes.com/2008/07/18/plaxo-linkedin-facebook-ent-tech-cx_ng_0718bmightyplaxo.html); Ted Mininni, "Brand New Thinking: Put It in Cultural Context," MarketingProfs.com, June 3, 2008 (www.marketingprofs.com/8/brand-new-thinking-cultural-context-mininni.asp).

online communities go by a variety of names, including portals, exchanges, and e-hubs, and make possible the real-time exchange of information, money, products, and services. Globally, the number of e-marketplaces for businesses is extensive.

E-marketplaces can be independent trading communities or private exchanges. Independent e-marketplaces typically focus on a specific product or service, or serve a particular industry. They act as a neutral third party and provide an online trading platform and a centralized market that enable exchanges between buyers and sellers. Independent e-marketplaces charge a fee for their services and exist in settings that have one or more of the following features:

- Thousands of geographically dispersed buyers and sellers
- Frequently changing prices caused by demand and supply fluctuations
- Time sensitivity due to perishable offerings and changing technologies
- Easily comparable offerings between a variety of suppliers

The Value of YouTube

2006 Google acquired YouTube

$1.65 billion Price Google paid for YouTube

70 million YouTube's worldwide audience

marketing meter

Source: Andrew Ross Sorkin, "YouTube sold for $1.65 billion," *Milwaukee (Wisconsin) Journal Sentinel*, October 10, 2006 (www.jsonline.com/story/index.aspx?id=511072).

Well-known independent e-marketplaces include PaperExchange (paper products), PlasticNet (plastics), Altra Energy (electricity, natural gas, and crude oil), and MRO.com (maintenance, repair, and operating supplies). Small business buyers and sellers, in particular, benefit from independent e-marketplaces. These e-marketplaces offer suppliers an economical way to expand their customer base and reduce the cost of purchased products and services.

Large companies tend to favour private exchanges that link them with their network of qualified suppliers and customers. Private exchanges focus on streamlining a company's purchase transactions with its suppliers and customers. Like independent e-marketplaces, they provide a technology trading platform and central market for buyer–seller interactions. They are not a neutral third party, however, but represent the interests of their owners.

Quadrem is an e-marketplace for the mining industry that now accounts for over $1.3 billion. It was set up by 14 of the world's most prominent mining, minerals, and metals companies "as a one-stop solution to specifically meet the e-procurement needs of the natural resource industry. Taking this vision and turning it into a reality, we have developed into a fully functional global eMarketplace, with 19 shareholders, thousands of sellers and hundreds of buying locations, located across the globe. . . . We are available 24 × 7 × 365 to address our customers' needs."[18] Figure 4–8 diagrams how Quadrem facilitates its e-marketplace.

Figure 4–8
This diagram from Quadrem's website shows the efficiency of e-marketplaces

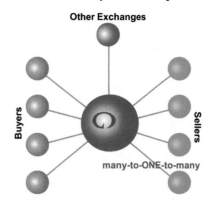

The most ambitous e-marketplace yet devised is Covisint, which is expected to revolutionize the worldwide automotive industry. Owned principally by General Motors, Ford, and Chrysler, Covisint will be the world's largest exchange when it is fully operational and will process $750 billion in transactions annually.

Online Auctions in Organizational Markets

Online auctions have grown in popularity among organizational buyers and business marketers. Many e-marketplaces offer this service. Two general types of auctions are common: a traditional auction and a

Figure 4–9
How buyer and seller participants and price behaviour differ by type of online auction

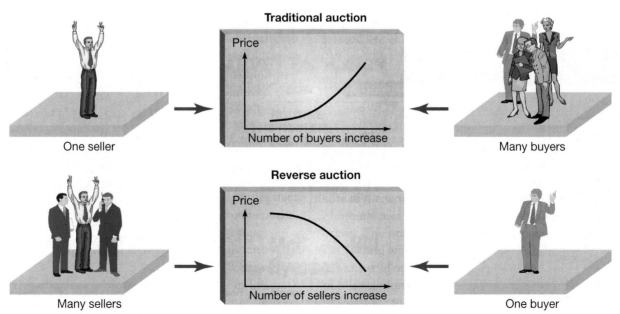

reverse auction.[19] Figure 4–9 (see page 77) shows how buyer and seller participants and price behaviour differ by type of auction. Let's look at each auction type more closely to understand the implications of each for buyers and sellers.

In a traditional auction a seller puts an item up for sale and would-be buyers are invited to bid in competition with each other. As more would-be buyers become involved, there is an upward pressure on bid prices. Why? Bidding is sequential—that is, bidders bid in order, one at a time. Prospective buyers observe the bids of others and decide whether or not to increase the bid price. The auction ends when a single bidder remains and "wins" the item with its highest price. Traditional auctions are frequently used to dispose of excess merchandise. For example, Dell Computer sells surplus, refurbished, or closeout computer merchandise at its dellauction.com website.

A reverse auction works in the opposite direction from a traditional auction. In a reverse auction, a buyer communicates a need for a product or service and would-be suppliers are invited to bid in competition with each other. As more would-be suppliers become involved, there is a downward pressure on bid prices for the buyer's business. Why? Like traditional auctions, bidding is sequential and prospective suppliers observe the bids of others and decide whether or not to decrease the bid price. The auction ends when a single bidder remains and "wins" the business with its lowest price. Reverse auctions benefit organizational buyers by reducing the cost of their purchases. As an example, General Electric, one of the world's largest companies, has its own Global eXchange Services unit, which runs online reverse auctions for the company. It claims that it saved $780 million on the purchase of $6 billion worth of products and services.[20]

Clearly, buyers welcome the lower prices generated by reverse auctions. Some suppliers also favour the reverse auction process because it gives them a chance to capture business that they might not have otherwise had because of a long-standing purchase relationship between the buyer and another supplier. On the other hand, suppliers argue that reverse auctions put too much emphasis on prices, discourage consideration of other important buying criteria, and threaten supply partnership opportunities.[21]

ask yourself

1. What are e-marketplaces?

2. How do traditional auctions and reverse auctions affect bid prices?

Summary...*just the facts*

- Organizational buyers are divided into four different markets: industrial, reseller, government, and non-profit. There are about 1.6 million industrial firms, 376,000 resellers, 7,800 government units, and 83,000 non-profit (charitable) organizations in Canada.

- Measuring industrial, reseller, government, and non-profit markets is an important first step for firms interested in determining the size of markets. The North American Industry Classification System (NAICS) is a convenient starting point to begin this process.

- Many aspects of organizational buying behaviour are different from consumer buying behaviour. Some key differences between the two include demand characteristics, number of potential buyers, buying

objectives, buying criteria, size of the order or purchase, buyer–seller relationships and partnerships, and multiple buying influences within companies.

- The three types of buying situations, or buy classes, are the straight rebuy, the modified rebuy, and the new buy. These range from a routine reorder to a totally new purchase.

- The stages in an organizational buying decision are the same as those for consumer buying decisions: problem recognition, information search, alternative evaluation, purchase decision, and post-purchase behaviour.

- The buying centre concept is central to understanding organizational buying behaviour. Knowing who makes up the buying centre and the roles they play in making purchase decisions is important in marketing to organizations. The buying centre usually includes a person from the purchasing department and possibly representatives from R&D, engineering, and production, depending on what is being purchased. These people can play one or more of five roles in a purchase decision: user, influencer, buyer, decider, or gatekeeper.

● Online buying is prevalent in industrial, reseller, and government markets. Globally, the number of e-marketplaces for businesses is extensive. Online auctions are commonly used by organizational buyers and business marketers.

Key Terms and Concepts...*a refresher*

business marketing *p. 64*
buy classes *p. 74*
buying centre *p. 72*
derived demand *p. 68*
e-marketplaces *p. 75*

fluctuating demand *p. 69*
inelastic demand *p. 69*
North American Industry Classification System (NAICS) *p. 67*
organizational buyers *p. 64*

organizational buying behaviour *p. 72*
reverse auction *p. 78*
supply partnership *p. 71*
traditional auction *p. 78*

chapter 5

market Research

Marketing that encourages consumers to purchase a product, buy a service, or support an idea works because it addresses consumers' needs. These needs, however, change as consumers alter their expectations, or become aware of new interests and trends. Market research is an area used by marketers to help provide insights into the lives of consumers. This information is then used to make better decisions and provide clear direction. This chapter focuses on market research, explaining its role, its uses,

and its strengths and limitations. We start the chapter by gaining some practical insights into the industry from Luke Sklar, partner and founder of the market research company, Sklar Wilton & Associates (SW&A). SW&A was founded in 1986 and has grown to include four main partners and a number of associates. Its clients are some of the most respected organizations in Canada, including, among others, Mars, Cara, J.M. Smuckers, Maple Leaf Foods, HMV, and Rogers. Heinz, its first client in 1986, continues to work closely with SW&A today.

SW&A works in partnership with its clients bringing them a fact-based approach to marketing decision-making. The firm provides market research information, marketing insights, and strategic direction to clients, assisting in the decision-making process. Although market research is its passion and focal point, SW&A also helps companies use this information to make sound decisions in the areas of strategy development, branding, and innovation. SW&A prides itself on being passionate about its clients' businesses.

SW&A's attitude to market research clearly acknowledges that research for the sake of research is an expensive proposition that does not yield results. Luke Sklar firmly believes that research should be evaluated on the basis of the value that it brings to an organization, and that it should be treated with the same rigour and return on investment as any other investment decision. Sklar emphasizes,

LEARNING OBJECTIVES

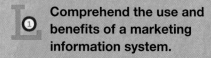 **L1** Comprehend the use and benefits of a marketing information system.

L2 Understand the importance and challenges of market research to companies.

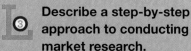 **L3** Describe a step-by-step approach to conducting market research.

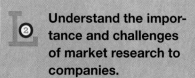

L ④ **Explain how secondary and primary data are used in marketing.**

L ⑤ **Explain the uses of market research tools such as questionnaires, observations, experiments, and panels.**

L ⑥ **Consider the future of market research.**

"Research that confirms or denies smart ideas is worth more than the research that searches aimlessly for insights." He explains that marketers need to understand that consumers cannot provide all the answers and identify where to take a business. They cannot provide visionary leadership, but they can provide useful insights as to what is important in their lives and how these factors can impact on a business. Marketers need to have a vision for their businesses and use market research to help make smarter decisions and avoid the pitfalls of mistakes.

Luke Sklar points to two well-known market research gaffes that demonstrate the limitations of market research and the importance of asking the right questions. The first example relates to Coca-Cola's New Coke, and the second instance refers to the Sony Walkman. New Coke was introduced in late April 1985 in Canada and the U.S. as a new and improved version of the traditional Coca-Cola beverage. It was touted as a sweeter Coke that people preferred to their traditional Coca-Cola, and even liked better than Pepsi. The product was launched with a media frenzy that had people heading to the stores to try the new product. This positive exposure soon backfired as consumers voiced their complaints that their regular Coca-Cola had now been replaced by this New Coke. Consumers were in an uproar over the disappearance of their beloved Coca-Cola and started hoarding the old beverage. The old Coca-Cola even surfaced on the black market, and the company was barraged with complaints about

the new product. In a little over two months, bowing to public pressure, Coca-Cola pulled New Coke off the shelves and replaced it with the old formula. Why the mistake? Coca-Cola did its homework, asked its consumers about the new product, and conducted extensive market research for over two years. The answer is that researchers forgot to ask one key question: Can we replace your current Coca-Cola with this new beverage? It's all about asking the right questions.

Sony Walkman is another interesting example of research gone wrong. The product, eventually so successful, initially failed in concept tests as the research focused on new technology rather than on consumers' love of music. Research failed to provide insights into the life of teenagers and how their love of music, and their appetite to listen to it anywhere and anytime, could drive this category. Again, it's all about asking the right questions.

Luke Sklar reminds us that market research is not just about an evaluation of numbers and statistics. It is a combination of art and science with the art coming into play when deciding what the research results really mean, and how they can be usefully applied to a business decision. Luke reminds us that successful research needs vision, hypotheses, instincts, and energy. He emphasizes that the best researchers have diverse backgrounds, rooted in areas other than research, that give them the mental flexibility and creative thinking skills needed to capture opportunities for their clients and provide useful insights and recommendations. 🍎

Marketing Information Systems and Market Research

Consumer insights can stimulate interesting ideas.

Market research helps marketers understand their consumers and make fact-based decisions.

LO ① Companies are constantly in need of information. They need to know the state of the economy, the moves their competitors are planning, and their customers' wants, needs, and preferences. Information can be an important competitive advantage for firms, as well as a key marketing tool and strategic benefit.

Changes in technology present managers with an abundance of information and the challenge is to determine which information is the most useful in making sound decisions. Information is used by marketers to reduce the risk of making a poor decision, so gathering the correct information and data is crucial to the smooth operation of a business.

> ## *Information can be an important competitive advantage for firms, as well as a key marketing tool and strategic benefit.*

marketing information system (MIS)
A set of procedures and processes for collecting, sorting, analyzing, and summarizing information on an ongoing basis

market research
The process of collecting and analyzing information in order to recommend actions to improve marketing activities

Information presents itself to companies in two different ways: (1) a marketing information system, and (2) market research projects. Many companies have a **marketing information system (MIS)**, which is a set of procedures and processes for collecting, sorting, analyzing, and summarizing information on an ongoing basis. The MIS may collect information on market conditions, competitive marketing actions, and local sales figures, and then analyzes it to provide a current market assessment. Separately, companies will often have a need for specific information that is not available through an MIS. Companies then turn to market research projects to help answer questions that will lead to sound business decisions. This chapter deals with market research, identifies the types of research tools available, and explains the steps that are taken to complete a market research study.

What Is Market Research?

L2 **Market research** is formally defined as the process of collecting and analyzing information in order to recommend actions to improve marketing activities.[1] Although market research isn't perfect at predicting consumer reaction, it can reduce the risk and uncertainty of making poor decisions. It can provide managers with the facts they can use to make sound decisions. Good marketing decisions are often the result of managers using their vision, knowledge, and experience, together with clear market research information.

Market research is not an easy undertaking. Gleaning accurate information from consumers can be difficult. If a researcher asks the wrong questions, or fails to investigate an important insight, the research results will be inaccurate. Sometimes the situation may be personal and respondents are often loathe to share private information with strangers. Other times, consumers are not necessarily truthful or are unsure about their choices. Ask a respondent about different pricing options and inevitably they may suggest a lower price. Ask a respondent about a new product they have never seen, and it is often difficult for them to conceptualize the item. As demonstrated by Luke Sklar's example of the Sony Walkman, market researchers often face difficulties when asking consumers about new, unknown products.

The task of market research is to overcome these challenges and obtain accurate information with which marketers can make sound decisions. Researchers work hard to ensure that they undertake their research using scientific methods and a methodical approach. They diligently plan their research methodology so

Marketing ▸ tip

"You need to know 'a day in the life of your consumer.' You need to know their pain points and delight points—what makes them tick."

Luke Sklar, partner, Sklar Wilton & Associates Ltd.

exploratory research
Preliminary research conducted to clarify the scope and nature of the marketing problem

descriptive research
Research designed to describe basic characteristics of a given population or to clarify their usage and attitudes

causal research
Research designed to identify cause-and-effect relationships among variables

that insights are not missed, the samples are representative of the target market, and costs are minimized for the client. This all occurs while ensuring that the research is reliable and valid.

Let's look at the different types of market research and how market research is collected.

Research Classifications

Research can be classified into three basic areas: (1) exploratory research, (2) descriptive research, and (3) causal research. Each serves a different function and uses different techniques.

Exploratory Research Preliminary research conducted to clarify the scope and nature of the marketing problem is referred to as **exploratory research**. It is generally carried out to provide the researcher with a better understanding of the dimensions of the problem. Exploratory research is often conducted with the expectation that subsequent and more conclusive research will follow. For example, the Dairy Farmers of Canada, an association representing dairy producers in the country, wanted to discover why milk consumption was declining in Canada. They conducted a search of existing literature on milk consumption, talked to experts in the field, and even conducted preliminary interviews with consumers on why they were drinking less milk. This exploratory research helped the association crystallize the issues, and identify areas that required more detailed follow-up.

Descriptive Research Research designed to describe basic characteristics of a given population or to clarify their usage and attitudes is known as **descriptive research**. Unlike exploratory research, with descriptive research the researcher has a general understanding of the marketing problem and is seeking more conclusive data that answers particular questions. Examples of descriptive research include providing more detailed profiles of product purchasers (e.g., the characteristics of the Canadian health food store shopper), describing the size and characteristics of markets (e.g., the types of products sold in the Canadian pizza restaurant market), detailing product usage patterns (e.g., how frequently people use bank machines), or outlining consumer attitudes toward particular brands (e.g., Canadian attitudes toward national, private, and generic brands). Magazines, radio stations, and television stations almost always do descriptive research to identify the characteristics of their audiences in order to present it to prospective advertisers. As a follow-up to its exploratory research, the Dairy Farmers of Canada conducted descriptive research to determine the demographic characteristics of milk consumers, current usage patterns, and consumer attitudes toward milk consumption.

Causal Research Research designed to identify cause-and-effect relationships among variables is termed **causal research**. In general, exploratory and descriptive research normally precedes causal research. With causal research there is typically an expectation about the relationship to be explained, such as predicting the influence of a price change on product demand.

Typical causal research studies examine the effect of advertising on sales, the relationship between price and perceived product quality, and the impact of a new package on sales. When the Dairy Farmers of Canada conducted their descriptive research on milk consumers, they discovered that many people believed milk was too fattening and too high in cholesterol. The association felt that these beliefs might be related to the overall decline in milk consumption in Canada. To test this assumption, they conducted some causal research that included running a TV campaign stating that milk was healthy and essential to a person's diet. In their research tracking studies, they found that the TV campaign changed consumer attitudes toward milk which, in turn, increased milk consumption.

Market research is useful in many different ways for a company. We have talked about it helping to identify consumer habits or intentions, but it can also be used to assess opportunities, evaluate new ideas, understand behaviour, analyze competitor and market situations, and troubleshoot problems. It is important that we think of market research as a tool that not only assists with problems and opportunities but also provides information for other key marketing decisions.

Procter & Gamble (P&G) is a company that believes in using market research and the power of advertising to drive its business. When creating new ads, it routinely looks to prior advertising research it has conducted, and tests its new creative ideas to ensure that they are compelling and are clearly communicated to consumers. Its recent personal hygiene print ads for Crest Pro-Health Rinse (shown opposite) and Crest Pro-Health Toothpaste are typical examples of P&G's approach to advertising in the personal hygiene category. The ads typically use scientific data to support P&G's claims (e.g., kills germs in laboratory tests), showcase the product, and use simple, crisp, and clinical visuals. Toothpaste ads generally use the seal of the Canadian Dental Association

Marketers use carefully researched facts in ads.

New Advertising Research Centre

The Quebec City–based international marketing communications firm Cossette has set up the Cossette University Research Centre in conjunction with the University of Ottawa. The centre was created with the goal of advancing research in advertising. Over the next few years, Cossette will be working with Luc Dupont, professor in the communications department at the University of Ottawa and an advertising and communications expert, to conduct research on past studies and campaigns to identify what makes an advertisement effective. The research will also evaluate the impact of new broadcast platforms now available in the communications industry.

Phase one of the partnership will focus on the study of the effectiveness of advertising using the archives of the Tracking Efficiency Study by Impact Research. These archives are the equivalent of almost 4,000 studies conducted since 1980. Phase one will expand the criteria normally used to assess this effectiveness by reviewing the advertising media weight together with the linguistic, graphic, and iconic items used in the ads. Phase two will deal with understanding the impact of new broadcasting platforms. Analysis, surveys, and interviews will better define the influence of new platforms such as blogs, social networking sites, Internet radio, mobile phones, and Internet streaming. The results will provide a

more detailed outline of the choices available to advertisers today.

In addition to creating the Cossette University Research Centre, Cossette has created a $3,000 study grant, which is awarded annually to a qualifying master's student recognized for outstanding advertising research. This grant will be awarded for the next five years. The funds are to be used by the recipient to further their research on a subject linked to the advertising industry. ●

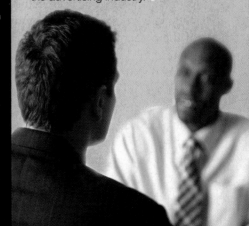

Source: Gail Chiasson, "Cossette Partners with the University of Ottawa to Establish Advertising Research Centre," *Pubzone*, May 8, 2008, accessed at www.pubzone.com/newsroom/2008/1x080507x062508.cfm; Cossette, "Cossette Partners with the University of Ottawa to Establish a Research Centre," *Cossette News*, May 7, 2008, accessed at www.cossette.com/www/news_cruc20080507.php?Sec=d3; Terry Poulton, "Cossette, U of Ottawa creating research centre," *Media in Canada*, May 14, 2008, at www.mediaincanada.com/articles/mic/20080514/cossette.html.

to add further cred-
ibility to the mes-
sage. These factors are not left
to chance. Years of advertising
research in these categories
play a key role in determining
advertising effectiveness.

Let's look at the Insurance Corporation of British Columbia (ICBC) as
an example. This Crown corporation
is responsible for providing auto
insurance and administering driver
licensing and vehicle registration
for drivers in British Columbia. It is
committed to reducing injuries and
fatalities, and has spent millions of
advertising dollars to encourage British Columbians to drive more safely.
Looking at the large amount of money
spent on advertising, ICBC realized it needed to
know whether the anti-speeding ads had a positive
effect on speeders. Did the ads change the speeders'
behaviour? This was its definition of the problem.
For ICBC, the immediate research objectives were to
determine whether its ads were working. At the start
of the project it was important for the researcher and
the ICBC to acknowledge that if the ICBC intended
to continue airing the anti-speeding ads, regardless
of the research results, then the research was not
worth conducting.

The Six-Step Market Research Approach

LO③ Effective market research is not left to chance. A
systematic approach ensures that the research is
done thoroughly, all elements are considered, and
the results are accurate. Here is a basic six-step approach
that is used to conduct market research studies:

1. Define the problem/issue/opportunity.

2. Design the research plan.

3. Conduct exploratory research.

4. Collect quantitative research information.

5. Compile, analyze, and interpret data.

6. Generate report and recommendations.

Figure 5–1 shows this sequence of steps, and in the
next few pages we will discuss these steps in detail.

Step 1: Define the Problem/ Issue/Opportunity

The first step in the market research process is to
clearly define the problem, issue, or opportunity. This
is often posed as a question that needs to be answered.
Most market researchers would agree with the saying that "a problem well-defined is half-solved," but
they know that defining a problem is a difficult task.
If the objectives are too broad, the problem may not
be tangible. If the objectives are too narrow, the value
of the research results may be seriously lessened. This
is why market researchers spend so much time pre-
cisely defining a marketing problem and writing a formal proposal that describes the research task.[2] Part of
Step 1 also includes clarifying the research objectives.
Objectives are specific, measurable goals the decision
maker seeks to achieve. Common research objectives
are to discover consumer needs and wants, and to
determine why a product is not selling.

Figure 5–1
The basic market research process

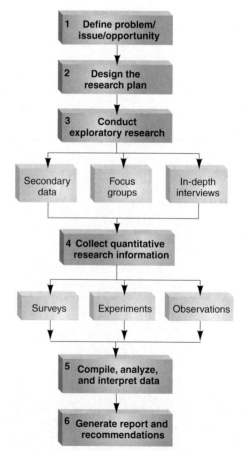

Step 2: Design the Research Plan

The second step in the market research process involves identifying what approach will be taken to complete the research project. This specifically includes identifying what information is needed, how it will be collected, and whether a sampling plan is needed. Let's look at these three areas:

Information Requirements

Often, market research studies collect data that is interesting, but not relevant to the task at hand. In ICBC's situation, it might be nice to know the colour of cars more likely to speed, but this information was not relevant to its research study. The challenge was to determine whether the ads encouraged speeders to slow down. The research needed to focus on collecting information that would allow the corporation to determine whether to continue with the speeders' ad campaign. The ICBC needed to understand where best to get this information. Clearly, speeders could tell the ICBC what it needs to know, but how do you define a speeder? Is it a driver who has received a speeding ticket in the past two years, or a driver with three or more speeding tickets in the past year? Maybe drivers who had not received a speeding ticket, but who admitted to consistently driving over the speed limit, should also be included? ICBC had to define who could effectively provide this information.

Collection Methods

In order to collect data in an organized fashion, it is important to have a data collection plan. There are scientific considerations and operational issues that the researcher must take into consideration. Determining *how* to collect useful market research data is often as important as actually collecting the data. Researchers can purchase the information from a pre-existing study, or conduct their own research using a variety of data collection methods such as in-depth personal interviews, focus groups, telephone surveys, mall intercepts, online questionnaires, or direct mail surveys.

If you were the market researcher working on the ICBC project, you may be faced with some questions for which answers were difficult to determine:

- Will drivers actually reveal their speeding habits?
- Will drivers be able to determine whether advertising affects their road behaviour?

To ensure accurate answers are obtained, you need to carefully select a research methodology that encourages respondents to answer truthfully. The method you choose is critical to obtaining accurate results. In this case, it may be more helpful to conduct focus groups or personal interviews, rather than telephone interviews where the responses cannot be as easily probed.

Canadian market researchers rely on their training, experience, and judgment to make the appropriate methodology decisions. They can also turn to their professional association, the Professional Marketing Research Society, which provides resources and training sessions for its members. Their monthly publication, *Imprints*, is also a source of Canadian market research information.

Sampling

Sampling is an important factor in the research design stage. A researcher's sampling plan indicates who is to be sampled, how large the sample should be, and how sampling units will be selected. Rarely does a research project involve a complete census of every person in the research population, because of its time and cost. So sampling is used. **Sampling** is the process of gathering data from a subset of the total population, rather than from

> *Rarely does a research project involve a complete census of every person in the research population, because of its time and cost.*

probability sampling Selecting a sample so that each element of a population has a specific known chance of being selected

non-probability sampling Selecting a sample so that the chance of selecting a particular element of a population is either unknown or zero

all members of that particular population. A sample, then, is a subset from a larger population.

A properly selected sample should be representative of the population being researched, however, errors can occur in sampling, and thus the reliability of the data can sometimes be an issue. Savvy researchers know that the first and most critical sampling question for researchers to ask is: Who is to be sampled? Another key question concerns the sample size: How big should the sample be? The final question of the sampling plan concerns how to select the sample?

There are two basic sampling techniques: probability and non-probability sampling. **Probability sampling** involves precise rules to select the sample so that each element of the population has a specific known chance of being selected. For example, if your university wants to know how last year's 1,000 graduates are doing, it can put their names into a bowl and randomly select 100 names of graduates to contact. The chance of being selected—100 out of 1,000, or 1 in 10—is known in advance, and all graduates have an equal chance of being contacted. This procedure helps to select a sample (100 graduates), that should be representative of the entire population (the 1,000 graduates), and allows conclusions to be drawn about the population being researched.

Non-probability sampling involves the use of arbitrary judgment by the market researcher to select the sample so that the chance of selecting a particular element of the population is either unknown or zero. If your university decided to talk to 100 of last year's graduates, but only those who lived closest to the institution, many

class members would be arbitrarily eliminated. This would introduce a bias, or possible lack of representativeness, which likely means that conclusions cannot be accurately drawn about the entire graduating class. Non-probability samples are often used when time and budgets are limited, and are most often used for exploratory research purposes. In general, market researchers use data from such samples with caution. They can furnish valuable information, but the results should not be assumed to represent the overall population.

ask yourself

1. How do research objectives relate to marketing actions?

2. What different methods can be used to conduct market research?

3. What are the differences between a probability and non-probability sample?

Step 3: Conduct Exploratory Research

Exploratory research is preliminary research conducted to clarify the scope and nature of a marketing problem. It is done to ensure that the researcher has not overlooked a key insight that is important to the rest of the study. Exploratory research is often conducted with the expectation that subsequent and more conclusive quantitative research may follow. Most researchers will usually conduct some basic exploratory research during the early stage of the research process. The extent of the exploratory research will depend on the magnitude of the problem as well as its complexity. If the researcher decides to conduct exploratory research, he or she has three basic tools from which to choose: (1) secondary data analysis, (2) focus group research, and (3) in-depth interviews. Focus group

qualitative research A form of research that uses focus groups and in-depth interviews to provide insightful and directional information that is not statistically accurate

secondary data Facts and figures that have already been recorded by a third party

primary data Information that is newly collected for a project

research and in-depth interviews are part of a form of research called **qualitative research**, which provides insightful and directional information, with the knowledge that it is not statistically accurate. In this manner, it is not usually used to draw firm conclusions, but rather to provide insights.

Let's look at a fictitious example. The marketing manager for cranberry juice at Ocean Spray is considering exporting cranberry juice to Asian countries. He needs to determine whether this is a viable opportunity but is concerned that these consumers may not be interested in cranberries because they are not usually grown outside of North America, and they are virtually unknown in Asia. This may, however, present an opportunity to sell something unique in the

market. One of the major stumbling blocks is that the word "cranberry" does not exist in any of the Asian languages. Exploratory research would be advisable in this situation, starting with secondary research to find out whether any information is available on beverage consumption in Asia. This may be followed by focus group research to probe attitudes and opportunities in this area.

Secondary Data Exploratory research can include **secondary data**, which is divided into two parts: (1) *internal data* that exists within a company such as sales reports, and (2) *external data* from published sources outside the organization. A general rule is to obtain secondary data first, and then collect **primary data**, newly collected data specifically for the project. This is because secondary data is generally lower in cost and readily available. Nonetheless, these advantages must be weighed against these possible disadvantages: (1) the secondary data may be out of date; (2) the definitions or categories may not be right for the project; and (3) the data may not be specific enough. (See Figure 5–2.)

Statistics Canada, the federal government's statistical agency, publishes a wide variety of useful reports, such as census data that includes information

Figure 5–2
Information sources

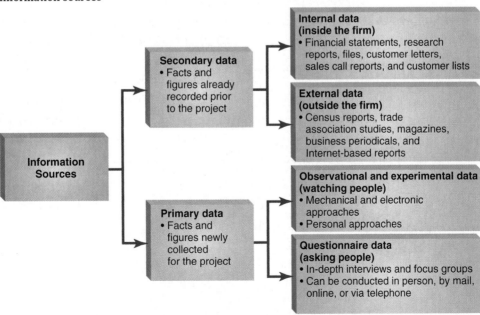

"A POPULAR EXPLORATORY RESEARCH TECHNIQUE IS THE FOCUS GROUP."

Leading Saturday Newspapers

The Print Measurement Bureau (PMB) provides secondary data on newspapers and magazines in Canada.

Ranking	Newspaper	Circulation
1	Toronto Star	632,000
2	The Globe and Mail	412,000
3	Le Journal de Montréal	310,000
4	National Post	231,000
5	Toronto Sun	155,000
6	Le Journal de Québec	126,000

Source: *2008 PMB Topline Report*, Canadian Print Measurement Bureau, accessed at www.pmb.ca/public/e/pmb2008/PMB2008_topline.pdf.

Maclean's *using published secondary data from the Audit Bureau of Circulations to promote sales*

provide this information to companies. Often, a portion of this information is provided at no charge, with more in-depth information provided for a price. Similarly, data on the market share of products and services is available for marketers to purchase to help track the competition. Figure 5–3 shows some of these information sources.

Online resources are also invaluable. Here are a few online resources that are used by marketers. Visit these sites to gain an understanding into the information that is available. In many instances, you can download a short snapshot of their latest information, read a synopsis of a study, and sign up for free online newsletters. Their more-detailed studies are typically not provided free of charge.

- Audit Bureau of Circulations: www.accessabc.com
- BBM Canada: www.bbm.ca
- Government of Canada: www.canada.gc.ca
- Industry Canada (formerly Strategis): www.ic.gc.ca
- Ipsos Canada: www.ipsos.ca
- Newspaper Audience Databank: www.nadbank.com
- Print Measurement Bureau: www.pmb.ca
- Radio Marketing Bureau: www.rmb.ca
- SEDAR: www.sedar.com
- Statistics Canada: www.statcan.gc.ca
- Television Bureau of Canada: www.tvb.ca

on the number of people per household, their age, gender, ethnic background, income, occupation, and education. Statistics Canada also publishes a wide range of other statistical reports that are used extensively by businesses across the country. These reports include information on the following:

- Economic indicators
- International trade
- Agriculture
- Manufacturing
- Environment
- Health
- Education
- Culture and leisure
- Tourism and travel
- Government
- Justice and crime

There are many other sources of secondary information other than Statistics Canada that are used by the marketing industry. Third-party organizations audit the circulation of magazines, newspapers, and TV shows and

Research on the impact of the writers' strike on TV viewing

Watching the same 72%

Watching less 25%

Watching more 3%

marketing meter

Source: Terry Poulton, "Carat surveys effect of writers' strike on US viewers," *Media in Canada*, January 30, 2008, accessed at www.mediaincanada.com/articles/mic/20080130/carat.html?word=online&word=surveys.

Figure 5–3
Selected sources of secondary data

SELECTED GUIDES, INDEXES, AND DIRECTORIES
Business Periodical Index
Canadian Almanac and Directory
Canadian Business Index
Canadian News Index
Canadian Periodical Index
Canadian Statistics Index
Canadian Trade Index
Directory of Associations in Canada
Fraser's Canadian Trade Directory
Predicasts Index
Scott's Directories
Standards Periodical Directory
Ulrich's International Periodicals Directory

SELECTED PERIODICALS AND NEWSPAPERS
Advertising Age
Adweek
American Demographics
Business Horizons
Canadian Business
Canadian Consumer
Forbes
Fortune
Harvard Business Review
Journal of Advertising
Journal of Advertising Research
Journal of Consumer Research
Journal of Marketing
Journal of Marketing Management
Journal of Marketing Research
Journal of Personal Selling and Sales Management
Journal of Retailing
Journal of Small Business
Marketing Magazine

Marketing & Media Decisions
Marketing News
Progressive Grocer
Sales and Marketing Management
The Globe and Mail
The Financial Post
The Financial Post Magazine
The Wall Street Journal

SELECTED STATISTICS CANADA PUBLICATIONS
Annual Retail Trade
Canadian Economic Observer
Canada Yearbook
Family Expenditure Guide
Market Research Handbook
Statistics Canada Catalogue

SELECTED TRADE SOURCES
ACNielsen
Audit Bureau of Circulations (ABC)
BBM Canada
Conference Board of Canada
Dun & Bradstreet Canada
Financial Post Publishing
Find/SVP
Gale Research
Ipsos Canada
MacLean Hunter Research Bureau
MapInfo Canada
Newspaper Audience Databank (NADbank)
Predicasts International
Print Measurement Bureau (PMB)
R. L. Polk
Radio Marketing Bureau (RMB)
Television Bureau of Canada (TVB)

---

focus group
A research technique where a small group of people (usually six to ten) meet for a few hours with a trained moderator to discuss predetermined areas

in-depth interview
A detailed interview where a researcher questions an individual at length in a free-flowing conversational style in order to discover information that may help solve a marketing problem

---

Focus Group Research A popular exploratory research technique is the focus group. A **focus group** is an informal interview session in which six to ten people are brought together in a room with a moderator to discuss topics surrounding the market research problem. The moderator poses questions and encourages the individuals to discuss the issues. Often, the focus-group sessions are watched by observers through one-way mirrors, and the sessions are videotaped. Participants are always informed that they are being observed and/or taped.

The ICBC research study we have discussed earlier in this chapter included focus groups where participants were shown the anti-speeding ads and probed on their attitudes and responses to these messages. The research suggested an association between personality and speeding. This exploratory research stage was followed by quantitative research with a larger group of people to confirm the personality/speeding linkage and to further understand the effectiveness of the ICBC advertising campaign with these people.

Another example of how focus group research has been used is with Britain's Lewis Woolf Griptight, a manufacturer of infant and toddler products. This firm conducted focus groups with consumers about possible brand names. U.K. consumers rejected the name "Griptight" because they thought it sounded like "carpet glue, a denture fixative, a kind of tire," but they liked the name Kiddiwinks, a much friendlier term for a child's product.

In-Depth Interviews Another exploratory research technique used to obtain primary data involves the use of in-depth interviews. **In-depth interviews** are detailed individual interviews where the researcher questions an individual at length in a free-flowing conversational style in order to discover information that may help solve the marketing problem. Sometimes these interviews can take a few hours, and they are often recorded.

quantitative research
Statistically reliable information that uses observational and/or questioning techniques

observational research
Obtained by watching how people behave either in person, or by using a machine to record the event

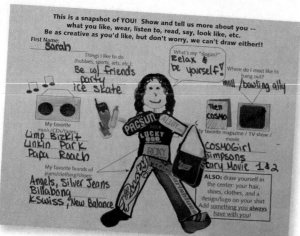

Teenagers visually express their interests for market researchers.

General Mills used in-depth interviews to better market its Hamburger Helper product. When the product was first introduced, sales were not brisk. Initial instructions called for cooking half a pound of hamburger separately from the noodles, and later adding it to the noodles. In-depth interviews revealed that consumers didn't think the recipe called for enough meat and that they didn't want the hassle of cooking in two different pots. As a result, the recipe for Hamburger Helper was changed to include a full pound of meat with all the ingredients cooked together in one pot.[3]

Other exploratory research techniques are used to try to spot consumer

ask yourself

1. Why do researchers use exploratory research?

2. What is the difference between secondary and primary data?

3. What are some advantages and disadvantages of secondary data?

trends. For example, Teenage Research Unlimited had teenagers complete a drawing to help discover what teenagers like, wear, listen to, and read.[4] Other companies hire "cool hunters," people with tastes far ahead of the curve, to identify the "next big thing" likely to sweep popular culture. Skechers uses this method to anticipate teenage girls' fashion and footwear trends.[5]

Step 4: Collect Quantitative Research Information

LO 5 Further research can be conducted using quantitative research through observational and/or questioning techniques. The main advantage is that quantitative research is designed to be statistically accurate and is more reliable than exploratory research. The main disadvantage is that quantitative research is far more costly and time consuming to collect. See Figure 5–4 (on page 93) for more detail about the advantages and disadvantage of quantitative research techniques.

Observational research is obtained by watching how people behave either in person, or by using a machine to record the event. National TV ratings, such as those provided by BBM Nielsen Media Research Inc. are examples of electronic observational data collected

Tostitos Uses Market Research

Marketing **NewsFlash**

Tostitos conducted market research that showed that women love Tostitos products but prefer to make their own dips. In 2008, in response to this market research, Tostitos launched a national recipe program to give women simple snack solutions. These recipes can be seen in their TV ads and are available on their website (www.tostitos.ca). Each recipe takes under 10 minutes to make, giving consumers the ability to make simple, homemade appetizers that they can enjoy with Tostitos products.

According to Melise Boisvert, marketing manager for Tostitos, "What they want are time-sensitive, really easy to make, simple solutions that they can whip up and serve to guests." Consumers can search on Tostitos.ca for more than 40 recipes. These recipes can be searched by ingredient, occasion, or preparation method. Each recipe takes under 10 minutes to make, giving consumers the ability to make the simple and homemade appetizers they desire, while still integrating the Tostitos products.

Source: Kristin Laird, "Chips and Clicks for Tostitos Recipes," *Marketing* magazine, May 5, 2008, accessed at www.marketingmag.ca/english/news/marketer/article.jsp?content=20080 505_777333_2469.

Figure 5–4
Quantitative research—How do the techniques compare?

TECHNIQUE	ADVANTAGES	DISADVANTAGES
Observation	• Flexible • May indicate things a consumer cannot articulate clearly	• Does not indicate why consumers behave as they do • Different researchers may interpret behaviour differently
Surveys/personal interviews	• Large numbers of people can be asked a standard set of questions • Interviewers can probe to get in-depth answers • Questions can be administered via e-mail, mail, telephone, the Internet, or in person	• Interviewers can bias results • Mail or e-mail surveys may be completed mainly by those with a bias • Can be very expensive and time consuming
Panels	• Can track changes in consumer behaviour over time	• Original participants needed for consistency • Can be difficult to keep consumers in the panel
Experiments	• Researchers able to change some key factors and measure the results	• Can be expensive • Time consuming • Results can be difficult to interpret
Test markets	• Allow a company to launch products or promotional campaigns in a controlled area • Can monitor and make adjustments • Can avoid the costly failures of products launched nationally	• Tells competitors what a company is doing • Requires as much effort as a major roll-out • Can be expensive • Time consuming

questionnaire
A means of obtaining information by posing questions in person, through the mail, the telephone, e-mail, fax, or the Internet

by a "people meter." The people meter is a box that is attached to TV sets, VCRs, cable boxes, and satellite dishes in a panel of homes across the country. It has a remote control that operates the meter when a viewer begins and finishes watching a TV program. Finally, it stores and then transmits the viewing information each night to BBM Nielsen Media Research Inc.[6]

Personal observation is both useful and flexible, but it can be costly and unreliable when different observers report different conclusions in watching the same event. An example of how observation research is used can be seen with Aurora Foods. Aurora Foods observes how consumers bake cakes in its test kitchens to find out whether baking instructions on their cake boxes are understood.

The second principal way of gathering quantitative information from consumers is by asking questions. Questions can be standardized and asked to a large number of people, as in a survey or personal interview. Personal interviews allow researchers to get in-depth answers.

Questions are often posed in research projects through questionnaires. **Questionnaires** can be administered in person, through the mail, the telephone, e-mail, fax, or the Internet. In choosing between these alternatives, the market researcher has to make important trade-offs to balance costs against the expected quality of information obtained. Personal interviews have the major advantage of enabling the interviewer to ask probing questions and get reactions to visual materials. However, this approach is very costly. Mail surveys have low response rates, and are usually biased because those most likely to respond have had positive or negative experiences. Telephone interviews allow flexibility, but are increasingly difficult to complete due to call display features. Fax and Internet surveys are restricted to respondents having the technologies but are becoming popular methods of gathering information.[7]

> **PERSONAL INTERVIEWS ALLOW RESEARCHERS TO GET IN-DEPTH ANSWERS.**

Two additional environments in which observations and questionnaires are sometimes used are panels and experiments. Market researchers often want to know if consumers change their behaviour over time, so they take successive measurements of the same people. A panel is a sample of consumers or stores from which researchers take a successive series of measurements. For example, the NPD Group collects data about consumer purchases such as apparel, food, and electronics from its "Online Panel," which consists of over 600,000 individuals worldwide. With this information, a firm can measure consumers switching behaviour from one brand to another.

A marketing experiment involves changing a variable involved in a customer purchase to find out what happens. Ideally, the researcher changes just one element, usually, one of the factors in the marketing mix, and keeps all the other variables constant. This is often done to test different promotional offers with consumers to gauge differences in response rates. Large companies often use a form of experiment known as a test market to determine whether consumers will buy a new product or brand, or shop at a new store concept. These test markets are conducted in a small localized region over a period of a few months. In 1988, Wal-Mart opened three experimental supercenters as a test market to gauge consumer acceptance before deciding to open others. Today, Wal-Mart operates over 1,250 supercenters internationally.[8]

Step 5: Compile, Analyze, and Interpret Data

After data has been collected, it has to be compiled, analyzed, and summarized in order to turn it into actionable information. The researcher must know how to analyze the data and what tools to use. There are many statistical packages and functions that can make this task easier. Market researchers face the challenge of synthesizing and simplifying pages of data into clear charts with relevant observations and conclusions that can be used by marketers to address

the problems, challenges, and opportunities they face with their businesses.

Step 6: Generate Report and Recommendations

Once the data has been analyzed, the researcher will discuss the results with the marketing manager and prepare a report to communicate the research findings. The report will include recommendations that address the marketing challenge. It is important to understand that marketing data and information have little value unless they are translated into findings and recommendations that lead to marketing action. Managers generally prefer clear, concise reports with the key findings highlighted, including relevant charts, graphs, and tables of data.

In our example of the ICBC, the corporation's final research report pointed out that the people who like speeding resisted the ads. The research told the ICBC that its advertising dollars were not well spent and recommended a change.[9]

ask yourself

1. Which survey provides the greatest flexibility for asking probing questions: mail, telephone, or personal interview?

2. What is the difference between a panel and an experiment?

Wal-Mart test-marketed its supercenters before deciding to open others.

The Future of Market Research

Today's marketer has extensive sources of information available on the competition, the market, and the consumer. This information can come from secondary sources or primary sources to help marketers make fact-based decisions. Technology is facilitating the gathering of this information, with more and more individuals having easy access to the Internet. (The search engine Google alone enjoys over 22 million hits a month.) This extensive use of the Internet makes online research more practical and reliable for market researchers.

This sea of information presents its own challenges as marketers find they need to adopt strategies and approaches to filter out the unreliable and useless information from the critical and actionable facts that can drive their business. In all instances, marketers need to remember that market research should be actionable and that the decisions to purchase a study, or embark upon a market research project, should be evaluated as any investment decision. A marketer needs to weigh the costs of conducting the research against the expected results and actions that can evolve. In all instances, marketers need to work with the market researcher as a team, ensuring that the objectives are clear, the process efficient, and the decisions cost effective.

Top Internet Sites

According to research conducted by comScore, Inc., the following were the Internet sites visited most often in Canada during March 2008.

Ranking	Site	Total Unique Visitors (000)
1	Google sites	22,436
2	Microsoft sites	22,341
3	Yahoo! sites	16,215
4	Facebook.com	15,513
5	eBay	13,821
6	Wikipedia sites	11,222

Source: "Top 25 Properties by Number of Canadian Unique Visitors," comScore Media Metrix, accessed at http://comscore.com/press/data/top_canadian_properties.asp.

Research Supports Pepsi Sponsorship

Marketing NewsFlash

In recent years, digital platform extensions to on-air television shows have been pitched by media companies as a way to keep viewers engaged, both with the medium and with advertisers. In keeping with this idea, soft-drink marketer Pepsi has embraced several media extensions offered by MTV, based on MTV research that shows consumer engagement grows with each digital platform. In 2007, MTV expanded its digital presence to include its hit prime-time series *The Hills* and was joined by Pepsi as a sponsor. Pepsi sponsored the show, its website, and its virtual world, creating exclusive branded content for the virtual world such as Pepsi vending machines and Pepsi-branded clothing.

Data collected by MTV in the "Multiscreen Engagement Case Study" showed that Pepsi's positive brand image increased among fans who watched the show and browsed *The Hills* content online, where Pepsi also ran spots and banners. Among the fans who watched only the on-air version of the show, roughly 50 percent said that Pepsi promotes music events/music artists. Less than 30 percent said that the brand was in touch with youth culture.

These numbers increased dramatically among fans who watched the TV show and used the online digital platform to enter *The Hills* virtual world. Ninety percent of those viewers said that Pepsi promotes music/music artists, and nearly 70 percent considered the brand to be in touch with youth culture. In MTV's virtual world, Pepsi was the best-selling product of 2007.

Source: Steve McClellan, "'The Hills' Is Alive," Adweek.com, May 5, 2008, accessed at www.adweek.com/aw/content_display/news/media/e3i26f1bfd408799a20c5f12f2e18a726fa.

Summary...*just the facts*

- Market research is the process of defining a marketing problem or opportunity, systematically collecting and analyzing information, and recommending actions to improve an organization's marketing activities.

- The first step in the research process is describing the problem, issue, or opportunity and establishing the research objectives.

- The second step involves designing the research plan. This involves identifying the required information and designing methods to gather it.

- During the third step, exploratory research is conducted.

- The fourth step involves collecting quantitative research information.

- The fifth step is when the data is analyzed and interpreted.

- The final step is when the information is translated into a report that includes research highlights, necessary details, and recommendations for future actions.

Key Terms and Concepts...*a refresher*

causal research *p. 84*
descriptive research *p. 84*
experiment *p. 94*
exploratory research *p. 84*
focus group *p. 91*
in-depth interview *p. 91*
market research *p. 83*

marketing information system
   (MIS) *p. 83*
non-probability sampling *p. 88*
objectives *p. 86*
observational research *p. 92*
panel *p. 94*
primary data *p. 89*

probability sampling *p. 88*
qualitative research *p. 89*
quantitative research *p. 92*
questionnaire *p. 93*
sampling *p. 87*
secondary data *p. 89*
test market *p. 94*

Check out the Online Learning Centre at **www.mcgrawhill.ca/olc/thecore**
for chapter application questions, discussion activities, Internet exercises, and video cases.

6

segmentation
and
TARGETING

Target marketing, market segmentation, and product positioning are basic driving forces in the world of marketing. Understanding these concepts is critical to comprehending how marketing functions. Rob Morash, director of Atomic Skis Canada, takes us into the world of sports marketing and explains how Atomic Skis segments the market for ski equipment, and how the company uses this information to better market its products to various target groups. Atomic Skis is owned by Amer Sports Canada, a division of Finnish company Amer Sports Inc., which also sells Wilson tennis goods, Suunto precision watches, and Salomon skis. Atomic sells top quality lines

of alpine skis, boots, bindings, and ski accessories, as well as snowboards and cross-country ski equipment. Its products are sold nationally through sporting goods retailers, independent ski stores, snowboard retail outlets, and ski resorts.

Atomic Skis has established a top quality reputation, built from over 50 years in the business where it is recognized for its association with top-level, World Cup athletes, and for bringing fresh, innovative ideas to the everyday skier. Rob Morash explains that knowing its customers is critical, and that an in-depth understanding of the unique needs of each market segment is required to bring the right product to market. Rob Morash tells us that, "In addressing the winter sports market, we have to spend as much time as possible actually at the hills, with skiers and snowboarders, in order to observe and understand how and where they use the product." The experts at Atomic Skis check whether their consumers are skiing on groomed runs or on deeper snow, and what kind of punishment their equipment takes in the terrain-parks with sliding rails and jumps. Atomic Skis realizes it can't market the same standard product to everyone. The company analyzes each target market and designs products and programs to meet the specific requirements of each segment, ensuring they meet market expectations.

Ten years ago, the marketing of ski equipment in Canada was limited two main groups: (1) recreational skiers and (2) high-performance racers. However, the profile of the Canadian skier has changed dramatically in the last decade, driven by an aging population, a wider age spread in the different target groups, a heightened interest in fashion, and evolving equipment technology. Atomic Skis now competes for market share in four main categories: (1) freestyle skiers, (2) recreational skiers, (3) snowboarders, and (4) high-performance racers. In order

L 1 Explain market segmentation and its relevance to marketing.

L 2 Understand the different forms of market segmentation.

L 3 Comprehend the steps involved in segmenting a market.

L 4 Be able to create a target market profile.

L 5 Know how to position a product in the market and develop a positioning map.

to complete effectively in these categories, Atomic Skis focuses on understanding the skill levels of skiers, determining what drives their purchases, and gaining insights into their lifestyles. Atomic Skis conducts detailed consumer analyses to guide the development of new products, and to ensure that its marketing programs reach consumers on a personal level, on the ski hill, at retail, and at home. This way, the firm's advertising, promotion, retail merchandising, event marketing, and athlete-sponsorship programs are uniquely tailored to appeal to each target market.

The target markets for these segments are primarily differentiated on the basis of gender and age (demographics), lifestyle and fashion (psychographics), and product usage/benefit (behaviouristics). Let's look at each segment and see how they differ.

- **The freestyle skier.** This market is a young group of free-spirited males who are rebellious, have a defiant attitude, and are interested in music, video games, and socializing with friends. They are 15 to 25 years old, and are recreational skiers with specific equipment needs for half-pipes and jumps. Fashion is an important driver for this target group.

- **The female recreational skier.** These are adult women with children who have returned to the ski slopes with their families. They are family oriented, social, and nurturing. They are recreational skiers interested in fashionable equipment, designed specifically for women.

- **Snowboarders.** This target market is similar to the freestyle skier, but with a more rebellious streak. For this group, independence is a basic requirement, and they have unique equipment needs for snowboards, and want to make a fashion statement.

- **High-performance racers.** These are the high-performance athletes, males and females, looking for reliable, leading-edge equipment. Their focus is on training, and fashion is far less important.

For each of these segments, Atomic Skis has developed specific products and marketing-mix programs that mesh with the profile of each target group. Snowboarders, for example, have a need to be different, and their products are not even sold in ski shops, but instead through specific snowboard stores. Similarly, the female

CHARLEY AGER | ATOMIC TEAM RIDER. THUG.
WWW.ATOMICFREESKIING.COM

PRO TEAM: CHARLEY AGER, TOM GOLEZEL, SVEN KUEENLE, P.Y. LEBLANC, TRAVIS REDD, ASHLEY SABA, JODSI WELLS

recreational skier has specific advertising campaigns focused on fashion, while the needs of high-performance racers are mainly equipment based, with fashion playing a secondary role in communication messages.

Let's look in detail at the freestyle skiing market segment to find out how Atomic Skis uses target market information to build its business. To cater to this group of high-spirited, independent thinkers, Atomic Skis pulled together a program that met their needs to be different, to have the right equipment, and to make a rebellious fashion statement. Atomic Skis designed the Thug skis with this in mind and added base reinforcements so that the equipment could better weather the aggressive jumps for which it is used. The name was selected to appeal to the target market, and the graphics on the skis were carefully created with unusual, youthful images to appeal to the target market's rebellious streak. The marketing communication program used freestyle athletes from the X Games to add further credibility with this target group, and an advertising campaign used edgy graphics and elite athletes in a poster-like rendering to create impact. The ads ran in youth-targeted ski magazines.

This marketing program kept the target market needs in the forefront to ensure that all elements of the marketing mix met the freestyle skier's needs and expectations. Rob Morash, a sports-marketing expert with experience in sports-marketing agencies and companies such as Nike and Bauer Hockey, understands the importance of having all elements of the marketing mix meet the needs of a specific target group. For the freestyle skier, if the graphics on the skis were uneventful, or the advertising campaign expected and conservative, the program would not have reached these skiers in a meaningful way and resulted in sales. Rob Morash emphasizes that marketers use this coordinated approach to segment the market, to position their products to appeal to consumer needs, and to drive consumer purchases. Rob Morash is a sports enthusiast and avid skier who combines his passion on the ski slopes with marketing expertise to successfully match consumer needs with product development and marketing programs. His example of Thug skis shows us that the marketing mix needs to be relevant and well coordinated in order to meet consumer needs. This is an example of meaningful market segmentation in practice. 🍎

Market Segmentation

The essence of market segmentation, target markets, and product positioning is based on two important facts. First, consumers have diverse needs, and a single product cannot satisfy everyone. Second, companies have finite amounts of money, and it needs to be spent efficiently and effectively on those consumers who are most likely to purchase the product. Marketers do not want to waste their resources by focusing on all consumers with the hope that someone may be interested in their product offering. The market is too competitive for this to work, and there is an abundance of information on consumers that can help effectively channel resources.

In simple terms, a market segment means a piece of the market. In the marketing world there are two main market segments: the **consumer market** and the **business market**. The consumer market consists of goods, services, and ideas that a person can purchase for their own personal use. The business market involves products that are purchased either to run a business or to be used as a component in another good or service. How a product is classified depends on its usage. Let's look at some examples to clarify this point. A person buys a new computer in order to e-mail friends, surf the Internet, and download music for entertainment. A company buys new computers to upgrade technology in the office to ensure its business runs efficiently. The products are exactly the same. In the first instance, the computer is a consumer product for personal use; in the second instance, the computer is a business product for the office. There are many other similar examples, but it is important to understand that many products are tailored specifically for one market or the other, and not necessarily both. Heavy machinery used for landscaping is not a consumer product, and a comic book is not a business product.

Formally, **market segmentation** involves aggregating prospective buyers into groups that have common needs and respond similarly to marketing programs. These groups are relatively homogeneous and consist of people who are fairly similar in terms of their consumption behaviour, attitudes, and target market profiles.

There is normally more than one firm vying for the attention of prospective buyers in a market. This has resulted in marketers following a strategy of **product differentiation** to position their products apart from the competition in the eyes of consumers. It is important to note that product differentiation does not mean a product has to be better than the competition. Marketers position their products as best they can to meet the needs of their target consumers. Sometimes this may mean adding a unique feature; other times this may mean minimizing all costs to provide a cheaper alternative to the market.

The Core: Chapter 6

Market segmentation, target marketing, and product positioning are interdependent.

In simple terms, a market segment means a piece of the market.

Forms of Market Segmentation

There are a number of different approaches companies can take to segment the market. Whether a company is in the business-to-business market or the consumer market, it can follow a mass marketing, segmented marketing, niche marketing, or individualized marketing approach.

Mass Marketing This approach exists in a limited capacity today due to the competitiveness of the market and the need for marketers to specifically address consumer needs with their offerings. Mass marketing involves a product being marketed to the entire market with no differentiation at all. Examples can be found in the utilities area with items such as natural gas being marketed with no differentiation from either a product or marketing perspective. Propane for gas barbecues also follows this approach to segmentation, in both the business and consumer markets. In the consumer

market, one can buy small propane gas tanks for outdoor barbecues; in the business-to-business market, companies such as Superior Propane, sell bulk propane to businesses, filling super-sized, permanent tanks with propane.

Segment Marketing This form of market segmentation is the most common form of segmentation followed by large companies. Segment marketing involves designing different products and services to meet the needs of different target groups. Examples of this approach can be seen in the breakfast cereal category with companies such as General Mills

Koodo's Youth Market

Telus Corporation recently launched Koodo Mobile, a discount cellphone service targeted to the price-conscious youth market segment. Studies have shown that many young Canadians only want a cellphone for the purposes of talking and texting, not requiring more expensive long-term contracts and network access fees. This new program promotes simplicity, with only three handsets and three ready-made plans to choose from. Customers can also create custom plans.

Telus hopes to attract a new, younger consumer base with the introduction of Koodo. Advertisements for the service have aired during youth-oriented programming such as MTV's *The Hills* and have been placed near universities and shopping malls to attract this market segment.

In order to make its advertising stand out Koodo created a campaign reminiscent of 1980s work-out programs, complete with a spandex-wearing aerobics instructor leading classes in talking and texting. These ads emphasise the lower cost of Koodo Mobile, promising to help users in the youth market segment "drop that bill bulge."

Marketing NewsFlash

Sources: David Brown, "Koodo is working out," *Marketing* magazine, March 31, 2008, accessed at http://markettingblog.blogspot.com/2008/03/koodo-is-working-out.html; David George-Cosh, "Telus' Koodo Mobile brand launched," *Financial Post*, March 18, 2008, accessed at http://network.nationalpost.com/np/blogs/fpposted/archive/2008/03/18/telus-koodo-mobile-brand-launched.aspx; Lisa Hannam, "Is Koodo campaign a good fit?" *Marketing* magazine, April 4, 2008, accessed at http://markettingblog.blogspot.com/2008/04/is-koodo-campaign-good-fit.html; Roberto Rocha, "Koodos to Telus," *The Gazette*, April 3, 2008, accessed at www.canada.com/montrealgazette/news/business/story.html?id=0b384d47-a6bd-442d-919c-38a37abf094b.

and Kellogg's, or in the beverage industry with organizations such as Coca-Cola and PepsiCo.

Let's examine Kellogg's approach to market segmentation. Kellogg's has a host of breakfast cereals that appeal to different market segments. If we look at the cereal market in general there are products that appeal to different demographic and psychographic groups. For example, there are adult-oriented, healthy cereals; fun, pre-sweetened children's cereals; and wholesome family cereals that are neither too healthy nor too sweet. In 1906, Kellogg's started the cereal business as the Battle Creek Toasted Corn Flake Company with only one product, Corn Flakes. This product was marketed to everyone, and Kellogg's followed a mass-marketing approach. Now, generations later, Kellogg's is a company with multiple cereal products that appeal to different market segments, and it now follows a segment-marketing approach, developing different products to meet the needs of different target groups. For example, for the health-oriented adult, Kellogg's has All Bran, Special K, and Muslix. For families who demand fun, pre-sweetened cereals, Kellogg's offers Froot Loops, Mini-Wheats, and Frosted Flakes. For wholesome family goodness, consumers can choose from Rice Krispies, Corn Flakes, and Corn Pops.

Each product not only caters to the specific product needs of individual target markets but also has its own marketing programs to ensure that each target groups' needs are properly met. If you look at the packages for these products, they reflect the different target market interests and needs. Froot Loops, for example has a fun package that uses bright colours and a cartoon character to appeal to young families. All Bran, targeting an older, more serious group, has more subdued graphics, muted tones, and a clear focus on dietary needs. Similarly, each product's promotional programs are designed to speak to each target group in a different manner. All Bran ads are serious in tone, focus on nutrition, and are placed in consumer-oriented magazines such as *Canadian Gardening*, geared to older adults. Froot Loops, on the other hand, is geared to young families and if considering advertising, may use print ads to appeal to parents with young families.

> **A SEGMENTED APPROACH IS ALSO FOLLOWED BY COMPANIES IN THE BUSINESS-TO-BUSINESS MARKET.**

A segmented approach is also followed by companies in the business-to-business market. This is evident in the food-service industry where companies create specific products to meet the needs of their large customers. A company such as Bick's pickles may create pickles for a large fast-food chain, designed to meet this key account's specifications. The product would be sliced in a particular fashion to meet the specific requirements of this chain; it would be flavoured to meet their specifications, and it may be packaged in plastic packaging to fit the equipment needs of the fast-food outlets. Bick's pickles may also create a customized pickle product for another key account. This time the product may be packed in small glass jars, with a particular spice for a retail food chain, and packaged under the retailer's brand name. In both these business-to-business instances, customized products are being created for the company's key accounts. In the business-to-business market, the market is often segmented by the needs of key accounts.

Niche Marketing The type of market segmentation that allows a company to focus its efforts on a limited segment in the market is called **niche marketing**. Staying with the cereal market, Kashi Company is following the niche-marketing approach, concentrating its efforts on cereals with all-natural ingredients. Kashi does not try to sell to all market segments like Kellogg's does, but instead sells a line geared to health

Kashi uses a niche market segmentation approach.

enthusiasts. Kashi's product line includes whole-grain varieties, high-fibre options, and organic varieties.

In the business-to-business market, a company such as Miller Dallas, a career transition firm, only services the niche market of executives and professionals who have lost their jobs. The firm provides specialized services to this niche on behalf of the former employer, supporting the executives and professionals in their job search. The marketing efforts at Miller Dallas consist of seminars, newsletters, website communication, and personal selling to organizations that may be a source of referrals or may require its services.

Individualized Marketing

New technology has welcomed **individualized marketing** as a segmentation option for marketers. The Internet allows marketers to use database technology to track consumer purchases and predict interests and future purchases. This enables a marketer to customize offers and, in some cases, products that fit individual needs.

Marketers are rediscovering today what previous generations knew running a general store a century ago. Every customer is unique, has particular wants and needs, and requires special care from the seller. Efficiencies in manufacturing and marketing during the past century made mass-produced goods so affordable that most customers were willing to compromise their individual tastes and settle for standardized products. Today's Internet ordering, flexible manufacturing, and marketing processes have made individualized market segmentation possible, tailoring goods or services to the tastes of individual customers.

Dell uses this approach to marketing its technology products to both the consumer and business markets. In the consumer market, it allows consumers to customize their purchases to meet individual needs. Dell's three-day deliveries, from time of order placement, are made possible by restricting its computer line to only a few basic models and stocking a variety of each. This gives customers a good choice with quick delivery. In the business-to-business market, Dell also offers a customized approach to its customers, providing the same custom-order approach, with the addition of leasing arrangements if requested.

Some companies in the service industry follow similar approaches by tracking individual preferences and sending offers that meet individual consumer requirements. If you use the same travel agent, visit the same restaurant, or buy concert tickets from the same online services, over time these companies will recognize and predict your needs, sending you information, offers, or special services that meet your requirements. For example, if you purchase vintage DVDs from Amazon.ca, the site may start sending you product alerts when similar products enter their portfolio.

The key to successful product differentiation and market segmentation strategies is finding the ideal balance between satisfying a customer's individual wants and being able to do this profitably. A company will go to the trouble and expense of segmenting its markets when it expects this will ultimately increase its sales, profits, and return on investment.

ask yourself

1. What are the advantages of a segment marketing approach to market segmentation?

2. What is product differentiation?

3. What are the disadvantages of individualized market segmentation?

Canada's career transition consulting firm of choice for executives and senior professionals.

Miller Dallas
OUR BUSINESS IS YOUR FUTURE

ABOUT US | PEOPLE | APPROACH | TESTIMONIALS | KNOWLEDGE | SEMINARS | CONTACT

"Developing the life skill of 'thriving in transition' is a very necessary and valuable tool for executives in the current corporate environment—Miller Dallas are the Sherpa guides for this mountain pass."

Daryl Wilson
President and CEO, Hydrogenics Inc.

Servicing a niche in the business-to-business market

"The market in Canada is very competitive, which results in promotional resources being spread across several market segments, often diminishing their impact on any one group."

Rob Morash, director, Atomic Skis

Steps in Market Segmentation

Segmenting a market requires a number of skills. A marketer needs to combine strong analytical skills, sound strategic thinking, an understanding of the consumer, a vision on where the market is heading, and how this all fits with the company's direction. The process of segmenting a market for both the consumer and business-to-business market is divided into eight steps, which can be seen in Figure 6–1.

1. *Review company objectives.* Objectives need to be clear and quantifiable. They should include sales, revenue, and profit targets, but also a qualitative element such as gaining a new threshold in the market.

2. *Identify consumer/customer needs and common characteristics in the market.* This should be done from a consumer/customer perspective, looking at what drives the category and what future trends are evolving. Marketers should be able to easily identify common interests and evolving trends by analyzing what products currently exist in the category, which areas of the market are expanding and shrinking, and where consumer/ customer interests lie. Looking to other countries sometimes provides interesting ideas of where potential future interests may lie.

3. *Cluster common consumer/customer variables to create meaningful market segments.* A marketer needs to stand back from the market and look for clusters of products that identify common consumer/customer interests, usage patterns, and prevailing attitudes. New areas of interest should not be overlooked as these may point to evolving segments. These clusters will identify the segments that exist in the market. Sometimes there is overlap between segments, and other times the segments are not well defined, but this is merely a reflection of the consumers/customers who can be fickle and non-committal.

   It is very important during this step to review the market from a consumer/customer perspective and not from a product perspective. For example, if we continue to review the cereal market, we may group products into those that contain whole grains and establish this as a segment. However, if we look at this category from a consumer perspective, we would see whole-grain products as only one of many appealing to health-conscious, adult consumers. The segment is in fact better defined, and more meaningful to marketers, when identified as appealing to health-conscious adults.

   A group of students was asked to review the cold cereal market, to cluster consumer needs into possible market segments, and to give product examples for each segment. They came up with four main clusters that addressed their needs for health, taste, and nutrition, which are shown in Figure 6–2 (see page 106).

Figure 6–1
The eight-step process for segmenting a market

STEPS IN MARKET SEGMENTATION

1. Review company objectives.
2. Identify consumer/customer needs and common characteristics in the market.
3. Cluster common consumer/customer variables to create meaningful market segments.
4. Conduct SWOT analyses on the segments to determine strengths, weaknesses, opportunities, and threats.
5. Identify the segment that best meets company objectives.
6. Identify marketing programs and budget requirements needed for this segment.
7. Create a sales forecast for this segment.
8. Conduct a profit-and-loss financial analysis for this segment.

Figure 6–2
Identifying consumer clusters

CONSUMER CLUSTERS EXAMPLE: COLD CEREALS

CONSUMER CLUSTER	CLUSTER ATTITUDES	PRODUCT EXAMPLES
Adults with dietary needs	• Feeling healthy • Taste is secondary	• All Bran • Fibre First
Adults focused on taste and nutrition	• Nutrition is key • Taste is important • Not health fanatics	• Oatmeal Crisp • Muslix
Families looking for fun and taste	• Family-oriented • Want kids to eat breakfast • Taste is important • Nutrition is not as important as taste	• Froot Loops • Nesquik
Families focused on wholesome goodness	• Taste and nutrition both important • Good family health is key	• Cheerios • Rice Krispies

4. *Conduct a SWOT analysis on the segments to determine strengths, weaknesses, opportunities and threats.* A **SWOT analysis** can be conducted on many different areas in marketing. It is very useful when analyzing the market as it can identify opportunities and whether a company has the strength to compete in a segment that may already be well served by the competition. SWOT stands for *strengths, weaknesses, opportunities,* and *threats.* The strengths and weaknesses refer to the internal areas of a company or a product/brand. Examples may be the product image, its quality, or lack of advertising spending. The opportunities and threats look to areas outside the company such as the competition, consumer trends, or technology. It is important to involve a number of people when conducting a SWOT analysis so that different perspectives and ideas are captured.

5. *Identify the segment that best meets company objectives.* At this point in the process, a marketer sifts through the facts and ideas that have surfaced during the SWOT analysis and assesses the opportunities and threats in relation to company objectives. A market segment may surface as particularly interesting at this point.

6. *Identify marketing programs and budget requirements needed for this segment.* If a particular segment has surfaced as an area of interest, it will require further investigation. This will include a

> " SWOT STANDS FOR STRENGTHS, WEAKNESSES, OPPORTUNITIES, AND THREATS. "

full financial evaluation of the market to assess the costs of doing business, to identify what programs are required to support an initiative, and to recognize what resources are needed to adequately compete in this segment.

7. *Create a sales forecast for this segment.* Once a thorough market assessment has been conducted, a marketer is tasked with forecasting the sales potential for this segment, which should also consider anticipated competitive reactions.

8. *Conduct a profit-and-loss financial analysis for this segment.* The marketing programs, budget requirements, and sales forecasts are put together with projected costs to determine what level of profits can be achieved in this market segment. A projected profit-and-loss statement is created to assess the financial viability of doing business in this

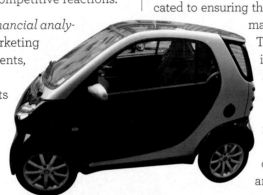

Who is the target market for the Smart car?

market segment. Marketers often work with financial analysts to determine these costs. Once the financial analysis is complete, marketers have the information they need to make rational decisions on whether they can achieve company objectives by conducting business in this market segment.

Target Market Profiles

L④ Marketers need to have a clear understanding of what drives their consumers, what delights them, and what does not. This helps marketers develop meaningful consumer products, design programs that meet consumer needs, and communicate to consumers in the manner to which they are accustomed. Developing an accurate target market profile is crucial to the success of all marketing initiatives as it drives all elements of the marketing mix. This profile is created by marketers, updated periodically as new information or research studies surface, and included in an area dedicated to ensuring this information is readily available to marketers as they work on the business. Target market profiles are usually included in annual marketing plans and in strategic documents that relate to this specific product.

Marketers define their target markets by looking at four main variables: (1) geographics, (2) demographics, (3) psychographics, and (4) behaviouristics. In marketing, all these variables are identified to clearly describe a target market so that when a marketer develops programs to meet this target group's needs, there is no confusion as to what drives this target market. Figure 6–3 (see page 109) clearly outlines these four variables.

Geographics

A **geographic** descriptor of a target market looks at where a target market lives using variables such as country, region, province, city size, and type of location such as urban, suburban, or rural. Marketers often find that Canadians differ in terms of needs or preferences based on where they live. An example is found in the flour industry: Consumers in Western

geographics
Where a target market lives using variables such as country, region, province, city size, and types of location such as urban, suburban, or rural

Canada tend to buy larger packages than in Ontario and Quebec due to a greater incidence in baking. Another example is with a product like the Smart car, which is small and compact and geared to urban dwellers. The target market for this car mainly resides in urban centres.

Demographics

One of the easiest factors to determine is the demographic profile of a target market. This includes identifying ranges for age, gender, family life-cycle, income, occupation, education, ethnic background, and home ownership for the main target market. This information can be identified through a company's market research information, and other secondary data sources such as Statistics Canada. An example where demographics play a leading role in a target market profile is with the Centrum vitamin brand. Centrum markets many of its products based on age and gender requirements. Centrum Select 50+ is formulated for adults over 50 years of age; Centrum Materna is a pre-natal vitamin created for pregnant women; and Centrum Junior is geared to children between the ages of 2 and 12. Products such as newspapers with all their different sections even have different target market profiles for different sections. The sports section has higher readership among male target groups, while the life section has higher readership among female target markets.

Psychographics

Psychographics is one of the most difficult variables to identify for marketers. It involves understanding consumer attitudes to life, their personalities, general interests, opinions, and activities. This information is generally based on primary research the marketer has conducted to gather insights on their consumers. Psychographic variables are central to understanding the delight points of consumers, and what gives them that extra spark. Image-based products gear much of their marketing efforts to these psychographic variables. The fragrance industry, for example, relies heavily on psychographics, as do many soft drink companies. Reflect for a minute on Coca-Cola, positioned as a traditional, refreshing soft drink rooted in old-fashioned Americana. Now think of Pepsi-Cola, marketed as the energetic cola for those with a youthful attitude to life. The products may only vary slightly in taste, but their target markets differ immensely in their attitudes, interests, and opinions. Coca-Cola and Pepsi-Cola use psychographics as a main variable in their marketing efforts.

Behaviouristics

This element directly refers to how consumers use the product. Behaviouristics looks at why consumers buy a product, the product benefit, how the product is used, and whether consumers are brand loyal in their purchase behaviour. Usage rate also plays a role in this information. The cellphone industry often uses

Canadian Business **Magazine Demographics** (ages 12+)

Total Readers **985,000**

Men **71%**

Average Age **43**

Average Annual Household Income **$93,310**

marketing meter

Source: "Advertise with Us: Your *Canadian Business* Competitive Advantage," *Canadian Business* website, accessed at www.canadianbusiness.com/canadian_business_magazine/advertisers/index.jsp.

Figure 6–3

Segmentation variables and breakdowns for Canadian consumer markets

TARGET MARKET PROFILES		
CATEGORIES	**VARIABLES**	**TYPICAL BREAKDOWNS**
Geographics	Region	Atlantic; Quebec; Ontario; Prairies; British Columbia
	City or census metropolitan area (CMA) size	Under 5,000; 5,000–19,999; 20,000–49,000; 50,000–99,999; 100,000–249,000; 250,000–499,999; 500,000–999,000; 1,000,000–3,999,999; 4,000,000+
	Density	Urban; suburban; rural
	Climate	Cold; warm
Demographics	Age	Infant; under 6; 6–11; 12–17; 18–24; 25–34; 35–49; 50–64; 65+
	Gender	Male; female
	Family size	1–2; 3–4; 5+
	Stage of family life cycle	Young single; young married, no children; young married, youngest child under 6; young married, youngest child 6 or older; older married, with children; older married, no children under 18; older single; other older married
	Income	Under $10,000; $10,000–19,999; $20,000–29,999; $30,000–39,999; $40,000–54,999; $55,000–74,999; $75,000+
	Occupation	Professional; managerial; clerical; sales; labourer; student; retired; housewife; unemployed
	Education	Grade school or less; some high school; high school graduate; some college; college graduate
	Ethnic background	Country of origin
	Home ownership	Own home; rent home
Psychographics	Personality	Gregarious; compulsive; extroverted; introverted
	Lifestyle (Goldfarb Segments)	Structured; discontented; fearful; assured; resentful; caring (see Chapter 3)
Behaviouristics	Benefits sought	Nutrition; entertainment; status
	Usage rate	Light user; medium user; heavy user
	User status	Non-user; ex-user; prospect; first-time user; regular user
	Loyalty status	None; some; medium; strong

behaviouristics to market to their customers, focusing on the key benefits consumers require in a cellphone. Telus Mobility, for example, markets cellphone services to young adults who want text messaging, instant messaging, and Facebook. Rogers, on the other hand, often promotes its BlackBerry phones to the business user, emphasizing, among other things, that the phones are enabled with Microsoft programs such as Word, Excel, Internet Explorer, and PowerPoint.

An example of how usage rate plays a role in marketing can be seen with the fast-food industry. Research indicates that for every $1 spent by a light user in a fast-food restaurant, a heavy user spends over $5.[1] Marketers may focus on the heavy user in this market to yield a greater return on investment.

Often students wonder why it is important to identify all these variables when describing a target market. If someone is buying a piece of chewing gum, what is the relevance of their income level, or where they live? In fact, usually only a few elements in a target market profile are the main determinants as to why

a consumer purchases a product. Nonetheless, all variables need to be included in the target market profile as this profile is used extensively in various aspects of marketing. If elements are missing, crucial errors could be made. For example, the target market profile is used extensively when creating an advertising

Demographic Profile for Sympatico/MSN Sports Channel

Gender	Men	64.9%
Age	35–64	52.8%
Household Income	$60,000/year	50.7%
Household Size	3+ people	53.2%

Source: Sympatico/MSN website, Advertising home, accessed at http://advertise.sympatico.msn.ca/channels/sports.

program. The consumer insights are used to help develop campaigns that talk to the target group, and media is bought against this target market profile.

Let's assume we are marketing a video on hockey heroes and are considering an online campaign to market to consumers. The Sympatico/MSN website (www.sympatico.msn.ca) is suggested as an option for running banner ads on its sports page. If we navigate to the advertising area of the MSN site and look at its sports section, it provides us with demographic information on the target market of this site. It tells us that there are 42,000 daily visitors interested in gathering sports information as they communicate and connect with others. Visitors are mostly male, live in Ontario, reside in households with one to three members and with a household income over $60,000.[2] If the target market profile for the hockey video matched all these variables, then this site would be an appropriate advertising vehicle. However, if the marketers failed to include income information, and the advertising agency assumed it was below $30,000 per year for the target group, then this site may have erroneously been overlooked. It is important to include all the target market information as completely as possible to avoid errors.

Product Positioning

One of the central elements in marketing is product positioning. Marketers position products in the market to appeal to certain target groups and to present a particular image relative to the competition. **Product positioning** refers to the image of the product you want to establish in consumers' minds relative to the competition. Marketers create **positioning statements** to clearly and simply outline the positioning of a product. These statements are used to crystallize the image for marketers so that they can devise all the elements of the marketing mix to align with the product's positioning. This is very

Psychographic Interests of Generation Y

Generation Y is made up of young adults aged 18 to 28. A 2007 study by Forrester Research showed their psychographic TV viewing habits to include the following:

- Watching TV programs on the Internet
- Multi-tasking while watching TV
- Recording TV or time shifting
- Spending 10 hours per week on the Internet
- Spending 11 hours per week watching regular TV
- Visiting Facebook and YouTube websites

Source: "TV Still Tops with Gen Y... For Now," *Marketing* magazine, November 13, 2008, accessed January 6, 2009, at www.marketingmag.ca/english/news/marketer/article.jsp?content=20081112_172150_12392.

important, otherwise the product will present a confusing image to consumers who will then not understand its relevance and will not buy it. Similar to a target market profile, a positioning statement is generally included in an annual marketing plan and in relevant strategic documents.

Positioning statements are simple, clear, and focused. They identify the main reasons the target market buys the product and what sets it apart in the market. It is important to understand that a product's positioning is reflected in all areas of the marketing mix. One needs to look at each element of the marketing mix in order to accurately determine its positioning in the market.

ask yourself

1. What are the steps involved in market segmentation?

2. What elements are included in demographics?

3. What is the difference between psychographics and behaviouristics?

Marketing ▶ tip

"Marketers need to recognize that a single product cannot be all things to all people. They need to develop a strong positioning that is relevant to their particular consumers."

Rob Morash, director, Atomic Skis

A Healthy Twist for Clearly Canadian Beverages

Clearly Canadian Beverage Corporation, one of the pioneers of the alternative beverage industry, has begun a comeback in the beverage market with the launch of a new line of drinks targeted to a health-conscious psychographic. Clearly Canadian gained popularity in the late 1980s with its line of sparkling, flavoured waters, but lost footing in the market over recent years as competitors such as Coca-Cola and Pepsi entered the flavoured water/iced tea/energy drink race. In 2006, Brent Lokash joined the

company as president and began a campaign to bring Clearly Canadian back into the beverages game.

In January 2007, the company launched a line of energy, vitamin, and flavoured waters called Natural Enhanced Waters. The line, featuring drinks such as dailyEnergy, dailyVitamin, and dailyHydration, is marketed toward 18- to 45-year-olds. In addition to this new line, Clearly Canadian recently acquired DMR Food Corporations, an organic snack company, and My Organic Baby, Inc., an organic baby food company.

Clearly Canadian also signed endorsement deals with Canadian professional athletes, including Steve Nash, two-time most valuable player in the National Basketball Association, and Justin Morneau, the 2006 most valuable player in Major League Baseball's American League. One of the most innovative moves that Clearly Canadian is making in its relaunch is the announcement by Lokash that the company is filming a reality series showcasing the company's business as it stages its return to the market.

Sources: Clearly Canadian Brands, "Clearly Canadian Beverages Receives First Orders from Major Canadian Supermarket Chains for New 1 Liter Sparkling Flavored Water Format," News Release, April 28, 2008, accessed at www.integratir.com/newsrelease.asp?news=2131020991&ticker=CCBEF&lang=EN; Eve Lazarus, "Clearly a Comeback?" *Marketing* magazine, April 16, 2008, accessed at www.marketingmag.ca/english/news/marketer/article.jsp?content=20070329_69482_69482.

Students were asked to research Kashi cereal by visiting the company's website, seeing it in a store setting, trying the product, examining its packaging, and reviewing its print ads. The students came up with the following statement, which clearly and simply expresses the potential positioning of this product: "Kashi cereal is positioned in the cold cereal market as a great-tasting, all-natural, whole-grain cereal perfect for people who want to lead healthy lives. It focuses on all-natural ingredients."

Positioning statements are this clear and focused. They average a short paragraph and identify four elements: (1) the product name, (2) the category in which the product competes, (3) one or two main reasons that the target market buys the product (product benefits), and (4) what sets the product apart from the competition.

In the business-to-business market, products and services are also positioned to appeal to a target market and to set themselves apart from the competition. If we examine the Miller Dallas career transition firm and direct our efforts towards that firm's website, we can clearly see its positioning reflected on its homepage. It states that Miller Dallas is "Canada's career transition consulting firm of choice for executives and senior professionals." The company is positioning itself as the top firm for senior business professionals in Canada.

repositioning
A revamping of the product and its marketing mix to more accurately meet consumer needs

Repositioning

Companies rarely change a product's positioning but do so when long-term changes in consumer trends require a shifting of the product to more accurately meet consumer needs. Repositioning is often done with a revamping of the product and the various elements of the marketing mix. McDonald's is a recent example

> ## POSITIONING STATEMENTS ARE SIMPLE, CLEAR, AND FOCUSED.

of a repositioning effort that includes interior and exterior store design, healthier menu choices, product ingredient changes, new website components, and focused advertising messages. We see trans fats being eliminated from McDonald's products, healthy choices included on the menu, nutrition calculators appearing on its website, and the store ambience being modified to be more comfortable and inviting. McDonald's is repositioning itself as a more engaging fast-food restaurant, offering not only the healthier food choices consumers are demanding but also an environment where a more comfortable setting is available.

Positioning Maps

Positioning maps, also known as perceptual maps, are visual representations of how products or product groups are positioned within a category to consumers/customers. Positioning maps can visually represent categories within a market, or more specifically,

Nothing like a fresh new look for spring.

Brighten things up this season with a great lowfat snack. Try a scrumptious Fruit 'n Yogurt Parfait at McDonald's®. It's delicious and has only 2g of fat per serving. Visit goodfoodchoices.ca for nutrition information.

At participating McDonald's restaurants in Canada.
©2008 McDonald's

m
i'm lovin' it®

Health food choices are part of McDonald's revamped menu.

product and brand offerings within a specific segment. Positioning maps are useful tools for marketers as they can reveal gaps in the market where consumers may be under-served, while also highlighting the competitive nature of the category.

Positioning maps need to clearly identify the two most important attributes that drive purchases in a category. One must be able to assess these attributes objectively from a consumer perspective. One might rush to immediately identify price as a key variable, but generally, this is a less important feature, evaluated by consumers once a short list of attributes on which they initially evaluate a purchase are identified. Let's make this clearer with two examples. First, in the cereal market, nutrition and sweetness might be key attributes used by parents of young children to evaluate product offerings. (Price would come into play later in the purchase decision.) These factors of nutrition and sweetness can be objectively used to evaluate products in the category, and identify how one is positioned against

McDonald's repositioning is reflected in its new store designs.

another. In a second example, if one is looking at this category from the perspective of very health-oriented consumers, one might set different parameters to evaluate the product offerings. Natural ingredients and fibre content may instead play a central role in the consumer's decision to purchase a cereal, and these variables would be used by marketers for a positioning map. The variables will change depending on what is important to a specific target group. In all instances, the variables will need to be objective and measurable for marketers to use.

How is this beverage positioned in the market?

In the business-to-business market, positioning statements and positioning maps are equally important. Again, looking at Miller Dallas, a positioning map for the career transition industry may look at two main variables: (1) the seniority of clients, and (2) the level of personalized service provided.

Figure 6–4 (see page 114) shows a positioning map for the beverage industry using the measurable variables of nutrition and age. The positioning map

shows milk, tea, sports drinks, fruit juices, and soft drinks rated relative to each other on these key elements. We can see diet drinks are geared to adults, while milk shakes appeal to teenagers.

Positioning maps can identify opportunities to launch new product offerings in the market. Staying with the beverage industry, in 2008, V8 introduced a line of high-fibre beverages called V8 V-Plus. These products are vegetable-based, come in two varieties, high fibre and high fibre/low sodium, and are promoted as providing two healthy servings of vegetables and natural prebiotics in every glass. What gap in the market did V8 identify before it created this product? Where would you place this type of product on the beverage positioning map?

Similarly, Nestlé Pure Life introduced a line of Green Tea Refreshers offering the purity of water enhanced with green tea. What opportunity did Nestlé recognize in the market? Create your own positioning map for V-Plus and Nestlé Pure Life Green Tea Refreshers in the beverages market.

What gap in the market does this product fill?

McDonald's Makeover

Marketing NewsFlash

McDonald's has begun transforming its Canadian restaurants—changing the traditional bright decor into a contemporary, cozy, coffeehouse-like atmosphere complete with fireplaces, leather chairs, and plasma-screen televisions. These makeovers are being done both to mark the chain's 40th anniversary in Canada and to help the restaurants meet the changing needs of its customers. McDonald's had redecorated 150 locations by the end of 2007, and plans to perform the makeover on 500 stores across the country by 2010.

The company is replacing the traditional red-and-brown rooftops with natural and cultured brick and stone exteriors, and the tiled interiors will be replaced with designs utilizing fabric, wood, granites, bamboo, birch, and limestone, among other materials. The restaurants will feature cushioned booths and accented lighting, and some locations will offer Wi-Fi. Restaurants will have a high-traffic area for customers dashing in and out, as well as the newly appointed areas for those patrons who want to relax over their food.

McDonald's is also making changes to its menu, introducing healthier and more diverse options in addition to changing the look and feel of its restaurants. ●

Sources: Rob Roberts, "McDonald's goes all Starbucks on us," *National Post*, September 13, 2007, accessed at http://network.nationalpost.com/np/blogs/toronto/archive/2007/09/13/mcdonald-s-goes-all-starbucks-on-us.aspx; Thulasi Srikanthan, "McDonald's outlets getting comfy look," *Toronto Star*, September 13, 2007, accessed at www.thestar.com/Business/article/256023.

Figure 6–4
A positioning map to suggest a strategy for positioning beverages

POSITIONING MAP FOR THE BEVERAGE CATEGORY

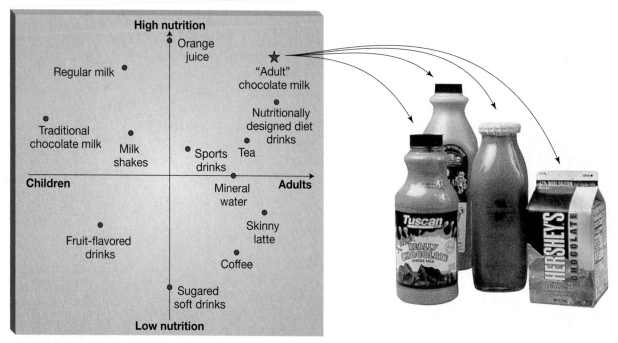

Market Segmentation, Target Markets, and Product Positioning in Practice

Segmentation, target markets, and positioning are fundamental concepts central to how marketers run their businesses. When creating marketing plans and developing marketing ideas to increase sales, marketers immediately look to how their products are positioned in the market, consult with positioning statements, and then use the target market profiles to ensure all elements are true to the image of their products. A mistake in this area could mean losing your consumers and clouding the image of your product in the market. Marketers are careful to ensure that all elements of the marketing mix are well coordinated to meet the product's positioning and target market expectations.

Market segmentation helps marketers place their product offerings in the context of a competitive market. It allows them to see the bigger picture from a consumer perspective, and to focus on how competitors are servicing their needs. A market segmentation analysis also allows a marketer to identify gaps in the market, and determine where future opportunities may lie.

Marketers like Rob Morash at Atomic Skis use these approaches to ensure that their product offerings and marketing programs are fresh, relevant, and focused. This approach helps them maintain a competitive edge in the market and stay in touch with the latest new trends that surface. Market segmentation, target markets, and positioning are keystones in the world of marketing.

ask yourself

1. What is product positioning?

2. What is the purpose of a positioning statement?

3. Why do marketers use positioning maps?

> A MARKET SEGMENTATION ANALYSIS ALSO ALLOWS A MARKETER TO IDENTIFY GAPS IN THE MARKET, AND DETERMINE WHERE FUTURE OPPORTUNITIES MAY LIE.

Summary...*just the facts*

- Market segmentation involves aggregating prospective buyers into groups that have common needs and who respond similarly to marketing programs.

- In the marketing world there are two main market segments: (1) the consumer market and (2) the business marketing approaches.

- Companies segment the market using mass marketing, segmented marketing, niche marketing, or individualized marketing.

- Segmenting the market involves eight steps that require analytical skills, strategic thinking, an understanding of the consumer, a vision on where the market is heading, and how this fits with company objectives.

- Marketers define their target markets by looking at four main variables: (1) geographics, (2) demographics, (3) psychographics, and (4) behaviouristics.

- Geographics looks at where a target market lives using variables such as country, region, province, city size, and types of location such as urban, suburban, or rural.

- Demographics includes identifying ranges for age, gender, family life-cycle, income, occupation, education, ethnic background, and home ownership.

- Psychographics involves understanding consumer attitudes to life, their personalities, general interests, opinions, and activities.

- Behaviouristics looks at why consumers buy a product, the product benefit, how the product is used, and whether consumers are brand loyal in their purchase behaviour. Usage rate also plays a role in this information.

- Product positioning refers to the image of the product in consumers' minds relative to the competition.

- Marketers create positioning statements to clearly and simply outline the positioning of a product.

- Repositioning includes a shifting of the product and its marketing mix to more accurately meet consumer needs.

- Positioning maps are otherwise known as perceptual maps. They visually represent how products or product groups are positioned within a category to consumers.

Key Terms and Concepts...*a refresher*

behaviouristics *p. 108*
business market *p. 101*
consumer market *p. 101*
demographics *p. 108*
geographics *p. 107*
individualized marketing *p. 104*

market segmentation *p. 101*
mass marketing *p. 102*
niche marketing *p. 103*
positioning maps *p. 112*
positioning statement *p. 110*
product differentiation *p. 101*

product positioning *p. 110*
psychographics *p. 108*
repositioning *p. 111*
segment marketing *p. 102*
SWOT analysis *p. 106*

CHAPTER 7

Products and Brands

Marketers understand that meeting customer needs is central to successfully marketing a product, a service, or an idea. In this chapter we explore products and brands more thoroughly to understand how they are marketed and look to Ken Derrett, vice president and chief marketing officer for the San Diego Chargers National Football League (NFL) franchise to explain how products are marketed in the world of sports and entertainment. Ken Derrett is a well-established Canadian sports marketer with prior experience as the managing director for the National Basketball Association (NBA) in Canada. He has also managed Labatt Breweries' sports and entertainment properties and directed the business operations for the CFL's Grey Cup. Over the last few years, Derrett has managed the marketing of the San Diego Chargers.

LEARNING OBJECTIVES

L1 Distinguish between goods and services.

L2 Understand the total product concept.

L3 Differentiate between products, product lines, and product mixes.

L4 Identify the ways consumer and business goods and services are classified.

Ken Derrett explains that sports marketing for the San Diego Chargers is multi-faceted and involves the marketing of emotions to connect the "product"—its team, players, and organization—to a loyal fan base. Fans want to be entertained and to support their football team and athletes. It is imperative to create meaningful bonds with the fans so that they become, and remain, loyal supporters. This bond encourages fans to attend home games, watch live broadcasts, and support team events. Ken Derrett recognizes that the best way to showcase a product, in this case the San Diego Chargers, is by filling the stadium and having a strong television audience.

Marketing the team revolves around the fact that there are only ten home games, each one meticulously planned as a major event to keep the fans, the team, the community, and the media all interested, involved, and loyal to the San Diego Chargers. A home game typically includes pre-event build-up with the media, game-day event marketing with the fans, in-game promotions for attendees, and post-game public and media relations. Pre-event support typically starts a week before the scheduled game and focuses on building momentum and excitement with the media and the fans. Marketing efforts are mainly directed toward the media, who will relay what is new, what is different, and what to watch in the upcoming game. The purpose is to heighten awareness of the home game in the community and to drive fans to the stadium or encourage them to enjoy the game with their friends and family through TV broadcasts.

L₅ Explain the elements of branding and how these can be protected.

L₆ Understand the different types of brands that exist in the market.

L₇ Apply product and brand knowledge to ongoing marketing strategies.

Game day involves a full schedule of events, staged to ensure that fans have an enjoyable experience and return to support their team the following home game. Tailgate parties kick off the event in the stadium parking lot, which is full by 11 a.m., although the game does not actually start until 1:15 p.m. Eighteen thousand cars fill the parking areas with friends and family who locate close to each other to socialize. They bring chairs, barbecues, and satellite TVs, making a full day of the football game, which becomes enjoyable for adults and kids alike. The marketers of the San Diego Chargers organize various events to keep the fans engaged: large-screen TVs broadcast live NFL games from other cities; live radio broadcast booths are set up, allowing fans to be part of the pre-game hype and experience a radio broadcast first-hand; and power parties are set up in the area with bands playing music to build momentum for the game. Fans come dressed in their team colours and sing organized chants and team songs throughout the morning in the parking lot.

Inside the building, food-service concessions are well situated to provide a variety of options for the fans and to add to a pleasurable experience. As the fans enter the stadium, a giveaway is handed out, which may be a game schedule, a team calendar, a team poster, or a rally towel, used as reminders of the event and the next home game.

During the game, the football action takes over but spare moments are filled by the home team's cheerleaders, various promotions on the Jumbotron, and the halftime show. The halftime show traditionally includes a highlight package from other NFL games, an interactive fan event on the field, and marching bands or youth football mini-games. Once the game concludes, the stadium and parking lot design become central to a positive fan experience. It is important that fans can exit the venue as quickly as possible, maintaining a pleasurable experience that will encourage them to return.

Ken Derrett spearheads the marketing of the San Diego Chargers to ensure that home games are events to remember and to build a loyal fan base in the community. The San Diego Chargers football team is a sports and entertainment product that is being marketed to satisfy the needs of its target market. In this case, the target market is multi-faceted. There is the target market at the stadium, the target market watching the games on TV, and the community and media groups who also need to be targeted to ensure a strong fan base is developed and maintained throughout the season. The marketers at the San Diego Chargers understand that their product, the team, needs to connect emotionally with its fans to keep them loyal and interested. They leave nothing to chance and manage the marketing of the team to keep fans coming back. Marketing ensures that the game is not just about the sport of football, but also about a multitude of events that are fun, engaging, and memorable for all who attend. 🍎

Types of Products

L❶ The essence of marketing lies in managing and developing products that meet the needs of a target market. In marketing, a **product** is a good, a service, or an idea consisting of a bundle of tangible and intangible attributes. Tangible attributes include physical characteristics such as colour or sweetness, and intangible attributes include those aspects of a product that can't be "touched," such as the way driving a Porsche may make you feel, or how a product makes you healthier. Products can include a variety of things such as breakfast cereals, public transportation, or the emergency services provided by a hospital. The San Diego Chargers is an example of a product in the sports and entertainment area facing the challenges of managing intangible elements to keep fans coming back.

The Core: Chapter 7

There are many levels of product.

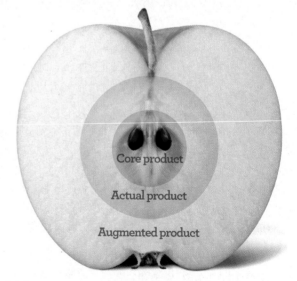

Core product

Actual product

Augmented product

It is important to manage all levels of a product to be competitive.

What type of product is being marketed by the ROM?

Products are divided into three main categories: (1) non-durable goods, (2) durable goods, and (3) services. Non-durable goods are items that do not last and that are consumed only once, or for a limited number of times. Examples of non-durable goods are food products and fuel. A durable good is a product that lasts for an extended period of time and encompasses items such as appliances, automobiles, and stereo equipment. Services are defined as intangible activities, benefits, or satisfactions offered for sale, such as banking, visits to a doctor, taking a vacation, going to a movie, or taking an educational course. In the services industry, it is useful to distinguish between a company's primary service and its supplementary services. A bank's primary service may be providing bank accounts, but it also offers supplementary services such as parking, ABMs, foreign exchange, monthly statements, and so on. Supplementary services often allow services to differentiate their offerings from competitors while adding value for consumers. Key categories of supplementary services include information, delivery, consultation, order taking, billing, and payment options.[1] Canada has a strong service-based economy with services comprising of approximately 70 percent of its gross domestic product (GDP).[2]

It is important to realize that most products cannot be defined as "pure goods" or "pure services." In fact, in today's marketplace, firms often combine goods and services to offer a more competitive product to consumers. Many goods are augmented with intangible services such as warranties, websites, or online support. Services also use goods to ensure a more complete offering to consumers. A college or university, for example, provides educational services, but it also provides graduates with a hard-copy diploma and transcripts. IBM Canada is an example of a company that combines goods and services to satisfy its customers. IBM sells computer software to businesses, together with expert consulting and training services for its clients.

As companies look at what they bring to market, there is a range from the tangible to the intangible, or goods-dominant to service-dominant. This is defined as the service continuum and demonstrated in Figure 7–1 (see page 120) where the services continuum for a number of products is shown. Teaching, nursing, and the theatre are intangible, service-dominant activities, while salt, neckties, and dog food are goods-dominant. Fast-food restaurants are in the middle of the service continuum, offering a combination of both tangible and intangible goods and services—the food is the tangible good, while the courtesy, cleanliness, speed, and convenience are the intangible services they provide.

The Uniqueness of Services

There are four unique elements to services: intangibility, inconsistency, inseparability, and inventory. These four elements are referred to as the *four Is of services.*

Intangibility Services are intangible, that is, for the most part, they can't be held, touched, or seen before the purchase

non-durable good
An item that does not last and is consumed only once, or for a limited number of times

durable good
An item that lasts over an extended number of uses

services
Intangible activities, benefits, or satisfactions offered for sale

service continuum
A range from tangible goods to intangible services

decision. In contrast, before purchasing a physical good, a consumer can touch a box of laundry detergent, kick the tire of an automobile, or sample a new beverage. Services tend to be more performance oriented and, as experiences, cannot be tried before they are purchased. To help consumers assess and compare services, it is important for marketers to demonstrate the benefits of using the service. Examples are movie trailers that are used to provide samples of a film, and testimonials from customers of other services to provide proof of satisfaction.

Inconsistency Developing, pricing, promoting, and delivering services is challenging because the quality of a service is often inconsistent as it is dependent on the people who provide it. Quality can vary with each person's capabilities, experience, motivation, and even personality. One day the Toronto Blue Jays baseball team may have a great game, and then the next day they may have a very disappointing showing. Similarly, you may have a very successful stay at one location of a Travelodge hotel, but then have a terrible experience at another Travelodge hotel due to the standards of the staff at that location.

Inseparability A third difference between services and goods, and related to problems of consistency, is inseparability. In most cases, the consumer cannot (and does not) separate the deliverer of the service from the service itself. For example, in the non-profit industry, the quality of an educational institution may be high, but if a student has difficulty interacting with

Figure 7–1
The service continuum

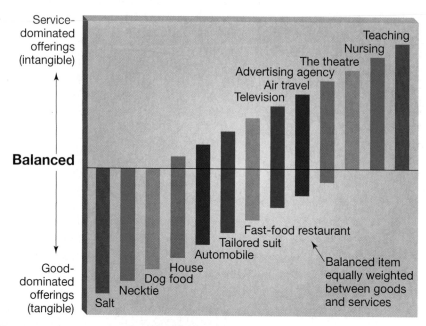

Travel and tourism services, such as those in Canada's wine regions, are intangible.

certain instructors, the student may not be satisfied with the educational experience. Similarly, if a surgeon has a poor bedside manner, this immediately reflects poorly on the hospital, which may in fact be excellent.

Inventory The inventory of services differs from that of goods due to the nature of the products. Inventory problems exist with goods because sales forecasts may be inaccurate, warehousing is expensive, and in some cases items are perishable. In the service industry, issues arise due to the fluctuating demand for services throughout the day and the difficulty in assessing the manpower needed to service these needs. Idle production capacity is expensive and arises in the service industry when a service is made available at times when there is little demand. **Idle production capacity** refers to when the supply of the service exceeds its demand. To deal with this issue, the service industry often uses many part-time employees who are paid an hourly wage and are

In today's marketplace, firms often combine goods and services to offer a more competitive product to consumers.

scheduled to work shifts. This is clearly demonstrated in a grocery store setting where the number of cashiers varies depending on the time of day and day of the week. The number of cashiers at 2.30 p.m. during the week will be far less than the number of cashiers available at noon due to the number of shoppers expected at these times.

Product Elements

The Total Product Concept

Marketers view products as having three different layers: the core product, the actual product, and the augmented product. The more complex and expensive the product, the more intricate the layers used to differentiate the product from the competition. Figure 7–2 shows how these layers work together. The *core product* refers to the fundamental benefit that a consumer derives from having the product. In the case of a bicycle, the core benefit may be the transportation it provides, or the pleasure of participating in a leisurely sport. For a service such as a massage, the core benefit may be the relaxation it provides.

The *actual product* is the physical good or the service that a consumer purchases when buying a product. It includes the product's branding, design, and features. With a bicycle, a consumer purchases a piece of equipment, directly associated with a brand name, design, and features. With a massage, the actual product is the massage itself and the time spent having a trained and expert massage therapist relax a client's muscles. In this instance, one may think that branding has no role to play. On the contrary, in the case of a massage, the brand becomes either the name of the massage therapist or the organization providing massage therapy services.

> MARKETERS VIEW PRODUCTS AS HAVING THREE DIFFERENT LAYERS: THE CORE PRODUCT, THE ACTUAL PRODUCT, AND THE AUGMENTED PRODUCT.

Finally, the *augmented product* refers to the additional features and attributes that accompany a product, such as a warranty, a service contract, delivery options, installation assistance, or a website used to distinguish the product from competitive offerings. For a bicycle, this may be a warranty, while for a massage there may in fact be no augmented product layer. Generally, augmented product layers exist for more expensive purchases such as cars, computers, or TVs, and are not part of a simple purchase such as a chocolate bar or a newspaper.

Packaging

Marketers need to pay attention to a product's packaging and label, which, for many products, is an integral part of the product. A package and its label provide purchasers with detailed information and face-to-face communication at the time when a purchase is being made. In 2008, Sun-Rype redesigned its beverage packaging to showcase its "real fruit" positioning and to communicate emphatically its "Real Fruit Goodness." This redesigned package uses vivid photography to create a colourful splash at retail and to communicate its freshness and health benefits to consumers. You can have a look at Sun-Rype's redesign at www.sunrype.ca.

Figure 7–2
The total product concept applied to a bicycle

THE TOTAL PRODUCT CONCEPT		
LAYER	**DESCRIPTION**	**EXAMPLE (BICYCLE)**
Core product	What the product does for the customer—the benefits derived from using the product	Provides transportation and leisure activity
Actual product	The physical good or service, including the branding, design, and features that the consumer receives	A branded product, with a metal frame, two wheels, and a seat
Augmented product	Additional features or benefits that accompany the product, such as a warranty, a service contract, delivery options, installation, or a website	Warranty or repair contract

Product Lines and Product Mixes

L⊙³ Marketers often manage groups of products that are closely related under an umbrella product line and brand name. A **product line** is a group of products with the same product and brand name that are directed to the same general target market and are marketed together. Examples of a product line are the different flavour varieties sold under the original line of Gatorade products, including lemon-lime, fruit punch, orange, strawberry-kiwi, and cool blue. Looking at the non-profit service industry, the product line at Toronto's Hospital for Sick Children consists of inpatient hospital care, outpatient physician services, and medical research.

Each product line contains specific *product items* that can be identified by their variety or size. The Downy fabric softener product line, for example, comes in 20-ounce and 40-ounce sizes, with each size identified as a separate stock keeping unit (SKU). Each SKU is has its own identification number (UPC code), which is scanned for inventory and pricing purposes. Product lines are part of a company's product mix. **Product mix** refers to the combination of product lines marketed by a company. Figure 7–3 (see page 123) looks at some of Nike's products, dividing the product mix into three main categories: shoes, clothing, and equipment. Under each category are a number of different product groupings such as basketballs, watches, and sunglasses in the equipment category. Each product grouping may contain a number of product lines marketed under different brand names. Figure 7–3 also shows Nike's product width and product depth. The

A Facelift for Sun-Rype

Sun-Rype has begun a fresh new campaign based on introducing its new packaging to its current consumers, while also growing its brand awareness in a new market. The brand has revitalized its product design by introducing a new bottle for Sun-Rype's juices—1.36 litre plastic bottles with a newly contoured shape that was customized to better meet consumer demands. The new bottles are easy to hold and to pour, more convenient to store, and are resealable. In addition, the new bottles are not made with the apparently harmful chemical Bisphenol A.

Along with the packaging redesign, Sun-Rype has unveiled a new advertising campaign, with an additional push in Ontario, where the Kelowna, B.C.-based brand is less well known. The campaign focuses on the no added sugar, no artificial flavours or colours, all-natural appeal of the company's juice products, as well as the redesigned bottles. The campaign uses print and television advertising with animated fruit to emphasize the freshness of the product; the campaign also features the updated bottles. Kiosks in Toronto malls have also been set up so that visitors can have their picture taken, with the resulting image created by using the images of fruit. ●

Marketing NewsFlash

Sources: Annette Bourdeau, "Sun-Rype keeps it real," *Strategy* magazine, May 2008, accessed, at www.strategymag.com/articles/magazine/20080501/creativesunrype.html; Gail Chiasson, "Sun-Rype Supports New Juice Packaging by National Campaign," *Pubzone*, April 18, 2008, accessed, at www.pubzone.com/newsroom/2008/1x080416x050828.cfm; Eve Lazarus, "Sun-Rype Heads East," *Marketing* magazine, April 18, 2008, accessed at www.marketingmag.ca/english/creative/regionalshowcase/article.jsp?content=20080502_161813_7340.

Figure 7-3
Some of Nike's products explained

PRODUCT MIX AND PRODUCT DEPTH AT NIKE

← Width of product mix →

↕ Depth of product mix

PRODUCT MIX		
Product category: shoes	**Product category: clothing**	**Product category: equipment**
Running	T-shirts	Sunglasses
Basketball	Shorts	Golf gear
Training	Socks	Bags, backpacks
Sandals	Hoodies	Basketball
Tennis	Sweatshirts	Watches
Lifestyle	Yoga wear	Sport monitoring items
Soccer	Track pants	Sport audio equipment
Walking	Jackets	
Baseball		

width of a company's product mix refers to the number of different categories offered by the company. The **depth** of a company's product mix refers to the variety of product offerings within a product category, product group, or product line.

Procter & Gamble uses this same concept of multiple product lines to market a wide selection of products to consumers. In the laundry detergent category, for instance, Procter & Gamble markets at least six different product lines: Tide, Ivory, Gain, Era, Dreft, and Cheer. Each product line itself carries many different product sizes, varieties, and formats. The Tide website at www.tide.com illustrates the wide range of products offered under the umbrella Tide brand and the extensive product depth within most categories. Visit the Procter & Gamble website (www.pg.com) and examine its product mix, product width, and product depth.

ask yourself

1. Explain the difference between non-durable goods, durable goods, and services.

2. What elements make services unique?

3. What is included in the total product concept?

The Classification of Consumer and Business Products

L4 Products are classified as either consumer or business products depending on their usage. **Consumer products** are purchased by the ultimate consumer for their own personal use, while **business products** (also called *industrial goods* or *organizational products*) are purchased either to run a business or to be used as a component in another product or service. In many instances, the differences are obvious: Oil of Olay face moisturizer and the Ontario Science Centre are examples of consumer products, while a cement mixing truck is primarily a business product. Some products, however, are both consumer and business products depending on their usage. A Canon printer can be classified as a consumer product when purchased as a final product for personal use, or it can be classified as a business product when purchased by an organization to help run a business. Consumer and business products consist of numerous types of products as explained in further detail below.

Consumer Products

Convenience, shopping, specialty, and unsought products are the four different types of consumer goods that exist in the market. These items differ in terms of the amount of effort a consumer puts into making a purchase, and how often the items are purchased.

Convenience products are inexpensive items that a consumer purchases

The product line for RUB-A-535 heat wraps consists of back, neck, shoulder, and wrist wraps.

product width
The number of different categories offered by the company

product depth
The variety of product offerings within a product category, product group, or product line

consumer products
Products purchased for their own personal use by the ultimate consumer

business products
Products that are purchased either to run a business or to be used as a component in another product or service

convenience products
Items purchased frequently that are inexpensive and require minimum risk and shopping effort

frequently with minimal shopping effort. If the product does not meet expectations, there is little risk because the product is inexpensive and easy to purchase. Examples of convenience products are bread, newspapers, or items purchased at a vending machine. **Shopping products** are items for which the consumer comparison-shops, assessing the attributes and prices of different products and brands. These types of products require a greater investment of shopping time, are more expensive than convenience products, and require a greater assurance of purchase satisfaction.

Examples are jeans, books, and items such as TVs. **Specialty products** are items that require considerable time and effort to purchase. They tend to be more expensive products needed for special occasions. They include specialty brands, and require high purchase satisfaction. Examples of specialty products include a Rolex watch or taking a cruise with Norwegian Cruise Lines. **Unsought products** are items that the consumer either does not know about, or is not interested in purchasing. Examples of unsought products may be diapers for a person who does not have a baby or epilepsy medication for a person who does not suffer seizures.

The manner in which a consumer good is classified depends on the individual. One person may view a camera as a shopping product and quickly visit a couple of stores before deciding on a brand to purchase. A friend, however, may view a camera as a specialty good, looking for a high-end camera for their photography hobby. This may result in extensive shopping at high-end camera shops for a specific type of camera. It is important to understand that although many products are clearly separated into one category or another, people in different stages of life will classify products differently. Figure 7-4 (see page 125) generally compares the different types of consumer products and how their marketing mixes may vary depending on the type of product.

Business Products

A major characteristic of business products is that their sales are often directly related to the sales' levels of the final product they are manufacturing or offering for sale. For example, if consumers' demand for Ford cars

> ## SOME PRODUCTS ARE BOTH CONSUMER AND BUSINESS PRODUCTS DEPENDING ON THEIR USAGE.

increases, the company's demand for industrial-grade paint and car stereo equipment, both business products, will also increase. Business products may be classified as production or support goods.

Production Goods Items used in the manufacturing process that become part of the final product are production goods. These include raw materials, such as grain or lumber, or component parts, such as door hinges used by Ford in its car doors.

Support Goods The second class of business products is support goods, which are items used to assist in producing other goods and services. Support goods include installations, accessory equipment, supplies, and services.

- *Installations* consist of buildings and fixed equipment. Industrial buyers purchase these assets through sales representatives, who often submit competitive bids.

- *Accessory equipment* includes tools and office equipment and is usually purchased in small-order sizes by buyers. As a result, sellers of industrial accessories use distributors to contact and deal directly with a large number of buyers.

- *Supplies* are the business equivalent of consumer convenience goods and consist of products that are used continually such as stationery, paper clips, and brooms. These are purchased with little effort as price and delivery are the key considerations.

Rolex watches are a specialty good.

Figure 7–4
Classification of consumer products

	TYPE OF CONSUMER PRODUCT			
	CONVENIENCE	SHOPPING	SPECIALTY	UNSOUGHT
Purchase behaviour of consumers	Frequent purchases; little time and effort spent shopping	Occasional purchases; needs to comparison shop	Infrequent purchases; needs extensive time to search and purchase	Very infrequent purchases; some comparison shopping
Brand loyalty of consumers	Aware of brand, but will accept substitutes	Prefer specific brands, but will accept substitutes	Very brand loyal; will not accept substitutes	Will accept substitutes
Product	Newspapers, chocolate bars, soft drinks, bread	Cameras, TVs, briefcases, clothing	Wedding dresses, luxury items such as Rolex watches	Insurance products, such as life and disability insurance
Price	Inexpensive	Fairly expensive	Usually very expensive	Varies
Place (distribution)	Widespread; many outlets	Large number of outlets	Very limited	Often limited
Promotion	Emphasis on price, availability, and awareness	Emphasis on differentiation from competitors	Emphasis on uniqueness of brand and status	Emphasis on awareness

brand
A name or phrase uniquely given by a company to a product to distinguish it from the competition

brand equity
The favourable associations and experiences that a consumer has with a brand resulting from the consumer's exposure and interaction with the brand over time

- *Services* are intangible activities needed to assist the business in its operations and in producing its goods and services. This category can include transportation services, maintenance and repair services, and advisory services such as tax or legal counsel.

ask yourself

1. What is the difference between consumer products and business products?

2. What are the four main types of consumer goods?

3. What are the classifications of business products?

Branding

LO5 Selecting a memorable brand name is an important factor in the marketing of a product. A **brand** is a name or phrase uniquely given by a company to identify its product(s) and to distinguish the product(s) from the competition. These names are often created in tandem with associated brand-marks or logos, designed to visually represent the brand to consumers and to build brand recognition. Over the long term, the support that goes into marketing a brand results in strong brand associations for the brand and a certain degree of consumer loyalty to the product. This creates **brand equity**, which is formally described as the favourable associations and experiences that a consumer has with a brand, resulting from the consumer's exposure and interaction with the brand over time. BlackBerry is a well-known brand name that has evolved over the last few years in the smartphone category. It enjoys such strong brand equity and usage that in the rare instance that its service is not functioning, this makes the news headlines.

Brand equity is the result of considerable marketing investment and needs to be protected. Patents, copyrights, and trademarks are used to protect products, brands, and processes from unethical infringement and use. Patents are used to legally protect new technologies, unique processes, or specific formulations from other companies that may wish to benefit from their use. In Canada, patents currently protect the owner for a period of 20 years, providing maintenance fees are paid during this time. After 20 years, this patent then becomes available to the market.

Copyrights are used to legally protect the written word, sound recording, or form of communication from being copied by others. It covers music, literature, and performances, and can include slogans. Trademarks are used by businesses to protect brands and their images from usage by others. Trademarks are limited to a period of 15 years, but can be renewed by their owners to maintain their investment. A trademark legally protects a brand name, and the combination of its logo, colours, fonts, and various combinations that exist for use in a particular category, and part of the world. If trademarks are to be used in foreign countries, the owner is

wise to register an application for that country. Companies hold separate trademarks for each version of a brand name and its associated graphics and logo. For a brand to be trademarked, a company needs to first conduct a trademark search to ensure the trademark is not already owned by another company. If the trademark is available, and not challenged, then the brand and its associated design and logos can be legally registered in the company name. Care must be taken to renew these trademarks as required to ensure they do not expire. Information on trademarks in Canada can be seen at the Canadian Intellectual Property Office website at www.cipo.ic.gc.ca. Here you can easily conduct a search of the trademark database and its registered trademarks. The Canadian Intellectual Property Office provides information on which trademarks are registered, when they were registered, and who owns the trademark.

An interesting trademark infringement case was recently disputed by the owners of the Scrabble trademark, Hasbro and Mattel, and those who brought the board game to the Internet with the popular Scrabulous game. Hasbro owns the trademark for the Scrabble game from at least 1953 and issued a number of takedown notices to Scrabulous.com, which enjoyed 50,000 daily users. This online version of the game used a version of the Scrabble trademark and game without permission from the trademark owners (see Marketing NewsFlash, opposite).

Brand Loyalty

Just how much do consumers like a particular brand? Will they choose another if their first choice is not available, or will they insist on finding their brand? These are brand loyalty decisions. The degree of attachment that a consumer has to a particular brand tells a marketer about their **brand loyalty**. Consumers that readily switch brands depending on price,

Canada's Top 10 Iconic Brands (2007)

Ranking	Brand	Value ($ millions)
1	Cirque du Soleil	880
2	Ski-Doo	293
3	CBC	283
4	Roots	134
5	Toronto Maple Leafs	95
6	Montreal Canadiens	87
7	Calgary Stampede	52
8	IMAX	50
9	CN Tower	23
10	Terry Fox	15

Source: John Gray, "Canada's top 10 iconic brands," Canadian Business Online, July 18, 2007, accessed at www.canadianbusiness.com/managing/strategy/article.jsp?content=20070619_125930_5932.

generally have very little brand loyalty. Consumers with a stronger brand attachment may have some brand loyalty, but may easily brand switch if the brand is not available. A brand's most loyal consumers will insist on purchasing their brand of choice, and will postpone a purchase if the brand is not available. Most people have different degrees of brand loyalty depending on the product, brand, or category. Consider the products you purchase, and determine where you have strong brand loyalty and where you have very little.

Brand Personality

Marketers recognize that brands offer more than product identification and a means to distinguish their products. Successfully established brands take on a **brand personality**, a set of human characteristics associated with a brand name.[3] Research shows that consumers often assign personality traits to products—traditional, romantic, rugged, sophisticated, rebellious—and choose brands that are consistent with their own or desired self-image. Through advertising, marketers often associate a brand with a personality that conveys certain emotions or feelings for the brand. For example, the personality traits associated with Pepsi-Cola are youthful in spirit and exciting, while with Dr Pepper, the personality traits are nonconforming, unique, and fun.

Brand Name

When we say Sony, Porsche, Pepsi, or Adidas, we typically do not think about how

Problems with the Scrabble Trademark?

In July of 2006, brothers Rajat and Jayant Agarwalla created a game called Scrabulous, an online version of the popular Hasbro and Mattel-owned word game Scrabble. (Hasbro owns the rights to Scrabble in Canada and the United States, and Mattel owns the rights in the rest of the world.) In 2007, the Agarwalla brothers made their game available as an application on the social networking site Facebook, where it soon became one of the top-ten most popular Facebook applications. Soon after, Hasbro and Mattel sent cease-and-desist letters to Facebook on the grounds that Scrabulous infringed upon the companies' trademark and copyright for the game Scrabble. Hasbro proceeded to launch a lawsuit against the two brothers in U.S. Federal Court.

This action by the companies soon sparked an intense reaction from fans of the application that protested the action by creating "Save Scrabulous" groups on Facebook, one of which had more than 5,000 members in January 2008. Many of the online users shared anecdotes regarding their love of the online game, some saying that they

Focus on Ethics

had never heard of or played Scrabble before discovering Scrabulous. Playing the game online had encouraged them to buy physical Scrabble sets and play outside of Facebook as well, giving some credence to the idea of Scrabulous as a form of viral marketing. The Agarwallas themselves say that they are fans who created Scrabulous out of love for the board game when they couldn't find a suitable online version.

In mid-2008, the Agarwalla brothers revised their Scrabulous application with the new game Wordscraper, which has new rules and circular tiles. A few months later, Hasbro announced that it was dropping the lawsuit. ●

Sources: "Facebook asked to pull Scrabulous game," *CBCnews.ca*, January 16, 2008, accessed, at www.cbc.ca/technology/story/2008/01/16/tech-scrabulous.html; Mathew Ingram, "Viral marketing or trademark theft?" *The Globe and Mail*, January 16, 2008, accessed, at www.theglobeandmail.com/servlet/story/RTGAM.20080116.WBmingram20080116132835/WBStory/WBmingram/?page=rss&; Matt Semansky, "How Do You Spell 'D-I-L-E-M-M-A'?" *Marketing* magazine, April 14, 2008, accessed, at www.marketingmag.ca/english/news/marketer/article.jsp?content=20080414_71238_71238; Chris Sorensen, "Scrabble makers want Scrabulous scrapped," *Toronto Star*, January 16, 2008, accessed, at www.thestar.com/Business/article/294676; "Scrabble knockoff returns," Associated Press, July 31, 2008, accessed at www.theglobeandmail.com/servlet/story/RTGAM.20080731.wgtscrabulous0731/BNStory/Technology/home.

companies determined these brand names. Selecting a successful brand name can be an arduous and sometimes expensive process. Companies can spend thousands of dollars developing and testing a new brand name. Intel, for example, spent US$60,000 developing the Pentium brand name for its microchips.[4] Here are some key points to consider when determining a good brand name:

- *The name should suggest the product benefits.* This is demonstrated by brand names such as Easy Off (oven cleaner), PowerBook (laptop computers), and *American Idol* (TV show), which all clearly describe the product benefits. Care should be taken to review how the brand name translates into other languages to avoid future pitfalls. The 7Up brand name, for example, roughly translates into "death through drinking" in a local dialect in Shanghai, China, which clearly does not positively influence sales in this region.[5]

- *The name should be memorable, distinctive, and positive.* A number of new brands have been introduced over the last few years with distinctive brand names such as iPod, Google, and Xbox. All these names are very distinctive and were entirely unique and unknown when first introduced. Today, these brand names have high awareness in Canada and enjoy very strong brand recognition.

- *The name should fit the company or product image.* The brand names iPod, Google, and Xbox all reflect the products they portray. iPod suggests something high-tech and small; Google is a fun, casual word associated with creativity (doodle);

> ## *The degree of attachment that a consumer has to a particular brand tells a marketer about their brand loyalty.*

and Xbox is a strong, crisp brand name associated with a video console (box) and the forbidden nature of something new and on the edge (X).

- *The name should have the ability to be legally protected.* A brand name must be "trademarkable" to protect a company's investment. If the brand name is too generic, or the trademark is owned by another company, the brand name cannot be trademarked. For example, you cannot trademark the name "Bottled Water," as it is not unique enough to warrant a trademark. Increasingly, brand names also need a corresponding website address, which can complicate name selection. An interesting example existed for a teenager in Victoria, British Columbia, named Mike Rowe who set up the website www.MikeRoweSoft.com to promote his web-design business. The software giant Microsoft demanded that Mike give up the domain name because it violated the Microsoft trademark. This generated negative publicity for Microsoft, which backed down and reached a settlement with Mike Rowe, who renamed his site www.MikeRoweForums.com.[6]

- *The name should be simple.* The brand names iPod, Google, and Xbox are all simple names to spell and remember. This makes them more memorable and helps build brand equity.

ask yourself

1. In what instances are patents, copyrights, and trademarks used?

2. Explain the concepts of brand equity and brand loyalty.

3. What are components of a good brand name?

Number of Branded Products Appearing in Movies Released in 2008

Sex and the City — **94** brands

Iron Man — **42** brands

The Dark Knight — **17** brands

Kung Fu Panda — **0** brands

marketing meter

Source: Brandchannel.com, "Leading brand appearances this year," *Brandcameo—brands*, 2008, accessed, at www.brandchannel.com/brandcameo_brands.asp?brand_year=2008#brand_list.

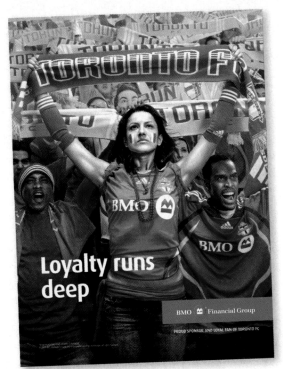

In sports marketing, brand loyalty is a primary marketing objective.

Types of Brands

There are three types of brands: (1) manufacturer's brands, (2) private label brands, and (3) generic brands. This is easily understood by looking at the pharmaceutical industry and over-the-counter pain medications.

A **manufacturer's brand** is one that is owned and produced by the manufacturer. Tylenol is the manufacturer's brand created by Johnson & Johnson and sold to drugstores throughout Canada. They in turn display the product on their shelves and sell it at retail to consumers. Johnson & Johnson invested considerable time and effort into researching, creating, and marketing this brand. When initially launched, this product was protected by a patent, but as mentioned earlier a patent is restricted to a limited number of years, currently 20 years in Canada. Once a patent expires, other manufacturers can produce a similar product. At Shoppers Drug Mart, the retail price for 325mg of regular strength Tylenol is currently $9.49 for 100 tablets.

A **private label brand**, otherwise known as a store brand, is a brand that is owned by a retailer that contracts its manufacturing to major suppliers and then sells the product at its own retail stores. A private label brand provides a retailer with the opportunity to offer its customers a less expensive alternative to a manufacturer's brand. Private label products are generally sold at lower prices than manufacturer's brands due to the absence of high listing fees to get the product on the shelf, and its lower marketing and product development costs. An example of a private label product in the over-the-counter pain reliever category is Shoppers Drug Mart's Life Brand Acetaminophen. Life Brand is one of Shoppers Drug Mart's private label brands used to compete directly with other over-the-counter pharmaceutical products. In this instance, Life Brand Acetaminophen competes directly with Tylenol, whose main ingredient is also acetaminophen. The current retail price for 325 mg of regular strength Life Brand Acetaminophen is $5.99 for 100 tablets, considerably less than a similar-size container of Tylenol priced at $9.49.

One of the most successful private label brands in Canada is that of President's Choice. This brand was introduced in 1975 by Loblaw Companies Ltd. as an upscale private label, selling a unique array of products that could not be found in other Canadian supermarkets. In the early years, Dave Nichol was Loblaw's initial spokesperson for the brand, now replaced by Galen Weston Jr., Loblaw's executive chairman and latest TV spokesperson who espouses the virtues of their products and how they are relevant to Canadian consumers. President's Choice products can be found at Loblaw Companies' stores such as No Frills, Fortinos, Loblaws, Valu-Mart, and the Real Canadian Superstore.

A **generic brand** has no branding at all and is produced as a cheap alternative to a manufacturer's brand and to a private label brand. A generic brand typically highlights the main product ingredient as a means of selling the product. Although a less expensive alternative to other branded products, a generic product lacks the brand equity and product recognition that is enjoyed by both manufacturer and private label brands. Outside of the pharmaceutical area, generic products can often be found at dollar stores for products such as dishwashing liquid with no associated brand name. In the over-the-counter

manufacturer's brand
A brand owned and produced by the manufacturer

private label brand
Otherwise known as a store brand, a brand owned by a retailer that contracts its manufacturing to major suppliers, and then sells the product at its own retail stores

generic brand
A product that has no branding and is produced as a cheap alternative to manufacturer's and private label brands

New TV Spokesperson for President's Choice

Marketing **NewsFlash**

Galen G. Weston, the executive chairman of Loblaw Companies Ltd., is now the face of Loblaw's private label products (under the brand names President's Choice and No Name) and Loblaw stores. Following advertising tradition that uses company executives as spokespeople (for example, Chrysler commercials with Lee Iacocca, Sleep Country Canada ads with Christine Magee, and Dave Nichol's spots for President's Choice products), the company decided to feature a top executive in its advertising as a way to show consumers that the company shares and represents their interests.

Beginning in 2007, Loblaw began its new marketing campaign featuring Weston, a campaign that was further expanded in 2008 and 2009 with the creation of other new commercials. New commercials featured Weston walking through fields and orchards, noting that Loblaw is the biggest buyer of Canadian produce in the country as he praises locally grown food. The demand for fresh, locally grown produce has risen in recent years, and Loblaw has become a part of this, with in-store events that feature local goods, and displays and banners depicting Weston.

Loblaw also created new advertisements for its President's Choice organic baby food line, featuring Weston and the young children of Loblaw employees. Studies have shown that Canadian mothers prefer to feed their families fresh organic foods, and this new advertising campaign was designed to show that Loblaw meets this need. The latest 2009 ads show Weston comparing the price of Loblaw No Name products to national brands, again showing consumers that the company has their interests in mind. ●

Sources: David Brown, "Weston Does Baby Talk in New PC Ad," *Marketing* magazine, January 9, 2008, accessed, at www.marketingmag.ca/english/news/marketer/article.jsp?content=20080506_120006_8908; Canwest News Service, "Loblaw's pushes local produce in ad campaign," *Calgary Herald*, August 22, 2008, accessed, at www.canada.com/calgaryherald/news/calgarybusiness/story.html?id=200afffe-7e59-4384-a1dd-922e99c24838; Dana Flavelle, "Spotlight turns on Galen G," *Toronto Star*, June 22, 2007, accessed, at www.thestar.com/article/228200; Hollie Shaw, "Local produce key to new Loblaw push," *Financial Post*, August 21, 2008, accessed, at www.financialpost.com/scripts/story.html?id=737699.

---

individual brand
When a company uses a brand name solely for a specific product category

family brand
When a company uses a brand name to cover a number of different product categories

pain reliever category, a generic product competing directly with Tylenol and Life Brand Acetaminophen is a product called Apo-Acetaminophen produced by Apotex Inc., Canada's largest generic drug manufacturer.

The prescription drug medication category also uses many cheaper generic drug products to substitute well-known higher priced prescription items whose patents have expired. In 2008, Apotex Inc. addressed an ethical dilemma faced by many developed countries around the world: the high cost of lifesaving prescription drugs. Apotex went through the Canadian Access to Medicines Regime (CAMR), which provides a framework for cheaper generic versions of *patented* drugs to become available for critical health care needs in developing countries. These countries cannot afford expensive branded, patented medicines, and their citizens have been unable to benefit from the latest pharmaceutical developments. Through this process, Apotex Inc. was successfully awarded a contract by the Rwandan government to sell them Apo-TriAvir, a generic version of a lifesaving AIDS drug. Under the provisions of CAMR, Apotex Inc. can sell the generic product to eligible developing countries but not in Canada until the drug's patent has expired. Apo-TriAvir is being sold at cost to the Rwandan government by Apotex Inc. for 19.5 cents (US) per pill versus a comparable drug regime at $6.[7]

Brands are classified as either individual brands or family brands depending on whether their name has been extended to cover more than one product category. An **individual brand** is when a company uses a brand name solely for a specific product category. Yop, the yogourt drink produced by Yoplait, Ultima Foods Inc., is an example of an individual brand that is currently used solely for this milk-based beverage. A **family brand** is when a company uses a brand name to cover a number of different product categories. The brand name Crest, although initially used only for toothpaste, is now used by Procter & Gamble for toothpaste, toothbrushes, mouthwash, and teeth-whitening products. Google is a similar example. When first introduced, and for a number of years, this individual brand was used solely to identify its search engine. Over the last few years, the Google brand has been extended into a family brand that encompasses not only its search engine but also Google Images, Google Video, Google Earth, Google Toolbar, Google Calendar, and many other Google products.

ask yourself

1. Explain the difference between a private label and a manufacturer's brand.

2. What type of pricing differences would you expect to see for a manufacturer's brand, a private label brand, and a generic brand for products within the same category?

3. What are the advantages and disadvantages of using a family brand rather than an individual brand to launch a new product?

A Practical Look at Marketing Products and Brands

L○7 A marketer's responsibility is to market products and brands to bring revenue into a company, or in the for-profit sector, to secure profits. Annually, a marketer creates marketing plans for the upcoming year to formalize which programs need to be implemented to secure these revenue and profit requirements. These plans review each element of the marketing mix, detailing their required activities and their impact on revenues and profits. These plans ultimately revolve around managing the product, ensuring that it meets consumer needs and that it lives up to its positioning in the market.

Despite the existence of a marketing plan, the world of marketing is dynamic and ever-changing, and requires a marketer to constantly evaluate planned programs against changing needs and to ultimately recommend necessary changes. The marketing environment is constantly changing and marketers need to anticipate competitive moves and work to ensure that all programs are current, competitive, and in line with the latest consumer trends.

> *A marketer's responsibility is to market products and brands to bring revenue into a company.*

Managing a product requires a marketer to wear many hats. On an ongoing basis, a marketer needs to analyze daily sales numbers, review profit targets, be alerted to changes in product costs, be in contact with the sales force, and understand changes in the selling environment. A marketer must also be aware of market research insights, understand consumer interests, and work with a team to create meaningful marketing programs. Examples of how a marketer practically manages products are as follows: If a food-product marketer plans to introduce a new plastic container, but realizes that there is a consumer movement away from these items due to health concerns, this marketer would most likely recommend against this planned program. Similarly, a marketer of an SUV may decide to delay the introduction of a new model due to the high price of gasoline and consumers' movement toward more fuel-efficient vehicles. In addition, if a product's profits are under pressure due to a sudden increase in the cost of manufacturing, then an expensive advertising campaign may be delayed or modified to reduce expenditures in an attempt to reach short-term profit targets. If a competitor unexpectedly reduces prices, then a marketer will need to determine whether their product pricing needs to be adjusted and how this may impact on profits.

In addition to managing these types of issues that arise as the year unfolds, a marketer must look to the future of the brand to ensure its relevancy to consumers. Product marketers manage the current competitive environment while also working on future programs

Private Label Products Market Share (by value)

Europe	23%
North America	16%
Emerging Markets	6%
Asia Pacific	4%
Latin America	2%
Global	17%

Source: Clare Nishikawa and Jane Perrin, "Private Label Grows Global," *Consumer Insight,* Winter 2005, AC Nielsen, p. 21, accessed at http://us.acnielsen.com/pubs/documents/2005_ci_q4_privatelabel.pdf.

and products for the upcoming years. In marketing, nothing remains static, and currently three main areas of interest are surfacing as areas where marketers need to be involved. Firstly, we see marketers in Canada and around the world investing in "green" conservation programs and new technologies to meet consumer demands in this area. A second area of interest for Canadian marketers is the increasingly multicultural composition of our society. This is demonstrated in the home language of people in Canada, which for 30 percent of the population is neither solely English nor French.[8] Marketers look to ensure that their products are relevant to these cultural groups and constantly examine the need to communicate their programs in a variety of languages. A third area of interest for marketers in Canada is the impact of the Internet on consumers' purchasing behaviour and the way it is changing how people communicate. Marketers look to how the music industry misread the impact of music downloads, and are cautious to not overlook consumers' ability to control the market and its dynamics.

In practical terms, the managing of a product requires marketers to intimately understand the dynamics of the marketplace in which they function, and to be

able to quickly assess the financial impact of any changes that are needed to maintain a product's competitiveness and relevancy in the market. Marketers need to be able to react quickly, recommending necessary changes to marketing plans, and to put in place contingency plans to support the product. Managing a product is not a static event but a process that is constantly changing, requiring marketers to use their analytical skills, creativity, and strategic understanding of the brand and the competition to keep it moving forward. In all instances, being true to a product's positioning, meeting consumer needs, and implementing competitive marketing programs helps to ensure products are well managed and have longevity.

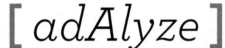

[*adAlyze*]

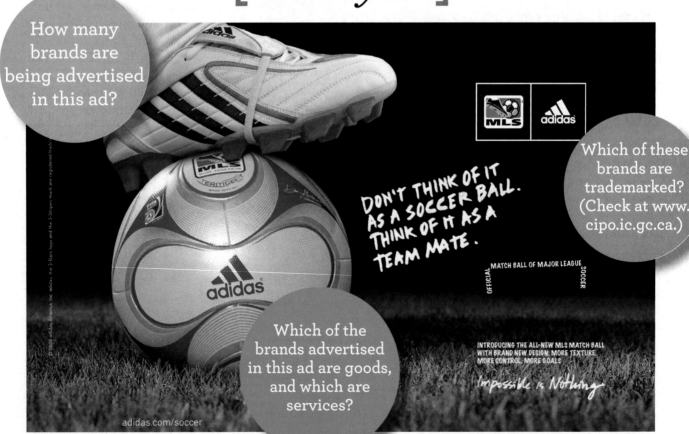

Summary...*just the facts*

- "Product" is a term used in marketing to designate non-durable goods, durable goods, and services that are marketed. Some products are a combination of both goods and services.

- There are four unique elements to services: intangibility, inconsistency, inseparability, and inventory. These four elements are referred to as the *four Is of services*.

- The total product concept includes the core product, the actual product, and the augmented product.

- Product mix is the combination of product lines managed by a company. The width of the product mix refers to the number of different categories offered by the company. The depth of the product mix refers to the number of product groups and product lines offered by a company within each category.

- Consumer products are classified into convenience products, shopping products, specialty products, and unsought products.

- Business products are classified into production or support goods. Production goods include raw materials and components parts, while support goods include installations, accessory equipment, supplies, and services.

- A brand is a name or phrase used to identify a product and to distinguish it from the competition. Brand equity is the result of the positive experiences consumers have with the brand over time and results in brand loyalty.

- Trademarks are used to legally protect brands. Patents are used to protect unique processes, and copyrights are used to protect the written or spoken word.

- Brands are categorized as manufacturer's brands, private label brands, and generic brands.

- Companies may restrict a brand name for use with a single product line, thus using an individual brand, or may extend a brand name to encompass a number of different product categories, resulting in the creation of a family brand.

Key Terms and Concepts...*a refresher*

brand *p. 125*
brand equity *p. 125*
brand loyalty *p. 126*
brand personality *p. 127*
business products *p. 123*
consumer products *p. 123*
convenience products *p. 123*
copyrights *p. 126*
durable good *p. 119*
family brand *p. 130*

generic brand *p. 129*
idle production capacity *p. 120*
individual brand *p. 130*
manufacturer's brand *p. 129*
non-durable good *p. 119*
patents *p. 126*
private label brand *p. 129*
product *p. 118*
product depth *p. 123*
product line *p. 122*

product mix *p. 122*
product width *p. 123*
service continuum *p. 119*
services *p. 119*
shopping products *p. 124*
specialty products *p. 124*
trademarks *p. 126*
unsought products *p. 124*

Check out the Online Learning Centre at **www.mcgrawhill.ca/olc/thecore**
for chapter application questions, discussion activities, Internet exercises, and video cases.

New Product Development

This chapter looks at new products, how they are developed, and the importance of managing the product life cycle for the long-term viability of a company. Ian Gordon, senior vice president at Loblaw Companies Ltd, manages product innovation for President's Choice and provides interesting insights into this important aspect of marketing. He provides a glimpse into the marketing of Loblaw's President's Choice Blue Menu line of products.

Ian Gordon, a seasoned marketer with a passion for food, has an extensive marketing background with companies such as Frito Lay, Unilever, Robin Hood Multifoods, and the advertising agency ACLC. Ian Gordon's perspective on product innovation is that for product innovation to succeed, it must be built around a consumer insight that is easily recognizable by consumers themselves. He cautions that many product innovations fail because the focus is on the innovation itself, rather than on how it needs to come together in a meaningful way for consumers. Ian Gordon emphasizes that rarely do marketers get it entirely right the first time, and marketers and companies must understand that it is the journey of product innovation that can make the product successful over time. During this journey, marketers must be willing to listen and apply the consumer insights they learn, making adjustments to the product's marketing mix to improve the product and its relevancy to consumers. Marketers in the for-profit world of business must not lose sight of the fact that their ultimate aim is to generate profits for the company.

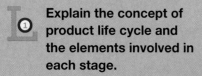
 Explain the concept of product life cycle and the elements involved in each stage.

 Understand how product life cycles are extended.

L₃ Differentiate between different types of new products.

Ian Gordon explains that companies have different approaches to product innovation. President's Choice has a team-based approach that includes chefs, nutrition researchers, registered dieticians, nutritionists, product developers, quality assurance specialists, regulatory affairs experts, and marketers. This team keeps its fingers on the pulse of the Canadian consumer, conducting research to identify trends, interests, and changes in attitudes. They also follow shopping trends within their store environment to alert the company to potential opportunities. Importantly, the company recognizes the benefits of traveling the world to borrow and perfect top-quality taste experiences with new food ideas for the Canadian palate.

President's Choice Blue Menu line of foods demonstrates how product innovation is about the journey, and that success stems from crafting a product, and then finessing the elements of the marketing mix over time so that it is meaningful to consumers. The President's Choice Blue Menu line was not always the success that it is today. It was initially introduced as the Too Good To Be True (TGTBT) line. While the line had an average performance, it offered consumers a

L4 Describe the adoption curve of new products.

L5 Explain why new products succeed or fail.

L6 Detail each step in the new product development process.

product life cycle
The stages that a new product goes through starting with introduction and evolving into growth, maturity, and decline

confusing proposition. The name was too long, the products inconsistently linked to the brand, and consumers were unclear on its relevance and significance to their food purchases. The company recognized an opportunity to relaunch the line in a more meaningful way to consumers and finesse each element of the marketing mix so that it worked to best communicate the line's benefits. The line was revamped to focus on only healthy food choices and boosted into the forefront of the President's Choice array of products under a new brand name: PC Blue Menu.

PC Blue Menu revamped the TGTBT line by changing the name and only including product offerings that had meaningful consumer benefits. The PC Blue Menu line concentrates only on healthier food choices that taste good. Each product in the line is either lower in fat (or contains good fats), lower in calories, provides more fibre, contains soy protein, or has less sodium than regular food choices. Under this directive, the PC Blue Menu line has evolved to include snack foods, pasta, cereals, soups, frozen entrees, and beverages.

In addition to revising the product line and creating a new brand for the TGTBT line, the PC marketers analyzed other elements of the marketing mix, revamping them as necessary to ensure that they worked to clearly communicate the brand's proposition. The package was given a new distinctive blue design with graphics that clearly focused consumers on the products' point of difference and the new brand name. Marketing communications were retooled to present a clearer message than the previous TGTBT line. A new "PC Insider's Report," focused on healthier eating, was created with the PC Blue Menu line front and centre. This provided the line with a detailed forum to showcase the new brand, communicate specific product health benefits, highlight the line's consumer relevance, and focus on its appetite appeal. Strong in-store displays accompanied this launch, merchandising the new line of products at retail. The PC Blue Menu line was launched with a meaningful, cohesive product line, a new brand name, a revitalized package design, and a marketing communications vehicle that reached consumers at home and in the store environment. The journey of product innovation thus moved the TGTBT line into the new brand of PC Blue Menu products.

Ian Gordon from Loblaw Companies Ltd. says, "It is about learning from your mistakes and applying the learning." He emphasizes that innovation is not just about new products themselves but also about the journey to craft the new products and all the elements of the marketing mix that must come together to make the innovations real and meaningful. "Innovation is about the journey, not the 'Eureka,'" says Ian Gordon, as he passionately talks about the marketing of the PC Blue Menu line. 🍎

The Product Life Cycle

L❶ The concept of the **product life cycle** describes the stages that a new product goes through, starting with its initial introduction into the marketplace and moving through to stages of growth, maturity, and decline. The concept of product life cycle is used by many marketers to help manage a product from its initial launch through to its eventual decline. Marketers try to manage products so that they do not reach the decline stage. Instead, products are revamped, retooled, and repositioned to meet evolving consumer needs and competitive challenges. This approach was clearly demonstrated with the PC TGTBT line that was relaunched under the PC Blue Menu line.

Figure 8–1 traces the curve of a product life cycle by plotting a product's sales and profits over time. The curves change in response to the competitive environment and to consumers' demand for the innovation.

The Core: Chapter 8

New products can add vitality to a company.

Product life cycles need to be managed to meet evolving trends.

Figure 8–1
Product life cycle

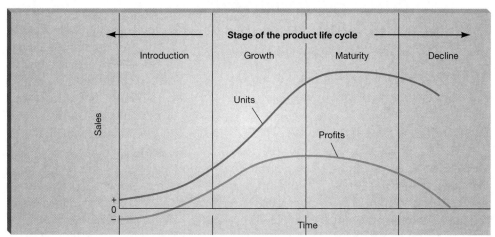

Initially, during the introduction stage, a product enjoys minimal sales, profits, and competition, but then with time, propelled by marketing programs, a product moves into a period of rapid growth and profit increases. As the competition becomes more severe, consumers are presented with competitive products, which cause a product's sales and profits to flatten out and eventually, if not addressed by a marketer, decline. The length of each stage in the product life cycle depends on the product, the category, and how it is being marketed. An example of how marketers use the product life cycle can be seen with the example of Sony and how, as an industry leader, it first introduced the CD player (in conjunction with Philips) as the new digital format replacing record players. Before the product was launched, Sony had already mapped out the product life cycle for the innovation, looking at least five years into the future to identify what new product innovations would be needed at that time to stay ahead of the competition. Initially, during the introductory stage, Sony and Philips provided the technology free to the industry to facilitate its adoption as the new technology of choice. This was closely accompanied by the launch of CD players and CDs, followed sequentially by the portable CD Walkman, in-car stereos, and jukeboxes. The introduction of actual music CDs was also carefully orchestrated to gain consumer confidence and acceptance by the music industry.[1]

Another more recent example can be seen with the introduction of the Apple iPod. Think about the elements of the marketing mix that were used when the iPod was first introduced and how they changed over time as new versions of the product rolled out. During its introductory stage, the iPod was a uniquely designed product and was priced at a premium level in the market. It was advertised extensively to consumers but its distribution levels were not initially high and it could not be found at all retailers. As the product moved through the different stages of its life cycle, new versions of the iPod were introduced, such as the iPod Mini, the iPod Nano, the video iPod, and the iPod Touch. Pricing levels were also reduced during these stages of the life cycle, and distribution levels were improved, with products becoming more widely available at retail. The iPod brand continues to be managed through its product life cycle with efforts concentrating on using technological upgrades to keep it relevant with consumers and to ensure that it does not go into the decline stage of the product life cycle.

Companies such as Sony and Apple carefully introduce and manage the life cycle of their new products and brands to make them as successful as possible.

Top Worldwide Brand Rankings (2008)

Ranking	Brand	Brand Value (US$ millions)
1	Coca-Cola	66,667
2	IBM	59,007
3	Microsoft	59,031
4	GE	53,086
5	Nokia	35,942
6	Toyota	34,050

Source: Interbrand, "Best Global Brands: 2008 Rankings," accessed at www.interbrand.com/best_global_brands.aspx.

In many instances, as we saw with both Sony and Apple, new products are launched with the associations of familiar brand names. This provides new products with the familiar brand equity and trust that already resonates with consumers. A familiar brand name can give a new product an initial boost with consumers who may be unfamiliar with the innovation and may require some reassurance to purchase the product. Check the rankings of the world's top brands listed in this chapter and you will realize that many of these top brand names lend themselves to a host of familiar products that were introduced over time.

In the following sections, we look at each stage of the product life cycle in more detail to appreciate how marketers use this concept to manage their products profitably (see Figure 8–2 on page 140). It is important to understand that this concept is widely used by marketers in many different ways. It is most often used to help manage products, but it can also be used to manage brands, and in some instances, to analyze an industry in general.

Introduction Stage

The introduction stage of the product life cycle occurs when a product is first introduced to its intended target market. During this period, sales grow slowly, and profits are minimal. Low profit levels are typically the result of three things: (1) slow sales growth, (2) high research and development costs incurred to bring the product to market, and (3) high levels of marketing spending needed to launch the new product. The marketing objective during this stage is to create consumer awareness and stimulate trial for the new product.

This stage is characterized by little competition and a lack of consumer awareness about the product. Radical new categories or technological innovations also come with the added challenge of needing to educate consumers on the existence and relevancy of the category itself. During this stage,

> *Distribution can often be a challenge during the introduction stage of the product life cycle because channel members may be hesitant to carry a new product that is unproven.*

companies often spend heavily on advertising and use other promotional tools to build awareness and trial among consumers. The other elements of the marketing mix are also carefully crafted to ensure that they are in step with the product launch and to add to its success.

During the introduction stage, pricing is typically high, but there are instances when a low pricing approach is used to encourage rapid acceptance of the product. A high initial price is called a *price skimming strategy* and is used by companies to help recover research and development costs. This approach takes advantage of the price insensitivity of early adopters. If a company uses a low price to enter the market, this is referred to as a *penetration pricing strategy* and is used to encourage rapid acceptance of an innovation or to combat a competitive threat.

Distribution can often be a challenge during the introduction stage of the product life cycle because channel members may be hesitant to carry a new product that is unproven. Listing fees may also present themselves as an expensive proposition for marketers who often experience retailers charging to recover their costs of listing, shelving, and merchandising a new product in their stores.

Growth Stage

The growth stage of the product life cycle sees an increase in competition and a rapid rise in sales and profits. The market is flooded with competing brands, which thrusts the category and its products into the forefront. This results in new consumers being enticed into the category and the resultant increase in sales and profits.

In this competitive arena, marketers focus their programs on differentiating their products from competitive offerings. New features are added to the original design, and product proliferation often occurs. Pricing levels are generally lowered to become more competitive, and distribution becomes more consistent. Promotion at this stage becomes more product specific, with advertising

TSN Keeps Its Product Line Fresh

In a nationwide survey conducted in 2007–2008 by Roper Reports Canada, TSN was named the leading sports network in Canada in a number of categories, in many places leading other sports networks by a very wide margin. TSN helps to maintain its lead by keeping its product line fresh and relevant with its broadcasts of the NHL, International Hockey, the Olympic Games, the CFL, and the Season of Champions Curling, among many others.

Roper Reports surveyed 1,200 Canadian adults ages 18 and up between November 16, 2007, and February 15, 2008.

TSN was chosen as the "Channel most enjoy watching" by 42 percent of the survey's respondents, beating out competing American networks (ABC, NBC, CBS, FOX), which gathered a combined 16 percent of sports viewers' votes. CBC followed these at 14 percent, Rogers Sportsnet at 11 percent, and The Score at 9 percent. TSN also swept the "Best channel for watching sports" category, taking in 46 percent of the votes, followed by the U.S. networks with 14 percent, The

Score at 12 percent, CBC with 11 percent, and Rogers Sportsnet at 9 percent. *SportsCentre*, TSN's news and information program, helped the network to be named the "Best channel for sports news," with 48 percent of the vote. TSN's French-language counterpart, RDS, took 45 percent of the votes to be declared "Best channel for sports news" in the Quebec market. TSN also won the category of "Best overall quality of sports coverage."

These percentages can come as no surprise to the network, given that TSN has been voted into the top slots since the survey began in 1998.

Sources: CNW Group, "TSN Is No. 1 with Canadian Sports Fans, According to National Audience Survey," *Newswire.ca*, April 16, 2008, accessed, at www.newswire.ca/en/releases/archive/April2008/16/c6088.html; Jesse Kohl, "TSN/RDS rank highest in Roper survey," *Media in Canada*, April 17, 2008, accessed, at www.mediaincanada.com/articles/mic/20080417/sportsnets.html.

---

playing a key role in focusing consumers toward specific brands.

Looking at the iPod, during the growth stage of its product life cycle we saw new versions being introduced, such as the slimmer iPod Nano. We also saw marketing efforts being directed toward iTunes, recognizing this service as a form of differentiation, and understanding the need to expand the array of songs being made available for digital downloads.

Maturity Stage

The maturity stage of the product life cycle is characterized by a slowdown of growth in both the sales and profit areas. Competitors are well established and fewer new consumers enter the market. Marketing focuses on gaining market share and uses pricing as a key promotional tool. This results in decreased profits for the market as a whole and also for individual products.

The maturity stage is generally the longest stage in the product life cycle with marketers focusing their efforts on ensuring the product does not go into decline. Marketers use short-term promotional tactics such as consumer promotions to encourage consumers to purchase the product. Product innovation can also become a priority at this stage as marketers try to reposition products in the market and revamp product lines to be more competitive and relevant to consumers' needs. The purpose of this renewed focus on innovation is to try to take the product back into the growth or early maturity stage of the product life cycle, as we have seen repeatedly with the different iterations of the iPod introduced over time.

Cellphone Ringtones (2007)

Price of Apple ringtone
99 cents

Price of Rogers/Bell, Much Music, or MTV ringtone
$3 99

Amount spent globally on ringtones by cellphone users
$13.7 billion U.S. per year

marketing meter

Source: "Gartner Says Consumer Spending on Mobile Music Will Surpass US$32 Billion by 2010," Gartner Research press release, January 23, 2007, accessed at www.gartner.com/it/page.jsp?id=500295.

Numerous well-established products are in the maturity stage of the product life cycle; examples include Heinz Ketchup, Hellmann's Mayonnaise, and Kraft Dinner. What do marketers of these products do to maintain their product relevancy in these categories and to stop them going into decline? Packaging changes, product modifications, and extended usage approaches are often used to keep them relevant.

Let's look at some less-conventional products and examine how they manage their product life cycles. Television networks and individual TV shows are also products that need to be managed. Unlike products in the food industry, these services have relatively short product life cycles and go into decline when they are no longer interesting to viewers. At this point, the network typically replaces the show with a new, probably unknown program. The risk of managing these products is relatively high, with many new shows not lasting more than a single season and requiring the network to constantly monitor its program ratings. TSN is an example of a successful Canadian specialty network that continually brings new programming to its viewers. TSN will periodically upgrade its studios, bring in new announcers, and add new programming from around the world as needed. This keeps its product fresh and interesting. TSN uses research from the Roper Reports Canada public opinion firm to monitor how viewers perceive the network and its programming relative to other sports networks and then to react accordingly. TSN has consistently ranked as number one with sports viewers since Roper Reports started the survey in 1998.[2] Marketers in many industries use similar tracking studies to monitor changing perceptions and attitudes with their consumers. These studies need to be conducted periodically, often annually, for changes to be perceptible over time.

Decline Stage

The decline stage of the product life cycle occurs when sales and profits consistently decline. Frequently, a product enters this stage when products become obsolete due to technological innovation or changes in consumer needs. The word-processing capability of personal computers pushed typewriters into decline, CDs replaced records in the music industry, and DVDs replaced VHS tapes. In the TV broadcast industry, shows in the decline stage are generally discontinued as with programs such as the teenage show *The OC*. Many reality shows, such as *The Apprentice*, are also in decline and will be or have been discontinued. *Survivor* is an example of a reality show that manages to inject an element of newness into each season, keeping it popular with its viewers. An interesting example in this industry is the show *90210*, which is currently being resurrected and relaunched with a new story line after many years of hiatus.

A company will follow one of two strategies to handle a declining product, either deleting the product, as seen in the television entertainment industry, or harvesting the product, as sometimes seen in the food industry. Deletion is when a product is discontinued, while **harvesting** is when a company keeps the product but reduces marketing support in an attempt to reap some minor profits at this stage. The cola beverage industry

Figure 8–2

Managing the stages of the product life cycle

MANAGING THE STAGES OF THE PRODUCT LIFE CYCLE

STAGE IN PRODUCT LIFE CYCLE	INTRODUCTION	GROWTH	MATURITY	DECLINE
Competition	Few competitors	More competitors enter the market	Many competitors	Reduced competition, with some competitors leaving the market
General marketing objective	Increase awareness	Differentiation	Brand loyalty	Product rationalization
Product	Focus on one product, often unique	Introduce more features	Ensure full product line and innovate with new ideas	Retain only best sellers or discontinue
Price	Use a skimming or penetration strategy	Prices are slowly reduced	Price discounts	Very low prices
Place (distribution)	Limited distribution	Distribution is increased	Full distribution	Distribution is reduced
Promotion	Focus on building awareness with advertising	Stress points of difference from the competition	Focus on pricing and sales promotion	Only minimal promotion, if any
Profit	Minimal, if any	Increasing profit that reaches the maximum	Maximized profits that level off	Decreasing and minimal profits

often harvests its poor-selling products for a short period of time before replacing them with newer, more relevant flavours. Vanilla Coke, Diet Coke with Lime, and Black Cherry Vanilla Coke are examples of this approach.

Shape of the Product Life Cycle

The length of a product life cycle varies according to the industry, the competition, technological innovation, and approaches to marketing the product. Television shows such as *The Apprentice* may follow a consistent product life cycle curve as illustrated by the *generalized life cycle* shown in Figure 8–1 (see page 137). This consistent curve however does not always apply to all products. Other products, such as cellphones, have very short product life cycles, moving from introduction to decline in only about 18 months, prompted by technological innovation and fashion. Other products, such as Heinz Ketchup, have extensive product life cycles that have continued for years, driven by marketing approaches to keep the product relevant. Figure 8–3 shows four different product life cycle curves, which apply to different types of products. These products and their life cycles can be categorized into four main areas: (1) high-learning products, (2) low-learning products, (3) fashion products, and (4) fad products.

A high-learning product is one for which significant education of the customer is required and for which there is an extended introductory period. DVDs are examples of such a product. The DVD technology required consumers to understand the advantages of the new technology and then adopt it while also deciding on what to do with their VHS players and cassettes. It also required the entertainment industry to adopt this new technology for its movie releases instead of the traditional VHS format. It took considerable time for consumers and the industry to fully adopt this technology, resulting in an extended introductory period for DVDs.

In contrast, a low-learning product has a short introductory stage in the product life cycle. In these instances, the benefits of purchasing these products are self-evident and very little learning is required. An example of a successful low-learning product is Gillette's MACH3 razor, which required little education on behalf of consumers. Introduced in mid-1998, MACH3 sales results were very positive, with $1 billion in sales achieved in a short three-year period.[3]

The product life cycle for a fashion product is cyclical. The length of the cycle will vary, but it is relatively short, going from introduction to decline generally within a two-year period, only to resurface again a few years later. Life cycles for fashion products most often appear in men's and women's clothing.

A fad refers to a product with a very short product life cycle. It typically experiences immediate rapid growth, followed by an equally rapid decline, with no real maturity stage at all. These products tend to be novelties. Children's toys often fall into this category.

Figure 8–3
Alternate product life cycles

A. High-learning products

B. Low-learning products
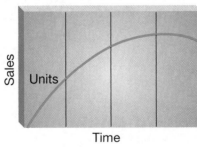

C. Fashion products
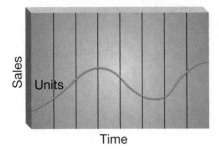

D. Fad products
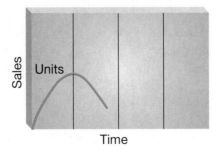

---

high-learning product
Significant consumer education is required for these products, which have an extended introductory period

low-learning product
Little consumer education is required resulting in a short introductory stage for the product

fashion product
The life cycle for fashion is relatively short and cyclical going from introduction to decline within two years, only to resurface again a few years later

fad Novelty products with very short product life cycles that experience immediate rapid growth, followed by an equally rapid decline

ask yourself

1. What are the four stages in the product life cycle? How do they differ in terms of sales and profits?

2. How do high-learning and low-learning products differ?

3. What is the shape of the product life cycle for a cellphone in today's marketplace?

Extending the Product Life Cycle

L2 It is important for a firm to manage its products through their life cycles, profitably extending and prolonging their relevance in the market. Product life cycles can be extended in a number of ways, namely by (1) targeting current users with extended usage strategies, (2) targeting new consumers through new marketing approaches, (3) revitalizing a product with product improvements and line extensions, (4) repositioning a product, (5) introducing a new product, and (6) finding new uses for a product. It is important to realize that a combination of these approaches is most often used to keep products fresh and relevant.

Targeting Current Users with Extended Usage Strategies

This approach is typically used by marketers for products with strong brand equity and a loyal consumer base. Current consumers are encouraged to consume more of the product in a variety of new ways. In the food industry, Knorr soup follows this approach by encouraging its users to not only consume the product as a soup but also to use it as an ingredient in main dish recipes. Another example is Rice Krispies, which often promotes its cereal usage as a baking ingredient for Rice Krispies Squares. Follow the links at www.kelloggs.ca to see the extended usage recipes used to market Rice Krispies.

Targeting New Consumers through New Marketing Approaches

Companies may decide that their current product is under-represented with certain consumer groups and may see an opportunity to target these consumers. Marketers are often cautious, and somewhat reluctant, to follow this approach as it can be an expensive proposition that yields few results. This approach is currently being followed by Coca-Cola with the 2007 introduction of Diet Coke Plus in the U.S., a new beverage fortified with vitamins and minerals. Time will tell whether this approach helps Coca-Cola reach the health-conscious consumer.

Knorr keeps its product lines fresh with new items and marketing campaigns.

Revitalizing a Product with Product Improvements and Line Extensions

Product improvements are often used by marketers to ensure that products remain competitive, to appeal to evolving needs, and to address new trends in the market. Examples can be seen in the food industry where marketers are addressing consumers' demand for smaller portion sizes and less fattening foods. Many companies have added line extensions and product modifications to meet this need. In the chocolate industry, for example, Cadbury introduced Cadbury Thins, a smaller, thinner chocolate bar, while Aero launched its Singles product as smaller single sticks of chocolate to meet this same downsizing trend. Toblerone recently introduced Toblerone Tiny, a miniature-size triangular bar, individually wrapped, with multiple products packed together in a high-quality bag. Similar approaches can be seen in the snack food area with products such as Doritos selling super-mini packages to meet this trend.

In the entertainment/service industry, there is evidence of similar product-improvement strategies with teams such as the National Hockey League's Pittsburgh Penguins franchise encouraging fans to attend its games more frequently. The marketers of the Pittsburgh Penguins are currently revitalizing their franchise with improvements to a new arena, which will be available in 2010. The new arena will be outfitted with a multitude of high-tech items of interest to the team's male fan base, including video-game consoles and on-demand TV replays in the luxury suites.[4]

Some of the most successful and long-lasting Canadian brands use this product-improvement and line-extension approach to extend their product life cycles. The *Globe and Mail's Report on Business* and Interbrand provide a ranking of the top Canadian brands every two years. The 2008 report rates BlackBerry as the number one Canadian brand. This brand created the smartphone market ten years ago, and through a continuous improvement strategy, has managed to continuously extend its product life cycle and dominate the smartphone industry in 135 countries around the world.[5]

New Pittsburgh Arena Meets Youth Demographic

Marketing NewsFlash

The Pittsburgh Penguins are working to make their new arena as exciting as the hockey that's taking place inside. Toward this end, the team and the Pittsburgh Technology Council (PTC) have announced a partnership that will explore technologies and advancements to be used in the team's new arena. The PTC will join the Penguins in a search for southwestern Pennsylvania's most innovative technologies. Meetings of the PTC and team representatives have emphasized that the new arena facility will be used as a venue for events other than just Penguins' games, allowing the

PTC member companies to see the numerous advantages that could come from allowing their technologies and services to be used as part of the new arena.

The Penguins and the PTC are investigating technologies and services for the facility such as on-demand televised replays and touch-screen food menus in luxury suites, video technology throughout the arena, video-gaming stations, and electronic ticketing. The Penguins also want to look into creating interactive seat finders and maps in the new arena and to investigate ways to communicate with fans with disabilities. Inspired by Seattle

Mariners baseball games, where fans can use their cellphones to order food and drinks from concession stands, the concessionaire Aramark has also been exploring new technology for the new arena, looking into services that would allow fans to use their game tickets to buy food items and merchandise. The Penguins hope that these innovations will help maintain the interest of their younger and more technologically inclined fan base, as well and make sporting experience more enjoyable for all.

Sources: Mark Belko, "The future is now for technology at Penguins' new arena," *Post-Gazette Now*, May 13, 2008, accessed, at www.post-gazette.com/pg/08134/881292-61.stm; "Pittsburgh Penguins Seek Innovations for New Arena Via The Pittsburgh Technology Council," *PRNewswire*, May 12, 2008, accessed, at www.prnewswire.com/cgi-bin/stories.pl?ACCT=104&STORY=/www/story/05-12-2008/0004811398&EDATE=.

Top 10 Canadian Brands (2008)

Ranking	Brand	Brand Value (C$ million)
1	BlackBerry	5,607.7
2	RBC	4,141.1
3	TD Canada Trust	3,779.6
4	Shoppers Drug Mart	3,137.5
5	Petro-Canada	3,132.6
6	Manulife	2,550.9
7	Bell	2,537.0
8	Scotiabank	1,870.4
9	Canadian Tire	1,828.5
10	Tim Hortons	1,604.6

Source: Interbrand, *Competing in the Global Brand Economy: Best Canadian Brands 2008*, June 2008, accessed, at www.ourfishbowl.com/images/surveys/BestCanadianBrands2008.pdf.

Repositioning a Product

Once a product has reached its maturity stage, it often needs an injection of newness to help focus the market on the product and to provide it with a renewed competitive advantage to face its competition. Many products appear tired at this stage and require a renewed focus. This can be achieved through new product development initiatives and/or repositioning the product to more readily meet changing consumer needs. Knorr is a well-known brand name built on a tradition of powdered soup mixes and beef or chicken stock cubes used to flavour old-fashioned recipes. Many years ago, the product had become tired and needed to be associated with more contemporary approaches to cooking. The brand was revitalized with new products and new packaging to bring it into the forefront and make it relevant, presenting it as a brand that enhances the taste of cooking. We can see a continuation of this approach today with Knorr's most recent marketing approach, which focuses its contemporary products on its "Eat in Colour" theme. Knorr products are creatively shown to "brighten up" a meal with colourful combinations of ingredients, aromas, and flavours. This approach is reflected not only in its TV and print advertising campaigns but also

through the new products it has introduced over time to bring this fresh, current feeling to the brand. The line includes items such as Mediterranean Inspirations, Sides Plus Veggies, and Simply Broth soups. The revitalized brand can be seen on the company's website at www.knorr.ca.

Introducing a New Product

Adding a new product can provide the focus that a mature product needs, bringing it back in the product life cycle to either the growth or early maturity stage. Apple has done this successfully by introducing new versions of its iPod product regularly. Cellphone manufacturers similarly follow this approach, ensuring that these products remain fresh and pertinent with new introductions every 18 months or so. In categories where technological change is not so prevalent, this approach is a little more difficult to manage, but Knorr is a good example with its Sides Plus Veggies product, which also contributes to a repositioning for the brand. Another example is Kellogg's, which recently introduced its Corn Pops and Froot Loops cereals in new, fun, snack packs for children's lunch boxes. Do you consider these two examples as new products or as line extensions? Check out their websites at www.knorr.ca and www.kelloggs.ca to determine your point of view.

Is this a new product or a line extension?

Finding New Uses for a Product

Finding new uses for an existing product is not a simple task, as many products do not lend themselves to this approach. Arm & Hammer is an exception, and an example of a product that has managed to take its 155-year-old baking soda brand from a baking ingredient to a product that is recommended to eliminate odours, to assist in the unblocking of sinks, and to clean various household items.

ask yourself

1. What six approaches can be used to extend a product's life cycle?
2. If you were the marketer of a large SUV, what approach would you use today to extend its product life cycle?
3. The Froot Loops Fun Pack To Go was recently introduced by Kellogg's. What approach is being used to extend the product life cycle of the Froot Loops product?

> *"New products are the lifeblood of a company, helping to make products relevant and bring future revenues into the company."*

minor innovations Minor product modifications that require no adjustments on behalf of the consumer

continuous innovations New products with more than just a minor product improvement, but that do not require radical changes by the consumer

New Product Innovation

LO 3 New products are the lifeblood of a company, helping to make products relevant and to bring future revenues into the company. There are many types of new products ranging from a slight product modification to a more radical innovation. How new products are categorized depends on the degree of newness involved, and how much time a consumer needs to learn how to use the product. Based on these factors, we classify innovations as (1) minor innovations, (2) continuous innovations, and (3) radical innovations (see Figure 8–4).

Minor innovations refer to minor product modifications that require no adjustments on behalf of the consumer. Marketing a minor modification requires marketers to generate awareness of the innovation and to continue to market along current lines. Consumers do not need to be educated on how to use the product.

These types of innovations are relatively common and can be seen in the instances of new and improved detergents and diapers that frequently surface in the market. A new product currently being introduced that fits into this category is Guinness Christmas Puddings, which will be imported into Canada as a slight adaptation of the traditional festive dessert.[6]

Continuous innovations refer to those new products that include more than just a minor product improvement but do not require radical changes by consumers. Continuous innovations are not common and require extensive product development work on behalf of the company. Marketers must invest in marketing communications programs to launch these types of innovative products to ensure that their benefits are front and centre, and that consumers can easily understand how the new product works.

Figure 8–4
Degree of product innovation

	MINOR INNOVATION	CONTINUOUS INNOVATION	RADICAL INNOVATION
Definition	Requires no new learning by consumers	Changes consumer's normal routine but does not require totally new learning	Requires new learning and consumption patterns by consumers
Examples	New improved detergents or diapers	Electric toothbrushes or digital cameras	Personal digital assistants (PDAs) or MP3 players
Marketing emphasis	Gain consumer awareness and wide distribution	Advertise points of difference and benefits to consumers	Educate consumers through advertising, product trial, and personal selling; public relations can play a major role

Guinness Christmas Puddings— Success or Failure?

Recently, English baker Coles Traditional Foods developed a Christmas pudding made with Guinness, the famous Irish beer created in 1759 by Dublin-based brewer Arthur Guinness. Guinness is a popular product worldwide, sold in almost 150 countries.

The Markham, Ontario-based company TFB & Associates Ltd. brought Cole's line of Guinness Christmas puddings from Britain to Canada in 2008, with plenty of time for consumers to stock up before the year's holiday season. The product was exclusively available in Canada, and only from TFB & Associates, who are well-known importers of British products such as Fisherman's Friend medicated lozenges.

The Christmas pudding is infused with Guinness beer to create a rich, dark pudding with a distinctive flavour and a very moist texture. Made with pure Guinness and dried fruits, the puddings are matured to allow the flavour to develop. The Guinness and dried fruits marinate for 24 hours before being mixed with breadcrumbs, ground almonds, and citrus peel to create the Christmas pudding. ●

Source: Gail Chiasson, "Since It's Only Eight Months to Christmas: Guinness Christmas Pudding," *Pubzone*, April 30, 2008, accessed, at www.pubzone.com/newsroom/2008/1x080429x081143.cfm.

Marketing **NewsFlash**

---

radical innovations
New products that involve the introduction of a product that is entirely new and innovative to the market

adoption curve
The sequential diffusion and acceptance of an innovation into the market by consumers

Sony's introduction in 2008 of its "Smile Shutter" face detection technology is an example of a continuous innovation for its digital cameras. This new technology allows a camera to automatically take photos of a person when a smile is detected. Triaminic's introduction of its Flowing Vapours portable vapour fan is another example of a continuous innovation for the decongestant brand.

Radical innovations are the least common form of innovation. They involve the introduction of a product that is entirely new to the market. The success of these products is dependent on the education of the consumer, usually through extensive advertising and public relations efforts. Public relations can add credibility to a radical innovation with the media encouraged through launch events, press kits, and press releases to discuss the product in its broadcasts or publications. This can result in considerable media coverage, which can boost sales by giving the public an objective and credible point of view. Examples of radical innovations are Crest Whitestrips and the BlackBerry smartphone, when they were first launched.

New Flowing Vapors helps soothe my little pup so he can huff, and he can puff, and blow things right down.

The Flowing Vapours fan is an example of a continuous innovation.

The Adoption Curve

The success of a new product and how quickly it is adopted by consumers in the market is demonstrated in Figure 8–5 (see page 147), which shows the **adoption curve**. The adoption curve takes the point of view that some consumers are more ready than others to buy a product

BRILLIANT SMILE. BRILLIANT PHOTO.

A GREAT SMILE MAKES A GREAT PHOTO. With visibly whiter teeth after just three days, Crest Whitestrips Premium will help you take your brightest holiday photos yet. Satisfaction guaranteed.

Crest

Crest Whitestrips are an example of a radical innovation.

innovation. Research shows that 2.5 percent of the population are innovators, risk takers who readily purchase innovative products; 13.5 percent are considered early adopters, another group that will accept a new offering sooner rather than later; and another 16 percent of the population are the laggards who are either reluctant or late purchasers of the innovation. In the middle of the pack are the early and late majority, each comprising of approximately 34 percent of the population. Once accepted by the innovators and early adopters, the adoption of new products moves on to the early majority, late majority, and finally laggards. Marketers try to move the product from the innovators through to the early majority as soon as possible to quickly reap the benefits of increased sales and profits.

An example of how the adoption curve applies to new product diffusion can be seen in the pharmaceutical industry where companies often target the innovators and early adopters to encourage other people in the industry to more readily accept an innovation. To achieve this, manufacturers of new pharmaceutical products often initially target leading hospitals, clinics, and physicians that are widely respected in the medical field. The adoption of the new products by these innovators will add credibility to the products and help speed up their diffusion in the industry.

Why New Products Succeed or Fail

LO 5 We all know the new product success of PC Blue Menu, and are familiar with successful new brands such as Google, Xbox, and iPod,

yet only one in ten new products are successful over time. It is important at this point to remember the insight that Ian Gordon from Loblaw Companies Ltd. gives us on how to successfully craft new products. He reminds us that it is the *journey* of new product innovation that makes new products successful over time. He states that marketers are tasked to implement meaningful changes to the marketing mix based on listening and reacting to consumers, and not to be only focused on the innovation itself.

Reasons for New-Product Failures   Using the research results from several studies[7] on new product successes and failures, we can identify critical marketing factors that often spell failure for new product launches:

1. *Insignificant point of difference.* Shown as one of the most important factors, a distinctive and meaningful point of difference is essential for a new product to compete in the market. In the mid-1990s, General Mills introduced Fingos, a sweetened cereal flake about the size of a corn chip, to compete in the snack market. Consumers were supposed to snack on them dry, but this did

Figure 8–5
The adoption curve

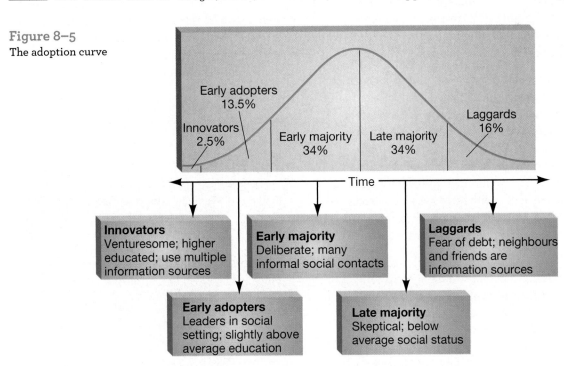

not occur as consumers were not presented with a meaningful reason for purchasing Fingos over other snacks in the market.[8]

2. *Incomplete new concept definition*. Ideally, before a new product is developed it needs a well-defined, consumer-based reason for being. Its consumer insights must be clearly identified. If these areas are not clearly outlined, the new products will have no meaningful positioning in the market.

3. *Insufficient market attractiveness*. Market attractiveness refers to a product having strong consumer appeal in a market with both growth and profit potential. Often, a target market can be too small or too competitive to result in a profitable entry. In the early 1990s, Kodak discontinued its Ultralife lithium battery with its 10-year shelf life, as the market accounted for less than 10 percent of the batteries sold in North America and was not a viable long-term proposition.

4. *Inadequate marketing support*. Companies often launch products with little marketing support or a marketing mix that does not adequately support the innovation. The President's Choice TGTBT line of products (discussed in this chapter's opening vignette) points to a marketing mix that required revamping and more support for consumers to fully comprehend its benefits. The revamped PC Blue Menu line provided this needed support for product success.

5. *Insensitivity to critical customer needs*. Ignoring a critical consumer insight can kill a product, even though the general concept may be well accepted. For example, the Japanese, like the British, drive on the left side of the road, resulting in right-hand-drive vehicles on their roads. Until 1996, North American car makers continued to sell left-hand-drive options to Japan with little success. Contrast this with the German car manufacturers, that successfully exported right-hand-drive models for a number of their brands to this market.[9]

6. *Bad timing*. A product can suffer negative consequences if it is introduced too soon, too late, or at a time when consumer tastes are shifting. An example exists in the aircraft industry. In March 2001, Boeing announced it would start the multibillion-dollar development of its Sonic Cruiser, designed to cross oceans with over 400 passengers at almost the speed of sound. However, the tragic attacks of September 11, 2001, caused such a decline in air travel that the project was postponed.[10]

7. *Limited access to buyers*. It is often difficult to obtain the necessary distribution to reach a target market. Consumer products typically need a retailer to list and display their products in-store, but this distribution network is not always readily available. A new product may have tested well with consumers, but if a retailer will not list the product, its distribution will be limited.

Looking at an example of product failures, Kimberly Clark's Avert Virucidal tissues lasted ten months in a test market in upstate New York before being pulled from the shelves. The product claimed to contain vitamin C derivatives that were scientifically designed to kill cold and flu germs. The reasons for failure relate to the product name and a lack of credibility in the product claims. People did not believe the anti-viral claims and found the "cidal" in the name unappealing and reminiscent of the negative words *suicidal* and *homicidal*. Therefore, reviewing the possible reasons for failure, the tissue probably failed due to *insufficient market attractiveness* and *inadequate marketing support*. One wonders whether the product could have been a success if launched under a different name and with a different positioning. Perhaps the journey of product development required more time and adjustments to become successful.

ask yourself

1. Describe the three types of product innovation and explain which ones are most common.

2. How does the adoption curve apply to the diffusion of new products in the marketplace?

3. What are the main reasons that new products fail?

New Product Development

Developing and launching new products is an expensive undertaking with a high risk of failure. Research costs are high, as is the time and effort spent on developing prototypes and marketing materials. Product launches may also include expensive listing fees required to secure retail distribution. Product failure can result in expensive product write-offs and a lack of future credibility in the market. Hundreds of thousands of dollars are often at stake. In order to avoid expensive product failures, companies can use a number of different approaches to developing these new products. These range from providing clear strategic direction, to creating particular company structures, and to instituting rigorous product development processes. We look at these areas in more detail in the sections that follow.

Approaches to New Product Development

Strategic Direction   From a strategic point of view, companies can follow different approaches to innovation (see Figure 8–6). It is somewhat dependent on the degree of risk and investment that companies are willing to take. The most common forms of innovation take either a market penetration or product development slant, focusing on current consumers with promotional tactics (market penetration), or looking to develop a new product for these current consumers (product development). Higher risk considerations include either a market development or diversification strategy, which take the more expensive approach of targeting new markets with either current products (market development), or moving out into new arenas with totally new products (diversification).

Hewlett-Packard's cross-functional teams reduce new product development time.

Company Structure   Companies use different structures to encourage innovation. Some companies, such as Loblaw Companies Ltd., use teams to help marshal successful new products to Canadian consumers. President's Choice has a *team-based approach* that includes chefs, nutrition researchers, registered dieticians, nutritionists, product developers, quality assurance specialists, regulatory affairs experts, and marketers. A clear example can also be seen with Hewlett-Packard (HP), which uses cross-functional teams to develop new products. Each team is made up of a small number of people from different departments, all responsible for achieving the same goals. These HP teams consist of individuals from research and development, marketing, sales, manufacturing, and finance, simultaneously working together to achieve a single goal.

> **COMPANIES USE DIFFERENT STRUCTURES TO ENCOURAGE INNOVATION.**

Figure 8–6
Strategic approaches to innovation

Markets	PRODUCTS	
	Current	**New**
	Market Penetration	**Product Development**
Current	Finding ways to make current products appeal to current customers	Reaching current customers with a new product
	Market Development	**Diversification**
New	Reaching new customers with a current product	Reaching new customers with a new product

Other companies may follow a more *individualized approach*, appointing a new product development manager to concentrate entirely in this area. In other instances, *full departments* are tasked with this responsibility, or new product development is included in the role of the general marketer. In some instances, *new venture teams* are used to concentrate on all innovation projects for the company, which could include new products, new processes, or new business ventures.

Regardless of the formal structure, new product development success ultimately requires the expertise of people with different specializations and from varied backgrounds to ensure that the best product ideas are developed. These experts are either fully involved in the process from the start, or brought in along the way to contribute to the journey.

The New Product Development Process

In order to avoid expensive product failures, companies use rigorous product development processes to minimize the risk. Each step in the process requires an individual or team to assess whether the project is still viable and should continue down the road to innovation. The **new product development process** includes the seven steps shown in Figure 8–7 and summarized in Figure 8–8 (see page 151), starting with a clearly defined strategy. This is followed by a number of brainstorming, research, product development, and business analysis steps. A successful trip down this road faces many twists and turns, and any new product development team needs to be flexible, creative, and responsive to the insights learned at each step.

Step 1: New Product Development Strategy
New product development success relies on many factors. Having a clear definition and understanding of what you are trying to achieve with the innovation is one of the most important building blocks in this process. A

new product development strategy involves setting the new product strategic direction for the company as a whole, and the precise objectives for the project at hand. There must be consistency between the two.

An example can be seen with Procter & Gamble which in 2000 refocused its new product development strategy from "new-to-the-world" products and brands, to evolving current brands such as Crest, Tide, and Pampers with new initiatives. The result was products such as Crest Whitestrips for teeth whitening and Crest SpinBrush for better dental care. These innovations helped boost global sales for the Crest brand by 50 percent within two years.[11]

Step 2: Idea Generation
Once the purpose and direction for the product development project is clarified, the second step of **idea generation** comes into play. This includes brainstorming sessions focused on participants coming up with new ideas for the project at hand. It is important for these brainstorming sessions to include individuals who are creative, have different experiences, and have differing areas of expertise. This should stimulate a more varied and interesting pool of ideas.

Brainstorming sessions can result in a host of interesting ideas, but for this approach to work, participants must be willing to share their most ludicrous or boring ideas with the group. Participants need to be open-minded, energetic, flexible, and willing to build on each other's ideas. Often, companies hire an outside moderator, skilled in these types of sessions, to promote creativity sessions that render results. As a rule of thumb, it takes at least 60 ideas to generate an inspired idea with some potential.

Step 3: Screening and Evaluation
The third stage of the new product development process, **screening and evaluation**, attempts to reduce the

Figure 8–7

Steps in the new product development process

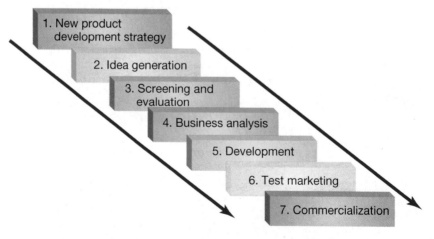

1. New product development strategy
2. Idea generation
3. Screening and evaluation
4. Business analysis
5. Development
6. Test marketing
7. Commercialization

Figure 8–8
Elements in each stage of the new product development process

STAGE OF PROCESS	PURPOSE OF STAGE	MARKETING INFORMATION AND METHODS USED
New product development strategy	Identify new-product development focus that meets company objectives	Company objectives; SWOT analysis of company/product/brand
Idea generation	Brainstorm new ideas	Ideas from employees, co-workers, and consumers
Screening and evaluation	Evaluate product ideas and develop concepts	Internal evaluation of technical requirements, external concept tests
Business analysis	Identify the product's features and its marketing strategy, and make financial projections	Product's key features and anticipated marketing mix; assessment of production, legal, and profitability issues
Development	Create the prototype, and test it internally at the company and externally with consumers	Internal company assessments and external tests on product prototypes
Test marketing	Test the product and marketing strategy in the marketplace on a limited scale (if necessary)	Test marketing in defined areas
Commercialization	Launch and fully market the product in the marketplace	Implement all areas of the marketing mix; possible regional rollout

array of brainstorming ideas down to a manageable list of promising concepts. Ideas are initially screened internally by the new product development team, which eliminates ideas that do not meet the objectives, as well as those that are clearly not feasible. The short list of ideas is then developed by the team into concepts. A concept is a more detailed idea, couched in consumer terms with more particulars for clarification. A concept is then presented to consumers for initial feedback in the form of a concept test. This presents consumers with a short descriptive paragraph and an accompanying visual.

Concept tests are external evaluations of the new product idea, rather than the actual product itself. Several key issues are addressed during concept testing, such as how the customer perceives the product, who would use it, and how it would be used. The purpose of these evaluations is to get feedback on the strengths and weaknesses of the concepts, and understand what further modifications are required. Concept tests will result in some concepts being eliminated and others surfacing as more promising opportunities that require further investigation. One may ask why product prototypes are not presented to consumers

business analysis
Financial projections on the impact of bringing the new product to market and selling it in the future

development
The new product idea is turned into a prototype for further consumer research and manufacturing tests

at this point. Product prototypes are typically expensive to develop, and a basic concept test avoids this unnecessary expense. It is also premature to develop a product prototype before a final concept is determined.

Once a clear concept has surfaced during this stage, further research is required to determine the specific elements of the marketing mix that will help the product succeed in the marketplace. Consumers need to be probed on elements such as pricing, brand names, and advertising ideas.

Step 4: Business Analysis

After the concept tests have determined which product, or line of products, are strong new product candidates, the **business analysis** step is necessary. This involves conducting financial projections on bringing the new product to market and selling it in the future. Typical financial projections for a new product cover a three-year period, and often look five years into the future. Financial projections involve sales and revenue forecasts, cost projections, and budget requirements for marketing support. Marketers need to initially establish the positioning of the product in the market and what marketing elements are needed for a successful launch. The new product is also studied to determine whether it can, and should, be protected with a patent, trademark, or copyright.

The business analysis step requires marketers to determine market share projections, price points, cost parameters, special discounts, distribution requirements, research needs, and all the marketing communications programs needed to ensure product success. Marketers also need to understand whether the product will require an investment in new machinery and whether it will cannibalize the sales of existing products. At this point in the new product development process, marketers are checking the commercial viability of the new product. This requires strong analytical skills and the ability to understand the dynamics of the market. A marketer must also be able to anticipate competitive reactions, and foresee target market needs.

The business analysis stage results in profit projections. Marketers review these projections, taking a realistic view of the product and the market to decide whether the concept has real financial merit. Often at this stage, one can easily take an optimistic view, but it is important for marketers to be as realistic as possible and consider severe competitive reactions to their launch. If the product can meet sales, profit, and market share targets, then the new product development process will continue onto the next step. If not, marketers may reassess the concept, going back to consumers to conduct further research. It is important for marketers at this point to stop the process if the concept has little merit and weak profit forecasts. This is usually the last checkpoint before significant resources are invested in creating a *prototype*, a full-scale operating model of the product.

> *"The business analysis stage results in profit projections."*

Step 5: Development

New product ideas that survive the business analysis step proceed to actual **development**, turning the idea into a prototype for further consumer research and manufacturing tests. This step is considerably complex, involving laboratory and consumer tests to ensure that the product consistently meets legal and quality control requirements. Manufacturing trials are also conducted to eliminate manufacturing problems and to reduce costs.

This step can be time consuming with some products requiring extensive testing before they can be safely brought to market. Pharmaceutical products,

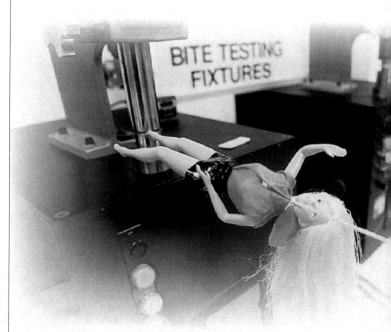

children's toys, cars, and food products that require shelf-life tests are examples that fall into this category. Mattel, for example, extensively tests its Barbie dolls to ensure that their heads cannot be detached from their bodies by small children biting on the head. Testing involves clamping the doll's head in steel jaws and pulling on the doll's head with a wire. Similarly, car manufacturers crash-test cars to determine safety standards.

The advantage of the development step is that it allows marketers to take actual product prototypes into consumer research. This may be needed to further probe elements of the marketing mix. In some instances, ambivalence may still exist on the subtleties of brand names, packaging, and pricing. Advertising campaigns may also require feedback on the clarity of the communication.

Step 6: Test Marketing Test marketing involves offering a product for sale on a limited basis in a defined geographic area. This test is done to determine whether consumers will actually buy the product, and to what extent. Marketers may use this opportunity to test different marketing approaches to support the product. Only about a third of test markets are successful enough for the product to move onto the next step and be fully launched into the market.

In Canada, test markets are conducted in cities such as London, Edmonton, and Moncton. These cities are good candidates as their population is representative of Canada in general. The media in these cities is also isolated, meaning that a company can advertise and test special promotions and be able to measure their success. Using tracking systems by firms such as AC Nielsen, marketers can correlate local advertising campaigns to in-store purchases by using data from store scanners.

The main drawbacks of test markets are that they are expensive to conduct and they immediately alert the competition. Competitors can easily sabotage test markets by altering their own pricing and marketing support to render the test market as unsuccessful. These issues are so real that many marketers do not embark on test markets, relying on research to provide good direction for a full product launch.

Technology is assisting marketers by creating simulated test markets through a number of software programs. An emerging trend uses virtual reality testing that allows marketers to present consumers with a range of experiences such as simulated store environments that allow product interaction. Elumens Corporation has developed VisionDome, which can accommodate up to 45 people at a time and provide them with an interactive 3-D experience.[12]

test marketing
Offering a new product for sale on a limited basis in a defined geographic area to assess its success

commercialization
When the new product is brought to market with full-scale production, sales, and marketing support

ask yourself

1. What occurs in the screening and evaluation step of the new product development process?

2. What is the purpose of the business analysis step in the new product development process?

3. What are the advantages and disadvantages of a test market?

Step 7: Commercialization Commercialization is the step when the new product is brought to market with full-scale production, sales, and marketing support. Companies proceed very carefully at the commercialization stage because this is the most expensive stage for most new products. To minimize the risk of financial failure, many companies use regional rollouts, introducing the product sequentially into geographical areas of the country to allow production levels and marketing activities to build gradually. Grocery product manufacturers and some telephone service providers are examples of firms that use this strategy.

Marketing plays a crucial role in the success of a new product, and marketers need to intimately understand their consumers and what is important to their purchase decisions. Each element of the marketing mix needs to be carefully crafted to help make a new product successful. The example of the PC Blue Menu line evolving from the TGTBT line of President's Choice products reminds us that all elements play a crucial role in new product success.

> ## "TO MINIMIZE THE RISK OF FINANCIAL FAILURE, MANY COMPANIES USE REGIONAL ROLLOUTS."

Summary...*just the facts*

- Product life cycles are the stages that a new product goes through from its initial introduction through to growth, maturity, and decline.

- The shapes of a product life cycle vary depending on the industry, the competition, technological innovation, and the marketing of the product.

- Product life cycles can be extended through various marketing techniques, which encourage new and current users to keep purchasing the product and use it in new ways.

- There are many types of new products ranging from slight product modifications, to more innovative changes, to the more radical innovations we see in the market.

- The adoption curve shows the sequential diffusion and acceptance of an innovation into the market by consumers.

- New products must have a distinct point of difference to enjoy long-term success in the market.

- From a strategic point of view, companies can follow a combination of approaches to innovation including market penetration, product development, market development, and diversification.

- The new product development process follows seven steps: (1) new product development strategy, (2) idea generation, (3) screening and evaluation, (4) business analysis, (5) development, (6) test marketing, and (7) commercialization.

adoption curve *p. 146*
business analysis *p. 152*
concept tests *p. 151*
commercialization *p. 153*
continuous innovations *p. 145*
development *p. 152*
fad *p. 141*
fashion product *p. 141*

harvesting *p. 140*
high-learning product *p. 141*
idea generation *p. 150*
low-learning product *p. 141*
minor innovations *p. 145*
new product development
 process *p. 150*

new product development
 strategy *p. 150*
product life cycle *p. 136*
radical innovations *p. 146*
screening and evaluation *p. 150*
test marketing *p. 153*

Check out the Online Learning Centre at **www.mcgrawhill.ca/olc/thecore**
for chapter application questions, discussion activities, Internet exercises, and video cases.

Pricing

Pricing is a complex issue in marketing, requiring both analytical and strategic thinking. Marketers must have a clear understanding of what prices the market will bear, how competitors will react, and what their target market is willing to pay. Marketers need to have a tight grasp on their product costs so that accurate profit forecasts can be made.

Judith Shaw is a successful small business owner who understands that getting your facts right is the key to success. With a strong background in market research, Shaw found her entrepreneurial spirit by following her dream and passion to run her own small business. Nearly Famous Enterprises Inc. was launched in 1989 as a home-based business, expanding into a thriving company which now has 8 warehouse employees and 17 sales representatives. Nearly Famous Enterprises has Canadian distribution rights to a number of U.S. product lines in the gift, card, stationary, toy, and souvenir categories. These products are sold through retailers such as Hallmark, Indigo/Chapters, Mastermind Toys, PharmaSave, and Value Drug Mart.

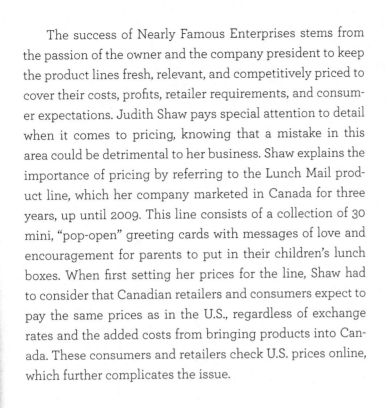

The success of Nearly Famous Enterprises stems from the passion of the owner and the company president to keep the product lines fresh, relevant, and competitively priced to cover their costs, profits, retailer requirements, and consumer expectations. Judith Shaw pays special attention to detail when it comes to pricing, knowing that a mistake in this area could be detrimental to her business. Shaw explains the importance of pricing by referring to the Lunch Mail product line, which her company marketed in Canada for three years, up until 2009. This line consists of a collection of 30 mini, "pop-open" greeting cards with messages of love and encouragement for parents to put in their children's lunch boxes. When first setting her prices for the line, Shaw had to consider that Canadian retailers and consumers expect to pay the same prices as in the U.S., regardless of exchange rates and the added costs from bringing products into Canada. These consumers and retailers check U.S. prices online, which further complicates the issue.

Shaw points out that there are many hidden costs to bringing products into Canada from the U.S. There are the obvious factors such as exchange rate fluctuations, but Shaw explains that for companies such as Nearly Famous Enterprises, which bring items across the U.S. border, there are also brokerage fees required to get the products into Canada, applicable GST taxes, fuel surcharges due to rising gas prices, high freight and transportation costs that transport companies levy when the destination is in Canada, and duties that may apply to a number of products coming into the country. These hidden costs for products such as Lunch Mail can add 12 percent to 18 percent to the cost of each pack of 30 cards. Shaw explains that she has no control over these hidden costs and needs to accurately estimate any changes that she foresees in the near future because retailers do not readily accept price increases mid-year. With the volatility of exchange rates, the uncertainty of world financial markets, and the ever unpredictable price of gas, these hidden costs become major uncontrollable variables for businesses such as Nearly Famous Enterprises and can have an enormous impact on profits.

When Judith Shaw set her prices for Lunch Mail, she considered what consumers and retailers were likely to pay, her costs from the U.S. supplier, and then the hidden costs to bring the products into Canada. The line was launched into the Canadian market in January 2005 and sold across the country at a retail price of $5.50 for a pack of 30 cards. Always thinking ahead, Shaw fully expects that the product will receive a wholesale price due to higher labour charges being experienced in China and the U.S., and the impact of rising petroleum prices. Shaw tells us that, "In the world of business you always have to keep moving, changing your mix and anticipating your next move." She constantly assesses the marketplace in terms of trends and demographic needs, ensuring that her company has the products to satisfy changing demands, and then she sets a price where she can make a profit. She never takes her eye off the pricing issue, knowing that a mistake could have dire consequences for her company.

What does the future hold for Nearly Famous Enterprises? The firm is moving on from the Lunch Mail products, refreshing its lines with fresh new items that meet the trends they see in the market. The company is introducing a line of gifts and cards, designed for people to give to grandparents—a growing area due to the aging of the baby boomers. The line includes Brag Books, Ultra-Sound Greetings, Sweet Something Frames, Holiday Keepsakes, and Treasured Portrait Frames. Regardless of the product line, Shaw has gathered her facts and will set her prices to meet consumer and retailer needs and so that her company can make a profit. Visit the business's website at www.nearlyfamous.ca.

Chapter 9 introduces the all-important question of pricing, and its many implications for marketing. This topic focuses on the price element of the 4Ps that make up the marketing mix. 🍎

Nature and Importance of Price

L◯₁ The price paid for goods and services goes by many names. You pay *tuition* for your education, *rent* for an apartment, *interest* on a bank credit card, and a *premium* for car insurance. Your dentist or physician charges you a *fee*, a professional or social organization charges *dues*, and airlines charge a *fare*. And what you pay for clothes or a haircut is termed a *price*.

What Is a Price?

These examples highlight the many and varied ways that price plays a part in our daily lives. From a marketing viewpoint, **price** is the money or other considerations, including other goods and services, exchanged

The Core: Chapter 9

Pricing has many implications for marketing.

Marketers need to know how pricing impacts their target market and their competitors.

for the ownership or use of a product. Recently, Wilkinson Sword exchanged some of its knives for advertising used to promote its razor blades. This practice of exchanging goods and services for other goods and services rather than for money is called barter. These transactions account for billions of dollars annually in domestic and international trade.

For most products, money is exchanged. However, the amount paid is not always the same as the list, or quoted, price because of discounts, allowances, and extra fees. While discounts, allowances, and rebates make the effective price lower, other marketing tactics raise the real price. One new pricing tactic is to use "special fees" and "surcharges." This practice is driven by consumers' zeal for low prices combined with the ease of making price comparisons on the Internet. Buyers are more willing to pay extra fees than a higher list price, so sellers use add-on charges as a way of having the consumer pay more without raising the list price. Examples of such special fees include a Telus Mobility "system licensing charge" and "911 emergency service access charge" that increase the monthly cellphone bill, or an environmental surcharge on new tires and batteries for cars in some provinces.

All these different factors that increase or decrease the price are put together in a "price equation," which is shown for several different products in Figure 9–1.

Suppose that you decide you want to buy a Bugatti Veyron, the world's fastest production car, which can move you from 0 to 100 kmph in 2.5 seconds with a top speed of 422 kmph. The Veyron has a list price of $1.5 million. However, if you put $500,000 down now and finance the balance over the next year, you will receive

a rebate of $100,000 off the list price. For your 2000 Honda Civic DX 4-door sedan that has 100,000 kilometres and is in fair condition, you are given a trade-in allowance of $4,350.[1]

The finance fee on the $500,000 down is $41,974 and a $5,000 destination charge to ship the car from Europe.

Applying the price equation (as shown in Figure 9–1) to your purchase, your final price is:

$$\text{Final price} = \text{List price} - (\text{Incentives} + \text{Allowances}) + \text{Extra fees}$$
$$= \$1,500,000 - (\$100,000 + \$4,350) + (\$41,974 + \$5,000)$$
$$= \$1,442,624$$

Are you still interested in buying this car?

Figure 9–1
The price of three different purchases

ITEM PURCHASED	PRICE EQUATION			
	PRICE	= LIST PRICE	INCENTIVES AND − ALLOWANCES	+ EXTRA FEES
New car bought by an individual	Final price	= List price	− Rebate Cash discount Old car trade-in	+ Financing charges Special accessories Destination charges
Term in university bought by a student	Tuition	= Published tuition	− Scholarship Other financial aid	+ Special activity fees
Merchandise bought from a wholesaler by a retailer	Invoice price	= List price	− Quantity discount Cash discount Seasonal discount Functional or trade discount	+ Penalty for late payment

Price as an Indicator of Value

From a consumer's standpoint, price is often used to indicate value when it is compared with the perceived benefits such as quality, durability, and so on of a product or service. Specifically, **value** is the ratio of perceived benefits to price,[2] or

$$\text{Value} = \frac{\text{Perceived benefits}}{\text{Price}}$$

This relationship shows that for a given price, as perceived benefits increase, value increases. For example, if you're used to paying $13.99 for a medium pizza, wouldn't a large pizza at the same price be more valuable? Conversely, for a given price, value decreases when perceived benefits decrease.

In a survey of home furnishing buyers, 84 percent agreed with the statement: "The higher the price, the higher the quality."[3] For example, Kohler introduced a walk-in bathtub that is safer for children and the elderly. Although priced higher than conventional step-in bathtubs, it has proven very successful because buyers are willing to pay more for what they perceive as the benefit of extra safety.

Creative marketers, aware that consumers often compare value between competing products, engage in *value pricing*. Value pricing is the practice of increasing a product's benefits while maintaining or decreasing price. "Super-sizing" at fast-food restaurants is one example; here, value comes from getting "more bang for your buck."

Price in the Marketing Mix

Pricing is a critical decision made by a marketing executive because price has a direct effect on a firm's profits. This is apparent from a firm's **profit equation**:

Profit = Total revenue − Total cost
       = (Unit price × Quantity sold) − Total cost

What makes this relationship even more complicated is that price affects the quantity sold, as illustrated with demand curves later in this chapter, because the quantity sold sometimes affects a firm's costs because of efficiency of production, price also indirectly affects costs. Thus, pricing decisions influence both total revenue (sales) and total cost, which makes pricing one of the most important decisions marketing executives face.

> *Creative marketers, aware that consumers often compare value between competing products, engage in value pricing.*

General Pricing Approaches

LO2 A key to a marketing manager's setting a final price for a product is to find an "approximate price level" to use as a reasonable starting point. Four common approaches to helping find this approximate price level are demand-oriented, cost-oriented, profit-oriented, and competition-oriented approaches (see Figure 9–2 on page 161). Although these approaches are discussed separately below, some of them overlap, and an effective marketing manager will consider several in searching for an approximate price level.

Demand-Oriented Approaches

Demand-oriented approaches emphasize factors underlying expected customer tastes and preferences more than such factors as cost, profit, and competition when selecting a price level.

Skimming Pricing   A firm introducing a new product can use *skimming pricing,* setting the highest initial price that those customers really desiring the

Figure 9–2
Four approaches for selecting an approximate price level

Demand-oriented approaches	Cost-oriented approaches	Profit-oriented approaches	Competition-oriented approaches
• Skimming • Penetration • Prestige • Odd-even • Target • Bundle • Yield management	• Standard markup • Cost-plus	• Target profit • Target return on sales • Target return on investment	• Customary • Above, at, or below market • Loss leader

product are willing to pay. These customers are not very price sensitive because they weigh the new product's price, quality, and ability to satisfy their needs against the same characteristics of substitutes. As the demand of these customers is satisfied, the firm lowers the price to attract a more price-sensitive segment. Thus, skimming pricing gets its name from skimming successive layers of "cream," or customer segments, as prices are lowered in a series of steps.

In early 2003, many manufacturers of flat-screen TVs were pricing them at about $5,000 and using skimming pricing because many prospective customers were willing to buy the product immediately at the high price. Over time, prices of flat-screen TVs have dropped considerably.

Penetration Pricing Setting a low initial price on a new product to appeal immediately to the mass market is *penetration pricing*, the exact opposite of skimming pricing. Nintendo consciously chose a penetration strategy when it introduced the Nintendo Wii, its popular video game console.

In some situations, penetration pricing may follow skimming pricing. A company might price a product high at first to attract price-insensitive consumers. After the company has earned back the money spent on research and development and introductory promotions, it uses penetration pricing to appeal to a broader segment of the population and increase market share.[4]

Prestige Pricing Although consumers tend to buy more of a product when the price is lower, sometimes the reverse is true. If consumers are using price as a measure of the quality of an item, a company runs the risk of appearing to offer a low-quality product if it sets the price below a certain point. *Prestige pricing* involves setting a high price so that quality- or status-conscious consumers will be attracted to the product and buy it. Rolls-Royce cars, Chanel perfume, and Cartier jewellery have an element of prestige pricing in them and may not sell as well at lower prices than at higher ones.[5]

Odd-Even Pricing Suppose that Sears offers a Craftsman radial saw for $599.99, and Zellers sells Windex glass cleaner on sale for 99 cents. Why not simply price these items at $600 and $1, respectively? These firms are using *odd-even pricing*, which involves setting prices a few dollars or cents under an even number. The presumption is that consumers see the Sears radial saw as priced at "something over $500" rather than "about $600." The effect this strategy has is psychological: $599.99 *feels* significantly lower than $600—even though there is only one cent difference. There is some evidence to suggest this does work. However, research suggests that overuse of odd-ending prices tends to mute its effect on demand.[6]

The Cost of Illegally Downloaded Music

Number of unpaid downloaded files annually **1.6** billion

Estimated lost revenue **$1.6** billion

Percentage of teenagers (in a U.K. survey) who would not pay to download music **58** percent

marketing meter

Sources: "The Problem (Ontario edition)," *Toronto Star*, February 20, 2008; Kevin Parrish, "Fewer People Downloading Music Illegally," Tom's Guide, October 13, 2008, www.tomsguide.com/us/Music-Illegal-Download-MP3,news-2755.html.

The Alligator's New Look

Marketing NewsFlash

The Lacoste alligator (actually a long-misidentified crocodile) has long been a symbol of preppy fashion, a staple of country clubs and tennis courts. Tennis player Rene Lacoste marketed the first-ever polo shirt in the 1930s, and the "alligator shirt" was at its most popular in the U.S. in the late 1970s and early 1980s. The brand lost its high standing shortly after that period, and the then-owner of the brand, General Mills, cut the prices and the quality of the product, depositing the shirts at discount retailers such as Wal-Mart. The U.S. rights to the logo (rebranded as Izod) were sold back to the Lacoste family by General Mills in 1992. The brand continued to suffer from poor sales in the U.S. until 2002, when Robert Siegel, Dockers creator and former Levi Strauss executive, came on board at Lacoste USA and revitalized the brand.

Siegel raised prices, added new designs, and made the clothes harder to find at retail, removing the shirts from non-luxury retailers like T.J. Maxx and a number of Macy's locations, narrowing distribution to high-end shops such as Neiman Marcus, Barneys, and Nordstrom. Siegel also borrowed a page from such retailers as Burberry and Coach, opening free-standing Lacoste boutiques in affluent shopping districts along both U.S. coasts and in Texas. One of Siegel's goals was to turn Lacoste into a high-end brand, not just a preppy emblem, and since Siegel began his overhaul of Lacoste USA, North American revenues grew 70 percent in 2005, after a 125 percent rise in 2004, demonstrating the success of his plan.

Sources: Greg Lindsay, "The Alligator's New Look: A phenomenal U.S. turnaround has positioned Lacoste to move past polo shirts," Business 2.0, Vol. 7, Iss. 3 (April 2006): 68; Eric Wilson, "Made preppy crocodile global symbol," Montreal Gazette, March 23, 2006, p. C6.

Target Pricing Manufacturers will sometimes estimate the price that the ultimate consumer would be willing to pay for a product. They then work backward through markups taken by retailers and wholesalers to determine what price they can charge for the product. This practice, called *target pricing*, results in the manufacturer deliberately adjusting the composition and features of a product to achieve the target price to consumers. Canon uses this practice for pricing its cameras, as does Heinz for its complete line of pet foods.[7]

Bundle Pricing A frequently used demand-oriented pricing practice is *bundle pricing*, which is the marketing of two or more products in a single "package" price. For example, Air Canada offers vacation packages that include airfare, car rental, and hotel. Bundle pricing is based on the idea that consumers value the package more than the individual items. This is due to benefits received from not having to make separate purchases as well as increased satisfaction from one item in the presence of another. Bundle pricing often provides a lower total cost to buyers and lower marketing costs to sellers.[8]

Yield Management Pricing Have you ever been on an airplane and discovered the person next to you paid a lower price for her ticket than you paid? Annoying, isn't it? But what you observed is *yield management pricing*, the charging of different prices to maximize revenue for a set amount of capacity at any given time.[9] Airlines, hotels, and car rental firms engage in capacity management by varying prices based on time, day, week, or season to match demand and supply.

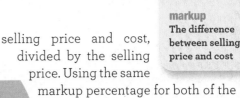

markup
The difference between selling price and cost

selling price and cost, divided by the selling price. Using the same markup percentage for both of the above approaches will result in a different selling price (see the example in Figure 9–3).

Consider the example of a product that is produced by a manufacturer and sold to a wholesaler, who in turn sells it to a retailer, who then sells it to a consumer. The product will be subjected to a series of markups as shown below.

ask yourself

1. What is the profit equation?
2. What is the difference between skimming and penetration pricing?
3. What is odd-even pricing?

Cost-Oriented Approaches

With cost-oriented approaches, a price is more affected by the cost side of the pricing problem than the demand side. Price is set by looking at the production and marketing costs and then adding enough to cover direct expenses, overhead, and profit.

Standard Markup Pricing In order to make a profit, firms sell their products at a price that exceeds their costs of producing or sourcing the items and the costs of marketing them. Conventionally, the difference between the selling price of an item and its cost is referred to as the **markup** and this is normally expressed as a percentage.

Manufacturers commonly express markup as a percentage of cost, which is the difference between selling price and cost, divided by cost. This is also referred to as *standard markup*. Manufacturers use this approach because they are concerned most of the time with costs.

Parties who buy and resell products, for example wholesalers and retailers, are nearly always dealing with selling prices. They often express markup as a percentage of price, which is the difference between

Manufacturer's cost:	$50.00
Markup % (based on cost):	40%
Markup $:	$20.00
Selling price to wholesaler:	**$70.00**
Wholesaler cost:	**$70.00**
Markup% (based on price):	15%
Markup $:	$12.35
Selling price to retailer:	**$82.35**
Retailer cost:	**$82.35**
Markup % (based on price):	35%
Markup $:	$44.34
Retailer selling price:	**$126.69**

This may surprise you to find out that a product costing $50 to produce can end up costing a consumer more than twice that much when bought at a retailer, but this is not unusual. It is important to remember that markup is necessary at each stage so that companies involved can cover their costs of purchasing the item, can pay to market it to the next stage in the distribution channel, and can generate some profit. The markups shown would be representative of some items such as designer furniture.

Figure 9–3
Markup examples

MARKUP TABLE BASED ON SELLING PRICE	$	%
Selling price	$75.00	100%*
− (minus) Cost	$60.00	80%
= (equals) Markup	$15.00	20%

* Price is always 100% when markup is relative to price.

MARKUP TABLE BASED ON COST	$	%
Selling price	$72.00	120%
− (minus) Cost	$60.00	100%**
= (equals) Markup	$12.00	20%

** Cost is always 100% when markup is relative to cost.

This percentage markup varies depending on the type of retail store (such as furniture, clothing, or grocery) and on the product involved. High-volume products usually have smaller markups than do low-volume products. Supermarkets such as Loblaws and Safeway mark up staple items like sugar, flour, and dairy products 10 percent to 25 percent, whereas they mark up discretionary items like snack foods and candy 25 percent to 47 percent. These markups must cover all expenses of the store, pay for overhead costs, and contribute something to profits. For supermarkets, these markups, which may appear very large, can result in only a 1 percent profit on sales revenue.

Cost-Plus Pricing

Many manufacturers, professional services, and construction firms use a variation of standard markup pricing. *Cost-plus pricing* involves summing the total unit cost of providing a product or service and adding a specific amount to the cost to arrive at a price. Cost-plus pricing is the most commonly used method to set prices for business products.[10] Increasingly, however, this method is finding favour among business-to-business marketers in the service sector. For example, the rising cost of legal fees has prompted some law firms to adopt a cost-plus pricing approach. Rather than billing business clients on an hourly basis, lawyers and their clients agree on a fixed fee based on expected costs plus a profit for the law firm. Many advertising agencies now use this approach. Here, the client agrees to pay the agency a fee based on the cost of its work plus some agreed-on profit.[11]

Profit-Oriented Approaches

A company may choose to balance both revenues and costs to set price using profit-oriented approaches. These might either involve setting a target of a specific dollar volume of profit or expressing this target profit as a percentage of sales or investment.

Target Profit Pricing   When a firm sets an annual target of a specific dollar amount of profit, this is called *target profit pricing*. For example, if you owned a picture frame store and wanted to achieve a target profit of $7,000 in the coming year, how much would you need to charge for each frame? Because profit depends on revenues and costs, you would have to know your costs and then estimate how many frames you would sell. Let's assume, based on sales in previous years, you expect to frame 1,000 pictures next year. The cost of your time and materials to frame an average picture is $22, while your overhead expenses (rent, manager salaries, and so on) are $26,000. Finally, your goal is to achieve a profit of $7,000. How do you calculate your price per picture?

$$\text{Profit} = \text{Total revenue} - \text{Total costs}$$
$$= (\text{Pictures sold} \times \text{Price/picture}) -$$
$$[(\text{Cost/picture} \times \text{Pictures sold}) + \text{overhead cost}]$$

Solving for price per picture, the equation becomes:

$$\text{Price/picture} = \frac{\text{Profit} + [(\text{Cost/picture} \times \text{Pictures sold}) + \text{overhead cost}]}{\text{Pictures sold}}$$

$$= \frac{\$7,000 + [(\$22 \times 1,000) + \$26,000]}{1,000}$$

$$= \frac{\$7,000 + \$48,000}{1,000}$$

$$= \$55 \text{ per picture}$$

Clearly, this pricing method depends on an accurate estimate of demand. Because demand is often difficult to predict, this method has the potential for disaster if the estimate is too high. Generally, a target profit pricing strategy is best for firms offering new or unique products, without a lot of competition. What if other frame stores in your area were charging $40 per framed picture? As a marketing manager, you'd have to offer increased customer value with your more expensive frames, lower your costs, or settle for less profit.

Target Return-on-Sales Pricing   Firms such as supermarkets often use *target return-on-sales pricing* to set prices that will give them a profit that is a specified percentage—say, 1 percent—of the sales volume. This pricing method is often used because of the difficulty in establishing a benchmark of sales or investment to show how much of a firm's effort is needed to achieve the target.

Target Return-on-Investment Pricing

Firms such as General Motors and many public utilities use *target return-on-investment pricing* to set prices to achieve a return-on-investment (ROI) target, such as a percentage that is mandated by its board of directors or regulators. For example, a hydro utility may decide to seek 10 percent ROI. If its investment in plant and equipment is $50 million, it would need to set the price of hydro to its customers at a level that results in $5 million a year in profits.

Competition-Oriented Approaches

Rather than emphasize demand, cost, or profit factors, a company's approach may be based on an analysis of what competitors are doing.

Customary Pricing For some products where tradition, a standardized channel of distribution, or other competitive factors dictate the price, *customary pricing* is used. Candy bars offered through standard vending machines have a customary price of a dollar, and a significant departure from this price may result in a loss of sales for the manufacturer. Hershey typically has changed the amount of chocolate in its candy bars depending on the price of raw chocolate, rather than vary its customary retail price so that it can continue selling through vending machines.

> ## AMONG WATCH MANUFACTURERS, ROLEX TAKES PRIDE IN EMPHASIZING THAT IT MAKES ONE OF THE MOST EXPENSIVE WATCHES YOU CAN BUY—A CLEAR EXAMPLE OF ABOVE-MARKET PRICING.

Above-, At-, or Below-Market Pricing The "market price" of a product is what customers are generally willing to pay, not necessarily the price that the firm sets. For most products, it is difficult to identify a specific market price for a product or product class. Still, marketing managers often have a subjective feel for the competitors' price or the market price. Using this benchmark, they then may deliberately choose a strategy of *above-, at-,* or *below-market pricing*.

Among watch manufacturers, Rolex takes pride in emphasizing that it makes one of the most expensive watches you can buy—a clear example of above-market pricing. Manufacturers of national brands of clothing such as Christian Dior and retailers such as Holt Renfrew deliberately set higher prices for their products than those seen at Sears.

iTunes in Battle with Wal-Mart

Marketing **NewsFlash**

The price of a song downloaded on iTunes has begun to cost the music industry. Given the constant problems that the music industry faces from music piracy and lowered revenues, it has long maintained that the 99-cent-per-track price that iTunes charges is too low. The industry will soon have another blow against it, as retailer Wal-Mart announced in early 2008 that it would reveal a plan to sell certain albums for as low as US$5. It also announced that it might introduce a tiered pricing system for its CD sales, with hit albums retailing for $10—matching iTunes price—and other CDs selling from $5 to $12.

Wal-Mart is considering these steps as it looks to lose its position as the largest North American music seller to iTunes by the end of 2008. Wal-Mart hopes to hold on to its position by changing its prices to better match those of iTunes (whose rise in popularity is influenced by its low prices), but this measure could possibly damage the music industry.

Source: Vito Pilieci, "Wal-Mart, iTunes heat up music battle; retail giant ready to sell CDs for as little as $5; report says Apple could be No. 1 seller," *The Ottawa Citizen*, March 4, 2008, p. D1.

Large mass-merchandise chains such as Sears and The Bay generally use at-market pricing. These chains often are seen as establishing the going market price in the minds of their competitors. They also provide a reference price for competitors that use above- and below-market pricing.

In contrast, a number of firms use below-market pricing. Zellers is one retailer that positions itself this way. Manufacturers of generic products and retailers that offer their own private brands of products ranging from peanut butter to shampoo deliberately set prices for these products about 8 percent to 10 percent below the prices of nationally branded competitive products such as Skippy peanut butter or Herbal Essences shampoo.

Loss-Leader Pricing For a special promotion, retail stores deliberately sell a product below its regular price to attract attention. The purpose of this loss-leader pricing is not to increase sales but to attract customers in hopes they will buy other products as well, particularly the discretionary items with large markups. For example, Wal-Mart sells CDs at a very low retail price to attract customers to their stores.

Dramatic iPhone Price Decrease

Date	Price (US$)
June 2007	$599
September 2007	$399

Sources: Bridget Carey, "Dropping iPhone price = angry Apple customers," *The Miami Herald*, September 6, 2007, http://miamiherald.typepad.com/cache_carey/2007/09/dropping-iphone.html; Rhys Blakely, "Apple cuts third off price of its iPhone 68 days after launch," *The Times*, September 7, 2007, http://business.timesonline.co.uk/tol/business/industry_sectors/technology/article2398965.ece.

Estimating Demand and Revenue

LO 3 Basic to setting a product's price is the extent of customer demand for it. Marketing executives must also translate this estimate of customer demand into estimates of revenues the firm expects to receive.

Fundamentals of Estimating Demand

Newsweek decided to conduct a pricing experiment at newsstands in 11 cities. In one city, newsstand buyers paid $2.25. In five other cities, newsstand buyers paid the regular $2.00 price. In another city, the price was $1.50, and in the remaining four cities it was only $1.00. By comparison, the regular newsstand price for a competing magazine, *Time*, was $1.95. Why did *Newsweek* conduct the experiment? According to a *Newsweek* executive, "We wanted to figure out what the demand curve for our magazine at the newsstand is."[12]

The Demand Curve A **demand curve** shows the number of products that will be sold at a given price. Demand curve D1 in Figure 9–4A shows the newsstand demand for *Newsweek* under the existing conditions. Note that as price falls, more people decide to buy and unit sales increase. But price is not the complete story in estimating demand. Economists emphasize three other key factors:

1. *Consumer tastes*. These depend on many factors such as demographics, culture, and technology. Because consumer tastes can change quickly, up-to-date marketing research is essential.

2. *Price and availability of similar products*. The laws of demand work for one's competitors, too. If the price of *Time* magazine falls, more people will buy it. That then means fewer people will buy *Newsweek*. *Time* is considered by economists to be a substitute for *Newsweek*. Online magazines are also a substitute—one for which availability has increased tremendously in recent years. The point to remember is that as the price of substitutes falls or their availability increases, the demand for a product (*Newsweek*, in this case) will fall.

3. *Consumer income.* In general, as real consumer income (allowing for inflation) increases, demand for a product also increases.

The first of these two factors influences what consumers *want* to buy, and the third affects what they *can* buy. Along with price, these are often called *demand factors,* or factors that determine consumers' willingness and ability to pay for goods and services. It is often very difficult to estimate demand for new products, especially because consumer likes and dislikes are often so difficult to read clearly.

Movement along versus Shift of a Demand Curve

Demand curve D_1 in Figure 9–4A shows that as the price is lowered from $2.00 to $1.50, the quantity demanded increases from 3 million (Q_1) to 4.5 million (Q_2) units per year. This is an example of a *movement along a demand curve* and assumes that other factors (consumer tastes, price and availability of substitutes, and consumer income) remain unchanged.

What if some of these factors change? For example, if advertising causes more people to want *Newsweek,* newsstand distribution is increased, or if consumer incomes rise, then the demand increases. Now the original curve, D_1 (the blue line in Figure 9–4B), no longer represents the demand; a new curve must be drawn (D_2). Economists call this a *shift in the demand curve*—in this case, a shift to the right, from D_1 to D_2. This increased demand means that more *Newsweek* magazines are wanted for a given price: At a price of $2, the demand is 6 million units per year (Q_3) on D_2 rather than 3 million units per year (Q_1) on D_1.

What price did *Newsweek* select after conducting its experiment? It kept the price at $2.00. However, through expanded newsstand distribution and more aggressive advertising, *Newsweek* was later able to shift its demand curve to the right and charge a price of $2.50 without affecting its newsstand volume.

Price Elasticity of Demand

Marketing managers must also pay attention to *price elasticity,* a key consideration related to the product's demand curve. Price elasticity refers to how sensitive consumer demand and the firm's revenues are to changes in the product's price.

A product with *elastic demand* is one in which a slight decrease in price results in a relatively large increase in demand, or units sold. The reverse is also true: With elastic demand, a slight increase in price results in a relatively large decrease in demand. Marketing experiments on cola, coffee, and snack foods show them often to have elastic demand. So marketing managers may cut price to increase the demand, the units sold, and total revenue for one of these products, depending on what competitors' prices are. The demand for many consumer products is elastic—think jeans, DVDs, and car stereos.

Figure 9–4
Illustrative demand curves for *Newsweek*

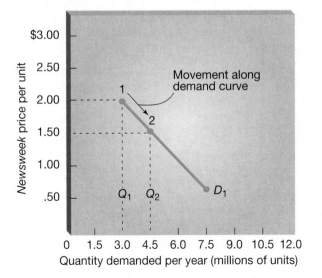

A Demand curve under initial conditions

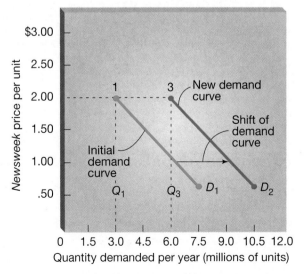

B Shift in the demand curve with different conditions

In contrast, a product with *inelastic demand* means that slight increases or decreases in price will not significantly affect the demand, or units sold, for the product. Products and services considered as necessities, such as electricity, usually have inelastic demand. What about gasoline for your car? Will an increase of a few cents per litre cause you to drive fewer kilometres and buy less gasoline? No? Then you're like millions of other consumers, which is why gasoline has inelastic demand. This means that an increase of a few cents per litre may have a relatively minor impact on the number of litres sold, and may actually increase the total revenue of the gasoline producer. Inelastic demand is usually a relatively short-term phenomenon. Consumers, when they are faced with high prices for something they have to have, will seek out an alternative, and/or producers will see an opportunity to develop a new product. A hybrid car is, in some ways, a producer's response to high gas prices. Or maybe you could learn to love the bus!

ask yourself

1. What is loss-leader pricing?

2. What are three demand factors other than price that are used in estimating demand?

3. What is the difference between movement along a demand curve and a shift in a demand curve?

Fundamentals of Estimating Revenue

While economists may talk about "demand curves," marketing executives are more likely to speak in terms of "revenues generated." Demand curves lead directly to an essential revenue concept critical to pricing decisions: **total revenue**. As summarized in Figure 9–5, total revenue (TR) equals the unit price (P) times the quantity sold (Q). Using this equation, let's recall our picture frame shop and assume our annual demand has improved so that we can set a price of $100 per picture and sell 400 pictures per year. So,

$$TR = P \times Q$$
$$= \$100 \times 400$$
$$= \$40,000$$

This combination of price and quantity sold annually will give us a total revenue of $40,000 per year. Is that good? Are you making money, making a profit? Total revenue is only part of the profit equation that we saw earlier:

Total profit = Total revenue − Total cost

The next section covers the other part of the profit equation: cost.

Determining Cost, Volume, and Profit Relationships

L4 While revenues are the monies received by the firm from selling its products or services to customers, costs or expenses are the monies the firm pays out to its employees and suppliers. Marketing managers often use break-even analysis to relate revenues and costs, topics covered in this section.

The Importance of Controlling Costs

Understanding the role and behaviour of costs is critical for all marketing decisions, particularly pricing decisions. Many firms go bankrupt because their costs get out of control, causing their total costs to exceed their total revenues over an extended period of time. This is why sophisticated marketing managers make pricing decisions that balance both their revenues and costs.

Figure 9–5
Total revenue concept

Total revenue (TR) is the total money received from the sale of a product. If

TR	=	Total revenue
P	=	Unit price of the product
Q	=	Quantity of the product sold

Then

TR = P × Q

Figure 9–6
Total cost concept

Fixed cost (FC) is the sum of the expenses of the firm that are stable and do not change with the quantity of product that is produced and sold. Examples of fixed costs are rent on the building, executive salaries, and insurance.

Variable cost (VC) is the sum of the expenses of the firm that vary directly with the quantity of product that is produced and sold. Examples are the direct labour and direct materials used in producing the product. Variable cost expressed on a per unit basis is called *unit variable cost (UVC)*.

$$TC = FC + VC$$

Total cost (TC) is the total expense incurred by a firm in producing and marketing the product. Total cost is the sum of fixed cost and variable cost.

Three cost concepts are important in pricing decisions: total cost, fixed cost, and variable cost (Figure 9–6).

Break-Even Analysis

LO ⑤ Marketing managers often employ an approach that considers cost, volume, and profit relationships, based on the profit equation. Break-even analysis is a technique that analyzes the relationship between total revenue and total cost to determine profitability at various levels of output. The *break-even point (BEP)* is the quantity at which total revenue and total cost are equal. Profit comes from any units sold after the BEP has been reached. In terms of the definitions in Figure 9–6,

$$BEP_{Quantity} = \frac{\text{Fixed cost}}{\text{Unit price} - \text{Unit variable cost}}$$

Calculating a Break-Even Point Consider again your picture frame store. Suppose that you wish to identify how many pictures you must sell to cover your fixed cost at a given price. Let's assume demand for your framed pictures has increased, so the average price customers are willing to pay for each picture is $100. Also, suppose your fixed cost (FC) has grown to $28,000 (for real estate taxes, interest on a bank loan, and other fixed expenses) and unit variable cost (UVC) for a picture is now $30 (for labour, glass, frame, and matting). Your break-even quantity ($BEP_{Quantity}$) is 400 pictures, as follows:

$$BEP_{Quantity} = \frac{\text{Fixed cost}}{\text{Unit price} - \text{Unit variable cost}}$$

$$= \frac{\$28,000}{\$100 - \$30}$$

$$= 400 \text{ pictures}$$

The row shaded in blue in Figure 9–7 shows that your break-even quantity at a price of $100 per picture is

Figure 9–7
Calculating a break-even point for a picture frame store

QUANTITY OF PICTURES SOLD (Q)	PRICE PER PICTURE (P)	TOTAL REVENUE (TR) = (P × Q)	UNIT VARIABLE COST (UVC)	TOTAL VARIABLE COST (TVC) = (UVC × Q)	FIXED COST (FC)	TOTAL COST (TC) = (FC + TVC)	PROFIT = (TR − TC)
0	$100	$0	$30	$0	$28,000	$28,000	−$28,000
200	100	20,000	30	6,000	28,000	34,000	−14,000
400	100	40,000	30	12,000	28,000	40,000	0
600	100	60,000	30	18,000	28,000	46,000	14,000
800	100	80,000	30	24,000	28,000	52,000	28,000
1,000	100	100,000	30	30,000	28,000	58,000	42,000
1,200	100	120,000	30	36,000	28,000	64,000	56,000

400 pictures. At less than 400 pictures your picture frame store incurs a loss, and at more than 400 pictures it makes a profit. Figure 9–7 also shows that if you could double your annual picture sales to 800, your store would make a profit of $28,000—the row shaded in brown in the figure.

Figure 9–8 shows a graphic presentation of the break-even analysis, called a *break-even chart*. It shows that total revenue and total cost intersect and are equal at a quantity of 400 pictures sold, which is the break-even point at which profit is exactly $0. You want to do better? If your frame store could double the quantity sold annually to 800 pictures, the graph in Figure 9–8 shows that you can earn an annual profit of $28,000, as shown by the row shaded in brown in Figure 9–7.

Applications of Break-Even Analysis

Because of its simplicity, break-even analysis is used extensively in marketing, most frequently to study the impact on profit of changes in price, fixed cost, and variable cost. The mechanics of break-even analysis are the basis of the widely used electronic spreadsheets offered by computer programs such as Microsoft Excel that permit managers to answer hypothetical "what if" questions about the effect of changes in price and cost on their profit.

Pricing Objectives and Constraints

With such a variety of alternative pricing strategies available, marketing managers must consider the pricing objectives and constraints that will impact their decisions. While pricing objectives frequently reflect corporate goals, pricing constraints often relate to conditions existing in the marketplace.

Identifying Pricing Objectives

Pricing objectives specify the role of price in an organization's marketing and strategic plans. To the extent possible, these pricing objectives are carried to lower levels in the organization, such as in setting objectives for marketing managers responsible for an individual brand. These objectives may change, depending on the financial position of the company as a whole, the success of its products, or the segments in which it is doing business. H. J. Heinz, for example, has specific pricing objectives for its Heinz ketchup brand that vary by country.

Profit Three different objectives relate to a firm's profit, which is often measured in terms of return on investment (ROI). These objectives have different implications for pricing strategy. One objective is *managing for long-run profits*, in which a company—such as many Japanese car or TV set manufacturers—gives up immediate profit in exchange for achieving a higher market share. Products are priced relatively low compared to their cost to develop, but the firm expects to make greater profits later because of its high market share.

A *maximizing current profit* objective, such as for a quarter or year, is common in many firms because the targets can be set and performance measured quickly. North American firms are sometimes criticized for this short-run orientation. As noted earlier, a

ask yourself

1. What is the difference between fixed costs and variable costs?

2. What is a break-even point?

Figure 9–8

Break-even analysis graph for a picture frame store

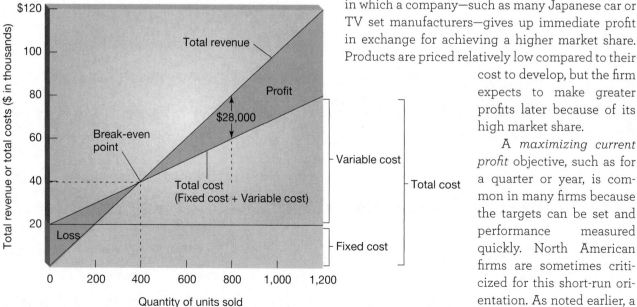

target return objective occurs when a firm sets a profit goal (such as 20 percent for return on investment), usually determined by its board of directors. These three profit objectives have different implications for a firm's pricing objectives.

Another profit consideration for firms such as movie studios and manufacturers is to ensure that those firms in their channels of distribution make adequate profits. For example, Figure 9–9 shows where each dollar of your movie ticket goes. The 51 cents the movie studio gets must cover its profit plus the cost of making and marketing the movie. Although the studio would like more than 51 cents of your dollar, it settles for this amount to make sure theatres and distributors are satisfied and willing to handle its movies.

Sales As long as a firm's profit is high enough for it to remain in business, an objective may be to increase sales revenue, which will in turn lead to increases in market share and profit. Cutting price on one product in a firm's line may increase its sales revenue but reduce those of related products. Objectives related to sales revenue or unit sales have the advantage of being translated easily into meaningful targets for marketing managers responsible for a product line or brand.

Market Share Market share is the ratio of the firm's sales to those of the industry (competitors plus the firm itself). Companies often pursue a market share objective when industry sales are relatively flat or declining. Although increased market share is a primary goal of some firms, others see it as a means to increasing sales and profits.

Volume Many firms use volume, the quantity produced or sold, as a pricing objective. These firms often sell the same product at several different prices, at different times, or in different places in an attempt to match customer demand with the company's production capacity. Using volume as an objective can sometimes be misleading from a profit standpoint. Volume can be increased by using sales incentives (lowering prices, giving rebates, or offering lower interest rates). By doing this, the company chooses to lower profits in the short run to sell its product quickly.

Survival In some instances, profits, sales, and market share are less important objectives of the firm than mere survival. Air Canada has struggled to attract passengers with low fares and aggressive promotions to improve the firm's cash flow. This pricing objective has helped Air Canada to stay alive in the competitive airline industry.

Social Responsibility A firm may forgo higher profit on sales and follow a pricing objective that recognizes its obligations to customers and society in general. Gerber supplies a specially formulated product free of charge to children who cannot tolerate foods based on cow's milk.

Figure 9–9
Where each dollar of your movie ticket goes

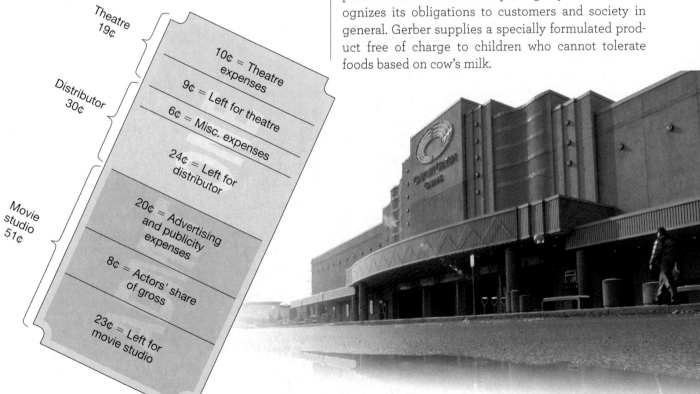

Theatre
19¢

Distributor
30¢

Movie studio
51¢

10¢ = Theatre expenses
9¢ = Left for theatre
6¢ = Misc. expenses
24¢ = Left for distributor
20¢ = Advertising and publicity expenses
8¢ = Actors' share of gross
23¢ = Left for movie studio

Identifying Pricing Constraints

Factors that limit the range of price a firm may set are **pricing constraints**. Consumer demand for the product clearly affects the price that can be charged. Other constraints on price vary from factors within the organization to competitive factors outside it.

Demand for the Product Class, Product, and Brand   The number of potential buyers for a product class (cars), product (sports cars), and brand (Bugatti Veyron) clearly affects the price a seller can charge. So does whether the item is a luxury, like a Bugatti Veyron, or a necessity, like bread and a roof over your head.

Newness of the Product: Stage in the Product Life Cycle   The newer the product and the earlier it is in its life cycle, the higher the price that can usually be charged. The high initial price is possible because of limited competition in the early stage. Sometimes, such as when nostalgia or fad factors are present, prices may rise later in the product's life cycle. Collectibles such as a Wayne Gretzky hockey jersey can experience skyrocketing prices. One of Gretzky's jerseys, from a 1980s Edmonton Oilers game, was sold for $45,000.[13]

The jersey pictured here is a replica and sells for $200 at the NHL online store; however, the original of this jersey, signed by Gretzky, sold in an online auction for $26,000. Publishing competitive prices on the Internet has revolutionized access to price comparisons for both collectors and buyers and has also created a very competitive marketplace.

> **One of Gretzky's jerseys, from a 1980s Edmonton Oilers game, was sold for $45,000.**

Breakdown of Gasoline Prices

Profit: 2 percent

Refining and marketing costs: 16 percent

Taxes: 35 percent*

Crude costs: 47 percent

*Federal and provincial governments receive over $14 billion per year in gasoline taxes.

Source: "The Facts on Gasoline Pricing," Canadian Automobile Association, accessed at www.caa.ca/mini%20sites/gasprice/pricing.html.

Cost of Producing and Marketing the Product   In the long run, a firm's price must cover all the costs of producing and marketing a product. If the price doesn't cover these costs, the firm will fail; so in the long run, a firm's costs set a floor under its price.

Competitors' Prices   When a firm sets its prices, an important consideration is the prices being charged by the competition. As we talked about previously, a firm has three choices: It can charge a higher price, the same price, or a lower price than its competitors. Each choice conveys a message to customers.

A high price signifies that the firm believes its offering represents a higher value in comparison to competing products—value being quality, brand image, benefits and unique features offering extra benefits, or something as simple as instant availability. Sony is known as a firm that typically prices higher than most of its competitors. Consumers wanting quality will pay a higher price.

Charging the same price as the competition means that the firm is relying on some aspect other than price to position and differentiate its products in the minds of customers—that differentiation may be a unique attribute, widespread availability, or an intensive marketing campaign. Thinking again of consumer electronics, Panasonic, JVC, and Sharp are examples of manufacturers whose prices are close for similar products. Consumers typically buy these brands on the basis of some unique attribute of the product, or because they prefer to deal with a specific retailer.

Lower prices can be a challenge, but many firms rely on this strategy. From the company standpoint, lower prices can mean lower profits on each sale, which may need to be offset by larger volume sales. In addition, larger volumes can result in production efficiencies and lower costs. Less well-known brands and some of the larger manufacturers such as RCA use this strategy. For consumers, the lower prices often mean forgoing some aspect such as quality or brand image.

The decision to charge a certain price is impacted by marketing and pricing objectives. If winning market share is an objective, lower prices may be the solution. If being perceived as the "best brand" is an objective, higher prices may be part of the answer. Being known as a *market leader* based on pricing is a title that could be ascribed to firms using either strategy.

Charging prices in line with the competition earns firms the title of *market follower*. This is a conscious choice of many smaller firms manufacturing and selling similar or often the same products. Emphasis is shifted away from price to some other aspect of the marketing mix.

There are occasions where other objectives override any consideration of competitor pricing, such as selling off discontinued models or time-sensitive items (summer-vacation packages, for example).

Legal and Ethical Considerations

Deciding on a final price is a complex process. In addition to the considerations we have just presented, there are laws and regulations that also play a role in the price decision. We will look at four of the most prominent considerations.

Price Fixing When competitors collaborate and conspire to set prices, they agree to increase, decrease, or stabilize a price for the benefit of some competitors. This is called *price fixing*, and it is illegal—the *Competition Act* prohibits this practice. Price fixing usually occurs where price is the most important factor in the marketing mix. Some drug companies and gas companies have been found to be involved in this practice.

Price Discrimination If different prices are charged to different customers for the same or very similar goods and the same terms, *price discrimination* has occurred. The *Competition Act* prohibits this, but in order for a firm to be charged with the offence, there has to be evidence of a "practice" of price discrimination—that is, that it is not just a one time or occasional event.

Deceptive Pricing Price offers that mislead the consumer are considered *deceptive pricing*, and this is prohibited under the *Competition Act*. Figure 9–10

Figure 9–10
Most common deceptive pricing practices

DECEPTIVE PRACTICE	DESCRIPTION
Bait and switch	A firm offers a very low price for a product (the bait), and when consumers come to purchase it, they are persuaded to buy a more expensive product (the switch). Uses techniques such as downgrading the advertised item or not having it in stock.
Bargains conditional on other purchases	A firm advertises "buy one, get one free" or "get two for the price of one." If the first items are sold at the regular price, this is legal. If the price for the first items is inflated for the offer, it is not.
Price comparisons	Advertising "retail value $100—our price $85" is deceptive if a substantial number of stores in the area are not using the $100 price—in other words, if it is not the "going price." Advertising "below manufacturer's suggested list price" is deceptive if no sales occur at the manufacturer's list price. Advertising that the price is reduced 50% is deceptive if the item was not offered for sale at the higher price for a substantial previous period of time.
Double ticketing	When more than one price tag is placed on an item, it must be sold at the lower price; this practice is not illegal, but the law requires that the lower price be charged.

shows the most common deceptive pricing practices. Many companies across the country have been accused of deceptive pricing, but it can be difficult to police and the laws are hard to enforce. Often regulators rely on the ethical standards of those making and publicizing pricing decisions. The Canadian Code of Advertising Standards provides guidelines for various aspects of promotion, and pricing is one of these; advertising industry members are expected to follow this Code and to self-regulate (ensure that they and their colleagues adhere to the Code).

Predatory Pricing Charging a very low price for a product with the intent of undercutting competitors and possibly driving them out of the market is called *predatory pricing*. After the competitors have been driven out, the offending firm raises its prices. If a company can genuinely operate more efficiently than others, and this lets them offer its products at a lower price, should this be classified as predatory pricing? No! It's not easy to prove that the intent of the

No Ifs, Ands or Buts.

Truth is an essential part of any successful ad campaign. Smart advertisers have known this for years. That's why the advertising industry created the *Canadian Code of Advertising Standards* more than 40 years ago. Since then the *Code* has set the standards for acceptable advertising in Canada. It helps ensure that the ads you see and hear are truthful, fair and accurate. Check it out for yourself. Because the more you know about advertising, the more you get out of it.

Learn about the *Code* at:
www.adstandards.com

ASC Advertising Standards Canada

lower price is to eliminate a competitor, and that the prices set are unreasonably and artificially low, so there are many more charges of predatory pricing than there are convictions.

Global Pricing Strategy

Global companies face many challenges in determining a pricing strategy as part of their worldwide marketing effort. Individual countries, even those with free trade agreements, may place considerable competitive, political, and legal constraints on the pricing flexibility of global companies. For example, Wal-Mart was told by German antitrust authorities that the prices in its stores were too low, relative to competitors, and faced a fine for violating the country's trade if the prices weren't raised![14]

Pricing too low or too high can have dire consequences. When prices appear too low in one country, companies can be charged with dumping, a practice subject to severe penalties and fines. Dumping occurs when a firm sells a product in a foreign country below its domestic price or below its actual cost. A recent trade dispute involving U.S. apple growers and Mexico is a case in

Retailer Fined $1.2 Million for Misleading Sale Prices

The sale price that consumers see in the stores might not always be the deal that it seems. Menswear retailer Grafton-Fraser Inc. and its CEO Glenn Stonehouse agreed recently to pay a $1.2 million penalty to settle an advertising case regarding misleading sale prices. The federal Competition Bureau found that Grafton-Fraser "had significantly inflated the regular price of certain garments sold in its stores, resulting in an overstatement of

the savings to consumers when these garments were on sale." The retailer joins other merchants, including Suzy Shier, Sears Canada Ltd., and Forzani Group Ltd., that the Competition Bureau found to be inflating an item's regular price and thereby overstating the savings of the sale price.

Grafton-Fraser, the Competition Bureau found, was tagging garments with both a regular price and a sale price, however, the items did not sell "in any significant

quantity or for any reasonable period of time at the regular price," the Bureau said. Grafton-Fraser runs more than 180 stores across the country. These stores operate under several names, among them Tip Top Tailors, George Richards Big & Tall, and Grafton & Co. ●

Focus on Ethics

Sources: Marina Strauss, "Grafton-Fraser fined for misleading sale prices," *The Globe and Mail*, July 28, 2006, p. B8; "Retailer fined $1.2 million for misleading ad," *Toronto Star*, July 28, 2006, p. D2.

point. Mexican trade officials claimed that U.S. growers were selling their red and golden delicious apples in Mexico below the actual cost of production. They imposed a 101 percent tariff on U.S. apples, and a severe drop in U.S. apple exports to Mexico resulted. Later negotiations set a price floor on the price of U.S. apples sold to Mexico.[15]

When companies price their products very high in some countries but competitively in others, they face a grey market problem. A **grey market**, also called *parallel importing*, is a situation where products are sold through unauthorized channels of distribution. A grey market comes about when individuals buy products in a lower-priced country from a manufacturer's authorized retailer, ship them to higher-priced countries, and then sell them below the manufacturer's suggested retail price through unauthorized retailers. Many well-known products have been sold through grey markets, including Olympus cameras, Seiko watches, IBM personal computers, and Mercedes-Benz cars. Parallel channels are not strictly illegal in Canada, but there are mounting legal challenges to them. Parallel importing is legal in the United States. It is illegal in the European Union.[16]

▼

ask yourself

1. What is the difference between pricing objectives and pricing constraints?
2. Explain what bait and switch is and why it is an example of deceptive pricing.

Setting a Final Price

L7 The final price set by the marketing manager serves many functions. It must be high enough to cover the cost of providing the product *and* meet the objectives of the company. Yet it must be low enough that customers are willing to pay it. But not too low, or customers may think they're purchasing an inferior product. Confused? Setting price is one of the most difficult tasks the marketing manager faces, but four generalized steps are useful to follow.

Step 1: Select an Approximate Price Level

Before setting a final price, the marketing manager must understand the market environment, the features and customer benefits of the particular product, and the goals of the firm. A balance must be struck between factors that might drive a price higher (such as a profit-oriented approach) and other forces (such as increased competition from substitutes) that may drive a price down.

Marketing managers consider pricing objectives and constraints first, and then choose among the general pricing approaches—demand-, cost-, profit-, or competition-oriented—to arrive at an approximate price level. This price is then analyzed in terms of cost, volume, and profit relationships. Break-even analyses may be run at this point, and finally, if this approximate price level "works," it is time to take the next step: setting a specific list or quoted price.

grey market
Situations where products are sold through unauthorized channels of distribution

Step 2: Set the List or Quoted Price

A seller must decide whether to follow a one-price or flexible-price policy.

One-Price Policy A *one-price policy* involves setting one price for all buyers of a product or service. For example, Saturn Corporation uses this approach in its dealerships and features a "no haggle, one price" price for its cars. Some retailers such as Dollarama have married this policy with a below-market approach and sell everything in their stores for $1!

Flexible-Price Policy In contrast, a *flexible-price policy* involves setting different prices for products and services depending on individual buyers and purchase situations in light of demand, cost, and competitive factors. Dell Computer adopted flexible

Marketing ▶ tip

"When the economy gets weak, it doesn't scare me because I know more customers are coming through the door."

Kevin Kane, owner of 21 Great Canadian Dollar Store
franchises, in Leader Post, October 21, 2008

pricing as it continually adjusts prices in response to changes in its own costs, competitive pressures, and demand from its various personal computer segments (home, small business, corporate, and so on). "Our flexibility allows us to be [priced] different even within a day," says a Dell spokesperson.[17]

Flexible pricing is not without its critics because of its discriminatory potential. For example, car dealers have traditionally used flexible pricing on the basis of buyer-seller negotiations to agree on a final price. Is it any wonder that 60 percent of prospective car buyers dread negotiating the price?

Step 3: Make Special Adjustments to the List or Quoted Price

L⑧ When you pay $1 for a bag of M&Ms in a vending machine or receive a quoted price of $10,000 from a contractor to renovate a kitchen, the pricing sequence ends with the last step just described: setting the list or quoted price. But when you are a manufacturer of M&M candies and sell your product to dozens or hundreds of wholesalers and retailers in your channel of distribution, you may need to make a variety of special adjustments to the list or quoted price. Wholesalers also must adjust list or quoted prices they set for retailers. Three special adjustments to the list or quoted price are discounts, allowances, and geographical adjustments.

Discounts *Discounts* are reductions from list price that a seller gives a buyer as a reward for some activity of the buyer that is favourable to the seller. Four kinds of discounts are

Toro uses seasonal discounts to stimulate consumer demand and smooth out seasonal manufacturing peaks and troughs.

especially important in marketing strategy: quantity, seasonal, trade (functional), and cash.[18]

- *Quantity discounts.* To encourage customers to buy larger quantities of a product, firms at all levels in the channel of distribution offer quantity discounts, which are reductions in unit costs for a larger order. For example, an instant photocopying service might set a price of 10 cents a copy for 1 to 24 copies, 9 cents a copy for 25 to 99, and 8 cents a copy for 100 or more. Because the photocopying service gets more of the buyer's business and has longer production runs that reduce its order-handling costs, it is willing to pass on some of the cost savings in the form of quantity discounts to the buyer.

- *Seasonal discounts.* To encourage buyers to stock inventory earlier than their normal demand would require, manufacturers often use seasonal discounts. A firm such as Toro that manufactures lawn mowers and snow blowers offers seasonal discounts to encourage wholesalers and retailers to stock up on lawn mowers in January and February and on snow blowers in July and August—months before the seasonal demand by ultimate consumers. This enables Toro to smooth out seasonal manufacturing peaks and troughs, thereby contributing to more efficient production. It also rewards wholesalers and retailers for the risk they accept in assuming increased inventory carrying costs and gives them the benefit of having supplies in stock at the time they are wanted by customers.

- *Trade (functional) discounts.* To reward wholesalers and retailers for marketing functions they will perform in the future, a manufacturer often gives trade, or functional, discounts. These reductions off the list or base price are offered to resellers in the channel of distribution on the basis of where they are in the channel and the marketing activities they are expected to perform in the future.

Traditional trade discounts have been established in various product lines such as hardware, food, and pharmaceutical items.

Although the manufacturer may suggest trade discounts, the sellers are free to alter the discount schedule depending on their competitive situation. Suppose that a manufacturer quotes prices in the following form:

List price – $100, less 30/10/5

The first number in the percentage sequence (in this example, 30/10/5) always refers to the retail end of the channel, and the last number always refers to the wholesaler or jobber closest to the manufacturer in the channel. The trade discounts are simply subtracted one at a time. This price quote shows that $100 is the manufacturer's suggested retail price:

◆ For the retailer, 30 percent of the suggested retail price ($100 × 0.3 = $30) is available to cover costs and provide a profit;

◆ Wholesalers closest to the retailer in the channel get 10 percent of their selling price ($70 × 0.1 = $7); and

◆ The final group of wholesalers in the channel (probably jobbers) that are closest to the manufacturer get 5 percent of their selling price ($63 × 0.05 = $3.15).

Thus, starting with the manufacturer's retail price and subtracting the three trade discounts shows that the manufacturer's selling price to the wholesaler or jobber closest to the manufacturer is $59.85 (see Figure 9–11).

● *Cash discounts.* To encourage retailers to pay their bills quickly, manufacturers offer them cash discounts. Suppose that a retailer receives a bill quoted at $1,000, 2/10 net 30. This means that the bill for the product is $1,000, but the retailer can take a 2 percent discount ($1,000 × 0.02 = $20) if payment is made within 10 days and send a cheque for $980. If the payment cannot be made within 10 days, the total amount of $1,000 is due within 30 days. It is usually understood by the buyer that an interest charge will be added after the first 30 days of free credit.

Retailers provide cash discounts to consumers as well, to eliminate the cost of credit granted to consumers. These discounts take the form of discount-for-cash policies.

Allowances   Allowances—like discounts—are reductions from list or quoted prices to buyers for performing some activity.

● *Trade-in allowances.* A new car dealer can offset the list price of that new Toyota Camry by offering you a trade-in allowance of $500 for your old Honda. A trade-in allowance is a price reduction given when a used product is part of the payment on a new product. Trade-ins are an effective way to lower the price a buyer has to pay without formally reducing the list price.

● *Promotional allowances.* Sellers in the channel of distribution can qualify for promotional allowances for undertaking certain advertising or selling activities to promote a product. Various types of allowances include an actual cash payment or an extra amount of "free goods" (as with a free case of pizzas to a retailer for every dozen cases purchased). Frequently, a portion of these savings is passed on to the consumer by retailers.

Figure 9–11
How trade discounts work

Geographical Adjustments Geographical adjustments are made by manufacturers or even wholesalers to list or quoted prices to reflect the cost of transportation of the products from seller to buyer. The two general methods for quoting prices related to transportation costs are FOB origin pricing and uniform delivered pricing.

- *FOB origin pricing.* FOB means "free on board" some vehicle at some location, which means the seller pays the cost of loading the product onto the vehicle that is used (such as a barge, railroad car, or truck). FOB origin pricing usually involves the seller's naming the location of this loading as the seller's factory or warehouse (such as "FOB Montreal" or "FOB factory"). The title and ownership to the goods passes to the buyer at the point of loading, so the buyer becomes responsible for picking the specific mode of transportation, for all the transportation costs, and for subsequent handling of the product. Buyers farthest from the seller face the big disadvantage of paying the higher transportation costs.

- *Uniform delivered pricing.* When a uniform delivered pricing method is used, the price the seller quotes includes all transportation costs. It is quoted in a contract as "FOB buyer's location," and the seller selects the mode of transportation, pays the freight charges, and is responsible for any damage that may occur because the seller retains title to the goods until delivered to the buyer.

Step 4: Monitor and Adjust Prices

Rarely can a firm set a price and leave it at that. As you have learned, there are many constraints that affect setting prices, and the firm has objectives that it also takes into account. Things change both in the external business environment and within the firm itself; as a result, prices need to be reviewed and revised if necessary. A key activity is the monitoring of competitor activity, legislative changes, economic conditions, and—the ultimate measure— consumer demand! These factors, and their potential impact on the firm's ability to achieve its marketing goals, have to be examined and action taken when necessary.

ask yourself

1. Why would a seller choose a flexible-price policy over a one-price policy?

2. What is the purpose of (a) quantity discounts and (b) promotional allowances?

Summary...*just the facts*

- Price is the money or other considerations exchanged for the ownership or use of a product or service. Although price typically involves money, the amount exchanged is often different from the list or quoted price because of allowances and extra fees.

- Consumers use price as an indicator of value when it is paired with the perceived benefits of a good or service. Sometimes, price influences consumer perceptions of quality itself; at other times, consumers make value assessments by comparing the costs and benefits of substitute items.

- Four general approaches for finding an approximate price level for a product or service are demand-oriented, cost-oriented, profit-oriented, and competition-oriented pricing.

- Demand-oriented pricing approaches stress consumer demand and revenue implications of pricing and include seven types: skimming, penetration, prestige, odd-even, target, bundle, and yield management.

- Cost-oriented pricing approaches emphasize the cost aspects of pricing and include two types: standard and cost-plus pricing.

- Profit-oriented pricing approaches focus on a balance between revenues and costs to set a price and include three types: target profit, target return-on-sales, and target return-on-investment pricing.

- Competition-oriented pricing approaches emphasize what competitors or the marketplace are doing and include three types: customary; above-, at-, or below-market; and loss-leader pricing.

- A demand curve shows the maximum number of products consumers will buy at a given price and for a given set of (a) consumer tastes, (b) price and availability of other products, and (c) consumer income. When any of these change, there is a shift in the demand curve.

- It is necessary to consider cost behaviour when making pricing decisions. Important cost concepts include total cost, variable cost, and fixed cost. An essential revenue concept is total revenue.

- Break-even analysis shows the relationship between total revenue and total cost at various quantities of output for given conditions of price, fixed cost, and variable cost. The break-even point is where total revenue and total cost are equal.

- Pricing objectives, which specify the role of price in a firm's marketing strategy, may include pricing for profit, sales revenue, market share, unit sales, survival, or some socially responsible price level.

- Pricing constraints such as demand, product newness, costs, competitors, other products sold by the firm, and the type of competitive market restrict a firm's pricing range.

- Given an approximate price level for a product, a manager must set a list or quoted price by considering factors such as one-price versus a flexible-price policy.

- List or quoted price is often modified through discounts, allowances, and geographical adjustments. The pricing environment needs to be monitored continually.

Key Terms and Concepts...*a refresher*

break-even analysis *p. 169*
demand curve *p. 166*
dumping *p. 174*
fixed cost *p. 169*
grey market *p. 175*

markup *p. 163*
price *p. 158*
pricing constraints *p. 172*
pricing objectives *p. 170*
profit equation *p. 160*

total cost *p. 169*
total revenue *p. 168*
value *p. 160*
variable cost *p. 169*

Distribution
AND *Supply Chain*

The business of marketing touches on a wide range of elements that impact on consumers' willingness to buy a product and subsequently return to purchase another in the future. Although not top-of-mind with students, distribution and supply chain are key variables in the marketing mix that can impact on this decision. This chapter looks at this area, explaining its challenges and relevance to businesses today. We start by looking at the success of Sleep Country Canada and how it uses distribution as a distinct point of difference in the market. The role

of supply chain has also been central in the growth of its business, allowing it to expand and become the leading mattress retailer in Canada.

In 1994 Sleep Country Canada was created by three partners: Christine Magee, Stephen Gunn, and Gad Lownds. It started with four stores and a single warehouse in Vancouver and is now the number one mattress retailer in Canada. It is run by a group of professionals who have created a culture of highly trained, caring people who operate professionally in a unique atmosphere that is friendly and supportive. Sleep Country Canada prides itself on providing top-quality service for its customers from the very start of a sale, right down to the delivery of a product. Christine Magee, president of Sleep Country Canada explains that their motto is "To under-promise and to over-deliver by giving customers an exceptional experience." She explains that at Sleep Country Canada it is all about providing an exceptional experience to every customer, in every store, in every region, each and every day.

Product delivery is a key variable used by Sleep Country Canada to uniquely set itself apart from the competition. Sleep Country Canada recognizes that final product delivery is crucial to cementing the Sleep Country experience in the home. They understand that their delivery personnel enter a person's most private space, the bedroom, and that this needs to be done courteously and with sensitivity. All delivery personnel are carefully screened to ensure that they have the right attitude to deal with customers, and are trained to reflect Sleep Country Canada's commitment to excellence. All new delivery personnel work with an experienced employee to learn the approach. Three-hour delivery windows are scheduled with customers, cellphones are used by delivery personnel, door-hang-tags are provided for customers who missed a delivery, and boot protectors are used to ensure that a home is not sullied during the delivery process. Mostly unique to the industry, all Sleep Country Canada delivery personnel are employed by Sleep Country Canada. In this manner, Sleep Country Canada ensures that their

LEARNING OBJECTIVES

L₁ Explain what is meant by a marketing channel and the value created by intermediaries.

L₂ Explain the differences between marketing channels for consumer goods and those for business goods.

L₃ Understand the use of multichannel marketing.

L₄ Differentiate between types of vertical marketing systems.

L5 Describe the factors considered by marketing executives when selecting and managing a marketing channel.

L6 Discuss supply chain and logistics management and how they relate to marketing strategy.

L7 Explain the two concepts of logistics management in a supply chain.

commitment to quality service is provided throughout the customer experience, from the initial in-store experience to the final in-home delivery.

Meeting customer needs from start to finish is the cornerstone of Sleep Country Canada's success. The experience is carefully planned so that a customer's experience is positive before, during, and after the sale. Staff are knowledgeable and polite, stores are bright and attractive, and delivery is professional and convenient. But there is more behind-the-scenes that goes into Sleep Country Canada's success: the company's supply chain. None of these pieces could fall smoothly into place if Sleep Country Canada's supply chain did not ensure that all elements work seamlessly together to provide customers with the products they order in the professional manner they expect.

Christine Magee explains how the firm's supply chain works. Sleep Country Canada manages its business on a regional basis, working hand-in-hand with its manufacturers to become a dominant player in the market before it expands into other areas. It works with major North American mattress manufacturers such as Simmons, Sealy, Serta, Spring Air, Kingsdown, Select Comfort, and Tempur, ordering products as needed through their regional distribution centres. These major manufacturers have just-in-time manufacturing and inventory systems, which frees up capital for Sleep Country Canada that would otherwise be tied up in expensive inventory. When a customer buys a mattress at Sleep Country Canada, it initially checks its own distribution centres for stock availability. In most instances the stock is pre-committed, and Sleep Country Canada then places the order with the local manufacturer. This supplier then manufactures and delivers the product within two to three days to Sleep Country Canada's distribution centre. At this point, Sleep Country Canada delivers the product to its customers, giving the entire process a four-day turnaround. Sleep Country Canada's distribution system takes over during the final delivery stage, using a logistics software system to route trucks and to plan deliveries. Deliveries are based on postal codes and organized around a centrally located warehouse that serves a given area. This software helps efficiently route the deliveries and, importantly, sets the packing plan for the truck so that merchandise is packed in a last-on/first-off fashion. Not leaving anything to chance, Sleep Country Canada also uses this delivery data for sales leads to identify areas that are underserved by Sleep Country Canada.

Sleep Country Canada uses an integrated system to manage its supply chain and distribution systems. These systems help ensure that unnecessary costs are not added to the business, which in turn allows it to direct its marketing efforts into offering quality products and services. Sleep Country Canada goes the extra step in its business, using top-quality service and personalized delivery as a point of difference to attract customers and keep them coming back year after year. The company's efficient supply chain and focus on customer needs allows them to do this effectively. As Christine Magee says, and demonstrates through Sleep Country Canada's approach to business, "Why buy a mattress anywhere else?"

Chapter 10 focuses on the concept of distribution—getting the product to the customer—the place P of the 4Ps that make up the marketing mix. 🍎

Nature and Importance of Marketing Channels

L1 Reaching potential buyers is obviously a critical part of successful marketing. Buyers benefit from well-structured and efficient distribution systems. The route to do this is direct in some cases and indirect in others.

What Is a Marketing Channel?

You see the results of distribution every day. You may have purchased Lay's Potato Chips at Mac's convenience store, a book through chapters.indigo.ca, or Levi's jeans at Sears. Each of these items was brought to you by a marketing channel of distribution, or

The concept of distribution is all about getting the product to the customer.

Marketers understand the value of the supply chain to perform activities required to deliver a good or service to customers.

simply a marketing channel, which consists of individuals and firms involved in the process of making a product or service available.

Marketing channels can be compared with a pipeline through which water flows from a source to an endpoint. Marketing channels make possible the flow of goods from a producer, through intermediaries, to a buyer. There are several types of intermediaries—and specific names or terms for each type—and, as shown in Figure 10–1, they perform various functions.[1] Some intermediaries actually purchase items from the producer, store them, and resell them to buyers. For example, Krave's Candy Company produces Clodhoppers candy and sells it to wholesalers. The wholesalers then sell the candy to supermarkets and retailers, which in turn sell it to consumers. Other intermediaries, such as brokers and agents, represent sellers but do not actually ever own the products; their role is to bring a seller and buyer together. Real estate agents are examples of this type of intermediary.

Value Created by Intermediaries

The importance of intermediaries is made clear when we consider the functions they perform and the value they create for buyers.

Functions Performed by Intermediaries

Intermediaries make possible the flow of products from producers to ultimate consumers by performing three basic functions (see Figure 10–2 on page 184).

(see Figure 10–2 on page 184)

- *Transactional function.* Intermediaries perform a transactional function when they buy and sell goods or services. But an intermediary such as a wholesaler also performs the function of sharing risk with the producer when it stocks merchandise in anticipation of sales. If the stock is unsold for any reason, the intermediary—not the producer—suffers the loss.

- *Logistical function.* The logistics of a transaction (described at length later in this chapter) involve the details of preparing and getting a product to buyers. Gathering, sorting, and dispersing products are some of the logistical functions of the intermediary—imagine the various fruits and vegetables displayed at your local grocery store!

- *Facilitating function.* Finally, intermediaries perform facilitating functions that, by definition, make a transaction *easier* for buyers. For example, Sears issues credit cards to consumers so that they can buy now and pay later.

All three groups of functions must be performed in a marketing channel, even though each channel member may not participate in all three. Channel members often negotiate about which specific functions they will perform. Sometimes disagreements result, and a breakdown in relationships among channel members

marketing channel
The set of individuals or firms involved in the process of making a product available

intermediaries
Individuals or firms performing a role in the marketing channel, involved in making a product available

Figure 10–1
Terms used for marketing intermediaries

TERM	DESCRIPTION
Middleman	Another name for intermediary
Agent or broker	Any intermediary with legal authority to act on behalf of another channel member (for example, a manufacturer)
Wholesaler	Any intermediary who sells to other intermediaries, usually to retailers—this term usually applies to intermediaries who deal in consumer goods
Retailer	An intermediary who sells to consumers
Distributor	A general term used to describe intermediaries who perform a variety of functions, including selling, maintaining inventories, extending credit, and others—usually used for those in business markets
Dealer	A general term that can mean the same as a distributor, a retailer, or a wholesaler

Figure 10–2

Marketing channel functions performed by intermediaries

TYPE OF FUNCTION	ACTIVITIES RELATED TO FUNCTION
Transactional function	• *Buying*: Purchasing products for resale • *Selling*: Contacting potential customers, promoting products, and seeking orders • *Risk taking*: Assuming business risks in the ownership of inventory
Logistical function	• *Selection:* Putting together a selection of products from several different sources • *Storing*: Assembling and protecting products at a convenient location • *Sorting*: Purchasing in large quantities and dividing into smaller amounts • *Transporting*: Physically moving a product to customers
Facilitating function	• *Financing*: Extending credit to customers • *Marketing information and research*: Providing information to customers and suppliers, including competitive conditions and trends

occurs. This happened when Pepsi-Cola's bottler in Venezuela switched to Coca-Cola. Given the intermediary's logistical role—storing and transporting Pepsi to Venezuelan customers in this case—Pepsi-Cola either had to set up its own bottling operation to perform these marketing channel functions, or find another bottler, which it did.[2]

Consumer Benefits from Intermediaries

Consumers also benefit from the actions of intermediaries. Having the goods and services you want, when you want them, where you want them, and in the form you want them is the ideal result of marketing channels. In more specific terms, marketing channels help create value for consumers through these five utilities: time, place, form, information, and possession.

- *Time utility* refers to having a product or service when you want it. For example, FedEx provides next-morning delivery.

- *Place utility* means having a product or service available where consumers want it, such as having a Petro Canada gas station located on a long stretch of a provincial highway.

- *Form utility* involves enhancing a product or service to make it more appealing to buyers. For example, Compaq Computer delivers unfinished PCs to dealers, which then add memory, chips, modems, and other parts, based on consumer specifications.

- *Information utility* means providing consumers with the information they need to make an informed choice; information-packed websites and user manuals provide this type of utility.

- *Possession utility* involves efforts by intermediaries to help buyers take possession of a product or service, such as providing various ways for payment to be made for a product—by credit card, debit card, cash, or cheque.

ask yourself

1. What is meant by a marketing channel?

2. What are the three basic functions performed by intermediaries?

Wal-Mart Unveils Plan to Reduce Packaging

In September 2006, Wal-Mart unveiled a planned initiative to reduce its overall packaging by 5 percent and in doing so prevent millions of pounds of trash from being thrown away and reaching landfills. Wal-Mart planned to start the plan in 2008, measuring its worldwide suppliers (numbering over 60,000) on their ability to develop packaging that conserves natural resources. The retailer introduced a packaging scorecard to private-label suppliers that will allow Wal-Mart buyers to learn about alternative, sustainable packaging options and influencing what products that they stock.

In 2007, Wal-Mart made tools available to the company's suppliers so that they could measure how using the new material-saving processes have helped them use less packaging, using more effective materials in their packaging, and better sourcing the materials. The overall plan is projected to save 667,000 metric tons of carbon dioxide from being released into the atmosphere, equal to keeping 323,800 tons of coal and more than 66 million gallons of diesel fuel from being burned. Wal-Mart stands to save US$3.4 billion from this initiative. The global packaging industry also stands to save nearly US$11 billion from the 5 percent reduction in the supply chain.

Sources: "Wal-Mart Launches 5-Year Plan to Reduce Packaging," GreenBiz.com, September 25, 2006, www.greenbiz.com/news/2006/09/25/wal-mart-launches-5-year-plan-to-reduce-packaging; "Wal-Mart goes green on packaging," BBC News, September 22, 2006; http://news.bbc.co.uk/2/hi/business/5372660.stm.

Channel Structure and Organization

A product can take many routes on its journey from producer to buyer, and marketers search for the most efficient route from the many alternatives available. As you'll see, there are some important differences between the marketing channels for consumer goods and those for business goods.

Marketing Channels for Consumer Goods and Services

Figure 10–3 (see page 186) shows the four most common marketing channel configurations for consumer goods and services. It also shows the number of levels in each marketing channel, that is, the number of intermediaries between a producer and ultimate buyers. As the number of intermediaries between a producer and buyer increases, the channel is viewed as increasing in length. The producer → wholesaler → retailer → consumer channel is longer than the producer → consumer channel.

Channel A in Figure 10–3 represents a *direct channel* because a producer and ultimate consumers deal directly with each other. Many products and services are distributed this way. A number of insurance companies sell their financial services using a direct channel and branch sales offices. The online store justwhiteshirts.com designs and produces high-quality men's shirts that are sold online and by catalogue to consumers around the world. Because there are no intermediaries with a direct channel, the producer must perform all channel functions.

The remaining three channel forms are *indirect channels* because intermediaries are inserted between the producer and consumers and perform numerous channel functions. Channel B, with a retailer added, is most common when the retailer is large and can buy in large quantities from a producer or when the cost of inventory makes it too expensive to use a wholesaler. Automobile manufacturers use this channel, with a local car dealer acting as a retailer. Why is there no wholesaler? So many variations exist in the product that it would be impossible for a wholesaler to stock all the models required to satisfy buyers; in addition, the cost of maintaining an inventory would be too high. Large retailers such as Sears, 7-Eleven, and Safeway buy in sufficient quantities to make it cost effective for a producer to deal with only a retail intermediary. Sleep Country Canada, as described in the opening vignette, is an example of a retailer that buys directly from manufacturers.

Adding a wholesaler in channel C is most common for low-cost, low-unit value items that are frequently purchased by consumers, such as candy, confectionary items, and magazines. For example, Mars sells its line of candies to wholesalers in case quantities; wholesalers can then break down (sort) the cases so that individual retailers can order in boxes or much smaller quantities.

Channel D, the most indirect channel, is employed when there are many small manufacturers and many small retailers and an agent is used to help coordinate a large supply of the product. Mansar Products, Ltd., is a Belgian producer of specialty jewellery that uses agents to sell to wholesalers, which then sell to many small retailers.

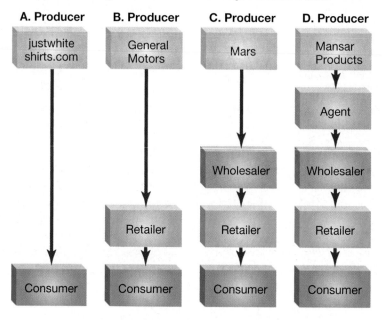

Figure 10–3

Common marketing channels for consumer goods and services

Marketing Channels for Business Goods and Services

The four most common channels for business goods and services are shown in Figure 10–4 (see page 187). In contrast with channels for consumer products, business channels typically are shorter and rely on one intermediary or none at all because business users are fewer in number, tend to be more concentrated geographically, and buy in larger quantities. For these reasons, business channels can be served directly or by a limited number of intermediaries.

Channel A, represented by IBM's large, mainframe computer business, is a direct channel. Firms using this kind of channel maintain their own sales force and perform all channel functions. This channel is employed when buyers are large and well defined, the sales effort requires extensive negotiations, and the products are of high unit value and require hands-on expertise in terms of installation or use. Bombardier and Airbus Industries would be other examples.

Channels B, C, and D are indirect channels with one or more intermediaries to reach industrial users. In channel B an *industrial distributor* performs a variety of marketing channel functions, including selling, stocking, and delivering a full product assortment and financing. In many ways, industrial distributors are like wholesalers in consumer channels. Caterpillar relies on industrial distributors to sell and service its construction and mining equipment in almost 200 countries.

Channel C introduces another intermediary, an agent, who serves primarily as the independent selling arm of producers and represents a producer to industrial users. For example, Stake Fastener Company, a producer of industrial fasteners, has an agent call on industrial users rather than employing its own sales force.

Channel D is the longest channel and includes both agents and distributors. For instance, Culligan, a producer of water treatment equipment, uses agents to call on distributors who sell to industrial users.

Electronic Marketing Channels

The marketing channels that we have just discussed for consumer and business goods and services are not the only routes to the marketplace. Advances in electronic commerce have opened new avenues for reaching buyers and creating customer value.

Interactive electronic technology has made possible **electronic marketing channels**, which employ the Internet to make goods and services available to consumers or business buyers. A unique feature of these channels is that they can combine electronic and traditional intermediaries to create time, place, form, and possession utility for buyers.[3]

Figure 10–5 (see page 188) shows the electronic marketing channels for books (Amazon.ca), travel reservation services (Travelocity.ca), and personal computers (Dell.ca). Are you surprised that they look a lot like common marketing channels? An important reason for the

dual distribution
Arrangement whereby a firm reaches buyers by using two or more different types of channels for the same basic product

Figure 10–4
Common marketing channels for business goods and service

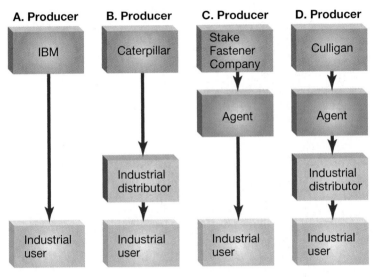

similarity resides in channel functions detailed in Figure 10-2 (see page 184). Electronic intermediaries can and do perform transactional and facilitating functions effectively and at a relatively lower cost than traditional intermediaries because of efficiencies made possible by information technology. However, electronic intermediaries are incapable of performing elements of the logistical function, particularly for products such as books and automobiles. This function remains with traditional intermediaries or with the producer, as seen with Dell and its direct channel.

Many services are distributed through electronic marketing channels, such as travel services marketed by Travelocity.ca, financial securities by Royal Bank, and insurance by Metropolitan Life. Software, too, can be marketed this way. However, many other services such as health care and auto repair still involve traditional intermediaries.

Multiple Channels and Strategic Alliances

In some situations producers use **dual distribution**, an arrangement whereby a firm reaches different buyers by employing two or more different types of channels for the same basic product. For instance, GE sells its large appliances directly to home and apartment builders but uses retail stores, including

Wal-Mart, to sell to consumers. In some instances, firms pair multiple channels with a multibrand strategy. This is done to minimize cannibalization of the firm's family brand and to differentiate the channels. For example, Hallmark sells its Hallmark greeting cards through Hallmark stores and select department stores, and its Ambassador brand of cards through discount and drugstore chains.

A recent development in marketing channels is the use of *strategic channel* alliances, whereby one firm's marketing channel is used to sell another firm's products.[4] An alliance between Kraft Foods and Starbucks is a case in point. Kraft distributes Starbucks coffee in North American supermarkets and internationally.

Strategic alliances are popular in global marketing, where the creation of marketing channel relationships is expensive and time consuming. For example, General Mills and Nestlé have an extensive alliance that spans 70 international markets from Brazil to Poland to Thailand.

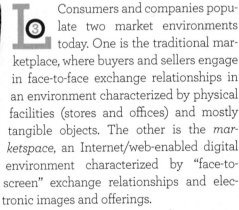

"Kraft distributes Starbucks coffee in North American supermarkets and internationally."

Multichannel Marketing to the Online Consumer

Consumers and companies populate two market environments today. One is the traditional marketplace, where buyers and sellers engage in face-to-face exchange relationships in an environment characterized by physical facilities (stores and offices) and mostly tangible objects. The other is the *marketspace*, an Internet/web-enabled digital environment characterized by "face-to-screen" exchange relationships and electronic images and offerings.

The existence of two market environments has benefited consumers tremendously. Today, consumers can shop for and purchase a wide variety of products and services in either market environment. Many consumers now browse and buy in both market environments, and more are expected to do so in the future. With so many consumers browsing and buying in two market environments,

multichannel marketing
Blending of different communication and delivery channels that are mutually reinforcing in attracting, retaining, and building relationships with customers

few companies limit their marketing programs exclusively to the traditional marketplace or to the online marketspace. Today, it is commonplace for companies to maintain a presence in both market environments. This dual presence is called *multichannel marketing*.

Integrating Multiple Channels with Multichannel Marketing Companies often employ multiple marketing channels for their products and services. Multichannel marketing bears some resemblance to dual distribution. For example, different communication and delivery channels are used, such as catalogues, kiosks, retail stores, and websites. However, the resemblance ends at this point. **Multichannel marketing** is the *blending* of different communication and delivery channels that are *mutually reinforcing* in attracting, retaining, and building relationships with consumers who shop and buy in the traditional marketplace and in the online marketspace. Multichannel marketing seeks to integrate a firm's communication and delivery channels, not differentiate them. In doing so, consumers can browse and buy anytime, anywhere, any way, expecting that the experience will be similar regardless of

Figure 10–5
Examples of electronic marketing channels

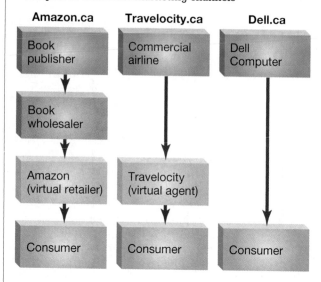

channel. At Eddie Bauer, for example, every effort is made to make the apparel shopping and purchase process for its customers the same in its retail stores, through its catalogues, and at its website. According to an Eddie Bauer marketing manager, "We don't distinguish between channels because it's all Eddie Bauer to our customers."[5] We will discuss the retail slant on this practice further in Chapter 11.

Reebok Website Allows Brand to Spend More Time with Consumers

Marketing NewsFlash

Online shopping was once a simple convenience, a way for consumers to browse and purchase their favourite items without leaving their living rooms. It was an online catalogue and little else. As the marketing world has changed, however, companies' websites have become interactive shopping experiences designed to make the customer feel as though they are personally being taken care of in a physical store.

Reebok is one such company, having recently introduced a new version of its website, one that gives their customers a personalized shopping experience. Visitors can create a profile, ranking how interested they are in a range of sports including basketball, football, and running. By setting a favourite colour, users can set the website to show products in those colours by default. Users have a visual shopping cart that remains with them as they shop, allowing them to keep track of what they've

added, and the site provides a one-page check-out process. In addition to these features, shoppers will be able to view further details about particular items on the website and locate it in a physical retail store. Later, the site will make user comments possible—the site was designed with Reebok's hopes to expand the site in the future.

Sources: "REEBOK: New Reebok.com website allows the brand to spend more time with consumers whilst driving brand and commerce," *M2 Presswire*, June 12, 2008; "Reebok's new website meets performance targets – claim," *Internet Business News*, June 13, 2008; "Reebok prepares to unleash its revamped global website," *New Media Age*, April 24, 2008, p. 3.

Implementing Multichannel Marketing

It should not be surprising to you that not all companies use websites for multichannel marketing the same way. Different companies apply the value-creation capabilities of Internet/web technology differently depending on their overall marketing program. Websites can play multiple roles in multichannel marketing because they can serve as either a communication or delivery channel, or as both. There are two general types of websites, classified based on their intended purpose: transactional websites and promotional websites.

Transactional websites are essentially electronic storefronts. They focus mainly on converting an online browser into an online, catalogue, or in-store buyer using website design elements. Transactional websites are most common among store and catalogue retailers and direct-selling companies, such as Tupperware. The Gap, for instance, generates more sales volume from its website than from any one of its stores, except for one.[6]

Retailers and direct-selling firms have found that their websites, while cannibalizing sales volume from stores, catalogues, and sales representatives, attract new customers and influence sales. Consider Victoria's Secret, specialty retailer of intimate apparel for women aged 18 to 45. Almost 60 percent of its website customers are men, most of whom generate new sales volume for the company.[7] Sears' website is estimated to account for millions of dollars worth of Sears in-store appliance sales. Why? Sears

customers first research appliances online before visiting a store.[8]

> *The Gap generates more sales volume from its website than from any one of its stores, except for one.*

Transactional websites are used less frequently by manufacturers of consumer products. A recurring issue for manufacturers is the threat of channel conflict and the potential harm to trade relationships with their retailing intermediaries. Still, manufacturers do use transactional websites, often cooperating with retailers. For example, Ethan Allen, the furniture manufacturer, markets its product line at www.ethanallen.com whenever feasible. Ethan Allen retailers fill online orders and receive 25 percent of the sales price. For items shipped directly from the Ethan Allen factory, the store nearest the customer receives 10 percent of the sales price.[9]

In addition, Ethan Allen, like other manufacturers, typically lists stores on its website where consumers can shop for and buy its merchandise. More often than not, however, manufacturers employ multichannel channels, using websites as advertising and promotional vehicles.

Promotional websites have a different purpose than transactional sites: No actual selling takes place on them, but they showcase products and services and provide information.

Global Channel Strategy

Distribution is of critical importance in global marketing. The availability and quality of retailers and wholesalers as well as transportation, communication, and warehousing facilities are often determined

Survey Shows Reasons for Using Internet

Use	Number of Users
Purchasing products and services*	Nearly 50 percent
Information seeking	77 percent

*Most purchased goods and services: Books, stocks and bonds, clothes, music, and travel arrangements

Sources: Charles Zamaria and Fred Fletcher, *Canada Online! The Internet, Media and Emerging Technologies: Uses, Attitudes, Trends and International Comparisons*, Canadian Internet Project, September 2008, www.cipic.ca/en/docs/2008/CIP07%20CANADA%20ONLINE-HIGHLIGHTS.pdf.

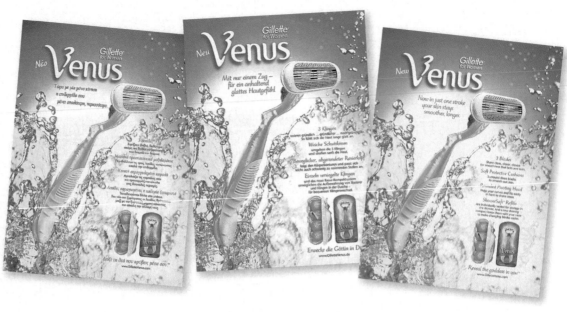

Gillette delivers the same global message whenever possible, as shown in the Gillette for Women Venus ads from Greece, Germany, and Canada.

by a country's economic infrastructure. Figure 10–6 outlines the channel through which a product manufactured in one country must travel to reach its destination in another country. The first step involves the seller; its headquarters is responsible for the successful distribution to the ultimate consumer.

The next step is the channel between two nations, moving the product from one country to another. Intermediaries that can handle this responsibility include resident buyers in a foreign country, independent merchant wholesalers who buy and sell the product, or agents who bring buyers and sellers together.

Once the product is in the foreign nation, that country's distribution channels take over. These channels can be very long or surprisingly short, depending on the product line. In Japan, fresh fish go through three intermediaries before getting to a retail outlet. Conversely, shoes go through only one intermediary. The sophistication of a country's distribution channels increases as its economic infrastructure develops. Supermarkets are helpful in selling products in many nations, but they are not popular or available in many others where culture and lack of refrigeration dictate shopping on a daily rather than a weekly basis. For example, when Coke and Pepsi entered China, both had to create direct distribution channels, investing in refrigerator units for small retailers.

Vertical Marketing Systems

The traditional marketing channels described so far represent a network of independent producers and intermediaries brought together to distribute goods and services. However, channel arrangements have emerged for the purpose of improving efficiency in performing channel functions and achieving greater marketing effectiveness. These arrangements are called vertical marketing systems. **Vertical marketing systems** are professionally managed and centrally coordinated marketing channels designed to achieve channel economies and maximum marketing impact.[10] Figure 10–7 (see page 191) depicts the major types of vertical marketing systems: corporate, contractual, and administered.

Corporate Systems The combination of successive stages of production and distribution under a single ownership is a *corporate vertical marketing system*. For example, a producer might own the intermediary at the next level down in the channel. This practice, called *forward integration*, is exemplified by Polo/Ralph Lauren, which manufactures clothing and also owns apparel shops. Other examples of forward integration include Goodyear and Sherwin Williams. Alternatively, a retailer might own a manufacturing

Figure 10–6
Channels of distribution in global marketing

operation, a practice called *backward integration*. For example, Safeway supermarkets operate their own bakeries and have a subsidiary company, Lucerne Foods, that produces a wide variety of food products for their stores. Some of these products are sold as Safeway brand, and some under the Lucerne name. Another example of backwards integration is Tiffany & Co., the exclusive jewellery retailer, which manufactures about half of the fine jewellery items for sale through its 150 stores and boutiques worldwide.

Companies seeking to reduce distribution costs and gain greater control over supply sources or resale of their products pursue forward and backward integration. Many companies favour contractual vertical marketing systems to achieve channel efficiencies and marketing effectiveness.

Tiffany & Co. and H&R Block represent two different types of vertical marketing systems. Read the text to find out how they differ.

Contractual Systems   Under a *contractual vertical marketing system*, independent production and distribution firms combine their efforts on a contractual basis to obtain greater functional economies and marketing impact than they could achieve alone. Contractual systems are the most popular among the three types of vertical marketing systems. They account for about 40 percent of all retail sales.

Three variations of contractual systems exist. Wholesaler-sponsored voluntary chains involve a wholesaler that develops a contractual relationship with small, independent retailers to standardize and coordinate buying practices, merchandising programs, and inventory management efforts. With the organization of a large number of independent retailers, economies of scale and volume discounts can be achieved to compete with chain stores. IGA is an example of a wholesaler-sponsored voluntary chain.

Figure 10–7
Types of vertical marketing systems

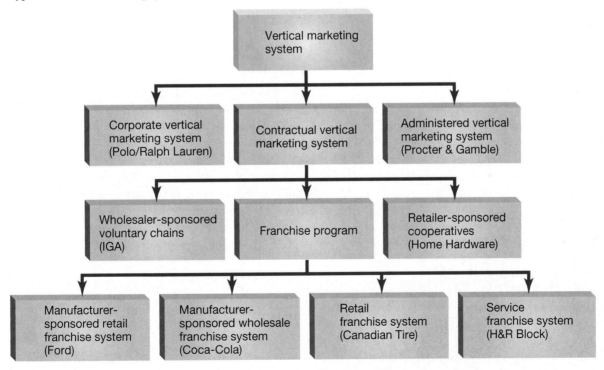

American Apparel Practises Backward Integration

Marketing NewsFlash

American Apparel started out as a T-shirt wholesaler, producing and selling in bulk to printers and other designers. The popularity of the brand has risen in recent years in the general retail market, with the company opening store locations in 11 countries worldwide with yearly sales reaching US$300 million in 2004. It is also the largest manufacturer still making its shirts in America.

One of the most successful elements of American Apparel's business is its use of backward integration—the company is its own supplier. American Apparel manufactures its own products in its Los Angeles plant—one of the largest apparel factories in America. The brand's founder Dov Charney has described the benefits of this process: "I can cut on Monday, sew Tuesday through Thursday, and ship on Friday. If I used offshore labour, that would take me 90 days." Although Charney is not opposed to outsourcing, he finds that the close-to-home approach is the logical one for his company right now as it allows the brand to quickly adapt to customers' wants and provides a rapid turnaround—demands can be met in American Apparel stores shortly after their need is known. Charney has also stated that, were he to build factories overseas, he would do so only to provide for that local market and he would pay his workers U.S. wages. ●

Sources: Janet Forgrieve, "Shirt shop sells apparel made in America," *Rocky Mountain News*, May 7, 2005, accessed at http://americanapparel.net/presscenter/articles/20050507rm.html; "American Apparel: A Made-In-U.S.A. Success," CBS News, February 4, 2006, accessed at www.cbsnews.com/stories/2007/02/04/sunday/bios/main2430121.shtml; Joellen Perry and Marianne Lavelle, "American Apparel," *U.S. News & World Report*, May 17, 2004, accessed at http://americanapparel.net/presscenter/articles/20040517usnews.html.

franchising
Contractual arrangement in which a parent company (the franchiser) allows an individual or firm (the franchisee) to operate a certain type of business under an established name and according to specific rules

Retailer-sponsored cooperatives exist when small, independent retailers form an organization that operates a wholesale facility cooperatively. Member retailers then concentrate their buying power through the wholesaler and plan collaborative promotional and pricing activities. Home Hardware is an example of a retailer-sponsored cooperative.

The most visible variation of contractual systems is **franchising**, a contractual arrangement between a parent company (a franchiser) and an individual or firm (a franchisee) that allows the franchisee to operate a certain type of business under an established name and according to specific rules.

Four types of franchise arrangements are most popular. *Manufacturer-sponsored retail franchise systems* are prominent in the automobile industry, where a manufacturer such as Ford licenses dealers to sell its cars subject to various sales and service conditions. *Manufacturer-sponsored wholesale franchise systems* appear in the soft-drink industry, where Pepsi-Cola licenses wholesalers (bottlers) that purchase concentrate from Pepsi-Cola and then carbonate, bottle, promote, and distribute its products to supermarkets and restaurants. *Retail franchise systems* are provided by firms that have designed a unique approach for selling merchandise to consumers. Canadian Tire and McDonald's represent this franchising approach.

Service franchise systems exist when franchisers license individuals or firms to dispense a service under a trade name and specific guidelines. An example is H&R Block tax services. Service franchise arrangements are the fastest-growing type of franchise.

Administered Systems By comparison, *administered vertical marketing systems* achieve coordination at successive stages of production and distribution by the size and influence of one channel member rather than through ownership. Procter & Gamble, given its broad product assortment ranging from disposable diapers to detergents, is able to obtain cooperation from supermarkets in displaying, promoting, and pricing its products. Wal-Mart can obtain cooperation from manufacturers in terms of product specifications, price levels, and promotional support, given its position as the world's largest retailer.

Channel Choice and Management

L⑤ Marketing channels not only link a producer to its buyers but also provide the means through which a firm executes various elements of its marketing strategy. Therefore, choosing a marketing channel is a critical decision.

Factors in Choosing a Marketing Channel

Marketing executives consider three questions when choosing a marketing channel and intermediaries:

1. Which channel and intermediaries will best reach the target market?

2. Which channel and intermediaries will best serve the needs of the target market?

3. Which channel and intermediaries will lead to the most cost-efficient and profitable results?

Target Market Coverage Achieving the best coverage of the target market requires attention to the density—that is, the number of stores in a given geographical area—and type of intermediaries to be used at the retail level of distribution. Three degrees of distribution intensity exist: intensive, exclusive, and selective.

Intensive distribution means that a firm tries to place its products and services in as many outlets as possible. Intensive distribution is usually chosen for convenience products or services, such as candy, newspapers, and soft drinks. For example, Coca-Cola's retail distribution objective is to place its products "within an arm's reach of desire."

Exclusive distribution is the extreme opposite of intensive distribution because only one retail outlet in a specified geographical area carries the firm's products. Exclusive distribution is typically chosen for specialty products or services such as specialty automobiles, some women's fragrances, men's and women's apparel and accessories, and yachts. Sometimes retailers sign exclusive distribution agreements with manufacturers and suppliers.

Selective distribution lies between these two extremes and means that a firm selects a few retail outlets in a specific geographical area to carry its products. Selective distribution combines some of the market coverage benefits of intensive distribution with the control measures possible with exclusive distribution. For this reason, selective distribution is the most common form of distribution intensity. It is usually associated with products such as Rolex watches, Levi's jeans, and Samsung flat-panel TVs.

Satisfying Buyer Requirements A second objective in channel design is gaining access to channels and intermediaries that satisfy at least some of the interests buyers might have when they purchase a firm's products or services. These requirements fall into four categories: information, convenience, variety, and pre- or post-sale services.

intensive distribution
A firm tries to place its products or services in as many outlets as possible

exclusive distribution
Only one retail outlet in a specific geographical area carries the firm's products

selective distribution
A firm selects a few retail outlets in a specific geographical area to carry its products

Global Availability of Fast Food

Restaurant	Number of Countries Worldwide
McDonald's	118
Burger King	67

Sources: "International Franchising Information," McDonald's website, accessed at www.mcdonalds.com/corp/intlfranchinfo.html; "BK Worldwide," Burger King website, accessed at www.burgerking.com/bkglobal.

Information is an important requirement when buyers have limited knowledge or desire specific data about a product or service. Properly chosen intermediaries communicate with buyers through in-store displays, demonstrations, and personal selling. Electronics manufacturers such as Apple and Sony have opened their own retail outlets, with highly trained personnel to inform buyers about their products and how they can meet the buyers' needs.

Convenience has multiple meanings for buyers, such as proximity or driving time to a retail outlet or hours of operation. For example, Mac's convenience stores, with outlets nationwide, many of which are open 24 hours a day, satisfy this interest for buyers. Candy and snack food firms benefit by gaining display space in these stores.

For other consumers, convenience means a minimum of time and hassle. Jiffy Lube and Mr. Lube, which promise to change engine oil and filters quickly, appeal to this aspect of convenience. Another example of convenience is Sleep Country Canada, as described in the opening vignette, which promises delivery to the customer in four days.

Variety reflects buyers' interest in having numerous competing and complementary items from which to choose. Variety is seen in both the breadth and depth of products carried by intermediaries, which enhances their attractiveness to buyers. Thus, manufacturers of pet food and supplies seek distribution through Canada's largest pet store, Petcetera, which offers over 10,000 pet products.[11]

Services provided by intermediaries are an important buying requirement for products such as large household appliances that require delivery, installation, and credit. Therefore, Whirlpool seeks dealers that provide such services.

Steve Jobs, Apple's CEO, is one person who believes that computer retailers have failed to satisfy the buying requirements of today's consumer. Believing that "Buying a car is no longer the worst purchasing experience; buying a computer is number one," he launched Apple stores.[12]

Profitability   The third consideration in designing a channel is profitability, which is determined by the revenues earned minus cost for each channel member and for the channel as a whole. Cost is the critical factor of channel profitability. These costs include distribution, advertising, and selling expenses. The extent to which channel members share these costs determines the profitability of each member and of the channel as a whole.

Channel Relationships: Conflict and Cooperation

Unfortunately, because channels consist of independent individuals and firms, there is always potential for disagreements concerning who performs which channel functions, how profits are distributed, which products and services will be provided by whom, and who makes critical channel-related decisions. These channel conflicts necessitate measures for dealing with them.

Conflict in Marketing Channels   Channel conflict arises when one channel member believes another channel member is engaged in behaviour that prevents it from achieving its goals. Two types of conflict occur in marketing channels: vertical conflict and horizontal conflict.[13]

Vertical conflict occurs between different levels in a marketing channel, for example, between a manufacturer and a wholesaler or between a wholesaler and a retailer. Three sources of vertical conflict are most common. First, conflict arises when a channel member bypasses another member and sells or buys products direct, a practice called **disintermediation**. Such a conflict emerged when Jenn-Air, a producer of kitchen appliances, decided to terminate its distributors and sell direct to retailers. Second, disagreements over how profits are distributed among channel members produce conflict. This happened when Compaq Computer Corporation and one of its dealers disagreed over how price discounts were applied in the sale of Compaq's products. A third conflict situation arises when manufacturers believe wholesalers or retailers are not giving their products adequate attention. For example, H. J. Heinz Company found itself in a conflict situation with supermarkets in Great Britain when the supermarkets promoted and displayed private brands at the expense of Heinz brands.

Horizontal conflict occurs between intermediaries at the same level in a marketing channel, such as between two or more retailers or two or more wholesalers that handle the same manufacturer's brands. For instance, the launch of Elizabeth Taylor's Black Pearls fragrance by Elizabeth Arden was put on hold when some upscale department store chains refused to stock the item once they learned that mass merchants would also carry the brand. Elizabeth Arden subsequently introduced the brand only through department stores.[14]

Cooperation in Marketing Channels Conflict can have disruptive effects on the workings of a marketing channel, so it is necessary to secure cooperation among channel members. One means is through a *channel captain*, a channel member that coordinates, directs, and supports other channel members. Channel captains can be producers, wholesalers, or retailers. Procter & Gamble assumes this role because it has a strong consumer following in brands such as Crest, Tide, and Pampers. Therefore, it can set policies or terms that supermarkets will follow. Wal-Mart and Home Depot are retail channel captains because of their strong consumer image, number of outlets, and purchasing volume.

A firm becomes a channel captain because it is the channel member with the ability to influence the behaviour of other members.[15] Influence can take four forms. First, economic influence arises from the ability of a firm to reward other members because of its strong financial position. Microsoft Corporation and Toys "Я" Us have such influence. Expertise is a second source of influence. Third, identification with a particular channel member creates influence for that channel member. For instance, retailers may compete to carry the Anne Klein line, or clothing manufacturers may compete to be carried by The Bay or Holt Renfrew. In both instances, the desire to be associated with a channel member gives that firm influence over others. Finally, influence can arise from the legitimate right of one channel member to direct the behaviour of other members. This situation occurs under contractual vertical marketing systems where a franchiser can legitimately direct how a franchisee behaves.

logistics
Activities that focus on getting the right amount of the right products to the right place at the right time at the lowest possible cost

Logistics and Supply Chain Management

L⑥ A marketing channel relies on logistics to make products available to consumers and industrial users. **Logistics** involves those activities that focus on getting the right amount of the right products to the right place at the right time at the lowest possible cost. The performance of these activities is *logistics management,* the practice of organizing the cost-effective flow of raw materials, in-process inventory, finished goods, and related information from point of origin to point of consumption to satisfy *customer requirements.*[16]

Three elements of this definition deserve emphasis. First, logistics deals with decisions from the source of raw materials to consumption of the final product—that is, the *flow* of the product. Second, those decisions have to be *cost-effective.* While it is important to drive down logistics costs, there is a limit: A firm needs to drive down logistics costs as long as it can deliver expected *customer service,* while satisfying customer requirements. The role of management is to see that customer needs are satisfied in the most cost-effective manner. When properly done, the results can be spectacular. Procter & Gamble is a case in point. Beginning in the 1990s, the company set out to meet the needs of consumers more effectively by collaborating and partnering with its suppliers and retailers to ensure that the right products reached store shelves at the right time and at a lower cost. The effort was judged a success when, during an 18-month period, Procter & Gamble's retailers recorded a US$65 million savings in logistics costs while customer service increased.[17]

The Procter & Gamble experience is not an isolated incident. Companies now recognize that getting

ask yourself

1. What are the three degrees of distribution intensity?

2. What are the three questions marketing executives consider when choosing a marketing channel and intermediaries?

the right items needed for consumption or production to the right place at the right time in the right condition at the right cost is often beyond their individual capabilities and control. Instead, collaboration, coordination, and information sharing among manufacturers, suppliers, and distributors are necessary to create a seamless flow of goods and services to customers. This perspective is represented in the concept of a supply chain and the practice of supply chain management. The opening vignette on Sleep Country Canada describes how it works hand-in-hand with its manufacturers to ensure customer satisfaction.

Supply Chains versus Marketing Channels

A **supply chain** is a series of firms that perform activities required to create and deliver a good or service to consumers or industrial users. It differs from a marketing channel in terms of the firms involved. A supply chain is longer and includes suppliers who provide raw material inputs to a manufacturer as well as the wholesalers and retailers who deliver finished goods to you. The management process is also different. **Supply chain management** is the integration and organization of information and logistics activities across firms in a supply chain for the purpose of creating and delivering goods and services that provide value to consumers. The relation among marketing channels, logistics management, and supply chain management is shown in Figure 10–8. An important feature of supply chain management is its use of sophisticated information technology that allows companies to share and operate systems for order processing, transportation scheduling, and inventory and facility management.

Sourcing, Assembling, and Delivering a New Car: The Automotive Supply Chain

All companies are members of one or more supply chains. A supply chain is essentially a series of linked suppliers and customers in which every customer is, in turn, a supplier to another customer until a finished product reaches the ultimate consumer. Even a simplified supply chain diagram for carmakers shown in Figure 10–9 (see page 197) illustrates how complex a supply chain can be.[18] A carmaker's supplier network includes thousands of firms that provide the 5,000 or so parts in a typical automobile. They provide items ranging from raw materials such as steel and rubber to components, including transmissions, tires, brakes, and seats, to complex subassemblies and assemblies such as in chassis and suspension systems that make for a smooth, stable ride. Coordinating and scheduling material and component flows for their assembly into actual automobiles by carmakers is heavily dependent on logistical activities, including transportation, order processing, inventory control, materials handling, and information technology. A central link is the carmaker supply chain manager, who is responsible for translating customer requirements into actual orders and arranging for delivery dates and financial arrangements for automobile dealers.

Logistical aspects of the automobile marketing channel are also an important part of the supply chain. Major responsibilities include transportation (which involves the selection and management of external carriers—trucking, airline, railroad, and shipping companies—for cars and parts to dealers), the operation of distribution

Figure 10–8
How distribution channels work: the relationships between supplier networks, marketing channels, logistics management, and supply chain management

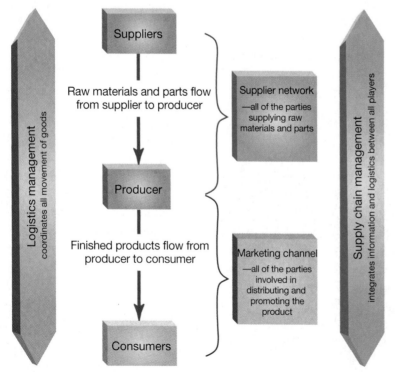

Figure 10–9
The automotive supply chain

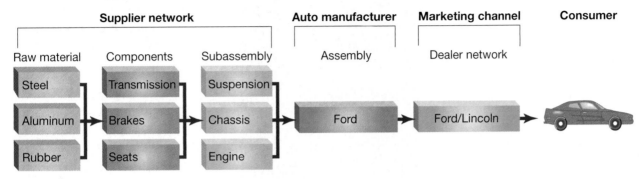

centres, the management of finished goods inventories, and order processing for sales. Supply chain managers also play an important role in the marketing channel. They work with extensive car dealer networks to ensure that the right mix of automobiles is delivered to each location. In addition, they make sure that spare and service parts are available so that dealers can meet the car maintenance and repair needs of consumers. All of this is done with the help of information technology that links the entire automotive supply chain. What does all of this cost? It is estimated that logistics costs represent 25 percent to 30 percent of the retail price of a typical new car.

Supply Chain Management and Marketing Strategy

The automotive supply chain illustration shows how logistics activities are interrelated and organized across firms to create and deliver a car for you. What's missing from this illustration is the linkage between a specific company's supply chain and its marketing strategy. Just as companies have different marketing strategies, they also manage supply chains differently. The goals to be achieved by a firm's marketing strategy determine whether its supply chain needs to focus on being more responsive or more efficient in meeting customer requirements.

Aligning a Supply Chain with Marketing Strategy There are a variety of supply chain configurations, each of which is designed to perform different tasks well. Marketers today recognize that the choice of a supply chain follows from a clearly defined marketing strategy and involves three steps:[19]

1. *Understand the customer.* To understand the customer, a company must identify the needs of the customer segment being served. These needs, such as a desire for a low price or convenience

of purchase, help a company define the relative importance of efficiency and responsiveness in meeting customer requirements.

2. *Understand the supply chain.* Second, a company must understand what a supply chain is designed to do well. Supply chains range from those that emphasize being responsive to customer requirements and demand to those that emphasize efficiency with a goal of supplying products at the lowest possible delivered cost.

3. *Harmonize the supply chain with the marketing strategy.* Finally, a company needs to ensure that what the supply chain is capable of doing well is consistent with the targeted customer's needs and its marketing strategy. If a mismatch exists between what the supply chain does particularly well and a company's marketing strategy, the company will either need to redesign the supply chain to support the marketing strategy or change the marketing strategy. The bottom line is that a poorly designed supply chain can do serious damage to an otherwise brilliant marketing strategy.

How are these steps applied and how are efficiency and response considerations built into a supply chain? Let's briefly look at how two market leaders—Dell

Computer Corporation and Wal-Mart, Inc.—have harmonized their supply chain and marketing strategy.

Dell Computer Corporation: A Responsive Supply Chain

The Dell marketing strategy targets customers who want to have the most up-to-date personal computer equipment customized to their needs. These customers are also willing to wait to have their customized personal computer delivered in a few days, rather than picking out a pre-packaged model at a retail store; and pay a reasonable, though not the lowest, price in the marketplace. Given Dell's market segments, the company has the option of choosing either an efficient or a responsive supply chain. An efficient supply chain may use inexpensive but slower modes of transportation, emphasize economies of scale in its production process by reducing the variety of PC configurations offered, and limit its assembly and inventory storage facilities to a single location, say Austin, Texas, where the company is headquartered. If Dell opted only for efficiency in its supply chain, it would be difficult if not impossible to satisfy its target customer's desire for rapid delivery and a wide variety of customizable products. Dell instead has opted for a responsive supply chain. It relies on more expensive express transportation for receipt of components from suppliers and delivery of finished products to customers. The company achieves product variety and manufacturing efficiency by designing common platforms across several products and using common components. Dell operates manufacturing facilities in the U.S., Brazil, Ireland, Malaysia, and China to assure rapid delivery. Dell also has invested heavily in information technology to link itself with suppliers and customers.

Wal-Mart, Inc.: An Efficient Supply Chain

Now let's consider Wal-Mart. Wal-Mart's marketing strategy is to be a reliable, lower-price retailer for a wide variety of mass consumption consumer goods. This strategy favours an efficient supply chain designed to deliver products to consumers at the lowest possible cost. Efficiency is achieved in a variety of ways. For instance, Wal-Mart keeps relatively low inventory levels, and most inventory is stocked in stores available for sale, not in warehouses gathering dust. The low inventory arises from Wal-Mart's use of *cross-docking*—a practice that involves unloading products from suppliers, sorting products for individual stores, and quickly reloading products onto its trucks for a particular store. No warehousing or storing of products occurs, except for a few hours or, at most, a day. Cross-docking allows Wal-Mart to operate only a small number of distribution centers to service its vast network of Wal-Mart Stores, Supercentres, and Sam's Club warehouse stores, which contributes to efficiency. On the other hand, the company runs its own fleet of trucks to service its stores.

This does increase cost and investment, but the benefits in terms of responsiveness justify the cost in Wal-Mart's case. Wal-Mart has invested significantly more than its competitors in information technology

> *Wal-Mart keeps relatively low inventory levels, and most inventory is stocked in stores available for sale, not in warehouses gathering dust.*

to operate its supply chain. The company feeds information about customer requirements and demand from its stores back to its suppliers, which manufacture only what is being demanded. This large investment has improved the efficiency of Wal-Mart's supply chain and made it responsive to customer needs.

RFID, which stands for radio frequency identification, is a tag that is incorporated in a product for tracking purposes. RFID improves the efficiency of inventory tracking and management. Wal-Mart has already asked its suppliers to use RFID. Wal-Mart says that RFID will result in a 30-percent reduction of out-of stock items and less excess inventory in the supply chain.[20] Some suppliers have complied but many to date have not. The cost of using this new technology is the reason for them not going ahead.

Three lessons can be learned from these two examples. First, there is no one best supply chain for every company. Second, the best supply chain is the one that is consistent with the needs of the customer segment being served and complements a company's marketing strategy. And finally, supply chain managers are often called upon to make trade-offs between efficiency and responsiveness on various elements of a company's supply chain.

Two Concepts of Logistics Management in a Supply Chain

L⑦ The objective of logistics management in a supply chain is to minimize total logistics costs while delivering the appropriate level of customer service.

Total Logistics Cost Concept

For our purposes **total logistics cost** includes expenses associated with transportation, materials handling and warehousing, inventory, stockouts (being out of inventory), order processing, and return goods handling.[21] Note that many of these costs are interrelated so that changes in one will impact the others. For example, as the firm attempts to minimize its transportation costs by shipping in larger quantities, it will also experience an increase in inventory levels. Larger inventory levels will not only increase inventory costs but should also reduce stockouts. It is important, therefore, to study the impact on all of the logistics decision areas when considering a change.

Customer Service Concept

Because a supply chain is a *flow*, the end of it—or *output*—is the service delivered to customers. Within the context of a supply chain, **customer service** is the ability of logistics management to satisfy users in terms of time, dependability, communication, and convenience. As suggested by Figure 10–10 (see page 200), a supply chain manager's key task is to balance these four customer service factors against total logistics cost factors.

Time In a supply chain setting, time refers to *order cycle* or *replenishment* time for an item, which means the time between the ordering of an item and when it is received and ready for use or sale. The various elements that make up the typical order cycle include recognition of the need to order, order transmittal, order processing, documentation, and transportation. A current emphasis in supply chain management is to reduce order cycle time so that the inventory levels of customers may be minimized. Another emphasis is to make the process of reordering and receiving products as simple as possible, often through inventory systems called *quick response* and *efficient consumer response* delivery systems. For example, at Wal-Mart stores, point-of-sale scanner technology records each day's sales. When

ask yourself

1. What is the principal difference between a marketing channel and a supply chain?

2. The choice of a supply chain involves what three steps?

total logistics cost
Expenses associated with transportation, materials handling and warehousing, inventory, stockouts, order processing, and return goods handling

customer service
Ability of logistics management to satisfy users in terms of time, dependability, communication, and convenience

Figure 10–10

Supply chain managers balance total logistics cost factors against customer service factors

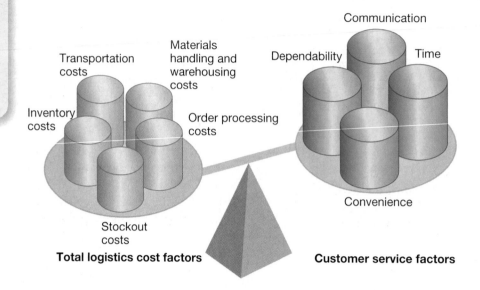

stock falls below a minimum level, a replenishment order is automatically produced. Vendors receive the order, which is processed and delivered promptly.[22]

Dependability
Dependability is the consistency of replenishment. This is important to all firms in a supply chain—and to consumers. How often do you return to a store if it fails to have in stock the item you want to purchase? Dependability can be broken into three elements: consistent lead time, safe delivery, and complete delivery. Consistent service allows planning (such as appropriate inventory levels), whereas inconsistencies create surprises. Intermediaries may be willing to accept longer lead times if they know about them in advance and can thus make plans.

Communication
Communication is a two-way link between buyer and seller that helps in monitoring service and anticipating future needs. Status reports on orders are a typical example of communication between buyer and seller.

Convenience
The concept of convenience for a supply chain manager means that there should be a minimum of effort on the part of the buyer in doing business with the seller. Is it easy for the customer to order? Are the products available from many outlets? Will the seller arrange all necessary details, such as transportation? This customer service factor has promoted the use of **vendor-managed inventory (VMI)**, whereby the *supplier* determines the product amount and assortment a customer (such as a retailer) needs and automatically delivers the appropriate items.

Campbell Soup's system illustrates how VMI works.[23] Every morning, retailers electronically inform the company of their demand for all Campbell products and the inventory levels in their distribution centres. Campbell uses that information to forecast future demand and determine which products need replenishment based on upper and lower inventory limits established with each retailer. Trucks leave the Campbell shipping plant that afternoon and arrive at the retailer's distribution centres with the required replenishments the same day.

ask yourself

1. What is the logistics management objective in a supply chain?

2. A manager's key task is to balance which customer service factors against which logistics cost factors?

Summary...*just the facts*

- A marketing channel consists of individuals and firms involved in the process of making a product or service available for use by consumers or business users.

- Intermediaries make possible the flow of products and services from producers to buyers by performing transactional, logistical, and facilitating functions. At the same time, intermediaries create time, place, form, and possession utility.

- In general, marketing channels for consumer products and services contain more intermediaries than do channels for business products and services. In some situations, producers use Internet, multiple channels and strategic channel alliances to reach buyers.

- The prevalence of consumer shopping online, as well as buying in retail stores, has made multichannel marketing popular. Multichannel marketing is the blending of different communication and delivery channels that are mutually reinforcing in attracting, retaining, and building relationships with consumers who shop and buy in the traditional marketplace as well as in the online marketspace.

- Not all companies approach multichannel marketing the same way. A major difference in approach is the use of transactional websites and promotional websites.

- Vertical marketing systems are channels designed to achieve channel function economies and marketing impact. A vertical marketing system may be one of three types: corporate, administered, or contractual.

- Channel design considerations are based on the target market coverage sought by producers, the buyer requirements to be satisfied, and the profitability of the channel. Target market coverage comes about through one of three levels of distribution density: intensive, exclusive, and selective distribution. Buyer requirements are evident in the amount of information, convenience, variety, and service sought by

consumers. Profitability—of each channel member and the channel as a whole—is largely affected by costs and whether or not costs can be shared by members.

- Conflicts in marketing channels are inevitable. Vertical conflict occurs between different levels in a channel. Horizontal conflict occurs between intermediaries at the same level in the channel.

- Logistics involves those activities that focus on getting the right amount of the right products to the right place at the right time at the lowest possible cost. Logistics management includes the coordination of the flows of both inbound and outbound goods, an emphasis on making these flows cost effective, and customer service.

- A supply chain is a sequence of firms that perform activities required to create and deliver a good or service to consumers or industrial users. Supply chain management is the integration and organization of information and logistics across firms for the purpose of creating value for consumers.

- The goals to be achieved by a firm's marketing strategy determine whether its supply chain needs to be more responsive or efficient in meeting customer requirements. Marketers today recognize that the choice of a supply chain involves three steps: (1) understand the customer, (2) understand the supply chain, and (3) harmonize the supply chain with the marketing strategy.

- The objective of logistics management in a supply chain is to minimize logistics costs while delivering maximum customer service. Minimizing total logistics cost must be weighed against specifying an acceptable customer service level that must be maintained. Although key customer service factors depend on the situation, important elements of the customer service program are likely to be time-related dependability, communications, and convenience.

Key Terms and Concepts...*a refresher*

channel conflict *p. 194*
customer service *p. 199*
disintermediation *p. 194*
dual distribution *p. 187*
electronic marketing
    channels *p. 186*
exclusive distribution *p. 193*

franchising *p. 192*
intensive distribution *p. 193*
intermediaries *p. 183*
logistics *p. 195*
marketing channel *p. 183*
multichannel marketing *p. 188*
selective distribution *p. 193*

supply chain *p. 196*
supply chain management *p. 196*
total logistics cost *p. 199*
vendor-managed inventory
    (VMI) *p. 200*
vertical marketing systems *p. 190*

Retailing
and *Wholesaling*

Retailing is an area that constantly evolves and adapts to changing consumer needs. Most recently, a new shopping centre concept, the *lifestyle centre,* emerged in response to an aging baby-boomer population and their needs for a more selective shopping experience. Anne Morash, vice president of development for The Cadillac Fairview Corporation Limited, has extensive experience in shopping centre development, and provides us with a glimpse into lifestyle centres through Cadillac Fairview's newly launched shopping centre, the Shops at Don Mills. Cadillac Fairview leads the way in Canada's commercial real estate market with innovative concepts spanning over 50 years. It focuses on high-quality retail centres and office properties, owning many landmark shopping centres such as the Toronto Eaton Centre, the Toronto-Dominion Centre, Le Carrefour Laval in Quebec, the Chinook Centre in Calgary, and the Pacific Centre in Vancouver. It prides itself on developing exciting shopping concepts by continually monitoring the consumer environment, anticipating trends, needs, and opportunities. The company is known for innovation.

Anne Morash explains that lifestyle centres are designed with the discriminating shopper in mind, not rich but discerning. The concept is a visually pleasing combination of shops, plazas, fountains, parks, and recreational areas to create an atmosphere borrowed from old-fashioned European high streets. This new style mall sees shopping as part purchase and part recreation. It is an open-air concept that combines brand-name boutiques, supermarkets, a selection of restaurants, and areas for socializing—all in a visually pleasing, village-style collection of small stores in a traditional street layout, with one landlord.

LEARNING OBJECTIVES

 Understand the benefits that retailing provides for the consumer.

 Explain retailing strategy and the different ways to classify retail outlets.

 Understand non-store retailing and its role in the retail world.

L4 Describe why consumers shop and buy online, what they purchase, and how marketers influence online purchasing behaviour.

L5 Explain how the retail mix is modified over the life cycle of the retail store.

L6 Describe the types of wholesalers and the functions they perform.

The lifestyle centre evolved from retail trends that see consumers wanting a choice of shopping experiences. Cadillac Fairview learned that on the one hand consumers want large malls with a variety of expected big-box stores, and on the other hand, they want smaller, more personal shopping areas and an increased number of sit-down restaurants where they can relax and socialize. The Shops at Don Mills appeals to the latter, and is a response to an educated, more affluent, and older female shopper.

The Shops at Don Mills is a lifestyle centre, opening in April 2009, that replaces the traditional and rather weathered Don Mills Centre. Cadillac Fairview sees this project as something special, a pioneering effort in the retail mall environment, resulting in one of the first lifestyle centres in Ontario. Anne Morash says, "This is a new breed of shopping centre that goes beyond just shopping. It is a destination that provides the opportunity for people to live, work, play, and of course, shop." Skeptics question the validity of an outdoor concept in a country where the winters are long, cold, and severe. But Morash explains, "It is the rain that keeps people away, not the cold and the snow. Shopping continues unless there are emergency weather conditions. Canadians are used to walking outside and, in fact, enjoy it!" Morash explains that the new pedestrian shopping concept does provide some weather protection with its large canopies adorning the shops and that the concept has been a success in parts of North America with similar climates.

Cadillac Fairview has designed the Shops at Don Mills so that shopping is not seen as a chore, but instead as an experience that is focused, pleasing, and convenient. It appeals to the shopper who does not enjoy aimless shopping but prefers a distinctive location where shopping, dining, and casual socializing come together at a single destination. Gone are the movie theatres and stores selling low-priced goods. The Shops at Don Mills contains only the best-in-class "A" stores with retailers providing their best designs, layout, and staff. Stores are selected so that shoppers can enjoy the shopping experience and spend time in other amenities such as restaurants. The food-court concept is replaced with five full-service discerning restaurants, a much higher number than the traditional one or two seen in regular malls. The Shops at Don Mills complex has pedestrian streets, fountains, streetscapes, a park, a town square, a post office, and an ice rink—all on 40 acres of land with office, residential, and retail space. Cadillac Fairview expects the Shops at Don Mills to cater to a substantial amount of pedestrian shoppers from the local neighbourhood, as well as shoppers from nearby areas. The clientele is expected to make frequent visits to the centre—more than once a week—for smaller purchases rather than the traditional once-a-week shopping spree for a full load of groceries. Morash explains, "Developers are building a new generation of retail environments to serve the needs of both the individual consumer and the broader community. The emergence of these lifestyle centres is simply the next step in the evolution of retail." You can see more about this innovative shopping centre at www.shopsatdonmills.ca.

Chapter 11 continues with the concept of distribution—creating a place where the customer can access the product—the place P of the 4Ps that make up the marketing mix. 🍎

The Value of Retailing

L○₁ **Retailing** includes all activities involved in selling, renting, and providing goods and services to ultimate customers for personal, family, or household use.

Retailing is an important marketing activity. Retailing engages the consumer; it provides a place for showcasing products and creates interest and excitement. Shopping is not only a way to acquire necessities but also a social activity and often an adventure—retailing makes this possible. Producers and consumers are brought together through retailing actions, and retailing also creates customer value and has a significant impact on the economy. To consumers, the value of retailing is in the form of utilities

Retailing involves creating a place where the customer can access the product.

Marketers understand that retailers rely on wholesalers to provide selection and availability of product.

Figure 11–1
Which company best represents which utilities?

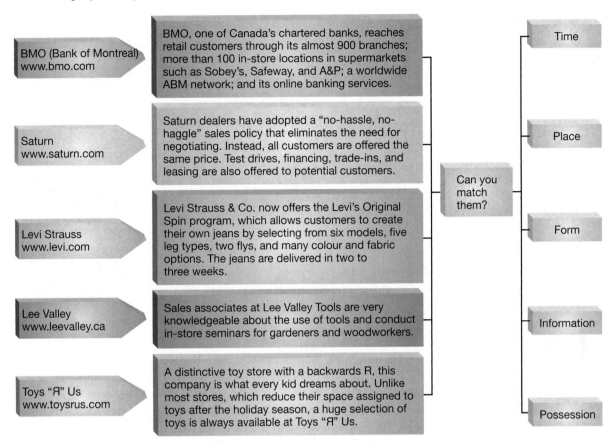

BMO (Bank of Montreal)
www.bmo.com

BMO, one of Canada's chartered banks, reaches retail customers through its almost 900 branches; more than 100 in-store locations in supermarkets such as Sobey's, Safeway, and A&P; a worldwide ABM network; and its online banking services.

Saturn
www.saturn.com

Saturn dealers have adopted a "no-hassle, no-haggle" sales policy that eliminates the need for negotiating. Instead, all customers are offered the same price. Test drives, financing, trade-ins, and leasing are also offered to potential customers.

Levi Strauss
www.levi.com

Levi Strauss & Co. now offers the Levi's Original Spin program, which allows customers to create their own jeans by selecting from six models, five leg types, two flys, and many colour and fabric options. The jeans are delivered in two to three weeks.

Lee Valley
www.leevalley.ca

Sales associates at Lee Valley Tools are very knowledgeable about the use of tools and conduct in-store seminars for gardeners and woodworkers.

Toys "Я" Us
www.toysrus.com

A distinctive toy store with a backwards R, this company is what every kid dreams about. Unlike most stores, which reduce their space assigned to toys after the holiday season, a huge selection of toys is always available at Toys "Я" Us.

Can you match them?

Time

Place

Form

Information

Possession

provided, which were discussed in Chapter 10. Retailing's economic value is represented by the number of people employed in retailing as well as by the total amount of money exchanged in retail sales.

Consumer Utilities Offered by Retailing

The utilities provided by retailers create value for consumers. Time, place, form, information, and possession utilities are offered by most retailers in varying degrees, but one utility is often emphasized more than others. Look at Figure 11-1 to find out how well you can match the retailer with the utility being emphasized in the description.

Placing minibanks in supermarkets, as the Bank of Montreal does,[1] puts the bank's products and services close to the consumer, providing place utility. By offering financing or leasing and taking used cars as trade-ins, Saturn makes the purchase easier and provides possession utility. Form utility—production or alteration of a product—is offered by Levi Strauss & Co. as it creates Original Spin jeans to meet each customer's

specifications. Finding toy shelves well stocked year-round is the time utility dreamed about by every child (and many parents) who enters Toys "Я" Us. Many retailers offer a combination of the four basic utilities. Some supermarkets, for example, offer convenient locations (place utility) and are open 24 hours (time utility). In addition, consumers may seek additional utilities such as entertainment, recreation, or information.[2]

The Canadian Retail Scene

Maybe you have had a job in retail. Many students get their first taste of employment by working in a store or restaurant. Retail is a vibrant and important part of the Canadian economy. Retailers develop strong ties with Canadians by generating more than 2 million jobs. In fact, the retail trade represents Canada's second largest labour force.[3]

In 2007, $413 billion in retail sales were recorded in Canada.[4] The largest ten Canadian retailers, ranked in descending order, are Loblaws, Alimentation Couche-Tard, Sobeys, Jean Coutu, Metro, Shoppers Drug Mart, Canadian Tire, Hudson's Bay Company, Jim Pattison Group, and Rona.[5]

Look at the chart in Figure 11–2, which tells us that 53 percent of dollars spent in retail go to food and automobile-related products and services.[6] It follows logically that the three largest retailers in the country are predominantly in the food business.

While there are many retail chains that dot the country, the retail industry is dominated by small businesses. Over 50 percent of the retailers in Canada have less than 10 employees.[7] It is an industry that operates with tight margins. It is very susceptible to economic fluctuation, and the competition is fierce. Visit your local mall and notice the turnover in stores!

The Global Retail Picture

Retailing is also a very important factor in the global economy, and it is a difficult retail climate for store owners. In the past few years, the worldwide economy has been challenged by issues such as terrorism, economic downturn, reduced tourism, political crises, and low consumer confidence. All of these issues translate into lower sales for retail. At the same time, consumers are more savvy and empowered, and it is more difficult to gain and maintain their loyalty. Profits have to be worked at very diligently. Technology is making the industry more sophisticated and streamlined, and

Figure 11–2

Retail sales ($billions) for 2007 in Canada by commodity group

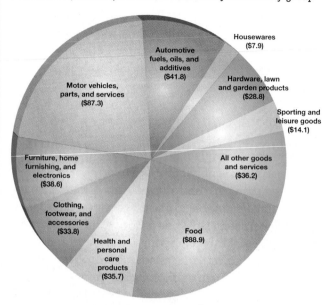

Source: Statistics Canada, CANSIM table 080-0018, December 2007.

consolidation makes some competitors large and very powerful. It is a demanding and thorny business.

Not all countries have experienced the soft demand and market challenges that have characterized the

Tim's Takes on America

Marketing NewsFlash

Tim Hortons is definitely not a struggling brand in its native Canada. There is a Tim Hortons restaurant for every 12,500 Canadians, an overwhelming number, especially when compared to its competitor McDonald's (one restaurant for every 21,000 Americans) and Dunkin' Donuts (with one outlet for every 56,000 Americans). With its 2,800 Canadian stores, Tim Hortons controls 80 percent of the coffee, doughnut, and tea market in Canada, and moves up to 90 percent for coffee alone. The fast-food chain is North America's fourth largest.

Tim Hortons has accomplished these numbers without a significant presence in the United States, but it has been attempting an expansion for several decades. In 2005, executives predicted that there would be 500 locations in the U.S. by 2007. There are presently only 400. The biggest issue affecting Tim Hortons presence in the U.S. is the lack of brand awareness and recognition. The restaurants' U.S. locations are within driving distance of the Canadian border, and two failed Florida locations were built in the southern state to capitalize on vacationing Canadians. The geography

of the existing stores shows that the chain loses brand recognition the further it gets from Canada, and this causes business to suffer. The idea of U.S. expansion is not an impossible one, however. Tim Hortons has been more successful in the U.S. than any other Canadian restaurant chain. There is a slowly developing Tim Hortons following in the U.S., and executives hope that the use of word-of-mouth advertising will help in the chain's growth. The company hoped to build 110 new locations in the northeast U.S. in 2008. ●

Sources: Jason Kirby, "Tim's takes on America," *Maclean's*, Vol. 121, Iss. 11 (March 24, 2008), pp. 32–33; Janet Whitman, "Tim Hortons' Toughest Foe; With 2,100 stores in the region, New England is Dunkin' Donuts turf," *National Post*, February 23, 2008, p. FP3; Ian Austen, "Northern Overexposure," *The New York Times*, September 8, 2007, p. C1.

major industrialized nations. Some of the developing countries or emerging markets in Asia and Eastern Europe are experiencing solid growth and are developing modern types of retailing. China, India, and Russia are seen as some of the biggest growth opportunities for retail in the next few years.

On a global scale, who is biggest? Wal-Mart! In 2006, Wal-Mart recorded sales of US$345 billion, and the next largest retailer, Carrefour, trailed at US$98 billion. A study of the top 250 global retailers by the firm Deloitte Touche Tohmatsu ranks the world's biggest in the retail industry. Of the top 250 firms, 93 are American and 91 are located in Europe (see Figure 11–3 on page 208).

The chart accompanying Figure 11–3 tells an interesting story: Most of the top 10 global retailers have a presence in many parts of the globe.

of retail offerings the customer has to choose from. This provides a challenge to retailers. It is no longer enough to appeal to customers; now the retailer has to interest, delight, and wow customers so that they will become loyal customers.

How do we define target markets? The most common descriptors are geographics, demographics, psychographics, and behaviouristics. Retailers study these factors and adjust their retail mix accordingly. McDonald's and Subway look at demographics—population, family, and age characteristics—to determine where new restaurants should be located and what formats to offer. Retailers such as Zellers and Canadian Tire look at consumers' trends and tastes and adjust their product offerings and store composition to match customer preferences. Office Depot and Shoppers Drug Mart have adjusted their store hours to respond to the behaviour of consumers; many now prefer to shop and do errands in the evening after working during the day.

Classifying Retail Outlets

For manufacturers, consumers, and the economy, retailing is an important component of marketing that has several variations. Because of the large number of alternative forms of retailing, it is easier to understand the differences among retail institutions by recognizing that outlets can be classified in several ways. First, form of ownership distinguishes retail outlets on the basis of whether individuals, corporate chains, or contractual systems own or control the outlet. Second,

Retailing Strategy

LO 2 Retailing involves many decisions and considerations, for example, deciding what type and format of retail presence to launch, determining who the target market will be, and deciding on a marketing mix to suit the particular retail concept. In this section we look at the issues in selecting a target market, the different types or classifications of retail to consider, the factors and components of the retail marketing mix, and the growing phenomenon of non-store retailing.

Selecting a Target Market

The first task in developing a retail strategy is to define a target market, describing it in detail. In Chapter 6 we discussed in detail how to segment a market and then how to choose the targets to focus on. Without customers, even the best-conceived retail concept is nothing, so focusing on customers is the guiding principle of successful retail businesses. This focus involves understanding wants and needs, knowing customer preferences, analyzing behaviour, and deciding how to craft all of the dimensions of the retail concept to appeal to the targeted customer. Look at any mall or shopping district, and you will see the varied selection

McDonald's and Subway look at demographics— population, family, and age characteristics—to determine where new restaurants should be located and what formats to offer.

Figure 11-3
Where do we find the top retailers in the world? Who are they?

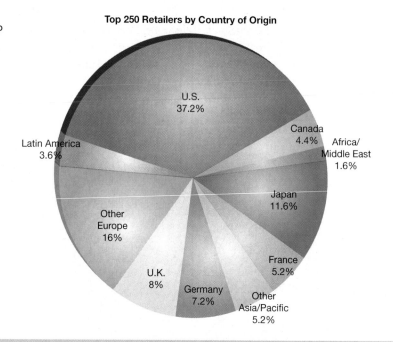

Top 250 Retailers by Country of Origin

- U.S. 37.2%
- Canada 4.4%
- Africa/Middle East 1.6%
- Japan 11.6%
- France 5.2%
- Other Asia/Pacific 5.2%
- Germany 7.2%
- U.K. 8%
- Other Europe 16%
- Latin America 3.6%

RANK	COUNTRY OF ORIGIN	NAME OF COMPANY	2006 SALES (US$ MILLIONS)	COUNTRIES OF OPERATION
1	U.S.	Wal-Mart	$344,992	Argentina, Brazil, Canada, China, Costa Rica, El Salvador, Guatemala, Honduras, Nicaragua, Germany, Japan, Mexico, Puerto Rico, U.K., U.S.
2	France	Carrefour	$97,861	Algeria, Argentina, Belgium, Brazil, Chile, China, Colombia, Dominican Republic, Egypt, France, Guadeloupe, Greece, Indonesia, Italy, Japan, Malaysia, Martinique, Oman, Poland, Portugal, Qatar, Romania, Saudi Arabia, Singapore, Spain, Switzerland, Taiwan, Thailand, Tunisia, Turkey, UAE
3	U.S.	Home Depot	$90,837	Canada, China, Mexico, Puerto Rico, U.S., Virgin Islands
4	U.K.	Tesco	$79,976	China, Czech Republic, Japan, Hungary, Republic of Ireland, Malaysia, Poland, South Korea, Taiwan, Thailand, Turkey, U.K.
5	Germany	Metro	$74,857	Austria, Belgium, Bulgaria, China, Croatia, Czech Republic, Denmark, France, Germany, Greece, Hungary, India, Italy, Japan, Luxembourg, Moldova, Morocco, Netherlands, Poland, Portugal, Romania, Russia, Serbia and Montenegro, Slovakia, Spain, Sweden, Switzerland, Turkey, Ukraine, U.K., Vietnam
6	U.S.	Kroger	$66,111	U.S.
7	U.S.	Target	$59,490	U.S.
8	U.S.	Costco	$58,963	Canada, Japan, South Korea, Mexico, Puerto Rico, Taiwan, U.K., U.S.
9	U.S.	Sears	$53,012	Canada, Guam, Puerto Rico, U.S., Virgin Islands
10	Germany	Schwarz Unternehmens Treuhand KG	$52,422	Austria, Belgium, Bulgaria, Croatia, Cyprus, Czech Republic, Denmark, Finland, France, Germany, Greece, Hungary, Republic of Ireland, Italy, Luxembourg, Netherlands, Norway, Poland, Portugal, Romania, Slovakia, Spain, Sweden, U.K.

Source: "2008 Global Powers of Retailing," Deloitte Touche Tohmatsu/*Stores*, January 2008, accessed at www.nxtbook.com/nxtbooks/nrfe/stores-globalretail08.

Marketing ▶ tip

level of service is used to describe the degree of service provided to the customer. Three levels of service include self-, limited-, and full-service retailers. Finally, the type of **merchandise mix** describes how many different types of products a store carries and in what assortment. The alternative types of outlets are discussed in greater detail in the following pages.

Form of Ownership

Independent Retailer   One of the most common forms of retail ownership is the independent business, owned by an individual. Small independent retailers account for more than 60 percent of the total retail trade in Canada. They tend to be retailers such as bakeries, sporting goods stores, jewellery stores, or gift stores. Other types of small independent retailers include restaurants, automotive supply stores, bookstores, paint stores, flower shops, and women's accessories outlets. The advantage of this form of ownership for the owner is that he or she can be his or her own boss. For customers, the independent store can offer convenience, quality personal service, and lifestyle compatibility.[9]

Corporate Chain   A second form of ownership, the corporate chain, involves multiple outlets under common ownership. If you've ever shopped at The Bay, Sears, or Loblaws, you've shopped at a chain outlet.

Market Shares of the Canadian Food Market

Loblaws	34.9 percent
Wal-Mart	2.6 percent

Source: *Marketing* magazine, November 26, 2007, p. 66.

In a chain operation, centralization of decision making and purchasing is common. Chain stores have advantages in dealing with manufacturers, particularly as the size of the chain grows. A large chain can bargain with a manufacturer to obtain good service or volume discounts on orders. Loblaws' large volume makes it a strong negotiator with manufacturers of most products. The buying power of chains is obvious to consumers who compare prices at chain stores with other types of stores. Consumers also benefit in dealing with chains because there are multiple outlets with similar merchandise and consistent management policies.

Contractual System   Contractual systems involve independently owned stores that band together to act like a chain. The three kinds described in Chapter 10 are retailer-sponsored cooperatives, wholesaler-sponsored voluntary chains, and franchises. One retailer-sponsored cooperative is Home Hardware, which is a collection of independent hardware and home-renovation stores across Canada. Home Hardware actually created its own wholesale operation to take full advantage of dealings with manufacturers and suppliers. As a cooperative, members can take advantage of volume discounts commonly available to chains and also give the impression of being a large chain, which may be viewed more favourably by some consumers. Wholesaler-sponsored voluntary chains such as Independent Grocers' Association (IGA) try to achieve similar benefits.

As noted in Chapter 10, in a franchise system, an individual or firm (the franchisee) contracts with a parent company (the franchiser) to set up a business or retail outlet. McDonald's, Holiday Inn, and Blockbuster Video all offer franchising opportunities. The franchiser usually assists in selecting the store location, setting up the store, advertising, and training personnel. In addition, the franchiser provides step-by-step procedures for the major aspects of the business and guidelines for the most likely decisions a franchisee will confront. The franchisee pays a one-time franchise fee and an annual royalty, usually tied to the store's sales.

Franchise fees paid to the franchiser can range from $10,000 for a Church's Chicken to $45,000 for a McDonald's restaurant franchise. When these fees are combined with other costs, such as building and equipment, the total investment becomes much higher. Figure 11–4 (see page 210) shows five franchises that operate across Canada, and indicates the range of investment required and the number of units operating. By selling franchises, an organization reduces the cost of expansion, although they lose some control. A good franchiser concentrates on enhancing the image and reputation of the franchise name.[10]

Level of Service

Most customers perceive little variation in retail outlets by form of ownership. Rather, differences among retailers are more obvious in terms of level of service. In some department stores, such as Zellers, very few services are provided. Some grocery stores, such as No Frills, have customers bag the food themselves. Other outlets, such as Holt Renfrew, provide a wide range of customer services from gift wrapping to wardrobe consultation.

Self-Service   Self-service is at the extreme end of the level-of-service continuum because the customer performs many functions and little is provided by the outlet. Home building-supply outlets and gas stations are often self-service. Warehouse stores such as Costco, usually in buildings several times larger than a conventional store, are self-service with all nonessential customer services eliminated. Several new forms of self-service include FedEx's placement of self-service package shipping stations in retail stores and office buildings, and self-service scanning systems currently in use in Loblaws, Home Depot, Wal-Mart, and other retailers.

Limited Service   Limited-service outlets provide some services, such as credit and merchandise return, but not others, such as alterations to clothes. General merchandise stores such as Zellers, Shoppers Drug Mart, and Ikea are usually considered limited-service outlets. Customers are responsible for most shopping

activities, although salespeople are available in departments such as cosmetics, home office, and consumer electronics.

Full Service   Full-service retailers, which include most specialty stores and department stores, provide many services to their customers. Holt Renfrew, a Canadian specialty fashion retailer with nine stores across the country, is very committed to exemplary customer service. Its stores feature more salespeople on the floor than other similarly sized stores, and Holt Renfrew offers a national concierge service, as well as personal shopping in each store. Employees are trained in customer follow-up, and many call their clients to advise them of new merchandise and send thank-you notes after purchase. With an eye kept fixed on customers and their evolving needs, Holt Renfrew is a leader in merchandise assortments and in innovations in customer services.[11]

Merchandise Mix

Retail outlets also vary by their merchandise mix, the key distinction being the breadth and depth of the items offered to customers (see Figure 11–5 on page 212). **Depth of product line**

Figure 11–4
Selected franchises and key issues

FRANCHISE	TYPE OF BUSINESS	TOTAL # OF UNITS	# OF UNITS FRANCHISED	% OF UNITS FRANCHISED	# OF UNITS IN CANADA	INVESTMENT REQUIRED (IN US$)
McDonald's	Fast food outlet	30,189	22,179	73%	1,320	$506,000–$1,630,000
Sylvan Learning Centres	Educational services provider	1,015	875	86%	75	$121,000–$219,000
Century 21	Real estate	6,585	6,585	100%	323	$12,000–$522,000
Church's Chicken	Chicken restaurant	1,229	761	62%	80	$194,000–$750,000
Second Cup	Coffee retailer	399	391	98%	399	$90,000–$335,000

Holt Renfrew Pampers Customers

According to Euromonitor International, baby-boomer Canadians (those aged 40 to 59) earned nearly double what their counterparts in the 27-to-39 age bracket did in 2006. Boomers are also more selective consumers. Although they have more disposable income, they are choosier about where and how to spend it, and they expect a greater level of quality and customer service from the stores they patronize. To keep up with this important demographic, many retailers are changing their stores, improving customer service, adding new merchandise, and providing special store features.

Customers have long known the Toronto-based retailer Holt Renfrew & Co. Ltd. for providing luxury products. In order to capitalize on the selective wallets of boomer shoppers, the company has made several baby boomer–friendly changes to its stores, emphasizing customer service and comfort. Holt Renfrew offers such services as an in-store spa, concierge service, and a gourmet restaurant. The merchant also offers a complimentary personal shopper service, a feature that has proved so popular that the retailer has doubled the number of personal shoppers over the past two years. Holt Renfrew has experienced unprecedented sales growth since implementing these changes. ●

Sources: Holt Renfrew website, www.holtrenfrew.com/holts/pages/services/services.dot?language_id=1; "Holt Renfrew Optimizes Store Experience," *Chain Store Age*, Vol. 84, Iss. 3 (March 2008), p. 62; Hollie Shaw, "Why do it when others can?" *National Post*, October 5, 2008, p. FP8.

means that the store carries a large assortment of each item, such as a shoe store that offers running shoes, dress shoes, and children's shoes. **Breadth of product line** refers to the variety of different items a store carries, such as women's clothing, men's clothing, children's clothing, cosmetics, and housewares.

Depth of Line Stores that carry a large assortment (depth) of a related line of items are limited-line stores. Sport Chek sporting goods stores carry considerable depth in sports equipment ranging from golf accessories to running shoes. Stores that carry tremendous depth in one primary line of merchandise are single-line stores. La Senza, a nationwide chain, carries great depth in women's lingerie. Both limited- and single-line stores are often referred to as *specialty outlets*.

Specialty outlets focus on one type of product, such as electronics (Future Shop), office supplies (Staples Business Depot), or books (Chapters-Indigo) at very competitive prices. These outlets are referred to in the trade as category killers because they often dominate the market. Chapters-Indigo, for example, controls a large percentage of the retail book market in Canada.

Breadth of Line Stores that carry a broad product line, with limited depth, are referred to as *general merchandise stores*. For example, large department stores such as The Bay, Sears, and Zellers carry a wide range of different types of products but not unusual sizes. The breadth and depth of merchandise lines are important decisions for a retailer. Traditionally, outlets carried related lines of goods. Today, however, **scrambled merchandising**, offering several unrelated product lines in a single store, is common. The modern drugstore carries food, cosmetics, camera equipment, magazines, paper products, toys, small hardware items, and pharmaceuticals. Supermarkets rent carpet-cleaning equipment, operate pharmacy departments, and sell flowers.

Scrambled merchandising is convenient for consumers because it eliminates the number of stops required in a shopping trip. However, for the retailer

Staples Business Depot is a category killer in office supplies.

> **breadth of product line** The variety of different items a store carries
>
> **scrambled merchandising** Offering several unrelated products lines in a single retail store

intertype
competition
Competition
between very dis-
similar types of
retail outlets

retailing mix
The goods and
services, physical
distribution, and
communications
tactics chosen by
a store

Figure 11–5

Breadth versus depth of merchandise lines

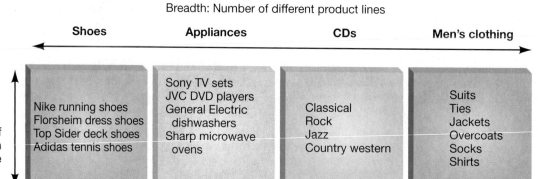

Breadth: Number of different product lines

| Shoes | Appliances | CDs | Men's clothing |

Depth: Number of
items within each
productline

Shoes: Nike running shoes, Florsheim dress shoes, Top Sider deck shoes, Adidas tennis shoes

Appliances: Sony TV sets, JVC DVD players, General Electric dishwashers, Sharp microwave ovens

CDs: Classical, Rock, Jazz, Country western

Men's clothing: Suits, Ties, Jackets, Overcoats, Socks, Shirts

this merchandising policy means that there is competition between very dissimilar types of retail outlets, or **intertype competition**. A local bakery may compete with a department store, discount outlet, or even a local gas station. Scrambled merchandising and intertype competition make retailing more challenging.

Retailing Mix

The marketing mix, or the 4 Ps (product, price, place, and promotion), are used in retail just as they are in other businesses, but with some unique considerations. In this section we look at the **retailing mix**, which includes product and service considerations, retail pricing, physical location factors, and communications, as shown in Figure 11–6 (see page 213). All of these components of the mix focus on the consumer. In retail it is often said that the consumer is king, and treating them that way is a winning idea for successful retailing.

Products and Services One of the first decisions that retailers make is what they are going to sell. Usually both services and products are offered. A department store such as The Bay sells many products—from clothing to housewares—and also provide services such as bridal registries. Magicuts provides services such as haircuts, colouring, and styling, but also sells hair care products. The balance between products and services involves a trade-off between costs and customer satisfaction. Retailers decide where their concentration will be—on convenience, goods, or service offerings—and what their target customers will most value.

ask yourself

1. Centralized decision making and purchasing are an advantage of _____ ownership.

2. What are some examples of stores with scrambled merchandising?

3. Would a shop for big men's clothes carrying pants in sizes 40 to 60 have a broad or deep product line?

In the previous section we talked about decisions to be made regarding the breadth and depth of the product assortment. Merchandise selection is one of the major attracting factors for customers, so choices and combinations must be made carefully and continually updated to reflect current trends and tastes. This involves finding sources of supply of the products, or having them manufactured, as well as managing inventory and warehousing.

Product and service strategy evolves over time. In retail stores in Canada, we have products available to us from all over the world. This makes a wide selection of choices for the consumer, but a significant challenge for the retailer. Think about food stores for a minute: In your shopping basket, you may have a mango from Mexico, cookies from England, spices from India, and rice from China. Imagine the task of the merchandiser who must decide which products to order from all over the globe, as well as how to store and display them.

Retail Pricing In setting prices for merchandise, retailers must decide on the markup, markdown, and timing for markdowns. The markup refers to how much should be added to the cost the retailer paid for a product to reach the final selling price. We discussed the calculation of markup in Chapter 9. The difference between the final selling price and retailer cost is called the gross margin.

Discounting a product, or taking a *markdown*, occurs when the product does not sell at the original price and an adjustment is necessary. Often, new models or styles

force the price of existing models to be marked down. Discounts may also be used to increase demand for related products.[12] For example, retailers might take a markdown on DVD players to increase sales of DVDs or reduce the price of cake mix to generate frosting purchases. The *timing* of a markdown can be important. Many retailers take a markdown as soon as sales fall off, to free up valuable selling space and obtain cash. However, other stores delay markdowns to discourage bargain hunters and maintain an image of quality. There is no clear answer, but retailers must consider how the timing might affect future sales.

Although most retailers plan markdowns, many retailers use price discounts as a part of their regular merchandising policy. Wal-Mart and Home Depot, for example, emphasize consistently low prices and eliminate most markdowns with a strategy often called *everyday low pricing*.[13] Consumers often use price as an indicator of product quality; however, the brand name of the product and the image of the store become important decision factors in these situations.[14]

A special issue for retailers trying to keep prices low is **shrinkage**, or breakage and theft of merchandise by customers and employees. What is surprising is that more than 50 percent of thefts are not made by consumers but by employees.

Off-price retailing is a retail pricing practice that is used by retailers such as Winners. **Off-price retailing** involves selling brand-name merchandise at lower than regular prices. The difference between the off-price retailer and a discount store is that off-price merchandise is bought by the retailer from manufacturers with excess inventory at prices below wholesale prices, whereas the discounter buys at full wholesale price but takes less of a markup than do traditional department stores. Because of this difference in the way merchandise is purchased by the retailer, selection at an off-price retailer is unpredictable, and searching for bargains has become a popular activity for many consumers. Savings to the consumer at off-price retailers are reported as high as 70 percent off the prices of a traditional department store.

Physical Location Another aspect of the retailing mix involves deciding where to locate the store and how many stores to have. Department stores, which started downtown in most cities, have followed customers to the suburbs, and in recent years more stores have been opened in large regional malls. Most stores today are near several others in one of five settings: the central business district, the regional centre, the community shopping centre, the strip, or the power centre.

The **central business district** is the oldest retail setting, the community's downtown area. Until the regional outflow to suburbs, it was the major shopping area, but the suburban population has grown at the expense of the downtown shopping area.

Regional shopping centres consist of 50 to 150 stores that typically attract customers who live or work within a 5- to 15-kilometre range. These large shopping

> ## "What is surprising is that more than 50 percent of thefts are not made by consumers but by employees."

shrinkage Breakage and theft of merchandise by customers and employees

off-price retailing Selling brand-name merchandise at lower than regular prices

central business district The oldest retail setting, the community's downtown area

regional shopping centres Consist of 50 to 150 stores that typically attract customers who live within a 5- to 15-kilometre range; often containing two or three anchor stores

Figure 11–6
The retailing mix

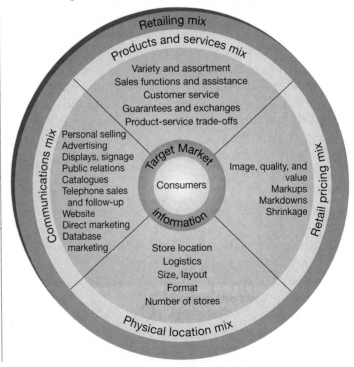

areas often contain two or three anchor stores, which are well-known national or regional stores such as Sears and The Bay. The largest variation of a regional centre is the West Edmonton Mall in Alberta. The shopping centre is a conglomerate of over 800 stores, seven amusement centres, 110 restaurants, and a 355-room Fantasyland hotel.[15]

A more limited approach to retail location is the community shopping centre, which typically has one primary store (usually a department store branch) and often about 20 to 40 smaller outlets. Generally, these centres serve a population of consumers who are within a 2- to 5-kilometre drive.

Not every suburban store is located in a shopping mall. Many neighbourhoods have clusters of stores, referred to as a strip location, to serve people who are within a 5- to 10-minute drive. Gas station, hardware, laundry, grocery, and pharmacy outlets are commonly found in a strip location. Unlike the larger shopping centres, the composition of these stores is usually unplanned. A variation of the strip shopping location is called the power centre, which is a large shopping strip with many national stores. Power centres are seen as having the convenient location found in many strip centres and the added power of national stores. These large strips often have two to five anchor stores plus a supermarket, which brings the shopper to the power centre on a weekly basis.[16]

This chapter's opening vignette focused on a new shopping centre concept called the lifestyle centre. It emerged in response to consumers' needs for a more selective shopping experience. The concept is a visually pleasing combination of shops, plazas, fountains, parks and recreational areas to create an atmosphere borrowed from old-fashioned European high streets.

Several new types of retail locations include carts, kiosks, and wall units. These forms of retailing have been popular in airports and mall common areas because they provide consumers with easy access and rental income for the property owner. Retailers benefit from the relatively low cost compared with a regular store.

Communications The elements of the retailing communication mix described in Figure 11–6 represent an exciting menu of choices for creating customer value in the marketplace. Each format allows retailers to offer unique benefits and meet particular needs of various customer groups. Today, retailers combine many of the formats to offer a broader spectrum of benefits and experiences. These multichannel retailers utilize and integrate a combination of traditional store and non-store formats such as catalogues, television, and online retailing. Chapters-Indigo, for example, created chapters.indigo.ca to compete with Amazon.ca. Similarly, Office Depot has integrated its store, catalogue, and Internet operations.

Integrated channels can make shopping simpler and more convenient. A consumer can research choices online or in a catalogue and then make a purchase online, over the telephone, or at the closest store. In addition, the use of multiple channels allows retailers to reach a broader profile of customers. While online retailing may cannibalize catalogue business to some degree, a web transaction costs about half

---

Canadian Tire Facts and Figures

Canadian Tire's retail sales that now come from the automotive category — **26%**

Average amount customers spend per trip to Canadian Tire — **$33.25**

Number of years the Canadian Tire Guy appeared in the retailer's television ads — **8**

marketing meter

Source: *Marketing* magazine, June 16, 2008, p. 42.

Average Sales per Square Foot

Store	Sales
The Bay	$155.54
Canadian Tire	$458.30

Source: *Marketing* magazine, April 30, 2007, p. 59.

as much to process as a catalogue order. Multichannel retailers also benefit from the synergy of sharing information among the different channel operations. Online retailers, for example, have recognized that the Internet is more of a transactional medium than a relationship-building medium and are working to find ways to complement traditional customer interactions.[17]

Non-store Retailing

LO③ Most of the retailing examples discussed earlier in the chapter, such as corporate chains, department stores, and limited- and single-line specialty stores, involve store retailing. Many retailing activities today, however, are not limited to sales in a store. Non-store retailing occurs outside a retail outlet through activities that involve varying levels of customer and retailer involvement. Forms of non-store retailing include automatic vending, television home shopping, and direct marketing (direct mail and catalogue retailing, telemarketing, and direct selling). Many traditional "brick and mortar" stores are involved in non-store retailing, making them "click and mortar" concepts; for example, Chapters-Indigo has developed chapters.indigo.ca, its online store. Dell Computers, in contrast, has no stores and relies mainly on non-store retailing for its consumer sales.

Automatic Vending Non-store retailing includes vending machines, which make it possible to serve customers when and where stores cannot. Maintaining and operating vending machines is expensive, so product prices in vending machines tend to be higher than those in stores. Typically, small convenience products are available in vending machines. In North America, some 60 percent of vending machines are soft-drink machines. In

Japan, however, products available in vending machines include dried squid, hair tonic, boxers, green tea, beer, CDs, books, clothing, and even music downloaded from a satellite transmission system. Sanyo Electric recently introduced a fully automated convenience store![18]

Improved technology will soon make vending machines easier to use by reducing the need for cash. In Europe, for example, Marconi Online Systems has installed 6,000 vending machines that allow consumers to pay for products using a cellphone. Similarly, the world's largest vending machine company, Canteen Vending Services, is testing a cashless system called FreedomPay, which allows consumers to wave a small wand in front of a sensor to make a purchase.

Another improvement in vending machines—the use of wireless technology to notify retailers when their machines are empty—is one reason automatic merchandising sales are expected to increase in the future.[19]

Television Home Shopping Television home shopping is possible when consumers watch a shopping channel on which products are displayed; orders are then placed over the telephone or the Internet. One popular network is The Shopping Channel, which has 24-hour programming and calls itself a broadcast retailer. A limitation of TV shopping has been the lack of buyer-seller interaction. New Internet technologies, however, now allow consumers to simultaneously shop, chat, and interact with their favourite show host while watching TV.[20]

Direct Marketing from a Retailing Perspective We talk in detail about direct marketing in Chapter 13; here we introduce the idea, as it is

ask yourself

1. Explain what shrinkage is.

2. A large shopping strip with multiple anchor stores is a _____ centre.

3. How do multichannel retailers make shopping simpler and more convenient?

telemarketing
Using the telephone to interact with and sell directly to consumers

an important form of retailing. In its simplest terms, direct marketing is an interactive process of marketing that uses advertising media or direct consumer contact to offer products or services. When a direct communication to a consumer or a business market is intended to generate a response from the recipient, direct marketing is the tactic being used.

Direct Mail and Catalogues Direct-mail and catalogue retailing is attractive because it eliminates the cost of a store and clerks. It costs a traditional retail store more than twice the amount to acquire a new customer than it costs a catalogue retailer. Why? Because catalogues improve marketing efficiency through segmentation and targeting. In addition, they create customer value by providing a fast and convenient means of making a purchase. In Canada, the amount spent on direct-mail catalogue merchandise continues to increase; internationally, spending is also increasing. IKEA delivers 130 million copies of its catalogue to 36 countries in 28 languages, including 5 million in Canada.[21]

One reason for the growth in catalogue sales is that traditional retailers such as Office Depot are adding catalogue operations. Another reason is that many Internet retailers such as Amazon.com have also added catalogues. As consumers' direct-mail purchases have increased, the number of catalogues and the number of products sold through catalogues have increased. A typical Canadian household now receives dozens of catalogues every year, and there are billions circulated around the world. The competition, combined with recent increases in postal rates, however, have caused

catalogue retailers to focus on proven customers rather than "prospects." Another successful new approach used by many catalogue retailers is to send specialty catalogues to market niches identified in their databases. L.L. Bean, a longstanding catalogue retailer, has developed an individual catalogue for fly-fishing enthusiasts. Lee Valley sends out specialized catalogues for hardware, woodworking, gardening, and Christmas.[22]

Telemarketing Another form of non-store retailing, called **telemarketing**, involves using the telephone to interact with and sell directly to consumers. Compared with direct mail, telemarketing is often viewed as a more efficient means of targeting consumers, although the two techniques are often used together. Sears Canada utilizes telemarketing to increase sales of extended warranty programs and other services. Communications companies such as Sprint and Bell Mobility telemarket new potential customers, and financial institutions such as HSBC and MBNA use telemarketing for customer follow-up and cross-selling. (Just in case you have not heard of these financial companies, here's a glimpse at who they are. HSBC, or the HSBC Group, is one of the largest banking and financial services organizations in the world, and over 100 years old, named from The Hongkong and Shanghai Banking Corporation Limited. MBNA is the largest independent credit-card issuer in the world; you may think that the letters MBNA should stand for some longer name, but apparently it does not.) Telemarketing has grown in popularity as companies search for ways to cut costs but still provide convenient access to their customers. According to the American Teleservices Association, annual telemarketing sales exceed US$500 billion.[23]

IKEA DELIVERS 130 MILLION COPIES OF ITS CATALOGUE TO 36 COUNTRIES IN 28 LANGUAGES, INCLUDING 5 MILLION IN CANADA.

As the use of telemarketing grows, consumer privacy has become a topic of discussion among consumers, governments, and businesses. Issues such as industry standards, ethical guidelines, and new privacy laws are evolving to provide a balance between the varying perspectives. In September 2008, the Canadian Radio-television and Telecommunications Commission (CRTC) instituted a National Do Not Call List (DNCL), which was created to enable Canadian consumers to reduce the number of unsolicited telemarketing calls they receive. Every year, thousands of Canadians raise concerns about receiving unwanted telemarketing calls.

Direct Selling Direct selling, sometimes called door-to-door retailing, involves direct sales of goods and services to consumers through personal interactions and demonstrations in their home or office. A variety of companies, including familiar names such as Avon, Tupperware, and Mary Kay Cosmetics, have created an industry with billions in sales by providing consumers with personalized service and convenience. However, sales have been declining as retail chains begin to carry similar products at discount prices and as the increasing number of dual-career households reduces the number of potential buyers who can be found at home.

In response to change, many direct-selling retailers are expanding into other markets. Avon, for example, already has 3 million sales representatives in 137 countries including Mexico, Poland, Argentina, and China.[24] Similarly, other retailers such as Amway (now also known as Quixtar), Herbalife, and Electrolux are rapidly expanding. More than 70 percent of Amway's US$7 billion in sales now comes from outside North America, and sales in Japan alone exceed sales in North America.[25] Direct selling is likely to continue to grow in markets where the lack of effective distribution channels increases the importance of door-to-door convenience and where the lack of consumer knowledge about products and brands will increase the need for a person-to-person approach.[26]

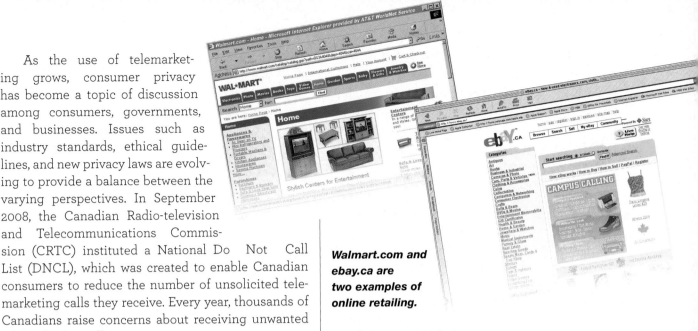

Walmart.com and ebay.ca are two examples of online retailing.

Online Retailing

L4 Online retailing allows customers to search for, evaluate, and order products through the Internet. For many consumers, the advantages of this form of retailing are the 24-hour access, the ability to comparison shop, the in-home privacy, and the variety. Studies of online shoppers indicated that men were initially more likely than women to buy something online. As the number of online households increased to more than 50 percent, however, the profile of online shoppers changed to include all shoppers. In addition, the number of online retailers grew rapidly for several years but then declined as many stand-alone, Internet-only businesses failed or consolidated. Today, there has been a melding of traditional and online retailers—"bricks and clicks"—that are using experiences from both approaches to create better value and experiences for customers. Wal-Mart in the U.S. has recently introduced "site-to-store" service that allows customers to order online and pick up the order without a shipping fee at the store of their choice. Experts predict that online sales will reach US$328 billion by 2010.[27]

Consumers can make online retail purchases in several different ways.

- They can pay dues and become members of an online discount service.
- They can use a shopping "bot" such as www.mysimon.com.
- They can go directly to online malls or online shopping directories (portals) such as www.retailcanada.com, which features more than 5,000 Canadian online stores.

ask yourself

1. Why are catalogue sales growing?

2. Where are direct-selling retail sales growing? Why?

- They can simply go to a specific online retailer's website.
- A final, and quickly growing, approach to online retailing is the online auction, such as www.ebay.ca, where consumers bid on more than 1,000 categories of products.

One of the biggest problems online retailers face is that nearly two-thirds of online shoppers make it to "checkout" and then leave the website to compare shipping costs and prices on other sites. Of the shoppers who leave, 70 percent do not return. One way online retailers are addressing this issue is to offer consumers a comparison of competitors' offerings. Online retailers are also trying to improve the online retailing experience by adding experiential, or interactive, activities to their websites, such as apparel stores' use of "virtual models" to involve consumers in the purchase process and help with product selection.[28] Car manufacturers such as BMW, Mercedes, and Jaguar encourage website visitors to "build" a vehicle by selecting interior and exterior colours, packages, and options and then view the customized virtual car.

Why Consumers Shop and Buy Online

Consumers typically offer six reasons why they shop and buy online: convenience, choice, customization, communication, cost, and control (see Figure 11–7).

- *Convenience.* Online shopping and buying is *convenient*, so websites must be easy to locate and navigate, and image downloads must be fast.
- *Choice.* There are two dimensions to choice: *selection*—numerous websites for almost anything consumers want—and *assistance*—interactive capabilities of Internet/web-enabled technologies assist customers to make informed choices.
- *Customization.* Internet/web-enabled capabilities make possible a highly interactive and individualized information and exchange environment for shoppers and buyers. Consumers get what they want and feel good about the experience.
- *Communication.* Communication can take three forms: marketer-to-consumer e-mail notification, consumer-to-marketer buying and service requests, and consumer-to-consumer chat rooms and instant messaging.[29]

As a group, online consumers, like Internet/web users, are evenly split between men and women and tend to be better educated, younger, and more affluent than the general population, which makes them an attractive market.

- *Cost.* Many popular items bought online can be purchased at the same price or cheaper than in retail stores. Lower prices also result from Internet/web-enabled software that permits *dynamic pricing*, the practice of changing prices for products and services in real time in response to supply and demand conditions.
- *Control.* Online shoppers and buyers are empowered consumers. They readily use Internet/web-enabled technology to seek information, evaluate alternatives, and make purchase decisions on their own time, terms, and conditions.

When and Where Online Consumers Shop and Buy Shopping and buying also happen at different times in the online marketspace than in the traditional marketplace.[30] About 80 percent of online retail sales occur Monday through Friday. The busiest shopping day is Wednesday. By comparison, 35 percent of retail store sales are registered on the

Figure 11–7

Why consumers shop and buy online

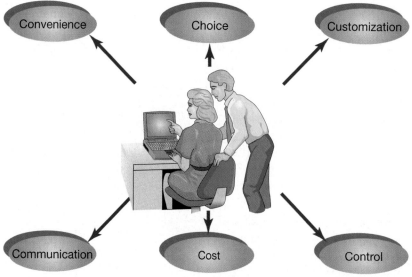

weekend. Saturday is the most popular shopping day. Monday through Friday online shopping and buying often occurs during normal work hours—some 40 percent of online consumers say they visit websites from their place of work, which partially accounts for the sales level during the workweek. Favourite websites for workday shopping and buying include those featuring event tickets, online periodical subscriptions, flowers and gifts, consumer electronics, and travel.

Websites offering health and beauty items, apparel and accessories, and music and video tend to be browsed and bought at home. Consumers are more likely to browse than buy online. Although 9 in 10 online consumers regularly shop in the marketspace of websites, over half (51 percent) confine their purchases to the traditional retail store marketplace.[31]

Describing the Online Consumer

Who are online consumers, and what do they buy? Why do they choose to shop and purchase products and services in the new marketspace rather than or in addition to the traditional marketplace? Cybershoppers, Netizens, and e-shoppers—whatever name you use for them—they do differ demographically from the general population, although over time they will likely become one and the same. Online consumers own or have access to a computer or an Internet/web-enabled device, such as a wireless cellular telephone. Nearly two out of every three Canadians accessed the Internet at least once a month, according to a Leger Marketing poll. This access may be via a computer at home with Internet/web access, although access is often possible at work or school.

Online consumers are the sub-segment of all Internet/web users who use this technology to research products and services and make purchases. Research indicates that about 80 percent of all adult Internet/web users have sought online product or service information at one time or another.[32] For example, some 70 percent of prospective travellers have researched travel information online, even though fewer than 25 percent have actually made online travel reservations. Over 40 percent have researched automobiles before making a purchase, but only 8 percent of users actually bought a vehicle online. About two-thirds of adult Internet/web users have actually purchased a product or service online at one time or another.

As a group, online consumers, like Internet/web users, are evenly split between men and women and tend to be better educated, younger, and more affluent than the general population, which makes them an attractive market. Even though online shopping and buying is growing in popularity, a small percentage of online consumers still account for a disproportionate share of online retail sales in North America. It is estimated that 20 percent of online consumers who spend $1,000-plus per year online account for 87 percent of total consumer online sales.[33]

What Online Consumers Buy

There is a lot marketers have to learn about online consumer purchase behaviour. Although research has documented the most frequently purchased products and services bought online, marketers also need to know why these items are popular. There are six general product and service categories that dominate online consumer buying today and for the foreseeable future, as shown in Figure 11–8 (see page 220).[34]

The Changing Nature of Retailing: The Retail Life Cycle

LO 5 Retailing is the most dynamic aspect of a channel of distribution. New retailers are always entering the market, searching for a new position that will attract customers. The reason for this continual change is explained by the retail life cycle.

The Retail Life Cycle

The process of growth and decline that retail outlets, like products, experience is described by the retail life cycle.[35] Figure 11–9 (see page 221) shows the retail life cycle and the position of various current forms of retail outlets on it. Early growth is the stage when a retail outlet first appears, with a major difference from existing competition. Market share rises gradually, although profits may be low because of start-up costs. In the next stage, accelerated development, both market share and profit achieve their greatest growth rates. Usually, multiple outlets are established as companies focus on the distribution element of the retailing mix. In this stage some later competitors may enter. Wendy's, for example, appeared on the hamburger chain scene almost 20 years after McDonald's had begun operation. The key goal for the retailer in this stage is to establish a dominant position in the fight for market share.

The battle for market share is usually fought before the maturity phase, and some competitors drop out of the market. New retail forms enter in the maturity phase, stores try to maintain their market share, and price discounting occurs. For example, when McDonald's introduced its Extra Value Meal, a discounted package of burger, fries, and drink, Wendy's followed with a Value Menu.

Wholesaling

Many retailers rely on intermediaries to provide them with selection and availability of the products sold in their retail operations. Many other businesses also use intermediaries to provide them with selection and availability plus value-added services for products that they need to operate their businesses. Those intermediaries are commonly called wholesalers and agents (described briefly in Chapter 10), according to the functions that they fulfill in the distribution process. In addition, there are manufacturers' sales offices operated by the original manufacturers of the products. All of these wholesaling intermediaries play an important role in the retailing process and in helping other businesses get the products they need.

Figure 11–8
Product and service categories for online shopping

TYPE OF PRODUCT OR SERVICE BOUGHT ONLINE	EXAMPLES	
1. Product information important, prepurchase trial not critical	Computers, computer accessories, books	
2. Audio or video demonstration important	CDs, DVDs, videos	
3. Items that can be delivered digitally	Software, travel reservations, financial brokerage services	
4. Unique items	Collectibles, gifts	
5. Regularly purchased items where convenience is important	Consumer packaged goods, grocery items	
6. Highly standardized products, price very important	Insurance (auto, home), home improvement products, toys, some casual clothing	

Merchant Wholesalers

Merchant wholesalers are independently owned firms that take title to—that is, they buy—the merchandise they handle. They go by various names, described in detail below. About 83 percent of the firms engaged in wholesaling activities are merchant wholesalers.

Merchant wholesalers are classified as either full-service or limited-service wholesalers, depending on the number of functions performed. Two major types of full-service wholesalers exist. General merchandise (or full-line) wholesalers carry a broad assortment of merchandise and perform all channel functions. This type

manufacturers' agents Work for several producers and carry non-competitive, complementary merchandise in an exclusive territory

selling agents Represent a single producer and are responsible for the entire marketing function of that producer

of wholesaler is most prevalent in the hardware, drug, and clothing industries. However, these wholesalers do not maintain much depth of assortment within specific product lines. Specialty merchandise (or limited-line) wholesalers offer a relatively narrow range of products but have an extensive assortment within the product lines carried. They perform all channel functions and are found in the health foods, automotive parts, and seafood industries.

Four major types of limited-service wholesalers exist. Rack jobbers furnish the racks or shelves that display merchandise in retail stores and perform all channel functions. They sell on consignment to retailers, which means they retain the title to the products displayed and bill retailers only for the merchandise sold. Familiar products such as hosiery, toys, housewares, and health and beauty aids are sold by rack jobbers. Cash and carry wholesalers take title to merchandise but sell only to buyers who call on them, pay cash for merchandise, and furnish their own transportation for merchandise. They carry a limited product assortment and do not make deliveries, extend credit, or supply market information. This wholesaler commonly deals in electric supplies, office supplies, hardware products, and groceries. Drop shippers, or desk jobbers, are wholesalers that own the merchandise they sell but do not physically handle, stock, or deliver it. They simply solicit orders from retailers and other wholesalers and have the merchandise shipped directly from a producer to a buyer. Drop shippers are used for bulky products such as coal, lumber, and chemicals, which are sold in large quantities. Truck jobbers are small wholesalers that have a small warehouse from which they stock their trucks for distribution to retailers. They usually handle limited assortments of fast-moving or perishable items that are sold for cash directly from trucks in their original packages. Truck jobbers handle products such as bakery items, dairy products, and meat.

Agents and Brokers

Unlike merchant wholesalers, agents and brokers do not take title to merchandise and typically provide fewer channel functions. They make their profit from commissions or fees paid for their services, whereas merchant wholesalers make their profit from the sale of the merchandise they have bought and resold.

Manufacturers' agents and selling agents are the two major types of agents used by producers. **Manufacturers' agents**, or manufacturers' representatives, work for several producers and carry non-competitive, complementary merchandise in an exclusive territory. Manufacturers' agents act as a producer's sales arm in a territory and are principally responsible for the transactional channel functions, primarily selling. They are used extensively in the automotive supply, footwear, and fabricated steel industries. By comparison, **selling agents** represent a single producer and are responsible for the entire marketing function of that producer. They design promotional plans, set prices, determine distribution policies, and make recommendations on product strategy. Selling agents are used by small producers in the textile, apparel, food, and home furnishing industries.

Figure 11–9
The retail life cycle

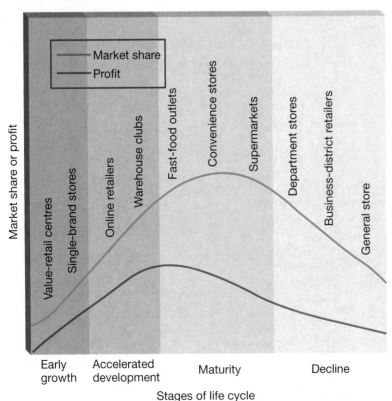

The Long-Distance Journey of a Fast-Food Order

Marketing **NewsFlash**

The days of yelling lunch orders into a tinny speaker hoping that they will be properly heard and understood by the person on the other end may be a thing of the past. A number of McDonald's restaurants are using remote call centres for their drive-thru orders. The company hopes that this plan will help to improve customer service, both by increasing order-processing speed and by allowing in-store employees to focus more of their attention on helping customers face-to-face.

A large amount of the complaints received by McDonald's are from customers who are unhappy with their drive-thru service, most often because they received the wrong order. The prevailing theory regarding drive-thru problems says that mistakes tend to come from the person taking the orders, not from the cooks themselves. By using call centre employees whose job is solely to take orders, McDonalds hopes to reduce the number of drive-thru mistakes. Orders are taken remotely, then sent back to the restaurants by Internet and are filled just inside the drive-thru window, a short distance from the customer who ordered them. This new system is not perfect—there are technology issues (customers are sometimes hard to hear), but it is showing itself to be effective. Employees at a call centre in Santa Monica, California, can take up to 95 orders an hour during peak times. ●

Sources: Matt Richtel, "The Long-Distance Journey of a Fast-Food Order," *The New York Times*, April 11, 2006, accessed at www.nytimes.com/2006/04/11/technology/11fast.html; Christine Lagorio, "Outsourcing Drive Thru? McDonalds Tests Use Of Remote Call Centers To Replace Order Windows," CBS News, accessed at www.cbsnews.com/stories/2005/03/11/national/main679730.shtml; "McDonald's could employ call centers to handle drive-thru," Associated Press, March 11, 2005, accessed at www.usatoday.com/tech/products/services/2005-03-11-mc-call-centers_x.htm.

---

brokers
Independent firms or individuals whose main function is to bring buyers and sellers together to make sales

Brokers are independent firms or individuals whose main function is to bring buyers and sellers together to make sales. Brokers, unlike agents, usually have no continuous relationship with the buyer or seller but negotiate a contract between two parties and then move on to another task. Brokers are used extensively in the real estate industry.

A unique broker that acts in many ways like a manufacturer's agent is a food broker, representing buyers and sellers in the grocery industry. Food brokers differ from conventional brokers because they act on behalf of producers on a permanent basis and receive a commission for their services. For example, food giant Nabisco uses food brokers to sell its candies, margarine, and Planters peanuts, but it sells its line of cookies and crackers directly to retail stores.

ask yourself

1. Where in the retail life cycle is market share usually fought between competitors?

2. What is the difference between merchant wholesalers and agents?

Manufacturer's Branches and Offices

Unlike merchant wholesalers, agents, and brokers, manufacturer's branches and sales offices are wholly owned extensions of the producer that perform wholesaling activities. Producers assume wholesaling functions when there are no intermediaries to perform these activities, customers are few in number and geographically concentrated, orders are large or require significant attention, or they want to control the distribution of their products. A *manufacturer's branch office* carries a producer's inventory and performs the functions of a full-service wholesaler. A *manufacturer's sales office* does not carry inventory, typically performs only a sales function, and serves as an alternative to agents and brokers.

Summary...*just the facts*

- Retailing provides customer value in the form of various utilities: time, place, form, information, and possession. Economically, retailing is important in terms of the people employed and money exchanged in retail sales.

- Retailing outlets can be classified along several dimensions: the form of ownership, level of service, or merchandise mix.

- There are several forms of ownership: independent, chain, retailer-sponsored cooperative, wholesaler-sponsored chain or franchise.

- Stores vary in the level of service they provide. Three levels are self-service, limited service, or full service.

- Retail outlets vary in terms of the breadth and depth of their merchandise lines. Breadth refers to the number of different items carried, and depth refers to the assortment of each item offered.

- Non-store retailing includes automatic vending, television home shopping, online retailing, and direct marketing (direct mail and catalogue retailing, telemarketing, and direct selling).

- Retailing strategy is based on the retailing mix, consisting of goods and services, retail pricing, physical location, and communications.

- In retail pricing, retailers must decide on the markup, markdown, and timing for the markdown. Off-price retailers offer brand-name merchandise at lower than regular prices.

- Online consumers represent a segment of all Internet/web users and differ demographically from the general population. Six general product and service categories are bought by online consumers. However, travel reservations, computer hardware and consumer electronics, media, and clothing and accessories account for the majority of consumer purchases. The increasing sales and number of people purchasing online suggest that the profile of the online consumer is becoming more and more like the profile of the consumer of the traditional marketplace.

- Consumers refer to six reasons they shop and buy online: convenience, choice, customization, communication, cost, and control. Marketers capitalize on these reasons using a variety of approaches, including electronic shopping agents (bots), web communities, viral marketing, and dynamic pricing.

- Retail store location is an important retail mix decision. The common alternatives are the central business district, a regional shopping centre, a community shopping centre, or a strip location. A variation of the strip location is the power centre, which is a strip location with multiple national anchor stores and a supermarket.

- Multichannel retailers use a combination of store and non-store formats.

- Like products, retail outlets have a life cycle consisting of four stages: early growth, accelerated development, maturity, and decline.

- Many retailers depend on the numerous types of intermediaries that engage in wholesaling activities.

- The main difference between the various types of wholesalers lies in whether or not they take title to the items they sell.

Key Terms and Concepts...*a refresher*

breadth of product line *p. 211*
brokers *p. 222*
central business district *p. 213*
community shopping centre *p. 214*
depth of product line *p. 210*
form of ownership *p. 207*
intertype competition *p. 212*
level of service *p. 209*

manufacturers' agents *p. 221*
merchandise mix *p. 209*
merchant wholesalers *p. 220*
multichannel retailers *p. 214*
off-price retailing *p. 213*
power centre *p. 214*
regional shopping centres *p. 213*
retail life cycle *p. 220*

retailing *p. 204*
retailing mix *p. 212*
scrambled merchandising *p. 211*
selling agents *p. 221*
shrinkage *p. 213*
strip location *p. 214*
telemarketing *p. 216*

Integrated Marketing Communications and

Interactive Marketing

Marketers increasingly use an integrated marketing communications approach, trying to reach consumers through a selection of the various media and tools they use to gather information and be entertained. CTV and *Canadian Idol* are examples of how product integration is used by marketers to hit these consumer touch points through the media of TV advertising, in-show product integration, online contests, and retail promotions. Mary Kreuk, vice president of marketing at CTV explains that this is done without compromising the integrity of the show, while also meeting clients' marketing objectives. Product integration involves companies signing sponsorship agreements with the show to provide them with product involvement in the actual show, together with advertising spots around the show itself. Product integration requires all parties to understand their role in the process and for the sponsors to understand that they have no editorial control. CTV makes all efforts to ensure that the sponsors are satisfied, but they will not compromise the integrity of the show for advertising purposes.

Canadian Idol, a family show watched by mothers and children, has run for six seasons and has a well-established reputation for successful and seamless product integration. For the 2007 season, sponsorship opportunities were secured for categories of interest to the show's target market: beauty products (Pantene), food products (Kraft and General Mills), financial services (TD Bank), cellphones (Telus), and charities (Ronald McDonald House). Individual sponsorship agreements varied depending on the client but often included pre-recorded and live on-air segments; website inclusion with contests, logos, and links; and sponsored advertising around the show. In some instances, retail contests were also involved. Although other sponsors, as noted above, were also involved in the show, we look more specifically at Pantene, Ronald McDonald House, and Telus as examples of product integration within this show.

Specifically, Pantene was involved with beauty make-overs, which focused on creating an interesting hairstyle and look for the idols. Pantene had a maximum of six pre-produced beauty make-over segments (60 seconds each) to ensure that the show maintained its integrity and vitality. A Pantene

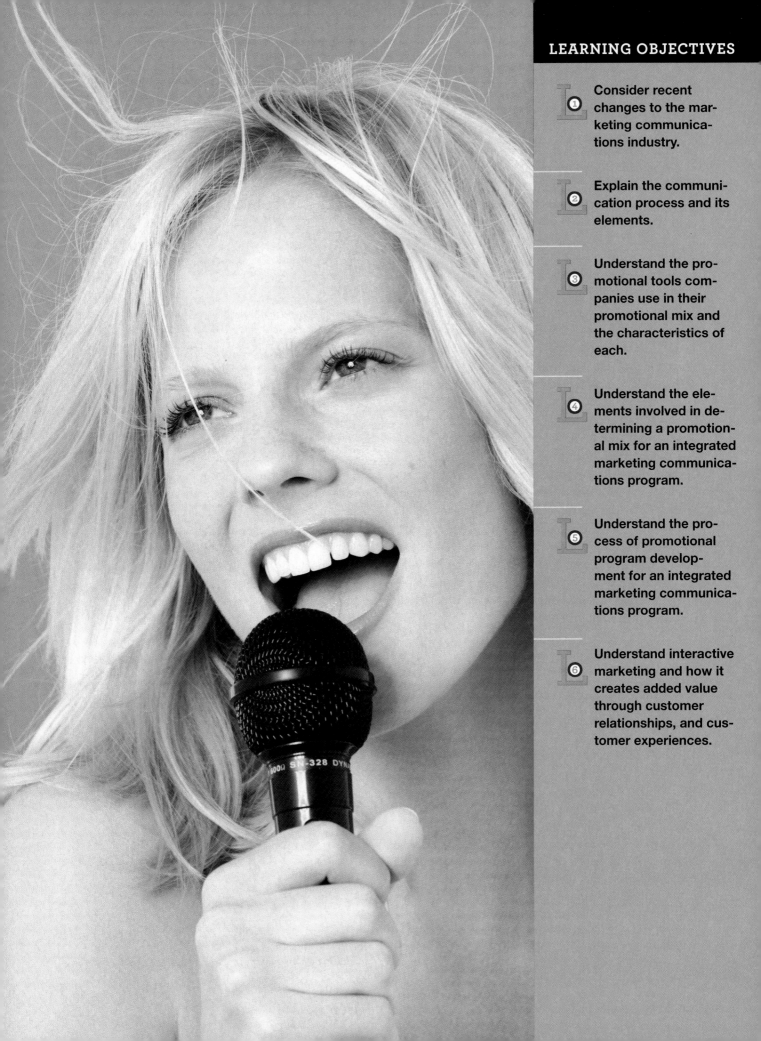

LEARNING OBJECTIVES

L1 Consider recent changes to the marketing communications industry.

L2 Explain the communication process and its elements.

L3 Understand the promotional tools companies use in their promotional mix and the characteristics of each.

L4 Understand the elements involved in determining a promotional mix for an integrated marketing communications program.

L5 Understand the process of promotional program development for an integrated marketing communications program.

L6 Understand interactive marketing and how it creates added value through customer relationships, and customer experiences.

Makeup Room was also involved with live outbreaks to the makeup room during the show to see last-minute hair and makeup preparations. Online integration continued this involvement with Pantene on the Get the Look & Tips web pages at www.idol.ctv.ca. Here, viewers could obtain instructions on how to create the looks that were created for the idols on TV. At the retail level, an in-store retail contest, "Meet the Idols," linked the product to the show and included point-of-sale material provided by Pantene. Finally, a tagged promotional spot played at the end of the *Canadian Idol* show stating, "Brought to you by Pantene."

Ronald McDonald House was the charity that CTV selected to support with this show. The intent was to raise awareness for the charity with pre-produced segments, and raise money for the cause with fundraising activities. The segments for Ronald McDonald House showed the idols interacting with the charity and visiting a newly donated location on Vancouver Island. In addition, online auctions for the charity ran at particular times during the season with on-air mentions pushing viewers to the *Canadian Idol* website to get involved and bid on an item. Furthermore, *Canadian Idol* produced a music track recorded by the top ten idols, making it available for sale to the general public. Proceeds from the sales went to Ronald McDonald House. At the retail level, McDonald's used signage in restaurants and tray liners to promote the *Canadian Idol* connection. Finally, public service advertisements for Ronald McDonald House ran around the show.

Telus was the cellphone provider integrated into the *Canadian Idol* show. Its sponsorship agreement included live on-air mentions and branded visual phone banners that appeared on-screen during the broadcast to provide viewers with phone numbers for voting purposes. Telus customers could text their vote to TELUS, with other customers provided with a 1-888 number. Viewers could also get their *Canadian Idol* ring tones and music downloads from Telus. Finally, Telus ran TV advertising spots around the show.

Mary Kreuk explains that for product integration to work it requires the clients, agencies, and producers to understand their role in the process. It is a time-consuming and costly task requiring involvement by the advertising agencies, public relations agencies, clients, outside production companies, and licensors. All groups need to work together with CTV marketing and production people who will not waver from the integrity of the show. Product integration requires a delicate balance that CTV is able to successfully make work!

This chapter provides the reader with an overview of the marketing communications process, introducing the promotional tools used in marketing. The focus is on the latest developments in marketing communications, specifically integrated marketing communications, followed by a review of interactive marketing. Chapter 13 provides a more detailed look at the separate promotional tools of advertising, sales promotion, public relations, personal selling, and direct response. 🍎

Developments in Marketing Communications

LO① The marketing communications industry has experienced numerous changes over the past few years due to the increased sophistication of digital media, the use of database technology, and the changing media habits of Canadians. If we look at the media landscape, the Internet now plays an integral role in most marketing campaigns, helping to meld programs into integrated marketing communications (IMC) programs that reach consumers through a variety of different media. Marketers increasingly turn to integrated

The Core: Chapter 12

The Internet is being integrated into marketing communications programs.

Integrated marketing communications' programs need to provide consistent messaging.

> *The Internet now plays an integral role in most marketing campaigns, helping to meld programs into integrated marketing communications programs.*

marketing communications campaigns to ensure that their messages reach a fragmented audience that uses individual media choices to gather information and be entertained. Integrated marketing communications refers to the design of a coordinated communications program using various communication tools to reach a target market with a consistent message. Increasingly as part of these campaigns, we see products being placed in TV shows and movies, viral campaigns surfacing on the Internet, and a variety of media choices being used to communicate messages. In addition, we see an increased involvement in customer loyalty programs that use sophisticated customer relationship management (CRM) tools to entice consumers to favour certain products and services (see Chapter 14).

Marketers need to consider the following developments in the industry. The Internet now accounts for over 9 percent of net advertising revenues, more than tripling since 2004 and closely approaching TV as the main forum for advertising (Figure 12–1). As part of this development, marketers are seeing social networks, online videos, blogs, podcasts, and video-sharing sites surfacing as important elements in the online advertising landscape. In fact, with the increased streaming of TV programming through the Internet, statistics now show that online video-viewing rivals traditional TV-viewing for many consumers. Marketers are not ignoring these developments and are increasingly including them in their communications programs in a variety of forms such as e-newsletters, promotional microsites, YouTube postings, and online ads.

In 2007, the Internet accounted for $1.24 billion in net advertising revenues, an increase of 23 percent versus the previous year, reflecting consumers' use of the Internet in their daily lives. This increase directly impacts other media where usage appears to be slightly waning. Print media is directly impacted by this development with many daily newspapers, consumer magazines, community newspapers, and trade publications seeing slight declines in readership and advertising revenues. Radio, although holding its own from a media perspective, is losing young listeners to digital

downloads and MP3 players. TV is also impacted by this increased use of the Internet, and we see more and more TV programs being streamed on the Internet. TV spots are also surfacing on these sites in online formats that are often abbreviated forms of the 30-second spot. In the direct mail arena, catalogues and direct mail pieces are expected to reduce their reliance on printed materials, which are an expensive proposition relative to using the Internet.

Separately, over the last few years we have seen a marked increase in marketing campaigns for the non-profit industry. This industry has become more competitive, with marketers realizing that they are competing for consumers' charitable donations. This non-profit segment has harnessed the power of the Internet, providing contributors with the ease of online donations and the ability to set up their own mini-fundraisers. In conjunction with this trend, we also see many for-profit companies having a heightened social awareness, evident in their promotional campaigns, which frequently have a charitable component as seen with CTV and Ronald McDonald House.

Ethics is surfacing as an issue in the Internet environment where anonymity allows unscrupulous individuals to misrepresent themselves to consumers. In particular, spam continues to plague people's e-mail with offers of pharmaceutical products and pornography. Also worrisome is the amount of phishing that occurs with spam

Figure 12–1

Relative importance of individual media to total media (based on net advertising revenue)

MEDIA	2004	2007
TV	26%	25%
Radio	11%	11%
Daily newspaper	16%	13%
Consumer magazines	6%	5%
Outdoor/transit	3%	3%
Internet	3%	9%
Catalogues/direct mail	13%	13%
Phone directories	10%	10%
Other print (religions, school, farm, trade publication, community newspaper, weekend supplement)	12%	11%
Total	100%	100%

Sources: *Canadian Media Directors' Council Media Digest 2008/2009*, p. 14, accessed at www.cmdc.ca/pdf/2008_09_media_digest.pdf.

Marketing ▶ tip

"The media industry continues to evolve as advertisers search for innovations to deliver their message to their customers. Broadcasters are eager to work with advertisers to find creative solutions in their quest!"

Mary Kreuk, vice president of marketing, CTV

e-mail purporting to come from reputable banks and other financial services. In these instances, personal financial information is requested so that it can be used for credit card fraud and identity theft. It is important to note that the Canadian Marketing Association (CMA) frowns on spam, viewing it as an unacceptable marketing practice. Members of the CMA are strongly advised not to use spam as part of their marketing programs, although permission-based e-mail is well regarded. It is important to make a distinction at this point between spam, which is unsolicited e-mail, and permission-based e-mail, which is when a recipient signs up to receive periodic electronic updates or newsletters from a company.

Maxwell House Coffee presents a leading-edge example of how marketing responds to such changes in the industry with a fully integrated marketing communications program. In April 2008, the company launched its "Brew Some Good" campaign with an innovative marketing communications program that scaled down its traditional TV-advertising budget, using the $200,000 in savings to support non-profit causes. The integrated marketing communications campaign used consumer touch points for the brand and created a campaign that would resonate with its target group. This included public relations, event marketing, sampling, TV advertising, print advertising, and an Internet component that used banner ads and its own microsite (www.brewsomegood.ca). The response was tremendous with press coverage in trade magazines (either online or in print), publications such as *Strategy* and *Canadian Business*, as well as on Internet marketing blogs and websites

such as Media in Canada (www.mediaincanada.com), *The Globe and Mail*, (www.theglobeandmail.com), *Pub-Zone* (www.pubzone.com), and the *National Post* (www.nationalpost.com). The campaign was also profiled on live broadcasts of Citytv and on its accompanying website. Within four months, Maxwell House received almost 2,000 nominations of non-profit organizations. Six worthy causes have been announced to date: the Mira Foundation, a guide/service dog foundation for the disabled; Regent Park School of Music, for inner-city youth; CARD, the Community Association for Riding for the Disabled; Little Women for Little Women (LW4LW), a charitable organization supporting the education of young girls in Afghanistan; Hope for Malawi, raising funds for the poor in Africa; and Ryan's Well Foundation, raising funds for clean water in under-developed nations. Fifteen more charitable recipients are to be announced.

The campaign coordinated advertising, public relations, and event marketing. A TV campaign simply showed a steaming cup of coffee, stating that the commercial cost only $19,000 compared to the average cost of $245,000. Viewers were asked where the savings should be spent and to nominate a good cause at www.brewsomegood.ca. The public relations and event marketing components were launched at the start of the campaign to dovetail with the TV ad. These initiatives included a free concert at specific subway stations in Toronto and Montreal where free subway tokens and cups of Maxwell House coffee were distributed to morning riders. In addition, $100,000 was donated by Maxwell House to Habitat for Humanity Canada to show its support for such charitable causes. The campaign continued in subsequent months with print and Internet ads and two TV spots encouraging consumers to do good deeds. These latter TV spots focused on two charities that received charitable donations from Maxwell House's *Brew Some Good* campaign: the Mira Foundation and the Regent Park School of Music. In addition, short informational videos on the Mira, CARD, and LW4LW foundations were created and posted on the www.brewsomegood.ca website.

A marketing trend of supporting non-profit causes

An online ad linked to www.brewsomegood.ca

Maxwell House's microsite at www.brewsomegood.ca

Free subway rides, concerts, and cups of coffee

The Communications Process

Communication is the process of conveying a message to others and requires six elements: a source, a message, a channel of communication, a receiver, the process of encoding, and the process of decoding the message[1] (see Figure 12–2 on page 230). The **source** may be a company or person who has information to share. The information sent, such as a description of a new cellular telephone, forms the **message**. The message is conveyed by means of a **channel of communication**, such as a salesperson, advertising media, or public relations tool. Consumers who read, hear, or see the message are the **receivers**. They respond by perhaps purchasing a product, and this response then goes back to the source as feedback.

Encoding and Decoding

Encoding and decoding are essential to communication. **Encoding** is the process of having the sender transform an idea into symbolic form, using words, pictures, symbols, and sounds. **Decoding** is the process of having the receiver take a set of symbols, words, pictures, and sounds and transform them into messages. Decoding is performed by the receivers according to their own frame of reference: their attitudes, values, and beliefs.[2]

The process of communication is not always a successful one. Errors in communication can happen in several ways. The source may not adequately transform the idea into an effective set of symbols, a properly encoded message may be sent through the wrong channel, or the receiver may not properly transform the set of symbols into the intended message. Although communication appears easy to perform, truly effective communication can be very difficult.

For the message to be communicated effectively, the sender and receiver must have a mutually shared **field of experience**, similar understanding and knowledge. Some communications problems occur when companies take their messages to cultures or target groups with different fields of experience.

Feedback

Figure 12–2 (see page 230) shows a line labelled *feedback loop*, which consists of a response and feedback. A **response** is the impact the message had on the receiver's knowledge, attitudes, or behaviours. **Feedback** is the flow of information to the source that indicates whether the message was decoded and understood.

communication Process of conveying a message to others

source Company or person who has information to share

message Information sent by a source to a receiver

channel of communication The means of conveying a message to a receiver

receivers Consumers who read, hear, or see the message sent by a source

encoding Process whereby the sender transforms an idea into symbolic form, using words, pictures, symbols, and sounds

decoding Process whereby the receiver takes a set of symbols, words, pictures, and sounds, and transforms them into messages

field of experience The experiences, perceptions, attitudes, and values that senders and receivers of a message bring to a communication situation

response The impact a message has on the receiver's knowledge, attitudes, or behaviours

feedback Communication flow from receiver back to the sender that helps the sender know whether the message was decoded and understood

Noise

Noise includes extraneous factors that can work against effective communication by distorting a message or the feedback received (Figure 12–2). At each stage of the communication process, factors can interfere with the message reaching its target as anticipated. Sometimes this occurs at the point where the receiver receives the message. Advertising clutter, where a large number of competing messages confront the receiver at one time, is a major cause of noise. Noise can also be a simple error, such as a printing mistake that affects the meaning of a newspaper advertisement or using words and pictures that fail to communicate the message clearly. Noise can occur when a salesperson's message is misunderstood by a prospective buyer due to a communication style that makes the message difficult to understand.

Figure 12–2
The communication process

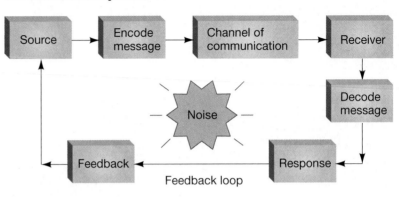

Promotional Tools

LO 3 Promotion consists of advertising, personal selling, sales promotion, public relations, and direct response. All of these elements can be used to inform prospective buyers about the product, to persuade them to try it, and to act as a reminder about the product. To communicate with consumers, a company can use one or more of these five promotional alternatives. Figure 12–3 (see page 231) summarizes the relative strengths and weaknesses of these five elements. The latest technologies allow all these elements to be tailored to suit specific target groups. TV ads can be created with slight modifications for different media channels, such as the Internet versus a traditional TV broadcast. Public relations specialists can create events to garner interest from a specific group of consumers. Sales promotions can be disseminated through the Internet using websites and permission-based newsletters to target different interest groups. Marketers are finding it increasingly more difficult to reach a mass target market by using only one media such as TV which is now fragmented along many different channels. Instead, they use an integrated marketing communications approach, which combines a number of media options suited to the target group, to more effectively communicate their message. Tailoring this message can make it considerably more effective.

Advertising

Advertising is a paid form of non-personal communication about an organization, good, service, or idea by an identified sponsor. The *paid* aspect of this definition is important because the space for the advertising message normally must be bought. An occasional exception is a public service announcement, where the

To communicate with consumers, a company can use one or more of five promotional alternatives: advertising, personal selling, public relations, sales promotion, and direct response.

Figure 12–3
Strengths and weaknesses of promotional tools

PROMOTIONAL TOOLS	STRENGTHS	WEAKNESSES
Advertising	• Efficient means for reaching large numbers of people • Many options for reaching different target groups	• High cost • Difficult to evaluate • High clutter • Low credibility
Personal selling	• Immediate feedback • Very persuasive • Can easily target messages • Can provide complex information • Easy to evaluate	• High cost per contact • Salespeople may not relay consistent messages
Public relations	• Often the most credible source in consumers' minds • Not costly	• Media coverage is not controllable • Message is not controllable • Difficult to evaluate
Sales promotion	• Effective at changing behaviour in the short run • Very flexible • Results are measurable	• Misredemption can occur • Can lead to promotion wars • Easily duplicated by competitors • Consumers may wait for a sales promotion before purchasing
Direct response	• Messages can be targeted • Facilitates customer relationships • Measurable results	• High cost • Negative customer reactions • Clutter • Requires a database to be done properly

advertising time or space is donated, usually for a non-profit organization or a community service.

Advertising can exist in many different forms of media. In the broadcast media, there is TV and radio. In the print media, there is newspaper and magazine. In the out-of-home media, there is billboard, poster, bus shelter, transit, washroom, and a variety of non-conventional modes such as aerial advertising. In the digital media, there are websites, Internet ads, electronic newsletters, and permission-based e-mails. Cellphones are surfacing as another form of media that delivers advertising messages, but this mode has yet to be widely accepted.

Advertising can be very expensive. A one-time, national rate for a full-page, four-colour ad in *Maclean's* magazine, for example, costs $35,630.[3] This magazine also has an accompanying website with which advertisers can also be involved through banner ads or sponsorships. Television ads are even more expensive with the average cost to produce a TV commercial running between $200,000 and $250,000. The cost of buying the TV media depends on when and where an advertiser wishes to run the spot. The costs vary based on supply and demand for the media time, and costs can run as high as $100,000 to $150,000 to run a 30-second spot during a top, prime-time, high-demand TV show. The number of minutes of TV advertising targeting children is regulated by the CRTC (Canadian Radio-television and Telecommunications Commission) to 4 minutes per half-hour, with the province of Quebec placing further restrictions by disallowing all advertising to children.

Attention! Blogs and Social Media

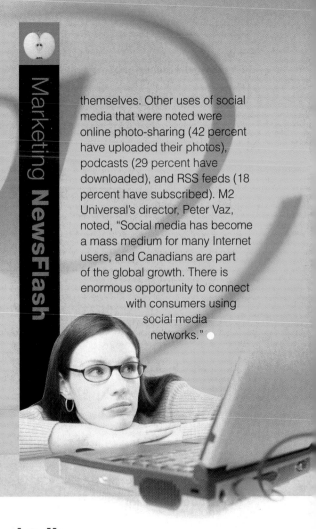

Marketing NewsFlash

Social media is now an essential part of the media environment. Internet users are becoming more and more attuned to social media, according to a survey by M2 Universal. The Toronto-based agency surveyed 1,500 Canadians and determined that social networks have continued to rise, becoming a crucial part of the growth of social media. The survey found that Facebook is the largest social network in Canada, leading with a 54 percent weekly reach. M2 Universal also found that 59 percent of Canadians online have joined social networking sites, and 52 percent have uploaded photos onto their profiles. In addition, 38 percent have installed an application to their profiles, and 20 percent have shared videos.

The survey also found that while blogs have become a part of the "online media diet," only 65 percent of Canadians online read blogs, compared to 73 percent globally. Additionally, only 23 percent of Canadians have created their own blogs.

The survey found that watching videos online currently rivals television viewing with 78 percent of Canadian Internet users having watched videos online and 27 percent having uploaded videos themselves. Other uses of social media that were noted were online photo-sharing (42 percent have uploaded their photos), podcasts (29 percent have downloaded), and RSS feeds (18 percent have subscribed). M2 Universal's director, Peter Vaz, noted, "Social media has become a mass medium for many Internet users, and Canadians are part of the global growth. There is enormous opportunity to connect with consumers using social media networks." ●

Source: Terry Poulton, "M2 Universal releases social media survey, May 2, 2008, accessed at www.mediaincanada.com/articles/mic/20080502/socialmedia.html.

---

personal selling
Two-way flow of communication between a buyer and seller, often in a face-to-face encounter, designed to influence a purchase decision

With advertising costs being so high, marketers often turn to market research to help ascertain the effectiveness of the message and to ensure that it will be seen and clearly understood.

There are several advantages to a firm using advertising in its promotional mix. It can be attention-getting and it can also communicate specific product benefits to prospective buyers. By paying for the advertising space, a company can control *what* it wants to say and, to some extent, to *whom* the message is sent. Advertising also allows a company to decide *when* to send its message, and *how often*. The non-personal aspect of advertising also has its advantages. Once the message is created, the same message can be sent to all receivers in a market segment. Advertising, however, has some disadvantages. As previously discussed, the costs to produce and place a message are significant, and the lack of direct feedback makes it difficult to know how well the message is received and whether the advertising is effective. In addition, research indicates that consumers are increasingly ignoring advertising messages and questioning the messages' credibility.

Personal Selling

The second major promotional alternative is **personal selling**, defined as the two-way flow of communication between a buyer and seller, designed to influence a purchase decision. Unlike advertising, personal selling is usually face-to-face communication between the sender and receiver, although telephone and electronic sales also exist. Why do companies use personal selling?

There are important advantages to personal selling, as summarized in Figure 12–3 (see page 231). A salesperson can control to *whom* the presentation is made. The personal component of selling has an advantage over advertising in that the seller can see or hear the potential buyer's reaction to the message and respond accordingly. If the feedback is unfavourable, or if there are questions, the salesperson can attempt to determine the reasons, modify the message, and respond.

The flexibility of personal selling can also be a disadvantage. Different salespeople can change the message resulting in an inconsistent message to the market. The high cost of personal selling is probably its major disadvantage. On a cost-per-contact basis, it is generally the most expensive of the five promotional elements.

public relations
Form of communication that seeks to influence the feelings, opinions, or beliefs held by customers, potential customers, stockholders, suppliers, employees, and the media about a company and its products or services

publicity
Communication about an organization that is non-personal and not paid for directly by the organization

Public Relations

Public relations is a form of communication that seeks to influence the feelings, opinions, or beliefs held by customers, prospective customers, stockholders, suppliers, employees, and the media about a company and its products or services.[4] Many tools such as special events, lobbying efforts, annual reports, and image management may be used by a public relations department, although publicity often plays the most important role.

Publicity is a public relations tool that is being used more and more by companies to influence public opinion. We describe it as a non-personal form of communication that is not paid for directly by the organization. How does it work? A company may prepare press kits, news releases, editorials, or stage events and interviews to attract media attention. The intent is for the media to run a favourable story about the item or the company. An advantage of publicity is credibility. When a message comes from a third party, it appears to be non-biased and objective. When you read a positive story about a company's product in the media, you tend to believe it, maybe more than you would believe an advertisement for the same product.

Three examples of how publicity has been positively used by organizations are outlined below:

- In 2003, the city of Vancouver won the right to host the 2010 Winter Olympics. Public relations efforts from the organizing committee encouraged the media to cover this news, which resulted in positive media exposure and increased awareness of Vancouver as a tourist destination.

- In 2008, Maple Leaf Foods had a major product recall due to some of their processed meats allegedly being contaminated with listeria. The company immediately communicated this product recall to the media who in turn broadcast this news, alerting consumers to this public health issue. Maple Leaf Foods themselves held news conferences to communicate with the public, ran newspaper ads to further draw attention to this public health issue, and posted broadcast announcements on YouTube. The lists of items involved in the product recall were posted on media websites and also on the Maple Leaf Foods' website. This approach helped curtail further consumption of the recalled food products.

- The Nova Scotia Department of Tourism and Culture produces an annual travel planner to send to those interested in visiting the province; the planner is also posted on www. novascotia.com. The planner lists restaurants and hotels in the province—invaluable publicity to

> ❝MANY TOOLS SUCH AS SPECIAL EVENTS, LOBBYING EFFORTS, ANNUAL REPORTS, AND IMAGE MANAGEMENT MAY BE USED BY A PUBLIC RELATIONS DEPARTMENT, ALTHOUGH PUBLICITY OFTEN PLAYS THE MOST IMPORTANT ROLE.❞

these establishments. The businesses mentioned in the planner do not pay to be included in it, but are listed because the tourism department staff have determined that they are good establishments. A business can purchase an ad in the publication, but this may not have the same impact as the positive publicity generated by the listing. In recent years, promotion for the province of Nova Scotia has increased substantially, with the media shining an extra spotlight on the province in articles that generate free publicity.[5]

Publicity has a downside too. The company has no control over what is published. The news media will not run a story that is not newsworthy, and it can put whatever spin it wishes on the story. A manufacturer can invite a news team to its headquarters to preview its revolutionary new exercise equipment and hope that it is featured on the 6:00 p.m. newscast, but there is no guarantee that this will happen. A media outlet may find an item newsworthy and plan to use it in an upcoming newscast, but if a more newsworthy event surfaces, then the item may be dropped.

Companies often have public relations staff, or use public relations agencies to build relationships with the media and prepare press releases, press kits, news conferences, and schedule interviews or stage events. These companies also evaluate the success of these approaches and monitor the media pickup of the story. Still, despite these well-orchestrated attempts to influence the media, companies ultimately have no control over what the media reports.

Sales Promotion

A fourth promotional element is **sales promotion**, a short-term offer of value designed to arouse interest in buying a good or service. Sales promotions are often used in conjunction with advertising, personal selling,

*A sales promotion from **CAA Magazine***

and direct response. They can be offered to intermediaries as well as to final consumers. Coupons, rebates, samples, and sweepstakes are just a few examples of the many types of sales promotions available. An example can be seen with the Canadian Automobile Association (CAA), which in its fall 2008 edition of *CAA Magazine* advertised a sales promotion that offered members special low prices on tickets to CFL football games.

The advantage of sales promotion is that the short-term nature of these programs, such as a coupon or sweepstakes with an expiration date, often increases sales for the specific period. Offering value to the consumer in terms of a cents-off coupon or rebate may also increase store traffic from consumers who are not store-loyal.[6] However, a disadvantage of sales promotion is that sales can drop off when the deal ends,[7] and advertising support is often needed to convert a customer who tried the product because of a sales promotion into a loyal customer.[8] If sales promotions are conducted continuously, they lose their effectiveness, with some customers delaying purchases until a coupon is offered. Sales promotions are reviewed in detail in Chapter 13.

Direct Response

Another promotional alternative, **direct response**, uses direct communication with consumers to generate a response in the form of an order, a request for further information, or a visit to a retail outlet.[9] The communication can take many forms, including face-to-face selling, direct mail, catalogues, telemarketing, direct response advertising (on television, on the radio, and in print), and online marketing. Like personal selling, direct response often consists of interactive communication. It also has the advantage of flexibility so that messages can be customized to meet the needs of specific target markets. Messages can be developed and adapted quickly to facilitate one-to-one relationships with customers.

While direct response has been one of the fastest-growing forms of promotion, it poses several challenges. First, most forms of direct response require a comprehensive and up-to-date database with information about the respondents. Developing and maintaining this database can be expensive and time consuming. In addition, growing concerns about privacy have led to a decline in response rates among some customer groups. Lastly, direct response can often include junk mail, which is seen as an environmental concern and a waste of natural resources. Companies with successful direct-response programs are sensitive to these issues and often use a combination of promotional tools to avoid these elements and to increase value for customers. The Internet is rapidly surfacing as a form of paperless direct response that companies can easily use to target individuals.

ask yourself

1. Explain the difference between advertising and publicity when both appear on television.

2. Which promotional element should be offered only on a short-term basis?

3. What are the challenges faced by the direct-response industry?

The IMC Promotional Mix

L❹ A firm's **promotional mix** is the combination of one or more of the promotional tools it chooses to use. In putting together the promotional mix, a marketer must consider several issues. Should advertising be emphasized more than personal selling? Should a promotional rebate be offered? Would public relations activities be effective? In other words, the combination of tools to be used and the importance placed on them has to be determined. These tools include advertising, personal selling, public relations, sales promotion, and direct response. Several factors affect such decisions: the type of product, the composition of the target audience for the promotion,[10] the stage of the product's life cycle, and the channel of distribution. This section reviews the concept of integrated marketing communications, and explains the relevancy of understanding the product's target audience, its product's life cycle, and its channel of distribution.

Integrated Marketing Communications

In the past, the promotional elements were regarded as separate functions handled by experts in separate departments. The sales force designed and managed its activities independently from the marketing department, and advertising, sales promotion, and public relations were often the responsibility of outside agencies or specialists. The result was often an overall communication effort that was not well coordinated and, in some cases, inconsistent. Today, the concept of designing a marketing communications program that coordinates all promotional activities to provide a consistent message to the target audience is referred to as **integrated marketing communications (IMC)**.

The Dairy Farmers of Canada have been using an integrated marketing communications approach to reach its target audience for cheese for several years. The 2008 campaign used a balance of TV advertising, magazine ads, billboards, Internet ads, websites, e-newsletters, podcasts, direct mail, sales promotions, and public relations efforts. All marketing communications efforts were associated with a theatrical theme of old-time musicals, and they worked together to encourage people to eat cheese. All the elements delivered a consistent message to the organization's target market.

promotional mix
Combination of one or more of the promotional tools—advertising, personal selling, public relations, sales promotion, and direct response—a firm uses to communicate with consumers

integrated marketing communications (IMC)
Concept of designing marketing communications programs that coordinate all promotional activities to provide a consistent message to the target audience

A Musical Campaign for Cheese

Marketing NewsFlash

In 2008, the Dairy Farmers of Canada embarked on a new integrated marketing communications campaign that promoted the increased usage of cheese among Canadians. Working with the advertising agency TAXI, a bold new initiative literally sang the praises of cheese with a campaign titled "All You Need is Cheese: The Musical." This campaign fully integrated a tongue-in-cheek musical theme through TV ads, radio spots, print ads, online banner ads, and a microsite. Cheese was also featured in the annual Milk Calendar distributed free to subscribers in many print publications, while the campaign also involved a consumer promotion that invited consumers to enter a contest to win a trip.

In-store signage promoted the virtues of cheese, while online banner ads on FoodTV.com, Wish.ca, Yahoo.ca, and Cityline.com pushed viewers through to the campaign's microsite (www.allyouneedischeese.ca). The TV campaign featured families singing familiar ditties from the 1970s and 1980s with new cheesy lyrics that encouraged viewers to add cheese to their meals. The tunes became almost jingle-like with their usage of words and melodies such as "Just a Little Bit," "Cheese Will Keep Us Together," and "Cheasy."

The microsite continued the integrated marketing communications musical theme onto its web pages. The website set a theatre-like scene, complete with marquee lights, dark black curtains, and spotlights to create an old-fashioned musical experience. Within the website, the tag line "All You Need is Cheese" was evident on every page with its familiar yellow background and bold white lettering, which prominently displayed the reversal of one of the "e" letters in the word cheese. Cleverly within the site, a brief musical greeting invited the viewer to select actors to star in a theatrical musical production. Viewers could choose from carrots, apples, pears, eggs, or mushrooms, just to name a few participants to star with cheese. Upon selection, the result was a musical ditty starring cheese and another food ingredient, together with links to recipes within the site. Podcasts on stories about fine cheese could also be accessed through the website as well as promotions and e-newsletters for subscribers.

The final promotional element was a series of print ads that ran in magazines such as *Today's Parent*, *Chatelaine*, *Canadian House & Home*, and *Wish*, as well as LCBO's *Food and Drink* magazine. The integrated marketing communications elements were also evident in these print ads through the same consistency of the messaging, all captured by the "All You Can Eat is Cheese" logo. Throughout this integrated marketing communications campaign the tone, theme, and visual treatment of the messaging linked each element together to create a campaign that was consistent, memorable, and impactful. ●

Sources: "Singing the Praises of Cheese," *Financial Post,* March 14, 2008, accessed at www.taxi.ca/index.cfm?siteid=80&pid=15203&newsid=1744; Gail Chiasson, "All You Need is Cheese: the Musical," *Pubzone,* March 12, 2008, accessed at www.taxi.ca/index.cfm?siteid=80&pid=15203&newsid=1745; and Kristin Laird, "Take it 'cheasy,' *Marketing Daily,* March 11, 2008, accessed at www.taxi.ca/index.cfm?siteid=80&pid=15203&newsid=1729.

The key to developing successful IMC programs is to use a process that makes it easy to design each element and ensure that they all work together to deliver a consistent message. After the program is finalized and put in place, the respective agencies and clients need to assess the success of the program. In an integrated marketing communications program, each element has a distinct role as well as a purpose in the overall campaign. For example, TV advertising might be used to build awareness, print advertising may be used to encourage product usage, sales promotion might be needed to generate product trial, direct mail may be required to create a database of the target market, and personal selling might be needed to complete the transaction. Each tool is used for a different reason and needs to be evaluated against that purpose and its contribution to the success of the overall marketing communications program.[11]

The Target Audience Marketing communications programs are used by marketers in both the consumer and in the business-to-business market. Consumer programs can be directed to the ultimate consumer, and in the business-to-business market, programs can be directed to a business buyer. Programs can also be targeted to intermediaries such as retailers, wholesalers, or distributors. In the case of consumer products, IMC promotional programs for well-established, profitable brands often use a combination of mass media, local media, public relations, and consumer promotions to effectively communicate with their target market. However, smaller brands may not always have the luxury of such large budgets and in this instance, may rely on regional programs and creativity to bring attention to their brands. The beer brand Grolsch is such an example where breakthrough humorous radio advertising was used in local markets to help boost volume by 10 percent.[12]

In the business-to-business market, personal selling often plays a more significant role in the IMC program than in the consumer market. The number of people targeted is typically smaller, and marketing programs tend to focus on services and solutions rather than on standardized products. In the business-to-business market, sales and marketing work cohesively together to meet target market needs. Advertising, sales promotion, and public relations programs tend to play a lesser role in this market than in the consumer market.

The Product Life Cycle As a product moves through its product life cycle, the promotional requirements needed in an IMC program to sustain volume and market share change. The market becomes increasingly more competitive over time, and the product may have unique features that it needs to publicize. Pricing plays a more significant role over time as do short-term consumer promotions that are needed to drive business and thwart the competition. Specifically, during each stage of the product life cycle we see the following promotional objectives and subsequent promotional tools:

- *Introduction stage.* The primary promotional objective during the introduction stage of the product life cycle is product awareness. In general, at this time marketers place a heightened emphasis on advertising in the IMC promotional mix, but personal selling is also used as an important means of communicating with

Consumer magazines can directly target female consumers

Purina Dog Chow: a product in the maturity stage of its life cycle

intermediaries and retailers. Sales promotions are also used to help simulate trial, while public relations is frequently used at this stage to help disseminate newsworthy information to the general public.

- *Growth stage.* The primary promotional objective during the growth stage is to persuade consumers to buy the product over a competitor's. The promotional IMC mix sees advertising being used to communicate brand differences, and personal selling being used to solidify the channel of distribution. Public relations plays a lesser role during this stage because the novelty of the product has worn off, resulting in a lack of newsworthiness for the media.

- *Maturity stage.* During the maturity stage the focus of the IMC program is to retain existing buyers and to encourage users of competitive products to switch brands. This stage is characterized by competitive pricing, and a proliferation of value-added offers designed to increase brand loyalty. Advertising plays a lesser role during this stage in the product life cycle, replaced by the short-term allure of sales promotion. Sales promotion, in the form of bonus packs, discounts, coupons, and contests surface as tools used to encourage brand loyalty.

- *Decline stage.* The decline stage of the product life cycle is usually a period where the product is discontinued, phased out, or, if appropriate, relaunched into an earlier stage of the product life cycle. The IMC objective during the decline stage is to minimize unnecessary spending on the product, maximize profits, and therefore typically reduce most promotional efforts on the product. Figure 12–4 (see page 238) shows how the promotional mix for Purina Dog Chow might change through its product life cycle.

> *Smaller brands may not always have the luxury of such large budgets and in this instance, may rely on regional programs and creativity to bring attention to their brands.*

Channel Strategies

Achieving full distribution is often difficult for a manufacturer to obtain. Promotional IMC strategies can assist in securing this needed distribution, alerting the distributor to the benefits of the product and its relevancy to their customers. In the consumer market a manufacturer needs to determine whether a portion of promotional funds should be directed to the wholesalers, distributors, or retailers, or whether funds should be earmarked for the consumer. In the business-to-business market, marketers need to determine whether IMC promotional programs should be limited to the ultimate buyers or whether a portion of the promotional efforts should be directed to the distributors or intermediaries. In short, the marketer needs to determine whether to use a push strategy,

Figure 12–4
IMC promotional considerations over the product life cycle of Purina Dog Chow

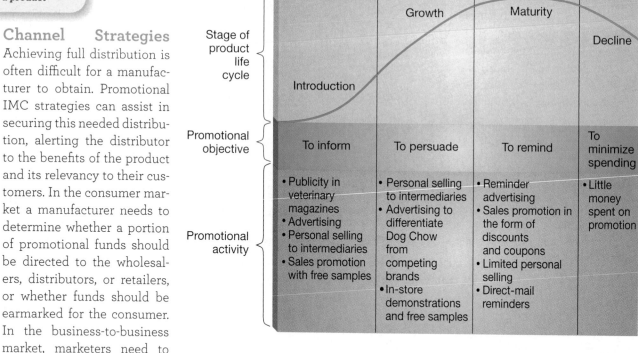

a pull strategy, or combination of both in its promotional programs.[13]

Figure 12–5 (see page 239) shows how a manufacturer uses a **push strategy**, directing the promotional mix to channel members to gain their cooperation

Grolsch—Building Business on a Small Budget

Grolsch beer is the number-one premium-beer brand in Holland, but before 2004 there was no advertising for the product in Canada, despite the beer's availability in drinking establishments and stores around the country. The brand's sales relied on word-of-mouth among consumers and on a sales team whose mission was to get the beer onto store shelves and into bars and restaurants. Growth without advertising was small, and customers had very little

knowledge about the brand itself. In order to improve awareness and sales in Canada, Grolsch embarked on an advertising campaign that emphasized the beer's heritage and authenticity. Grolsch had only a small advertising budget and needed to use creativity to break through the clutter of competing messages.

The company chose to focus on the brand's unique name and bottle creating a campaign that revolved around the simple tagline: "It could only be Grolsch." The media accompanying this

Marketing NewsFlash

tagline centred on Toronto, where Grolsch wanted to expand brand awareness. It used radio due to its ability to affordably reach several demographic groups. The use of the "popping" sound as the Grolsch swing-top bottle opened in the radio spots created an easily recognizable connection to the brand. As a result, sales grew beyond the projected 10 percent, ably demonstrating that brands without extensive advertising budgets can still create ad campaigns that increase brand awareness and improve sales. ●

Source: "Grolsch awareness grows 5-fold in one season," Radio Marketing Bureau Case Study, 2007, accessed at http://rmb.ca/uploadedFiles/Research/Case_Studies/Grolsch2007.pdf.

Figure 12–5
A comparison of push and pull promotional strategies

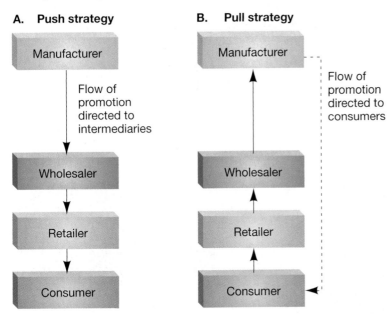

A. Push strategy

Manufacturer

Flow of promotion directed to intermediaries

Wholesaler

Retailer

Consumer

B. Pull strategy

Manufacturer

Flow of promotion directed to consumers

Wholesaler

Retailer

Consumer

through the channel. Pharmaceutical companies follow this approach with some of their products, now spending more than $1.2 billion annually to advertise prescription drugs directly to consumers.[14] This strategy is designed to encourage consumers to ask their physicians for a specific drug by name, thereby pulling it through the channel. Pfizer Canada used this approach with the prescription drug Viagra, creating TV commercials, specifically directed at consumers, to encourage them to contact their doctor about the pharmaceutical product.[15]

in ordering, stocking, and selling the product. In this approach, personal selling and sales promotions play major roles. Salespeople call on wholesalers to encourage orders and provide sales assistance. Sales promotions to intermediaries, such as case discount allowances (20 percent off the regular case price), are offered to stimulate demand. By pushing the product through the channel, the goal is to get channel members to promote it to their customers.

Figure 12–5 illustrates a **pull strategy**, which is used by marketers to direct promotional efforts toward ultimate consumers. The aim is to encourage consumers to ask a retailer for the product, thus pulling the product through the distribution channel. Seeing demand from ultimate consumers, retailers order the product from wholesalers, and thus the item is pulled

ask yourself

1. What promotional tools are most likely used during the introduction stage of the product life cycle?

2. Explain the differences between a push strategy and a pull strategy.

3. What are the benefits of an integrated marketing communications program?

Creating IMC Promotional Programs

LO 5 Because media costs are high, promotion decisions must be made carefully, using a systematic approach. The IMC promotion decision process involves developing, executing, and evaluating the promotion program as shown in Figure 12–6 (see page 240).

Developing the IMC Promotional Program

Developing the IMC promotional program requires a marketer to complete seven main steps: (1) specify the IMC objectives, (2) identify the target audience, (3) set

Figure 12–6
The IMC process

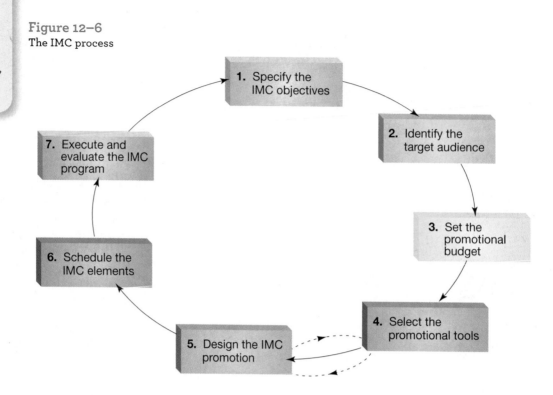

1. Specify the IMC objectives
2. Identify the target audience
3. Set the promotional budget
4. Select the promotional tools
5. Design the IMC promotion
6. Schedule the IMC elements
7. Execute and evaluate the IMC program

the promotional budget, (4) select the promotional tools, (5) design the IMC promotion, (6) schedule the IMC elements, and (7) execute and evaluate the IMC program. These steps are explained in further detail below.

Specifying the IMC Objectives   First, a decision must be reached on what the promotion should accomplish, and this should be set as the IMC promotional objective. Examples of objectives can be to increase awareness, to generate product trial, or to encourage repeat purchase. To set these objectives, marketers may look at consumer behaviour theory and set the objectives based on the **hierarchy of effects**. This is the sequence of stages a prospective buyer goes through from initial awareness of a product to eventual action, either trial or adoption of the product.[16] These stages are outlined below:

- *Awareness.* The consumer's ability to recognize and remember the product or brand name
- *Interest.* An increase in the consumer's desire to learn about some of the features of the product or brand
- *Evaluation.* The consumer's assessment of the product or brand on important attributes
- *Trial.* The consumer's actual first purchase and use of the product or brand
- *Adoption.* The consumer's continued purchase and use of the product or brand

For a totally new product, the sequence applies to the entire product category. For a new brand competing in an established product category, it applies to the brand itself. In either case, the hierarchy of effects can serve as a guideline for developing promotional objectives.

Identifying the Target Audience   After the IMC objectives are set, the second step in developing the promotion program is to identify the target audience to whom the promotional program is directed. The more a firm knows about its target audience's profile—including lifestyle, attitudes, and values—the easier it is to develop a promotional program. If a firm wanted to reach a consumer with television or magazine ads, it would be helpful to know what TV shows are watched or what magazines are read.

Marketing ▶ tip

"Totally understanding your target's profile is critical to driving results. A totally integrated program, off-target, is a waste of time and effort."

Mary Kreuk, vice president of marketing, CTV

Setting the Promotional Budget After setting the IMC promotional objectives and creating the target market profile, a company must decide how much to spend on the promotional effort. The promotional budgets needed to reach North American households are enormous. Six companies—General Motors, Philip Morris, Procter & Gamble, Ford, Pfizer, and Pepsi—each spend a total of more than US$2 billion dollars annually on promotion.[17] Determining the ideal amount for the budget is difficult, and several methods can be used.[18]

- *Percentage of sales.* In the percentage-of-sales budgeting approach, the amount of money spent on promotion is a percentage of past or anticipated sales. A common budgeting method,[19] this approach is often stated in terms such as "our promotion budget for this year is 3 percent of gross sales."

- *Competitive parity.* Competitive-parity budgeting matches the competitor's absolute level of spending or the proportion per point of market share.[20]

- *All you can afford.* Common to many small businesses, the all-you-can-afford budgeting method allows money to be spent on promotion only after all other budget items—such as manufacturing costs—are covered.

- *Objective and task.* The most accurate approach to budgeting promotional programs is the objective-and-task method. This approach involves the company determining its promotional objectives, outlining the programs required to meet these objectives, and then allocating the costs of respective programs.[21]

Of the various budgeting methods, only the objective-and-task method takes into account what the company wants to accomplish and requires that the objectives be specified.[22]

Selecting the Promotional Tools After a budget has been determined, the IMC tools can be selected (advertising, personal selling, public relations, sales promotion, and direct response). While many factors provide direction for selection of the appropriate mix, the large number of possible combinations of the promotional tools means that many combinations can achieve the same objective. Therefore, an analytical approach and experience are particularly important in this step of IMC program development. The specific mix can vary from using a single tool, to a comprehensive program that uses all forms of the promotional mix. It is important to assess the relative importance of the various tools as one element may deserve more emphasis than another and companies may be restricted by budget.

The Olympics is an example of a product that uses a comprehensive IMC program to market to consumers, companies, and governments. It uses personal selling and direct response efforts to generate support from governments, cities, companies, and athletes. It uses advertising, sales promotion, and sponsorship programs to target individuals, while public relations efforts are used to focus on positive media exposure.[23]

Designing the IMC Promotion The key component of a promotional program is the message. Many considerations go into creating a message that works. Marketers need to consider what information to convey, whether to use visuals, what music may be required, and how the message can be consistently communicated through the IMC promotional mix. The design of the promotion requires a creative strategy followed by the development of creative tactics. Part of the design includes deciding how to appeal to the target market and what approach may be the best. An ad for Catelli Whole Grain Pasta that targets mothers with young children may use a cute child in the advertisement to get attention, while an ad for Advil, which targets an aging population with arthritis, may use an edgier image to demonstrate how the product will relieve pain.

THE KEY COMPONENT OF A PROMOTIONAL PROGRAM IS THE MESSAGE.

Scheduling the IMC Elements After the design of the promotional program is complete, it is important to finesse the scheduling of each element so that the overall objectives are met. The promotion schedule describes the order in which each promotional tool is introduced and

Executing and Evaluating the IMC Program The ideal execution of a promotion program involves pre-testing its design before it is actually used to allow for changes and modifications that improve its effectiveness. Similarly, post-tests are recommended to evaluate the impact of each promotional element. Testing procedures for sales promotion and direct response efforts often focus on comparing different offers and their respective responses. To fully benefit from IMC programs, companies should create and maintain a test-result database that allows for comparison and provides facts for future decisions that will improve future promotional programs.

Carrying out the promotional program can be expensive and time consuming. There are IMC agencies in operation to help companies with these efforts. In addition, many advertising agencies design fully integrated IMC programs while also maintaining departments dedicated to advertising, sales, promotion, and direct response. The trend today is toward a long-term perspective in which all forms of promotion are integrated.[25]

the frequency of its use during the campaign. New Line Cinema, for example, designed a promotional program for its *Lord of the Rings* movie trilogy that started with movie-trailer advertising appearing on TV and in movie theatres. This was followed by a major merchandising effort in Burger King outlets, together with point-of-sale material to bring attention to the movie and its related merchandise. Overall, the scheduling of the various promotional elements was designed to first generate interest in the movie, then bring consumers into theatres, and finally encourage additional interest through merchandising.[24]

More recently, we can see the importance of promotional scheduling with Bell Canada. In 2008, Bell Canada was a major sponsor of the 2008 Olympic Summer Games in Beijing, launching its new "er" campaign to show its support of Canadian Olympic sports and to communicate that Bell was bettER and fastER. Bell ran print, outdoor, Internet, and TV advertising throughout the games. On the last day of the 2008 games, during the high-audience closing ceremonies, Bell ran a new TV spot focusing on the countdown to the 2010 Winter Olympics and its support of the event. This scheduling was very clever. It considered the high audience of these closing ceremonies, and the fact that typically Canadian viewers of these summer games are also supporters of the winter games. Other sponsors of the 2008 Olympic Summer Games, such as Rona and Wonder Bread Plus, also used the Games to communicate their support of Canadian athletes for the 2010 Winter Olympics in Vancouver.

ask yourself

1. What are the stages of the hierarchy of effects?

2. What common approaches are used to setting promotional budgets?

3. How have advertising agencies changed to help companies develop IMC programs?

Interactive Marketing

LO 6 Internet technology has had a major impact on the dynamics of the marketplace. The Internet empowers consumers to seek information, evaluate alternatives, and make purchase decisions on their own terms and conditions. At the same time, this technology has also challenged marketers to deliver to consumers *more* (selection, service, quality, enjoyment, convenience, and information) for *less* (money, time, and effort). The result is that the Internet has quickly transformed itself into a distribution channel that allows consumers to shop anytime and anywhere, 24/7. Marketers have responded by engaging in interactive and multichannel marketing. Let's review some interesting statistics before we embark upon understanding how companies create Internet marketing programs that create customer value, build customer relationships, and enhance customer experiences.[26]

In April 2008, Statistics Canada reported an increase in online sales for the sixth consecutive year (see Figure 12–7).[27] In 2007, total Internet sales reached an estimated $62.7 billion, an increase of 26 percent from 2006. Over the next few years, e-commerce is expected to continue this growth in both the consumer and business-to-business segment with the split of online sales in the private sector standing at 62 percent for the business market and 38 percent for the consumer market. Despite this growth, it is important to understand that online sales still account for only a small portion of total economic activity, less than 2 percent of total operating revenue for the private sector. Marketers, however, understand that they cannot ignore the sheer size of this market and its future potential. Its importance is reflected in the leap in Internet advertising revenues that were discussed earlier in the chapter and the fact that the Internet offers considerable advantages. These benefits include lowering costs, reaching new consumers, providing a wider assortment of products, and being able to better coordinate requirements with suppliers and customers.

Customer-Value and E-Commerce

The value of e-commerce for customers relates to operating hours, geographical constraints, product selection, interactivity, and customization.

Operating Hours Customers can purchase products at any time and from anywhere, accessing a greater range of products that may be difficult to locate. Indigo Books and Music Inc. is an example of a bricks-and-mortar retailer with stores under the Chapters, Indigo, Coles, and World's Biggest Bookstore names. It also provides consumers with the convenience of

Figure 12–7
Internet sales 2003–2007 (with or without online payment)

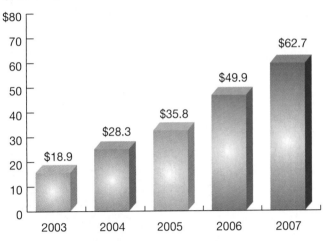

ONLINE SALES CONTINUE TO SHOW RAPID INCREASE
($ billions)

Source: Statistics Canada, *The Daily*, April 24, 2008, accessed at www.statcan.ca/Daily/English/080424/d080424a.htm.

online shopping at www.chapters.indigo.ca. This site allows for online shopping where visitors can browse through their products and order online easily, with delivery often guaranteed for the next business day. This online access is an important feature when one considers that some online retailers report 35 percent of their online orders are placed after traditional stores have closed, between 10 p.m. and 7 a.m.[28]

Geographical Constraints The Internet allows customers to access products from around the world at the click of a mouse. An online consumer can access Harrods, the upscale British department store, at www.harrods.com to shop for products as easily as a person living near the flagship store in London, England. If one wants to purchase a specialized product from the other side of the world, this can be done easily through the Internet. The travel and tourism

Online Advertising Spending in Canada

Source: *Canadian Media Directors' Council Media Digest 2008/2009*, p. 14, accessed at www.cmdc.ca/pdf/2008_09_Media_Digest.pdf.

industry has adapted to the use of the Internet with sophisticated reservation systems that overcome geographical barriers and often the need for an actual travel agent. Airlines such as Air Canada, hotels such as Travelodge, and online travel agents such as Expedia (www.expedia.ca) use sophisticated booking systems that allow individuals to review destinations around the world, easily compare prices, and with the aid of a credit card, book online. One has to only navigate to www.expedia.ca to see the many travel options that are now available. On this site, individuals can go to the "Perfect Trip" section to book flights, hotels, and car rentals, and save money by booking these features together. Alternatively, a visitor can take advantage of "Today's Top Deals," which encourages visitors to return daily to the site to review the latest offers. A number of other helpful features are also available such as "Last Minute Deals"; information from TripAdvisor, another online travel service; maps; and many "Handy Tools and Tips." Customer service is also available with a 24-hour customer service telephone line or via e-mail.

Product Selection

In many instances certain products cannot be easily found in a store and would require special ordering. Specialized DVDs or rare books are good examples of products that fall into this category. Alibris (www.alibris.com) is a website that specializes in books. (Alibris also carries DVDs, VHS cassettes, CDs, LPs, and other music and movie items.) Within this website, you can review rare and out-of-print books and link to sites where they can be purchased. These books cannot be found at traditional retailers, and the website provides customers with the convenience of easily finding and purchasing these rare items. For example, the site was recently selling an 1838 hard-copy book 25 water-colour sketches from the first printing of *Oliver Twist* by Charles Dickens. The site explained that the book's cover was in poor condition but that the sketches themselves were in good condition, each separated by an onion skin. Prices were also quoted.

Interactivity

Another advantage of e-commerce includes the interactivity it can provide. The Internet can facilitate customer service, and help consumers and companies to communicate seamlessly. An example of customer service over the Internet can be seen with the web-hosting company Netfirms (www.netfirms.ca). This company provides excellent customer service through its website by allowing visitors to have their questions answered in a variety of ways. Through instant messaging, customers can access a live customer service representative who will immediately answer questions. Alternatively, customers can use the site's e-mail inquiry system, or access the step-by-step documents and online tutorials.

Blogs have also surfaced on company websites as a means for companies to provide a forum for two-way communication with customers. General Motors was one of the first major companies to use blogs to communicate with its customers, realizing that this mode of communication could help keep them in touch with customer complaints while also providing a forum to communicate with the market. General Motors has a number of blogs that it uses for this purpose. Visit www.gmblogs.com to see examples of how this works in the automobile industry.

Most Active Internet Users (by country)

Ranking	Country	Hours/ User per Month
1	Canada	45.5
2	Israel	35.3
3	United Kingdom	34.9
4	Brazil	33.6
5	United States	32.4

Source: *Canadian Media Directors' Council Media Digest 2008/2009*, p. 64, accessed at www.cmdc.ca/pdf/2008_09_Media_Digest.pdf.

Customization Technology has progressed on the Internet to the extent that customers can often benefit from the customization of the products they are accessing. A simple example can be seen with websites such as MSN (www.msn.com) that allow users to customize their personal web pages to best suit their needs. Another example can be seen in the automobile industry where car manufacturers provide customers with the option to build their own car online, compare prices, and then visit the showroom for further information. Although few cars are actually purchased online, automobile manufacturers find this online interactivity to be an invaluable information-gathering tool for their potential customers. Visit www.honda.ca to see an example of this interactivity.

Components of Interactive Marketing

Interactive marketing involves two-way buyer–seller electronic communication in a computer-mediated environment where the buyer controls the type and amount of information received from the seller. Interactive marketing today is characterized by sophisticated choiceboards, collaborative filtering, and personalization systems that create customized responses to individual needs.[29] Let's review these terms in more detail.

- **Choiceboards.** These are interactive, Internet-enabled systems that allow individual customers to design their own products and services by answering a few questions. Typically, customers choose from a menu of products, services, prices, and delivery options.[30] Customers today can design their own computers with Dell Computer's online configuration, or create their own athletic shoe at www.niketown.com. Because choiceboards collect precise information

about the customer preferences, in time a company can better anticipate and fulfill customer needs.

- **Collaborative filtering.** This is a process that uses technology to automatically group people together who have similar preferences, buying intentions, and behaviour to predict future purchases. Think of it as customer segmentation on a website. For example, if two people who have never met buy the same books, collaborative filtering software is programmed to reason that these two buyers might have similar reading tastes and market to them in a similar manner.

- **Personalization.** This is the consumer-initiated selection of website content that is available on certain websites. Website portals such as Canada.com allow customers to personalize their home pages by selecting or deselecting certain types of information from their home page. Information that is often available for personalization may be for stock quotes, weather, TV schedules, horoscopes, or news items. Most customized sites ask consumers to register on the site by providing personal information such as age and gender. This process typically provides consumers with the option to "opt-in" and subscribe to free online newsletters and/or to make their information available to receive offers. This is called permission-based marketing.

Formally, **permission-based marketing** is the request for a consumer's consent (called "opt-in") to receive e-mail and promotions based on personal data supplied by the consumer. Permission-based marketing is a proven vehicle for building and maintaining customer relationships, provided it is properly used. Companies that successfully employ permission-based marketing use three rules.[31]

First, they make sure that opt-in customers only receive information that is relevant and meaningful. Second, they give customers the ability to opt out or change the type or timing of information. Finally, they assure customers that their name and profile will not

interactive marketing
Two-way buyer–seller electronic communications in a computer-mediated environment in which the buyer controls the kind and amount of information received from the seller

choiceboard
Interactive, Internet-enabled system that allows individual customers to design their own products and services

collaborative filtering
Process that automatically groups people with similar preferences, buying intentions, and behaviours to predict future purchases

personalization
Consumer-initiated practice of generating content on a marketer's website that is tailored to an individual's specific needs and preferences

permission-based marketing
Asking for a consumer's consent (called "opt-in") to receive e-mail and advertising based on personal data supplied by the consumer

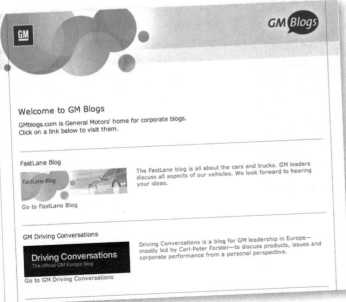

Welcome to GM Blogs
GMblogs.com is General Motors' home for corporate blogs. Click on a link below to visit them.

FastLane Blog
The FastLane blog is all about the cars and trucks. GM leaders discuss all aspects of our vehicles. We look forward to hearing your ideas.
Go to FastLane Blog

GM Driving Conversations
Driving Conversations is a blog for GM leadership in Europe—mostly led by Carl-Peter Forster—to discuss products, issues and corporate performance from a personal perspective.
Go to GM Driving Conversations

be sold or shared with others without their consent. In an online world, where spam is an increasing problem, permission-based marketing uses this approach to reassure consumers their information is secure.

Marketing on the Web

Simply putting information on a website is not enough to entice people to navigate to a site. Marketing programs need to be cleverly designed to direct consumers to an Internet site, and once there to surf the site and return numerous times to gather further information or to be entertained. The approaches to marketing on the web include a variety of choices. Often we see marketers use traditional media to drive people to websites for further information. This is the case with many print and TV ads, which include website addresses at the bottom of their ads. We can see an example of this with an ad for Ontario tourism, which directs readers to the website www.ontariotravel.net/fallcolour to order their Great Fall Drives booklet.

However, placing a website address at the bottom of an ad does not always drive consumers to a website, and other approaches can be used. A number of value-added approaches will drive people to a website such as opt-in newsletters, free "webinars" (web-based seminars), free online courses, and free e-books. In addition, a public relations approach can be used with press releases, and other articles posted on related websites to generate interest. Ads can also be placed on the Internet itself, targeting users on other related sites. In addition, one can use Internet solutions companies, such as Tribal Fusion and Google AdSense, which collect data on Internet usage by placing cookies on individual computers and using behavioural marketing models to place ads throughout the Internet on their related sites where Internet behaviour indicates a target market match. Check out www.tribal-fusion.com and www.google.com/adsense to see these companies' offerings.

Components of Good Web Design

There are seven basic components that can be included in a website and that need to be considered during the design stage

and included as appropriate for the task at hand. These elements are summarized in Figure 12–8 and defined as (1) context, (2) content, (3) community, (4) customization, (5) communication, (6) connection, and (7) commerce. Although every website has context and content, they differ in the use of the remaining five elements. Why? Websites have different purposes. For example, only websites that emphasize the actual sale of products and services include the commerce element, and websites that are used primarily for advertising and promotional purposes emphasize the communication element.

The design of a website is crucial to its success from both a content and visual perspective. The visual appeal of a website is very important as users decide on whether to enter a site in only a few short seconds. A website needs to be visually exciting; use simple, clean graphics; have uncluttered backgrounds; and use limited animation. A well-designed website should also have consistent and intuitive navigation that ideally takes the consumer to a point of interest in two or three clicks. The site should have fast-loading pages and provide useful, relevant external links to other sites. Other useful elements for commercial sites include a section for frequently asked questions (FAQs) and having a clear online purchasing process. Finally, allowing users to register on the site for value-added options is a useful online feature.

Webspeak for the Interactive Marketer

Internet and interactive technology has spawned a whole new vocabulary that marketers need to know. This is as follows:

- *Web communities.* Websites that allow people to meet online and exchange views on topics of common interest. The site iVillage.com is a web community for women and includes topics such as career management, personal finances, parenting, relationships, beauty, and health.

- *Spam.* Communication in the form of electronic junk mail or unsolicited e-mail. The prevalence of spam has prompted some online services, such as Hotmail, to institute policies and procedures to prevent spammers from spamming their subscribers, and many jurisdictions have anti-spamming laws.

- *Viral marketing.* An Internet-enabled promotional strategy that

THERE'S NO PLACE LIKE THIS FOR A CHANGE OF SCENERY

Let shades of amber, auburn and crimson guide you on a getaway to remember this fall in Ontario. The season is bountiful, ripe with local harvests and fresh produce just waiting to be savoured. Take an artisan tour and visit professional artists and craftspeople in their studios. There's no better time than autumn to plan the perfect escape in Ontario.

For great getaway ideas starting from $93 visit us online or call 1 800 ONTARIO for your Great Fall Drives booklet.

ONTARIO
Yours to Discover
ontariotravel.net/fallcolour

Figure 12–8
Web design elements that drive customer experience

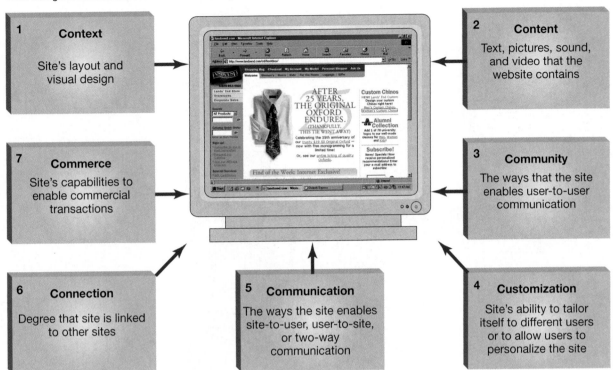

1 Context
Site's layout and visual design

2 Content
Text, pictures, sound, and video that the website contains

7 Commerce
Site's capabilities to enable commercial transactions

3 Community
The ways that the site enables user-to-user communication

6 Connection
Degree that site is linked to other sites

5 Communication
The ways the site enables site-to-user, user-to-site, or two-way communication

4 Customization
Site's ability to tailor itself to different users or to allow users to personalize the site

encourages individuals to forward marketer-initiated messages, such as links to ads and short video clips, to others via e-mail.

- *Portals.* Electronic gateways to the web that supply a broad range of news and entertainment, information resources, communication tools, and shopping services. Well-known portals include Yahoo!, Canada.com, and MSN.

- *Cookies.* Computer files that a marketer can direct onto the computer of an online user who visits the marketer's website. Cookies allow the marketer's website to record a user's visit, track visits to other websites, and store and retrieve this information in the future. Cookies also contain information provided by visitors, such as expressed product preferences, personal data, and financial information, including credit card numbers.

- *Blogs.* A web page where an individual posts personal opinions in a journal style, usually a reflection of the author's personality. Often a blog is updated daily.

- *Bots.* Derived from "robot," an electronic shopping agent that combs websites, to compare prices and product or service features.

- *Customerization.* Customizing not only a product or service, but also the marketing and shopping experience for each customer.

Interactive and Internet marketing are dynamic and exciting tools in the marketer's arsenal of IMC promotional considerations. In the next few years, we will see them increase in importance and usage. Consumers and marketers are locked in a dance of more technology, more service, and more expectations. Consumers become ever more demanding, wanting products and services immediately. They are savvy, selective, critical, and sceptical, and challenge marketers to strive for ever-improving interactive experiences.

ask yourself

1. What are the advantages that e-commerce provides?

2. What are the components of a good web design?

3. What are the seven components that can be included in a website design?

[*adAlyze*]

What is the role of the headline in this ad?

optimischt

What is the main message of this ad?

What makes this ad memorable?

It could only be

Summary...*just the facts*

- Communication is the process of conveying a message to others. It requires a source, a message, a channel of communication, a receiver, the process of encoding, and the process of decoding.

- Integrated marketing communications (IMC) uses a combination of promotional tools to reach a variety of consumer touch points. Promotional activities provide a consistent message across promotional tools.

- IMC promotional tools consist of advertising, personal selling, sales promotion, public relations, and direct response.

- The IMC promotional mix is selected based on target audience, product life cycle, and channel strategies.

- A push strategy involves directing promotional programs to intermediaries such as wholesalers and retailers.

- A pull strategy involves directing the promotional efforts to ultimate consumers.

- Creating IMC promotional programs involves (1) specifying the IMC objectives, (2) identifying the target audience, (3) setting the promotional budget, (4) selecting the promotional tools, (5) designing the IMC promotion, (6) scheduling the IMC elements, and (7) executing and evaluating the IMC program.

- Setting promotional objectives is based on the hierarchy of effects: awareness, interest, evaluation, trial, and adoption.

- Budgeting methods for marketing communications are percentage of sales, competitive parity, the all-you-can-afford approach, and the objective and task method.

- E-commerce provides marketers and customers with the following benefits: operating hours, geographical constraints, product selection, interactivity, and customization.

- Interactive marketing involves two-way buyer–seller electronic communication, which includes choiceboards, collaborative filtering, and personalization.

- Website creation needs to take seven elements into consideration: context, content, community, customization, communication, connection, and commerce.

Key Terms and Concepts...*a refresher*

advertising *p. 230*
channel of communication *p. 229*
choiceboard *p. 245*
collaborative filtering *p. 245*
communication *p. 229*
decoding *p. 229*
direct response *p. 234*
encoding *p. 229*
feedback *p. 229*
field of experience *p. 229*

hierarchy of effects *p. 240*
integrated marketing communications (IMC) *p. 235*
interactive marketing *p. 245*
message *p. 229*
noise *p. 230*
permission-based marketing *p. 245*
personalization *p. 245*
personal selling *p. 232*
promotion *p. 230*

promotional mix *p. 235*
public relations *p. 233*
publicity *p. 233*
pull strategy *p. 239*
push strategy *p. 238*
receivers *p. 229*
response *p. 229*
sales promotion *p. 234*
source *p. 229*

Promotional TOOLS

The area of promotion involves five key areas, advertising, sales promotion, public relations, direct marketing, and personal selling. We start this chapter by looking at one of these areas, advertising, and discuss the approach used by the advertising agency *doug agency inc.* to communicate with consumers. *doug agency* is a small Canadian advertising agency, with clients such as Clover Leaf Seafood, Olympus, York University, and the Art Gallery of Ontario. It was started in 2002 by Doug Robinson

with a view to creating a lean, nimble, creative boutique that champions and inspires creative thinking. Mike Welling, president at *doug agency*, explains that the firm's trademark logo is a barcode to remind clients that advertising is not about winning awards, but about selling products and sending credible brand messages. Their work fuses emotional and rational insights to create ads that start conversations. We look to their work for the non-profit organizations Oxfam and York University to understand their approach to advertising.

In 2007, *doug agency* was challenged, along with many other leading Canadian agencies, to raise Oxfam's profile in Canada and to build awareness of their charitable work and services. Specifically, the objective was to encourage individuals to sign an online petition to persuade the Government of Canada to invest in and support the development of public services in developing countries to improve local residents' quality of life. With an array of great causes competing for public attention, the challenge was to make this cause top-of-mind with individuals, create an emotional link to the cause, and provoke a call to action.

doug agency created a concept that revolved around the idea that a handwritten signature is a personal expression that can powerfully inspire and encourage people to do good. The print ads were simple and featured blank pieces of writing paper, subtly outlined and inscribed with a bold signature. Under the signature a brief analysis of the handwriting was used to evoke emotion, draw attention to the cause, create interest in the message, and point the reader to the tagline, "What does your signature say about you?" Readers were then

You are an emotional rock, impervious to life's hardships but it breaks your heart that 80 million children – mostly girls – don't get to go to school.

WHAT DOES YOUR SIGNATURE SAY ABOUT YOU?
Show you care about women's rights and global poverty. Health and education for all – sign on today. Go to www.oxfam.ca

Oxfam Canada

LEARNING OBJECTIVES

① Consider recent changes to the promotions industry.

② Understand the role of advertising, sales promotion, public relations, direct response marketing, and personal selling as tools in the communications mix.

③ Recognize the different types of advertising and the application of each.

④ Identify the various forms of media that can be used for advertising and explain the advantages and disadvantages of each.

⑤ Explain the different types of consumer-oriented and trade-oriented sales promotions.

⑥ Understand the concept of public relations and the various public relations tools.

⑦ Explain the types of direct response marketing tools available to marketers.

⑧ Recognize the developments in personal selling and the different approaches that can be taken.

challenged to go to the Oxfam website (www.oxfam.ca) to show that they cared by signing the petition. The concept was carried into TV where ads showed an animated signature, again directing people to the website. Washroom ads in the form of floor decals were also developed to draw attention to the squalor that can exist in developing countries and elicit an emotional response to drive people to the website. The floor decals showed a dirt trench with the tagline, "For over 2 billion people, a public washroom looks like this." A call to action was clearly stated underneath with the words, "Show you care. Sign on at www.oxfam.ca." Emotion and rational reasoning joined together to create an engaging statement and call to action. The floor decals were so well received that Oxfam in Berlin placed them at its office entrance! Mike Welling explains that this campaign is compelling as the message is brave, different, and memorable.

The marketing communications campaign *doug agency* created for York University further illustrates this single-minded approach to advertising with a campaign that both provokes and sends a competitive message. In this instance, *doug agency* jolts the reader with clear, crisp, oversized images that evoke curiosity and provide focus. The concept communicates that York University students are challenged to think, be inventive, and achieve heights that they may not have considered. The ads clinch the idea with the tagline "redefine the possible," a call to action to the intellectually curious. In the campaign's "cigarette" print ad, we see an oversized visual of a cigarette stub front and centre, followed by a few sentences explaining the York University doctrine. The result is a distinctive and

QUESTION EVERY ANGLE. STUDY EVERY ANGLE. RESEARCH EVERY ANGLE. WELCOME TO THE INTERDISCIPLINARY UNIVERSITY. AT YORK, WE BREAK DOWN TRADITIONAL BOUNDARIES AND BRING TOGETHER THINKERS FROM EVERY DISCIPLINE TO TACKLE REAL-WORLD ISSUES. PSYCHOLOGISTS, EDUCATORS AND KINESIOLOGISTS AT YORK ARE WORKING TO CONFRONT SCHOOLYARD BULLYING HEAD-ON. THE RESULTS SHOULD HELP EXPOSE THE SOCIAL REPERCUSSIONS OF BULLYING AND EXPLAIN HOW PEER PRESSURE CAN BE SO INFLUENTIAL ON A CHILD'S DEVELOPMENT. FOR FURTHER INFORMATION ABOUT THE INTERDISCIPLINARY UNIVERSITY, VISIT YORKU.CA.

YORK U
UNIVERSITE
UNIVERSITY
redefine THE POSSIBLE

compelling brand image for a relatively young university that competes against universities with decades of heritage and tradition.

In 2004, the campaign, now in its fourth year, received the gold medal for Best Program: Student Recruitment from the Canadian Council for the Advancement of Education. In 2006, it was presented with the grand gold medal as the Best North American University Recruitment Campaign by the Council for Advancement and Support of Education (CASE).

Mike Welling emphasizes that if you want your message to be noticed it must stand out from the crowd, and be simple, single-minded, and focused. *doug agency* strongly believes that creating emotional connections between brands, organizations, and individuals is what gets attention and builds loyalty and support. You can see more of the agency's work at www.dougagency.com. 🍎

Developments in Promotion

1 Chapter 13 provides a more detailed look at the separate promotional tools of advertising, sales promotion, public relations, direct response marketing, and personal selling. Each element is reviewed in detail, explaining how it is best used in marketing communications and what new developments have occurred over the last few years. In brief, the most important change we see in promotion involves the Internet, which now plays a more significant role in all these areas, providing marketers with a direct and affordable way to reach consumers. Increasingly, we see consumers purchasing products online for the convenience that this adds to their shopping experience. Database marketing is also surfacing as an increasingly important tool in marketing communications with many integrated programs using customer relationship management (CRM) programs to customize offers to their consumers. CRM is covered in more detail in Chapter 14.

The Core: Chapter 13

Promotional tools include advertising, sales promotion, public relations, direct response, and personal selling.

Promotional Tools

Promotional programs are created in line with target market interests.

In Chapter 12, we explained that marketing communications has experienced numerous changes over the last few years, increasingly following an integrated marketing communications (IMC) approach. This has been prompted by a fragmentation of media audiences and by consumers' increased use of the Internet and their need to use this platform to supplement their communications. The 2008 release of the Canadian Media Project's report *Canada Online!* (www.canadianinternetproject.ca) emphasizes that although the Internet is central to Canadians' lives, Canadians still use their traditional trusted media sources such as TV, radio, and newspaper, which have experienced marginal declines. The Internet has become a way for people to connect, and is being used to multi-task while using other forms of media. Consumers are frequently surfing the Internet while watching TV, or they may be listening to the radio while online. Internet penetration in Canada in 2007 reached 78 percent.[1] In terms of hours spent with the different forms of media, the Internet has surpassed TV, radio, and newspaper (Figure 13–1), but one needs to recognize the multi-tasking that occurs and the fact that consumers are increasingly watching TV programming on the Internet.

In this way, the Internet has changed the media landscape with most forms of media turning to the Internet to supplement their offerings with online elements. We see this with traditional newspapers, which have experienced slight declines in advertising revenues and have responded with strong Internet presence with their online editions. TV advertising, while appearing to hold its own with advertising revenues, is also succumbing to consumer desires to view programming on the Internet, and networks are increasingly streaming programs online together with advertising opportunities for marketers. In some instances, programming continues on

Figure 13–1
Canadians' media usage

WEEKLY HOURS SPENT WITH THE MEDIA		
MEDIA	**2004**	**2007**
Internet	13.0	17.0
TV	12.1	10.7
Radio	9.3	9.0
Newspaper	4.0	4.4

Source: Charles Zamaria and Fred Fletcher, *Canada Online! The Internet, Media and Emerging Technologies: Uses, Attitudes, Trends and International Comparisons,* Canadian Internet Project, September 2008, www.cipic.ca/en/docs/2008/CIP07%20CANADA%20ONLINE-HIGHLIGHTS.pdf.

Marketing tip ▶

"Marketers need to have clear consumer insights—otherwise communication messages become irrelevant and meaningless."

Mike Welling, **president, doug agency**

the Internet as a continuation of a TV show that has finished its traditional broadcast. We see this with some sports broadcasts and current-events shows. Magazines in turn have created websites providing users with extended content and daily updates. Radio seems to be holding its own due to its ability to satisfy marketers' desire to advertise locally. Radio stations now routinely use podcasts and live broadcasts on the Internet to appeal to consumers. The recent changes in media importance can be seen in Figure 12–1 on page 227.

Consumer promotions heavily integrate the Internet into their offers, often using microsites and e-mail database marketing approaches to affordably reach consumers. Direct response marketing similarly uses the Internet to market and communicate with shoppers, facilitated by online stores and offers sent directly to consumers' homes or e-mail boxes. Personal selling has also been impacted by the online environment. Database technology and CRM techniques provide sales experts with new communications tools and the ability to gather extensive data with which to better serve their customers.

Separate to the Internet influence, outdoor advertising is reaping the benefits of marketers realizing that consumers cannot switch off this particular media (unlike TV), and increasingly we see this element being used to build awareness of new product launches, which then dovetail into TV and print campaigns. In major cities, subway station domination has surfaced as an approach used by marketers to make an imposing statement. This approach sees marketers purchasing all the media in a subway station and plastering it with floor decals, stair-risers, posters, and billboards. Similarly, often the interior space of subway cars can be dominated by one advertiser, sometimes with the outside of the subway

"ALTHOUGH THE INTERNET IS CENTRAL TO CANADIANS' LIVES, CANADIANS STILL USE THEIR TRADITIONAL TRUSTED MEDIA SOURCES."

car also being wrapped with an advertiser's message. Cellphones are starting to play a minor role in marketing communications and we frequently see reality-TV shows use these devices for viewers to text-message a vote. Increasingly, we also see sales promotions asking consumers to use text messaging to enter contests.

Lastly, public relations is an area that is now being used more and more frequently by marketers to drive credible messages back to consumers. Marketers find that consumers tend to skip commercials by changing channels, leaving the room, or muting the sound. Consumers are also skeptical about the commercial messages they see, tending to tune them out as annoyances in their day. Public relations tries to influence the media to cover a story on a product, company, or issue in a credible, unbiased manner.

Developing the IMC Promotional Program

Effective promotional programs require careful planning and management. As discussed in Chapter 12 there are seven basic steps involved in the IMC promotional process: (1) specify the IMC objectives, (2) identify the target audience, (3) set the promotional budget, (4) select the promotional tools, (5) design the IMC promotion, (6) schedule the IMC elements, and (7) execute and evaluate the IMC program (see Figure 13–2). In this chapter we look in more detail at the specific communication tools available to marketers and any special considerations that need to be kept in mind.

Advertising

Advertising is everywhere! Think of all the ads that reach consumers every day. We have come to expect ads on television, and we know that magazines will be full of advertising. However, advertising has become more pervasive than this. A sticker on a banana, a poster in a washroom stall, a city bus painted with a product message, and a "logoed" coffee cup are all advertisements. **Advertising** is described as any paid form of non-personal communication about an organization, good, service, or idea by an identified sponsor. As discussed earlier, advertising has experienced many

Figure 13–2
The IMC promotional process follows sequential steps

The Promotional Process

1. Specify the IMC Objectives
2. Identify the Target Market
3. Set the Promotional Budget
4. Select the Promotional Tools
5. Design the IMC Promotion
6. Schedule the IMC Elements
7. Execute and Evaluate the IMC Program

changes over the past few years due to the impact of technology and the change in consumers' use of the media. This section reviews the special factors that need to be considered when advertising in Canada.

Advertising fulfills a number of tasks, including creating awareness, stimulating demand, conveying a product's positioning, reassuring the purchaser, and building brand loyalty. Rarely is advertising used alone. Sales promotion, direct response marketing, public relations, and sales force initiatives often accompany advertising to reinforce the message and create integrated marketing communications programs that communicate to consumers on many levels.

> *Advertising has experienced many changes over the past few years due to the impact of technology and the change in consumers' use of the media.*

movie lov**er**

An institutional ad that builds goodwill for Bell

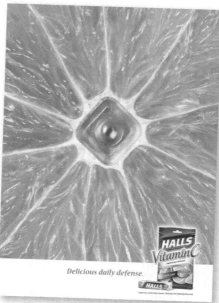

Delicious daily defense.

HALLS
VitaminC

HALLS

A product ad that creates awareness for Halls

uses. Understanding the target consumers—their lifestyles, attitudes, demographics, and usage patterns—is essential to developing advertising that will attract the attention and interest of the intended market. When Rethink Breast Cancer, a national charitable organization dedicated to fighting the disease, launched its marketing campaign, the target market was defined as women and men ages 18 to 34. This may sound strange to you, but the idea was for men to be aware of the disease and to encourage the women in their lives to take a proactive approach to it.[2] In 2007 and 2008, Rethink Breast Cancer partnered with many companies to garner support with these companies producing pink merchandise, or creating supportive ads for the cause during October, designated as Breast Cancer Awareness Month. In 2008, Telus supported the cause by selling pink BlackBerry smartphones and donating $25 for every purchase of the pink gadget.

Budget Considerations Advertising can be very expensive and marketers need to consider the costs of both creating the ads and purchasing the media when designing campaigns. Here are some costs to consider. While the costs of creating ads vary across media and are dependent on specific requirements, the production of radio and print ads can run on average upwards

When we think of advertising, we often think about product ads, however, advertising is also used to convey messages about organizations themselves. This form of promotion can be used effectively by both consumer and business-to-business marketers in both the profit and non-profit segments. Advertising in these sectors is used to influence people to view a product, organization, or cause in a positive light. Ideally, the advertiser wants the target market to purchase a product, to support a cause, or to pursue some other course of action. The challenge in today's environment is to break through the hundreds of competing promotional messages that reach consumers on a daily basis and stand out so that the message is remembered. There are basically two types of advertising: product advertising and institutional advertising. **Product advertisements** are focused on selling a good, a service, or an idea while **institutional advertisements** are focused on building goodwill and a positive image for an organization.

Key Considerations in Advertising Planning

Target Audience Considerations A key consideration in advertising planning is to correctly determine the target audience for the ads. This is central to creating a meaningful message but also to selecting the appropriate media that the target audience

M&Ms supports breast cancer research with pink products.

Figure 13–3
Relative importance of media in Canada (2007)

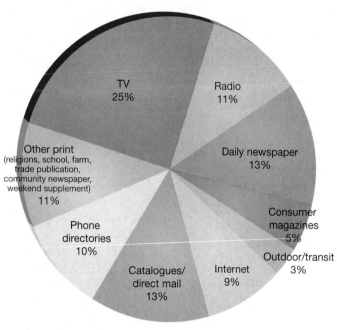

- TV 25%
- Radio 11%
- Daily newspaper 13%
- Consumer magazines 5%
- Outdoor/transit 3%
- Internet 9%
- Catalogues/direct mail 13%
- Phone directories 10%
- Other print (religions, school, farm, trade publication, community newspaper, weekend supplement) 11%

Source: *Canadian Media Directors' Council Media Digest 2008/2009*, p. 14, accessed at www.cmdc.ca/pdf/2008_09_media_digest.pdf

of $15,000 each, while the average cost of creating a 30-second TV commercial is approximately $200,000 to $250,000. All these costs exist before purchasing the actual media required to communicate the message. In fact, the most expensive part of running an advertising campaign is buying media space and time. To understand the magnitude of media advertising budgets, consider that the top 10 advertisers in Canada spent over $800 million in 2006. Procter & Gamble was the largest advertiser in Canada spending $172 million, followed by Rogers Communications at $106 million, and General Motors at $99 million.[3]

Media Considerations Every advertiser must select the advertising media in which to place its ads. Ads can be placed on TV, on the Internet, in newspapers and magazines, on the radio, and in a variety of out-of-home media such as billboards, bus shelters, and transit. Figure 13–3 shows the relative importance of the various forms of media in Canada.

In deciding where to place advertisements, a company has several media choices and a number of alternatives within each medium. Often, advertisers use a mix of media forms and vehicles to maximize exposure of the message to the target audience while also minimizing costs. These two conflicting goals of maximizing exposure and minimizing costs are of central importance to media planning. Media planning assesses which tools are the best to use based on (1) campaign objectives, (2) the media habits of the target market, (3) the target market profile, (4) the complexity of the message, (5) the costs of the media, and (6) budget constraints. Media can often be compared on the basis of CPM, the cost of reaching a thousand people, and GRPs, gross rating points, which weigh the potential reach and frequency of the media against its target market.

Design Considerations Although a marketer can use many different types of appeals to break through the clutter, common advertising appeals include fear, sex, humour, and other emotional approaches.[4] In today's world, with so much advertising clutter, it is increasingly difficult to get the attention of target markets. If an advertisement does not attract attention and convey a clear message, it will not be effective. Consider the ad for York University. It was created with a visually interesting image of a cigarette that begged the consumer to be curious about the ad's content, helping the ad break through the clutter. Consider the ad for Jackson-Triggs wines for the 2008 Toronto International Film Festival.

> *Advertising can be very expensive and marketers need to consider the costs of both creating the ads and purchasing the media when designing campaigns.*

Ranking of Top Advertisers in Canada

Rank	Company	Dollars ($ millions)
1	Procter & Gamble	$172
2	Rogers Communications	$106
3	General Motors	$99
4	Telus	$71
5	BCE	$61

Source: *Advertising Age*, November 20, 2006.

Creativity breaks through the clutter.

The ad breaks through the clutter by using a bold and beautiful image of grapes hanging in a vineyard. Close scrutiny cleverly reveals that the bunch of grapes is in fact made up of miniature movie reels—so fittingly creative for the placement of the ad in the film festival's official program.

Marketers must be careful to create ads that break through the clutter *and* also deliver a fitting message through the appropriate media. This will create meaningful links between the product and its target market. Nintendo did just this with its three ads featured in a 2007 issue of *Maclean's* magazine. These ads were designed with the magazine format in mind, requiring a media placement of three consecutive right-hand pages. The ads were very plain, in fact almost boring, featuring a flat illustration of a man's head with a cartoon-like caption. The caption, in oversized lettering, contained scrambled letters that the reader needed to decipher to understand the message. Cleverly, the ad promoted Nintendo's Brain Age computer-game activities for adults, designed to sharpen the mind. *Maclean's* was a clever media choice with its readership comprising of adults interested in staying sharp and informed.

Advertising Media Choices

L4 Marketers have a number of media options from which to choose. As previously mentioned, these choices are dependent upon not only campaign objectives but also the product, the target market, and budget. Figure 13-4 (see page 258) summarizes the advantages and disadvantages of the major forms of advertising—TV, Internet, newspaper, magazine, radio, and outdoor/transit. These media choices are described in more detail below with a focus on understanding the changes they are currently experiencing.

Television Television is a valuable medium because it communicates with sight, sound, and motion to get the attention of large target audiences. When ads are well designed and appropriately placed in the media, this tool can deliver very impactful and effective messages. Over the last few years, the media of TV has experienced numerous changes with the advent of many new channels. There are now 143 commercial TV channels, which has fragmented audiences so that they are now spread over a wider TV landscape. This makes it more difficult for marketers to target a wide section of the population by focusing on the major networks, which are experiencing declining audiences. This decline is particularly evident among young males, who often prefer to spend time on a computer watching streaming video, DVDs, or playing video games. Many viewers also point to the availability of video on demand and the questionable quality of TV programming as a reason for their changing viewing habits.

Marketers need to be aware that the effectiveness of TV advertising is being questioned by the fact that viewers frequently change channels when ads appear, and use personal video recorders (PVRs) such as TiVos to skip commercials. This problem is being compounded by the fact that more and more viewers are watching their TV programs online. To minimize commercial avoidance, many marketers and producers of TV programs are using product placement and story-line inclusion in TV shows. This has been done very effectively by CTV with its *Canadian Idol* program (see Chapter 12).

Many young consumers prefer to watch TV programs online, which

ask yourself

1. What are the steps involved in the IMC promotional process?
2. What is the difference between product and institutional advertising?
3. What key areas need to be considered when developing an advertising campaign?

Figure 13–4

Advantages and disadvantages of major advertising media

MEDIUM	ADVANTAGES	DISADVANTAGES
Television	Reaches extremely large audience; uses picture, print, sound, and motion for effect; can target specific audiences	High cost to prepare and run ads; short exposure time and perishable message; difficult to convey complex information
Internet	Video and audio capabilities; animation can capture attention; ads can be interactive and link to advertisers	Animation and interactivity require large files and more time to "load"; effectiveness is still undetermined
Newspapers	Excellent coverage of local markets; ads can be placed and changed quickly; ads can be saved; quick consumer response; low cost	Ads compete for attention with other newspaper features; short life span; poor color
Magazines	Can target specific audiences; high-quality colour; long life of ad; ads can be clipped and saved; can convey complex information	Long advance time needed to place ad; relatively high cost; competes for attention with other magazine features
Radio	Low cost; can target specific local audiences; ads can be placed quickly; can use sound, humour, and intimacy effectively	No visual element; short exposure time and perishable message; difficult to convey complex information
Outdoor/Transit	Low cost; local market focus; high visibility; opportunity for repeat exposures	Message must be short and simple; low selectivity of audience; criticized as a traffic hazard

Sources: William F. Arens, *Contemporary Advertising*, 8th ed. (New York: McGraw-Hill/Irwin, 2002), p. 291; and William G. Nickels, James M. McHugh, and Susan M. McHugh, *Understanding Business*, 6th ed. (Burr Ridge, IL: McGraw-Hill/Irwin, 2002), p. 493.

has prompted Canadian networks (including CBC, CTV, and Global) to stream many of their TV shows online after they have been broadcast on the airwaves. This is forcing TV stations to rethink their advertising model, which traditionally comprised of 30-second spots periodically interrupting TV programs. Online streaming video does not lend itself to this same format. Viewers' attention spans are very short on the Internet where a 30-second spot seems endless and particularly annoying. Research has shown that TV-type spots on the Internet lose their impact after about 10 seconds. Currently, the many TV programs that are being streamed on the Internet are being broken up into 10-minute segments for easy downloading and advertising placement. Commercials are shown at the start of some of the segments with many other ads placed on the TV website itself. Switching to a new segment of an episode forces a viewer back on a web page where other advertising messages exist in the form of banner

ads. CTV, for example, currently has full episodes of *Mad Men* and *Grey's Anatomy* streamed on its website in this fashion. Check out www.ctv.ca to see the format.

Another development in TV advertising is the length of TV commercials. This is being challenged by advertisers experimenting with shorter and longer versions of the traditional 30-second spot. More and more advertisers launch a campaign with a 30-second spot, reducing the length of the ad with clever edits down to a 15-second commercial. In 2007 and 2008, the Dairy Farmers of Canada successfully experimented with shorter ads of only five seconds each to capture the attention of tweens and young teenagers. Twenty-five of these short-format ads rotated on stations, pointing the target group to www.getaloadofmilk.ca for more information, contests, and interactive features. Longer format ads of over 30 seconds are rare on TV, but sometimes surface for major sporting events and award shows, which enjoy very

"There are now 143 commercial TV channels."

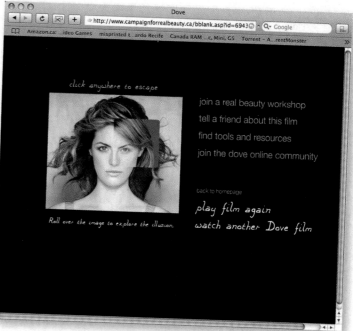

Marketing ▶

high audiences. These longer format ads also tend to appear in movie theatres, where marketers enjoy the fact that viewers cannot change the channel; on video-sharing sites such as YouTube; and on marketers' websites where expensive TV media does not have to be purchased.

Internet   A few years ago the Internet represented a relatively new media for advertisers, taking the form of annoying pop-up ads for viewers. Now advertising on the Internet has become more sophisticated, providing marketers with numerous opportunities to reach online audiences in a variety of different methods that are no longer annoying. The Internet is unique in that it can accommodate many different advertising forms such as visual-based banner ads, audio messages (podcasts), text-based ads (e-mail/newsletters), rich media formats that encompass video-type ads, and interactive messages that can have drop-down menus and built-in activities to engage viewers. Corporate websites and promotional microsites have also become part of the online media landscape, providing consumers with the ability to gather information and interact with the brand in ways never before available. All these options have prompted the emergence of **viral marketing**, where creative advertising campaigns are posted on websites for viewers to forward the links to their contacts so that the message spreads like a virus. The Dove Evolution campaign, created as part of Dove's Campaign for Real Beauty, became an instant success when the creators posted it on their YouTube account. It did the rounds of the Internet and captured the imagination of TV talk shows and marketing blogs around the world. To date, YouTube boasts more than 8 million views of this original promotional spot, which visually depicts how technology creates

an unrealistic and distorted vision of beauty. A viral Internet advertising approach circumvents the costs of traditional media, but there are no guarantees that an ad will capture people's imagination and go viral at all.

Search-word advertising is a totally new form of advertising that developed due to consumers' use of search engines such as Google to gather information and surf the Internet. Search-word advertising appears to the right, or to the top, of your search engine screen after a search has been placed. These ads are typically listed under the heading *sponsored links* or *sponsor results*. Companies that wish to appear on this list of sponsored links are listed in order, based on the highest bidder for a particular word search that was previously established with the host site. Typically, the advertiser then pays the search engine host, such as Google, every time someone clicks on that sponsored link. This is called **pay-per-click** and can become a very expensive proposition if not carefully managed by the advertiser. A number of ad networks

Dove Evolution captured people's imagination and went viral on the Internet.

ad networks Specialist agencies that provide assistance in the research and the development of Internet campaigns in areas such as search-word advertising, e-mail campaigns, and the placement of ads through cooperating sites

banner ads Online ads that can stretch across the top of a web page or be formatted as rectangles, big boxes, and skyscrapers

leaderboards Banner ads that stretch across the top of a web page

skyscrapers Banner ads that are tall, slim, and vertical and appear along the side of a web page

microsites Short-term promotional websites that focus on promotional offers or campaigns

permission-based e-mail When a recipient chooses to receive e-mail from an advertiser

spam Unsolicited e-mail that clutters the advertising landscape for legitimate campaigns

such as Google AdSense can assist in managing search-word advertising. **Ad networks** are specialist agencies that assist in Internet campaigns. They can perform a variety of functions, such as building search-word advertising campaigns, advising on e-mail campaigns, and managing behavioural Internet marketing programs, which place online ads throughout participating sites based on the surfing profile of IP addresses. Examples of these ad networks are Tribal Fusion, Canada.com, Google AdSense, and Yahoo!, just to name a few. In 2008, Microsoft Advertising launched its online ad network in Canada, Drive Performance Media (DRIVEpm), which can be seen at http://advertising.microsoft.com/canada/en/drivepm.

A common type of online advertising is the **banner ad**, which can take many forms. It can stretch across the top of a web page as a **leaderboard**, or be formatted as a *rectangle*, *big box*, or **skyscraper**, which is a tall, slim, vertical ad that appears along the side of a web page. The most successful banner ads are interactive in nature and commonly link to an advertiser's promotional website. Short-term promotional websites, which focus on a promotional offer or campaign, are referred to as **microsites**.

E-mail advertising is a common type of Internet advertising approach taking the form of either permission-based e-mail advertising (opt-in) or spam. **Permission-based e-mail** is when a recipient chooses to receive e-mail from an advertiser, while **spam** is unsolicited e-mail that clutters the advertising landscape for legitimate campaigns. The Canadian Marketing Association (CMA) strictly advises its members not to use spam as part of their marketing initiatives.

Newspapers Newspapers are an important advertising medium with excellent reach potential. Newspapers are the second largest form of advertising in Canada and used by many retailers and automobile manufacturers to reach local markets. There are three types of newspapers: daily paid circulation newspapers, free daily newspapers, and free community newspapers. The highest circulation

of a paid daily newspaper in Canada is the *Toronto Star* followed in order by *The Globe and Mail*, the *National Post*, and the *Toronto Sun*. The two free daily newspapers, *Metro* and *24 hours*, are enjoying high circulation numbers that rival the traditional paid circulation newspapers.[5] Community newspapers are published either weekly or monthly and are an excellent media choice for local retailers and for community events.

Paid circulation daily newspapers have been impacted by the Internet and the advent of free daily newspapers, both of which compete for advertising dollars. Daily newspapers have responded with Internet sites of their own, which contain added features for readers such as blogs, updates, archives, and expanded ad placement opportunities for marketers. It is important to understand that newspaper revenues have been severely impacted by online classified sites such as craigslist and eBay, as well as job-search websites such as Workopolis.com, which interestingly is partly owned by the *Toronto Star*.

Newspapers provide marketers with quick response times. An ad can be placed in a newspaper with a lead time of only two to four days. This allows advertisers to respond to competitive threats and to create ads that relate to current issues. Newspapers allow for detailed advertising copy, which consumers can save and retain for future reference. Newspaper ads are hampered by the fact that their life span is generally just one day and that they have poor colour reproduction, which may not be appropriate for high-quality products. Due to the flexibility in the size of ads and the availability of regional and national papers with local editions, this media can be appropriate for both large and small budgets.

Dove "Evolution" Goes Viral

In 2006, the advertising agency Ogilvy & Mather Canada created the viral video "Evolution" as part of Dove's campaign for real beauty. The 75-second short film was created to stimulate a dialogue on women's beauty, which is often distorted by the media. Time-lapse imagery and engaging music captured viewers' attention while they viewed an average-looking woman being digitally altered to become a beautiful billboard model. The piece ended with the message, "No wonder our perception of beauty is distorted."

The short film was posted on the Dove website (www.campaignforrealbeauty.ca), e-mailed to website subscribers, and posted on YouTube. It quickly went viral, capturing the imagination of both individuals and the media. The film spread across the Internet via personal e-mails, enjoyed millions of clicks (over 8 million to date) on YouTube, and was seen on popular websites such as MySpace and Google Video. The film topped the viral popularity chart (www.viralchart.com) and became the talk of the press, doing the rounds of news broadcasts and popular talk and entertainment shows such as *Ellen, The View, and Entertainment Tonight*. The film also created traffic spikes on the campaign for real beauty website.

The Dove "Evolution" short film eventually became a 60-second TV commercial, airing in a number of countries around the world. It went on to win numerous industry awards, such as the Film Grand Prix and Cyber Grand Prix at the prestigious international Cannes Advertising Festival, and a Gold and Best of Show at the Canadian Marketing awards. Ogilvy & Mather Canada values the media exposure of Dove "Evolution" at over US$150 million. At press time, "Evolution" could be seen in high definition at www.campaignforrealbeauty.ca, while "The Making of Evolution of Dove," could be seen on the YouTube website. ●

Sources: Raju Mudhar, "Dove's 'Evolution' ad wins at Cannes," *Toronto Star*, June 22, 2007, accessed at www.thestar.com/entertainment/article/228160; "Dove – Evolution," Ogilvy Toronto blog, October 11, 2006, accessed at http://meanwhile.wordpress.com/2006/10/11/dove-evolution-2; Brett McKenzie, "The Evolution of Evolution," ihaveanidea.org, accessed at www.ihaveanidea.org/articles/index.php?/archives/381-The-Evolution-of-Evolution.html.

Magazines Magazines provide advertisers with a high-quality media with which to reach their consumers. Magazines have adapted well to changes in the media landscape by providing added value through extra features and updated content on their websites. Magazines such *Canadian Living* and *Chatelaine* offer expansive recipe databases and in-depth coverage on topics related to their latest issues. *Maclean's* magazine website includes a number of exclusive online features such as blogs, quizzes, breaking news, forums, and RSS feeds.

The effectiveness of magazine advertising is impacted by the number of issues published per year, which limits the exposure of the ads and frequency with which they are viewed by readers. This is partly countered by the fact that magazines are kept and passed along to other readers who in turn see the ads. The infrequent publication of magazine issues means that marketers need to extend their advertising over many months and use multiple publications to effectively deliver the message. Using other forms of media will also greatly enhance the message. Magazine advertising allows for detailed information to be relayed to a target group, which can then keep the ad for future reference—a feature that cannot be replicated with TV or radio campaigns.

The Canadian Print Measurement Bureau (PMB) issues an annual topline report detailing circulation, readership, and target market information on leading Canadian magazines. The 2008 report shows that Canadian

Circulation of Top Canadian Daily Newspapers (Monday–Friday)

Ranking	Newspaper	Circulation
1	Toronto Star	438,000
2	The Globe and Mail	329,000
3	Metro Toronto	260,000
4	24 Hours	245,000
5	National Post	215,000
6	Toronto Sun	189,000

Source: *2008 PMB Topline Report,* Canadian Print Measurement Bureau, accessed at www.pmb.ca/public/e/pmb2008/PMB2008_topline.pdf.

magazines with the highest readership are *Reader's Digest* and *Canadian Living*.[6] Visit www.pmb.ca to see the latest topline results.

Magazine advertising is not inexpensive. For example, a full-page, colour ad for English Canada in *Reader's Digest* currently runs at $39,580. This cost, however, can be significantly reduced with smaller ads, quantity discounts, and by restricting the advertising to smaller geographical areas. In this manner, a national English half-page ad becomes less expensive at $27,705, while a half-page ad in British Columbia costs $8,325, and in Ontario, $14,475. These types of price breaks are available for different regions across Canada for a number of print vehicles. Rates are generally determined on the basis of circulation and readership.

Radio   Radio reaches 99 percent of Canadian households with adults over the age of 18 listening an average of 19 hours per week.[7] The main characteristics of this media are that it is local and that it has a relatively low production cost. This makes radio an affordable media for both small and large advertisers. Its primary disadvantages are that it is not a visual media and that it is not appropriate for all types of products. There are 1,238 commercial radio stations in Canada, many of which focus on specific listener interests, including categories such as news and talk, or music genres such as adult contemporary, country, contemporary hits, rock, classical, and the oldies. Stations also exist for specific ethnic groups, broadcasting their content in ethnic languages. Radio is being impacted by the Internet in that more and more listeners, particularly teenagers, are downloading music and listening to it on their MP3 players or computers. Radio stations have responded with simultaneous broadcasts through the Internet and podcasts for digital downloads. Satellite radio with its commercial-free programming is also available through XM Canada and Sirius Canada, but its monthly fee of at least $12.99 per month may make it a questionable long-term option in Canada.

Outdoor/Transit   Outdoor/transit advertising is a very effective medium for creating awareness and interest in a product, and can serve as an excellent reminder about products that currently exist in the market. Over the last few years, this media has experienced slight increases due to its participation in integrated marketing communications programs and the realization that this media cannot be turned off. New digital technology is surfacing in this medium with outdoor digital billboards appearing in major cities across Canada. Clear Channel Media manages many of these digital billboards, using LED screens that have full-motion video displays on 15-minute loops. Examples of these electronic billboards can be seen at Yonge and Dundas Square in Toronto where Clear Channel Media also manages Canada's first media tower. This media tower includes front-lit and back-lit billboards, full-motion, neon, and customized displays offering 20,000 square feet of advertising.

Outdoor/transit advertising includes billboards, back-lit posters, superboards (large billboards),

Top Magazines
(Readership of Canadian Editions)

Ranking	Magazine
1	*Reader's Digest*
2	*Canadian Living*
3	*Chatelaine*
4	*People*
5	*What's Cooking*
6	*Canadian Geographic*
7	*Canadian Health and Lifestyle*
8	*Canadian House & Home*
9	*Maclean's*
10	*Time*

Source: *2008 PMB Topline Report*, Canadian Print Measurement Bureau, accessed at www.pmb.ca/public/e/pmb2008/PMB2008_topline.pdf.

"MAGAZINE ADVERTISING IS NOT INEXPENSIVE."

Digital media tower at Yonge and Dundas Square in Toronto

mall posters, transit vehicles, transit shelters, digital signs, video signage/displays, wall banners, murals, and street-level columns. The most common form of outdoor advertising is billboard due to its ability to quickly reach a target audience and positively influence purchase.[8] The high visibility of this medium serves as a strong reinforcement for well-known products. It is a relatively low-cost, flexible alternative that can complement other media such as print or TV. A company can buy billboard advertising in desired geographical markets and select locations to meet target market needs. For instance, if a clothing company wants to reach high school students, ads can be placed on billboards close to schools and on transit shelters in the area. Transit advertising includes messages on the interior and exterior of buses, subway cars, and taxis. Selectivity is available to advertisers, who can buy space by neighbourhood or by bus route.

A disadvantage of outdoor/transit advertising is that the message has to be very short and visually enticing to work. Advertisers must also realize that outdoor advertising can be viewed by all segments of the population and therefore should not include messages that may be inappropriate for young children. When it comes to transit advertising, marketers need to understand that while it's a solid choice for many products, people may find it difficult to read advertising copy during rush hour. They are often standing shoulder to shoulder, hoping not to miss

Washroom ads are becoming increasingly common in restaurants, bars, colleges, and universities.

their transit stop, or paying attention to heavy traffic congestion while driving.

Other Media Traditional media has become more expensive and cluttered, encouraging advertisers to look at a variety of non-traditional advertising options, called *place-based media*. Messages are placed in locations that attract a specific target audience such as airports, doctors' offices, health clubs, washrooms in restaurants and bars, video screens at gas stations, and in elevators. Aerial advertising can often be seen over major metropolitan areas such as Toronto, Montreal, and Vancouver. Small airplanes or helicopters tow banners or giant billboards. Zoom media is an innovative company that manages washroom advertising, creating innovative designs that appeal to specific genders.

Sales Promotion

LO5 Sales promotion has become a key element of the promotional mix, now accounting for annual marketing expenditures. The distribution of marketing expenditures reflects the trend toward integrated promotional programs that include a variety of promotional elements. Selection and integration of the many promotional techniques requires a good understanding of the advantages and disadvantages of each kind of promotion.[9] There are two basic types of sales promotion: (1) consumer-oriented sales promotions and (2) trade oriented sales promotions.

Consumer-Oriented Sales Promotion

Directed to ultimate consumers, consumer-oriented sales promotions, or simply consumer promotions, are short-term marketing tools used to encourage immediate consumer purchase. They include incentives such as coupons, premiums, contests, sweepstakes, samples, continuity programs, point-of-purchase materials, and rebates.

Coupons

Coupons are consumer promotions that when redeemed at retail offer consumers a discounted price. Many Canadians are coupon users. In 2006, 3.6 billion coupons were distributed in Canada, and 100 million of them were redeemed—a 2.8 percent redemption rate. The average value of the coupons was $2.02, and consumers saved an estimated $135 million through coupon use.[10] Coupons can be distributed online, on-pack, through flyers, or on-shelf; their expiry dates may prompt increased purchases during a specific time period.

Premiums

Offers that provide consumers with merchandise in exchange for proof-of-purchase are called **premiums**. Sometimes a nominal price is charged to cover items such as shipping and handling. A self-liquidating offer is a type of premium that is charged to the consumer at cost to cover the cost of the item. Milk-Bone dog biscuits used a self-liquidating premium when it offered a ball toy for $8.99 and two proofs of purchase.[11] By offering a premium, companies encourage customers to buy the product more frequently and/or to use the product more often.

Contests

A contest is when consumers participate in an activity to win a prize. For example, Tim Hortons' "Roll Up the Rim to Win" contest gives away millions of prizes. Specially marked cups show an arrow directing the consumer to roll up the rim of the cup; they may find a "play again" message, or they may win one of the millions of prizes available. TV ads and in-store signage promote the contest.[12]

Sweepstakes

Consumer promotions that require participants to complete an entry form to enter a promotion to win an item are called **sweepstakes**. These are purely games of chance requiring no analytical or creative effort. Reader's Digest and Publisher's Clearing House are two of the better-promoted sweepstakes. Canada has federal and provincial rules covering sweepstakes, contests, and games to regulate their fairness and ensure that the chances of winning are accurately represented and that prizes are honestly awarded.

Samples

This promotional tool generally provides consumers with a free trial size of a product. This approach overcomes consumers' resistance to spend money on products they have never tried. When Mars changed its Milky Way Dark chocolate bar to Milky Way Midnight, it gave away more than 1 million samples to college and university students at nightclubs, campuses, and popular spring break locations. Awareness of the new candy bar reached 60 percent, resulting in a sales increase of 25 percent.[13]

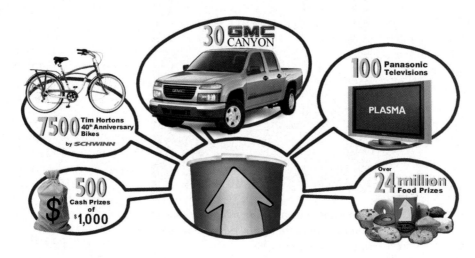

mislead consumers with their advertised offers. Misleading the consumer can result in negative consequences from Canadian regulatory bodies such as the Competition Bureau.

Trade-Oriented Sales Promotions

Trade-oriented sales promotions are promotional tools used to elicit support from wholesalers, distributors, or retailers. The two common approaches used are trade allowances/trade discounts, and cooperative advertising.

Continuity Programs Continuity programs are consumer promotions used to encourage and reward repeat purchases. Canadian Tire money is one of the oldest continuity programs in Canada. It rewards customers who pay in cash, or use a debit card, with Canadian Tire money for their purchases. This money can be used in-store on other purchases. Canadian Tire estimates that $30 million Canadian Tire money is floating around.[14] Other popular continuity programs today involve customer relationship management (CRM) and are successfully used by companies such as HBC with its HBC Rewards program, and Shoppers Drug Mart with its Optimum card. (Chapter 14 covers CRM in more detail.)

Point-of-Purchase Materials These items generally take the form of advertising signs or merchandising units that appear at the locations where the product is sold. They are often located in high-traffic areas near the cash register or the end of an aisle. They are designed to attract consumers' attention and encourage purchase.

Rebates A cash rebate offers consumers the return of money in the mail based on a proof-of-purchase of an item. This tool has been frequently used by computer retailers who advertise a low rebated price in their flyers, counting on many consumers not claiming the rebate. This is a term known as slippage. Marketers must be cautious if using this approach to not

Allowances and Discounts Price discounts offered in return for increasing inventories and/or temporarily reducing the retail price to consumers in the form of a "sale price" are called **trade allowances and discounts**. Common approaches are the merchandise allowance for displaying products, and the case allowance for price reductions.[15]

Cooperative Advertising In a **cooperative advertising** program, a manufacturer pays a percentage of the retailer's advertising expenses for advertising the manufacturer's products in their promotional materials such as flyers.

trade-oriented sales promotions Promotional tools used to elicit support from wholesalers, distributors, or retailers

trade allowances and discounts Price discounts offered in return for increasing inventories and/or temporarily reducing the retail price to consumers in the form of a "sale price"

cooperative advertising Advertising programs where a manufacturer pays a percentage of the retailer's advertising expenses for advertising the manufacturer's products in their promotional materials

ask yourself

1. What types of consumer promotions are available to marketers?

2. How do trade promotions differ from consumer promotions?

3. What trade promotional tools are used by marketers?

Public Relations

Public relations is a form of communication management that seeks to analyze and influence the image of an organization and its products and services. Public relations efforts may utilize a variety of tools and may be directed at many distinct audiences. While public relations personnel usually focus on communicating positive aspects of the business, they may also be called on to minimize the negative impact of a problem or crisis. Firestone, for example, recalled millions of tires after receiving complaints from consumers about product safety. Debates with Ford about the tire failures created a difficult situation for the Firestone public relations department.[16]

Public relations has a number of important strengths. Because the messages are usually finally delivered by the media, they tend to have more credibility than advertising, as they are seen as impartial. The cost of public relations is quite low in comparison to other promotional tools, and the exposure is often more focused. Targeting specific groups can be done quite easily, and different approaches can be taken with different publics. As a tool for creating and enhancing a firm's image, public relations can be very effective. If a positive article or news item comes out about a firm, it can be worth thousands or even millions of dollars in promotional value.

Public relations has a number of drawbacks. A firm cannot control the content of messages put out by the media, and the media are not interested in sending out free messages for advertisers. The media will cover events that are newsworthy. Marketers also need to realize that if the spin is negative, it can take a long time and involve significant costs to counteract negative images with the public.

Greenpeace Takes on Unilever

Focus on Ethics

A public relations nightmare descended upon Unilever, the company behind Dove's advertising campaign for real beauty, when Greenpeace accused Unilever of contributing to the destruction of orangutan habitats in Borneo. Greenpeace published a report accusing Unilever and its suppliers of contributing to global warming by being part of the clearance of rain forest in Indonesia. Greenpeace's report, called "Burning up Borneo," claims that Unilever's palm oil suppliers are companies that are destroying the Indonesian rainforest. Greenpeace says that Unilever is probably the largest corporate buyer of palm oil in the world, using up to 1 in every 20 litres that are produced in Indonesia to manufacture its products. Due to the resulting deforestation, Indonesia is now the third-largest emitter of greenhouse gases on the planet.

Despite this fact, Unilever is the chair of the Roundtable on Sustainable Palm Oil (RSPO). Established in 2002, the RSPO is a coalition that includes Oxfam, the World Wildlife Fund (WWF), manufacturers, and retailers, as well as plantation owners. The Roundtable has created criteria for sustainable palm oil production, but according to Greenpeace, there is still no certified environmentally sustainable palm oil on the market.

Greenpeace protesters demonstrated at Unilever's offices across Europe, and in particular in the United Kingdom at its Port Sunlight factory and its London headquarters. There, dressed as orangutans, protesters handed out materials and screeched at employees.

Since the demonstrations, Unilever has addressed Greenpeace's concerns, stating that it is committed to finding solutions to the issue and sourcing all sustainable palm oil by 2015. Unilever has agreed to stop buying palm oil that originates from deforested areas and to support Greenpeace's call for a moratorium on deforestation in Indonesia. On November 11, 2008, Unilever accepted its first delivery of certified sustainable palm oil. ●

Sources: "Orang-utans swing into action to stop Dove destroying rainforests for palm oil," Greenpeace UK, April 21, 2008, accessed at www.greenpeace.org.uk/blog/forests/orang-utans-swing-into-action-to-stop-dove-destroying-rainforests-for-palm-oil-20080421; David Batty, "Unilever targeted in orang-utan protest," *The Guardian*, April 21, 2008, accessed at www.guardian.co.uk/environment/2008/apr/21/wildlife?gusrc=rss&feed=environment; Charles Clover, "Unilever accused over rainforest destruction," *The Daily Telegraph*, April 21, 2008, accessed at www.telegraph.co.uk/earth/main.jhtml?xml=/earth/2008/04/21/eauni121.xml; "November 2008: Unilever buys first batch of certified sustainable palm oil," Unilever press release, accessed at www.unilever.com/sustainability/news/november2008unileverbuysfirstbatchofcertifiedsustainablepalmoil.aspx; "Dove's story: how you're helping to change Unilever's mind on palm oil," Greenpeace UK blog, May 1, 2008, accessed at www.greenpeace.org.uk/blog/forests/unilever-agrees-plans-for-palm-oil-moratorium-20080501.

Public Relations Tools

Public relations activities should be planned and made part of an organization's integrated marketing communications effort and used in an ethical manner. In developing a public relations campaign, several tools and tactics are available to the marketer including press releases, press conferences, special events, and company reports.

Press Releases The most frequently used public relations tool is the press release, which is an announcement written by the organization and sent to the media.

Press Conferences A second common publicity tool is the press conference, when representatives of the media are invited to an informational meeting with the company. Advanced materials and press releases are often distributed ahead of time. This tool is often used when negative publicity has occurred or in instances of high public interest or concern. This was the case with the listeria contamination issue that surfaced with Maple Leaf Foods in 2008.

Special Events A growing area of public relations involves the creation, or support, and publicizing of special events such as company-sponsored seminars, conferences, sports competitions, or entertainment events. The goal of event sponsorship is to create a forum to disseminate company information or to create brand identification to members of the target audience. For example, the 2008 Canadian Open tennis championship was primarily sponsored by Rogers, thus it was known as the Rogers Cup, and Cadillac Fairview lent its support in 2008 to the Childhood Cancer Foundation Candlelighters Canada, creating positive publicity for the organization and necessary funds for the charity. An interesting approach was

recently seen in 2008 with the introduction of the PawsWay Pet Discovery Centre by Purina, a major manufacturer of pet food in Canada. This new centre provides animal lovers with information on animal care and a facility with fun, interactive exhibits for pet owners and their animals to enjoy. This initiative garnered positive response in the media, which showcased the facility on a number of local news programs.

Company Reports Finally, the development of media such as annual reports, brochures, newsletters, and videos about the company and its products are also public relations tools. These materials provide information to target publics and often generate publicity.

ask yourself

1. What are the advantages and disadvantages of using public relations?
2. What is a press release?
3. What role do company reports play in public relations?

Direct Response Marketing

L7 Direct response marketing is a promotional tool that uses direct communication with consumers to encourage them to place an order, request more information, or visit a store. Direct response marketing has many forms and utilizes a variety of media. Several forms of direct response marketing exist such as direct mail, catalogues, direct response TV, telemarketing, e-marketing, and direct selling. The Internet often plays a major role in direct response marketing, facilitating the information gathering and purchase process with CRM software allowing marketers to track consumers' purchases and customize offers that suit their needs. (See Chapter 14 for more about CRM.)

Direct Mail This involves the use of standardized mail services to elicit funds and/or send offers to a recipient. Direct mail can be either *addressed*, including the recipient's name, or *unaddressed*, sent blank to a household or business.

> "THE INTERNET OFTEN PLAYS A MAJOR ROLE IN DIRECT RESPONSE MARKETING."

Purina's Pet Community & Discovery Centre

I n September 2007, Purina PetCare Canada announced the creation of the Purina PetCare Legacy. The Legacy is a special fund dedicated to the support of initiatives in the pet community, as well as to the education of and advocacy for pets and pet owners. The first major project of the Legacy is the Pet Community & Discovery Centre, which opened its doors in the spring of 2008. The centre is located at Toronto's Harbourfront Centre site. The 16,000-square-foot centre is a pet-friendly, pet-accessible venue, focused on education and the encouragement of responsible pet ownership. It features dog- and cat-related exhibits, events, and activities. Mary Siemiesz, executive director of the Purina PetCare Legacy, says, "The Purina PetCare Legacy was born from the special role our pets play every day and helps us to do more for the pet community—helping more pet lovers and their four legged friends." The Legacy also focuses its efforts on service-dog training programs, providing support for programs such as the Dog Guides of Canada.

Marketing NewsFlash

Purina research shows that 51 percent of Canadian households have a dog or a cat, and Purina makes great efforts to recognize the importance that pets play in their owners' lives. Purina is currently the number-two pet food company in Canada. ●

Sources: Lucy Saddleton, "Purina's Pet Advocate," *Strategy*, May 2008, accessed at www.strategymag.com/articles/magazine/20080501/whopurina.html?word=new&word=products; "Purina PetCare Legacy, Purina website, accessed at www.purina.ca/about/legacy.aspx; "The New Face of Purina's Community Spirit," press release, Nestlé Purina PetCare Canada, September 12, 2007, accessed at http://newswire.ca/en/releases/archive/September2007/12/c7955.html.

Catalogues   These visual compilations of products are provided to consumers in either the traditional print form, and made available in-store, or online through a company website. IKEA successfully uses all these direct response marketing approaches with its catalogue.

Direct Response TV   This includes three basic forms. A company can sell directly to consumers by using a shopping channel. Alternatively, companies can use long-format commercials (over 12 minutes in length) known as infomercials, or companies can sell directly to viewers with traditional length commercials that use toll-free numbers for viewers to order a product via telephone or through a website.

Telemarketing   This direct response marketing form uses the telephone to raise funds or encourage consumers to buy a product. This format is often considered the most annoying form of marketing by consumers, prompting the Canadian Radio-television and Telecommunications Commission (CRTC) to launch a Do Not Call List. Launched in 2008, this list allows consumers to register their phone numbers and be taken off telemarketers' phone lists. The effectiveness of this approach is questionable as registered charities, newspapers, and companies with a commercial relationship with the household in the past 18 months are exempt.

E-marketing   This form of direct response marketing uses electronic technology to market to consumers. Typically, this approach involves the use of online stores, permission-based e-mail messages, and online ads. Marketers face the challenge of creating marketing programs that drive consumers to their website. This may involve the use of other forms of traditional media.

Direct Selling   This includes a variety of approaches ranging from door-to-door sales to the inclusion of other direct response marketing tools such as telemarketing, direct mail, or e-mail marketing. Personal selling is discussed in more detail later in this chapter.

One of the most telling indicators of the power of direct response marketing is how it is used by consumers. Over half of the Canadian population has ordered merchandise or services by phone or mail, and millions have purchased from TV direct response offers. The Internet is also having a major impact, and catalogue shopping is also popular, with about 20 percent of adults making a purchase from a catalogue each year.[17]

The value of direct response marketing for sellers can be described in terms of the responses it generates.[18] **Direct orders** are the result of offers that contain all the information necessary for a prospective buyer to make a decision to purchase and complete the transaction. Club Med, for example, has used direct e-mail offers to sell "last-minute specials" to people in its database. The messages, which were sent midweek, describe rooms and air transportation available at a 30 percent to 40 percent discount if the customer can make the decision to travel on such short notice.[19] **Lead generation** is the result of an offer designed to generate interest in a product or service and a request for additional information. Finally, **traffic generation** is the outcome of an offer designed to motivate people to visit a business. Mitsubishi mailed a sweepstakes offer to 1 million prospective buyers to encourage them to visit a Mitsubishi dealer and test drive the new Galant. The names of prospects who took test drives were entered in the sweepstakes to win a Galant, a trip to Hawaii, and large-screen TVs as prizes.[20]

Information technology and database management are the driving forces in any direct response marketing program. Databases are the result of organizations' efforts to collect demographic, media, and purchase profiles of customers so that direct response marketing tools—such as catalogues—can be directed at specific customers.

Marketers need to have an ethical approach to direct response marketing, ensuring they are not misleading consumers by making unsubstantiated claims or providing products and services that do not meet regulatory requirements. Marketers also need to adhere to privacy laws and ethical marketing practices. Visit the Canadian Marketing Association's website (www.the-cma.org) for the association's code of ethics and guidelines for direct response marketing practices in Canada.

ask yourself

1. What are the main forms of direct response marketing?

2. What are the three types of responses generated by direct response marketing activities?

3. Which association in Canada provides guidelines for the direct response marketing industry?

NOVA SCOTIA.COM

CANADA POSTES
POST CANADA
Postage paid / Port payé si posté
if mailed in Canada / au Canada
Business Reply Mail / Correspondance-
réponse d'affaires
3893472   01

1000012827-B3J3E4-BR01

NOVA SCOTIA TOURISM
PO BOX 2408 STN CENTRAL
HALIFAX NS   B3J 9Z9

You're just two hours away from our natural beauty and renowned hospitality.

Board a direct flight in Toronto or Ottawa and you could be enjoying authentic Nova Scotia cuisine in under two hours. To discover more and get you one step closer to your dream vacation, visit novascotia.com. The incredible packages and deals you will find there will make your visit to Nova Scotia even better.

TO START PLANNING
your Nova Scotia vacation today, be sure to order your FREE copy of the 2008 Doers' and Dreamers' Travel Guide.

Nova Scotia Tourism uses direct mail to attract visitors.

Personal Selling

In Canada, more than 4 million people are employed in sales- and service-related positions.[21] Included in this number are manufacturing sales personnel, real estate brokers, stockbrokers, and salesclerks who work in retail stores. In reality, virtually every occupation that involves customer contact has an element of personal selling. For example, lawyers, accountants, bankers, and recruiters perform sales-related activities. Many executives in major companies have held sales positions at some time in their careers. Selling often serves as a stepping stone to marketing roles and top management positions, as well as being a career path in itself.

Personal selling serves three major roles in a firm's overall marketing effort. First, salespeople are the critical link between the firm and its customers. This role requires salespeople to match company interests with customer needs to satisfy both parties in the exchange process. Second, salespeople *are* the company, in a consumer's eyes. They represent what a company is, or attempts to be, and are often the only personal contact a customer has with the company. Third, personal selling may play a dominant role in a firm's marketing program. Avon, for example, spends almost 40 percent of its total sales dollars on selling expenses.

As the critical link between the firm and its customers, salespeople can create customer value in many ways. Salespeople can create value by easing the customer's purchase decision-making process, and by being close to the customer, salespeople can identify creative solutions to customer problems.

Customer value is made possible by **relationship selling**, the practice of building ties to customers based on a salesperson's attention and commitment to customer needs over time. Relationship selling involves mutual respect and trust among buyers and sellers. It focuses on creating long-term customers, not a one-time sale.[22] A recent survey of 300 senior sales executives revealed that 96 percent consider "building long-term relationships with customers" to be the most important activity affecting sales performance. Companies such as Bell, National Bank, IBM Canada, and Kraft Canada have made building relationships a core focus of their sales effort.[23]

Relationship selling represents another dimension of customer relationship management. It emphasizes the importance of learning about customer needs and tailoring solutions to customer problems as a means of creating customer value.

Personal selling involves the two-way flow of communication between a buyer and seller, often in a face-to-face encounter, designed to influence a person's or group's purchase decision. However, with advances in telecommunications, personal selling also takes place over the telephone, via video teleconferencing, and

Perceived Benefits of Conducting Business on the Internet (as reported by private sector enterprises, 2007)

Lower costs 30%

Reduced time to market 19%

Reaching new customers 36%

marketing meter

Source: "Electronic commerce and technology," *The Daily*, Statistics Canada, April 24, 2008, accessed at www.statcan.ca/Daily/English/080424/d080424a.htm.

"SALESPEOPLE CAN CREATE CUSTOMER VALUE."

through Internet-enabled links between buyers and sellers.

Broadly speaking, two types of personal selling exist: order taking and order getting. While some firms use only one of these types of personal selling, others use a combination of both.

Order Taking

Typically, an **order taker** processes routine orders or reorders for products that were previously sold by the company to existing customers. The primary responsibility of order takers is to preserve an ongoing relationship with existing customers and maintain sales.

Two types of order takers exist. *Outside order takers* visit customers, arrange displays, and replace inventory stocks of resellers, such as retailers or wholesalers. For example, Frito-Lay salespeople call on supermarkets, neighbourhood grocery stores, and other establishments to ensure that the company's line of snack products is in adequate supply. *Inside order takers,* also called *order clerks* or *salesclerks,* typically answer simple questions, take orders, and complete transactions with customers. Many retail clerks are inside order takers. Inside order takers are often employed by companies that use *inbound telemarketing,* the use of telephone numbers that customers can call to obtain information about products or services and make purchases.

Order Getting

An **order getter** sells in a conventional sense by identifying prospective customers, providing customers with information, persuading customers to buy, closing sales, and following up on customers' use of a product or service. Order takers can be inside (an automobile salesperson) or outside (a Xerox salesperson). Order getting involves a high degree of creativity and customer empathy. This type of personal selling is typically required for complex or technical products, so extensive product knowledge and sales training are necessary. An order getter acts as a problem solver who identifies how a particular product or service may satisfy a customer's need.

Order getting is not a 40-hour-per-week job. Industry research indicates that outside order getters, or field service representatives, work about 48 hours per week. As shown in Figure 13–5 (see page 272), 54 percent of their time is spent selling and another 13 percent is devoted to customer service calls. The remainder of their work is occupied by getting to customers and performing numerous administrative tasks.[24]

Order getting by outside salespeople is expensive. It is estimated that the average cost of a single field sales call is almost $170, factoring in a salesperson's compensation, benefits, and travel-and-entertainment expenses.[25] This cost illustrates why outbound telemarketing is so popular today. *Outbound telemarketing* is the practice of using the telephone rather than personal visits to contact customers. A significantly lower cost per sales call (in the range of $20 to $25), and little or no field expenses are the reasons for its widespread appeal. Outbound telemarketing has grown significantly over the past decade, despite legislative controls aimed at setting standards for its use and growing opposition by consumer groups.[26]

We mentioned at the beginning of this section that many firms employ both order takers and order getters. If we view this as a continuum, some salespeople will be strictly order takers, and this means that they will be at one end of the continuum; other salespeople will be at the opposite end, as they will be strictly order getters.

A salesperson determines stock requirements.

> **order taker**
> Salesperson who processes routine orders or reorders
>
> **order getter**
> Salesperson who sells in a conventional sense by identifying prospective customers, providing customers with information, persuading customers to buy, closing sales, and following up on customers' use of a product or service

Figure 13–5

How outside order-getting salespeople spend their time each week

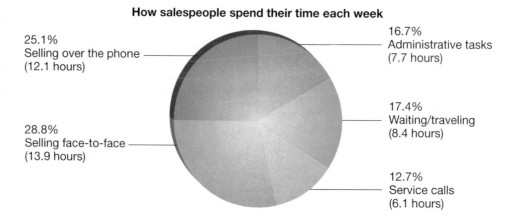

How salespeople spend their time each week

25.1%
Selling over the phone
(12.1 hours)

16.7%
Administrative tasks
(7.7 hours)

28.8%
Selling face-to-face
(13.9 hours)

17.4%
Waiting/traveling
(8.4 hours)

12.7%
Service calls
(6.1 hours)

Most sales jobs require both activities, and depending on the percentage of each, they would place on the continuum somewhere between the two extremes.

Selling is a complicated activity that involves building buyer–seller relationships. Although the salesperson–customer interaction is essential to personal selling, much of a salesperson's work occurs before this meeting and continues after the sale itself. The **personal selling process** consists of six stages: prospecting, pre-approach, approach, presentation, close, and follow-up (Figure 13–6).

A critical concern for salespeople is in handling objections. *Objections* are reasons for not making a purchase commitment or decision. Some objections are valid and are based on the characteristics of the product or service or price. However, many objections reflect prospect skepticism or indifference. Whether valid or not, experienced salespeople know that objections do not put an end to the presentation, rather, techniques can be used to deal with objections in a courteous, ethical, and professional manner.[27]

Developments in the Sales Industry

Technology is presenting its own set of challenges and opportunities for salespeople in Canada. In fact, personal selling and sales force management are undergoing a technological revolution with the integration of technology into customer relationship management processes. We look at some of these changes that impact on the sales industry.

Sales Force Computerization Computer technology has become an integral part of field selling. For example, salespeople for Godiva Chocolates use their laptop computers to process orders, plan

calls, forecast sales, and communicate with Godiva personnel and customers. In a head-office buyer's office, such as at The Bay, a salesperson can calculate the order cost (and discount), transmit the order, and obtain a delivery date within minutes from Godiva's order processing department.[28] Toshiba America Medical System salespeople use laptop computers to provide interactive presentations for customers to see elaborate three-dimensional animations, high-resolution scans, and video clips of the company's products and satisfied customers. Toshiba has found this application to be effective both for sales presentations and for training its salespeople.[29]

Technological advancements allow salespeople to work out of their homes.

Figure 13–6
Stages and objectives in the personal selling process

STAGE	OBJECTIVE	COMMENTS
1. Prospecting	Search for and qualify prospects	Start of the selling process; prospects generated through advertising, referrals, and cold canvassing
2. Preapproach	Gather information and decide how to approach the prospect	Information sources include personal observation, other customers, and company salespeople
3. Approach	Gain prospect's attention, stimulate interest, and make transition to the presentation	First impression is critical; gain attention and interest through reference to common acquaintances, a referral, or product demonstration
4. Presentation	Begin converting a prospect into a customer by creating a desire for the product or service	Different presentation formats are possible; involving the customer is critical; responding to objections is key; a professional ethical approach is needed
5. Close	Obtain a purchase commitment from the prospect and secure a customer	Salesperson asks for the order; different approaches include the trial close and assumptive close; trial close can be used at any stage
6. Follow-up	Ensure that the customer is satisfied with the product or service	Resolve any problems faced by the customer to ensure customer satisfaction and future sales possibilities

Sales Force Communication Technology has also changed the way salespeople communicate with customers, sales support staff, and management. Smartphones such as a BlackBerry are facilitating the transfer of information for salespeople who can now speak to clients, e-mail information, and easily access documents from these mobile devices. In turn, these devices make it easier for clients to contact salespeople with queries or issues they may have.

Perhaps the greatest impact on sales force communication is the application of Internet-based technology. Today, salespeople are using their company's intranet for a variety of purposes such as accessing marketing presentations, account information, technical papers, and competitive profiles.

ask yourself

1. What is the main difference between an order taker and an order getter?

2. What percentage of an order-getting salesperson's time is spent selling?

3. What are the stages in the personal selling process?

[*adAlyze*]

What other forms of media could be used to communicate this message?

What information in this ad may be useful for a public relations campaign?

A freshly cracked egg every morning. What English muffins are wearing this season.

How could this advertising campaign be extended into a sales promotion?

Because even your breakfast has excellent taste. Made with a freshly cracked Canada Grade A egg, the Egg McMuffin® is a sandwich worth flaunting. And with 6g of fat when you hold the processed cheese and margarine, there's never been a better time to enjoy one. Visit mcdonalds.ca for nutrition information.

©2008, McDonald's

Summary...*just the facts*

- Promotional tools include advertising, sales promotion, public relations, direct response marketing, and personal selling.
- Advertising can be classified as either product or institutional.
- Media decisions are based on the target audience, the type of product, the nature of the message, the campaign objectives, and budget.
- Advertising messages can be placed on TV, on the Internet, in newspapers, in magazines, on the radio, and using outdoor forms of media.
- A sales promotion can be either a consumer promotion or a trade promotion.

- Consumer promotional tools include coupons, premiums, contests, sweepstakes, samples, continuity programs, point-of-purchase displays, and rebates.
- Trade promotions include trade allowances, discounts, and cooperative advertising.
- Public relations initiatives include press releases, press conferences, special events, and company reports.
- Direct response marketing tools are direct mail, catalogues, direct response TV, telemarketing, e-marketing, and direct selling.
- The personal selling process consists of six stages; prospecting, pre-approach, approach, presentation, close, and follow-up.

Key Terms and Concepts...*a refresher*

ad networks *p. 260*
advertising *p. 254*
banner ads *p. 260*
consumer-oriented sales promotions *p. 264*
cooperative advertising *p. 265*
direct orders *p. 269*
institutional advertisements *p. 255*
leaderboards *p. 260*
lead generation *p. 269*
microsites *p. 260*

order getter *p. 271*
order taker *p. 271*
pay-per-click *p. 259*
permission-based e-mail *p. 260*
personal selling *p. 270*
personal selling process *p. 272*
premiums *p. 264*
press conference *p. 267*
press release *p. 267*
product advertisements *p. 255*
relationship selling *p. 270*

search-word advertising *p. 259*
skyscrapers *p. 260*
spam *p. 260*
sweepstakes *p. 264*
trade allowances and discounts *p. 265*
trade-oriented sales promotions *p. 265*
traffic generation *p. 269*
viral marketing *p. 259*

Check out the Online Learning Centre at **www.mcgrawhill.ca/olc/thecore**
for chapter application questions, discussion activities, Internet exercises, and video cases.

chapter 14

Customer

Over the last few years, customer relationship management (CRM) has surfaced as a valuable tool rooted in database technology, allowing marketers to use specific purchase information on individual customers to customize offers and mould retail concepts. Loyalty programs are used by many CRM programs to drive their business. Neil Everett, senior vice president and chief marketing officer of Alliance Data takes us on a journey through the complex world of CRM. Everett has a breadth of experience in CRM, including

loyalty programs for Shoppers Drug Mart Optimum card and the Air Miles reward program. Alliance Data Loyalty Services runs a group of companies specializing in loyalty programs. The firm concentrates on three areas of this industry: (1) Air Miles reward program, (2) consulting services, and (3) market research. Alliance uses customer database research to provide insights and recommendations to their clients on how to innovatively build their business. Alliance works with leading North American brands in the grocery, financial services, petroleum, and hospitality industries.

Neil Everett explains that in CRM there are two basic approaches that involve the use of loyalty cards to collect data on consumer purchases. The simplest form of CRM focuses on using customer purchase data to encourage the purchase of additional items and services from a participating sponsor. In its wider application, CRM uses customer data to refocus store layout, in-store merchandising, product mix, and service levels to better suit customer needs and company objectives. Raw customer data is analyzed and analytical models are used to cluster information and provide insights into individual purchase interests and shopping habits.

This is how it works. Neil Everett tells us that customers are encouraged to obtain loyalty cards such as Air Miles, which provide the retailer with purchase information. The loyalty program then analyzes customer data, looking for consistent behaviours in individual purchases to understand trigger points. Offers are then tailored to the individual to encourage increased purchases and share of wallet with the retailer. Everett elaborates with an example: Air Miles data for a particular customer may indicate that a customer is price-sensitive and buys healthy food. The data may place the customer in a specific "solution segment," where particular offers are used to encourage

LEARNING OBJECTIVES

 Understand the concept of customer relationship management (CRM).

 Understand how CRM entails cultural changes.

 Describe customer retention and give examples of various loyalty programs.

Relationship *management*

make it count ™

4 Understand the concepts of data mining and customer lifetime value.

5 Describe the pros and cons of retaining marginal customers.

6 Describe the process of customer reacquisition.

additional purchases with this retailer. Offers that focus on healthy foods and price discounts may work here. More sophisticated CRM professionals may take this data to another level, using modelling programs to slot the shopper into a life stage to better understand their needs and what type of offers may work to increase purchases. For example, from the person's purchase data, CRM may classify the shopper as a baby boomer, indicating they are probably interested in travel, health, and financial services. Offers structured around these areas may work. Everett emphasizes that a CRM professional needs to understand, on an individualized basis, (1) consumer interests, (2) projected share of wallet, (3) offer structures that will work, and (4) how best to communicate with the shopper—e-mail, direct mail, or in-store. Well-structured offers can render a 30 percent to 40 percent response rate, a high level relative to direct mail at approximately 2 percent.

Shoppers Drug Mart with its Optimum card is considered "best in class" for CRM, and leading edge in its use of CRM to drive consumer in-store purchases. The company uses purchase data to learn what drives its consumers, to find out what will keep them loyal to Shoppers Drug Mart, and then to ensure that its stores are best suited to meet customer needs. Air

Miles, with more than 9 million active cardholders, runs another top loyalty program that is used by two-thirds of Canadian households. Air Miles cardholders earn travel, leisure, and entertainment rewards by buying products and services at sponsor locations. Points can be redeemed for movie passes, family attractions, electronic merchandise, travel, sports and recreation items, and travel. Air Miles runs its programs through BMO Bank of Montreal, RONA, Shell, Sport Chek, The Shoe Company, A&P, Sobeys, Safeway, IGA, and airmilesshops.ca. Additional Air Miles reward miles can be collected by using the BMO Mosaik Air Miles MasterCard, or an American Express Air Miles credit card. Cardholders receive quarterly statements with redemption updates, special offers, e-newsletters, and targeted mailings.

Neil Everett reminds us that CRM can target consumers with laser-point accuracy, and is considered the way of the future for marketers. CRM offers efficient programs that can be measured for effectiveness, evaluated for their return on investment, and then modified to drive better business results. You can find out more about the Alliance Data Loyalty Services at www.loyalty.com and www.alliancedata.com.

This chapter's focus is on customer relationship management (CRM), and its three components: customer acquisition, customer retention, and customer reacquisition. 🍎

Customer Relationship Management

Marketers use customer relationship management tools to create marketing programs that satisfy customers.

L❶ **Customer relationship management (CRM)** is the overall process of building and maintaining profitable customer relationships by delivering superior customer value and satisfaction.[1]

CRM focuses on using information about customers to create marketing programs that result in customer satisfaction. The heart of a CRM program is information technology and database systems. However, for CRM to be successful there must be attitude changes in the organization. This point will be covered in the next few pages. CRM originally started out as a tool to help the sales force keep track of customers and prospects.

A large corporation may spend tens of millions of dollars on a CRM system. Among the big suppliers are Oracle, SAP, and IBM; dozens of other companies specialize in components such as telephone call centre technology, database software, and Internet systems. The whole idea is to customize each system to a specific company's needs.

Customer relationship management involves three stages: customer acquisition, customer retention, and customer reacquisition.

Call your local bank about your chequing account and you may discover that the person on the phone is looking at a screen that summarizes your previous calls and displays information about your mortgage and credit card as well. That's an example of CRM. Log on to Amazon.ca and you may find a personalized list of suggested books based on your previous purchases, as well as books that have appealed to readers who have bought the same books as you. That's another example of CRM.

Generally, CRM is seen as a system for funnelling information to one place that otherwise would be dispersed in a big company. This allows all employees to access one customer profile instead of bits and pieces of information about the customer scattered throughout the company. This means collecting information from phone centres, Internet sites, and contacts by salespeople with customers and prospective customers—from any **touch point**.

Here is an example of a company using CRM and touch points to maintain profitable relationships with its customers. Canadian Pacific Hotels (CP Hotels) was not well regarded by business travelers, a notoriously demanding and diverse group to serve, but also very lucrative and much coveted by other hotel chains. By investing time and money in learning what

would most satisfy this segment, the company discovered that customers wanted recognition of their individual preferences and lots of flexibility with check-ins and check-outs. CP Hotels mapped each step of the guest experience from check-in to check-out, and set a standard of performance for each activity. Even small additions, such as free local calls or gift shop discounts, required significant changes in information systems. Along the way, the management structure was revamped so that each hotel had a champion with broad cross-functional ability to ensure that the hotel lived up to its ambitious goals.[2]

Ideally, CRM information is analyzed to gain insight into each customer's needs and behaviour, and then it is used to improve the customer's dealings with the company. This can be as simple as freeing the customer from having to repeat his mailing address every time he places an order, to something like being able to instantly tell the customer the status of a shipment. The analysis might guide promotion efforts so that the customer receives mailings, calls, e-mails, or website advertising tailored to his likes.

CRM Entails Cultural Changes

L2 CRM databases allow companies to get closer to their customers to establish a mutually beneficial relationship. A company's failure with CRM is often the result of approaching CRM as a software project rather than an overall company strategy. A company may spend millions of dollars on software, but doesn't bother changing the cultural attitudes of the organization. A company may be looking for a quick fix for its problems. Companies feel that if they

CRM Expenditure Projections

Projected worldwide CRM software revenue in 2008 **$7.8** billion

Expected worldwide CRM software revenue in 2012 **$13.3** billion

Satisfaction with CRM results **Less than 50%**

marketing meter

Source: Source: Barney Beal, "Gartner: CRM spending looking up," CRM News, April 29, 2008, accessed at http://searchcrm.techtarget.com/news/article/0,289142,sid11_gci1311658,00.html; Shamus McGillicuddy, "CRM projects fail because users say 'no thanks,'" *CIO News*, October 18, 2007, accessed at http://searchcio.techtarget.com/news/article/0,289142,sid182_gci1277542,00.html.

The Power of Moms

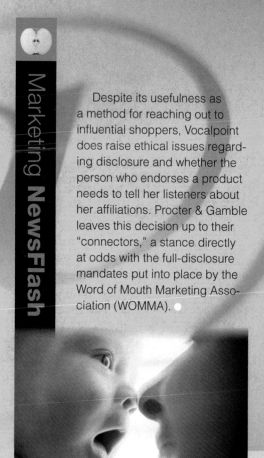

Marketing NewsFlash

Word-of-mouth advertising is a potent tool utilized in a new program launched in 2006 by Procter & Gamble (P&G). Vocalpoint is a unique advocacy program that focuses on getting moms to pass on information about P&G products to people they know. The company has recruited 600,000 moms, ranging in age from 28 to 45 years, who were handpicked because of the ages of their children (under 19) and their social connections through sports, church, theatre, and volunteer work. Vocalpoint volunteers speak to 25 to 30 other women throughout the day, while "average moms" speak to about five. These volunteers receive products (both Procter & Gamble products and products from other companies) to test and comment about them each week on the program's website. The testers also receive free samples and coupons. By using word-of-mouth, P&G hopes to eliminate the confusion of normal advertising by using personal endorsements. Vocalpoint's CEO Steve Knox has said of the plan, "We know that the most powerful form of marketing is an advocacy message from a trusted friend."

Despite its usefulness as a method for reaching out to influential shoppers, Vocalpoint does raise ethical issues regarding disclosure and whether the person who endorses a product needs to tell her listeners about her affiliations. Procter & Gamble leaves this decision up to their "connectors," a stance directly at odds with the full-disclosure mandates put into place by the Word of Mouth Marketing Association (WOMMA).

Sources: Diane Francis, "P&G's army of 'moms,'" *National Post*, July 7, 2006. p. FP6; Robert Berner, "I Sold It Through The Grapevine," *Business Week*, May 29, 2006, p. 32; "News Round up: Buzz-marketing network," *Brand Strategy*, April 10, 2006, p. 6.

---

purchase CRM software, their problems will disappear. For example, if a company has poor customer service, no amount of CRM software by itself will solve the problem. CRM requires a top-down long-run commitment by management. For example, if employees see that management treats them with little respect, there is no incentive for employees to treat customers with respect. The cultural attitudes of the organization must change internally to what is called a CRM culture if the company is really interested in instituting positive customer service. Management must learn to "walk the talk." A good example of a company that practises what it preaches is WestJet. Every employee takes ownership in what they do. They have a heightened sense of customer service responsibility uncharacteristic of many employees. WestJet has a series of ads that focuses on WestJet's theme of ownership..

Employees who take ownership in what they do have a heightened sense of customer service responsibility.

The average business executive goes into CRM thinking it's about technology. If cultural attitudes don't change, employees won't use the system. Without employees using the system, the software becomes useless. The most senior levels of management need to embrace the business strategy of CRM and move the message and tactics of CRM throughout the organization. CEOs need to get the message out to their VPs and have them get it out to their managers, down to supervisors, and down to the front line.

A CRM culture does not come in a box of software. Before installing the tools of CRM, companies need to make sure that they are on their way to establishing a CRM culture. Here are some questions to assess how close the company is to developing a CRM culture.[3]

● Does the company's vision and mission statement reflect a customer-centric sentiment?

- What percentage of employees can state the company's vision or mission statement?
- Do employees complain about customers?
- To what degree do employees feel that they are rewarded (recognition, promotion, compensation) for behaving in a way that has the customer's interests at heart?
- Would the company feel comfortable talking to 10 randomly chosen customers about their sales and after-care experience?

The company should consider the answers to these questions to evaluate the state of the firm's cultural attitudes. The benefits of implementing CRM software are greater if the company adopts a CRM culture.

Customer Acquisition

Part of the definition of CRM focuses on building customer relationships. Data-driven programs can examine the profiles of a company's most-popular customers and use these characteristics to find prospective customers. After a company has found commonalities among profitable customers, it can use this information to accurately target potential customers with the same profile.

Customer Retention

loyalty programs
Programs specifically designed for customer retention

L3 The CRM definition includes maintaining profitable customer relationships. A company that builds strong relationships with customers will retain these customers, resulting in more sales and profits than the company would have if it focused only on getting new customers. It's important to note that making a sale to a current customer is way less expensive than making a sale to a new customer.

Listening to customers is as important as—if not more important than—talking to them. Some business-to-business (B2B) companies are now making a special effort to ask customers when and how they would like to be contacted by the company. This information is placed in a database so that it is readily available. This practice shows respect for loyal customers' time and allows companies to direct the brand communication in a way that is appropriate.

The increased profitability that is associated with customer retention is due to several factors that occur after a relationship has been established with a customer.[4]

- The cost of acquiring a customer occurs only at the beginning of a relationship, so the longer the relationship, the lower the amortized cost.
- Long-term customers tend to be less inclined to switch, and also tend to be less price-sensitive.
- Long-term customers may initiate word-of-mouth activity and referrals.

Loyalty Programs

One way to retain customers is through **loyalty programs**. It should be noted that all customers should be rewarded, but not all customers are the

ask yourself

1. What is customer relationship management all about?
2. What is the difference between customer acquisition and customer retention?

same. In most product categories, a small number of heavy users account for a large percentage of a brand's sales and profits. Heavy users are customers who buy an above-average amount of a given brand. According to Pareto's Rule, a marketing rule of thumb named after Italian economist Vilfredo Pareto, 80 percent of a brand's sales come from 20 percent of its customers. Heavy users should be rewarded differently than light users. The implication here is to take special care of the 20 percent by offering them better rewards than the remaining 80 percent. Databases allow companies to do more than merely recognize their customers. Companies that surprise and delight their high-profit customers with reward programs are more likely to keep these customers in the long run.

The oldest and best-known loyalty program in Canada is Canadian Tire money. The Air Miles reward program is Canada's largest loyalty program; Air Miles can be earned through more than 100 different sponsors, and there are almost 1,000 different rewards that can be redeemed. BMO Bank of Montreal offers an Air Miles–sponsored program, and CIBC offers an Aeroplan program.

Another large Canadian loyalty program that has been around for a long time is HBC Rewards, first started by Zellers under the name Club Z. Loblaws offers the President's Choice Financial MasterCard, with which consumers can get PC points that can be redeemed for groceries. Finally, the Shoppers Drug Mart Optimum card is a very successful loyalty program. Loyalty programs have become a way for one company to differentiate itself from another.

An example of a loyalty program that recognizes Virgin Atlantic's best customers is its clubhouse in London's Heathrow Airport. Virgin's $21 million clubhouse is an expansive 27,000-square-feet lounge with an equally expansive range of ways for Virgin customers to indulge themselves. In the spa, the customer can get a manicure or pedicure as well as a facial, wet shave, and shoulder massage. With three dining options, refreshments are always at the ready. A customer can while away the time by playing retro video games, watching movies on a 16 × 5 foot screen in the cinema, or heading upstairs to the rooftop garden. The

library offers quiet nooks, standard office supplies, and an antique refectory table that came straight from the home of Virgin Chairman Richard Branson.[5]

Another example of a loyalty program is Starwood Hotels & Resorts, which has such brands as Sheraton and Westin. The chain offers a different twist on personalizing a loyalty program. As well as the usual system of accumulating points that can be redeemed for free rooms, preferred-guest program members can use their points to bid for special experiences. The Moments program allows members to take part in online auctions to bid for "insider access" to red-carpet premieres, closed rehearsals with top musicians, private dinners with celebrity chefs, or rounds of golf with PGA Tour pros.[6]

In addition to rewarding customers, loyalty programs provide businesses with a wealth of information about their customers. This information is the raw material for data mining, which is discussed in the next section.

Data Mining

How does a company use the reams of information in their databases? One answer is data mining. Data mining is an efficient way to sort through large amounts of data to find relationships between variables. It is a process of analyzing customer patterns and insights to make better marketing decisions. Data mining can spot trends and other nuggets of information that the company may not have been aware of. Data mining can help marketers with customer

In addition to rewarding customers, loyalty programs provide businesses with a wealth of information about their customers.

segmentation. This chapter's opening vignette provides good examples of loyalty programs and how customer information is used.

All the data about customers is stored in a central place, called the **data warehouse**. A data warehouse can be looked at as an electronics library where all the information is indexed. Once the data warehouse brings the data together, the company uses data mining techniques to find insights about customers.

An example of using data mining is in the grocery industry. Supermarkets should identify the most profitable ways to build and maintain loyal customer relationships. Data-mining techniques are used in an effort to help them understand their customers' shopping behaviour.[7]

For example, one grocery chain in the U.S. discovered through data mining that men who bought diapers on Thursday also tended to buy beer at the same time. Further analysis showed that these shoppers typically did their weekly grocery shopping on Saturdays. On Thursday they only bought a few items. The retailer concluded that they purchased the beer to have it available for the upcoming weekend. The grocery chain used this information in various ways to increase sales. For example, they moved the beer display closer to the diaper display.

Another example of data mining is the banking industry. Data-mining techniques can identify the bank's best customers. Information stored in the database can then build a complete profile of these customers. The profile can then be used in promotions to more accurately target this group, and to target potential customers with a similar profile.

> **data warehouse**
> A central repository of an organization's electronically stored data
>
> **customer lifetime value** The potential sales that will be generated by a customer if that customer remains loyal to that company for a lifetime

ask yourself

1. What is Pareto's Rule?
2. Give some examples of loyalty programs.
3. What is data mining?

Customer Lifetime Value

In customer relationship management, a company focuses on its relationship with customers with the ultimate goal of creating an unbreakable bond with its customers. Companies are starting to focus on the value of a customer if that customer remains loyal to the firm over the customer's lifetime. This is referred to as the **customer lifetime value**.

The Popularity of Loyalty Cards

Marketing **NewsFlash**

Loyalty card programs are becoming increasingly popular among the 18-to-34 age demographic, and especially among teenaged girls. Marketers are discovering that attempts to attract young Canadians to join retail loyalty programs are proving more successful with young women than with teenaged boys. A survey conducted by Youth Culture Group found that while only 55 percent of teenage males ages 13 to 19 belonged to a loyalty program, almost 73 percent of teenage girls in the same age range were program members. A similar survey conducted by Youthography noted the loyalty programs that 19- to 26-year-olds belonged to, with Air Miles leading with nearly 72 percent of those surveyed, followed by the Shoppers Drug Mart Optimum card (50 percent), Hudson's Bay Co.'s HBC Rewards (44 percent), La Senza (20 percent), and the Student Price Club discount card (15 percent).

Loyalty programs are a part of life for more than just the youth market. A 2008 survey found that 86 percent of Canadians belong to at least one loyalty program, averaging 2.5 retail programs, 2 financial programs, and 1.5 travel programs per consumer. The Shoppers Drug Mart Optimum card, one of the most popular programs, is now seven years old and has more than seven million active users, mainly adult women.

Sources: Paul Brent, "In cards, youth insist on choices; Women opt for many cards and focus on clothing, while men have fewer cards but specific interests," *Toronto Star*, April 10, 2008, p. U2; Vinay Menon, "Stuck in the points chase," *Toronto Star*, September 11, 2008, p. A2; Natalia Williams, "Overall Brand of the Year: We love Shoppers. What's not to love about a store that dares to offer an experience?" *Strategy* magazine, November 2006, p. 38.

Carl Sewell, a successful GM dealer-owner, looks at each customer as an investment. If he can provide each customer with excellent customer service, that customer will likely remain loyal to Carl's dealership in the future. In a sense, that customer may have a lifetime value to Carl of hundreds of thousands of dollars. Knowing this, Carl keeps a correct perspective in dealing with customers.[8]

For example, a customer came to pick up his car after servicing and noticed that his tennis racquet, which he had left in the car, was gone. Under normal circumstances, a dealer would say that it is not responsible for items left in a car. Carl Sewell, on the other hand, went over to the customer and apologized for the mishap. He then proceeded to write a cheque for replacement of the racquet. Carl surmised that it was not worth jeopardizing an investment of hundreds of thousands of dollars over the price of a tennis racquet.

A concept very close to customer lifetime value is share of wallet. CRM techniques can help marketers get a larger share of a customer's purchases from that company. Here's an example of how a bank can increase its share of wallet. The bank that holds a customer's mortgage and chequing account may learn at some point that the customer has children and may then try to sell the customer a registered education savings plan. Another example of a company increasing share of wallet is Shoppers Drug Mart. A customer with an Optimum card who purchases cosmetics may receive further mailings from Shoppers that offer coupons for related cosmetic products.

Customer Service Component of CRM

Customer relationship management entails building and maintaining profitable customer relationships. For this to happen, customer service must be addressed. According to the TD Canada Trust customer loyalty poll, more Canadians want customer service and more are getting it, even if it's just a friendly smile.[9]

But if they don't receive positive customer service, they may not be coming back. Businesses are constantly looking for ways to show customers that they care, such as through reward programs. Many customers appreciate the perks, but according to the findings of the TD Canada Trust loyalty poll, customers want to be treated

Marketing ▶

"They [loyalty programs] are customer relationship management programs that work. And they are also good for consumers."

Randy Williams, president and CEO of Tourism Industry Association of Canada, in National Post, April 10, 2008

well. When asked which form of appreciation they are most interested in, 49 percent ranked "just good customer service" as number one. This was followed by just 18 percent who cited reward programs. According to the results, respondents' definition of good service was friendly staff followed by quick and helpful service.

The Worth of Retaining Marginal Customers

L⑤ CRM allows firms to use information technology to quantify the value of individual customers in terms of sales and profits. High-value customers are provided with better privileges, discounts, or other inducements. CRM analysis shows that a small proportion of customers contribute to a large percentage of profits, and that many customers are unprofitable. Many firms are beginning to jettison or fire their low-value customers and are focusing their time on their high-valued customers. For example, in July 2007, CNN reported that Sprint had dropped about 1,000 customers who were calling the customer-care centre too frequently—40 to 50 times more than the average customer every month over an extended period.[10]

Firing low-value customers seems to be a common-sense approach, but in some cases there is a danger. If a company is left with only high-value customers, this leaves the company open to poaching by competitors if they are aware of its customer base.

CRM and Customer Reacquisition

L⑥ Companies are realizing that losing a customer means more than losing a sale. It means losing the entire future stream of purchases that the customer would make over a lifetime of patronage. Customers stop buying from a company for a variety of reasons. Very often, the reasons can be poor customer service

ask yourself

1. Why is customer lifetime value important for companies to calculate?

2. What does share of wallet mean?

WestJet Walks the Talk

A company's corporate culture can have an important influence on how consumers see them. WestJet is an example of one such company that through its treatment of its employees has helped to improve its customer service. The airline, ranked as a top employer on Mediacorp's annual "Canada's Top 100 Employers" list, has the most admired corporate culture in Canada, according to several studies. The airline is known as a workplace with a friendly atmosphere, with employees known for their enthusiasm. WestJet focuses on creating a "culture of ownership and empowerment" for its employees, with 85 percent of employees owning WestJet shares.

Front-line employees have the authority to make customer-service decisions, with company programs designed to help these employees to make decisions that are good both for their customers and for the company. The corporate language that the airline uses, with employees known as "people" or "WestJetters" and passengers known as "guests," helps the customer-friendly culture.

WestJet uses a reward system to ensure that their employees provide an excellent level of customer service. WestJet's call centre receives more than 5 million calls a year, and by implementing an incentive program for its agents, the company has raised its standards for guest services.

The system monitors calls, with every agent having up to 10 calls a month monitored and rated for friendliness, knowledge, and their ability to take control of the call. The agent receives a graded report of the calls, detailing what went right and what can be improved. Agents receive individual training or salary raises depending on their performance. "The higher the customer service rating for our calls, the more people buy from us," WestJet says of these initiatives. ●

Sources: Shannon Klie, "Workplace culture flying high," *Canadian HR Reporter*, Vol. 20, Iss. 6 (March 26, 2007): p. 1; Joe Castaldo, "Just be nice," *Canadian Business*, Vol. 79, Iss. 20 (October 9–22, 2006): p. 140; Norma Ramage, "Be Our Guest," *Marketing* magazine, Vol. 112, Iss. 17 (September 10, 2007): p. 6.

as opposed to something inherently wrong with the brand. The first step in customer recovery is to find the customer who is in jeopardy of being lost to the company. The longer customers stay away from a business, the less likely they are to return. Because customer databases capture purchases, computers can be programmed to periodically examine transaction frequencies and create a list of all customers who have not made a purchase within a set period of time. Because each customer generally has a certain purchase frequency, software can determine when each customer's purchase frequency has been broken. After lapsed customers are identified, the next step is to contact them to determine why they have stopped buying.[11] If the problem is resolved, the lapsed customer may become a very loyal customer because the firm has shown interest in the customer.

Survey of Retail Staff Shows Lack of Customer Service Skills

Percentage of staff who do not smile: 25.9%

Percentage of staff who do not meet customers' needs: 26.4%

Percentage of staff who fail to give a friendly comment once the transaction is complete: 25.8%

Source: "Insight customer service: It helps to know the score," *Marketing Week*, January 5, 2006, p. 22.

ask yourself

1. What were the results of the TD Canada Trust customer loyalty poll?

2. What does firing a customer mean?

[*adAlyze*]

Which need is the advertiser appealing to with this ad?

Is the ad attention-getting?

Is it clear which target market the ad is appealing to?

Summary...*just the facts*

- Customer relationship management (CRM) focuses on using information about customers to build and maintain profitable customer relationships.

- A company's failure with CRM is often the result of approaching CRM as a software project rather than as an overall company strategy.

- One way to retain customers is through loyalty programs. It should be noted that all customers should be rewarded, but not all customers are the same. In most product categories, a small number of heavy users account for a large percentage of a brand's sales and profits.

- Data mining is an efficient way to sort through large amounts of data to find relationships between variables.

- Companies are starting to focus on the value of a customer if that customer remains loyal to the firm over the customer's lifetime.

- The customer service component of CRM is crucial to its success.

- Many firms are beginning to jettison or fire their low-value customers and are focusing their time on their high-valued customers.

- Companies are instituting customer reacquisition programs to prevent losing customers.

Key Terms and Concepts...*a refresher*

customer lifetime value *p. 283*
customer relationship management
   (CRM) *p. 278*

data mining *p. 282*
data warehouse *p. 283*
loyalty programs *p. 281*

Pareto's Rule *p. 282*
share of wallet *p. 284*
touch point *p. 279*

Marketing & Strategic Planning

Strategic planning is a continuous process used by large and small organizations to help ensure that they meet organizational objectives over a three- to five-year period. Both the profit and the not-for-profit industries use this approach to help achieve their long-term visions and to satisfy stakeholders' requirements. To better understand strategic planning, we look at its implementation in one not-for-profit organization: Humber River Regional Hospital.

Humber River Regional Hospital (HRRH) is one of Ontario's largest regional acute-care hospitals, located in the northwest area of Toronto. In 2001, HRRH developed a five-year corporate plan setting its vision to become "*the hospital of choice . . . committed to patient needs.*" In 2006, the hospital embarked on a process to update this plan and set a revised strategic direction for the next five years. HRRH needed to address changes in the industry, such as the establishment of Local Health Integration Networks, and to ensure that the hospital and its services continued to meet community needs in collaboration with other health care providers.

The strategic planning process for HRRH covered an eight-month period. It was a process of collaboration and community involvement, ensuring that all interest groups were represented and heard. The process was guided by a steering committee of board members, medical staff, and senior managers who gathered and analyzed information, drafted documents for feedback and created a five-year strategic plan that met community requirements. The process was facilitated by Agnew Peckham, a health care consulting firm specializing in hospital planning. The process went through the following steps:

- **Background analysis.** A thorough analysis was conducted on community demographics, local health care needs, and the utilization of HRRH hospital services.

LEARNING OBJECTIVES

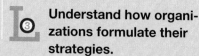

L1 Describe how strategy is developed at the corporate, business unit, and functional levels in an organization.

L2 Explain the concepts of business, mission, and goals and why they are important in organizations.

L3 Understand how organizations formulate their strategies.

L④ Describe the strategic marketing process and its three key phases: planning, implementation, and evaluation.

- **SWOT analysis.** An assessment of HRRH strengths, weaknesses, opportunities, and threats was conducted based on the background analysis.

- **Information gathering.** The opinions of managers, staff, and medical personnel on the future direction of HRRH were gathered with focus groups, online questionnaires, and drop-off boxes.

- **Draft strategic plan document.** A draft of the strategic plan was created by Agnew Peckham based on the background analysis, SWOT analysis, and information gathering.

- **Planning retreat.** A planning retreat, facilitated by Agnew Peckham, was conducted away from the daily distractions of work to allow participants to provide feedback and suggestions on the draft strategic plan.

- **Priority setting.** Hospital clinical planning groups were provided with the draft strategic plan and asked to set their priorities, aligning them with the direction of the strategic plan.

- **Final priorities.** Final priorities for the next five years were set by the steering committee based on input from the hospital clinical planning groups.

- **Final strategic plan.** Agnew Peckham finalized the strategic plan, which was approved by the hospital's Board of Directors.

As a result of this thorough planning process, HRRH created a five-year strategic plan that considered the input of all interest groups, set a vision for its future, and helped the organization focus on its five-year objectives and priorities. The vision sets the hospital as being "... *the hospital of choice ... committed to patient and family needs.*" Its mission focuses on "*providing quality primary patient care for a diverse urban community.*"

As one might expect, its priorities include quality patient care and the safe and efficient delivery of health care services. Priorities also address accountability, support services, and implementation of the new acute-care facility. However, one might not have anticipated that the hospital's priorities also include creating a workplace of distinction and strengthening HRRH's image in the community. The strategic planning process helped HRRH address areas that may not have been top-of-mind when the process first started. This is an example of strategic planning that works!

Chapter 15 describes how organizations set their mission and overall direction and link these activities to marketing strategies. As consumers become more concerned about a company's impact on society, marketing strategy may need to be linked to the social goals of the company's mission statement. Chapter 15 focuses on strategic planning and the role it plays in the marketing process. 🍎

Organizations and Their Levels of Strategy

LO 1 Large organizations today are extremely complex. All of us deal in some way with huge organizations every day, so it is useful to understand the two basic kinds of organizations and the levels that exist in them and their link to marketing.

Today's organizations can be divided into business firms and not-for-profit organizations. A *business firm* is an organization that serves its customers in order to earn a profit. **Profit** is the excess of revenues over costs, the reward to a business for the risk it undertakes in offering a product for sale. In contrast to business firms, a *not-for-profit organization* is an organization that serves its customers but does not have profit as an organizational goal. For simplicity, however, we use the terms *firm, company, corporation,* and *organization* to cover both business and not-for-profit operations.

The Core: Chapter 15

Successful companies link corporate missions and goals to marketing strategies.

The strategic marketing process helps marketers develop programs around a company's impact on society.

Figure 15–1
The three levels of strategy in organizations: corporate, business unit, and functional

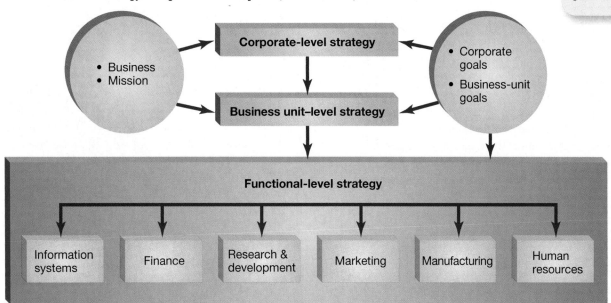

Levels in Organizations and How Marketing Links to Them

A strategy is a plan of action to achieve specific goals. All organizations should have a strategic direction— that is, they should have an idea of what they hope to achieve and how they plan to achieve it. Marketing not only helps set the direction but also helps the organization get there. Figure 15–1 illustrates the three levels of strategy in an optimal organization.

The *corporate level* is where top management directs overall strategy for the entire organization. Multimarket, multiproduct firms such as General Electric or Unilever really manage a group of different businesses, variously termed strategic business units (SBUs), strategic business segments, or product-market units (PMUs).[1] Each of these units markets a set of related products to a clearly defined group of customers. Management at the corporate level focuses on the interests of the shareholders of the firm, as measured by stock performance and profitability. The *business unit level* is where business unit managers set the direction for individual products and markets. Strategic direction is more specific at the business unit level of an organization. For less complex firms with a single business focus, the corporate and business unit strategies may merge.

At the *functional level*, each business unit has marketing and other specialized activities such as finance, manufacturing, or human resources. The name of a *department* generally refers to its specialized function, such as the marketing department or information systems department. At the functional level, the strategic direction becomes very specific and focused.

In a large corporation with multiple business units, marketing may be called on to assess consumer trends as an aid to corporate planning. At the business unit level, marketing may be asked to provide leadership in developing a new, integrated customer service program across all business units. At the functional level, marketing may implement an advertising campaign.

Strategy Issues in Organizations

Organizations need a reason for their existence—and a direction. This is where their business, mission, and goals converge. We'll discuss each below. As shown in Figure 15–1, business and mission apply to the corporate and business unit levels, while goals relate to all three levels.

The Business   Organizations like the Red Cross and your university exist for a purpose—to accomplish something for someone. At the beginning, most organizations have clear ideas about what "something" and "someone" mean. But as the organization grows over time, often its purpose becomes fuzzy and continually unclear.

This is where the organization repeatedly asks some of the most difficult questions it ever faces: What business are we in? Who are our customers? What offerings should we provide to give these customers value? One guideline in defining the company's business: Try to understand the people served by the organization and the value they receive, which emphasizes the critical customer-driven focus that successful organizations have.

In a now-famous article, Harvard professor Theodore Levitt cited railroads as organizations that had

mission
Statement of the organization's purpose and direction

a narrow, production-oriented statement of their business: "We are in the railroad business!" This narrow definition of their business lost sight of who their customers were and what their needs were. Railroads saw only other railroads as competitors and failed to design strategies to compete with airlines, barges, pipelines, trucks, bus lines, and cars. Railroads would probably have fared better over the past century by recognizing they are in "the transportation business."[2]

With this focus on the customer, Disney is *not* in the movie and theme park business, but rather it *is* in the business of entertainment, creating fun and fantasy for customers.

The Mission   By understanding its business, an organization can take steps to define its **mission**, a statement of the organization's scope, often identifying its customers, markets, products, technology, and values. Today, often used interchangeably with *vision*, the *mission statement* frequently has an inspirational theme—something that can ignite the loyalty of customers, employees, and others with whom the organization comes in contact.

To explore strange new worlds, to seek out new life and new civilizations, to boldly go where no one has gone before.

This continuing mission for the starship *Enterprise*, as Gene Roddenberry wrote it for the *Star Trek* adventure series, is inspirational and focuses the advanced technology, strong leadership, and skilled crew of the *Enterprise* on what is to be accomplished.

Focus on Ethics

Consumer Confusion over Green Products

While consumers want the companies that they buy from to be socially and environmentally responsible, the current push for "green" products has left some Canadian consumers doubtful. According to a study done by Gandalf Group (commissioned by Bensimon Byrne), 75 percent of Canadians believe that "environmental claims are marketing ploys," and 65 percent said that "companies overuse the term 'green.'" Sixty-five percent of those surveyed said that they don't understand why green products are more expensive,

while the same percentage believes that companies only claim that certain products are green so that they can raise the price, regardless of how the product is made. Confusion about green marketing is keeping consumers from making environmentally friendly choices.

The ethical practices of corporations are increasingly becoming an important part of how consumers make buying decisions. No longer satisfied with just the quality of the products themselves, consumers are factoring in the company's reputation as being a good corporate citizen when they

choose a company to patronize, according to an online survey conducted by TNS Canadian Facts. This survey showed that 49 percent of Canadians said that they would likely refuse to purchase products from companies that they have heard negative things about. Nearly 28 percent of those surveyed reported that over the past six months, they have refused to buy from a company that they believed had a poor reputation. Among the survey's other findings was that the company's reputation in consumers' minds was almost as important as classic elements such as price, value, and customer service. ●

Sources: Kristin Laird, "Confusion reigns about green marketing: study," *Marketing* magazine, July 29, 2008, accessed at www.marketingmag.ca/english/news/marketer/article.jsp?content=20080728_181849_5256; Chris Daniels, "The ring of truth," *Marketing* magazine, June 11, 2007, accessed at www.marketingmag.ca/english/news/agency/article.jsp?content=20070611_69775_69775; Kristin Laird, "Corporate reputation nearly as important as product price for many shoppers," *Marketing* magazine, August 5, 2008.

Disney is not in the movie and theme park business, but rather it is in the business of entertainment, creating fun and fantasy for customers.

goals (objectives)
Targets of performance to be achieved within a specific time frame

market share
Ratio of a firm's sales to the total sales of all firms in the industry

This inspiration and focus appears in the mission of many organizations, such as the Canadian Red Cross:

> We help people deal with situations that threaten their survival and safety, their security and well-being, their human dignity, in Canada and around the world.

Organizations must connect not just with their customers but with all their *stakeholders*. Stakeholders are the people who are affected by what the company does and how well it performs. This group includes employees, owners, and board members, as well as suppliers, distributors, unions, local communities, governments, society in general, and, of course, customers. Communicating the mission statement is an important corporate-level marketing function. Some companies publish their mission statement on their website or in their annual reports. One British Columbia company has its mission statement on a huge wall poster in its manufacturing facility, and every employee reads and signs it!

Goals Goals or objectives take an organization's mission and translate it into targeted levels of performance to be achieved within a specific time frame. These goals measure how well the mission is being accomplished. As shown in Figure 15–1 (see page 291), goals exist at the corporate, business unit, and functional levels. All lower-level goals must contribute to achieving goals at the next higher level.

Business firms can pursue several different types of goals:

- *Profit*. Classic economic theory assumes that a firm seeks to get as high a profit as possible.
- *Sales*. A firm may elect to maintain or increase its sales level even though profitability may not be maximized.
- *Market share*. A firm may choose to maintain or increase its market share, sometimes at the expense

of greater profits if industry status or prestige is a desired goal. **Market share** is the ratio of sales revenue of the firm to the total sales revenue of all firms in the industry, including the firm itself.

- *Quality*. A firm may target the highest quality, as Rolex does with its luxury wristwatches.
- *Customer satisfaction*. Customers are the key to an organization's success, so their perceptions and actions are of vital importance. Their satisfaction can be measured directly with surveys or tracked with data such as number of customer complaints or percentage of orders shipped within 24 hours of receipt.
- *Employee welfare*. A firm may recognize the critical importance of its employees by having an explicit goal stating its commitment to good employment opportunities and working conditions.
- *Social responsibility*. A firm may seek to balance conflicting goals of consumers, employees, and stockholders to promote overall welfare of all these groups, even at the expense of profits. Firms manufacturing products abroad increasingly seek to be "good global citizens" by paying reasonable wages and reducing pollution from their manufacturing plants.

Many organizations (for example, museums, symphony orchestras, and private schools) do not seek profits as a primary goal. These organizations strive to serve consumers as efficiently as possible. Government agencies also perform marketing activities in trying to achieve their goal of serving the public good.

ask yourself

1. What are the three levels of organization in today's large corporations?
2. What is the purpose of an organization's mission?
3. How should an organization's goals relate to its mission?

Marketing ▶ tip

"Canadians are eager to make choices that will benefit the environment. But cost, cynicism and confusion about green marketing efforts are prohibiting them from making those choices."

Jack Bensimon, president of Bensimon Byrne, in Marketing magazine, July 29, 2008

Setting Strategic Directions

L 3 Setting strategic directions involves answering challenging questions: Where are we now? Where do we want to go? How will we get there?

A Look Around: Where Are We Now?

Asking an organization where it is at the present time involves identifying its customers, competencies, and competitors. More detailed approaches of assessing "where are we now?" include SWOT analysis, discussed later in this chapter, and environmental scanning (Chapter 2). These may be done at each of the three levels in the organization.

Customers Tilley Endurables is a Canadian retailer that knows that its customers appreciate the fine hats and travel clothing that Tilley makes. Tilley provides an example of a clear focus on customers. Its stores and website give a remarkable statement about its commitments to customer relationships and the quality of its products. The Tilley guarantee for its legendary hats has always been an unconditional one: "Tilley Hats will be replaced free if they ever wear out, mildew, or shrink." The same guarantee applies to some of their shorts, vests, jackets, pants, and skirts. They are replaced free if they ever wear out.[3]

The crucial point: Strategic directions must be customer-focused and provide genuine value and benefits to existing and prospective customers.

Competencies "What do we do best?" asks about an organization's competencies—an organization's special capabilities, including skills, technologies, and resources that distinguish it from other organizations. Exploiting these competencies can lead to success.[4] In Tilley's case, its competencies include an obsession

---

Apple's Massive Launch of iPhone 3G

Date	Countries Included
July 11, 2008	Launch of iPhone 3G in 21 countries: Australia, Austria, Belgium, Canada, Denmark, Finland, Germany, Hong Kong, Ireland, Italy, Japan, Mexico, the Netherlands, New Zealand, Norway, Portugal, Spain, Sweden, Switzerland, the United Kingdom, and the United States (1 million units sold during first weekend)
July 17, 2008	France
August 22, 2008	22 countries (largest release since iPhone 3G launch): Argentina, Chile, Colombia, Czech Republic, Ecuador, El Salvador, Estonia, Greece, Guatemala, Honduras, Hungary, India, Liechtenstein, Macau, Paraguay, Peru, the Philippines, Poland, Romania, Singapore, Slovakia, and Uruguay
By end of 2008	Goal of 70 countries and 10 million units sold

Sources: Dan Moren, "iPhone 3G now available in 22 other countries," *Macworld*, August 22, 2008, accessed at www.macworld.com/article/135164/2008/08/iphone3g_countries.html; Maria Kiselyova and Anastasia Teterevleva, "iPhone sales seen at 3.5 million in two years: source," The Vancouver Sun, August 22, 2008.

---

with quality. To quote the founder Alex Tilley, "I'll make travel clothing! I'll make it the best in the world! And then I'll make it even better!" Tilley Endurables is one of the last remaining companies to manufacture all its products in Canada.[5]

Competitors In today's global competition, the lines among competitive sectors are increasingly blurred. For example, Loblaws competes directly with other supermarkets such as Sobeys and Safeway. At the same time, it also competes against mass merchandisers such as Wal-Mart, which also carry groceries, and it competes with warehouse clubs such as Costco. Loblaws also carries many pharmacy items, which puts it into direct competition with pharmacies such as Shoppers Drug Mart and Pharma Plus. Shoppers Drug Mart carries many lines of cosmetics, which puts it into direct competition with department stores such as The Bay, which traditionally carries cosmetics.

Growth Strategies: Where Do We Want to Go?

Knowing where the organization is at the present time enables managers to set a direction for the firm and commit resources to move in

that direction. Two techniques to aid in these decisions are the business portfolio analysis and the market-product analysis.

Business Portfolio Analysis Developed by the Boston Consulting Group (BCG), *business portfolio analysis* uses quantified performance measures and market growth to analyze a firm's strategic business units as though they were a collection of separate investments.[6] While used at the business unit level here, this so-called BCG analysis has also been applied at the product line or individual product or brand level. This kind of portfolio analysis is very popular; most large firms have used it in some form.

BCG, a leading management consulting firm, advises its clients to locate the position of each of its SBUs on a growth-share matrix (Figure 15–2). The vertical axis is the *market growth rate*, which is the annual rate of growth of the specific market or industry in which a given SBU is competing. The horizontal axis is the *relative market share*, defined as the sales of the SBU divided by the sales of the largest firm in the industry.

BCG has given specific names and descriptions to the four resulting quadrants in its growth-share matrix based on the amount of cash they generate for or require from the firm:

- *Cash cows* are SBUs that typically generate large amounts of cash, far more than they can invest profitably in their own product line. They have a dominant share of a slow-growth market and provide

Figure 15–2

Boston Consulting Group growth-share matrix for a strong, diversified firm showing some strategic plans

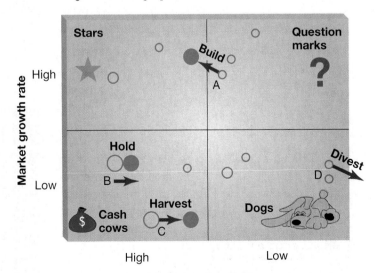

Nintendo Captures Adult Market

Marketing NewsFlash

Nintendo of Canada is seeking to target new demographics of video-game players. With the introduction of the Wii Fit, Nintendo hopes to redefine the video game. The Wii Fit is a balance-board type console that allows the user to choose from more than 40 activities such as yoga and skiing, and then gives the user a real workout. The console also calculates body mass index (BMI) by measuring the user's weight and centre of gravity. The Wii Fit can be used by people of all ages—children and their mothers, fathers, and grandparents—but it is the adult segment of the user population that Nintendo hopes to attract. To ensure that this desired demographic is aware of the product, Nintendo set up stations in malls around Vancouver, Toronto, and Montreal to allow people to test the Wii Fit, and placed advertisements in magazines such as *Canadian Living* and *Best Health*. Ads also ran during adult-centric TV programs such as *Oprah* and *Grey's Anatomy*.

The Wii Fit is also demonstrating to adults that it is more than just a children's game, as it becomes part of a growing trend of using video games as fitness and rehabilitative tools for adults. Many seniors' residences have begun to buy the Wii Fit for their recreation centres. The console is both a physical and a social benefit to the residents, helping them to keep up their coordination and fitness levels. Hospitals have also begun to use the Wii Fit in their rehabilitation units, as the activities aid in the recovery of balance, coordination, and strength for patients with brain injuries. The multiple uses of the Wii Fit and its games are opening doors for Nintendo into a variety of new markets.

Sources: Terry Poulton, "Wii Fit arrives with energetic push," *Media in Canada*, May 21, 2008, accessed at www.mediaincanada.com/articles/mic/20080521/nintendo.html?word=nintendo&word=wii; Joanne Hatherly, "Seniors get active and hooked on Wii, *The Vancouver Sun*, August 18, 2008, accessed at www.canada.com/vancouversun/news/arts/story.html?id=75e4ff46-d3be-46f7-b530-5f6c2d2b40be.

---

cash to pay large amounts of company overhead and to invest in other SBUs.

- *Stars* are SBUs with a high share of high-growth markets that may need extra cash to finance their own rapid future growth. When their growth slows, they are likely to become cash cows.

- *Question marks* or *problem children* are SBUs with a low share of high-growth markets. They require large injections of cash just to maintain their market share, and even more to increase it. Their name implies management's dilemma for these SBUs: choosing the right ones to invest in and phasing out the rest.

- *Dogs* are SBUs with a low share of low-growth markets. Although they may generate enough cash to sustain themselves, they do not hold the promise of ever becoming real winners for the firm. Dropping SBUs that are dogs may be required, except when relationships with other SBUs, competitive considerations, or potential strategic alliances exist.[7]

The circles in Figure 15–2 show the current SBUs in a strong, diversified firm. The area of each circle is proportional to the corresponding SBU's annual sales revenue.

Management often makes conscious decisions on what role each SBU should have in the future and either injects or removes cash from it. Four alternative strategies are available for each SBU. The firm can invest more in the SBU to *build* its share (SBU A in Figure 15–2), as Fujitsu has done with its tablet PC computer product lines. Or it can invest just enough to *hold* the SBU's share at about its current level (SBU B in Figure 15-2). Or it can *harvest* the SBU (SBU C

Marketing ▶ *tip*

"If you had to call a winner right now, it would be the Nintendo Wii, because it's demolishing the other platforms."

Ricardo Torres, senior editor of the California-based online magazine Gamespot, in Marketing magazine, January 15, 2007

Strategies emerging from a business portfolio analysis: Fujitsu builds its tablet PC business while Procter & Gamble divests its Duncan Hines cake mix line to Aurora Foods.

in Figure 15-2), trying to milk its short-term cash flow even though it may lose share and become a dog in the longer run. Finally, the firm can *divest* the SBU (SBU D) by phasing it out or actually selling it to gain cash, as Procter & Gamble did by selling its Duncan Hines cake mix line to Aurora Foods.

Market-Product Analysis

Firms can also view growth opportunities in terms of markets and products. Think of it this way: For any product there is both a current market (consisting of existing customers) and a new market (consisting of potential customers). And for any market, there is a current product (what they're now using) and a new product (something they might use if it were developed). Four possible market-product strategies are shown in Figure 15-3.

As Unilever attempts to increase sales revenues of its Ben & Jerry's business, it must consider all four of the alternative market-product strategies shown in Figure 15-3. For example, it can try to use a strategy of *market penetration*—increasing sales of present products in its existing markets, in this case by increasing sales of Ben & Jerry's present ice cream products to consumers. There is no change in either the basic product line or the market served, but increased sales

are possible—either by selling more ice cream (through better promotion or distribution) or by selling the same amount of ice cream at a higher price to its existing customers.

Market development, which here means selling existing Ben & Jerry's products to new markets, is a reasonable alternative. Australia, for example, is a good possible new market.

An expansion strategy using *product development* involves selling a new product to existing markets. When Ben and Jerry's launched sorbet and frozen yogurt products, the firm was following a product development strategy. Figure 15-3 shows that the firm could try leveraging the Ben & Jerry's brand by selling its own frozen yogourt in North America.

Diversification involves developing new products and selling them in new markets. This is a potentially high-risk strategy for Ben & Jerry's—and for most firms—because the company has neither previous production experience

Figure 15–3
Four market-product strategies: alternative ways to expand sales revenues for Ben & Jerry's

| Markets | PRODUCTS | |
	Current	New
Current	**Market penetration** Selling more Ben & Jerry's super premium ice cream in North America	**Product development** Selling a new product such as frozen yogourt under the Ben & Jerry's brand in North America
New	**Market development** Selling Ben & Jerry's super premium ice cream in Australia for the first time	**Diversification** Selling a new product such as breakfast cereal in China for the first time

How can Ben & Jerry's identify new ice cream flavours and social responsibility programs that contribute to its mission? The text describes how the strategic marketing process and its SWOT analysis can help.

nor marketing experience on which to draw. For example, in trying to sell a Ben & Jerry's brand of breakfast cereal in China, the company has expertise neither in producing cereals nor in marketing to consumers in China.

Which strategies will Ben and Jerry's follow? Keep your eyes, ears, and taste buds working to discover the marketing answers!

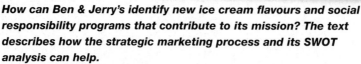

ask yourself

1. What are competencies and why are they important?

2. What is business portfolio analysis?

3. What are the four market-product strategies?

period of time, such as one year or five years. This chapter's opening vignette focuses on the strategic marketing process in a regional hospital. Both profit and not-for-profit industries use this approach to help achieve their long-term visions and to satisfy stakeholders' requirements.

The following sections give an overview of the strategic marketing process that puts Chapters 1 through 14 of this book in perspective.

The Strategic Marketing Process

After an organization assesses where it's at and where it wants to go, it must work out how it will get there. Specifically, it must decide:

- How to allocate resources;
- How to convert plans into actions; and
- How results compare with plans, and whether deviations (results that differ from expectations) require new plans and actions.

This approach is used in the **strategic marketing process**, whereby an organization allocates its marketing mix resources to reach its target markets and achieve its goals. This process is divided into three phases: planning, implementation, and evaluation (Figure 15–4).

The strategic marketing process is so central to the activities of most organizations that they formalize it as a **marketing plan**, which is a road map for the marketing activities of an organization for a specified future

Strategic Marketing Process: The Planning Phase

As shown in Figure 15–4, the planning phase of the strategic marketing process consists of the three steps shown at the top of the figure: situation analysis, market-product focus and goal setting, and the marketing program. Let's use the recent marketing planning experiences of several companies to look at each of these steps.

Step 1: Situation (SWOT) Analysis The essence of a **situation analysis** is taking stock of the firm or product's past performance, where it is now, and where it is headed in light of the organization's plans and the external factors and trends affecting it. The situation analysis box in Figure 15–4 is the first of the three steps in the planning phase.

A **SWOT analysis** describes an organization's appraisal of its internal **S**trengths and **W**eaknesses and its external **O**pportunities and **T**hreats. Both the situation and SWOT analyses can be done at the level of the

Figure 15–4
The strategic marketing process

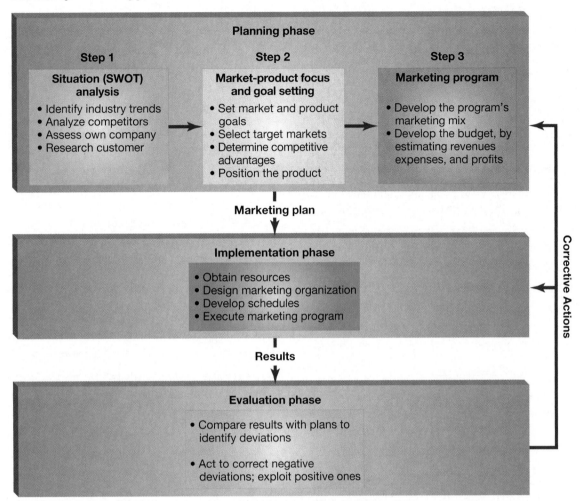

entire organization, the business unit, the product line, or the specific product. As an analysis moves from the level of the entire organization to the specific product, it, of course, gets far more detailed. For small firms or those with basically a single product line, an analysis at the firm or product level is really the same thing.

The SWOT analysis is based on a detailed study of the four areas shown in step 1 of the planning phase of the strategic marketing process (see Figure 15–4). Knowledge of these areas forms the foundation on which the firm builds its marketing program:

- Identifying trends in the firm's industry.
- Analyzing the firm's competitors.
- Assessing the firm itself.
- Researching the firm's present and prospective customers.

Let's assume you are the Unilever vice president responsible for integrating Ben & Jerry's into Unilever's business. You might do the SWOT analysis shown in Figure 15–5. Note that your SWOT table has four cells formed by the combination of internal versus external factors (the rows) and favourable versus unfavourable factors (the columns) that summarize Ben & Jerry's strengths, weaknesses, opportunities, and threats.

A SWOT analysis helps a firm identify the strategy-related factors in these four cells that can have a major effect on the firm. The goal is not simply to develop the SWOT analysis but to translate the results of the analysis into specific actions to help

A SWOT analysis helps a firm identify the strategy-related factors in these four cells that can have a major effect on the firm.

the firm grow and succeed. The ultimate goal is to identify the critical factors affecting the firm and then build on vital strengths, correct glaring weaknesses, exploit significant opportunities, and avoid or prepare for disaster-laden threats. That is a big order.

The Ben and Jerry's SWOT analysis in Figure 15–5 can be the basis for these kinds of specific actions. An action in each of the four cells might be:

- *Build on a strength.* Find specific efficiencies in distribution with Unilever's existing ice cream brands.

- *Correct a weakness.* Recruit experienced managers from other consumer product firms to help stimulate growth.

- *Exploit an opportunity.* Develop a new line of low-fat yogourts to respond to consumer health concerns.

- *Avoid or prepare for a disaster-laden threat.* Focus on less risky international markets, such as Mexico.

Step 2: Market-Product Focus and Goal Setting Determining which products will be directed toward which customers (step 2 of the planning phase in Figure 15–4) is essential for developing an effective marketing program (step 3). This decision is often based on **market segmentation**, which involves considering prospective buyers in terms of groups, or segments. These groups have common needs and will respond similarly to a marketing action. Ideally, a firm can use market segmentation to identify the segments on which it will focus its efforts—its target market segments—and develop one or more marketing programs to reach them.

Goal setting involves setting measurable marketing objectives to be achieved. For a specific market, the goal may be to introduce a new product—such as Toyota's launch of its hybrid car, the Prius. For a specific brand or product, the goal may be to create a promotional campaign or pricing strategy

that will get more consumers to purchase. (Think of all those commercials touting the auto industry's popular 0 percent financing?) For an entire marketing program, the objective is often a series of actions to be implemented over several years.

Using the strategic marketing process shown in Figure 15–4 (see page 299), let's examine step 2 by way of using Sleep Country Canada as an example:

- *Set marketing and product goals.* Based on listening to what is important to customers, Sleep Country Canada offers lots of choice in mattresses. It also makes each experience before, during, and after the sale an enjoyable one for the customer. One of its marketing goals may be to increase its market share by a certain percentage in the retailing mattress business in Canada. It's important to quantify the percentage so that the company can measure whether it successfully meets its goals.

- *Select target markets.* Sleep Country Canada targets consumers who want a quality mattress as well as a positive customer service experience.

- *Determine competitive advantages.* **Competitive advantages** are those characteristics of a product that make it superior to competing substitutes. Sleep Country Canada offers the mattress purchaser

Figure 15–5
Ben & Jerry's: A SWOT analysis

Location of Factor	TYPE OF FACTOR	
	Favourable	**Unfavourable**
Internal	**Strengths** • Prestigious, well-known brand name among North American consumers • Major share of the super premium ice cream market • Can complement Unilever's existing ice cream brands • Widely recognized for its social responsibility actions	**Weaknesses** • Danger that B&J's social responsibility actions may add costs, reduce focus on core business • Need for experienced managers to help growth • Flat sales and profits in recent years
External	**Opportunities** • Growing demand for quality ice cream in overseas markets • Increasing demand for frozen yogourt and other low-fat desserts • Success of many firms in extending successful brand in one product category to others	**Threats** • Consumer concern with fatty desserts; B&J customers are the type who read new government-ordered nutritional labels • Competes with giant Pillsbury and its Häagen-Dazs brand • International downturns increase the risks for B&J in European and Asian markets

Figure 15–6
Elements of the marketing mix that comprise a cohesive marketing program

an enjoyable customer service experience unparalleled in this market. It offers clean, bright stores; sleep experts who put the customer's comfort and budget needs first; and courteous delivery people.

- *Position the product.* Sleep Country Canada is positioned as a mattress specialist that offers quality products with the added benefit of courteous and knowledgeable staff, an attractive in-store setting, and a convenient delivery service.

Details in these four elements of step 2 provide a solid foundation to use in developing the marketing program—the next step in the planning phase of the strategic marketing process.

Step 3: Marketing Program
Activities in step 2 tell the marketing manager which customers to target and which customer needs the firm's product offerings can satisfy— the *who* and *what* aspects of the strategic marketing process. The *how* aspect—step 3 in the planning phase—involves developing the program's marketing mix and its budget.

Figure 15-6 shows components of each marketing mix element that are combined to provide a cohesive marketing program. For Sleep Country Canada, the marketing mix activities can include the following:

- *Product strategy.* Offer consumers one of the largest selections of top, name-brand mattresses.
- *Price strategy.* Offer consumers a low-price guarantee. If consumers find a comparable product at a competitor that is equal to or lower than Sleep Country Canada's price, the company will beat that figure by 5 percent.
- *Promotion strategy.* Sleep Country Canada uses mass media advertising to communicate its unique retail experience to prospective and current customers.
- *Place (distribution) strategy.* Sleep Country Canada is conveniently located in five Canadian provinces with 133 stores in total (as of 2009).[8]

Top 3 Brands in *Business Week's* Annual Ranking of the 100 Best Global Brands

Source: "Best Global Brands: 2008 Rankings," accessed at www.interbrand.com/best_global_brands.aspx.

Putting a marketing program into effect requires that the firm commit time and money to it, prepare a sales forecast, and establish a budget that must be approved by top management.

Strategic Marketing Process: The Implementation Phase

A firm's marketing plan is the result of the many hours spent in the planning phase of the strategic marketing process. Implementation, the second phase of the strategic marketing process, involves carrying out the marketing plan that emerges from the planning phase. If the firm cannot put the marketing plan into effect—in the implementation phase—the planning phase was a waste of time. Figure 15-4 (see page 299) shows the four components of the implementation phase: obtaining resources, designing the marketing organization, developing schedules, and actually executing the marketing program designed in the planning phase.

ask yourself

1. What is the difference between a strength and an opportunity in a SWOT analysis?

2. What is market segmentation?

3. What are competitive advantages and why are they important?

ask yourself

Obtaining Resources Most companies have numerous options for growth. But such growth requires an investment. Corporate leadership within an organization determines the best options for growth and how they should be funded.

Designing the Marketing Organization A marketing program needs marketing staff to implement it. Figure 15-7 (see page 303) shows the organization chart of a typical manufacturing firm, giving some details of the marketing department's structure. Four managers of marketing activities are shown to report to the vice president of marketing. Several regional sales managers and an international sales manager may report to the manager of sales. This marketing organization is responsible for converting marketing plans to reality.

Developing Schedules Effective implementation requires developing appropriate schedules and determining specific deadlines for the creation

---

Famous Canadian Brands

Marketing **NewsFlash**

Canada is not often considered a country with a great deal of brand power. It lacks a reputation for producing strong brands like Coca-Cola or Budweiser, and the brands that it distributes globally are often not connected to Canada in their consumers' minds. This reputation might soon be a thing of the past, however. In their new book *Ikonica: A Field Guide to Canada's Brandscape*, authors Jeannette Hanna and Alan Middleton argue that Canadian brands are prospering both in Canada and abroad, and that many brands are poised for

further success in the increasing global market.

Hanna argues that Canadian brands are succeeding globally, citing examples like Umbra, McCain Foods, Aldo Shoes, Cirque du Soleil, and BlackBerry, but that the companies blend in so well with the local marketing environments that consumers outside of Canada don't realize the products' origin, and people inside of Canada don't realize how well the brands are doing. Hanna and Middleton say in their book that "This country's real handicap is that we don't celebrate or study our greatest

successes; instead, we shrug them off as lucky breaks or freaks of nature." One of the things the authors talk about in the book is that, ironically, the great Canadian international success stories are chameleons. McCain is one of the largest food producers in the world, but in England it's seen as an English brand, and in India, it's an Indian brand. That ability to be chameleon-like is the secret to McCain's success. Where American companies bring their American-ness with them, Canadians have the ability to embed themselves. ●

Sources: John Gray, "Q&A: Branding experts Jeannette Hanna and Alan Middleton," *Canadian Business*, June 16, 2008, accessed at www.canadianbusiness.com/managing/ceo_interviews/article.jsp?content=20080616_198717_198717; Jeremy Lloyd, "Homegrown ikons," *Marketing* magazine, April 28, 2008, accessed at www.marketingmag.ca/english/news/marketer/article.jsp?content=20080513_091107_8520.

Figure 15–7
Organization of a typical manufacturing firm, showing a breakdown of the marketing department

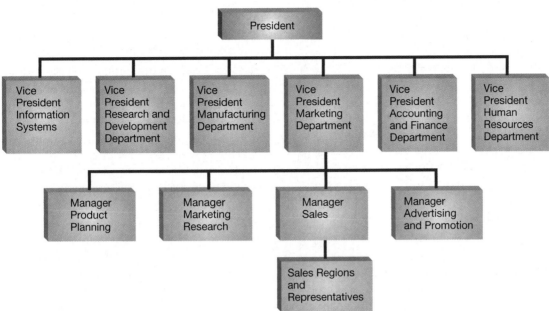

and execution of marketing activities. For example, if a company wants to place an ad in *Time* magazine, it must reserve space a month prior to the date that the ad appears in the magazine. Also, the company must allow time for creating and producing the ad.

Executing the Marketing Program Marketing plans are meaningless unless they are put into action. This requires attention to detail to both marketing strategies and marketing tactics. A marketing strategy is the means by which a marketing goal is to be achieved, usually characterized by a specified target market and a marketing program to reach it. Although the term strategy is often used loosely, it implies both the end sought (target market) and the means to achieve it (marketing program).

To implement a marketing program successfully, hundreds of detailed decisions are often required, such as writing ads or setting prices. These decisions, called marketing tactics, are detailed day-to-day operational decisions essential to the overall success of marketing strategies.

Strategic Marketing Process: The Evaluation Phase

The evaluation phase of the strategic marketing process seeks to keep the marketing program moving in the direction set for it. Accomplishing this requires the marketing manager to compare the results of the marketing activities with the goals laid out in the marketing plans to identify deviations and to act on these deviations—correcting negative deviations and exploiting positive ones.

Comparing Results with Plans When a company sets goals and then compares them to actual results, it needs to research the reasons for the differences. Where plans are exceeded, the company determines the drivers of this success and identifies ways to build on them as it moves forward. When there is a shortfall (actual results less than planned—often referred to as the *planning gap*), the company has to "fill in" this planning gap with a revised marketing program and possibly new goals.

Acting on Deviations Sometimes, the marketing program falls short of its goals. When this occurs, managers need to take corrective action. This is called correcting a negative deviation. But when actual results are far better than the plan called for, creative managers find ways to exploit the situation. This is called exploiting a positive deviation.

ask yourself

1. How would you distinguish a marketing strategy from a marketing tactic?

2. How do the objectives set for a marketing program in the planning phase relate to the evaluation phase of the strategic marketing process?

Summary...*just the facts*

- Today's large organizations, both business firms and not-for-profit organizations, are often divided into three levels: the corporate, business unit, and functional levels.

- Marketing has a role in all three levels by keeping a focus on customers and finding ways to add genuine customer value. At the lowest level, marketing serves as part of a team of functional specialists whose day-to-day actions actually involve customers and create customer value.

- Organizations exist to accomplish something for someone. To give itself focus, an organization continuously assesses its business, mission, and goals.

- Setting strategic directions for an organization involves asking "Where are we now?" to assess the organization's customers, competencies, and competitors. It also involves asking "Where do we want to go?" and using techniques like portfolio analysis and market-product analysis, and asking questions like "How will we get there?" that uses marketing plans.

- The strategic marketing process involves an organization allocating its marketing mix resources to reach its target markets using three phases: planning, implementation, and evaluation.

- The planning phase of the strategic marketing process has three steps, each with more specific elements: situation (SWOT) analysis, market-product focus and goal setting, and marketing program.

- The implementation phase of the strategic marketing process has four key elements: obtaining resources, designing the marketing organization, developing schedules, and executing the marketing program.

- The evaluation phase of the strategic marketing process involves comparing results with the planned targets to identify deviations and taking actions to correct negative deviations and exploit positive ones.

Key Terms and Concepts...*a refresher*

competitive advantages *p. 300*
goals *p. 293*
market segmentation *p. 300*
market share *p. 293*
marketing plan *p. 298*

marketing strategy *p. 303*
marketing tactics *p. 303*
mission *p. 292*
objectives *p. 294*
profit *p. 290*

situation analysis *p. 298*
strategic marketing process *p. 298*
strategy *p. 291*
SWOT analysis *p. 298*

This is your brain

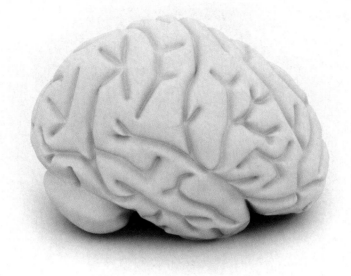

This is your brain on [istudy]

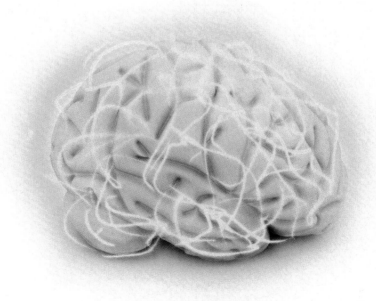

www.istudymarketing.ca

Boost your marketing knowledge

Glossary

Numbers following the definitions indicate pages where the terms were identified. Consult the index for further page references.

absolute poverty A minimum level of subsistence that no family should be expected to live below. (221)

achieved status A social position that a person attains largely through his or her own efforts. (107, 209)

activity theory An interactionist theory of aging that suggests that those elderly people who remain active and socially involved will be best adjusted. (310)

ad networks Specialist agencies that provide assistance in the research and the development of Internet campaigns in areas such as search-word advertising, e-mail campaigns, and the placement of ads through cooperating sites (260)

adoption curve The sequential diffusion and acceptance of an innovation into the market by consumers (146)

advertising Any paid form of nonpersonal communication about an organization, good, service, or idea by an identified sponsor (230, 254)

attitude Tendency to respond to something in a consistently favourable or unfavourable way (50)

baby boomers Generation of people born between 1946 and 1964 (27)

back translation Retranslating a word or phrase back into the original language by a different interpreter to catch errors (60)

banner ads Online ads that can stretch across the top of a web page or be formatted as rectangles, big boxes, and skyscrapers (260)

behaviouristics Why consumers buy a product, the product benefit, how they use it, and whether they are brand loyal in their purchase behaviour (108)

beliefs Consumer's perceptions of how a product or brand performs (50)

brand A name or phrase uniquely given by a company to a product to distinguish it from the competition (125)

brand equity The favourable associations and experiences that a consumer has with a brand resulting from the consumer's exposure and interaction with the brand over time (125)

brand loyalty Favourable attitude toward and consistent purchase of a single brand over time; the degree of consumer attachment to a particular brand (50, 126)

brand personality Set of human characteristics associated with a brand name (127)

breadth of product line The variety of different items a store carries (211)

break-even analysis Sum of the expenses of the firm that vary directly with the quantity of products that is produced and sold (169)

brokers Independent firms or individuals whose main function is to bring buyers and sellers together to make sales (222)

business analysis Financial projections on the impact of bringing the new product to market and selling it in the future (152)

business market Products that are purchased either to run a business or to be used as a component in another product or service (101)

business marketing Marketing to firms, governments, or not-for-profit organizations (64)

business products Products that are purchased either to run a business or to be used as a component in another product or service (123)

buy classes Three types of organizational buying situations: straight rebuy, modified rebuy, or new buy (74)

buying centre Group of people in an organization who participate in the buying process (72)

causal research Research designed to identify cause-and-effect relationships among variables (84)

central business district The oldest retail setting, the community's downtown area (213)

channel conflict Arises when one channel member believes another channel member is engaged in behaviour that prevents it from achieving its goals (194)

channel of communication The means of conveying a message to a receiver (229)

choiceboard Interactive, Internet-enabled system that allows individual customers to design their own products and services (245)

collaborative filtering Process that automatically groups people with similar preferences, buying intentions, and behaviours to predict future purchases (254)

commercialization When the new product is brought to market with full-scale production, sales, and marketing support (153)

communication Process of conveying a message to others (229)

community shopping centre Retail location that typically has one primary store and 20 to 40 smaller outlets, serving a population of consumers within a 2- to 5-kilometre drive (214)

competitive advantages Those characteristics of a product or service that make it superior to competing substitutes (301)

competitive forces Alternative products that can satisfy a specific market's needs (34)

concept tests External consumer evaluations where a new product idea is presented as a written description with an accompanying visual (151)

consumer behaviour Actions a person takes when purchasing and using products and services (42)

consumer market Consists of products, ideas, and services that a person can purchase for personal use (101)

consumer-oriented sales promotion Short-term marketing tools used to encourage immediate consumer purchase (264)

consumer products Products purchased for their own personal use by the ultimate consumer (123)

continuous innovations New products with more than just a minor product improvement, but that do not require radical changes by the consumer (145)

convenience products Items purchased frequently that are inexpensive and require minimum risk and shopping effort (123)

cooperative advertising Advertising programs where a manufacturer pays a percentage of the retailer's advertising expenses for advertising the manufacturer's products in their promotional materials (265)

copyrights Used to legally protect the written word, sound recording, or form of communication from being copied by others (126)

corporate social responsibility (CSR) When organizations voluntarily consider the well-being of society by taking responsibility for how their businesses impact consumers, customers, suppliers, employees, shareholders, communities, the environment, and society in general (14)

cross-cultural analysis Study of similarities and differences among consumers in two or more societies (59)

cultural symbols Objects, ideas, or processes that represent a particular group of people or society (60)

culture A set of values, ideas, and attitudes that are learned and shared among the members of a group (56)

customer lifetime value The potential sales that will be generated by a customer if that customer remains loyal to that company for a lifetime (283)

customer relationship management (CRM) The overall process of building and maintaining profitable customer relationships by delivering superior customer value and satisfaction (13, 278)

customer service Ability of logistics management to satisfy users in terms of time, dependability, communication, and convenience (199)

customer value The unique combination of benefits received by targeted buyers that includes quality, price, convenience, on-time delivery, and both before-sale and after-sale service (6)

customs Norms and expectations about the way people do things in a specific country or culture (59)

data mining A process of analyzing customer patterns and insights to make better marketing decisions (282)

data warehouse A central repository of an organization's electronically stored data (283)

decoding Process whereby the receiver takes a set of symbols, words, pictures, and sounds, and transforms them into messages (229)

demand curve Graph relating quantity sold and price, which shows how many units will be sold at a given price (166)

demographics The statistical data on a population according to characteristics such as age, gender, income, occupation, education, and ethnic background (26, 108)

depth of product line The size of the assortment of each item a store carries (210)

derived demand Demand for industrial products and services driven by demand for consumer products and services (68)

descriptive research Research designed to describe basic characteristics of a given population or to clarify their usage and attitudes (84)

development The new product idea is turned into a prototype for further consumer research and manufacturing tests (152)

direct competitors Similar products sold in the same category (34)

direct orders The result of direct response marketing offers that contain all the information necessary for a potential buyer to make a decision to purchase and complete the transaction (269)

direct response Promotional element that uses direct communication with consumers to generate a response in the form of an order, a request for further information, or a visit to a retail outlet (234)

discretionary income Money that consumers have left after paying taxes and buying necessities (33)

disintermediation Channel conflict that arises when a channel member bypasses another member and sells or buys products direct (194)

disposable income Balance of income left after paying taxes; income that is used for spending and savings (33)

dual distribution   Arrangement whereby a firm reaches buyers by using two or more different types of channels for the same basic product (187)

dumping   Occurs when a firm sells a product in a foreign country below its domestic prices or below its actual cost (174)

durable good   An item that lasts over an extended number of uses (119)

economy   The collective income, expenditures, and resources that affect the cost of running a business or a household (32)

electronic marketing channels   Channels that use the Internet to make goods and services available to consumers or business buyers (186)

e-marketplaces   Online trading communities that bring together buyers and supplier organizations (75)

encoding   Process whereby the sender transforms an idea into symbolic form, using words, pictures, symbols, and sounds (229)

exchange   The trade of things of value between buyers and sellers so that each benefits (9)

exclusive distribution   Only one retail outlet in a specific geographical area carries the firm's products (193)

experiential marketing   Creating opportunities for consumers to directly interact with brands (13)

experiment   In marketing, changing a variable involved in a customer purchase to find out what happens (94)

exploratory research   Preliminary research conducted to clarify the scope and nature of the marketing problem (84)

fad   Novelty products with very short product life cycles that experience immediate rapid growth, followed by an equally rapid decline (141)

family brand   When a company uses a brand name to cover a number of different product categories (130)

family life cycle   A family's progression from formation to retirement,

with each phase bringing distinct needs and purchasing behaviours (55)

fashion product   The life cycle for fashion is relatively short and cyclical going from introduction to decline within two years, only to resurface again a few years later (141)

feedback   Communication flow from receiver back to the sender that helps the sender know whether the message was decoded and understood (229)

field of experience   The experiences, perceptions, attitudes, and values that senders and receivers of a message bring to a communication situation (229)

fixed cost   Firm's expenses that are stable and do not change with the quantity of product that is produced and sold (169)

fluctuating demand   Demand for business products and services fluctuates more than demand for consumer products and services (69)

focus group   A research technique where a small group of people (usually six to ten) meet for a few hours with a trained moderator to discuss predetermined areas (90)

form of ownership   Distinguishes retail outlets on the basis of whether individuals, corporate chains, or contractual systems own the outlet (207)

franchising   Contractual arrangement in which a parent company (the franchiser) allows an individual or firm (the franchisee) to operate a certain type of business under an established name and according to specific rules (192)

Generation X   People born between 1965 and 1976 (27)

Generation Y   People born between 1975 and 1995 (27)

generic brand   A product that has no branding and is produced as a cheap alternative to manufacturer's and private label brands (129)

geographics   Where a target market lives using variables such as country, region, province, city size, and types of location such as urban, suburban, or rural (107)

goals   Targets of performance to be achieved within a specific time frame (294)

good   A product you can touch and own (9)

grey market   Situations where products are sold through unauthorized channels of distribution (175)

gross income   Total amount of money made in one year by a person, household, or family unit, including taxes (33)

harvesting   When a company keeps a product but reduces marketing support in an attempt to reap some minor profits (140)

hierarchy of effects   Sequence of stages a potential buyer goes through: awareness, interest, evaluation, trial, and adoption (240)

high learning product   Significant consumer education is required for these products, which have an extended introductory period (141)

idea   A concept that typically looks for your support (9)

idea generation   Focuses on brainstorming sessions to prompt new ideas for the project at hand (150)

idle production capacity   When the supply of the service exceeds its demand (120)

in-depth interview   A detailed interview where a researcher questions an individual at length in a free-flowing conversational style in order to discover information that may help solve a marketing problem (91)

indirect competitors   Products competing for the same buying dollar in a slightly different, but related category (35)

individual brand   When a company uses a brand name solely for a specific product category (130)

individualized marketing   Involves customizing offers and, in some cases, products that fit individual needs (104)

inelastic demand   Demand for products does not change because of increases or decreases in price (69)

inflation A period when the cost to produce and buy products and services gets higher as prices rise (32)

institutional advertisements Advertisements focused on building goodwill or a positive image of an organization (255)

integrated marketing communications (IMC) Concept of designing marketing communications programs that coordinate all promotional activities to provide a consistent message to the target audience (235)

intensive distribution A firm tries to place its products or services in as many outlets as possible (193)

interactive marketing Two-way buyer–seller electronic communications in a computer-mediated environment in which the buyer controls the kind and amount of information received from the seller (245)

intermediaries Individuals or firms performing a role in the marketing channel, involved in making a product available (183)

intertype competition Offering several unrelated products lines in a single retail store (212)

involvement Personal, social, and economic significance of a purchase to the consumer (45)

leaderboards Banner ads that stretch across the top of a web page (260)

lead generation Result of direct response marketing offer designed to create interest in a product or a service and a request for additional information (269)

learning Behaviours that result from repeated experience or reasoning (49)

level of service The degree of service provided to the customer by self-, limited-, and full-service retailers (209)

logistics Activities that focus on getting the right amount of the right products to the right place at the right time at the lowest possible cost (195)

low learning product Little consumer education is required resulting in a short introductory stage for the product (141)

loyalty programs Programs specifically designed for customer retention (281)

macroeconomic forces The state of a country's economy as a whole (32)

manufacturers' agents Work for several producers and carry non-competitive, complementary merchandise in an exclusive territory (221)

manufacturer's brand A brand owned and produced by the manufacturer (129)

market Potential consumers with both the willingness and ability to buy (10)

market research The process of collecting and analyzing information in order to recommend actions to improve marketing activities (83)

market segmentation The aggregation of prospective buyers into groups that have common needs and respond similarly to marketing programs (101, 300)

market share Ratio of a firm's sales to the total sales of all firms in the industry (294)

marketing The process of planning goods, services, or ideas to meet consumer needs and organizational objectives. It includes the conception of these products and the pricing, promotion, and distribution programs designed to make a profit (9)

marketing channel The set of individuals or firms involved in the process of making a product available (183)

marketing concept The idea that an organization should strive to satisfy the needs of consumers while also trying to achieve organizational goals (12)

marketing environmental scan The process of continually acquiring information on events occurring outside the organization to identify trends, opportunities and threats to your business (25)

marketing information system (MIS) A set of procedures and processes for collecting, sorting, analyzing, and summarizing information on an ongoing basis (83)

marketing mix The 4 Ps—product, price, place, and promotion (6)

marketing orientation Focusing organizational efforts to collect and use information about customers' needs to create customer value (11)

marketing plan Road map for the marketing activities of an organization for a specified future period of time (299)

marketing process The process of (1) identifying consumer needs, (2) managing the marketing mix to meet these needs, and (3) realizing profits (8)

marketing strategy Means by which a marketing goal is to be achieved (303)

marketing tactics Detailed day-to-day operational decisions essential to the overall success of marketing strategies (303)

markup The difference between selling price and cost (163)

mass marketing The marketing of a product to the entire market with no differentiation at all (102)

merchandise mix How many different types of products a store carries and in what assortment (209)

merchant wholesalers Independently owned firms that take title to the merchandise they handle (220)

message Information sent by a source to a receiver (229)

microeconomic forces The supply and demand of goods and services and how this is impacted by individual, household, and company decisions to purchase (33)

microsites Short-term promotional websites that focus on promotional offers or campaigns (260)

minor innovations Minor product modifications that require no adjustments on behalf of the consumer (145)

mission Statement of the organization's purpose and direction (292)

monopolistic competition Type of competition where a large number of sellers compete with each other, offering customers similar or substitute products (35)

monopoly When only one company sells in a particular market (36)

motivation Energizing force that stimulates behaviour to satisfy a need (47)

multichannel marketing Blending of different communication and delivery channels that are mutually reinforcing in attracting, retaining, and building relationships with customers (188)

multichannel retailers Use a combination of traditional store formats and non-store formats such as catalogues, television, and online retailing (214)

new product development process Sequence of steps that a firm takes to develop a new product idea and take it to market (150)

new product development strategy Setting the new product strategic direction for the company as a whole, and the precise objectives for the project at hand (150)

niche marketing When a company focuses its efforts on a limited segment in the market (103)

noise Factors that can work against effective communication by distorting the message (230)

non-durable good An item that does not last and is consumed only once, or for a limited number of times (119)

non-probability sampling Selecting a sample so that the chance of selecting a particular element of a population is either unknown or zero (88)

North American Industry Classification System (NAICS) Provides common industry definitions for Canada, Mexico, and the United States (67)

objectives Specific measurable goals (86, 294)

observational research Obtained by watching how people behave either in person, or by using a machine to record the event (92)

off-price retailing Selling brand-name merchandise at lower than regular prices (213)

oligopoly Type of competition that occurs when a few companies control a market (36)

opinion leaders Individuals who have social influence over others (52)

order getter Salesperson who sells in a conventional sense by identifying prospective customers, providing customers with information, persuading customers to buy, closing sales, and following up on customers' use of a product or service (271)

order taker Salesperson who processes routine orders or reorders (271)

organizational buyers Manufacturers, wholesalers, retailers, and government agencies that buy goods and services for their own use or for resale (64)

organizational buying behaviour Process by which organizations determine the need for goods and then choose among alternative suppliers (72)

panel A sample of consumers or stores from which researchers take a series of measurements (94)

Pareto's Rule The concept that 80 percent of a brand's sales come from 20 percent of its customers (282)

patents Legally protect new technologies, unique processes, or formulations from usage by other companies for a period of 20 years (126)

pay-per-click A fee paid to the hosting website each time a listing or ad is clicked (259)

perceived risk Anxiety felt when a consumer cannot anticipate possible negative outcomes of a purchase (49)

perception Process by which someone selects, organizes, and interprets information to create a meaningful picture of the world (48)

perfect competition Type of competition where there are many sellers with nearly identical products and little differentiation (35)

permission-based e-mail When a recipient chooses to receive e-mail from an advertiser (260)

permission-based marketing Asking for a consumer's consent (called "opt-in") to receive e-mail and advertising based on personal data supplied by the consumer (245)

personal selling Two-way flow of communication between a buyer and seller, often in a face-to-face encounter, designed to influence a purchase decision (232, 270)

personal selling process Sales activities occurring before and after the sale itself, consisting of six stages: prospecting, pre-approach, approach, presentation, close, and follow-up (272)

personality A person's consistent behaviours or responses to recurring situations (47)

personalization Consumer-initiated practice of generating content on a marketer's website that is tailored to an individual's specific needs and preferences (245)

place Distribution channels and retailers required to sell the product (7)

positioning maps Visual representations of how products are positioned in a category to consumers (112)

positioning statement A tool that identifies the main reasons the target market buys a product and what sets it apart in the market (110)

power centre Large shopping strip with multiple anchor stores, a convenient location, and a supermarket (214)

premiums Consumer offers that provide consumers with merchandise in exchange for proof-of-purchase (264)

press conference A planned event where representatives of the media are invited to an informational meeting with the company (267)

press release An announcement written by an organization and sent to the media (267)

price Expected retail shelf price and sale price of the product; money or other considerations exchanged for the ownership or use of a good or service (7, 158)

pricing constraints Factors that limit the range of price a firm may set (172)

pricing objectives Expectations that specify the role of price in an organization's marketing and strategic plans (170)

primary data Information that is newly collected for a project (89)

private label brand Otherwise known as a store brand, a brand owned by a retailer that contracts its manufacturing to major suppliers, and then sells the product at its own retail stores (129)

probability sampling Selecting a sample so that each element of a population has a specific known chance of being selected (88)

product Attributes that make up a good, a service, or an idea, including product design, features, colour, packaging, warrantee, and service levels (7, 118)

product advertisements Asking for a consumer's consent (called "opt-in") to receive e-mail and advertising based on personal data supplied by the consumer (255)

product depth The variety of product offerings within a product category, product group, or product line (123)

product differentiation Involves positioning a product apart from the competition in the eyes of consumers (101)

product life cycle The stages that a new product goes through starting with introduction and evolving into growth, maturity, and decline (136)

product line A group of products with the same product and brand name that are directed at the same general target market and are marketed together (122)

product mix The combination of product lines offered by a company (122)

product positioning The image of the product you want to establish in consumers' minds relative to the competition (110)

product width The number of different categories offered by the company (123)

production orientation Focusing organizational efforts on the manufacture of goods (10)

profit The excess of revenues over costs, the reward to a business for the risk it undertakes in offering a product for sale (290)

profit equation Profit = Total revenue – Total cost (160)

promotion Communication tools needed to inform consumers about the product, including advertising, sales promotion, public relations, direct marketing, and personal selling (7, 230)

promotional mix Combination of one or more of the promotional tools—advertising, personal selling, public relations, sales promotion, and direct response—a firm uses to communicate with consumers (235)

psychographics Understanding consumer attitudes to life, their personalities, general interests, opinions, and activities (108)

public relations Form of communication that seeks to influence the feelings, opinions, or beliefs held by customers, potential customers, stockholders, suppliers, employees, and the media about a company and its products or services (233)

publicity Communication about an organization that is non-personal and not paid for directly by the organization (233)

pull strategy Directing the promotional mix at ultimate consumers to encourage them to ask the retailer for the product (239)

purchase decision process Stages that a buyer passes through when making choices about which products or services to buy (42)

push strategy Directing the promotional mix to channel members to encourage them to order, stock, and sell a product (238)

qualitative research A form of research that uses focus groups and in-depth interviews to provide good

insightful and directional information that is not statistically accurate (89)

quantitative research Statistically reliable information that uses observational and/or questioning techniques (92)

questionnaire A means of obtaining information by posing questions in person, through the mail, the telephone, e-mail, fax, or the Internet (93)

radical innovations New products that involve the introduction of a product that is entirely new and innovative to the market (146)

receivers Consumers who read, hear, or see the message sent by a source (229)

recession A time of slow economic activity with two consecutive periods of negative growth (32)

reference groups People to whom an individual looks as a basis for self-appraisal or as a source of personal standards (54)

regional shopping centres Consist of 50 to 150 stores that typically attract customers who live within a 5- to 15-kilometre range; often containing two or three anchor stores (213)

regulations Restrictions placed on marketing practices by government and industry associations (36)

relationship marketing When organizations create long-term links with customers, employees, suppliers, and other partners to increase loyalty and customer retention (11)

relationship selling Practice of building ties to customers based on a salesperson's attention and commitment to customer needs over time (270)

repositioning A revamping of the product and its marketing mix to more accurately meet consumer needs (111)

response The impact a message has on the receiver's knowledge, attitudes, or behaviours (229)

retail life cycle The process of growth and decline that retail outlets, like products, experience over time (220)

retailing All activities involved in selling, renting, and providing goods and services to ultimate consumers for personal, family, or household use (204)

retailing mix The goods and services, physical distribution, and communications tactics chosen by a store (212)

reverse auction Occurs when a buyer communicates a need for something and would-be suppliers bid in competition with each other (78)

sales orientation Focusing organizational efforts on selling as many products as possible (10)

sales promotion A short-term offer designed to arouse interest in buying a good or service (234)

sampling The process of gathering data from a subset of the total population rather than from all members of that particular population (87)

scrambled merchandising Offering several unrelated products lines in a single retail store (211)

screening and evaluation Reduces the list of brainstorming ideas down to a list of promising concepts (150)

search-word advertising Sponsored links that appear to the right, or to the top, of a search engine screen after a search has been placed (259)

secondary data Facts and figures that have already been recorded by a third party (89)

segment marketing Designing different products and services to meet the needs of different target groups (102)

selective distribution A firm selects a few retail outlets in a specific geographical area to carry its products (193)

selling agent Represent a single producer and are responsible for the entire marketing function of that producer (221)

service A good that is intangible, an activity, benefit, or satisfaction offered for sale that you cannot touch (9, 119)

service continuum A range from tangible goods to intangible services (119)

share of wallet The percentage of a customer's purchases that a company has in a specific product category (284)

shopping products Items that require comparison shopping between different brands and require an investment of shopping time (124)

shrinkage Breakage and theft of merchandise by customers and employees (213)

situation analysis Taking stock of a firm or product's past performance, where it is now, and where it is headed (299)

skyscrapers Banner ads that are tall, slim, and vertical and appear along the side of a web page (260)

societal marketing concept Focusing on the consumer and the well-being of society (15)

socio-cultural forces Cultural values, ideas, and attitudes, as well as society's morals and beliefs (30)

source Company or person who has information to share (229)

spam Unsolicited e-mail that clutters the advertising landscape for legitimate campaigns (260)

specialty products Items for special occasions that require a specific brand and considerable time and effort to purchase (124)

strategic marketing process Approach whereby an organization allocates its marketing mix (298)

strategy A plan of action to achieve specific goals (291)

strip location A cluster of stores serving people who live within a 5- to 10-minute drive (214)

subcultures Subgroups within a larger culture that have unique values, ideas, and attitudes (56)

supply chain Sequence of firms that perform activities required to create and deliver a product to consumers or industrial users (196)

supply chain management Integration and organization of information and logistics activities across firms in a supply chain for the purpose of creating and delivering goods and services that provide value to consumers (196)

supply partnership Demand for business products and services fluctuates more than demand for consumer products and services (71)

sweepstakes Consumer promotions that require participants to complete an entry form to enter into a promotion to win an item (264)

SWOT analysis Process by which a company can identify opportunities and whether it has the strength to compete in a segment that may already be well served by the competition (106, 299)

target market The specific group of existing and potential consumers to which a marketer targets its marketing efforts (6)

technological forces Inventions from applied science or engineering research (33)

telemarketing Using the telephone to interact with and sell directly to consumers (216)

test market A small localized region used to help determine whether consumers will buy a new product or brand, or shop at a new store concept (94)

test marketing Offering a new product for sale on a limited basis in a defined geographic area to assess its success (153)

total cost Total expenses incurred by a firm in producing and marketing a product; total cost is the sum of fixed cost and variable costs (169)

total logistics cost Expenses associated with transportation, materials handling and warehousing, inventory, stockouts, order processing, and return goods handling (199)

total revenue Total money received from the sale of a product (168)

touch point Any situation in which a customer comes into contact with a brand or company (279)

trade allowances and discounts Price discounts offered in return for increasing inventories and/or temporarily reducing the retail price to consumers in the form of a "sale price" (265)

trademarks Used to legally protect brands and their images from usage by others (126)

trade-oriented sales promotions Consumer promotions that require participants to complete an entry form to enter into a promotion to win an item (273)

traditional auction Occurs when a seller puts an item up for sale and would-be buyers bid in competition with each other (78)

traffic generation Outcome of direct response marketing offer designed to motivate people to visit a business (269)

unsought products Unknown items or those of no interest to the purchaser (124)

value The ratio of perceived benefits to price (160)

values Socially preferable modes of conduct or states of existence that tend to persist over time (59)

variable cost Sum of the expenses of the firm that vary directly with the quantity of products that is produced and sold (169)

vendor-managed inventory Inventory management system whereby the supplier determines the product amount and assortment a customer (such as a retailer) needs and automatically delivers the appropriate items (200)

vertical marketing systems Professionally managed and centrally coordinated marketing channels designed to achieve channel economies and maximum marketing impact (190)

viral marketing Creative advertising campaigns posted on websites for viewers to forward to their contacts so that the message spreads like a virus (259)

word of mouth People influencing each other in personal conversations (52)

Chapter Notes

Chapter 1

1. Personal interview with Jeremy Stonier, American Marketing Association website, February 5, 2003, accessed at www.marketingpower.com/live/content.php?Item_ID=4620.
2. John C. Narver, Stanley F. Slater, and Brian Tietje, "Creating a Market Orientation," *Journal of Market Focused Management*, no. 2 (1998), pp. 241–255; Stanley F. Slater and John C. Narver, "Market Orientation and the Learning Organization," *Journal of Marketing*, July 1995, pp. 63–74; and George S. Day, "The Capabilities of Market-Driven Organizations," *Journal of Marketing*, October 1994, pp. 37–52.
3. Philip Kotler, Gary Armstrong, and Peggy H. Cunningham, *Principles of Marketing*, Seventh Canadian Edition (Toronto: Pearson, 2008).
4. Gail Chiasson, "The Big Wild Wilderness Protection Movement Launches Social Networking Site," *PubZone*, May 6, 2008, accessed at www.pubzone.com/newsroom/2008/1x080505x063532.cfm.

Chapter 2

1. "2001 Census of Canada," Statistics Canada, www12.statcan.ca/english/census01/release/index.cfm; see also "2006 Census of Canada," Statistics Canada, www12.statcan.ca/census-recensement/index-eng.cfm.
2. "2006 Census: Age and sex," *The Daily*, Statistics Canada, July 17, 2007, accessed at www.statcan.gc.ca/daily-quotidien/070717/dq070717a-eng.htm.
3. "Money and the Canadian Family," The Vanier Institute, www.vifamily.ca.
4. "Births: 2006," Statistics Canada Catalogue no. 84F0210X, September 2008, accessed at www.statcan.gc.ca/pub/84f0210x/84f0210x2006000-eng.pdf.
5. Statistics Canada, Market Research Handbook, 63-224.
6. "Portrait of the Canadian Population in 2006, by Age and Sex, 2006 Census," Statistics Canada Catalogue no. 97-551-XIE, July 2007, p. 13, accessed at www12.statcan.gc.ca/english/census06/analysis/agesex/pdf/97-551-XIE2006001.pdf.
7. David K. Foot, *Boom, Bust & Echo: How to Profit from the Coming Demographic Shift* (Toronto: Macfarlane Walter & Ross, 1996).
8. "Getting Inside Gen Y," *American Demographics*, September 2001, p. 44.
9. "Portrait of the Canadian Population in 2006, by Age and Sex, 2006 Census," p. 13.
10. "Population and dwelling counts," *The Daily*, Statistics Canada, March 13, 2007, accessed at www.statcan.gc.ca/daily-quotidien/070313/dq070313a-eng.htm.
11. "Portrait of the Canadian Population in 2006, 2006 Census," Statistics Canada Catalogue no. 97-550-XIE, March 2007, p. 24, www12.statcan.ca/census-recensement/2006/as-sa/97-550/pdf/97-550-XIE2006001.pdf.
12. "2006 Census: Immigration, citizenship, language, mobility and migration," *The Daily*, Statistics Canada, December 4, 2007, accessed at www.statcan.gc.ca/daily-quotidien/071204/dq071204a-eng.htm.
13. U.S. Census Bureau, International Data Base, December 15, 2008, accessed at www.census.gov/cgi-bin/ipc/idbrank.pl.
14. Ibid.

Chapter 3

1. Personal interview with Ruth Klostermann, May 2008.
2. Terry Poulton, "ZO unveils results of Touchpoints ROI Tracker," *Media in Canada*, April 8, 2008, accessed at www.mediaincanada.com/articles/mic/20080408/touchpoints.html.
3. James F. Engel, Roger D. Blackwell, and Paul Miniard, *Consumer Behavior*, 9th ed. (Fort Worth, TX: Dryden Press, 1998).
4. For thorough descriptions of consumer expertise, see Joseph W. Alba and J. Wesley Hutchinson, "Knowledge Calibration: What Consumers Know and What They Think They Know," *Journal of Consumer Research*, September 2000, pp. 123–56.
5. For in-depth studies on external information search patterns, see Sridhar Moorthy, Brian T. Ratchford, and Debabrata Tulukdar, "Consumer Information Search Revisited: Theory and Empirical Analysis," *Journal of Consumer Research*, March 1997, pp. 263–77; and Joel E. Urbany, Peter R. Dickson, and William L. Wilkie, "Buyer Uncertainty and Information Search," *Journal of Consumer Research*, March 1992, pp. 452–63.
6. For an extended discussion on evaluative criteria, see Del J. Hawkins, Roger J. Best, and Kenneth A. Coney, *Consumer Behavior*, 8th ed. (New York: Irwin/McGraw-Hill, 2001), pp. 566–83.
7. John A. Howard, *Buyer Behavior in Marketing Strategy*, 2nd ed. (Englewood Cliffs, NJ: Prentice Hall, 1994), pp. 101, 128–89.
8. Jagdish N. Sheth, Banwari Mitral, and Bruce Newman, *Consumer Behavior* (Fort Worth, TX: Dryden Press, 1999), p. 22.
9. Frederick F. Reichheld and Thomas Teal, *The Loyalty Effect* (Boston: Harvard Business School Press, 1996); "What's a Loyal Customer Worth?" *Fortune*, December 11, 1995, p. 182; and Patricia Sellers, "Keeping the Buyers You Already Have," *Fortune*, Autumn–Winter 1993, p. 57. For an in-depth examination of this topic, see Werner J. Reinartz and V. Kumar, "On the Profitability of Long-Life Customers in a Noncontractual Setting: An Empirical Investigation and Implications for Marketing," *Journal of Marketing*, October 2000, pp. 17–35.
10. Rahul Jacob, "The Struggle to Create an Organization for the 21st Century," *Fortune*, April 3, 1995, pp. 90–99.
11. Lands' End website, www.landsend.com/cd/fp/help/0,1452,1_36877_36883_37024___,00.html?sid=6752072684971181040.
12. For an overview of research on involvement, see John C. Mowen and Michael Minor, *Consumer Behavior*, 6th ed. (Upper Saddle River, NJ: Prentice Hall, 2001), pp. 64–68; and Frank R. Kardes, *Consumer Behavior* (Reading, MA: Addison-Wesley, 1999), pp. 256–58.
13. For an overview on the three problem-solving variations, see Hawkins, Best, and Coney, *Consumer Behavior*, pp. 506–7; and Howard, *Buyer Behavior*, pp. 69–162.

14. Russell Belk, "Situational Variables and Consumer Behavior," *Journal of Consumer Research*, December 1975, pp. 157–63.

15. A. H. Maslow, *Motivation and Personality* (New York: Harper & Row, 1970).

16. Arthur Koponen, "The Personality Characteristics of Purchasers," *Journal of Advertising Research*, September 1960, pp. 89–92; Joel B. Cohen, "An Interpersonal Orientation to the Study of Consumer Behavior," *Journal of Marketing Research*, August 1967, pp. 270–78; and Rena Bartos, *Marketing to Women around the World* (Cambridge, MA: Harvard Business School, 1989).

17. Myron Magnet, "Let's Go for Growth," *Fortune*, March 7, 1994, p. 70.

18. Michael R. Solomon, *Consumer Behavior*, 5th ed. (Upper Saddle River, NJ: Prentice Hall, 2002), p. 61.

19. BMW website, www.bmw.com/generic/com/en/services/service/index.html?content=service_overview.html.

20. Martin Fishbein and I. Aizen, *Belief, Attitude, Intention and Behavior: An Introduction to Theory and Research* (Reading, MA: Addison-Wesley, 1975), p. 6.

21. Richard J. Lutz, "Changing Brand Attitudes through Modification of Cognitive Structure," *Journal of Consumer Research*, March 1975, pp. 49–59; "Pepsi's Gamble Hits Freshness Dating Jackpot," *Advertising Age*, September 19, 1994, p. 50; and "Every Which Way to Color, Whiten, Brighten," *Brandweek*, June 17, 2002, p. 558.

22. www.future.sri.com, downloaded January 3, 2002; Eric Arnould, Linda Price, and George Zinkham, *Consumers* (Burr Ridge, IL: McGraw-Hill/Irwin, 2002), pp. 285–90.

23. See, for example, Lawrence F. Feick and Linda Price, "The Market Maven: A Diffuser of Marketplace Information," *Journal of Marketing*, January 1987, pp. 83–97.

24. "Maximizing the Market with Influentials," *American Demographics*, July 1995, p. 42; also see, "I'll Have What He's Having," *American Demographics*, July 2000, p.

25. Representative recent work on positive and negative word of mouth can be found in Robert E. Smith and Christine A. Vogt, "The Effects of Integrating Advertising and Negative Word-of-Mouth Communications on Message Processing and Response," *Journal of Consumer Psychology* 4 (1995), pp. 133-51; Paula Bone, "Word-of-Mouth Effects on Short-Term and Long-Term Product Judgments," *Journal of Business Research* 32 (1995), pp. 213-23; Chip Walker, "Word of Mouth," *American Demographics*, July 1995, pp. 38-45; and Dale F. Duhan, Scott D. Johnson, James B. Wilcox, and Gilbert D. Harrell, "Influences on Consumer Use of Word-of-Mouth Recommendation Sources," *Journal of the Academy of Marketing Science*, Fall 1997, pp. 283-95.

26. For an extended discussion on reference groups, see Wayne D. Hoyer and Deborah J. MacInnis, *Consumer Behavior*, 2nd ed. (Boston: Houghton Miffin, 2001), chap. 15.

27. For an extensive review on consumer socialization of children, see Deborah Roedder John, "Consumer Socialization of Children: A Retrospective Look at Twenty-Five Years of Research," *Journal of Consumer Research*, December 1999, pp. 183-213.

28. This discussion is based on "The American Family in the 21st Century," *American Demographics*, August 2001, p. 20; and J. Paul Peter and Jerry C. Olson, *Consumer Behavior and Marketing Strategy*, 5th ed. (New York: Irwin/McGraw-Hill, 1999), pp. 341–43.

29. "Household Type, in Private Households, 2001 Counts, for Canada, Provinces and Territories," Statistics Canada, www12.statcan.ca/english/census01/products/highlight/PrivateHouseholds/Page.cfm?Lang=E&Geo=PR&Code=0&View=1a&Table=1&StartRec=1&Sort=2&B1=Counts.

30. Diane Crispell, "Dual-Earner Diversity," *American Demographics*, July 1995, pp. 32-37.

31. "There She Is . . . ." *American Demographics*, August 2001, p. 6; "Wearing the Pants," *Brandweek*, October 20, 1997, pp. 20, 22; and "Look Who's Shopping," *Progressive Grocer*, January 1998, p. 18.

32. "Call It 'Kid-fluence,'" *U.S. News & World Report*, July 30, 2001, pp. 32–33; "Special Report: Superstars of Spending," *Advertising Age*, February 20, 2001, pp. S1, S10; and Teen Research Unlimited, www.teenresearch.com, downloaded September 4, 2001.

33. Statistics Canada Catalogue # 97F0007XCB01007.

34. Danny Kucharsky, "French Lessons," *Marketing* magazine, March 27, 2006, p. 8.

35. "Canada's ethnocultural portrait: The changing mosaic," Statistics Canada, www12.statcan.ca/english/census01/products/analytic/companion/etoimm/contents.cfm.

36. For comprehensive references on cross-cultural aspects of marketing, see Paul A. Herbig, *Handbook of Cross-Cultural Marketing* (New York: Halworth Press, 1998); and Jean-Claude Usunier, *Marketing across Cultures*, 2nd ed. (London: Prentice Hall Europe, 1996). Unless otherwise indicated, examples found in this section appear in these excellent sources.

37. "McDonald's Adapts Mac Attack to Foreign Tastes with Expansion," *Dallas Morning News*, December 7, 1997, p. 3H; and "Taking Credit," *The Economist*, November 2, 1996, p. 75.

38. Patricia Adams, "Foreign aid corruption case puts Canada on trial," *National Post*, August 20, 1999.

39. These examples appear in Del I. Hawkins, Roger J. Best, and Kenneth A. Coney, *Consumer Behavior*, 8th ed. (Burr Ridge, IL: McGraw-Hill/Irwin, 2001), chap. 2.

40. "Greeks Protest Coke's Use of Parthenon," *Dallas Morning News*, August 17, 1992, p. D4.

41. "Global Thinking Paces Computer Biz," *Advertising Age*, March 6, 1995, p. 10.

Chapter 4

1. Peter LaPlaca, "From the Editor," *Journal of Business and Industrial Marketing*, Summer 1992, p. 3.

2. This figure is based on *Statistical Abstract of the United States: 2002*, 122nd ed. (Washington, DC: U.S. Census Bureau, 2002).

3. Nortel Networks website, www.nortelnetworks.com/corporate/technology/olh/index.html.

4. "FAA Announces Contract for New Workstations," *Dallas Morning News*, April 30, 1999, p. 16H; and "Canada's Manley Says Government Spending C$5 Bln Under Budget," Bloomberg.com, September 29, 2003.

5. "List of Canadian registered charities," Canada Revenue Agency website, www.cra-arc.gc.ca/tax/charities/online_listings/canreg_interim-e.html.

6. *2002 NAICS United States Manual* (Washington, DC: Office of Management and Budget, January 2002).

7. This listing and portions of the following discussion are based on F. Robert Dwyer and John F. Tanner, Jr., *Business Marketing*, 2nd ed. (Burr Ridge, IL: McGraw-Hill/Irwin, 2002); and Edward G. Brierty, Robert W. Eckles, and Robert R. Reeder, *Business Marketing*, 3rd ed. (Upper Saddle River, NJ: Prentice Hall, 1998).

8. "Latin Trade Connection," *Latin Trade*, June 1997, p. 72; and "Canadian firm wins contract to upgrade Cingular Wireless," *Amarillo Globe News*, March 7, 2002, www.amarillo.com/stories/030702/tex_toupgrade.shtml.

9. This discussion is based on James C. Anderson and James A. Narus, *Business Market Management* (Upper Saddle River, NJ: Prentice Hall, 1999); and Joseph P. Cannon and Christian Homburg, "Buyer–Supplier Relationships and Customer Firm Costs," *Journal of Marketing*, January 2001, pp. 29–43.

10. Thomas V. Bonoma, "Major Sales: Who Really Does the Buying?" *Harvard Business Review*, May–June 1982, pp. 11–19.

11. Ibid.

12. These definitions are adapted from Frederick E. Webster, Jr., and Yoram Wind, *Organizational Buying Behavior* (Englewood Cliffs, NJ: Prentice Hall, 1972), p. 6.

13. "Can Corning Find Its Optic Nerve?" *Fortune*, March 19, 2001, pp. 148–50.

14. Representative studies on the buy-class framework that document its usefulness include Erin Anderson, Wujin Chu, and Barton Weitz, "Industrial Purchasing: An Empirical Exploration of the Buy-Class Framework," *Journal of Marketing*, July 1987, pp. 71–86; Morry Ghingold, "Testing the 'Buy-Grid' Buying Process Model," *Journal of Purchasing and Materials Management*, Winter 1986, pp. 30–36; P. Matthyssens and W. Faes, "OEM Buying Process for New Components: Purchasing and Marketing Implications," *Industrial Marketing Management*, August 1985, pp. 147–57; and Thomas W. Leigh and Arno J. Ethans, "A Script-Theoretic Analysis of Industrial Purchasing Behavior," *Journal of Marketing*, Fall 1984, pp. 22–32. Studies not supporting the buy-class framework include Joseph A. Bellizi and Philip McVey, "How Valid Is the Buy-Grid Model?" *Industrial Marketing Management*, February 1983, pp. 57–62; and Donald W. Jackson, Janet E. Keith, and Richard K. Burdick, "Purchasing Agents' Perceptions of Industrial Buying Center Influences: A Situational Approach," *Journal of Marketing*, Fall 1984, pp. 75–83.

15. "Evolution, Not Revolution," *Forbes*, May 21, 2001, pp. 38–39; "Business Connections: The Wired Way We Work," *Newsweek*, April 30, 2001, p. 59; and "Behind the Crystal Ball," *The Industry Standard*, March 26, 2001, pp. 81–83.

16. This discussion is based on Mark Roberti, "General Electric's Spin Machine," *The Industry Standard*, January 22–29, 2001, pp. 74–83; "Smart Business 50," *Smart Business*, November 2000, pp. 121–50; and "Grainger Lightens Its Digital Load," *Industrial Distribution*, March 2001, pp. 77–79.

17. "Internet Trading Exchanges: E-Marketplaces Come of Age," *Fortune*, April 15, 2001, special section; "Private Exchanges May Allow B-to-B Commerce to Thrive after All," *The Wall Street Journal*, March 16, 2001, pp. B1, B4; and Steven Kaplan and Mohanbir Sawhney, "E-Hubs: The New B2B Marketplaces," *Harvard Business Review*, May–June, 2000, pp. 97–103.

18. Quadrem website, www.quadrem.com.

19. A major portion of this discussion is based on Robert J. Dolan and Youngme Moon, "Pricing and Market Making on the Internet," *Journal of Interactive Marketing*, Spring 2000, pp. 56–73; and "Auctions Have Taken the Internet by Storm," *Dallas Morning News*, January 25, 2001, pp. 1F, 9F.

20. Bob Tedeschi, "GE Has a Bright Idea," *Smart Business*, June 2001, pp. 86–91.

21. Sandy Jap, "Going, Going, Going," *Harvard Business Review*, November–December, 2000, p. 30.

Chapter 5

1. For an expanded definition, consult the American Marketing Association's website at www.marketingpower.com; for a researcher's comments on this and other definitions of marketing research, see Lawrence D. Gibson, "Quo Vadis, Marketing Research?" *Marketing Research*, Spring 2000, pp. 36–41.

2. Lawrence D. Gibson, "Defining Marketing Problems," *Marketing Research*, Spring 1998, pp. 4–12.

3. Cyndee Miller, "Kiddi Just Fine in the UK, But Here It's Binky," *Marketing News*, August 28, 1995, p. 8.

4. Michael J. McCarthy, "Stalking the Elusive Teenage Trend Setter," *The Wall Street Journal*, November 19, 1998, pp. B1, B10.

5. Roy Furchgott, "For Cool Hunters, Tomorrow's Trend is the Trophy," *The New York Times*, June 28, 1998, p. 10; and Emily Nelson, "The Hunt for Hip: A Trend Scout's Trail," *The Wall Street Journal*, December 9, 1998, pp, B1, B6.

6. "What TV Ratings Really Mean," Nielsen Media Research, pp. 1–8.

7. Joshua Grossnickle and Oliver Raskin, "What's Ahead on the Internet," *Marketing Research*, Summer 2001, pp. 9–13; and Gordon A. Wyner, "Life (on the Internet) Imitates Research," *Marketing Research*, Summer 2000, pp. 38–39.

8. Conversation with John Vavrik, director of the B.C. Centre for Strategic Management of Risk in Transportation.

Chapter 6

1. National Consumer Survey Choices 3 Cross tabulation Report: Fast-Food Restaurants (New York: Simmons Market Research Bureau, Spring, 2001).

2. Sympatico.msn.ca, "Advertise Sports," accessed at http://advertise.sympatico.msn.ca/channels/sports.

Chapter 7

1. "How to Separate Trends from Fads," *Brandweek*, October 23, 2000, pp. 30, 32.

2. "Gillette's Edge," *Brandweek*, May 28, 2001, p. 5.

3. This discussion is based on Kevin Lane Keller, *Strategic Brand Management*, 2nd ed. (Upper Saddle River, NJ: Prentice Hall, 2003); and Jennifer L. Aaker, "Dimensions of Brand Personality," *Journal of Marketing Research*, August 1997, pp. 347–56. See also, Susan Fournier, "Consumers and Their Brands: Developing Relationship Theory in Consumer Research," *Journal of Consumer Research*, March 1998, pp. 343–73.

4. Rob Osler, "The Name Game: Tips on How to Get It Right," *Marketing News*, September 14, 1998, p. 50; and Keller, *Strategic Brand Management*. See also Pamela W. Henderson and Joseph A. Cote, "Guidelines for Selecting or Modifying Logos," *Journal of Marketing*, April 1998, pp. 14–30; and Chiranjeev Kohli and Douglas W. LaBahn, "Creating Effective Brand Names: A Study of the Naming Process," *Journal of Advertising Research*, January–February 1997, pp. 67–75.

5. "A Survey of Multinationals," *The Economist*, June 24, 1995, p. 8.

6. Paul Thurrott, "The Fun Never Stops: Microsoft vs. MikeRoweSoft," *Windows IT Pro*, January 20, 2004, www.winnetmag.com/Article/ArticleID/41510/41510.html.

7. "Canadian Company Receives Final Tender Approval from Rwanda for Vital AIDS Drug," Apotex press release, May 7, 2008, accessed at www.apotex.com/PressReleases/20080507-01.asp?flash=Yes.

8. *Canadian Media Directors' Council Media Digest 2008/2009*, p. 6, accessed at www.cmdc.ca/pdf/2008_09_media_digest.pdf.

Chapter 8

1. C. Phocas, *The management of innovations with specific reference to the compact disc*. M.B.A. Dissertation, University of Bradford Management Centre, 1983.

2. "TSN is No. 1 with Canadian Sports Fans, According to National Audience Survey," CNW Group, April 16, 2008, accessed at www.newswire.ca/en/releases/archive/April2008/16/c6088.html.

3. "Gillette's Edge," *Brandweek*, May 28, 2001, p. 5.

4. Mark Belko, "The future is now for technology at Penguins' new arena," *Pittsburgh Post-Gazette*, May 13, 2008, accessed at www.post-gazette.com/pg/08134/881292-61.stm.

5. Interbrand, *Competing in the Global Brand Economy: Best Canadian Brands 2008*, June 2008, accessed at www.ourfishbowl.com/images/surveys/BestCanadianBrands2008.pdf.

6. Gail Chiasson, "Since It's Only Eight Months to Christmas: Guinness Christmas Pudding," *Pubzone*, April 30, 2008, accessed at www.pubzone.com/newsroom/2008/1x080429x081143.cfm.

7. R. G. Cooper and E. J. Kleinschmidt, "New Products—What Separates Winners from Losers?" *Journal of Product Innovation Management*, September 1987, pp. 169–84; Robert G. Cooper, *Winning at New Products*, 2nd ed. (Reading, MA: Addison-Wesley, 1993), pp. 49–66; and Thomas D. Kuczmarski, "Measuring Your Return on Innovation," *Marketing Management*, Spring 2000, pp. 25–32.

8. Greg Burns, "Has General Mills Had Its Wheaties?" *Business Week*, May 8, 1995, pp. 68–69.

9. John Gilbert, "To Sell Cars in Japan, U.S. Needs to Offer More Right-Drive Models," *Star Tribune*, May 27, 1995, p. M1.

10. "Sonic Sinker," *The Economist*, November 23, 2002, p. 58.

11. Robert Berner, "Why P&G's Smile Is So Bright," *Business Week*, August 12, 2002, pp. 58–60.

12. Christopher Ryan, "Virtual reality in marketing," *Direct Marketing*, April 2001, p. 57.

Chapter 9

1. Sue Zesiger Callaway, "Bachelor Meets Bugatti," *Fortune*, March 19, 2007, pp. 214-15; and www.bugatti.com.
2. Adapted from Kent B. Monroe, *Pricing: Making Profitable Decisions*, 3rd ed. (New York: McGraw-Hill, 2003).
3. Roger A. Kerin and Robert A. Peterson, "Throckmorten Furniture (A)," *Strategic Marketing Problems: Cases and Comments*, 9th ed. (Englewood Cliffs, NJ: Prentice Hall, 1998), pp. 235-45.
4. For the classic description of skimming and penetration pricing, see Joel Dean, "Pricing Policies for New Products," *Harvard Business Review*, November–December 1976, pp. 141-53. See also, Reed K. Holden and Thomas T. Nagle, "Kamikaze Pricing," *Marketing Management*, Summer 1998, pp. 31-39.
5. Jean-Noel Kapferer, "Managing Luxury Brands," *Journal of Brand Management*, July 1997, pp. 251-60.
6. "Why That Deal Is Only $9.99," *Business Week*, January 10, 2000, p. 36. For further reading on odd-even pricing, see Robert M. Schindler and Thomas M. Kilbarian, "Increased Consumer Sales Response through Use of 99-Ending Prices," *Journal of Retailing*, Summer 1996, pp. 187-99; Mark Stiving and Russell S. Winer, "An Empirical Analysis of Price Endings with Scanner Data," *Journal of Consumer Research*, June 1997, pp. 57-67; and Robert M. Schindler, "Patterns of Rightmost Digits Used in Advertised Prices: Implications for Nine-Ending Effects," *Journal of Consumer Research*, September 1997, pp. 192-201.
7. For an overview on target pricing, see Stephan A. Butscher and Michael Laker, "Market Driven Product Development," *Marketing Management*, Summer 2000, pp. 48-53.
8. Thomas T. Nagle and Reed K. Holden, *The Strategy and Tactics of Pricing*, 3rd ed. (Englewood Cliffs, NJ: Prentice Hall, 2002), pp. 243-49.
9. Ibid., pp. 237-39.
10. Peter M. Noble and Thomas S. Gruca, "Industrial Pricing: Theory and Managerial Practice," *Marketing Science* 18, no. 3 (1999), pp. 435-54.
11. George E. Belch and Michael A. Belch, *Introduction to Advertising and Promotion*, 5th ed. (New York: Irwin/McGraw-Hill, 2001), p. 93.
12. Frank Bruni, "Price of Newsweek? It Depends," *Dallas Times Herald*, August 14, 1986, pp. S1, S20.
13. Darren Rovell, "Jerseys from old-timers' game on the block," ESPN.com, December 4, 2003, http://espn.go.com/sportsbusiness/news/2003/1204/1678438.html.
14. "Stores Told to Lift Prices in Germany," *The Wall Street Journal*, September 11, 2000, pp. A27, A30.
15. "Rotten Apples," *Dallas Morning News*, April 7, 1998, p. 14A.
16. "When Grey Is Good," *The Economist*, August 22, 1998, p. 17; and Neil Belmore, "Parallel Imports and Grey Market Issues," The Canadian Institute, December 5-6, 2001.
17. "How Dell Fine-Tunes Its PC Pricing to Gain Edge in a Slow Market," *The Wall Street Journal*, June 8, 2001, pp. A1, A8.
18. For an extensive discussion on discounts, see Kent B. Monroe, *Pricing: Making Profitable Decisions*, 2nd ed. (New York: McGraw-Hill, 1990), chaps. 14 and 15.

Chapter 10

1. See Peter D. Bennett, ed., *Dictionary of Marketing Terms*, 2nd ed. (Chicago: American Marketing Association, 1995).
2. PepsiCo, Inc., Annual Report 1997.
3. This discussion is based on Bert Rosenbloom, *Marketing Channels: A Management View*, 6th ed. (Fort Worth: Dryden Press, 1999), pp. 452-58.
4. Johny K. Johansson, "International Alliances: Why Now?" *Journal of the Academy of Marketing Science*, Fall 1995, pp. 301-4.

5. "Eddie Bauer's Banner Time of Year," *Advertising Age*, October 1, 2001, p. 55.
6. Michael Krantz, "Click Till You Drop," *Time*, July 20, 1998, pp. 34-39.
7. *Multi-Channel Integration — The New Retail Battleground* (Columbus, OH: PricewaterhouseCoopers, March 2001).
8. "Don't Cut Back Now," *Business Week e-biz*, October 1, 2001, p. EB34.
9. *Fighting Fire with Water — From Channel Conflict to Confluence* (Cambridge, MA: Bain & Company, July 1, 2000).
10. For an overview of vertical marketing systems, see Lou Pelton, David Strutton, and James R. Lumpkin, *Marketing Channels*, 2nd ed. (Burr Ridge, IL: McGraw-Hill/Irwin, 2003), chap. 14.
11. Petcetera website, www.petcetera.ca.
12. "5 Down 95 to Go," www.apple.com, downloaded August 1, 2001; Apple Computer, press release, May 21, 2001; "Apple to Open Its First Retail Store in New York City," www.apple.com, downloaded July 20, 2002.
13. For an extensive discussion on channel conflict, see Anne T. Coughlan, Erin Anderson, Louis W. Stern, and Adel I. El-Ansary, *Marketing Channels*, 6th ed. (Upper Saddle River, NJ: Prentice Hall, 2001).
14. "Black Pearls Recast for Spring," *Advertising Age*, November 13, 1995, p. 49.
15. For an extensive discussion on power and influence in marketing channels, see Coughlan et al., *Marketing Channels*.
16. *What's It All About?* (Oakbrook, IL: Council of Logistics Management, 1993).
17. This example is described in David Sinchi-Levi, Philip Kaminsky, and Edith Sinchi-Levi, *Designing and Managing the Supply Chain* (Burr Ridge, IL: McGraw-Hill/Irwin, 2000), p. 5.
18. This discussion is based on Robyn Meredith, "Harder than the Hype," *Forbes*, April 16, 2001, pp. 188-94; Robert M. Monczka and Jim Morgan, "Supply Chain Management Strategies," *Purchasing*, January 15, 1998, pp. 78-85; and Robert B. Handfield and Earnest Z. Nichols, *Introduction to Supply Chain Management* (Upper Saddle River, NJ: Prentice Hall, 1998), chap. 1.
19. Major portions of this discussion are based on Sunil Chopra and Peter Meindl, *Supply Chain Management: Strategy, Planning, and Operations* (Upper Saddle River, NJ: Prentice Hall, 2001), chaps. 1-3; and Marshall L. Fisher, "What Is the Right Supply Chain for Your Product?" *Harvard Business Review*, March–April 1997, pp. 105-17.
20. "Wal-Mart Expands Commitment to RFID," *Material Handling Management*, May 2007, Vol. 62, Iss. 5, pg. 8.
21. For an extensive listing and description of total logistics costs, see James R. Stock and Douglas M. Lambert, *Strategic Logistics Management*, 4th ed. (Burr Ridge, IL: McGraw-Hill/Irwin, 2001).
22. Michael Levy and Barton A. Weitz, *Retailing Management*, 4th ed. (Burr Ridge, IL: McGraw-Hill/Irwin, 2001), pp. 335-36.
23. Fisher, "What Is the Right Supply Chain for Your Product?"

Chapter 11

1. Kenneth Cline, "The Devil in the Details," *Banking Strategies*, November–December 1997, p. 24; and Roger Trap, "Design Your Own Jeans," *The Independent*, October 18, 1998, p. 22.
2. Bank of Montreal website, www.bmo.com.
3. Retail Council of Canada website, www.retailcouncil.org/news/media/profile.
4. Statistics Canada, CANSIM table 080-0018, December 2007.
5. "2008 Global Powers of Retailing," Deloitte Touche Tohmatsu/Stores, January 2008, section 2, accessed at www.nxtbook.com/nxtbooks/nrfe/stores-globalretail08.
6. Statistics Canada, CANSIM table 080-0018, December 2007.
7. "Retail — The Heart of Every Community," Retail Council of Canada, accessed at www.retailcouncil.org/research/data/il/structure/jacobson/rcc_profile_2001.pdf.
8. "2008 Global Powers of Retailing."

9. "Retail Trade—Establishments, Employees, and Payroll," *Statistical Abstract of the United States*, 120th ed. (Washington, DC: U.S. Department of Commerce, Bureau of the Census, October 2000); and Gene Koretz, "Those Plucky Corner Stores," *Business Week*, December 5, 1994, p. 26.

10. "Franchise 500," *Entrepreneur*, January 2001; and Scott Shane and Chester Spell, "Factors for New Franchise Success," *Sloan Management Review*, Spring 1998, pp. 43–50.

11. "Holt Renfrew… One of the World's Leading Fashion and Lifestyle Shopping Experiences Benchmarked against the Best," Holt Renfrew website, accessed at www.holtrenfrew.com/english/history.

12. Francis J. Mulhern and Robert P. Leon, "Implicit Price Bundling of Retail Products: A Multiproduct Approach to Maximizing Store Profitability," *Journal of Marketing*, October 1991, pp. 63–76.

13. Gwen Ortmeyer, John A. Quelch, and Walter Salmon, "Restoring Credibility to Retail Pricing," *Sloan Management Review*, Fall 1991, pp. 55–66.

14. William B. Dodds, "In Search of Value: How Price and Store Name Information Influence Buyers' Product Perceptions," *Journal of Consumer Marketing*, Spring 1991, pp. 15–24.

15. Barry Brown, "Edmonton Makes Size Pay Off in Down Market," *Advertising Age*, January 27, 1992, pp. 4–5.

16. James R. Lowry, "The Life Cycle of Shopping Centers," *Business Horizons*, January–February 1997, pp. 77–86; Eric Peterson, "Power Centers! Now!" *Stores*, March 1989, pp. 61–66; and "Power Centers Flex Their Muscle," *Chain Store Age Executive*, February 1989, pp. 3A, 4A.

17. Ranjay Gulati and Janson Garino, "Getting the Right Mix of Bricks and Clicks," *Harvard Business Review*, May–June 2000, pp. 107–14; Marshall L. Fisher, Ananth Raman, and Anna Sheen McClelland, "Rocket Science Retailing Is Almost Here: Are You Ready?" *Harvard Business Review*, July–August 2000, pp. 115–24; Charla Mathwick, Naresh Malhotra, and Edward Rigdon, "Experiential Value: Conceptualization, Measurement and Application in the Catalog and Internet Shopping Environment," *Journal of Retailing*, Spring 2001, pp. 39–56; Lawrence M. Bellman, "Bricks and Mortar: 21st Century Survival," *Business Horizons*, May–June 2001, pp. 21–28; Zhan G. Li and Nurit Gery, "E-Tailing—for All Products?" *Business Horizons*, November–December 2000, pp. 49–54; and Bill Hanifin, "Go Forth and Multichannel: Loyalty Programs Need Knowledge Base," *Marketing News*, August 27, 2001, p. 23.

18. Ginny Parker, "Vending the Rules," *Time*, May 7, 2001, p. 24.

19. Julie Mitchell, "Electronic Payment Services Move beyond Tollbooths," *Investor's Business Daily*, August 30, 2001, p. 10; and Steve Scrupski, "Tiny 'Brains' Seen for Vending Machines," *Electronic Design*, December 1, 1998, p. 64F.

20. "Joe Namath, Franco Harris, Boomer Esiason, and Tim Brown Appear on Home Shopping Network during Super Bowl Week," *PR Newswire*, January 23, 2001; "Cover Girls Queen Latifah and Molly Sims Brush Up on Youth Volunteerism," *PR Newswire*, August 22, 2001; Carole Nicksin, "QVC Opens Up in Mall Space," *HFN*, August 20, 2001, p. 6; and Chris Wynn and Tim Adler, "Battle for UK Home-Shopping Viewers Hots Up as QVC Gets Heavyweight Rival," *New Media Markets*, May 11, 2001.

21. Vito Pilieci, "The IKEA Catalog: It's Bigger than the Bible," *Ottawa Citizen*, August 27, 2003, p. A1.

22. Lee Valley website, www.leevalley.com.

23. Donna Bursey, "Targeting Small Businesses for Telemarketing and Mail Order Sales," *Direct Marketing*, September 1995, pp. 18–20; "Inbound, Outbound Telemarketing Keeps Ryder Sales in Fast Lane," *Direct Marketing*, July 1995, pp. 34–36; "Despite Hangups, Telemarketing a Success," *Marketing News*, March 27, 1995, p. 19; Kelly Shermach, "Outsourcing Seen as a Way to Cut Costs, Retain Service," *Marketing News*, June 19, 1995, pp. 5, 8; and Greg Gattuso, "Marketing Vision," *Direct Marketing*, February 1994, pp. 24–26.

24. Nanette Byrnes, "The New Calling," *Business Week*, September 18, 2000, pp. 137–48.

25. Bill Vlasic and Mary Beth Regan, "Amway II: The Kids Take Over," *Business Week*, February 1, 1998, pp. 60–70.

26. Mathew Schifrin, "Okay, Big Mouth," *Forbes*, October 9, 1995, pp. 47–48; Veronica Byrd and Wendy Zellner, "The Avon Lady of the Amazon," *Business Week*, October 24, 1994, pp. 93–96; and Ann Marsh "Avon Is Calling on Eastern Europe," *Advertising Age*, June 20, 1994, p. 116.

27. "Order Online, Pick Up Items at Local Wal-Mart," *St. Petersburg Times*, May 23, 2007, p. 1D; and "Marketing Factbook: Online Retail Sales," *Marketing News*, July 15, 2006, p. 37.

28. "My Virtual Model Inc. Acquires EZsize," *PR Newswire*, June 21, 2001; Steve Casimiro, "Shop Till You Crash," *Fortune*, December 21, 1998, pp. 267–70; and De' Ann Weimer, "Can I Try (Click) That Blouse (Drag) in Blue?" *Business Week*, November 9, 1998, p. 86.

29. "What's so new about the 'New Economy'? Glad you asked," *Business 2.0*, August–September 2001, p. 84.

30. This discussion is based on "By the Numbers: Buying Breakdown," *The Wall Street Journal*, September 24, 2001, p. R4; "Factoids," *Research Alert*, November 17, 2000, p. 4; and Weiss, "Online America."

31. "NPD e-Visory Report Shows Offline Sales Benefit from Online Browsing," NPD Group, July 17, 2001.

32. This discussion is based on "Statistics: U.S. Online Shoppers," www.shop.org, downloaded September 14, 2001; "The Clicks-and-Bricks Way to Buy That Car," *Business Week*, May 7, 2001, pp. 128–30; and *The Next Chapter in Business-to-Consumer E-Commerce* (Boston: The Boston Consulting Group, March 2001).

33. "The 90/20 Rule of e-Commerce: Nearly 90% of Online Sales Accounted for by 20% of Consumers," Cyber Dialogue, press release, September 25, 2000.

Chapter 12

1. Wilbur Schramm, "How Communication Works," in Wilbur Schramm, ed., *The Process and Effects of Mass Communication* (Urbana, IL: University of Illinois Press, 1955), pp. 3–26.

2. E. Cooper and M. Jahoda, "The Evasion of Propaganda," *Journal of Psychology* 22 (1947), pp. 15–25; H. Hyman and P. Sheatsley, "Some Reasons Why Information Campaigns Fail," *Public Opinion Quarterly* 11 (1947), pp. 412–23; and J. T. Klapper, *The Effects of Mass Communication* (New York: Free Press, 1960), chap. VII.

3. *Canadian Media Directors' Council Media Digest 2008-2009*, p. 46, accessed at www.cmdc.ca/pdf/2008_09_Media_Digest.pdf.

4. Adapted from *Dictionary of Marketing Terms*, 2nd ed., Peter D. Bennett, ed. (Chicago: American Marketing Association, 1995), p. 231.

5. Nova Scotia Department of Tourism website, www.novascotia.com; and e-mail communication with Peggy Tibbo-Cameron, Tourism Partnership Council.

6. Kusum L. Ailawadi, Scott A. Neslin, and Karen Gedenk, "Pursuing the Value-Conscious Consumer: Store Brands versus National Brand Promotions," *Journal of Marketing*, January 2001, pp. 71–89.

7. B. C. Cotton and Emerson M. Babb, "Consumer Response to Promotional Deals," *Journal of Marketing* 42 (July 1978), pp. 109–13.

8. Robert George Brown, "Sales Response to Promotions and Advertising," *Journal of Advertising Research* 14 (August 1974), pp. 33–40.

9. Adapted from *Economic Impact: U.S. Direct Marketing Today* (New York: Direct Marketing Association, 1998), p. 25.

10. Siva K. Balasubramanian and V. Kumar, "Analyzing Variations in Advertising and Promotional Expenditures: Key Correlates in Consumer, Industrial, and Service Markets," *Journal of Marketing*, April 1990, pp. 57–68.

11. Don Schultz, "Objectives Drive Tactics in IMC Approach," *Marketing News*, May 9, 1994, pp. 14, 18; and Neil Brown, "Redefine Integrated Marketing Communications," *Marketing News*, March 29, 1993, pp. 4–5.

12. "Grolsch awareness grows 5-fold in one season," Radio Marketing Bureau Case Study, 2007, accessed at http://rmb.ca/uploadedFiles/Research/Case_Studies/Grolsch2007.pdf.

13. James M. Olver and Paul W. Farris, "Push and Pull: A One-Two Punch for Packages Products," *Sloan Management Review*, Fall 1989, pp. 53–61.

14. Fusun F. Gonul, Franklin Carter, Elina Petrova, and Kannan Srinivasan, "Promotion of Prescription Drugs and Its Impact on Physicians' Choice Behavior," *Journal of Marketing*, July 2001, pp. 79–90.

15. *Strategy* Magazine Agency of the Year winners, 2003, www.strategymag.com/aoy/2003/taxi/viagra.html.

16. Robert J. Lavidge and Gary A. Steiner, "A Model for Predictive Measurement of Advertising Effectiveness," *Journal of Marketing*, October 1961, p. 61.

17. "45th Annual Report: 100 Leading National Advertisers," *Advertising Age*, September 24, 2001, pp. S1–S26.

18. Don E. Schultz and Anders Gronstedt, "Making Marcom an Investment," *Marketing Management*, Fall 1997, pp. 41–49; and J. Enrique Bigne, "Advertising Budget Practices: A Review," *Journal of Current Issues and Research in Advertising*, Fall 1995, pp. 17–31.

19. John Philip Jones, "Ad Spending: Maintaining Market Share," *Harvard Business Review*, January–February 1990, pp. 38–42; and Charles H. Patti and Vincent Blanko, "Budgeting Practices of Big Advertisers," *Journal of Advertising Research* 21 (December 1981), pp. 23–30.

20. James A. Schroer, "Ad Spending: Growing Market Share," *Harvard Business Review*, January–February 1990, pp. 44–48.

21. James E. Lynch and Graham J. Hooley, "Increasing Sophistication in Advertising Budget Setting," *Journal of Advertising Research* 30 (February–March 1990), pp. 67–75.

22. Jimmy D. Barnes, Brenda J. Muscove, and Javad Rassouli, "An Objective and Task Media Selection Decision Model and Advertising Cost Formula to Determine International Advertising Budgets," *Journal of Advertising* 11, no. 4 (1982), pp. 68–75.

23. Don E. Schultz, "Olympics Get the Gold Medal in Integrating Marketing Event," *Marketing News*, April 27, 1998, pp. 5, 10.

24. "The Fellowship of the New Line," *PROMO*, September 2001, p. 84; and "Sneak Preview of Trailer for New Line Cinema's 'The Lord of the Rings: The Fellowship of the Ring,'" *PR Newswire*, September 21, 2001.

25. Kate Fitzgerald, "Beyond Advertising," *Advertising Age*, August 3, 1998, pp. 1, 14; Curtis P. Johnson, "Follow the Money: Sell CFO on Integrated Marketing's Merits," *Marketing News*, May 11, 1998, p. 10; and Laura Schneider, "Agencies Show That IMC Can Be Good for Bottom Line," *Marketing News*, May 11, 1998, p. 11.

26. Rafi A. Mohammed, Robert J. Fisher, Bernard J. Jaworski, and Aileen M. Cahill, *Internet Marketing: Building Advantage in a Networked Economy* (Burr Ridge, IL: McGraw-Hill/Irwin, 2002); and Yoram Wind, Vijay Mahajan, and Robert Gunther, *Convergence Marketing* (Upper Saddle River, NJ: Prentice Hall, 2002).

27. Statistics Canada, *The Daily*, April 24, 2008, accessed at www.statcan.ca/Daily/English/080424/d080424a.htm.

28. Michael Weiss, "Online America," *American Demographics*, March 21, 2001, pp. 53–60.

29. Mohammed et al., *Internet Marketing*.

30. Adrian J. Slywotzky, "The Age of the Choiceboard," *Harvard Business Review*, January–February 2000, pp. 40–41.

31. Alan Rosenspan, "Participation Marketing," *Direct Marketing*, April 2001, pp. 54–66.

Chapter 13

1. Charles Zamaria and Fred Fletcher, *Canada Online! The Internet, Media and Emerging Technologies: Uses, Attitudes, Trends and International Comparisons*, Canadian Internet Project, September 2008, www.cipic.ca/en/docs/2008/CIP07%20CANADA%20ONLINE-HIGHLIGHTS.pdf, p. 5.

2. "Ten Marketers That Mattered," *Marketing* magazine, December 16/23, 2002, p. 20.

3. *Advertising Age*, November 20, 2006.

4. Michael S. LaTour and Herbert J. Rotfeld, "There Are Threats and (Maybe) Fear-Caused Arousal: Theory and Confusions of Appeals to Fear and Fear Arousal Itself," *Journal of Advertising*, Fall 1997, pp. 45–59.

5. *2008 PMB Topline Report*, Canadian Print Measurement Bureau, accessed at www.pmb.ca/public/e/pmb2008/PMB2008_topline.pdf

6. Ibid.

7. *Canadian Media Directors' Council Media Digest 2008/2009*, p. 30, accessed at www.cmdc.ca/pdf/2008_09_media_digest.pdf.

8. Arch G. Woodside, "Outdoor Advertising as Experiments," *Journal of the Academy of Marketing Science* 18 (Summer 1990), pp. 229–37.

9. Magid M. Abraham and Leonard M. Lodish, "Getting the Most out of Advertising and Promotion," *Harvard Business Review*, May–June 1990, pp. 50–60; Steven W. Hartley and James Cross, "How Sales Promotion Can Work for and against You," *Journal of Consumer Marketing*, Summer 1988, pp. 35–42; Robert D. Buzzell, John A. Quelch, and Walter J. Salmon, "The Costly Bargain of Trade Promotion," *Harvard Business Review*, March–April 1990, pp. 141–49; and Mary L. Nicastro, "Break-Even Analysis Determines Success of Sales Promotions," *Marketing News*, March 5, 1990, p. 11.

10. "Coupon Fact Sheet for the Year 2006 – Coupon Use in Canada," Coupon Industry Association of Canada website, 2007, accessed at www.couponscanada.org/html/couponing_facts.html.

11. Carrie MacMillan, "Creature Features," *PROMO*, October 2001, p. 11; Dan Hanover, "Not Just for Breakfast Anymore," *PROMO*, September 2001, p. 10.

12. Tim Hortons website, www.timhortons.com.

13. "Best Activity Generating Brand Awareness/Trial," *PROMO*, September 2001, p. 51; and "Brand Handing," *PROMO's 9th Annual Sourcebook*, 2002, p. 32.

14. "On a Roll," *Marketing* magazine, July 1, 2002; and "Hey, Big Spender," *Marketing* magazine, January 14, 2002.

15. This discussion is drawn particularly from John A. Quelch, *Trade Promotions by Grocery Manufacturers: A Management Perspective* (Cambridge, MA: Marketing Science Institute, August 1982).

16. "Safetyforum.com and Public Citizen Report: NHTSA Forces Firestone to Recall Defective Tires, Expand Wilderness Ats Recall," *PR Newswire*, October 5, 2001; Cindy Skrzycki and Frank Swoboda, "Firestone Refuses Voluntary Recall," Safetyforum.com, July 20, 2001; Jim Suhr, "Tire Recall Response Time Defended," Safetyforum.com, August 10, 2000.

17. Eric Berkowitz, et al., *Marketing*, 5th Canadian Ed. (Whitby, ON: McGraw-Hill Ryerson, 2003).

18. Adapted from *Economic Impact: U.S. Direct Marketing Today* (New York: Direct Marketing Association, 1998), pp. 25–26.

19. Carol Krol, "Club Med Uses E-Mail to Pitch Unsold, Discounted Packages," *Advertising Age*, December 14, 1998, p. 40.

20. Jean Halliday, "Taking Direct Route," *Advertising Age*, September 7, 1998, p. 17.

21. "Labour force survey estimates (LFS), by full- and part-time students during school months, sex and age group, annual," Statistics Canada, Table 282-0095, May 2003.

22. For recent representative research on and commentary on relationship selling, see James Boles, Thomas Brashear, Danny Bellenger, and Hiram Barksdale, Jr., "Relationship Selling Behaviors: Antecedents and Relationship with Performance," *Journal of Business & Industrial Marketing* 15, no. 2/3 (2000), pp. 141–53; and Barton A. Weitz and Kevin D. Bradford, "Personal Selling and Sales Management: A Relationship Marketing Perspective," *Journal of the Academy of Marketing Science*, Spring 1999, pp. 241–54.

23. David W. Cravens, "The Changing Role of the Sales Force," *Marketing Management*, Fall 1995, pp. 49–57.

24. Christen Heide, *Dartnell's 31st Sales Force Compensation Survey 2000* (Chicago: The Dartnell Corporation, 2000), p. 176.

25. "What a Sales Call Costs," *Sales & Marketing Management*, August 2002, p. 80.

26. "Keep Calling!" *Sales & Marketing Report*, May 2001, p. 3.

27. For an extensive discussion of objections, see Charles M. Futrell, *Fundamentals of Selling* (New York: Irwin/McGraw-Hill, 2002), chap. 10.

28. Cravens, "The Changing Role of the Sales Force."

29. Robert L. Lindstrom, "Training Hits the Road, Part 2," *Sales & Marketing Management*, June 1995, pp. 10–14.

Chapter 14

1. Kotler et al., *Principles of Marketing,* 7th Canadian edition (Toronto: Pearson, 2008).

2. "Why Some Companies Succeed at CRM (and Many Fail)," Knowledge@Wharton, January 15, 2003, accessed at http://knowledge.wharton.upenn.edu/article.cfm?articleid=699.

3. The Ultimate CRM Guide.com website, www.ultimatecrmguide.com/crm-strategy/culture.

4. R. Buchanan and C. Gillies, "Value Managed Relationship: The Key to Customer Retention and Profitability," *European Management Journal*, Vol. 8, No. 4, 1990.

5. Lindsay Blakely, "Lounging in Style," *Business 2.0*, August 2007, p. 92.

6. "Hotels Encourage Loyalty with Perks," *National Post,* April 10, 2008, p.1, s5

7. Hokey Min, "Developing the Profile of Supermarket Customers through Data Mining," *Service Industries Journal,* October 2006.

8. Carl Sewell and Paul Brown, *Customers For Life,* Doubleday Publishing, 2002.

9. Eric Beauchesne, "Customers Want Friendly Service Most," *Star Phoenix,* June 20, 2008.

10. Knowledge @Wharton website, www.knowledge.wharton.upenn.edu.

11. Tom Duncan, *Principles of Advertising + IMC,* 2nd Edition (New York: McGraw-Hill/Irwin, 2005), p. 266.

Chapter 15

1. Roger A. Kerin, Vijay Mahajan, and P. Rajan Varadarajan, *Contemporary Perspectives on Strategic Marketing Planning* (Boston: Allyn & Bacon, 1990), chap. 1; and Orville C. Walker, Jr., Harper W. Boyd, Jr., and Jean-Claude Larreche, *Marketing Strategy* (Burr Ridge, IL: Richard D. Irwin, 1992), chaps. 1 and 2.

2. Theodore Levitt, "Marketing Myopia," *Harvard Business Review,* July - August 1960, pp. 45–56.

3. Tilley Endurables website, accessed at www.tilley.com/home.asp.

4. George Stalk, Phillip Evans, and Lawrence E. Shulman, "Competing on Capabilities. The New Rules of Corporate Strategy," *Harvard Business Review,* March–April 1992, pp. 57–69.

5. Tilley Endurables website, accessed at www.tilley.com/home.asp.

6. Adapted from "The Experience Curve Reviewed, IV. The Growth Share Matrix of the Product Portfolio" (Boston: The Boston Consulting Group, 1973).

7. Kerin, Mahajan, and Vardarajan, *Contemporary Perspectives*, p. 52.

8. "About Sleep Country," Sleep Country Canada website, accessed January 30, 2009, at www.sleepcountry.ca/default.asp?CName=about&Index=100.

[istudy] marketing
...do you?
McGraw-Hill Ryerson proudly presents
a new innovative study tool.
www.istudymarketing.ca

Credits

Name Index

Agarwalla, Jayant, 127
Agarwalla, Rajat, 127
Arens, William F., 258*f*
Austen, Ian, 206*f*

Barrett, Andrew, 2, 4, 5, 15
Batty, David, 266
Beal, Barney, 279
Belko, Mark, 143
Bensimon, Jack, 293
Berner, Robert, 280*f*
Blakely, Rhys, 166
Bosivert, Melise, 98
Branson, Richard, 282
Brent, Paul, 283*f*
Bridge, Andrew, 31
Brown, David, 102*f*, 130

Carey, Bridget, 166
Castaldo, Joe, 285*f*
Charney, Don, 192
Chiasson, Gail, 85*f*, 146, 236*f*
Clover, Charles, 266
Cooperberg, Lorne, 31

Daniels, Chris, 292*f*
Dell, Michael, 197
Denny, Charles, 214
Derrett, Ken, 116, 117, 118, 119, 122, 126, 132
Dickens, Charles, 244
Dupont, Luc, 85

Everett, Neil, 276, 278

Fedchum, Gerry, 69
Flavelle, Dana, 130
Fletcher, Fred, 189*f*, 253*f*
Ford, Rollin, 199
Forgrieve, Janet, 192*f*
Francis, Diane, 280*f*

George-Cosh, David, 102*f*
Gordon, Ian, 134, 135, 136, 142, 146, 154
Gray, John, 126*f*, 303*f*
Gretzky, Wayne, 172
Grossman, Naomi, 76*f*
Guinness, Arthur, 146
Gunn, Stephen, 180

Hanna, Jeannette, 302
Hannam, Lisa, 102*f*
Hatherly, Joanne, 297*f*

Iacocco, Lee, 130
Ingram, Matthew, 128*f*

Jobs, Steve, 194

Kane, Kevin, 176
Karpinski, Rich, 58
Kho, Nancy Davis, 58
Kincaid, David, 51
Kirby, Jason, 206*f*
Klie, Shannon, 285*f*
Klostermann, Ruth, 40, 42, 46
Knox, Steve, 280
Kohl, Jesse, 139
Kothawala, Anne, 27
Kreuk, Mary, 224, 226, 228, 240, 242

Lagorio, Christine, 222*f*
Laird, Kristin, 292*f*
Lavelle, Marianne, 192*f*
Lazarus, Eve, 111
Lindsay, Greg, 162
Lloyd, Jeremy, 70, 303*f*
Lokash, Brent, 111
Lownds, Gad, 180

Magee, Christine, 130, 180, 182

Martin, Brandy, 18
McClellan, Steve, 95*f*
McGillicuddy, Shamus, 279
McHugh, James M., 258*f*
McHugh, Susan M, 258*f*
McKenzie, Brett, 261
McKenzie, Deborah, 62, 65
Menon, Vinay, 283*f*
Middleton, Alan, 303
Mininni, Ted, 76*f*
Morash, Anne, 202, 204, 209
Morash, Rob, 98, 100, 102, 105, 110, 114
Moren, Dan, 294*f*
Morneau, Justin, 111
Mudhar, Raju, 261

Nash, Steve, 111
Nichol, Dave, 129, 130
Nickels, William G., 258*f*
Nighbor, Derek, 219
Nishikawa, Clare, 131

Parrish, Kevin, 161
Perrin, Jane, 131*f*
Perry, Joellen, 192*f*
Pilleci, Vito, 165
Pitts, Gordon, 66*f*
Poulton, Terry, 85*f*, 232*f*, 297*f*

Ramage, Norma, 285*f*
Richtel, Matt, 222*f*
Roberts, Rob, 113
Robinson, Doug, 250
Rocha, Robert, 102*f*
Roddenberry, Gene, 292
Rowe, Mike, 128

Saddleton, Lucy, 268*f*
Semansky, Matt, 8*f*, 127*f*
Shaw, Hollie, 130, 211*f*
Shaw, Judith, 156, 157, 158, 167
Shaw, Stephen, 282
Siegel, Robert, 152
Siemiesz, Mary, 268
Sklar, Luke, 80, 82, 83, 97, 99
Sorensen, Chris, 127*f*
Sorkin, Andrew Ross, 76*f*
Srikanthan, Thulasi, 113
Stonehouse, Greg, 174
Stones, David, 22, 24, 27, 34
Strauss, Marina, 174

Taylor, Elizabeth, 195
Tilley, Alex, 295
Torres, Ricardo, 296

Vaz, Peter, 232

Welling, Mike, 250, 251, 252, 253, 259, 264
Weston, Galen, Jr., 129, 130
White, Rick, 56
Whitman, Janet, 206*f*
Williams, Natalia, 283*f*
Williams, Randy, 284
Wilson, Eric, 162

Zamaria, Charles, 189*f*, 253*f*

share.

www.mcgrawhill.ca/olc/thecore

Company/Product Index

2008 Olympic Summer Games, 242
2010 Winter Olympics, 233, 242
24 Hours, 260, 261
7-Eleven, 185
7Up, 128

A&P, 205, 278
Absolut Vodka, 14
AC NIelsen, 153
ACLC, 134
Adidas, 127, 132, 212
Advertising Standards Canada
    (ASC), 36, 37
Advil, 50, 241
Aeroplan, 282
Agnew Peckham, 290
Air Canada, 162, 171, 244
Air Canada Centre, 11
Air Miles, 13, 276, 278, 282, 283
Airbus Industries, 186
airmilesshops.ca, 278
Aldo Shoes, 302
Alibris, 244
Alimentation Couche-Tard, 205
Alliance Data Loyalty Services, 276,
    278
Altra Energy, 77
Amazon, 104
Amazon.ca, 186, 214, 279
Amazon.com, 216
Amer Sports Canada, 98
American Apparel, 192
American Express, 47, 278
American Idol, 4, 128
American Teleservices
    Association, 216
Amway, 217
Anne Klein, 195
Apotex Inc., 130
Apple Computer, 5, 6, 43, 44, 56, 76,
    137, 138, 194
Arm & Hammer, 144
Art Gallery of Ontario, 250
AT&T, 60
Atomic Skis Canada, 98, 100, 102, 105,
    110, 114
Aurora Foods, 93, 297
Avon, 217, 270

Bank of Montreal, 205, 278, 282
Barnes & Noble, 48
Barney, 162
Battle Creek Toasted Corn Flake
    Company, 103
Bayer Corporation, 50
BBM Nielsen Media Research
    Inc., 90, 91, 92, 93
BCE, 256
Bear Mountain Resort, 17
Bell, 2, 4, 14, 144, 255, 270
Bell Canada, 242
Bell Mobility, 216
Ben & Jerry's, 297, 298, 299, 300
Bensimon Byrne, 292, 293
Best Health, 296
Better Business Bureau (BBB), 36, 37
BlackBerry, 64, 109, 125, 143, 144, 146,
    255, 302
Blockbuster Video, 209
BMO, 205, 278, 282
BMW, 49, 218
Boeing, 75, 148
Bombardier, 66, 70, 186
Boston Consulting Group, 295
Boy Scouts, 66
Breast Cancer Society of Canada, 255
British Airways, 45
Budweiser, 50, 303
Bugatti, 159, 172
Burberry, 162
Burger King, 47, 193, 242

CAA, 26
CAA Magazine, 234
Cadbury, 31, 143
Cadbury Adams, 18
Cadillac Fairview Corporation
    Limited, 202, 204, 209, 267
Calgary Stampede, 126
Calvin Klein, 36
Campbell's Soup, 142, 200
Canada Online, 253
Canada Revenue Agency, 66
Canada.com, 245, 247, 260
Canadian Automobile Association
    (CAA), 234
Canadian Automotive Parts
    Manufacturers Association, 69

Canadian Breast Cancer Foundation, 15
Canadian Business, 18, 108, 228
Canadian Cancer Society, 66
Canadian Council for the
    Advancement of Education, 252
Canadian Football League, 116
Canadian Gardening, 103
Canadian Geographic, 262
Canadian Health and Lifestyle, 262
Canadian House & Home, 262
Canadian Idol, 15, 17, 33–34, 224, 226, 257
Canadian Intellectual Property
    Office, 126
Canadian Living, 261, 262, 296
Canadian Marketing Association
    (CMA), 16, 36, 37, 228, 260, 269
Canadian Media Project, 253
Canadian Newspaper Association, 27
Canadian Open, 267
Canadian Pacific Hotels, 279
Canadian Parks and Wilderness
    Society, 16
Canadian Print Measurement
    Bureau, 261
Canadian Radio-television
    and Telecommunications
    Commission, 36
Canadian Red Cross, 293
Canadian Tire, 31, 144, 191, 192, 205,
    207, 214, 215, 265, 282
Cannes Advertising Festival, 261
Canon, 123, 162
Canteen Vending Services, 215
Cara, 80
CARD, 228
CARP, 30
Carrefour, 207, 208
Cartier, 161
Catelli, 241
Caterpillar, 186
CBC, 66, 126, 258
Centrum, 108
Century 21, 210
Chanel, 161
Chapters-Indigo, 211, 214, 215, 243
Chatelaine, 255, 261, 262
Chevron, 36
Childhood Cancer Foundation
    Candlelighters Canada
    (CCFC), 22, 24, 25, 27, 33, 34, 267

Chinook Centre, 202
Christian Dior, 165
Chrysler, 77, 130
Church's Chicken, 209, 210
CIBC, 15, 282
Cineplex Odeon, 10
Cingular Wireless, 69
Cirque du Soleil, 126, 302
Citizenship and Immigration
    Canada, 29f
CITY-TV, 228
Clairol, 49
Clear Channel Media, 262
Clearly Canadian Beverage
    Corporation, 111
Clover Leaf Seafood, 250
Club Med, 269
CN Tower, 11, 126
CNN, 284
Coach, 162
Coca-Cola, 11, 45, 50, 60, 82, 103, 108,
    111, 137, 142, 184, 190, 191, 193, 301,
    303
Coca-Cola Canada, 37
Coles, 243
Coles Traditional Foods, 146
Colgate-Palmolive, 51
Community Association for Riding
    for the Disabled, 228
Compaq Computer Corporation, 184,
    194
Competition Bureau, 36, 265
Consumer Reports, 42
Cool Whip, 255
Corona, 54
Cossette, 85
Costco, 50, 208, 210, 295
Council for the Advancement and
    Support of Education, 252
Covisint, 77
CP Hotels, 279
Crest, 146, 195
CRTC, 16, 36, 217, 231, 268
CTV, 15, 17, 33, 224, 226, 227, 228, 240,
    242, 257
Culligan, 186
Cyber Grand Prix, 261

Dairy Farmers of Canada, 84, 235–
    236, 258
David Suzuki Foundation, 31
DeBeers Canada, 29
Dell Computer, 58, 78, 104, 175, 176,
    187, 197–198, 215, 245
Dell.ca, 186
Deloitte Touche Tohmatsu, 207
Desperate Housewives, 34
Diesel, 36
Disney, 293
DMR Food Corporation, 111
Dockers, 162
Dog Guides of Canada, 268

Dollarama, 175
Dominos, 35, 68
Don Mills Centre, 204
Donna Karan, 48
Doritos, 143
doug agency inc., 250, 252, 253, 259,
    264
Dove, 259, 261, 266
Downy, 122
Dr. Pepper, 127
Duncan Hines, 297
Dunkin' Donuts, 206

Eastman Kodak, 58
Easy Off, 128
eBay, 95, 260
ebay.ca, 217
Eddie Bauer, 188
Edmonton Oilers, 172
Electrolux, 217
Electronic Engineering Times, 197
Elizabeth Arden, 195
Ellen, 261
Elumens Corporation, 153
Enterprise, 292
Entertainment Tonight, 261
Esso, 36
Ethan Allen, 189
Euromonitor International, 211
Expedia, 244

Facebook, 34, 76, 95, 109, 232
Fantasyland, 214
Fashion, 229
FedEx, 68, 184, 210
Fields, 15
Film Grand Prix, 261
Firestone, 266
Fisher Price, 11, 37
Fisherman's Friend, 146
Flick Off, 31
Florsheim, 212
Ford, 77, 191, 192, 197, 241, 266
Forrester Research, 110
Fortinos, 129
Forzani Group Ltd., 174
FreedomPay, 215
Frito Lay, 134
Fujitsu, 296
Future Shop, 211

Gamespot, 296
Gandalf Group, 292
Gatorade, 122
General Electric (GE), 45, 75, 78, 137,
    187, 212
General Mills, 91, 102, 147, 162, 187,
    224
General Motors, 34, 77, 165, 241, 244,
    256
George Richards Big & Tall, 174
Gerber, 171

Gillette, 141, 190
Girl Guides, 66
Global, 33, 258
Global eXchange Services, 78
Godiva Chocolates, 272
Good Housekeeping, 49
Goodyear, 190
Google, 95, 128, 130, 131, 147, 259, 261
Gossip Girls, 34
Government of Canada, 250
Government of Ontario, 31
Grafton & Co., 174
Grafton-Fraser Inc., 174
Great Canadian Dollar Store, 176
Greenpeace, 266
Grey's Anatomy, 258, 296
Grolsch, 237, 238
Gucci, 48
Guess, 36
Guinness Christmas Puddings, 145, 146

H&R Block, 191, 192
H.J. Heinz, 80, 170
Habitat for Humanity, 15
Haggar Clothing Co., 56, 57
Hallmark, 156, 187
Harley Davidson, 76
Harrods, 243
Hasbro, 126, 127
HBC, 14, 16, 265, 282, 283
Heart and Stroke Foundation, 9
Heathrow Airport, 282
Heinz, 80, 140, 141, 162
Hellmann's, 140
Herbal Essences, 166
Herbalife, 217
Heroes, 33
Hershey, 165
Hewlett-Packard (HP), 149
HMV, 80
HMV Canada Inc., 8
Holiday Inn, 209
Holt Renfrew & Co. Ltd., 47, 165, 195,
    210, 211
Home Depot, 195, 208, 210, 213
Home Hardware, 191, 192, 209
Home Outfitters, 15
Honda, 34, 159
Hongkong and Shanghai Banking
    Corporation Limited (HSBC), 216
Hope for Malawi, 228
Hotmail, 246
HSBC, 216
HSBC Group, 216
Hudson's Bay Company, 205, 283
Humber River Regional
    Hospital, 288–290

IBM, 58, 60, 137, 175, 186, 278, 301
IBM Canada, 62, 63, 64, 65, 119, 270
IGA, 191, 209, 278
IKEA, 210, 216, 268

IMAX, 126
Independent Grocers' Association (IGA), 209
Indigo, 243
Indigo Books and Music Inc., 243
Indigo/Chapters, 156
Insurance Corporation of British Columbia (ICBC), 86, 87, 91
Intel, 58, 71, 128
iPod, 128, 137, 138, 139, 147
   See also Apple Computer
Ipsos Reid, 53*f*
Ipsos Reid Canada, 15
iVillage.com, 246

J.M. Smuckers, 80
Jackson-Triggs, 256, 257
Jaguar, 218
Jean Coutu, 205
Jell-O, 255
Jenn-Air, 194
Jiffy Lube, 194
Jim Pattison Group, 205
Johnson & Johnson, 45, 56, 129
JVC, 172, 212

Kashi Company, 103, 104, 111
Kellogg Canada, 37
Kelloggs, 56, 70, 103, 144
Kenna Group, 282
Kimberly Clark, 148
Kingsdown, 182
Knight Rider, 33
Knorr, 144
Kodak, 148
Kodiak, 66
Kohler, 160
Koodo, 102
Kraft, 31, 35, 140, 187, 224, 263
Kraft Canada, 37, 270
Krave's Candy Company, 183
Kroger, 208

L.L. Bean, 216
La Senza, 211
Labatt Breweries, 116
Lacoste, 162
Lands' End, 45
Lay's, 182
Le Carrefour Laval, 202
Lee Valley Tools, 205, 216
Leger Corporate Reputation Survey, 4
Leger Marketing, 219
Levi Strauss & Co., 205
Levi's, 36, 182, 193, 205
Lewis Woolf Griptight, 91
LG Canada, 2, 4, 5, 8, 11, 14, 15, 19
Life Brand, 129, 130
LinkedIn, 76
Little Women for Little Women (LW4LW), 228

Loblaw Companies Ltd., 129, 130, 134, 135, 136, 142, 147, 149, 154, 164
Loblaws, 205, 209, 210, 282, 295
Local Health Integration Networks, 288
Lord of the Rings, 242
Loyalty Group, 13
Lucerne Foods, 191
Lunch Mail, 157, 158

M&M, 176
M2 Universal, 232
Mac's, 182, 194
Maclean's, 18, 214, 231, 257, 261, 262
Macy's, 162
Mad Men, 258
Magicuts, 212
Magna International Inc., 68, 69
Major League Baseball, 111
Mansar Products Ltd., 186
Manulife, 144
Maple Leaf Foods, 16, 80, 233, 267
Marconi Online Systems, 215
Marcus, 162
Marketing, 18, 30, 51, 56, 71*f*, 110, 111, 214*f*, 215*f*, 219, 282, 296
Mars, 80, 186, 265
Mary Kay Cosmetics, 49, 217
MasterCard, 59, 278, 282
Mastermind Toys, 156
Matchstick, 54
Material Handling Management (ii), 199
Mattel, 126, 127
Maxwell House Coffee, 15, 228, 229
MBNA, 216
McCain Foods, 302
McCormick & Co., 30
McDonald's, 48, 54, 59, 112, 113, 192, 193, 206, 207, 209, 210, 220, 222
McDonald's Restaurants of Canada, 37
Media in Canada, 228
Mediacorp, 285
Menu Foods, 71
Mercedes-Benz, 175, 218
Metro, 205, 208
Metro Toronto, 260, 261
Metropolitan Life, 187
Microsoft Corporation, 95, 109, 128, 137, 170, 195, 301
Milk-Bone, 264
Milky Way, 264
Miller Dallas, 104, 111, 113
Millward Brown Goldfarb, 51, 53*f*
Ming Pao, 58–59
Mira Foundation, 228
Mitsubishi, 269
Molson, 57
Montreal Canadiens, 126
Mountain Equipment Co-op, 6, 16
Mr. Lube, 194

MRO.com, 77
MSN, 245, 247
MTV, 95, 102
MuchMusic, 31
My Organic Baby Inc., 111
MySpace, 34, 261

Nabisco, 222
National Bank, 270
National Basketball Association, 111, 116–117
National Fluid Milk Processor, 49
National Football League, 116, 117, 118
National Hockey League, 143
National Post, 228, 260, 261, 280*f*, 284
Nearly Famous Enterprises Inc., 156, 157, 158, 167
Nestle, 7, 113, 187
Netfirms, 244
New Line Cinema, 242
Newsweek, 166, 167
Nieman Marcus, 162
Nike, 122, 123, 212
Nintendo, 161, 257, 296
Nissan Motor Company, 70
No Frills, 129, 210
Nokia, 137
Nordstrom, 162
Nortel Networks, 64, 69
Norwegian Cruise Lines, 124
Nova Scotia Department of Tourism and Culture, 233–234
Nova Scotia Tourism, 269
NPD Group, 94

O'Keefe, 57
Ocean Spray, 89
OECD, 32, 59
Office Depot, 207, 214, 216
Ogilvy & Mather Canada, 261
Oil of Olay, 123
Oliver Twist, 244
Olympics, 241
Olympus, 175, 250
Ontario Science Centre, 123
Ontario Tourism, 246
Oprah, 297
Oracle, 278
Organization for Economic Cooperation and Development (OECD), 32, 59
Oscar Meyer, 56
Oxfam, 250, 251, 266

Pacific Centre, 202
Pampers, 195
Panasonic, 43, 172
Pantene, 224, 226
PaperExchange, 77
Patak, 30
People, 262
Pepsi-Cola, 50, 51, 82, 95, 103, 108, 127, 184, 190, 192, 241

Petcetera, 194
Petro Canada, 36, 144, 184
Pfizer, 241
Pfizer Canada, 239
PGA, 282
Pharma Plus, 295
PharmaSave, 156
Philip Morris, 241
Philips, 137
Pittsburgh Penguins, 143
Pittsburgh Technology Council, 143
Pizza Hut, 35
Pizza Pizza, 6, 35
PlasticNet, 77
Polo/Ralph Lauren, 190, 191
Porsche, 118, 127
PowerBook, 128
President's Choice, 50, 129, 130, 134, 135, 136, 147, 148, 149, 154, 282
Procter & Gamble, 56, 60, 72, 75, 85, 123, 150, 191, 192, 195, 241, 256, 280, 297
Professional Marketing Research Society, 87
Promotion Marketing Association, 263
Provigo, 75
Publisher's Clearing House, 264
PubZone, 228
Purina, 237, 267, 268
Pussycat Dolls Present: Girlicious, 4

Quadrem, 77
Quixtar, 217

Radio Marketing Bureau, 28f
RBC, 144, 187
RCA, 173
Reader's Digest, 262, 264
Real Canadian Superstore, 129
Red Cross, 291
Redbook, 56
Reebok, 188
Regent Park School of Music, 228
Report on Business, 143
Retail Council of Canada, 219
retailcanada.com, 217
Rethink Breast Cancer, 255
Rice Krispies, 142
RIM, 64
Ritz, 229
Robin Hood Multifoods, 134
Rogers Communications, 2, 4, 14, 29, 80, 109, 245, 256, 267
Rolex, 124, 165, 193
Rolls-Royce, 161
Rona, 205, 242, 278
Ronald McDonald House Charities, 15, 17, 224, 226, 227
Roots, 126
Roots Canada, 31
Roper Reports Canada, 139, 140

Royal Bank, 144, 187
Royal Canadian Mint, 66
Royal Ontario Museum, 119
Rub A-535, 123
Ryan's Well Foundation, 228

Saab, 12
Safeway, 164, 185, 205, 278, 295
Salomon, 98
Samsung, 193
San Diego Chargers, 116, 117, 118, 119, 126, 132
Sanyo Electric, 215
SAP, 278
Saturn, 205
Schwarz Unternehmens Treuhand KG, 208
Scotiabank, 144
Scotts Miracle-Gro, 18
Scouts Canada, 66
Scrabble, 126, 127
Scrabulous, 127
Sealy, 182
Sears, 161, 165, 166, 182, 185, 208, 209, 211, 214
Sears Canada, 174, 216
Second Cup, 210
Seiko, 175
Select Comfort, 182
Serta, 182
Seven, 36
7-Eleven, 185
7Up, 128
Sharp, 172, 212
Shell, 36, 278
Sheraton, 282
Sherwin Williams, 190
Shoppers Drug Mart, 13, 129, 144, 205, 207, 210, 265, 276, 278, 282, 283, 284, 295
Simmons, 182
Sing Tao, 56
Sirius Canada, 262
Skechers, 92
Ski-Doo, 126
Skippy, 166
Sklar Wilton & Associates (SWA), 80, 83, 94
Sleep Country Canada, 130, 180, 182, 185, 194, 196
Smart car, 107, 108
Sobeys, 205, 278, 295
Sony, 5, 8, 43, 45, 56, 82, 83, 127, 137, 138, 146, 194, 212
Sport Chek, 211, 278
Spring Air, 182
Sprint, 216, 284
SRI International, 51
Stake Fastener Company, 186
Staples Business Depot, 211
Star Trek, 292
Starbucks, 187

Starwood Hotels & Resorts, 282
Statistics Canada, 26, 28f, 65f, 89, 90, 108, 206, 243
Strategy, 18, 228
Student Price Club, 283
Subway, 207
Sun-Rype, 121–122
Suunto, 98
Suzy Shier, 174
Swiss Chalet, 35
Sydney Opera House, 11
Sylvan Learning Centres, 210
Sympatico, 109, 110

T.J. Maxx, 162
Target, 208
TAXI, 236
TD Bank, 224
TD Canada Trust, 144, 284
Teenage Research Unlimited, 92
Telus, 2, 4, 14, 224, 226, 255, 256
Telus Mobility, 109, 159
Tempur, 182
Terry Fox, 126
Tesco, 208
TFB & Associates Ltd., 146
The Apprentice, 140
The Bay, 16, 166, 195, 209, 211, 212, 214, 215, 272, 295
The Daily Show, 34
The Gap, 189
The Globe and Mail, 143, 228, 260, 261
The Hills, 95
The Late Show with David Letterman, 4
The OC, 140
The Office, 33
The Shoe Company, 278
The Shopping Channel, 215
The Shops at Don Mills, 202, 204
The View, 261
Tide, 195
Tiffany & Co., 60, 191
Tilley Endurables, 294, 295
Tim Hortons, 14, 144, 206, 264
Tim Hortons Children Foundation, 14, 15
Time, 166, 262, 303
Tip Top Tailors, 174
Toblerone, 143
Top Sider, 212
Toro, 48, 176
Toronto Blue Jays, 120
Toronto City Hall, 11
Toronto Eaton Centre, 202
Toronto Hospital for Sick Children, 122
Toronto International Film Festival, 255, 256
Toronto Maple Leafs, 126
Toronto Star, 260, 261
Toronto Sun, 260, 261

Toronto-Dominion Centre, 202
Toshiba America Medical System, 272
Tostitos, 92
Touchpoints ROI Tracker, 40, 42
Tourism Industry Association, 284
Toy Industry Association, 10, 38
Toyota, 137, 301
Toys "R" Us, 195, 205
Travelocity.ca, 186, 187
Travelodge, 120, 244
Triaminic, 146
TripAdvisor, 244
TNS Canadian Facts, 292
TSN, 139, 140
Tupperware, 189, 217
Twitter, 76
Tylenol, 26, 49, 129, 130

U.S. Census Bureau, 30
Ultima Foods Inc., 130
Umbra, 303
Unilever, 134, 266, 297, 300
University of Ottawa, 24, 85

V8, 113
Valu-Mart, 129
Value Drug Mart, 156
Vanity Fair, 56

VIA Rail, 66
Viagra, 239
Vicks, 60
Virgin Atlantic, 282
Virgin Mobile Canada, 31
Visa, 59
Vocalpoint, 280
Volkswagen, 34

Wal-Mart, 72, 94, 162, 165, 166, 174,
    185, 187, 193, 195, 198–199, 207, 208,
    209, 210, 213, 295
Walmart.com, 217
Wendy's, 220
West Edmonton Mall, 214
Westin, 282
WestJet, 280, 285
Weyerhauser, 68
What's Cooking, 262
Whirlpool, 68, 194
Wii Fit, 297
Wikipedia, 95
Wilkinson Sword, 159
Wilson, 98
Windex, 161
Wonder Bread Plus, 242
Word of Mouth Marketing
    Association, 54, 55, 280

Wordscraper, 127
Workopolis.com, 260
World Wildlife Federation, 266
World Wildlife Fund, 9, 11
World's Biggest Bookstore, 243

Xbox, 128, 147
Xerox, 271
XM Canada, 262

Yahoo!, 95, 247, 260
Yonge and Dundas Square, 262
Yoplait, 130
York University, 250, 252, 256
Youth Culture Group, 283
Youthography, 283
YouTube, 34, 76, 227, 233, 259, 261
Yves St. Laurent, 48

Zellers, 6, 15, 161, 166, 207, 210, 211,
    282
ZenithOptimedia (ZO), 40, 42, 46
Zoom media, 263

Use [istudy] and save a tree...

McGraw-Hill Ryerson

www.istudymarketing.ca

Subject Index

above-market pricing, 165
accessory equipment, 124
actual product, 121
ad networks, 260
administered vertical marketing
   systems, 192–193
adoption curve, 146
advertising
   budget, 255
   Canadian advertising
     expenditures, 256*f*
   cooperative advertising, 265
   defined, 254
   described, 230–232
   designing the advertisement, 256–
     257
   institutional advertisements, 255
   media, selection of. *see* advertising
     media
   message appeal, 256–257
   objectives, 254
   product advertisements, 255
   program, development of, 254–263
   role of, 254
   scope of, 254
   target audience, identification, 255
advertising media
   different media alternatives, 257
   Internet, 259–260
   magazines, 261–262
   newspapers, 260–261
   outdoor media, 262–263
   place-based media, 263
   radio, 262
   television, 257–259
   viral marketing, 259–260
advertising program, development
   of, 254–263
Advertising Standards Canada, 37
agents, 221
all-you-can-afford budgeting
   approach, 241
allowances
   case allowance, 265
   described, 177
   finance allowance, 265
   merchandise allowance, 265
   promotional allowances, 177
   trade-in allowances, 177

   trade-oriented sales
     promotions, 265
alternatives, evaluation of, 43
analysis of data, 94
anchor stores, 214
antecedent states, 46
anti-corruption convention, 59
aspiration group, 54
assistance, 218
at-market pricing, 165
attitudes
   changes in, 30, 50
   defined, 50
   formation of, 50
attributes, 50
auctions, online, 77–78
augmented product, 121
automatic vending, 215
automotive supply chain, 196–197,
   197*f*
awareness, 240

baby boomers, 27
back translation, 60
backward integration, 191
bad timing, 148
balancing interests, 16–17
banner ads, 4, 260
barter, 159
behavioural learning, 49–50
behavioural segmentation, 108
below-market pricing, 165
Better Business Bureau (BBB), 37
blogs, 247
bots, 247
brand equity, defined, 125
brand loyalty, 50, 126–127
brand management
   brand equity, 125
   brand loyalty, 126–127
   brand personality, 127–128
brand name, defined, 127
brand personality, 127–128
branding, defined, 125
branding strategies
   family branding, 130
   individual branding, 130
breadth of product line, 211–212
break-even analysis

   applications of, 170
   break-even chart, 170
   break-even point (BEP), 169–170
   defined, 169
break-even chart, 170
break-even point (BEP), 169–170
bribes, 59
brokers, 221–222
budget
   advertising budget, 255
   all-you-can-afford budgeting
     approach, 241
   competitive parity budgeting
     approach, 241
   market segmentation, 106
   objective and task budgeting
     approach, 241
   percentage of sales budgeting
     approach, 241
   promotion budget, 240–241
bundle pricing, 162
business analysis, 152
business firm, 290
   see also organizations
business goods, 123, 124–125, 186, 187*f*
business marketing, 64, 65
   see also organizational markets
business markets, 101
   See also organizational markets
business portfolio analysis, 295–296
business unit level strategy, 291
business-to-business (B2B), 281
buy classes, 74–75
buyer requirements, 193–194
buyer-seller relationships, 71–72
buying centre
   buy classes, 74–75
   buyers, 74
   buying situations, 74–75
   deciders, 74
   defined, 72
   gatekeepers, 74
   influencer, 74
   modified rebuy, 74
   new buy, 75
   people in, 73
   roles in, 74
   straight rebuy, 74
   user, 74

Canada
  advertising expenditures, 256f
  business markets in, 65f
  environmental scan of, 26
  ethnic diversity in, 29
  Goldfarb psychographic market
    segments, 52f, 53f
  immigrants in, 29
  population shifts, 28
  recent polls, 28
  retailing in, 205–206
  urbanization in, 28
Canadian Code of Advertising
  Standards, 37, 174
Canadian Intellectual Property
  Office, 126
Canadian Marketing Association
  (CMA), 37
Canadian Radio-television and
  Telecommunications Commission
  (CRTC), 16, 36–37
careers, 17–18
carts, 214
case allowance, 265
cash and carry wholesalers, 221
cash cows, 296
cash discounts, 177
catalogue, 268
catalogue retailing, 216
category killers, 211
causal research, 84–86
central business district, 213
chain operations, 209
channel captain, 195
channel conflict, 190, 194
channel of communication, 229
channel strategies, 238–239
channels of distribution. See
  marketing channels
Chinese-Canadian subculture, 58
choiceboard, 245
cognitive learning, 50
collaborative filtering, 245
collateral materials, 267
commercialization, 154
communication
  benefits of packaging and
    labelling, 121
  channel of communication, 229
  customer service, and, 200
  decoding, 229
  defined, 229
  encoding, 229
  feedback, 229
  field of experience, 229
  integrated marketing
    communications, 235–236
  message, 229
  noise, 230
  online retailing, 218
  process, 230f
  receivers, 229

response, 229
  retailing mix, 214–215
  sales force automation, 273
  source, 229
community shopping centre, 214
company, 290
  see also organizations
company reports, 267
competencies, 294–295
competition
  defined, 34
  intertype competition, 212
  monopolistic competition, 34
  monopoly, 35
  oligopoly, 35
  perfect competition, 34
  types of competition, 34–35
Competition Act, 36, 173, 174
Competition Bureau, 36
competition-oriented pricing
  approaches
  above-market pricing, 165
  at-market pricing, 165
  below-market pricing, 165
  customary pricing, 165
  described, 165
  loss-leader pricing, 166
competitive advantages, 300
competitive forces, 34–35
competitive institutional
  advertisements, 255
competitive parity budgeting
  approach, 241
competitive products, 137, 138, 144,
  152
competitors
  identification of, 295
  prices of, 142
concept tests, 152
consumer behaviour
  attitudes, 50–52
  beliefs, 50
  consumer purchase decision
    process, 42–46
  culture, and, 57–59
  defined, 42
  family influence, 54–56
  learning, 49–50
  motivation, 47–48
  needs, 47–48
  opinion leaders, 52–54
  perception, 48–49
  personal influence, 52–54
  personality, 47–48
  psychographics, 51, 52f, 53f
  psychological influences, 46–52
  reference groups, 54
  situational influences, 46
  socio-cultural influences, 52–60
  subculture, and, 57–59
  values, 50–52
  word of mouth, 52

consumer goods, 123–125, 185, 187f
consumer income, 32–33, 33f, 167
consumer market, 101
consumer markets, segmenting
  of, 107–110
consumer needs
  action, and, 101
  difference of, within segments, 105
  discovery of, 5–6
  insensitivity to, and new-product
    failure, 148
  perception of need, 42
  satisfaction of, 5
  similarity of, within segments, 105
  vs. wants, 5
Consumer Packaging and Labelling
  Act, 36
consumer privacy, 217
consumer purchase decisions. See
  purchase decision process
consumer socialization, 54
consumer-oriented sales promotions
  contests, 264
  continuity programs, 265
  coupons, 264
  point-of-purchase displays, 265
  premiums, 264
  product placement, 265
  rebates, 265
  samples, 264
  sweepstakes, 264
consumers, 10
  see also ultimate consumers
  hierarchy of effects, 240
  online consumers, 218
  product life cycle, and, 141
  questioning, for primary data, 92–
    93
contests, 264
continuity programs, 265
continuous innovation, 145
contractual systems, 209–210
contractual vertical marketing
  system, 191–192
convenience goods, 123
convenience, and customer
  service, 200
cookies, 247
cooperative advertising, 265
copyrights, 126
core product, 121
core values, 51
corporate chains, 209
corporate culture, 279–281
corporate level strategy, 291
corporate regulatory body, 36
corporate vertical marketing
  system, 190–191
corporation, 290
  see also organizations
cost-oriented pricing approaches
  cost-plus pricing, 164

described, 163
standard markup pricing, 163–164
cost-plus pricing, 164
costs
  break-even analysis, 169–170
  control of, 168
  fixed cost, 169
  market segmentation, 105
  online retailing, 218
  packaging, 121
  pricing constraints, and, 172
  total cost, 169
  variable costs, 169
couples without children, 54
coupon fraud, 264
credibility, 233
cross-cultural analysis, 59
cross-docking, 198
cultural symbols, 60
culture
  changing attitudes and roles, 30
  defined, 30
  social force, as, 30
  socio-cultural influence, as, 57–59
customary pricing, 165
customer acquisition, 281
customer lifetime value, 283
customer reacquisition, 284–285
customer relationship management
  (CRM), 12–13, 227, 252
  corporate culture, 279–281
  customer acquisition, 281
  customer lifetime value, 283
  customer reacquisition, 284–285
  customer retention, 281
  customer service, 284
  data mining, 282–283
  data warehouse, 283
  database systems, 278
  defined, 278
  information technology, 278
  loyalty cards, 276
  loyalty programs, 276, 281–282
  marginal customers, 285
  Pareto's Rule, 282
  share of wallet, 284
  solution segment, 276
  touch point, 279
customer retention, 11, 281
customer satisfaction, 293
customer service, 284
  communication, 200
  convenience, 200
  defined, 199
  dependability, 200
  efficient consumer response
    delivery systems, 199
  quick response delivery
    systems, 199
  time and, 199
customer suggestions, 152
customer value, 6

customers, identification of, 294
customization, 218, 245, 247
customs, 59

data
  analysis of, 94
  collection, 87
  collection methods, 87–88
  defined, 89
  observational data, 92
  primary data, 89
  questionnaire data, 93
  secondary data, 89–90
data mining, 282–283
data warehouse, 283
database marketing, 12
database technology, 253
deals, 264
deceptive pricing practices, 173
deciders, 74
decision maker, 57
decline stage, 140–141, 237
decoding, 229
deletion, 140
demand
  demand curve, 166–167
  derived demand, 68
  elastic demand, 167
  estimates of, 166–167
  inelastic demand, 167
  price elasticity, 167–168
  pricing constraints, and, 172
  primary demand, 138
demand curve
  consumer income, and, 167
  consumer tastes and, 166
  defined, 166
  demand factors, 166
  examples, 167f
  movement along, vs. shift in, 167
  similar products, price and
    availability of, 166
demand factors, 166
demand-oriented pricing approaches
  bundle pricing, 162
  described, 160–162
  odd-even pricing, 161
  penetration pricing, 161
  prestige pricing, 161
  skimming pricing, 160–161
  target pricing, 162
  yield management pricing, 162
demographic segmentation, 108
demographics
  baby boomers, 27
  defined, 26
  ethnic diversity, 29
  Generation X, 27
  Generation Y, 27
  non-traditional families, 29
  online consumers, 219
  population shifts, 28

population trends, 26–28
department, 291
dependability, 200
depth of product line, 210–211
derived demand, 68
descriptive research, 84
desk jobbers, 221
deviations from plan, 304
diffusion of innovation, 141
direct channels, 186
direct competitors, 34
direct mail, 267
direct marketing
  described, 234
  direct orders, 269
  ethical issues, 269
  global issues, 269
  lead generation, 269
  retailing, in, 215–216
  technological issues in, 269
  traffic generation, 269
  value of, 269
direct orders, 269
direct response marketing, 253,
  267–269
  catalogue, 268
  direct mail, 267
  direct response TV, 268
  direct selling, 268
  e-marketing, 268–269
  internet, 268–269
  telemarketing, 268
direct response TV, 268
direct selling, 217
discontinuous innovation, 145–146
discounting, 212
discounts
  cash discounts, 177
  defined, 176
  functional discounts, 176–177
  quantity discounts, 176
  seasonal discounts, 176
  trade discounts, 176–177, 177f
  trade-oriented sales
    promotions, 265
discretionary income, 33
disintermediation, 194
disposable income, 33
dissociative group, 54
distribution, 2, 4
  dual distribution, 187
  exclusive distribution, 193
  intensity, 193
  intensive distribution, 193
  logistics. see logistics; logistics
    management
  marketing channels. see marketing
    channels
  multichannel retailers, 214
  selective distribution, 193
  supply chain management. see
    supply chain management

diversification, 297
dogs, 296
door-to-door retailing, 217
drive, 49
drop shippers, 221
dual distribution, 187
dumping, 174
durable goods, 119
dynamic pricing, 218
dynamically continuous
    innovation, 145

e-mail advertising, 260
e-marketing, 268–269
e-marketplaces, 75–76
economic forces, 32–33
economic protectionism, decline of
    defined, 32
    macroeconomic conditions, 32
efficient consumer response delivery
    systems, 199
efficient supply chain, 198
elastic demand, 167
electronic commerce
    (e-commerce), 217–219
electronic marketing channels, 186–
    187, 188f
electronic observation, 92
employee suggestions, 150
employee welfare, as goal, 293
encoding, 229
endorsements, 49
environment, 31
environmental forces
    demographics, 26–30
    competitive forces, 34–35
    consumer income, 32–33
    culture, 30
    economic forces, 32–33
    macroeconomic conditions, 32
    microeconomic forces, 33
    regulatory forces, 36–37
    social forces, 26–30
    technological forces, 33–34
environmental scanning
    Canada, environmental scan of, 26
    competitive forces, 34–35
    defined, 25
    economic forces, 32–33
    regulatory forces, 36–37
    social forces, 26–30
    technological forces, 33–34
equipment-based services, 124
estimates
    demand, of, 166–168
    revenue, of, 167
ethics. see also social responsibility
    balancing interests, 16
    coupon fraud, 264
    direct marketing, 269
    e-mail marketing, 269
    internet, 227–228

pricing, 173
ethnic diversity, 29
evaluation
    alternatives, of, 43
    consumers and, 240
    integrated marketing
        communications, 242
    new-product process, 150–154
    promotion program, 242
    strategic marketing process, 304
evaluative criteria, 43
event marketing, 13
everyday low pricing, 213
evoked set, 43
exchange, defined, 9
exclusive distribution, 193
experiential marketing, 13
experiments, 93
exploratory research
    conducting, 88–92
    described, 84
    focus groups, 90–91
    in-depth interviews, 91–92
    independent retailer, 209
extended problem solving, 46
external search, 42
external secondary data, 89–90

facilitating function, 183
fad products, 141
failure of new products, 147–148
family branding, 130
family decision making, 57
family influences
    consumer socialization, 54
    family decision making, 57
    family life cycle, 55
family life cycle, 55
family roles, 57
fashion products, 141
federal regulation, 36
feedback, 229
feedback loop, 229
field of experience, 229
final price
    allowances, 177–178
    approximate price level, 175
    discounts, 176
    flexible-price policy, 175–176
    geographical adjustments, 178
    list price, 175–176
    monitoring and adjusting, 178
    one-price policy, 175
    quoted price, 175–176
    special adjustments, 175–176
finance allowance, 265
firm. see organizations
fixed cost, 169
flexible-price policy, 175–176
fluctuating demand, 69
FOB origin pricing, 178
focus groups, 90–91

forecasting. see sales forecasts
form of ownership, 207–210
forward integration, 190
four Is of services, 119, 120
franchising, 192, 209
free trials, 49
French-Canadian subculture, 57–58
full department, 150
full-line wholesalers, 220
full-service retailers, 210
functional benefits of packaging, 121
functional discounts, 176–177
functional level strategy, 291

gatekeepers, 74
gender roles, 31
    socio-cultural forces, 31–32
general merchandise stores, 211
general merchandise
    wholesalers, 220
generalized life cycle, 141
Generation X, 27
Generation Y, 27
geographic segmentation, 107, 109
geographical adjustments, 178
global marketing
    direct marketing issues, 269
    retailing, 206–207
goal setting, 300–301
goals, 294
    see also objectives
Goldfarb psychographic market
    segments, 52f, 53f
goods. see also products
    business goods, 123, 124–125, 186,
        187f
    classification of, 123–125, 125f
    consumer goods, 123–125, 125f, 185,
        186f
    convenience goods, 123
    marketing of, 9
    production goods, 124
    shopping goods, 124
    specialty goods, 124
    support goods, 124
    unsought goods, 124
government markets, 66
government organizations, 294
government units, 66
grey market, 174, 175
gross income, 33
growth stage, 138–139, 237
growth strategies
    business portfolio analysis,
        295–296
    diversification, 297
    market development strategy, 298
    market penetration strategy, 297
    market-product analysis, 297
    product development expansion
        strategy, 297
guarantees, 49

habits, development of, 50
health and fitness, 31
hierarchy of effects, 240
hierarchy of needs, 48*f*
high-involvement purchases, 45–46
high-learning product, 141
horizontal conflict, 195

idea generation
  competitive products, 150
  customer suggestions, 150
  employee suggestions, 150
  research and development
    breakthroughs, 150
  supplier suggestions, 150
ideal self, 48
ideas, marketing of, 9
idle production capacity, 120
implementation phase (strategic
  marketing)
  execution of marketing
    program, 303
  marketing organization, design
    of, 302
  resources, obtaining, 302
  schedules, 302–303
income
  consumer income, 32–33, 33*f*
  discretionary income, 33
  disposable income, 33
  gross income, 33
inconsistency of services, 120
increasing use, 142
independent retailer, 209
in-depth interviews, 91–92
indirect channels, 186
indirect competitors, 35
individual branding, 130
individualized marketing, 104
industrial demand, 68
industrial distributor, 186
industrial goods, 123
industrial markets, 64–67
inelastic demand, 69, 167
inflation, 32
influencer, 57, 74
information gatherer, 57
information search, 42
information technology, 95
innovation, 145
innovators, 147
inseparability, 120
inside order taker, 271
insignificant point of
  difference, 148
installations, 124
institutional advertisements, 255
intangibility of services, 119
integrated marketing
  communications (IMC), 226, 253
  see also communications;
    promotion program

customization, 245
defined, 235
development of successful
  programs, 235–236
evaluation of, 242
geographical constraints, 243–244
internet, 227–228
product selection, 244
target audience, 236–237
intensive distribution, 193
interactive marketing
  choiceboard, 245
  collaborative filtering, 245
  commerce, 246
  customer-value creation, 243–245
  customization, 245
  defined, 245
  permission-based marketing, 245
  personalization, 245
  terminology, 247
interest, 240
intermediaries
  consumer benefits, 184
  defined, 183
  functions performed by, 184
  types of, 184*f*
  value created by, 183–184
internal search, 42
internal secondary data, 89
internet. *see also* marketspace
  advertising media, as, 259–260
  auctions, 77–78
  choice board, 245
  collaborative filtering, 245
  consumer purchase decision
    process, and, 44
  direct marketing, 268–269
  e-mail, 269
  e-marketplaces, 75–76
  electronic marketing
    channels, 186–187, 188*f*
  ethics, 227–228
  integrated marketing
    communications (IMC),
    227–228
  interactive marketing, 242–248
  multichannel marketing, and,
    189–190
  online retailing, 217–219
  organizational markets and online
    buying, 74–77
  permission-based marketing, 246
  personalization, 245
  portals, 247
  private exchanges, 77
  promotional websites, 189
  research tool, as, 95
  sales force communication, 272, 273
  terminology, 247
  transactional websites, 189
  viral marketing, 259–260
internet technology, 12

intertype competition, 212
introduction stage, 138, 237
inventory
  cross-docking, 198
  idle production capacity, and, 120
  services, of, 120
  vendor-managed inventory
    (VMI), 200
involvement, 45–46

joint decision making, 57

kickbacks, 59
kiosks, 214

labelling. *see* packaging
laggards, 147
language, 60
laws. *see* regulation
lead generation, 269
leaderboard, 260
learning
  behavioural learning, 49–50
  brand loyalty, 50
  cognitive learning, 50
  defined, 49
length of product life cycle, 141
level of service, 209
level of service of retail outlets, 210
lifestyle, 51
limited-line wholesalers, 221
limited problem solving, 46
limited-service outlets, 210
list price, 176
logistical function, 183
logistics
  cost-effective decisions, 195
  customer service and, 195
  defined, 195
  flow of product, and, 195
logistics management. *see also*
  supply chain management
  customer service concept, 199–200
  described, 195
  total logistics cost, 199
long-run profits, 170
loss-leader pricing, 166
low-involvement purchases, 45
low-learning product, 141
loyalty cards, popularity of, 283
loyalty programs, 276, 281–282

macroeconomic conditions, 32
magazines, 261–262
mail surveys, 93
manufacturer's branch office, 222
manufacturer's sales office, 222
manufacturer-sponsored retail
  franchise systems, 192
manufacturer-sponsored wholesale
  franchise systems, 192
manufacturers' agents, 221

marginal customers, 284
markdown, 212
market attractiveness, 147
market development strategy, 298
market-dominated sources of
information, 42
market follower, 173
market leader, 173
market modification, 142
market orientation, 11
market penetration strategy, 297
market-product analysis, 297
market-product focus, 300–301
market segmentation
approaches, 105
behavioural segmentation, 108
budget, 106
consumer markets, of, 107–110
costs of assigning to
segments, 105
criteria for forming segments, 105
defined, 101, 300
demographic segmentation, 108
forms of, 102–104
geographic segmentation, 107, 109
needs and actions, linking of, 101
psychographic segmentation, 108
sales forecast, 106
segmentation variables, 109f
simplicity of assigning to
segments, 105
SWOT analysis, 106
timing of, 102–103
market segmentation steps, 105–107
market segments
defined, 101
formation of, 105–107
multiple market segments, 102–
103
one product segments, 102–103
market share
defined, 293
goal, as, 293
pricing objective, as, 171
relative market share, 295
market testing, 153
marketing
consumer needs, and, 5–6
defined, 9
essence of, 5–8
evolution of, 12–13
influencing factors, 10–11
internet technology, 12
organizational strategy, and, 291
marketing action, feasibility of, 205
marketing channel choice
buyer requirements, 193–194
factors, 193–194
profitability, 194
target market coverage, 193
marketing channel management
channel captain, 195

channel conflict, 190, 194
cooperation in marketing
channels, 194–195
disintermediation, 194
horizontal conflict, 195
vertical conflict, 194
marketing channels
business goods and services, 186,
187f
channel strategies, 238–239
choice in, 193–194
consumer goods, 186f
consumer goods and
services, 185–186
defined, 183
direct channels, 186
dual distribution, 187
electronic, 186–187, 188f
indirect channels, 186
intermediaries, 183–184
management of. see marketing
channel management
multichannel marketing,
187–190
multiple channels, 187
strategic channel alliances, 187
structure and organization, 185–
190
supply chains, vs., 196
vertical marketing systems, 190–
193
marketing concept, 11, 15, 16
marketing information
marketing information systems
(MIS), 83
marketing research. see marketing
research
primary data, 89
requirements, 83
secondary data, 89–90
sources, 95f
marketing information systems
(MIS), 83
marketing mix, 8
defined, 6
elements of, 6–8, 302f
place (distribution). see
distribution
planning phase, in, 298
poor execution, and new-product
failures, 148
price. see pricing
product. see products
promotion. see promotion
retailing, in, 212–215
marketing organization, design
of, 302
marketing orientation stage, 11
marketing plan
defined, 298
deviations from plan, 303
results, vs., 303

marketing process
consumer behaviour, 42
distribution, 182, 202
environment, the, 25
introduction of, 8
market segmentation, 98
marketing information, 82
new product/service
development, 118
organizational consumers, 64
pricing, 158
product, services and brand
management, 134
promotion, 229
promotional tools, 254
strategic marketing planning
phase, and, 298
strategic planning, 290
target markets, 98
marketing program. see also
marketing mix
defined, 8
execution of, 303
marketing staff, for
implementation, 303
relationship marketing, and, 11–12
marketing research
benefits of, 83
causal research, 84–86
concepts, 87–88
defined, 83
descriptive research, 84
exploratory research, 84, 88–92
focus groups, 90–91
in-depth interviews, 91–92
information technology, and, 95
Internet research, 95
reliability, 83
research objectives, 86
sampling, 88
scope of, 83
types of, 84–86
validity, 83
marketing research process
data analysis, 94
described, 86f
exploratory research, 88–92
problem definition, 86
report and recommendations, 94
research plan design, 87–88
marketing strategies. see also
strategies
channel strategies, 238–239
defined, 303
market modification, 142
market penetration strategy, 297
new-product strategy
development, 150
product differentiation, 101
product modification, 142
product repositioning, 144
pull strategy, 239

push strategy, 238
supply chain management,
and, 197–199
marketing tactics, 303
markets
defined, 10
organizational markets. *see*
organizational markets
target market, 6
test markets, 94
types of competition markets,
34–35
marketspace, 187
customer relationships in, 245
customer-value creation in, 243–245
individuality in, 245
interactivity in, 244–245
terminology, 247
markup, 163–164, 212–213
mass marketing, 102, 230
maturity stage, 139–140, 237
membership group, 54
merchandise allowance, 265
merchandise mix
breadth of product line, 211–212
depth of product line, 210–211
intertype competition, 212
scrambled merchandising,
211–212
merchant wholesalers, 220
message, 229
microeconomic forces, 33
microsite, 4, 260
middle-aged married couples, 56
minor innovation, 145
mission, 292–293
modified rebuy, 74
monopolistic competition, 34
monopoly, 35
motivation, 47–48
movement along a demand curve, 167
multichannel marketing
defined, 188
implementation of, 189
online consumers, and, 189–190
promotional websites, 189
transactional websites, 189
multichannel retailers, 214
multiple channels, 187
multiple-family households, 55
multiple market segments, 102–103

needs
consumer needs. *see* consumer
needs
drive, 49
hierarchy of needs, 48f
personal needs, 47
physiological needs, 47
safety needs, 47
self-actualization needs, 48
social needs, 47

negative reinforcement, 49
new buy, 75
new markets, and product
repositioning, 144
new-product process
business analysis, 152
commercialization, 154
concept tests, 151
evaluation, 151
external approach, 151
idea generation, 151
internal approach, 151
market testing stage, 153
new-product strategy
development, 150
screening, 150
stages in, 151f
new-product strategy
development, 150
new products
actual development of, 153
adoption, factors influencing, 141
"business fit" of, 152
consumer needs, insensitivity
to, 148
economical access, lack of, 148
failures, marketing reasons
for, 147–148
features, reduced number of, 148
incomplete market and product
definition, 148
insignificant point of
difference, 147
market attractiveness, 148
marketing mix, poor execution
of, 148
poor product quality, 148
successful, 148
timing, 148
new use situations, 142
new users, 142
new venture teams, 149
newspapers, 260
niche marketing, 103–104
Nielsen ratings, 92, 93f
noise, 230
non-traditional families, 29
demographics, 29
nondurable goods, 119
nonprobability sampling, 88
nonstore retailing
automatic vending, 215
catalogue retailing, 216
direct selling, 217
door-to-door retailing, 217
telemarketing, 216–217
television home shopping, 215
North American Industry
Classification System
(NAICS), 67–68
not-for-profit organization. *see also*
organizations

described, 290
market, as, 66
objections, 272
objective and task budgeting
approach, 241
objectives
advertising, 254
defined, 86, 293
organizational objectives, 293
pricing objectives, 170–171
promotion objectives, 240
research objectives, 86
observational data, 92
odd-even pricing, 161
off-price retailing, 213
oligopoly, 35
one product segments, 102–103
one-price policy, 175
online advertising, 4
online auctions, 77–78
online consumers, 218
online retailing
advantages for consumers, 217–218
browsing vs. buying, 218
challenges of, 218
choice, 218
communication, 218
consumers' reasons for online
shopping, 218–219
control and, 218
convenience, 218
costs, 218
customization, 218
dynamic pricing, 218
online consumer, the, 218
what consumers buy, 219
when online consumers shop and
buy, 218
where online customers shop and
buy, 218
opinion leaders, 52–54
order clerks, 271
order cycle, 199
order getter, 271–272
order taker, 271
organizational buyers
defined, 65
online buying, 75
potential buyers, number of, 70
organizational buying
buyer-seller relationships, 71–72
characteristics of, 68–72, 69f
criteria, 70–71
demand characteristics, 68–69
objectives of, 70
potential buyers, number of, 70
reciprocal arrangements, 71–72
size of order or purchase, 69
supply partnerships, 71–72
organizational buying behaviour
buying centre, 72–75

defined, 72
stages in buying process, 72–73, 73f
organizational goods, 123
organizational markets
Canada, in, 65f
e-marketplaces, 75–76
government markets, 66
industrial markets, 64–67
measurement of, 67–68
nature and size of, 64–67
North American Industry
Classification System
(NAICS), 67–68
not-for-profit organizations, 66
online auctions, 77–78
online buying, 75–76
private exchanges, 77
reseller markets, 66
organizations
business firms, 290
competencies, identification
of, 294–295
competitors, identification of, 295
customers, identification of, 294
goals, 293
mission, 292–293
not-for-profit organization, 290
strategy issues, 291–293
strategy levels, 291
outbound telemarketing, 271
outdoor advertising, 253
outside order taker, 271

packaging, 121–122
communication benefits, 121
costs of, 121
customer value, and, 121–122
defined, 121
functional benefits, 121
perceptual benefits, 121
panels, 93
parallel importing, 175
Pareto's Rule, 282
patents, 126
pay-per-click, 259
payoffs, 59
penetration pricing, 138, 161
perceived risk, 49
percentage markup, 163–164
percentage of sales budgeting
approach, 241
perception
beliefs, 50
defined, 48
perceived risk, 49
selective perception, 49
perceptual benefits of packaging, 121
perceptual map, 112–113
perfect competition, 34
permission-based e-mail, 260
permission marketing, 246

personal influence, 52–54
personal interview surveys, 93
personal observation, 93
personal selling, 253
defined, 232–233, 270
forms of, 271–272
marketing, in, 270–272
order getter, 271–272
order taker, 271
relationship selling, 270
personal selling process, defined, 272
personal sources of information, 42
personal values, 50
personality, 48
personalization, 245
physical surroundings, 46
physiological needs, 47
place, 7
see also distribution
central business district, 213
community shopping centre, 214
power centre, 214
regional shopping centres, 213
retailing mix, in, 213–214
strip location, 214
place strategies. see distribution
planning gap, 303
planning phase (strategic marketing)
goal setting, 300–301
market-product focus, 300–301
marketing program, 301
situation analysis, 298–300
SWOT analysis, 298–300
point of difference, 147
point-of-sale material, 4
population shifts, 28
population trends, 26
portals, 247
positioning
perceptual map, 112–113
product positioning, 110–114
product repositioning, 144
positioning statements, 110
postpurchase behaviour, 44
power centre, 214
Precious Metals Marking Act, 36
predatory pricing, 174
premiums, 264
press conference, 267
press release, 267
prestige pricing, 161
price, 7
competitors' prices, 142
defined, 158
different names for, 158
final price, 176–178
indicator of value, as, 160
list price, 175
marketing mix, in, 160
profit equation, 160
quoted price, 175
price discrimination, 173

price elasticity of demand, 167–168
price equation, 159
price fixing, 173
pricing, 4
allowances, 177–178
break-even analysis, 169–170
cost concepts, 169–170
demand, estimating, 166–168
discounts, 176
dynamic pricing, 218
final price, 175–178
flexible-price policy, 175–176
FOB origin pricing, 178
geographical adjustments, 178
one-price policy, 175
predatory pricing, 174
price discrimination, 173
price fixing, 173
retailing mix, in, 212–213
revenue, estimating, 168
uniform delivered pricing, 178
pricing constraints
competitors' prices, 142
cost of production and
marketing, 172
deceptive pricing practices, 173–
174, 173f
defined, 172
demand and, 172
legal and ethical
considerations, 173–174
product life cycle stage, 172
pricing objectives
defined, 170
managing for long-run profits, 170
market share, 171
maximization of current profit, 170
profit, 170
sales, 171
social responsibility, 171
survival, 171
target return, 171
volume, 171
pricing strategies
above-market pricing, 165
at-market pricing, 165
below-market pricing, 165
bundle pricing, 162
competition-oriented
approaches, 165–166
cost-oriented approaches, 163–164
cost-plus pricing, 164
customary pricing, 165
demand-oriented
approaches, 160–162
everyday low pricing, 213
loss-leader pricing, 166
odd-even pricing, 161
penetration pricing, 138, 161
prestige pricing, 161
profit-oriented approaches,
164–165

skimming pricing, 138, 160–161
standard markup pricing, 163–164
target pricing, 162
target profit pricing, 164–165
target return-on-investment
    pricing, 165
target return-on-sales pricing, 165
yield management pricing, 162
primary data
advantages, 89
defined, 89
disadvantages, 89
electronic observation, 92
experiments, 93
observational data, 92
panels, 93
personal observation, 93
questioning consumers, 92–93
questionnaire data, 92
wording problems, 93f
primary demand, 138
print-based advertising, 4
privacy issues, 217
private exchanges, 77
probability sampling, 88
problem children, 296
problem definition in research
    objectives, 86
problem recognition, 42
problem solving
extended, 46
limited, 46
routine, 46
product, 4, 7
product advertisements, 255
product development expansion
    strategy, 298
product differentiation, 101
product life cycle
consumers, and, 141
decline stage, 140–141, 237
defined, 136
deletion, 140
depth of product line, 210–211
diffusion of innovation, 141
explanations of changes over
    product life, 136–137
fad products, 141
fashion products, 141
for high-learning product, 141
generalized life cycle, 141
growth stage, 138–139, 237
introduction stage, 138, 237
length of, 141
low-learning product, for, 141
management of, 142
market modification, 142
maturity stage, 139–140, 237
pricing constraints, 172
product modification, 142
product repositioning, 144
promotional mix, and, 237

shape of, 136, 141
various products, 141f
product line
breadth of product line, 211–212
depth of product line, 210–211
described, 122
product mix, 123
product modification, 142
product placement, 265
product positioning, 110–114
product repositioning, 144
product-market units (PMUs), 291
production goods, 124
production orientation stage, 10
products. see also goods
attributes, perceived changes
    in, 50
augmented product, 121
classification of, 123
competitive products, 152
core product, 121
defined, 118
deletion, 140
durable goods, 119
new products. see new products
nondurable goods, 119
product line, 122
product mix, 123
retailing mix, in, 212
services, combination of, and, 119–
    120
tangibility, degree of, 119
total product concept, 121–123
user, type of, 23
variations, 122
profit, 9
current profit maximization, 170
defined, 290
long-run profits, 170
organizational goal, as, 294
potential, and market
    segments, 105
pricing objective, as, 170
profit equation
break-even analysis, 169–170
costs, 169–170
described, 160
total revenue, 168
profit-oriented pricing approaches
described, 164
target profit pricing, 164–165
target return-on-investment
    pricing, 165
target return-on-sales pricing, 165
profitability, and marketing channel
    choice, 194
promotion, 7
communication process, 230–232
described, 229
interactive marketing, 242–248
tools. see promotional mix
promotion program. see also

integrated marketing
    communications (IMC)
design of promotion, 241
evaluation of, 242
execution of, 242
objectives, 240
promotion budget, 240–241
promotional tools, selection of, 241
scheduling, 241–242
target audience, identification
    of, 240
promotion strategies
channel strategies, 238–239
pull strategy, 239
push strategy, 238
promotional allowances, 177
promotional mix. see also advertising
decline stage, 237
advertising, 230–232
defined, 235
development of, 235–239
direct marketing, 234, 237
    see also direct marketing;
    growth stage, 237
integrated marketing
    communications, 235–236
introduction stage, 237
maturity stage, 237
personal selling, 232–233, 237
public relations, 233–234, 241
promotional program, 4
promotional websites, 189
promotions, 13
psychographic segmentation, 108
psychographics, 51, 52f, 53f
psychological influences
attitude formation, 50
learning, 49–50
motivation, 47
needs, 47
perception, 48–49
personality, 48
psychographics, 51, 52f, 53f
public relations, 4, 13, 266–267
collateral materials, 267
described, 233–234
press conference, 267
press release, 267
publicity, 233–234
special events, 267
tools, 267
public sources of information, 42
publicity, 233–234
pull strategy, 239
purchase decision process. see also
alternative evaluation; consumer
    behaviour
buying value, 44
decision, the, 44
defined, 42
described, 43f
influences on, 47f

information search, 42
Internet and, 44
involvement variations, 45–46
postpurchase behaviour, 44
problem recognition, 42
problem solving variations, 45*f*, 46
situational influences, 46
purchase task, 46
purchaser, 57
push strategy, 238

quality
goal, as, 293
poor product quality, and new-product failure, 148
quantity discounts, 176
question marks, 296
questionnaire data, 93
quick response delivery systems, 199
quoted price, 175–176

rack jobbers, 221
radical innovation, 146
radio, 262
radio frequency identification tag, 199
rebates, 265
receivers, 229
recession, 32
reciprocal arrangements, 71–72
reference groups, 54
regional shopping centres, 213
regulation
Competition Bureau, 36
defined, 36
federal regulation, 36
pricing, 173–174
self-regulation, 36–37
regulatory forces, 36
reinforcement, 49
relationship marketing, 11
defined, 11
marketing program, and the, 11–12
relationships, 11
relative market share, 295
reliability of marketing research, 83
reluctant purchasers, 147
repeat purchasers, 138
replenishment time, 199
repositioning, 110–111, 144
research and development breakthroughs, 149
research information. *see* marketing research
research plan
data collection, 87
data collection methods, 87–88
design of, 87–88
sources of data, 87
research report and recommendations, 94
reseller markets, 66

resources, obtaining, 302
response, 49, 229
responsive supply chain, 198
retail franchise systems, 192
retail life cycle, 219, 221*f*
retail locations
anchor stores, 214
carts, 214
central business district, 213
community shopping centre, 214
kiosks, 214
power centre, 214
regional shopping centres, 213
strip location, 214
wall units, 214
retail outlets
breadth of product line, 211–212
category killers, 211
classification of, 207–210
contractual systems, 209
corporate chains, 209
depth of product line, 211
form of ownership, 207–210
full service, 211
general merchandise stores, 211
independent retailer, 209
intertype competition, 212
level of service, 210
limited service, 210
merchandise mix, 211–212
scrambled merchandising, 211–212
self-service, 210
specialty outlets, 211
retail pricing
everyday low pricing, 213
markdown, 212
off-price retailing, 213
shrinkage issues, 213
retail sales, 206*f*
retailer-sponsored cooperatives, 192, 209
retailing
Canada, in, 205–206
consumer utilities of, 205
defined, 204
global market, 206–207
online retailing, 217–219
top retailers, 208*f*
value of, 204–207
retailing mix
communications, 214–215
defined, 212
multichannel retailers, 214
physical location, 213–214
pricing, 212–213
products and services, 212
retailing strategy
classification of retail outlets, 207–210
marketing mix, 212–215
nonstore retailing, 215–216
target market selection, 207–209

return on investment, 170
revenue
estimating, 168
total revenue, 168
reverse auction, 78
reverse marketing, 71
RFID, 199
risk takers, 147
roles, changes in, 30
routine problem solving, 46

safety needs, 47
sales as goal, 293
sales force automation
communication, 273
computerization, 272–273
defined, 272
sales force computerization, 272–273
sales forecast, 106
sales orientation stage, 10
sales promotions
allowances, 265
consumer-oriented sales promotions, 264–265
contests, 264
continuity programs, 265
cooperative advertising, 265
coupons, 264
deals, 264
defined, 234
discounts, 265
importance of, 163
point-of-purchase displays, 265
premiums, 264
product placement, 265
rebates, 265
samples, 264
sweepstakes, 264
trade-oriented sales promotions, 265
salesclerks, 271
samples, 264
sampling, 88
schedules for implementation, 303
scrambled merchandising, 211–212
screening, 150
seals of approval, 49
search word advertising, 259
seasonal discounts, 176
secondary data
defined, 89
external, 89–90
internal, 89
selected sources of, 89*f*
segment marketing, 102
segmentation of markets. *see* market segmentation
selection, 218
selective comprehension, 48
selective distribution, 193
selective exposure, 48
selective perception, 49

selective retention, 49
self-actualization needs, 48
self-concept, 48
self-regulation, 36–37
self-service outlets, 210
selling agents, 221
service continuum, 119–120, 119*f*
service franchise systems, 192
services. *see also* products
    business goods, 124
    classification of, 124
    defined, 119
    equipment-based services, 124
    four Is of services, 119–120
    goods, combination of, and, 119–120
    idle production capacity, and, 120
    inconsistency, 120
    inseparability, 120
    intangibility, 119
    inventory, 120
    marketing of, 9
    people, delivery by, 124
    retailing mix, in, 212
    service continuum, 119–120, 119*f*
    uniqueness of, 119
shape of product life cycle, 141
share of wallet, 284
shift in demand curve, 167
shopping goods, 124
shrinkage, 213
single-parent households, 55
single-person households, 55
site-to-store service, 217
situation analysis, 298–300
situational influences, 46
skimming pricing, 138, 160–161
skyscraper, 260
social forces and culture, 30
social needs, 47
social responsibility. *see also* ethics
    balancing interests, 15–16
    goal, as, 293
    pricing objective, as, 171
    societal marketing concept, 15
social surroundings, 46
societal marketing concept, 15
socio-cultural influences
    culture, 57–59
    defined, 30
    demographics, 26–28
    family influence, 55–56
    gender roles, 31–32
    opinion leaders, 52–54
    personal influence, 52–54
    reference groups, 54
    subculture, 57–59
    word of mouth, 52
solution segment, 276
source, 229
spam, 246, 260
special events, 267

specialty goods, 124
specialty merchandise
    wholesalers, 221
specialty outlets, 211
sponsor results, 259
sponsored links, 259
spouse-dominant decision making, 57
stakeholders, 293
standard markup pricing, 163–164
stars, 296
stimulus discrimination, 50
stimulus generalization, 49
straight rebuy, 74
strategic business units (SBUs), 291, 296
strategic channel alliances, 187
strategic marketing process
    defined, 298
    evaluation phase, 303
    implementation phase, 302–303
    marketing plan, 298
    planning phase, 298–302
strategic planning. *see also* strategic marketing process
    growth strategies, 295–297
    planning gap, 303
    strategic directions, developing, 294–298
strategies. *see also* strategic planning
    business unit level, 291
    business, the, 291–292
    corporate level, 291
    defined, 291
    functional level, 291
    goals, and, 294
    growth strategies, 295–298
    issues, in organizations, 291–293
    levels of, in organizations, 291
    marketing strategy. *see* marketing strategies
    mission, 292–293
strip location, 214
subcultures
    Chinese-Canadian subculture, 58
    defined, 57
    French-Canadian subculture, 57–58
supplier suggestions, 150
supplies, 124
supply chain
    automotive supply chain, 196–197, 197*f*
    defined, 196
    efficient supply chain, 198
    marketing channels, vs., 196
    order cycle, 199
    replenishment time, 199
    responsive supply chain, 198
supply chain management. *see also* logistics management
    described, 196
    marketing strategy, and, 197–199

total logistics cost vs. customer service factors, 200*f*
    vendor-managed inventory (VMI), 200
supply partnerships, 71–72
support goods, 124
survival, as pricing objective, 171
sweepstakes, 264
SWOT analysis, 294, 298–300
    market segmentation, 106

tangibility, degree of, 119
target audience, 240
target market, 2, 6
    coverage of, and marketing channel choice, 193
    defined, 6
    exclusive distribution, 193
    intensive distribution, 193
    retailing, in, 207–209
    selective distribution, 193
target pricing, 162
target profit pricing, 164–165
target return, 171
target return-on-investment pricing, 165
target return-on-sales pricing, 165
technological forces, 33–34
technology
    defined, 33
    direct marketing, and, 269
    impact on customers, 33–34
    marketing programs, 278
    sales force automation, 272–273
telemarketing, 216–217, 268, 271
telephone surveys, 87
television, 257–259
television home shopping, 215
temporal effects, 46
test marketing, 153
    concept tests, 151
    market testing, 153
    virtual reality testing, 153
test markets, 94
Textile Labelling Act, 36
time poverty, 31
time, and customer service, 199
timing of markdown, 213
timing of segmentation, 102–103
total cost, 169
total logistics cost, 199
total product concept, 121–123
total revenue, 168
touchpoint, 279
trade discounts, 176–177, 177*f*
trade-in allowances, 177
trade-oriented sales promotions
    allowances, 265
    cooperative advertising, 265
    defined, 265
    discounts, 265
trademarks, 126

traditional auction, 78
traditional family, 55
traffic generation, 269
transactional function, 183
transactional websites, 189
truck jobbers, 221
TV advertising, 4

ultimate consumers. *see also*
    consumers
    described, 10
uniform delivered pricing, 178
unsought goods, 124
usage instructions, 49
user, 57, 74, 123
utility, 205

validity of marketing research, 83
VALS Program, 51
value, 59
    assessment of, 43
    buying value, 44
    consumer behaviour, and, 50–52
    consumption or use, in, 44
    core values, 51
    direct marketing, of, 269
    intermediary-created value, 183–184
    personal values, 51
    price as indicator, 160
value pricing, 160
variable costs, 169
vending machines, 215
vendor-managed inventory (VMI), 200

vertical conflict, 194
vertical marketing systems
    administered vertical marketing
        systems, 192–193
    backward integration, 191
    contractual vertical marketing
        system, 191–192
    corporate vertical marketing
        system, 190–191
    defined, 190
    forward integration, 190
    franchising, 192
    manufacturer-sponsored retail
        franchise systems, 192
    manufacturer-sponsored wholesale
        franchise systems, 192
    retail franchise systems, 192
    retailer-sponsored
        cooperatives, 192
    service franchise systems, 192
    types of, 191*f*
    wholesaler-sponsored voluntary
        chains, 191
vibe-feedback technology, 4
viral marketing, 14, 246–247, 259–260
virtual reality testing, 153
visible minorities, 29
volume, as pricing objective, 171

wall units, 214
wants, 5
warranties, 49
web communities, 246

weblogs, 247
wholesaler-sponsored voluntary
    chains, 191, 209
wholesalers, 186
wholesaling
    agents, 221
    brokers, 221–222
    cash and carry wholesalers, 221
    desk jobbers, 221
    drop shippers, 221
    full-line wholesalers, 220
    general merchandise
        wholesalers, 220
    limited-line wholesalers, 221
    manufacturer's branch office, 222
    manufacturer's sales office, 222
    manufacturers' agents, 221
    merchant wholesalers, 220
    rack jobbers, 221
    selling agents, 221
    specialty merchandise
        wholesalers, 221
    truck jobbers, 221
women and time poverty, 31
word-of-mouth, 52
world trade. *see* global marketing

yield management pricing, 162

Improve your marketing game.

www.istudymarketing.ca